The Origins of Christianity

An Exploration

Étienne Nodet and Justin Taylor

École Biblique of Jerusalem

A Michael Glazier Book
THE LITURGICAL PRESS
Collegeville, Minnesota

A Michael Glazier Book published by The Liturgical Press

Cover design by David Manahan, O.S.B. Ivory carving; German ca. 1000; Fitzwilliam Museum, Cambridge.

An edition of this book in French has been published by Éditions du Cerf (Paris, 1998) under the title *Essai sur les origines du christianisme. Une secte éclatée*. ISBN 2-204-05819-X.

1 2 3 4 5 6 7 8

Library of Congress Cataloging-in-Publication Data

Nodet, Etienne.
The origins of Christianity : an exploration / Etienne Nodet and Justin Taylor.
p. cm.
"A Michael Glazier book."
Includes bibliographical references and index.
ISBN 0-8146-5862-8 (alk. paper)
1. Christianity—Origin. I. Taylor, Justin, 1943– II. Title.
BR129.N63 1998
270.1—dc21 98–5539
CIP

Contents

Preface

Christians have always had two basic rites which are complementary: baptism and the eucharist, the one giving access to the other. Our aim in this study is to pick out the distinctive features of the environment in which Christianity began by looking into the origin of these two institutions and at the link between them. The outcome can be stated very simply: the environment from which Christianity emerged was close to the Essenes, with whom baptism marked the successful conclusion of a process of initiation, and whose essential act as a community was a meal, principally of bread and wine taken in symbolic portions, which had an eschatological significance. At the heart of this sectarian culture, which was marginal to the rest of Judaism, a profound transformation took place, in which contact with Gentiles played a decisive role. The traditional institutional setting was preserved, as early Christian literature attests. For rites are of their nature stable and tend to persist even when their meaning has changed. Nonetheless, the group itself burst open, and from a sect became a universal church.

We use the word "sect" quite deliberately. Comparisons have often been made between the first Christians on the one hand and Philo's Therapeutae and Josephus' Essenes on the other, especially since the discoveries at Qumran (although ideas about the Essenes have perhaps been excessively determined by the community occupying that site, and especially by its apparently monastic character). These points of contact, reinforced by several areas of convergence with the rabbinic sources, have given rise to the idea that we have thus obtained a better knowledge of the general patrimony of Judaism at the time of Jesus. On the other hand, the data in question find only feeble echoes, if at all, in the Judaism described by Philo and Josephus. These authors set out to *publish* the realities of their religion. By contrast, Essenes, Christians and also Tannaites, the founders of the rabbinic tradition, appear marginal and highly traditional.

Furthermore, such groups did not, at least originally, publish their special rites and beliefs but kept them to themselves and transmitted them orally. A further sectarian feature was that each group or sub-group regarded itself as the true Israel, charged exclusively with restoring the Covenant. In other words, if there are similarities among these groups, it is because they are close to one another, but equally distant from governing circles.

So we are justified in taking these groups to be true "sects" and not simply "parties" to one or other of which Jews in general belonged or adhered (as Americans may be Democrats or Republicans). Viewed from outside, these groups looked all much the same. They, however, were intensely conscious of the variants, often minute, that differentiated each from its rivals. From this sectarian environment, we will argue, emerged both Christianity, claiming to be the universalist fulfilment of Judaism, and rabbinic Judaism, claiming to represent the nation. We shall trace the evolution—or rather revolution—that produced Christianity. The rise of rabbinic Judaism also represents an important development in which, by a process of selection and federation, Tannaite brotherhoods were transformed into schools within a comprehensive tradition. The impetus to this development was the need to take responsibility for the people as a whole after the disasters of 70 and 135 which destroyed the Jewish commonwealth.

We hope to show in what follows that these statements are well founded. The project was born and in part carried out in the context of a seminar on the Book of Acts conducted jointly by the co-authors at the École Biblique. Justin Taylor was trained in history, and has looked for facts and their causes; Étienne Nodet was trained in Judaic studies, and his special interest has been to look for traces of Jewish institutions in the expression of these facts. The enterprise has proved very stimulating, and the result is the present work, which is the fruit of close collaboration at every stage of composition; both authors are jointly responsible for the totality of opinions expressed.

The writing of this book would have been impossible without the patient help given so freely by the staff of the École Biblique library. We are also grateful to those friends, colleagues and students who have helped us with criticisms and suggestions as to both form and contents. We cannot mention all by name, but there is one who must not pass unnoticed. The tireless labor of Marie-Émile Boismard has provided the indispensable critical basis of our work; it is proof of his generosity of mind that he has encouraged us to exploit his findings independently, even when at times we come to different conclusions. Thanks are also due to Malcolm Lowe, who read the entire English text in draft and suggested a number of improvements. The remaining defects of the book, as well as the opinions expressed, remain the sole responsibility of the authors.

We have had to use many ancient sources, which often require technical explanations in order to interpret them. In the interests of keeping the main text as readable as possible, all such specialized discussion, as well as quotations in languages other than English, have been placed in the notes. In the last analysis, we are not writing about ancient history. On the contrary, we are deeply convinced that a better knowledge of how the Church began, can throw light on present day realities, especially at a time when the very notion of tradition is in crisis. We wish to share this conviction with our fellow Christians.

Jerusalem, May 1997 Étienne Nodet and Justin Taylor

Abbreviations

Only those works which are used most frequently are indicated in the list which follows. For the rest, the first reference is given in complete form in the corresponding note, and further references within the same chapter in abbreviated form.

1 QH,
11 QT, etc. — Documents from the Qumran caves; the most frequently cited are: 1 QH *(Hodayot/Thanksgiving Hymns)*, 1 QM *(War Scroll)*, 1 QS *(Rule of the Community/ Manual of Discipline)*, 1 QSa *(Rule of the Congregation/Messianic Rule)*, 4 QMMT *(Miqṣat maᶜaśeh ha-Torah)*, 4 QFl *(Florilegium)*, 11 QT *(Temple Scroll)*, CD *(Damascus Document)*. Except for 4 QFl, these texts exist in an English translation by Geza Vermes, *The Dead Sea Scrolls in English*, revised and extended fourth edition, London & New York, Penguin Books, 1995. All the non-biblical texts from Qumran, including those not yet published, are given in Spanish translation, with index of fragments by caves and available editions, by Florentino García Martínez, *Textos de Qumrán* (Col. Estructuras y Procesos), Madrid, Edit. Trotta, 1992; Eng. tr.: *The Dead Sea Scrolls Translated*, Leiden, Brill, 1992; Italian tr., revised and annotated: *Testi di Qumran* (Biblica. Testi e Studi, 4), Brescia, Paideia, 1996.

1 Q — Dominique Barthélemy & Joseph-T. Milik, *Qumran Cave 1* (DJD, 1), Oxford, Clarendon Press, 1962.

4 QMMT — Elisha Qimron & John Strugnell, *Qumran Cave 4. V – Miqṣat Maᶜaśeh ha-Torah* (DJD, 10), Oxford, Clarendon Press, 1994.

11 QT — Yigael Yadin, *The Temple Scroll*, Jerusalem, The Israel Exploration Society, 1983.

AASOR — The Annual of the American Schools of Oriental Research.

AB — Anchor Bible.

Ab — Tractate *Abot*, of the order *Neziqin* of the *Mishnah*.

AbRN A, B — Salomon Schechter, *Aboth de Rabbi Nathan*, New York, 1967[2] (Rec. א and ב).

AbZ — Tractate *ᶜAboda Zara*, of the order *Neziqin* of the *Mishnah*.

acc.	Accusative.
adj.	Adjective.
AGAJU	Arbeiten zur Geschichte des Antiken Judentums und des Urchristentums.
Ag. Ap.	Flavius Josephus, *Against Apion*; Greek text and English translation in Loeb Classical Library, London and Cambridge, Mass., William Heinemann and Harvard University Press, vol. I (transl. by H. St. J. Thackeray).
AGSU	Arbeiten zur Geschichte des Spätjudentums und Urchristentums.
AJ I–V	Étienne Nodet *& al.*, *Flavius Josèphe, les Antiquités juives. Livres I à III*, Paris, Cerf, 1992[2]; *Livres IV et V*, Paris, Cerf, 1995.
Albeck	Ḥanok Albeck, *Mishnah*, Tel-Aviv, Dvir, 6 vol., 1954.
ALGHJ	Arbeiten zur Literatur und Geschichte des Hellenistischen Judentums.
ANET	James B. Pritchard, *Ancient Near Eastern Texts Related to the Old Testament*. Princeton (N. Y.), Princeton University Press, 1969[3], XXVIII–710 p.
ANRW	*Aufstieg und Niedergang der römischen Welt.*
Ant.	Flavius Josephus, *Jewish Antiquities*; Greek text and English translation in Loeb Classical Library, London and Cambridge, Mass., William Heinemann and Harvard University Press, vol. IV–IX (transl. by H. St. John Thackeray, Ralf Marcus, Allan Wikgren & Louis H. Feldman). When the indication of a note follows a reference, it is to the edition described under *AJ* I–V.
AOAT	Alter Orient und Altes Testament.
Arak	Tractate *ʿArakhin*, of the order *Moʿed* of the *Mishnah.*
Aram.	Aramaic.
Arukh	Alexander Kohut, *Aruch completum,* 9 Vol., 1969.[2]
AT	Alexandrian Text (cf. WT).
Att.	Attic.
B (*e.g.*: *BYoma* 11b)	Babylonian Talmud *(Babli)*, tractate (including the "minor tractates" without corresponding *Mishnah*), usual pagination; there is an English translation of *The Babylonian Talmud*, ed. by I. Epstein, London, Soncino.
BA	Marguerite Harl e*t al.*, *La Bible d'Alexandrie, LXX : 1. la Genèse*, Paris, Éd. du Cerf, 1986; *2. l'Exode*, 1989; *3. le Lévitique*, 1988; *4. les Nombres*, 1994; *5. le Deutéronome*, 1992.
BabaQ, BabaM, BabaB	Tractates *Baba Qamma*, *Baba Meṣia*, *Baba Batra*, of the order *Neziqin* of the *Mishnah.*
BAH	Bibliothèque Archéologique et Historique.
BASOR	*Bulletin of the American Schools of Oriental Research.*
Bek	Tractate *Bekhorot*, of the order *Qodashim* of the *Mishnah.*
Ber	Tractate *Berakhot*, of the order *Zeraʿim* of the *Mishnah.*
Beṣa	Tractate *Beṣa*, of the order *Moʿed* of the *Mishnah.*
BETL	Bibliotheca Ephemeridum Theologicarum Lovaniensium.

Bik	Tractate *Bikkurim*, of the order *Zeraʿim* of the *Mishnah*.
BJPES	*Bulletin of the Jewish Palestine Exploration Society*.
BZAW	Beihefte zur Zeitschrift für die Alttestamentliche Wissenschaft.
CBQ	*Catholic Biblical Quarterly*.
CD	*The Damascus Document* (see the first entry).
cor.	Correction.
CRAIBL	*Comptes rendus de l'académie des inscriptions et belles-lettres*.
CRB	Cahiers de la Revue Biblique.
CRINT	Compendia Rerum Iudaicarum ad Novum Testamentum.
dat.	Dative.
DBS	Louis Pirot *et al.* (ed.), *Dictionnaire de la Bible, Supplément*. Paris, Letouzé & Ané, 1935.
Dem	Tractate *Demaʾi*, of the order *Zeraʿim* of the *Mishnah*.
ditt.	Dittography.
DJD(J)	Discoveries in the Judaean Desert (of Jordan); 10 volumes published (August 1994).
EB	Études Bibliques.
Ed	Tractate *ʿEduyot*, of the order *Neziqin* of the *Mishnah*.
Epstein	Jacob N. Epstein, *Maboʾ lenusaḥ hamišna*, Jerusalem, Magnes, 1964.[2]
err.	Error.
Erub	Tractate *ʿErubin*, of the order *Nashim* of the *Mishnah*.
ETH	Études de Théologie Historique.
fem.	Feminine.
Gk	Greek
Field	Fridericus Field, *Origenis hexaplorum quae supersunt*, Oxford, Clarendon, 1875. The indication "*deest* Field" signifies that there is no haxaplaric fragment for the passage under discussion.
FJ	Flavius Josephus, the person or his writings.
FRLANT	Forschungen zur Religion und Literatur des Alten und Neuen Testamentes.
gen.	Genitive.
GenR	Genesis Rabba *(Bereshit Rabba)*, first part of the *Mid Rabba*. Cited according to Yehuda Theodor, *Bereschit Rabba, mit kritischem Apparat und Kommentar*, Berlin, 1912. Completed and re-edited by Hanok Albeck, Jerusalem, 1955.[2]
Ginzberg	Louis Ginzberg, *The Legends of the Jews*, Philadelphia, 1909–1938, 7 vol.
Greek and Latin	Menaḥem Stern, *Greek and Latin Authors on Jews and Judaism*, Jerusalem, Magnes, 3 vol., 1974–1984.
hapl.	Haplography.
Heb.	Hebrew.
Hex.	Reading common to Aq., Sym. and Theod. (cf. Field).
homeot.	Homeoteleuton.
HRSup	Edwin Hatch & Henry A. Redpath, *A Concordance to the Septuagint. Supplement I*, Oxford, Clarendon, 1906.
HTR	*Harvard Theological Review*.
HUCA	*Hebrew Union College Annual*.

Ḥul	Tractate *Ḥulin*, of the order *Qodashim* of the *Mishnah.*
IDBSup	*Interpreter's Dictionary of the Bible, Supplementary Vol.*
IEJ	*Israel Exploration Journal.*
Institutions	Roland de Vaux, *Les Institutions de l'Ancien Testament,* Paris, Éd. du Cerf, 2 vol., 1990.[5]
Intertestament	André Dupont-Sommer & Marc Philonenko, *La Bible: écrits intertestamentaires*, Paris, *NRF*, 1987.
JANES	*Journal of the Ancient Near Eastern Society* (Columbia University).
Jastrow	Marcus Jastrow, *Dictionary of Talmud Babli, Yerushalmi, Midrashic Literature and Targumim*, New York, 1903 (reprinted many times).
JBL	*Journal of Biblical Literature.*
JJS	*Journal of Jewish Studies.*
JNES	*Journal of Near Eastern Studies.*
JQR	*Jewish Quarterly Review.*
JNST, SS	Journal for the Study of the New Testament, Supplement Series.
JSOT	*Journal for the Study of the Old Testament.*
JSOT, SS	Journal for the Study of the Old Testament, Supplement Series.
JSP	*Journal for the Study of the Pseudepigraphia.*
JThS	*Journal of Theological Studies.*
Jub(ilees)	*The Book of Jubilees*; there are English translations in R. H. Charles (ed.), *The Apocrypha and Pseudepigrapha of the Old Testament in English*, Oxford, Clarendon, 1913, vol. II, p. 1–82, and in James H. Charlesworth (ed.), *The Old Testament Pseudepigrapha*, Garden City, N.Y., Doubleday, 1985, vol. II, p. 35–142.
J.W.	Flavius Josephus, *The Jewish War*; Greek text and English translation in Loeb Classical Library, London and Cambridge, Mass., William Heinemann and Harvard University Press, vol. II–III (transl. by H. St. J. Thackeray).
Kel	Tractate *Kelim*, of the order *Tohorot* of the *Mishnah.*
Ker	Tractate *Keritut* (or: *Karetot*), of the order *Qodashim* of the *Mishnah.*
Ket.	*Ketib* (MT).
Ketub	Tractate *Ketubbot*, of the order *Nashim* of the *Mishnah.*
Kil	Tractate *Kilʾayim*, of the order *Tohorot* of the *Mishnah.*
L.A.	*The Letter of Aristeas*; there are English translations in R. H. Charles (ed.), *The Apocrypha and Pseudepigrapha of the Old Testament in English*, Oxford, Clarendon, 1913, vol. II, p. 83–122, and in James H. Charlesworth (ed.), *The Old Testament Pseudepigrapha*, Garden City, N.Y., Doubleday, 1985, vol. II, p. 7–34.
LDJ	Henry George Liddell, Robert Scott & Henry Stuart Jones, *A Greek-English Lexicon*, Oxford, 1940.[9]
Les Actes I–III	Marie-Émile Boismard & Arnaud Lamouille, *Les Actes des deux Apôtres I, II, III* (EB, N.S. 12–14), Paris, Gabalda, 3 vol. 1990.
Les Actes IV–VI	Justin Taylor, *Les Actes des deux Apôtres IV, V, VI* (EB, N.S. 23 & 30), Paris, Gabalda, vol. V 1994, vol. VI 1996, vol. IV in preparation.

Lieberman I	Saul Lieberman, *Greek in Jewish Palestine*, New York, 1942.
Lieberman II	Saul Lieberman, *Hellenism in Jewish Palestine*, New York, 1950.
Life	Flavius Josephus, *The Life*; Greek text and English translation in Loeb Classical Library, London and Cambridge, Mass., William Heinemann and Harvard University Press, (transl. by H. St. J. Thackeray).
Loeb	see under *Ant.*
LV	*Lumière et Vie.*
LXX (A, B, S)	Text of the Septuagint unless otherwise indicated, cited according to Alfred Rahlfs, *Septuaginta*, Stuttgart, 1935.
M (*e.g.*: *MPea* 3:2)	*Mishnah,* name of the tractate, chapter, particular *Mishnah*; there is an English translation of *The Mishnah*, by H. Danby, Oxford, Clarendon, 1933.
masc.	Masculine.
MaasSh	Tractate *Maʿaser Sheni*, of the order *Zeraʿim* of the *Mishnah.*
Maaserot	Tractate *Maʿaserot*, of the order *Zeraʿim* of the *Mishnah.*
Mak	Tractate *Makkot*, of the order *Neziqin* of the *Mishnah.*
Meg	Tractate *Megila*, of the order *Moʿed* of the *Mishnah.*
Meg Taan	Scroll *Megilat Taʿanit*, cf. Hans Lichtenstein, *Die Fastenrolle, eine Untersuchung zur jüdisch-hellenistischen Geschichte*, *HUCA* (8-9), 1931–1932. Cf. Strack I, IV, 3b.
MekhRI	*Mekhilta de-Rabbi Yishmaël*, cited by volume and page according to Jacob Z. Lauterbach, *Mekilta de-Rabbi Ishmael*, Philadelphia, 1933, 3 vol.
MekhSY	*Mekhilta de-Rabbi Shimʿon bar Yoḥaï*, cited according to Jacob N. Epstein & Ezra Z. Melamed, *Mekhilta d'Rabbi Šimʿon b. Jochai*, Jerusalem, 1955. Cf. Strack III, II, 3.
Men	Tractate *Menaḥot*, of the order *Qodashim* of the *Mishnah.*
MGWJ	*Monatsschrift für Geschichte und Wissenschaft des Judentums.*
Mid	Tractate *Midot*, of the order *Qodashim* of the *Mishnah.*
Mid Tan	*Midrash Tannaïm*, cf. David Hoffmann, *Midrasch Tannaim zum Deuteronomium*, Berlin, 1908.
Moore	George Foot Moore, *Judaism in the First Centuries of the Christian Era. The Age of Tannaim*, New York, 2 Vol., 1927 (reprinted many times).
Moulton	James H. Moulton & George Milligan, *The Vocabulary of the Greek New Testament, Illustrated from the Papyri and the Non-Literary Sources*, London, Hodder & Stroughton, 1914–1929.
MQaṭ	Tractate *Moʿed Qaṭan*, of the order *Moʿed* of the *Mishnah.*
ms., mss.	Manuscript(s).
MT	(Proto-)Massoretic Text *(ketib).*
n., nn.	Note, notes.
Naber	Flavii Iosephi *Opera omnia* (ed. Samuel A. Naber). 7 vol. Berlin, 1885–1895.
Naz	Tractate *Nazir*, of the order *Nashim* of the *Mishnah.*

Ned	Tractate *Nedarim*, of the order *Nashim* of the *Mishnah.*
Neg	Tractate *Negaʿim,* of the order *Tohorot* of the *Mishnah.*
neut.	Neuter.
Nid	Tractate *Nida*, of the order *Tohorot* of the *Mishnah.*
NJB	*The New Jerusalem Bible,* London and New York, Darton, Longman & Todd and Doubleday, 1985.
nom.	Nominative.
NovT	*Novum Testamentum.*
NT	New Testament.
NumbR	Numbers Rabba (*Bemidbar Rabba*), fourth part of the *Mid Rabba*. Cf. Strack III, IV, 7.
OBO	Orbis Biblicus et Orientalis.
Ohol	Tractate *ʾOholot (ʾAhilut),* of the order *Tohorot* of the *Mishnah.*
om.	Omit(ting), omission.
Orig.	In the Hexapla (cf. Field): text and/or modifications of Origen.
OT	Old Testament.
OTS	*Oudtestamentlische Studiën.*
par.	Parallel(s).
PAAJR	*Proceedings of the American Academy for Jewish Research.*
Para	Tractate *Para*, of the order *Tohorot* of the *Mishnah.*
Pea	Tractate *Peʾa*, of the order *Zeraʿim* of the *Mishnah.*
PEQ	*Palestine Exploration Quarterly.*
Philo	F. H. Colson & G. H. Whitaker (transl.), *Philo in Ten Volumes (and Two Supplementary Volumes)*, (The Loeb Classical Library), London and Cambridge, Mass., William Heinemann and Harvard University Press, 1927–1962.
PIASH	*Proceedings of the Israel Academy of Science and Humanity.*
plur.	Plural.
Praep. ev.	Karl Mras, *Eusebius Werke; VIII. Band: Die Praeparatio Euangelica*, Berlin, 1954–1956.
Ps.-Philo	Pseudo-Philo, trans. by M. R. James, *The Biblical Antiquities of Philo.* Prolegomenon by Louis H. Feldman, New York, Ktav, 1971.[2]
Qer.	*Qere* (MT).
Qid	Tractate *Qidushim*, of the order *Nashim* of the *Mishnah.*
rab. trad.	Rabbinic Tradition.
Rashi	Commentator of the Babylonian Talmud and the Massoretic Bible, cf. *Miqraot Gedolot, ad loc.*, or *B . . ., ad loc.*
RB	*Revue Biblique.*
REG	*Revue des Études Grecques.*
REJ	*Revue des Études Juives.*
RHR	*Revue d'Histoire des Religions.*
RQ	*Revue de Qumrân.*
RSh	Tractate *Rosh haShana*, of the order *Moʿed* of the *Mishnah.*
SamT	Samaritan Targum.
Sanh	Tractate *Sanhedrin*, of the order *Neziqin* of the *Mishnah.*
SBA	*Sitzungsberichte der Berliner Akademie.*
SC	Sources chrétiennes.

Schürer-Vermes — Emil Schürer, *The History of the Jewish People in the Age of Jesus Christ*, tr. & ed. by Geza Vermes *et al.*, Edinburgh, T. & T. Clark, 3 vol., 1973–1987.

Search — Étienne Nodet, *A Search for the Origins of Judaism. From Joshua to the Mishnah* (JSOT, SS 248), Sheffield, Sheffield Academic Press, 1997 (Eng. tr. by Ed Crowley of *Essai sur les origines du judaïsme*, Paris, Éd. du Cerf, 1992).

Shab — Tractate *Shabbat*, of the order *Moʿed* of the *Mishnah.*

SHAW — *Sitzungsberichte der Heidelberger Akademie der Wissenschaften.*

Shebi — Tractate *Shebiʿit*, of the order *Zeraʿim* of the *Mishnah.*

Shebu — Tractate *Shebuʿot*, of the order *Neziqin* of the *Mishnah.*

Sheq — Tractate *Sheqalim*, of the order *Moʿed* of the *Mishnah.*

SifDeut — Sifre Deuteronomy (*Sifre Debarim*). L. Finkelstein, *Siphre ad Deuteronomium H. S. Horovitzii schedis usis cum variis . . . .* Berlin, 1939. Cf. Strack III, II, 8.

SifNumb — Sifre Numbers (*Sifre Bemidbar*). H. S. Horovitz, *Siphre D'be Rab. Fasc. primus: Siphre ad Numeros adjecto Siphre zutta*. Leipzig, 1917. Cf. Strack III, II, 6.

Sifra — Sifra (Leviticus). I. H. Weiss, *Sifra debe Rab, huʾ sefer Torat Kohanim.* Wien, 1862. Cf. Strack III, II, 4.

sing. — Singular.

SJLA — Studies in Judaism in Late Antiquity.

SOR — B. Ratner, *Seder Olam Rabba. Die grosse Weltchronik*, Vilna, 1897. Cf. Strack III, VII, 1b.

Soṭa — Tractate *Soṭa*, of the order *Nashim* of the *Mishnah.*

SPB — Studia Post-Biblica.

STDJ — Studies on the Texts of the Desert of Judah.

Steinsalz — Adin Steinsalz, *Talmud Babli*, Jerusalem, Israel Institute for Talmudic Publications, 1971–. Complete (uncensored) text, vocalized, with Hebrew trans. and commentaries.

Strack — Hermann L. Strack & Günter Stemberger, *Einleitung in Talmud und Midrasch*, München, Beck, 1982.[7] English translation by Markus N.A. Bockmuehl, Edinburgh, T. &T. Clark, 1991.

StrB — Hermann L. Strack & Paul Billerbeck, *Kommentar zum neuen Testament aus Talmud und Midrasch*, München, 5 vol., 1922–1926.

Suk — Tractate *Sukkot*, of the order *Moʿed* of the *Mishnah.*

Syncellus — Georgius Syncellus, *Ecloga chronographica*, ed. A. A. Mosshammer, Leipzig, 1984. (The pagination of G. Dindorf, Bonn, 1829, is given between parentheses.)

Syr — Syriac translation of the Bible (peshiṭto, unless otherwise indicated).

T (*e.g.: TYomA* 4:2) — *Tosefta*, name of the tractate, chapter, *halakha* (ed. Zuckermandel).

Taan — Tractate *Taʿanit*, of the order *Moʿed* of the *Mishnah.*

Tam — Tractate *Tamid*, of the order *Qodashim* of the *Mishnah.*

targ. — The *targums*; for the Pentateuch, TOnq, TYer (fragmentary), TYon and TNeof.

TargP — Roger Le Déaut, *Targum du Pentateuque* (SC, 245, 246, 261, 271) Paris, 1978–1980. (Trans. and comm. of TYon and TNeof.)

ṬebY — Tractate *Ṭebul Yom*, of the order *Tohorot* of the *Mishnah.*

Tem — Tractate *Temura*, of the order *Qodashim* of the *Mishnah.*

Texte occidental — Marie-Émile Boismard & Arnaud Lamouille, *Le texte occidental des Actes des Apôtres. Reconstitution et réhabilitation* ("Synthèse," 17), Paris, Éd. Recherches sur les Civilisations, 1984.

TNeof — Targum "Neofiti," cf. Alejandro Díez Macho, *Neofiti I, Targum palestinense, ms. de la biblioteca vaticana* (Textos y Estudios, 7–11 et 20), Madrid, 1968–1979, 6 vol. (Translation and commentary, cf. *TargP.*)

TOnq — Targum of Onqelos, cf. Alexander Sperber, *The Bible in Aramaic. Vol. I: The Pentateuch according to Targum Onkelos*, Leiden, Brill, 1959.

Tos. — Tosafists, commentators of the Babylonian Talmud (successors of Rashi); articles in the margin of the text, indicated by an *incipit*. Their commentaries on the Pentateuch have also been collected.

Tosefta kifshuṭah — Saul Lieberman, *Tosefta kifshuṭah; A Comprehensive Commentary on the Tosefta*. New York, The Jewish Theological Seminary of America, 8 vol., 1955–1973.

TSAJ — Texte und Studien zum Antiken Judentum.

TUGAL — Texte und Untersuchungen zur Geschichte der Altchristlichen Literatur.

TWNT — *Theologisches Wörterbuch zum Neuen Testament.*

TYer — (fragmentary) Targum (Jerusalem), cf. *TargP.*

TYon (Pentateuch) — Targum of Pseudo-Jonathan ben Uzziel, cf. *TargP.*

TYon (Proph., Writ.) — (so called) Targum of Jonathan ben Uzziel, cf. *Rab. Bibl.* and Alexander Sperber, *The Bible in Aramaic. Vol. II, III, IVa*, Leiden, 1959–1973.

Urschrift — Abraham Geiger, *Urschrift und Übersetzungen der Bibel in ihrer Abhängigkeit von der innern Entwicklung des Judenthums*, Breslau, 1857.

var. — Variant.

Vig. Chr. — *Vigiliae Christianae.*

VT — *Vetus Testamentum.*

WMANT — Wissentschaftliche Monographien zum Alten und Neuen Testament.

WT — Western Text, cf. in particular *Les Actes* I (above) and *Texte occidental* (above).

WUNT — Wissentschaftliche Untersuchungen zum Neuen Testament.

Y (*e.g.*: *YYoma* 2:4, p. 41c) — Jerusalem Talmud (*Yerushalmi*), name of tractate, reference, folio and column of the *editio princeps*.

Yadin I, II, III — Yigael Yadin, *The Temple Scroll*, Jerusalem, Israel Exploration Society, 3 Vol., 1983.

Yeb	Tractate *Yebamot*, of the order *Nashim* of the *Mishnah*.
Yoma	Tractate *Yoma*, of the order *Moʿed* of the *Mishnah*.
Zab	Tractate *Zabim*, of the order *Tohorot* of the *Mishnah*.
ZAW	*Zeitschrift für die Alttestamentliche Wissenschaft*.
ZDPW	*Zeitschrift des Deutschen Palästina-Vereins*.
Zeb	Tractate *Zebaḥim*, of the order *Qodashim* of the *Mishnah*.
ZNW	*Zeitschrift für die Neutestamentliche Wissenschaft*.
ZThK	*Zeitschrift für Theologie und Kirche*.

Chapter I

Starting Points

When the Jewish historian Josephus mentions Jesus towards the end of the 1st century, he indicates some surprise that the race of Christians has outlasted its founder. The Pharisee Gamaliel, intervening in the trial of the apostles in Acts 5, also raises the question of the movement's survival. Such remarks were not out of place. At the end of St. John's Gospel, the first reaction of Peter and his companions, despite the extraordinary events that they have just experienced, is to go back to their former occupation of fishing. In fact, Jesus himself does not seem to have organized more than a circle of disciples, and the apostles fled at the time of his arrest. Something did, however, continue, under the sign of the Spirit; it was set in motion at Pentecost, in a scene which gave concrete expression to the mission confided to the disciples by Christ after his resurrection. At the same time there is a break in continuity, since Jesus' own activity hardly extended further than the Jewish world; it was only afterwards that the mission reached out to the Gentiles, thanks to conflicts aroused by the apostles' preaching within the bounds of Judaism.

The question of Christianity's relationship to Judaism is central. Already in the 2nd century, Christian writers were at pains to underline the evident superiority of Christianity: by fulfilling the Scriptures better than its rival, it showed that it was the true Israel which could now embrace the whole world in this final age. The Jews, by refusing, put themselves on the sideline, an interpretation which seemed to be confirmed by the ruin first of the Temple then of Jerusalem itself. This view of things can be regarded as traditional, in the sense that a religious tradition, operating as a collective memory, finds meaning in events and so, by definition, recognizes the continual working out of the divine plan. Not that such a phenomenon was new. When the little group of repatriates led by Ezra and Nehemiah heard the law of Moses proclaimed and signed a common engagement to observe it, they saw themselves as the true Israel, even though, in social terms, they were marginal.

In historical fact, things were certainly more complex in both cases, but the documents which have come down to us have all issued from normative traditions. This means that we see the events through a filter of interpretation which makes it difficult to reconstruct them. For example, the biographies of John the Baptist, Jesus or the apostles are still to a large extent open to discussion, and even the method to be adopted is under debate, while the sum of recognized facts remains rather meagre. This book is going to try a different approach, based on what might be called an analysis of institutions, which will examine not so much what is said but the form in which it is said. That form is determined by a culture, and in particular by habitual ways of acting. Of especial importance are rites, which bring together various elements in a rational way, and so constitute structures of meaning.

By way of introduction, instead of reviewing the numerous works which up to the present time have dealt with the origins of Christianity, this chapter and the following will define a starting point and a subject for investigation.[1] The starting point has two phases. First we shall look at the literary sources used in this study, the New Testament and the principal evidence for 1st century Judaism. Then we shall try to understand the meaning of two remarkable scenes in Acts, which feature baptism and the breaking of the bread. This leads to an investigation of these two institutions that are taken to be indicative of the environment in which Christianity arose, with a view to locating their Jewish roots. From these preliminary chapters arise a series of larger questions, detailed on pp. 123–125, which we need to discuss in order to throw light on baptism and the eucharist. The thorough study of these questions will lead us far afield, but will bring us back to the essential institutions. Five chapters (3–7) are devoted to this study: two to Jewish Galilee, one to the so-called "Jewish-Christians," another to the birth of the Christian mission, and the final chapter to the Covenant and the rites which give it expression. In our conclusion we sketch a brief synthesis and also point out various problems which await further study.

1. Despite having a similar title, the perspective adopted here, which is to choose the questions to be dealt with, is very different from that of the well-documented synthesis of Ramón Travijano Etcheverría, *Origines del Cristianesimo. El Trasfondo judío del cristianismo primitivo,* Salamanca, Universidad Pontificia, 1995, which presents the known facts from the Exile to the establishment of Catholicism.

I — Using the Sources

The classic sources, both Christian and Jewish, are well known. The purpose of this section is not to describe them but to make some comments about their nature and to introduce a fundamental distinction between the composition of a text and its publication, that is the moment when it escapes from the control of the author or group who produced it. A further distinction, less easy to handle when dealing with the ancient world, lies in the difference between the publication of a text and its authority. This difference is often hard to appreciate, for the authority of a text is initially derived from the reputation of those responsible for it. A good example of these realities is furnished by the *Letter of Aristeas*, which sets out to show that the Greek translation of the Pentateuch is not a private whim: on the contrary, it was ordered by the founder of the library of Alexandria and carried out by representatives of the twelve tribes of Israel appointed for this purpose by the high priest of Jerusalem. Thus, not only does the translation have all the religious and legal authority one could wish, but also its publication is supervised by official copyists in the setting of the best library of the time.

That is an exceptional case, but it provides a good illustration of the problem. For the biblical writings, publication and canonization are obviously two distinct phases, which in turn are quite distinct from the process of composition. On the other hand, further alteration and reworking cannot be totally excluded after publication, not even after canonization. It is well known that the text of the Hebrew Bible continued to evolve long after its translation into Greek.[2] That translation itself was not the only one, and various forms continued to evolve, more or less independently, until the diversity of Greek texts in the different churches at the end of the 2nd century alarmed Origen and prompted him to make a revision.

1. New Testament and Kerygma

The point here is not to discuss the literary origins of the various books of the NT, but rather to study what use the first Christians made of them.[3] Irenaeus, at the end of the 2nd century, was able to describe and defend something like the canon as we know it.[4] By his time, therefore,

2. Some examples will be discussed below, cf. chap. V, §II.3.

3. On the formation of the biblical canon (OT and NT), see Lee M. McDonald, *The Formation of the Christian Biblical Canon*, revised & expanded edition, Peabody (Mass.), Hendrickson, 1995.

4. Cf. Yves-Marie Blanchard, *Aux sources du canon, le témoignage d'Irénée* (Cogitatio Fidei, 175), Paris, Éditions du Cerf, 1993. Irenaeus does not make equal use of the synoptics: from Mark, "interpreter and companion of Peter," he cites only the prologue and

the conception of a canon was in existence, but the earlier position of Christian writers was quite different. Ignatius of Antioch, at the beginning of the 2nd century, sums up their attitude when he declares: "My documents are Jesus Christ; my unimpeachable documents are his cross and resurrection, and the faith that comes from him."[5] So, even if the composition of the books that form the NT was already well under way, there was as yet no *written* authoritative reference point. Ignatius speaks often of Christ, but refers to precise events only in succinct statements which are very close to the primitive kerygma—the proclamation of the saving death and resurrection—or which resemble those of the Roman Creed. He is therefore in the same situation as Paul, who he knows was a writer but whom he never quotes. On the other hand, he is well aware what a normative text is, since he knows and cites the OT, which he interprets typologically, thus assuring the continuity between the two covenants.

Fifteen years earlier, Clement of Rome made much use of the OT, fairly freely and most of the time, it seems, from memory. Sometimes he attributed the status of Scripture to texts which have since been lost, or to received interpretations of biblical passages, of a *pesher* type, which is not at all strange considering the Essene influences which can be found in his *Letter*.[6] As Christian Scripture he knows at most 1 Cor and recalls

---

the conclusion (in its long form); from Matt, he cites only the infancy narratives, the ministry of John the Baptist and the baptism of Jesus; from Luke, he cites the infancy narratives and various passages throughout the gospel, which seems to indicate a preference. But the words of Jesus which Irenaeus quotes, almost all out of their context, are for the most part to be found in Matt, with differences of vocabulary, suggesting a common source rather than direct borrowings. For Irenaeus, the Johannine writings are all of a piece and of true apostolic authority: he cites numerous passages of the gospel, with their context; he cites 1 and 2 John, but as a single epistle; he also cites numerous passages of Rev, which is in accordance with the Western tradition (cf. the Muratorian canon), whereas the Greek and Syriac traditions rejected it for a long time. The Pauline epistles are widely quoted by Irenaeus, especially Rom and Cor, but his extant writings show no knowledge of Heb (despite a somewhat vague remark by Eusebius, *Hist. eccl.* 5.26, who places at the end of the works of Irenaeus a "little book containing various discussions, where he mentions Heb and Wis"; the information is unsure, as the contents are oddly matched and the work has no title). He also shows no knowledge of 2 Pet, which is not surprising, or of Jas. As for Acts, Irenaeus makes frequent use of the Western Text (cf. below, §2).

5. On the other hand, he can be very severe towards the Judaizers, who claim to maintain the letter of Scripture, cf. *Philad.*, §8 f. He is in the same line as the polemic of Paul against Peter (Gal 2:1 f.). On the twofold tendency within the early community, cf. chap. V, §2.

6. Cf. Annie Jaubert, *Clément de Rome: Épître aux Corinthiens* (SC, 167), Paris, Éd. du Cerf, 1971, synthesis p. 48 f. and remarks passim. This point will be taken up in chap. II and VI.

the context of crisis in which it was written. He refers often to salvation in Jesus Christ, but, like Ignatius, without ever alluding to the facts of the life of Jesus. Only once does he cite words of Jesus (13:2), but the *logion* is not known in this form in the NT, which shows that for Clement there is no *official* text (although that does not, of course, exclude the existence of some documents). He speaks of Jesus only by way of the OT. Thus, when speaking of Christ as the suffering servant, he makes no direct reference to his life but uses only a biblical passage (the song of Isa 53:1-12). It is interesting to note that Heb 10:5 does exactly the same: "Coming into the world, Christ said: 'You did not want sacrifice or oblation, but you formed for me a body [. . .]' (Ps 40:7)."

The *Didache* knows and interprets the OT. It also quotes words of Jesus related to the Sermon on the Mount, but without a precise literary link with the Matthaean text, and a very similar version of the Lord's Prayer; there is probably a common origin in the liturgy. The *Epistle of Barnabas* is a Christian interpretation of traditions from the OT or related texts (*Enoch* is cited once as Scripture, which incidentally raises an interesting question concerning the constitution of the third part of the Hebrew Bible, the Writings). This interpretation is totally based on a typological reading of the OT, with several facts or words relating to Jesus, but in a rather stylized form and in any case without a literary link with the gospels as we know them. Polycarp of Smyrna, whose background is similar to that of Ignatius of Antioch, is familiar with the writings of Paul and makes a number of references to them. He has some knowledge of Matt, perhaps in the form of written notes (compilations of *logia*), but certainly not as a normative work. The *Shepherd* of Hermas belongs to the timeless world of apocalyptic and knows no Scripture apart from itself (cf. also Rev 22:18 f.).

This absence of normative Christian writing is confirmed by the ways in which the Gospel was transmitted. The *Didache* encourages respect for the one who proclaims the word of God (4:1), recommends the company of the saints, who are faithful witnesses, and warns against false teachers. Polycarp speaks of fidelity to the word handed down by tradition since the beginning, which makes it possible to refute those who deny the incarnation. For the *Shepherd*, false prophets can only be detected by their way of life. Papias, bishop of Hierapolis at the time of Ignatius and Polycarp, is known only through Eusebius (*Hist. eccl.* 3.39.1–7), who says that Papias made inquiry concerning the *words* of the apostles, who are named, but without indicating any evangelist; Papias insisted that the oral tradition was more useful to him than any writings. Eusebius thus confirms the direct sources, and his testimony concerning

Papias is all the more significant in that he disapproves of what he regards as the latter's lack of respect for the NT.

As for the Christians of Rome, the testimony of Josephus, a contemporary of Clement, is worth considering. His brief notice on Jesus (*Ant.* 18 §63 f.), the authenticity of which can be defended,[7] is characteristic: like the Christian authors, he has nothing precise to say about the life of Jesus. On the other hand, his statement that Jesus *himself* made disciples among both Jews and Greeks is an instructive anachronism, and in any case does not go well with the idea of a Messiah, who is above all a *national* liberator. Therefore the name of *Christos*, given by Josephus and necessary to explain the name of "Christian,"[8] does not seem to have for him any identifiable Messianic meaning.[9] In other words, by the time Josephus was gathering his information, "Christos" could pass for a surname, while the name of "Christian" had travelled a long way from its Messianic origins at Antioch some fifty years earlier[10] and taken on a meaning close to that which it has in the NT.[11] In fact, Josephus has no place for any idea of royal Messianism. In *Ant.* 6 §337, he credits David

7. Cf. Étienne Nodet, "Jésus et Jean-Baptiste selon Josèphe," *RB* 92 (1985), p. 312–348 & 497–524.

8. Perhaps pejoratively: "painted, plastered" (cf. chap. V, §I.2 in connection with makeup); FJ employs the term χριστός only one other time (*Ant.* 8 §137), in order to describe a plastered wall, which is the normal meaning, cf. chap. V, §II.2. However, the verb χρίω is that which he uses for the royal anointing (olive oil, cf. *Ant.* 6 §54 Saul, 6 §157 f. David, 7 §355 f. Solomon, 9 §106 Jehu, 9 §141 Joash), for the priestly anointing (rare essence, cf. *Ant.* 3 §198 et 4 §100), for the anointing of private persons (cf. *Life* §174), or even for plastering (*Ant.* 2 §221), but, unlike the LXX, he does not use the derived adjective in the sense of "anointed" (cf. chap. V, §II.3).

9. At least in a favorable sense. But, for a Roman ear, it could have had the negative connotation of criminal agitator; cf. chap. VI, §I.3, in connection with the expulsion of the Jews from Rome by Claudius, where we shall see that agitations "under the impulsion of Chrestus" preceded the application of the term "Christians" to Jesus' disciples. This argument of a pejorative meaning of *Christus* and *christianus* is developed by Erik Peterson, "Christianus," in: *Miscellanea Giovanni Mercati* (Studi e Testi, 121), Roma, Biblioteca Apostolica Vaticana, 1946, p. 355–372, who concludes for this reason that the contested expression ὁ Χριστὸς οὗτος ἦν ("He was Christos") in the "Testimonium Flavianum" is authentic. It is more than possible that FJ, writing in Rome, combines information from Christian sources with a very negative, even criminal connotation, but, with his habitual caution, he places no emphasis on it. In *Ant.* 20 §200, speaking of James as "brother of Jesus called Christos," he stays neutral, but a Roman ear might well have picked up "Jesus identified as Christus," *i.e.* identified as the author of the troubles.

10. Cf. Justin Taylor, "Why Were the Disciples First Called 'Christians' at Antioch? (Acts 11, 26)," *RB* 101 (1994), p. 75–94. The change in the meaning of χριστός is highly important, cf. below chap. VI, §I.3.

11. Where the identification of Jesus (risen) as "Lord" (of both Jews and Gentiles) has emptied the title "Christ" of its messianic content, cf. chap. VI, §IV.

with a posterity of twenty one generations,[12] ending at the exile. However, at the return from the exile, he does not give Zerubbabel any sort of Davidic or royal ancestry (*Ant.* 11 §13), unlike Luke 3:23-31, for whom Zerubbabel stands at the beginning of a second series of twenty one Davidic generations. It is clear, then, that for Josephus there is no Messianic promise linked to the Davidic dynasty.[13] In general, he avoids eschatology (cf. *Ant.* 10 §210), and has the greatest mistrust for zealot[14] nationalism, which, according to him, caused the downfall of Jerusalem and which he calls "brigandage."[15] For him the future of Judaism rests not with the monarchy,[16] but rather with the priesthood,[17] alone compatible with Roman sovereignty and capable, he believes, of preserving Jewish identity. In brief, Josephus could have had his information concerning Jesus from Christian circles in Rome, at the moment when they came to his attention, around 90, which would indicate that they then counted for something socially.[18]

12. Corresponding to the genealogy of 1 Chr 3:1-19, his probable source.

13. Cf. Kenneth E. Pomykala, *The Davidic Dynasty. Tradition in Early Judaism. Its History and Significance for Messianism*, Atlanta (Geo.), Scholars Press, 1995, p. 222 f.

14. Here and in what follows this term (written with lower case z) is not restricted to the faction so called by Josephus (*J.W.* 2 §160–161, etc.), but is taken in the very wide sense used by Martin Hengel, *The Zealots: Investigations into the Jewish Freedom Movement in the Period from Herod I until 70 A.D.*, Edinburgh, T.&T. Clark, 1985 (Eng. tr. of *Die Zeloten* [AGSU, 1], Leiden & Köln, 1961); it will be discussed in chap. VI, §I.2.

15. Cf. chap. III, §1.2; this terminology recurs in the NT, cf. chap. II, §I.4.

16. Unlike his opponent Justus of Tiberias, partisan of Agrippa II, cf. Alberto Barzano, "Giusto di Tiberiade," *ANRW* II.20.1 (1987), p. 337–358.

17. It is as a priest that he introduces himself (*Life* §1 f.), insisting on his genealogy, and mentioning only very briefly his adherence to the Pharisee party, which appears to be of recent date and certainly linked with the tendencies dominant at Rome (cf. chap. III, §IV). In fact, before his discovery of the social reality of Christianity at Rome, he had, about 75, written a very long account of the Essenes as a network of town-based communities, detailing their customs and rites, and the course of initiation which led to the ablution giving entry to the community (*J.W.* 1 §120 f.), in terms remarkably close to Acts, except for the matter of purity (cf. below, chap. VII, §IV); he seemed at the time to believe that that party had a future. Later, in his Pharisee phase (*Ant.* 18 §116 f.), he separates Jesus from John the Baptist, whom equally he knows only from the Christians, and gives only a brief description of the Essenes, purely in terms of philosophical doctrines, without rites or initiation process (*Ant.* 18 §18 f.). Among the reasons for such a change, there is certainly a renewed hope for the cult in Jerusalem (cf. chap. IV, §I.4), but probably also a recently conceived mistrust of the Essenes (cf. chap. IV, §I.1).

18. As remarked already by Henry St. John Thackeray, *Josephus: The Man and Historian* (Strook Lectures, 1928), New York, 1929 (repr. 1967), p. 128 f. Their resistance to the imperial cult which Domitian wanted to restore was important enough to warrant their (unnatural) alliance with senatorial circles in order to eliminate the emperor (96), cf. Philippe Pergola, "La condamnation des flaviens 'chrétiens' sous Domitien: persécution religieuse, ou répression à caractère politique?" *MEFAR* 90 (1978), p. 407–423.

In fact, his "testimony" is a slightly reworked version of a confession of faith, centered on the birth of Jesus according to the Spirit (Josephus wonders, by the way, if it can really be said that he is a man, a question which a Christian would not put in this way), his death under Pontius Pilate and his resurrection in accordance with the prophecies. So it is a kerygma, and even a sketch of what was to become the Apostles' Creed, whose origin is Rome, the apostles being in the first place Peter and Paul, the founding martyrs.[19] To sum up, the evidence provided by Josephus coincides with that of Clement: there is as yet no indication of *authoritative* Christian writings.

Such was the situation at Rome in the time of Clement and Josephus. With Justin, in the mid-2nd century, things have changed. According to the *First Apology*, the books about Jesus, referred to as "memoranda of the apostles," are read, together with the works of the prophets, at the Sunday assembly. The new state of affairs has a double aspect: there are now Christian texts of reference, and Justin, though still adhering to the primacy of the traditional (oral) kerygma, makes many allusions to the life of Jesus, and takes pains to situate his *logia* in a narrative context. However, the quotations do not match well the gospels as we know them, despite a certain preference for Luke, and a recent study by M.-É. Boismard[20] shows that these "memoranda of the apostles" are none other than a gospel harmony *(diatessaron)* in a form earlier than that attested by Tatian, the elements of which come from the canonical gospels but at an archaic stage of their development. In the *Dialogue with Tryphon*, the term "scripture(s)" always designates the OT, which is at the center of the debate, but Justin interprets it through gospel traditions of several kinds: collections of *logia* of Jesus, but without context; episodes obviously inspired by the gospel accounts, especially concerning John the Baptist, the nativity and the passion; explicit references to the "memoranda," which, according to Justin, Tryphon, though a Jew, could have consulted. Compared to the writers who preceded him, Justin attests two salient facts. One is the existence of Christian writings which are regulative, though they do not yet have the stature of incontestable Scripture (and it is not clear how far, in terms of territory, their authority extends).[21] The other is the complete absence of any reference to Paul or

19. Cf. chap. VI, §III.5.

20. M.-Émile Boismard, with Arnaud Lamouille, *Le Diatessaron: de Tatien à Justin* (EB, N. S. 15), Paris, Gabalda, 1992. See *RB* 101 (1994), p. 153–154. Cf. also Dominique Barthélemy, "Justin et le texte de la Bible," in: *Justin martyr: œuvres complètes* (Coll. Bibliothèque, 1), Paris, Brépols, 1994, p. 368 f.

21. Certain Jewish reactions in Judaea, at the beginning of the reign of Hadrian, indicate that Christian texts in Greek have recently made their appearance, cf. chap. V, §II.2.

Acts (the two perhaps inseparable), which would suggest that the canon is not yet fixed. Some commentators believe that Justin's silence about Paul is deliberate and due to his struggle against Marcionism regarded as a sort of radical Paulinism. Others suppose that Justin, who came from Palestine, would have been more inclined to defend Petrine positions, which would in any case make sense at Rome. These points of view are not mutually exclusive, since Paul's adversaries tried to label him as a heretic.

From all this it emerges that the appearance of authoritative Christian writings, as distinct from the works of individual Christians, followed well behind the oral transmission of the kerygma. This is still the state of things at the time of Irenaeus. For him, the tradition has four phases, to be carefully distinguished: the prophets have announced, Christ has established, the apostles have handed on, and the Church hands on throughout the entire world (*Demonstration*, §99). The first three terms designate the three classes of writings in the usual biblical order: OT, gospels, epistles. In *Against the Heresies*, Irenaeus thinks in terms of a structure which is alternately binary (OT/NT), in accordance with the tradition of typological exegesis, and ternary, by distinguishing the Lord from the apostles, i.e. the gospels from the rest of the NT. For Irenaeus, the binary structure is a theological synthesis, as he shows by his use of the word *testamentum*, whereas the ternary structure, which he prefers, corresponds to a significant literary fact, namely, the central place occupied by the life of Jesus (the gospels), surrounded by prophets coming before and after. However, the written text is not everything for him, for he accuses Marcion (1.27.2) of manipulating the gospel texts, or simply of giving too much attention to the letter (he cites Matt and Luke), to the detriment of a global view of the single Gospel, in relation to which the four booklets called gospels are only particular aspects. It goes without saying that his protest against abuse of the written word presupposes that authoritative texts were in existence.

To this end, he develops a highly structured notion of tradition. It has not only a content, but a power *(virtus)*,[22] which lies in the transmission

22. This term, which corresponds to δύναμις, has an interesting history. In Acts 18:24, Apollos is "powerful (δυνατός) in the Scriptures," that is, capable of giving inspired interpretations (cf. below, chap. VI, §II.1–2), or of uncovering their implications. Similarly, in 1 Cor 4:6 f., Paul, after recalling the maxim "nothing beyond what is written," distinguishes between the words of the proud and words spoken "with power": non-inspired words only create divisions, whereas "power," which alone establishes the kingdom of God, is a gift of the Spirit who makes the Scriptures speak in the present. For Jesus, signs and wonders are not themselves power but are what accredit him (cf. Acts 2:22). Josephus,

of the message. However many the languages in which it is conveyed, tradition is one, since it comes down from the apostles; in other words, the very act of handing on the faith assures the unity of the Scriptures. It is clear that for Irenaeus the kerygma is the central element in the living, that is oral, tradition,[23] which the heretics in one way or another reject. In the last analysis, what is at stake is the meaning of the life, deeds and words of Jesus.

Behind these debates and hesitations lies a central problem. If Jesus is regarded as a Teacher, then what he taught and the principal facts of his life will be of the highest importance; that is the view of the Jewish-Christians,[24] and of the Gnostics. If, on the other hand, the emphasis is placed on the kerygma, with the cross and resurrection at its heart, then the biography of Jesus assumes less importance, which does not, of course, exclude other, even precise, recollections.[25] The long time it took for the canonical gospels to emerge may even suggest that it was thought dangerous to *publish* the biography of Jesus. Not that, at the time of Justin or Irenaeus, the gospels had only been recently composed; no doubt there were written documents from the earliest times, but with the

---

presenting the Decalogue (*Ant.* 3 §90), explains τὰς δὲ δυνάμεις αὐτῶν δηλώσομεν, the underlying idea being that the other laws, which he is going to expound, are contained in them "potentially"; he does not say exactly how, but Philo, who starts from a similar principle, reorganizes the entire Law as an expansion of the Decalogue. In the Qumran texts, the inspired interpretation of things hidden in the Scripture (נסתר), and in particular their capacity to speak to the present, is a distinguishing mark of the community, whose teaching is esoteric, cf. the references in Laurence H. Schiffman, *The Halakha at Qumran* (SJL, 16), Leiden, Brill, 1975. It is the same mechanism which is at work in typological exegesis and, more generally, in the entire oral tradition of the first generations of Christians.

23. An interesting feature in Irenaeus is the quasi absence of gospel traditions concerning the passion and resurrection, whereas the kerygma consists precisely in the proclamation of those events. The same is true of the supposed Q source of the parts common to Matt and Luke, and of the proto-Mark reconstituted by M.-Émile Boismard, *L'évangile de Marc. Sa préhistoire* (EB, N.S. 26), Paris, Gabalda, 1994. This may not be a mere coincidence, even though a gospel without a passion narrative would more naturally come from Gnostic or Jewish-Christian circles, whom Irenaeus opposes.

24. This point will be developed when we come to deal with the succession to James and the observant Jewish bishops of Judaea, cf. chap. V, §III.2.

25. Paul passes on what he has received (1 Cor 11:2 f., Gal 1:9); he distinguishes clearly between what comes "from the Lord" and what he says as from himself (1 Cor 7:2-25, etc.); it is always a question of prescriptions and not of narratives. Cf. Birger Gerhardsson, *Memory and Manuscript* (ASNU, 22), Uppsala, 1961, p. 290 f. Jerome Murphy-O'Connor holds, with others, that Paul's epistles contain many allusions to Jesus' teaching, and even to its (rural) setting; at the same time, he admits that Paul's references to "the historical Jesus" are few and obscure, but insists that this does not mean that he had no "detailed knowledge of the gospel tradition" and appeals to the apostle's Christology to explain why he did not display all the knowledge he had; *Paul. A Critical Life*, Oxford, Clarendon, 1996, p. 91 f.

status of private notes, which explains why their texts remained somewhat fluid throughout the 2nd century. It is quite possible that the *harmony* attested by Justin was the trace of a first (abortive) attempt at publishing a text of reference, at least for internal use, in the form of a synthesis of venerable notes possessing apostolic authority; in any case, the documents which resulted in our gospels continued to evolve after the *harmony* was put together.

These considerations enable us to assess certain editorial observations on the written text which occur in the books of the NT.[26] Luke's is the gospel most used by Justin and Irenaeus, and his prologue has the general form of an historian's preface, comparable to that of Josephus' *Antiquities*. However, he declares that he is writing only after many others have already put order into the narratives. What is his subject? It concerns "that which has been fulfilled among us," which can be understood also, and more literally, as "*in* us." So, as well as an account of the events themselves, such as can be expected of any historian,[27] there is also the effect of their reception, which is what makes these events unique. Besides, there is a tradition, since the events have been handed down by the first witnesses, who are not simple spectators, but have been transformed by these events into active servants of the word. The fulfillment which Luke intends to set down in writing is derived from them. As for the addressee, Theophilus, he is assumed—as his name suggests—to have heard before he reads, but the reading will give stability and definition to what he has heard. Finally, it is noteworthy that this prologue does not specify any content, even though it is obviously a biography of Jesus, but concentrates solely on the status of the book, of the witnesses and of those to whom it is addressed.

According to 1 John 1:4, "we are writing to you that your joy may be made perfect," a declaration which puts a seal on a process of reception and transmission, described in terms of the bodily senses, resulting in communion between the writer and those addressed. Once again, there is no content to be verified, but simply the proclamation of eternal life,

26. There is a difference of nature, underestimated by Bultmann, between the oral and the written, cf. Werner H. Kelber, *The Oral and the Written Gospel*, Philadelphia, Fortress Press, 1983; id., "Jesus and Tradition: Words in Time, Words in Space," *Semeia* 65 (1994), p. 139–167, and the following discussion.

27. In Antiquity, the good historian is first and foremost a direct witness; secondarily, he uses the testimonies of others, oral or written, cf. Claus-Jürgen Thornton, *Der Zeuge des Zeugen. Lukas als Historiker der Paulusreisen* (WUNT, 56), Tübingen, J. C. B. Mohr (Paul Siebeck), 1991, p. 156–163. For Josephus, the biblical historian is a prophet, since the present can only be explained by the past, with the underlying idea of recurrence (cf. *J.W.* 1 §17 f., *Ag.Ap.* 1 §41 f. and 2 §16 f.).

confirmed in writing. A first conclusion to the epistle (5:13) redefines the purpose of the text, so that those addressed may know what they already possess: "I have written to you that you may *know* that you have eternal life, you who believe [. . .]"; in the same way, the prologue of Luke makes Theophilus expressly aware of what he has already. In 1 John 2:7-8, a time for writing is defined, in which the new commandment (declared now) meets the old (received from the beginning): there are brothers and sisters to love, and so a certain test of reality, involving truth or lies. Love of the brethren is, then, a problem (and why is the problem limited to them?). The old commandment, received from the beginning, can certainly be found elsewhere (Lev 19:18, a quotation which, like the person of Jesus, is absent, or at any rate outside the Johannine text). In reality, a crisis has made it necessary for Jesus Christ to come in water and blood, but its resolution is expressed in terms of eternal life and communion; the written text is not intended to give new information, but to call to mind an oral teaching (which is being forgotten).

John's gospel has two conclusions. John 20:30-31 indicates that what the book contains has been written "so that you may believe," but states just before, that Jesus worked many other signs. So to believe means "not to have seen," for the important thing is not to have seen the signs, but to recognize that Jesus is the Son of God. In fact, at the end of a long section on the signs, John 12:37 reaches the conclusion that they are unable to bring about belief. The signs cease after the arrival of the Greeks. The hour has come for Jesus to be glorified, that is, to die and be raised from the dead; in other words, Jesus has to move out of his own history, his own deeds and acts. By contrast, the written text as such is made up of signs of a quite different kind and of a quite different persuasive force. In the second conclusion (21:24) the "disciple whom Jesus loved" expressly testifies in writing; of him Jesus said only: "If I want him to remain until I come [. . .]." This permanence, in contrast to the death of Peter just foretold, is like that of the written text. Furthermore, the truthfulness of what has been written is attested by a projection of the intended readers into the text: "we know that his testimony is true." Once again, there is an external point of reference, which is oral. Finally there is a reflection about the absolute book, invading the entire cosmos, which would tell all there is to tell about Jesus, but would, of course, say nothing to anyone, for there would no longer be any room for a reader. So, by another path we return to the same point, that the text is selective: not only does the addressee have a place, but the biography is limited to what is needed "so that you may believe." In the same way, Jesus insists at length in the discourse after the Last Supper that he has to go away.

The written text is of necessity finite, just like the alphabet of which God is the master; the final injunction of Rev 22:18 f. forbids anything to be added or removed under pain of a curse, for respect for the text is equivalent to respect for the Law, (cf. Matt 5:17-19). It is a standard principle of conservation,[28] but also of limitation, excluding parallel traditions; the very notion of canon has its correlative in the "apocrypha," i.e. books which are meant to disappear. The ending of Rev puts a closure also on the NT as a collection. That it begins with the words "book of genesis" (Matt 1:1) is certainly not without significance: it is a collection defined by clear markers.[29]

All these passages show that the written text is a complement of oral transmission, and not its source. This is clearly seen under another aspect: in Rom 16:25, Paul concludes his letter by recalling the *gospel* which he announces and the *proclamation* of Jesus Christ, who is quite obviously absent. Both these technical terms evoke a terse, direct communication: a clarion call *(kerygma)* announcing good news *(euaggelion)*, one referring to the form, the other to the content of the message. The proclamation, however, goes much further than the information proclaimed,[30] which, in any case, cannot be verified, since it says nothing about the life of Jesus. By the same token, the one addressed bears the name of *catechoumenos* (Rom 2:18; Gal 6:6, etc.), that is to say, one in whom the proclamation has "echoed"; in the NT, it often causes an upheaval.[31] The same Paul also makes a clear distinction between the spoken and the written word. He

28. The same sanction is attached to the Septuagint, according to *L.A.* §311 ("Pronounce a curse, *according to usage*, against anyone who would modify a letter of the text"). The principle of the immutability of the written word features also in Deut 4:2; 13:1. For the historian, the principle of exact fidelity to the sources (evoked by Josephus, *Ant.* 1 §17) is also a canon received–and discussed–by Greek historiography, when the writer is not a direct witness (cf. Dionysius of Halicarnassus, *De Thucydide* §5, where he praises fidelity to sources, at the same time criticizing the naive servility of the mere compiler). However, the dominant view was that history, even though founded on facts, was a branch of rhetoric (Cicero, *De oratore* 2.51; Lucian, *Historia* §48). That corresponds well with the practice of Josephus (and with his explicit conviction, cf. *Ant.* 14 §1 s.), despite his preliminary declarations of conformity with his sources.

29. The center of the canon as we have it is not to be found in the death and resurrection of Jesus, but in geography: Acts, which highlights Peter and Paul, describes a progression from Jerusalem to Rome; then comes the synthesis constituted by the epistle to the Romans. We will show in chap. VI that the importance given to Rome is the trace of a *selection* operated in the interpretation of the heritage left by Jesus.

30. Compare Herbert Marshall McLuhan's formula "The medium is the message," *Understanding Media*, New York, McGraw Hill Book Co., 1964.

31. Cf. chap. VI, §III.2. In the classic method of teaching, the pupil learns by repeating (cf. also chap. I, §I.3). Here too, the "echo" leads to a repetition, which is none other than a confession of faith (ritualized in the rite of baptism).

explains that faith originates from hearing (Rom 10:17), but, in the exordium of his written composition (Rom 1:17), he is aware of going about a further procedure, which confirms and puts into perspective what has been heard: "the righteousness of God is revealed by faith to faith." Those to whom the written word is addressed are *already* believers.

These remarks lead to useful consequences for our task, which is to identify the environment from which the apostles went out on mission. First, if what is spoken and heard is primary, there follow relations of master and disciple and so questions of obedience. Then, the act of writing also implies a control, hence the various stages of canonization or revision of texts, and the reason why ancient translations may have escaped revision more easily than Greek texts. Finally, regarding the biographies of Jesus, i.e. the gospels, their publication supposes that they are in agreement with the kerygma, in other words that the Jesus whom their reader encounters is ultimately not the Teacher but the Risen One. That implies that they have undergone reworking inspired by the preaching of cross and resurrection, although the Teacher has left his traces in the text.

2. *The Western Text*

Problems of textual criticism occur throughout the NT. This is not the place to embark on a full-scale study of them, but only to look at certain aspects of Luke-Acts, following in the steps of M.-É. Boismard and A. Lamouille. The issue is the significance to be ascribed to the so-called "Western text" (WT) of these books.

a) Acts

In the case of Acts, there appear to be two relatively distinct forms of the entire book. One of these has been known since the 18th century (Griesbach) as the "Western" text, since two of its principal witnesses—a major Greek manuscript and the Old Latin translation—are of Western origin. The name, which we shall continue to use for its convenience, is misleading, since the witnesses to this form of the text are by no means confined to the West. The other text-type can fittingly be called "Alexandrian" (AT).[32]

32. For a recent overview and history of the question, cf. Peter Head, "Acts and the Problem of Its Text," in: Bruce W. Winter & Andrew D. Clarke (Ed.), *The Book of Acts in Its Ancient Literary Setting* (The Book of Acts in Its First Century Setting, 1), Grand Rapids-Carlisle, W. B. Eerdmans, 1993, p. 415–444. In general, the author's conclusions support the common opinion.

To take first the major ancient Greek manuscripts in uncial writing (capital letters only), the primary representatives of the AT are two 4th century codices, Sinaiticus (represented in the critical apparatus by the siglum א) and especially Vaticanus (B). The primary witness of the WT is usually taken to be the 5th century Codex Bezae (D). This ms. lacks three sections of the text of Acts (8:29-10:14; 22:10-20; 22:29–28:30), but contains, for the rest of the book, 800 words more than the usual published Greek texts based on the AT, which gives the WT its reputation as a long text. Constant witnesses to the WT are also ancient versions (especially Latin, Syriac, Coptic and Ethiopian), and readings of a "Western" type are to be found as well in ancient liturgical books and the writings of certain Fathers of the Church, including Irenaeus.

The relationship between these two text-types has long been the subject of speculation. As early as the 17th century, the suggestion was made[33] that Luke published two editions of Acts. This view has been championed in this century by F. Blass, who regarded the WT as Luke's first edition, which he subsequently revised to produce the apparently shorter AT. The distinctions that we made a little earlier, between composition, publication and canonization, make it possible to see how two types of the same text could remain in circulation at the same time, even within a fairly restricted environment where the text was regarded as authoritative, but not yet as definitive.

The opinion generally held by scholars today is the opposite of that proposed by Blass, namely that the WT is secondary to the AT and originated essentially in explanatory glosses. This consensus has, however, been challenged, and notably by Boismard and Lamouille.[34] They are by no means hostile to the AT, and indeed an important part of their work is aimed at restoring the purest form of this text, in the main following Vaticanus. However, their principal endeavor has been to "reconstitute" and "rehabilitate" the WT. These two verbs, which feature in the sub-title of their work, are highly significant and already indicate the nature of the project and hint at its results. The WT of Boismard and Lamouille is not simply Codex Bezae corrected or emended, despite the great antiquity of this important manuscript. On the contrary, they show that both it and other Greek manuscripts containing "Western" readings not infrequently bear the effects of an important recension of the WT, made, it seems, in the 2nd century, which sought to conform it more nearly to the AT.

33. Jean Leclerc, in a letter to Richard Simon, cf. the previous note.

34. Marie-Émile Boismard & Arnaud Lamouille, *Le Texte occidental des Actes des Apôtres, reconstitution et réhabilitation* (Études et Recherches sur les Civilisations, Synthèse 17), Paris, 1984.

Indeed, many of the long readings in D are revealed as conflations of true Western readings with others of an Alexandrian type. On the other hand, these authors give greater weight than is commonly given to the other kinds of witnesses, both ancient versions and patristic citations, which frequently translate or quote a Greek text earlier than that given by the majority of Greek mss.[35] From these elements they "reconstitute" the WT (while not claiming that all their results are equally certain).[36]

Now it is remarkable that the WT thus restored gives short readings—a feature which is generally regarded as being characteristic of the AT. Not only that, but, while the WT still contains a number of passages which are not in the AT, the reverse is also true, and the WT can be notably shorter than the corresponding AT. Furthermore, a close examination of the two texts not infrequently shows that the AT gives precisely the sort of facilitating readings—smoother transitions, more polished style, expressions easier to understand, more orthodox formulations—that would indicate a revised version. So a principal argument put for-

35. For a good definition of the method employed, cf. the fundamental article of Marie-Émile Boismard, "Critique textuelle et citations patristiques," *RB* 57 (1950), p. 383–408. The essential point is this: what is important is not the number of manuscripts, even ancient, which provide a given reading, but their descent. It is quite conceivable that the major Greek manuscripts that have come down to us, being official copies deposited in libraries, were the result of revisions and syntheses made by learned scribes; that is to say, they have undergone contamination. On the other hand, the older translations and citations (even if they are attested only by later mss), are less likely to have undergone such revisions. In particular, a normal sign of revision by a copyist is the appearance of glosses, which originate in marginal notes, whether from simply combining rival readings, or from the desire to lose nothing of what has been handed down. The result is longer readings, and hence the classic rule of textual criticism that, all else being equal, the shorter reading is the better. This rule is not, however, to be applied mechanically, since, when dealing with revisions, we also have to reckon with the possibility of deliberate omissions, whether for stylistic reasons or for other motives, including doctrinal censure. In other words, not all longer readings are secondary: it is necessary not simply to count the number of words but also to evaluate the two text forms. As for witnesses usually treated as secondary (translations, citations), M.-Émile Boismard, "Lectio brevior, potior," *RB* 58 (1951), p. 161–168, shows that this rule, which holds good when choosing among the readings offered by Greek mss, should be extended to those found in ancient translations and patristic citations, if they are shorter. The result of all this is not that we should systematically prefer a reading given by an ancient version or quotation over that given by the major Greek mss. Where, however, constantly recurring witnesses independently give an alternative reading, it has the right to be considered on its merits. On contamination, cf. Paul Maas, *Textual Criticism*, Oxford, Clarendon Press, 1958; Martin L. West, *Textual Criticism and Editorial Technique Applicable to Greek and Latin Texts*, Stuttgart, Teubner, 1973.

36. A study by Paul Tavardon, *Le texte alexandrin et le texte occidental des Actes des Apôtres. Doublets et variantes de structure* (CRB, 37), Paris, Gabalda, 1997, on the doublets in Acts shows also that the WT gives them in a "rougher" form, whereas the AT makes subtle changes which have the effect of smoothing the surfaces.

ward in favor of the primacy of the AT disappears. Furthermore, an inventory of more than 950 stylistic characteristics shows that the WT is perfectly Lucan. Taken all together, there are good reasons for accepting the thesis of Boismard and Lamouille that the WT is—or rather, represents—the Book of Acts as written by Luke, meaning by "Luke" here the writer of the Third Gospel, as explained below.

This conclusion has important consequences for the study of Acts. Boismard and Lamouille used their own findings about the text in order to elaborate a theory of the history of the composition of the book.[37] If the WT represents the original composition of Luke, then the AT represents a revision, either made by Luke himself, as Blass believed, or by another. But that is not all. Comparison between the two texts can, they claim, reveal pre-Lucan strata, whether used by Luke in his work of composition, or rejected by him but adopted by the reviser. Here again, Boismard and Lamouille challenge another assumption of recent scholarship,[38] that, whereas Luke undoubtedly drew on earlier sources in the composition of Acts, these have been so thoroughly digested and transformed into his own style that they are now irrecoverable. The same authors also come back to certain classical problems, such as the existence of doublets throughout the first chapters of the book, and the famous "we" passages in the last chapters. Finally, they give due weight to different authorial points of view which can be discerned.

They conclude that Luke reworked an already existing narrative (which, along with its author, goes by the name of "Acts I"), to produce the Book of Acts as we know it ("Acts II"—the revision being "Acts III"). The pre-Lucan work already had the broad lines of our Acts, with a mainly Petrine section followed by a Pauline part, but it also made use of texts which were already in existence and which certainly had their own literary history. For the Petrine part, Acts I followed and adapted a "Petrine Document" ("P Doc") which recounted the history of Jesus' disciples, mainly in Jerusalem, after the ascension, and for the Pauline section, the same writer made use of a "Travel Journal" which is the source of the "we" passages. This travel document may have been the work of the historical Luke, the companion of Paul in captivity (Phlm 24; Col 4:14; 2 Tim 4:11);[39] it is also possible that the same historical Luke was

37. Marie-Émile Boismard & Arnaud Lamouille, *Les Actes des deux Apôtres* (EB, NS 12–14), Paris, Gabalda, 3 vol., 1990. Referred to as *Les Actes* I, II or III.

38. In particular Jacques Dupont, *Les sources du Livre des Actes. État de la question*, Bruges-Paris, 1960.

39. Cf. Gregory E. Sterling, *History and Self-Definition. Josephos, Luke-Acts, and Apologetic Historiography* (Nov. Test. Suppl., 64), Leiden, Brill, 1992, who suggests that Luke is also the author of other material in Acts 13–28.

the author of the document called Acts I, which retraces the lines, and even imitates the style, of the Travel Journal when recounting the journeys of St. Paul. This "historical" Luke is probably to be distinguished from the "literary" Luke, the author of the Third Gospel and of Acts II. In that case, the attribution of earlier and fundamental elements in the work to the historical Luke explains the persistent and unanimous tradition which names him as the author of Acts.

Redactional phase	*Text-type*	*Supposed author*
Acts III	AT	Reviser
Acts II	WT	"Luke" (author of the gospel)
Acts I		(?) Luke (companion of Paul)
Sources used: P Doc,		
Travel Journal		(?) Luke (companion of Paul)

Schema of the redactional phases of Acts, linked with the two forms of the text.

The textual and literary conclusions of Boismard and Lamouille form the working hypothesis which is the starting point for an associated historical commentary.[40] By and large, they have not only stood the test of confrontation with historical evidence, but have also helped to solve some outstanding historical problems, and suggested fruitful lines of further research.

Even independently of the validity of the theory regarding the composition of Acts, the direct comparison between the WT and AT has turned out to be highly profitable. Many small differences, which are easily passed over or regarded as mere accidents of textual transmission, take on a new interest once the WT is held to be earlier, whereas the opposite hypothesis can see in them only insignificant variants or marks of careless editing.[41] In particular, the AT, viewed as a final revision, enables us to detect an important rewriting of Acts to make it conform to the realities of a later period in the life of the Church or to the conceptions that the Church then had of her own past. Following back down the line of

40. Justin Taylor, *Les Actes des deux Apôtres IV, V, VI* (EB, NS 23, 30, -.), Paris, Gabalda, vol. V 1994, vol. VI 1996, vol. IV in preparation. Referred to as *Les Actes* IV, V or VI.

41. It must be admitted that this opinion of the WT is not held by many at the present time, owing to the widely held equation of the WT with D, cf. Bruce M. Metzger, *A Textual Commentary on the Greek New Testament*, Stuttgart, United Bible Societies, 1994², p. 222–236. So, to avoid giving an impression of dogmatism, we refer the reader immediately to chap. VI, §I.3 and §II.1, which study certain characteristic passages of Acts 18–19 in which the differences between WT and AT can be appreciated.

successive reworkings of the narrative, we may even be able to recover some missing links in the history of the origins of Christianity. That is the exercise to which we shall devote our chapter VI.

b) Luke

The sort of work which has yielded such interesting results for Acts could possibly be done on other books of the NT, where "Western" readings are present, even if not on the scale of Acts. The first place to look, of course, would be the gospel of Luke, which was originally linked with Acts as two parts of a single work, and where it may be possible to reconstruct an integral WT prior to the AT. It has often been supposed that, for the composition of his gospel, Luke reworked a "proto-Luke," in which case Acts I could well be its continuation. Further upstream, the P Doc may turn out to prolong a primitive gospel which is the source of material common to our Luke and John.

Without entering on this vast program or defending any particular view of the synoptic problem, we will simply examine here two passages where the WT of Luke is especially instructive. The first case is the narrative of the Last Supper, where the WT—as attested by Codex Bezae and Latin and Syriac versions dating from the 2nd century—is remarkably short. By contrast, the AT is longer and is quite similar to the way in which the institution is narrated in 1 Cor 11:23 f., as a comparison of the texts reveals (see table).

Which of the two texts is earlier is a question long debated. The chief argument in favor of the long text (AT) is its great diffusion (all the ancient Greek mss except D). However, strictly on grounds of textual criticism, it has two fatal flaws: one is its remarkable similarity to 1 Cor 11 (but not to Matt and Mark, cf. the table chap. II, §II.5), which raises the suspicion of harmonization;[42] the other is a very clear attestation of the short text, as early as the 2nd century, by independent versions, which would suggest that the text that they translated enjoyed great authority and was in existence well before the major Greek uncial mss, which themselves are no earlier than the 4th century. In view of the principles recalled above, we should prefer the short text.[43] As for its content, we

42. With all the greater probability in that the final reviser of Acts (AT, Acts III) often has echoes of Paul, cf. *Les Actes* III:13 f.

43. Joachim Jeremias, *The Eucharistic Words of Jesus*, Philadelphia, Fortress, 1977 (Eng. tr. of *Die Abendmahlsworte Jesu*³, Göttingen, Vandenhoeck & Ruprecht, 1960, rev. 1964), p. 139 f. gives a complete survey of the question and takes up the discussion, which he widens to include the main short readings of the WT of Luke, and concludes that preference is to be given to the long text. He does, however, set out clearly the difficulties of

Luke 22 WT	Luke 22 AT	1 Cor 11
(19) And taking bread, he gave thanks, broke (it) and gave to them, saying: This is my body, given for you.	(19) And taking bread, he gave thanks, broke (it) and gave to them, saying: This is my body, given for you. Do this in memory of me. (20) And the cup in the same way after the meal, saying: This cup (is) *the new Covenant* in my blood, which is shed for you.	(23) The Lord Jesus, the night he was handed over, took bread, (24) and, giving thanks broke (it) and said: This is my body, for you. Do this in memory of me. (25) And in the same way the cup after the meal, saying: This cup is *the new Covenant* in my blood. Do this each time that you drink in memory of me.

will show later (chap. II, §II.1) that the short text fits better into the Lucan context, which knows only the "breaking of the bread," and that it avoids the command to repeat (absent also from Matt and Mark), which, in the paschal setting of the synoptic Last Supper, would have the effect of an invitation to repeat the Passover meal (which no ancient tradition attests; cf. chap. VII §I.3). That confusion is impossible in 1 Cor, which does not explicitly identify the Last Supper as a Passover meal.

---

this position and in the end, to explain the origin of the short text, appeals to a custom of abridging liturgical (sacred) texts, so as to avoid their profanation, a sort of *disciplina arcani*. The following objections could be made to this argumentation: 1. at the time we are considering, the texts had not yet, strictly speaking, been published, and remained largely an internal literature (cf. §1 above); 2. it seems strange that the same protection against profanation was not extended to all the narratives of institution (Matt, Mark, 1 Cor), say, in the 3rd century, at the time when published texts were being disseminated and the *disciplina arcani* was taking a more precise shape; 3. in fact, the rites are well protected in the NT, since no indication is given about how exactly they were celebrated (the eucharist is *not* the Passover meal), and they occur only in the course of the narratives. David Flusser, "The Last Supper and the Essenes," *Immanuel* 2 (1973), p. 202–206 (reprinted in: id, *Judaism and the Origins of Christianity*, Jerusalem, Magnes, 1988, p. 23–27), and more recently a communication (1997) from Bart D. Ehrman also conclude that the WT is primary.

The second passage that we will look at is, by way of contrast, a long variant of the WT, in Luke 6:1 f.:

> *Now, one sabbath* (WT adds δευτεροπρώτῳ, *"second-first") as he was going through the fields ready for harvest, his disciples were plucking ears of grain and eating them, after rubbing them in their hands. But some Pharisees said: "Why do you do that which is not permitted on the Sabbath day?"*

The principle of preferring the shorter text would, of course, lead us to eliminate the extra word as a gloss. There is, however, another principle of textual criticism, which is that, all else being equal, the more difficult text is to be preferred, and this is a case in point. For, far from being the sort of addition which seeks to make the text easier to understand, it is hard to see *a priori* what meaning to give to a "second-first" Sabbath. The only plausible explanation which has so far been suggested[44] is to interpret this term in the context of the calendar of the Book of *Jubilees*,[45] which is found also in the Qumran documents.[46] This calendar is both solar and weekly, with a year of 364 days, or exactly 52 weeks.[47] The year, divided into four quarters of 91 days (13 weeks, or two months of

44. Jean-Paul Audet, "Jésus et le 'calendrier sacerdotal ancien'; autour d'une variante de Luc 6,1," *Sciences Ecclésiastiques* 10 (1958), p. 361–383 has shown that this strange variant makes sense only in the calendar of *Jubilees*, but, convinced as he is that the WT is secondary, he has trouble in explaining how a detail of the Essene calendar could appear so late in Luke (2nd century), at a time when there is no sign of the use of such a calendar among the Christians.

45. The direct and indirect data are put together conveniently by Annie Jaubert, *La Date de la Cène. Calendrier biblique et liturgie chrétienne* (EB), Paris, Gabalda, 1957, p. 23 f. Cf. also Roger T. Beckwith, *Calendar and Chronology, Jewish and Christian. Biblical, Intertestamental and Patristic Studies* (AGAJU, 33), Leiden, Brill, 1996.

46. We shall see it again when we discuss the night at Troas (§II.2 below) and the date of the Last Supper (chap. II, §II.1).

47. As a result, there is an annual deviation of about 1.25 days. To catch up without breaking the rhythm of the Sabbaths, it is necessary to add a week from time to time. The shortest cycle at the end of which the deviation adds up to a whole number of weeks is 28 years, giving 5 weeks to add. The correction would be precise if the annual deviation were exactly 1.25 days, but in fact the method of catching up means that every 100 years there is about one day too many (cf. the Gregorian calendar which takes this into account), or, alternatively, at the end of three cycles, so after 84 years; since the unit of measurement is always the week, it would be necessary to subtract one week from the system of correction once in about every 21 cycles (588 years). We do not know what system of correction the Essenes used for a basic cycle of 28 years, and still less for the deviation every century, but it is interesting to note that the rab. trad., which uses a very different luni-solar calendar beginning in autumn (Tishri), has preserved a special blessing, said on 1 Nisan every 28 years (*BBer* 59b), expressing very clearly that it marks the return of the same astral conjunction. That shows plainly that the system of *Jubilees* functioned in reality and was not merely theoretical.

30 days and one of 31), always begins on a Wednesday (1 Nisan), so the eve of Passover (14 Nisan) is a Tuesday, and Pentecost falls on a Sunday, the 15th day of the third month. This supposes that the counting of the fifty days until Pentecost, from "the day after the Sabbath" according to Lev 23:15, begins not on 16 Nisan, as in the rabbinic tradition, which takes the day of Passover to be the Sabbath referred to, but from Sunday 26, that is to say, from the day after the Sabbath (here Saturday) which follows the end of the week of Unleavened Bread.[48] So it is the *second* Sabbath after Passover, but the *first* for the purposes of counting the days to Pentecost. In this sense it can be called the "second-first."

This explanation is plausible, but it can be improved. In fact, if the episode is supposed to occur just after Passover (around April), the corn is far from ripe, so what the disciples do is odd. It is worth noting then that the calendar of *Jubilees*, or at least one of its variants,[49] contains a series of successive Pentecosts (periods of fifty days), falling on a Sunday every seven weeks; on the first, the first-fruits of the wheat are offered (in the form of bread), on the second, the first-fruits of the grape (new wine, must), then of the olive (oil), etc. In such a system, the expression "second-first" can be understood even more simply as the *first* Sabbath of the *second* cycle, *i.e.* the Sabbath following the first Pentecost. In this setting, the disciples gather corn which has not yet been harvested at a time when it is properly ripe (in June), and, what is more, legally available, since the first-fruits of this same corn have just been presented. Attention can then be given to the Pharisees' question, that is to say on the observance of the Sabbath and the meaning of a symbolic transgression in order to eat the fruits of the new year, which is a metaphor for the coming of the Kingdom.[50]

Without the Essene literature, this variant would be perfectly unintelligible. In the NT, even taken together with later Christian texts, it can only be understood in terms of a remote Jewish context. It should, then, be regarded as original; in which case, its disappearance can easily be explained by the disuse in later Christianity of the calendar of reference.[51]

48. For more concerning the controversies over the date of Pentecost, see chap. VII, §III.1.

49. Attested among Philo's Therapeutae (cf. chap. VII, §III.2), and also in 11 QT 18–22 & 43, 4 QMMT A.

50. As emerges from another long reading of the WT in v. 5, where Jesus sees someone working on the Sabbath, and says: "If you know what you are doing, blessed are you; if you do not, you are accursed and a Law-breaker."

51. Other long variants of the WT of Luke will be mentioned below: 6:5, which has a rabbinic parallel (cf. chap. V, §II.1); 22:9 (cf. chap. II, §II.3).

3. Rabbinic Texts and Qumran Documents

These two collections are very different from one another. They do, however, have one thing in common: they were not intended to be published. In one case, there is a reforming sect, access to which is strictly controlled; in the other, emphasis is placed on the oral tradition, and so on the relationship of master and disciple. It is worth pointing out that the whole of rabbinic literature is pretty well unintelligible for an unprepared *reader*, with all the good will in the world: it takes for granted an oral teaching. We shall be able to put this common feature, namely esoteric teaching, into a context when we have taken a look at each of the two groups in turn.

Josephus describes at length the Essenes and their usages as one party among others, with several tendencies. Viewed from within, their intention is at once more precise and more ambitious. In the *Community Rule* (1 QS), which has a complex literary history,[52] the members are to separate themselves from perverse folk and begin by going into the desert, in order to rediscover the practice of the "first ordinances" (8:1-16a and 9:3–10:8a); thus it is a return to the sources, that is, to the gift of the Law at Sinai in the desert. At the same time there is an esoteric side which is stressed: the doctrines (in particular the times) must be hidden from the perverse (9:12 f.), that is, from anyone who does not belong to the group. The belief that the community alone has the true Covenant (5:8, 20; 6:15) is expressed in liturgical worship,[53] which had an eschatological dimension, as in the *Appendix to the Rule* (1 QSa) and the *Temple Scroll* (11 QT). The observance laid down is defined in relation to the law of Moses, but mediated by "what the prophets have revealed by the Holy

52. Cf. the analysis in four stages of Jerome Murphy-O'Connor, "La genèse littéraire de la *Règle de la Communauté*," *RB* 76 (1969), p. 528–549, and the additional remarks of Jean Pouilly, *La règle de la communauté de Qumrân. Son évolution littéraire* (CRB, 17), Paris, Gabalda, 1976.

53. Jerome Murphy-O'Connor, *RB* 75 (1968), p. 443–444, reviewing B. Gärtner, *The Temple and the Community in Qumran and the New Testament*, Cambridge University Press, 1965, holds that the ideal of prayer and an irreproachable life is sufficient to explain a special presence of God and that Temple symbolism is purely literary. This view is, however, too Pauline: for Paul, the community is a Temple (presence of God), and so the Christian life has in itself a sacrificial value (Rom 12:1; 1 Cor 3:16-17; Phil 2:17). J. Pouilly, *op. cit.*, p. 88 rightly thinks that there is more: restoration by observance of the covenant of Sinai, with Tent of Meeting in the desert (Exod 25:8, etc.); as well as a moral ideal, there is a continuation of ritual (in particular the "purity"), and the hope of a Temple restored and purified (cf. 11 QT), of a new Jerusalem (2 QJNar) and of a restoration for the priests (1 QSb 4:25-26). The fulfillment of the sacrifices is then the ultimate overall goal, which comes close to 1 Pet 2:5 (baptism makes the Christian a living stone of the Temple), for whom sacrifice remains also the goal (of the Temple), cf. Jerome Murphy-O'Connor, *Paul on Preaching*, London and New York, Sheed & Ward, 1964, p. 292, n. 6.

Spirit":[54] the community—and it alone—has the inspired interpretation, in continuity with the prophets.[55] In other words, the Law comprises two domains: laws which are clear and transparent, explicit in Scripture and accessible to all, and laws which are hidden and can be correctly interpreted only by the community.[56] The interpretation in question is indeed *scriptural*, but divinely inspired and taking account of changing circumstances. These laws remain internal and are handed on by the masters,[57] so are not, properly speaking, published. This means that the texts found in the caves near Qumran should be regarded as essentially private and incomplete memoranda, and not as published works, which may explain why many of the non-biblical documents among them do not have the appearance of finished products. Still, they have been carefully preserved, even if not in a *geniza*, which would show that they were regarded as important. Finally, among the solemn engagements undertaken by those admitted by the Essenes as new members, according to Josephus, is an oath not to divulge anything concerning the community (*J.W.* 2 §141).

The central element on which the precepts proper to the group converge, is the "purity," which is none other than a community meal taken in very strict conditions of purity,[58] and to which we will return (chap. II, §II.5). In the same way, the ancestors of the rabbinic tradition are described as eating profane food in a state of Levitical purity. This provides an intrinsic link which we will develop later on (chap. V, §I.1).

In the rabbinic tradition, the Torah, which is for "all Israel," comprises the written text and the oral tradition, the two pillars of which are respectively the Pentateuch and the *Mishnah*. The ultimate purpose of the Torah and the precepts is the acceptance of the "yoke of the Kingdom of Heaven" and the "yoke of the commandments," which *liberates* from the

54. There is therefore a very simple trinitarian structure: 1. God (in general, Creator); 2. Moses (in particular, with Covenant: Torah, Scriptures); 3. the Spirit (who applies Covenant, Torah, Scriptures to the present *in the community*, through prophets or authorized teachers). For the rabbinic tradition, inspiration properly speaking (prophetic) ceased with Scripture, but the masters have the monopoly of present-day interpretation (legal and/or homiletic); the structure remains ternary. This aspect will be developed in chap. VII, §IV.1.

55. And not the whole body of the people, cf. chap. V, §I.3 on proselyte baptism. The community claims to be the new people, the renewed Covenant, cf. chap. V, §I. A similar claim will be made in the NT by the first Christians, cf. chap. III, §II.1.

56. Respectively נגלה and נסתר, cf. the synthesis of Laurence H. Schiffman, *The Halakha at Qumran* (SJLA, 16), Leiden, Brill, 1975. Cf. also chap. V, §II.4.

57. Sages, who "cause to understand" (משכיל, cf. 1 QS 9:12 s.). Similarly among the Therapeutae, cf. Philo, *Vita contempl.* §31, 75.

58. Cf. Hannah K. Harrington, *The Impurity Systems of Qumran and the Rabbis. Biblical Foundations* (SBL Dissertation Series, 143), Atlanta (Georgia), Scholars Press, 1993, App. II.

yoke of nature.[59] The point of departure is expressed at the beginning of the tractate *Abot*: "Moses received the Torah from[60] Sinai, then transmitted it. . . ." Thus Sinai appears as an absolute beginning, both for the written and for the oral instruction. However, the distinction between written Torah and oral Torah, both having equal rank, appears clearly for the first time with Hillel and Shammai, so at the time of Herod (*BShab* 31a), that is, well after the rise of the Pharisees according to Josephus (*Ant.* 13 §171 f., at the time of John Hyrcanus). This is the period in which, according to rabbinic tradition, the internal controversies begin. Nowhere are the doctors said to be "inspired," except perhaps collectively.[61] Another passage speaks of irreducible differences between the oral and the written instruction (*MḤag* 1:8): "The *halakhot* [practical rules][62] for the dissolution of vows [or perhaps: "for prayer"] flourish in the air and have nothing in which they are rooted; the *halakhot* on the Sabbath, pilgrimage sacrifices, and sacrileges are like mountains hanging from a hair, with little Scripture and many *halakhot*; as for lawsuits, the service of the Temple, clean and unclean, forbidden unions, they have something to lean on. All these categories[63] are major areas of Torah."

The internal unity of the Torah finds expression only in the oneness of God who gave it. Nowhere is it expressed in terms of a *logical* coherence, which would amount to subordinating God to rational human thought. Outside homiletics, there is no trace of any attempt to reduce everything to simple principles, not even to the Decalogue, which is nevertheless the charter of the Covenant. According to tradition, the

59. *MBer* 2:2, cf. Ephraim E. Urbach, *The Halakha, Its Sources and Development*, Tel Aviv, 1984.

60. That is to say "starting from Sinai" (מסיני), and not "at Sinai": Sinai is the starting point of a process.

61. According to *TSoṭa* 13:2 (cf. *BYoma* 9a), the era of the prophets is closed, and "heavenly echoes" (בת קול, lit.: "echo," cf. Acts 2:2) have become the only direct channel of communication with God; for *BErub* 13b, a voice from heaven determined that the *halakha* would be as the School of Hillel, even though the School of Shammai is also divinely inspired. However, Yehoshua (end of the 1st cent., already mentioned in connection with Alexandrian methods) judges that the Torah is not in heaven but close to the heart (cf. Deut 30:12), and so that these echoes have no legal force (cf. *BBabaM* 59b); this is still the prevailing opinion. On the links between divination and this expression (which originally designated a voice heard without any speaker being seen), cf. Lieberman II:194 f.

62. The terms *halakha* and *agada (haggada)* are defined in chap. V, §II.4.

63. Understanding הן והן (lit: "the ones and the others") with *BḤag* 11b; the mss of the *Mishnah* and *YḤag* 2:7, p. 5b have הן הן (lit: "these are those that . . . ," *viz.* the last category), which *could* imply (but not necessarily) that the true *halakha* is that which has a scriptural basis, in which case there is a difficulty, cf. *Tosefta kifshuṭah* 3:470. This hesitation corresponds, however, to the twofold origin of the rab. trad., cf. chap. V, §III.1.

Torah contains 613 precepts;[64] they are not specified, but the important thing to note is that they are not put in any hierarchical order.

The differences from the Essenes are obvious. Yet the method of handing on teaching that is proper to the Tannaites allows a comparison to be made. The body of oral laws, or *Mishnah* in the broad sense,[65] has been known for a long time in written form, but, in the first centuries of our era, it was not supposed to be written down; yet we are told that the doctors wrote down all or part of the *Mishnah* for their private use.[66]

The contradiction is more apparent than real when the facts are looked at from the angle of *publication*. In the ancient world, when books were to be distributed rapidly, they were entrusted to specialized workshops where a number of copyists together wrote down a text which was dictated to them.[67] In the case of the Bible, however, it was necessary to copy a manuscript which was read and not dictated, because the holiness of the book was expressed even in details of spelling which were imperceptible to the ear;[68] such a process was certainly safer, but slower. Another way of publishing books, especially for those that were important and meant to last, was to deposit them in a temple, a library, or a public record office, where copies would be made, often bearing at the end a colophon indicating the origin and kind of the deposited *exemplar*.[69] The *Letter of Aristeas*, already referred to, can be regarded as a sort of expanded colophon, implying, in an exceptional case, the deposit of the original *and* of a translation.[70] Eusebius, who was an expert in bibliography, reports that Josephus was held in such esteem by the Romans that his works "were judged worthy of the libraries" (*Hist. eccl.* 3.9.2), that is

64. Or 365 prohibitions and 248 prescriptions (*BMak* 23b), cf. chap. V, §II.4.

65. Including the *Mishnah* properly so called (משנתנו "our *Mishnah*") and various other Tannaitic collections (*baraita*, from מתניתא ברייתא "external *Mishnah*"). The term designates the repetition, and so the teaching (cf. below); the related Aramaic term תנא (*tanna*, "repeater") appears towards the beginning of the 2nd century. In Greek, the Christian authors have translated δευτέρωσις, (in parallel with the LXX, which translates משנה תורה in Josh 8:32 by δευτερονόμιον), cf. Wilhelm Bacher, *Die exegetische Terminologie der jüdischen Traditionsliteratur*, Leipzig, 1899, I:122 f.

66. Cf. Epstein, p. 700 f.

67. Cf. Lieberman II:85 f.

68. Cf. *YMeg* 4:1, p. 74d (and *BMeg* 18b); to check the copy, it was pronounced while reading (and copying) according to the *ketib*, and not the *qere*. In Matt 5:18 Jesus insists on the letters which cannot be heard, thereby implying that the integral text and the correct reading are necessary, cf. chap. II, §I.4.

69. Cf. Elias J. Bickerman, "The Colophon of the Greek Book of Esther," *JBL* 63 (1944), p. 339–362.

70. Tertullian, *Apol.* §18, Justin, *I Apol.* 31.5.

to say, of imperial protection.[71] Rabbinic tradition refers to this usage rather freely when it records that Moses made thirteen copies of the Torah, one for each tribe and one to deposit in the Ark of the Covenant, expressly in order to prevent any counterfeit. Equally, when the Jews of Galilee hesitate to adopt the feast of Purim, for fear of divulging the Book of Esther, Mardochai and Esther in person declare that the narrative is "already deposited in the archives." In these legends,[72] the act of deposition is itself an act of publication, which places the text beyond further possibility of editing.[73] Nothing of the sort is to be found in the case of the *Mishnah*. Numerous talmudic discussions debate the text and sometimes correct it in the interpretation, but there is never any question of checking it from a written archival copy; variants are indicated only by expressions such as: "we teach (or: "some teach") [. . .], whereas others teach[74] [. . .]." These are the divergences typical of oral teaching. In other words, there is not yet an authoritative *written* publication.

What might an *oral* publication be? The *Mishnah* was known by heart and recited by a repeater *(Tanna)* in front of the masters, preferably without attempting to understand it, which was the best way of avoiding alterations.[75] This system is in fact the end result of a fairly complex process, which certain texts allow us to reconstruct in the context of school debates. The pupils had personal notes derived from various sources, and during an editing session, the master, with a view to sorting out[76] the tradition, asked them what they read in their notes and what they

71. In *Life* §363, FJ says himself that *J.W.* was published by order of Titus, at the expense of the public treasury.

72. Cf. *DtR* 9:9 et *YMeg* 1:7, p. 70d. The technical term is כתוב ומונח "written and deposited."

73. In *Meg Taan*, 4 Tammuz commemorates the abolition of a "book of decrees" of the Sadducees (who, according to FJ, receive only the written instruction), which has been "written and deposited" (כתוב ומונח); the editor supposes that the event took place in the reign of Alexandra Salome (76–67 B.C.), cf. Hans Lichtenstein, "Die Fastenrolle," *HUCA* 8 (1931), p. 295 f. However, the publication of certain Qumran documents shows that the צדוקים of the rab. sources often coincide with the "Zadokites" of CD, who are in fact a branch of the Essenes, cf. Yaakov Sussman, "The History of *Halakha* and the Dead Sea Scrolls—Preliminary Observations on *Miqṣat Maʿaṣeh ha-Torah* (4 QMMT)," *Tarbiz* 49 (1989), p. 11–76; the problem, which is new and not yet solved, is to know why Josephus' Sadducees and the sectarian Zadokites have the same name, and to distinguish them in the sources, cf. id., *Postscript*, in: 4 QMMT (DJD, 10), p. 200. Cf. also chap. III, §IV.

74. אנן תנינן, אית תניי תני etc., cf. Epstein, p. 76 f.

75. Cf. *BSoṭa* 22a. Likewise, in manuscripts generally, the involuntary (and meaningless) slips made by copyists are easier to pick up than learned corrections, revisions, etc., which are meant to improve the text, but cover over its previous state.

76. The terms employed are: סדר in Heb. (lit. "order"), תקן in Aram. (rendered by ישר in Heb.) and διορθοῦν in Gr., with the idea of correcting, cf. W. Bacher, *Terminologie*, I:204.

knew from his own teaching or from other traditions, and challenged them to discussion. In this way the different opinions and their sources were set out, including sometimes an earlier teaching of the master, who had since changed his mind. The first step was to distinguish the received traditions *(lemmata)* from the commentaries of the masters, which were more or less mixed together in the notes. In the second step, after debate,[77] the master fixed his own teaching in which he combined, with due consideration, the traditions *and* the commentaries which were to be maintained. Editing, properly speaking, consisted in having the result memorized by several repeaters present, who repeated it to one another.[78] At this point, the teaching thus prepared could "enter into the academy," which was the equivalent of "being deposited in a library." The sources allow the identification of several "editors" of this type, including Yehoshua, at the end of the 1st century, who was trained in the Alexandrian casuistic;[79] Aqiba, who promoted the literal Hebrew sense and the alignment of the written and oral instruction, at the beginning of

77. The question arises whether the famous "School of Hillel" and "School of Shammai" (בית הלל, בית שמאי), to which no doctor is ever clearly and properly attached (cf. Wilhelm Bacher, *Die Aggada der Tannaiten*, Straßburg, 1903, p. 11 f.), are not simply the results of organized debates, the class being divided into two camps arguing according to different methods. The Ancients were familiar with contradictory debates practiced as exercises in the schools of rhetoric, cf. Paolo Garuti, *Alle origini dell'omiletica cristiana. La lettera agli Ebrei. Note di analisi retorica* (Studium Biblicum Franciscanum, Analecta 38), Jerusalem, Franciscan Printing Press, 1995, p. 11–31, esp. p. 27–29.

78. A saying (*BErub* 54b) tells that Moses, regarded as the author of the oral tradition, used to recite the *Mishnah* thus edited (סדורה) to Aaron, his sons, the Elders, etc.; in this way the authority of Moses is conferred on this method of oral editing, which is essential. In fact, the different traditions and teachings which the Tannaites seek to put together are not in the first place the discoveries of any particular sage, but result from the coalescence of the traditions of different brotherhoods (all regarded as originating with Moses, cf. *YPea* 2:6, p. 17a). The building of this synthesis was undertaken after the war of 70 (Gamaliel II) then after that of 135 in Galilee, cf. chap. V, §I.2. All this esoteric teaching should be compared with the statement of 4 Esd 14:18-47, that Esdras, restoring the Law, wrote 94 books: the 24 of the canon *to be published* (corresponding to the MT), and 70 to be communicated only to the sages, in secret; the number 70, corresponding to the Elders of Num 11:16 and found also in the "70 aspects (ע' פנים) of the Torah," designates an oral teaching both stable and multiform, whether it was really written or not. These "books," endowed with the highest authority, are to be distinguished from another category of writings mentioned by FJ after the 22 official books, and which have a *lesser* authority because they are more recent. Here it is a question of a more or less definite list of annexed writings, like those preserved by the LXX or even the *Letter of Aristeas*; FJ makes the same use of them as he does of the Bible. On the Hebrew "canon," cf. chap. V, §II.3.

79. Cf. Lieberman II:92, with references and indications of the customs of Alexandrian editors. Yehoshua was one of those who congratulated Aquila on his literal translation of the Bible, cf. chap. V, §II.2.

the 2nd century; and Judah the Prince, who edited the *Mishnah* in its present form at the beginning of the 3rd century. In other words, the *Mishnah* went through several successive editions, not without controversies, and several layers can often be discerned.

A further important consequence of this technique is that at the moment of publication the editor lost control of his own work; *BAbZ* 35b says explicitly that it can no longer be changed. Even the editor cannot go back on what he himself has done: so it is reported (*YBabaM* 4:1, p. 9c) that Judah, after editing the *Mishnah*, wanted to make a change, but his own son opposed it. However, the repeaters had to be faithful and precise. The best were designated as "meticulous," the same term used by the scribes of Alexandria to designate a copy that had been checked;[80] the meticulousness consisted not only in repeating exactly the official teaching, but also in being able to add the oral notes indicating the authority of certain opinions, rather like critical scholia outside the text.[81] Here it is interesting to observe that in Acts 18:25 the oral teaching of Apollos, who came from Alexandria, is first described as "meticulous," then checked and corrected by Aquila and Priscilla, so that his sayings become "more meticulous"; Aquila and Priscilla act as "correctors" of an *oral* edition (cf. chap. VI, §II.1).

As for the notes of *halakha* which many possessed, they were only "secret scrolls"[82] or tablets,[83] without any authority other than that of their owner. Notes taken in the course of lectures or debates bore the name of "memoranda"; in particular, it was not possible to communicate them to a third party for direct study without oral teaching.[84] This reality and terminology throw light not only on the status of the Qumran documents, but also on that of the gospels. Justin, as we have seen, does not speak of "books," but always of "memoranda of the apostles"; they were therefore disciples' notes, enjoying at most the authority of the apostles, but not of Jesus (cf. 1 Cor 7:10 f.). We come back, by another way, to the primacy

80. דווקני, cf. *BYeb* 43a, corresponding to ἠκριβωμένη (βίβλος). The "corrector" (or editor) is the διορθωτής.

81. Cf. Epstein, p. 680.

82. *BShab* 6b, *BBabaM* 92a. The term used (מגילת סתרים) is found in the Qumran texts where it designates "secret teachings," *i.e.* not to be made public without control.

83. The term used, פנקס (pronounced *pinqas*, cf. *YMaas* 2:4, p. 49d, *BMen* 70a), is the transcription of πίναξ "tablet"; it later took on the sense of "notebook, personal collection." Sometimes the wall of the classroom was used as a writing surface, cf. *YKil* 1:1, p. 27a.

84. *BTem* 14b, which specifically states that to "write down the *halakha* is like burning the Torah"; according to *TShab* 13:4, it is the same for the blessings, cf. *Tosefta kifshuṭah* III:205.

of the oral teaching and the subordinate nature of the written text, which we have seen very clearly with Irenaeus.

We have been observing the features characteristic of the preservation of an oral teaching; they give it a private dimension totally different from the publications of Philo and Josephus which we will examine in a moment. They can very probably be projected on to the Essenes, by simple formal likeness. That raises the question of a possible relationship between the Essenes and the rabbinic traditions; such a relationship existed, as we will show by way of other approaches (chap. V, §I).

4. Philo and Josephus

One was a philosopher, the other an historian, but what they had in common was the intention to spread public knowledge of Scripture, duly provided with commentary, that is, to disseminate a tradition without any control over the reader. In both cases, the author was an important and well-known person, but has left no following that can be traced to him.

The relations between Philo and Christianity do not go back to the beginnings. It is true that Philo has more or less clear affinities with certain parts of the NT (John, Heb, Paul), but against a background of obvious differences.[85] Until the end of the 2nd century, no known Christian writing shows direct acquaintance with him. Eventually, he is rediscovered by the Alexandrians (Clement, Origen) who make explicit use of him, especially for their allegorical exegesis, and so ensure that his writings will be preserved. Then Eusebius gives him permanence *("Philo christianus")* by identifying the Therapeutae as proto-Christians, and by popularizing the legend of Philo's meeting with St. Peter at Rome. In the west, Jerome writes him up as one of the great Christian figures. But already in the 4th century, there begin to be suspicions of heresy, naturally in the context of contemporary quarrels, especially over Arianism, which also arose in Alexandria.

The question can be put another way. Was Philo's influence on Christianity more than purely ornamental or casual? In fact, the only mention of Alexandria in Acts concerns Apollos, "powerful in the Scriptures" (Acts 18:26); he knew "the things about Jesus" and the baptism of John, which is already something, but had to be taken in hand by Aquila, who taught him more precisely "the Way."[86] It almost seems as though

85. Cf. David T. Runia, *Philo in Early Christian Literature* (CRINT, III/3), Minneapolis, Fortress Press, 1993.

86. According to the WT, whereas the AT minimizes the difference and does not disclose the fact that Apollos received his teaching about Jesus at Alexandria. This passage is discussed in chap. VI, §II.1.

Alexandria is avoided, but if so, that should probably not be put down to problems over Gnosticism.[87] Philo's outlook is very different from that of the first Christians. For him, the Bible, or more exactly the Pentateuch, is not first and foremost a code, but a book of philosophy giving access to truth, which exists in the world of ideas.[88] Yet the empirical world is not false, but, being corruptible, is only part of the truth. The law of Moses, or *nomos*, is the law of the world, and has the unity of a *logos*; for that reason it begins with Creation. This view has Stoic roots, but is attached to the utopia of a future ideal city: in this sense, Philo is heir to Hellenism, which, from the time of Alexander the Great, sought to reduce the sphere of "barbarism" through cultural expansion. It follows that only the one who observes the Law is truly an inhabitant of the world, or *cosmopolitês*.[89] Further, it is necessary to show the profound unity of the Law, which Philo does by trying to bring everything back to the Decalogue, in which the number ten is itself unique.

In the prologue of his treatise on the Ten Commandments, Philo wonders why the Law was given in the desert. Indeed, for the Greek historians, the law is not an abstract entity; lawgivers were founders of cities and well established places of worship, or their successors. For example, Hecataeus of Abdera, writing in Egypt in the 3rd century B.C.,[90] mentions that Moses, being a lawgiver, founded Jerusalem; even Strabo, a contemporary of Herod and Philo, ignores the desert and regards Moses as an Egyptian priest who founded a new cult at Jerusalem.[91] Philo's question, then, is entirely to the point, for it was not normal that a law should not be strictly tied to a territory and its inhabitants. In reply, he puts forward various reflections about the deterioration of cities and the need to restore civilization from the desert (*Decalog.* §2 f.). The theme of the decadence

87. Cf. S. R. Llewellyn et al., *New Documents Illustrating Early Christianity*, 7, Macquarie University (N. S. W., Austr.), The Ancient History Documentary Research Centre, 1994, p. 245 f.

88. Cf. Yehoshua Amir, "The Decalogue According to Philo," in: Ben-Zion Segal & Gershon Levi (Eds.), *The Ten Commandments in History and Tradition*, Jerusalem, 1990, p. 121–160.

89. According to *Abrah.* §5, 16, 46, 261, 276, *Migrat.* §130, *Vita Mosis* 1 §28, 158, 162, *Spec. leg.* 4 §149–150, the vocation of the Law is to be the definitive legislation for every city. This vision is inspired by the Hellenistic ideal and is entirely different from the notion of the Noachide precepts, in force for all nations (since Noah), but distinct from the Covenant with Abraham and Moses, cf. chap. V, §II.

90. Cf. *Greek and Latin* I:26, citing Diodorus, *BH*, 40. 3. In the same spirit, Joshua acts as a lawgiver when he fixes a law on a slab during the consecration of an altar on Ebal-Garizim (Josh 8:32), or draws up a statute at the assembly at Shechem (24:25); the legislation is tied to a place.

91. *Geographus*, 16.2.35–37, cf. *Greek and Latin*, I:294 f.

of every civilization, with all its misdeeds concentrated in the city, is a commonplace taken over from Hesiod. Not so, however, Philo's explanation of why the law was given in the desert, since it pinpoints in history a revelation, that is, an intervention of God, even if that revelation consists in showing the profound reality of nature which has become opaque to human eyes. Further, history has for him a different meaning from that which it has for the Stoics. According to Philo, after the foundation of Jerusalem there was no exile, but rather a voluntary emigration in order to spread the Law to the ends of the earth;[92] at the same time, the flow of pilgrims back to the center assured the unity of the people. In his eyes, the effort of proselytism should continue, at least in theory.[93]

These views are obviously far removed from the outlook of the first disciples, who at first had no overall program, as we shall see at greater length (chap. VI): their mission expanded only through opposition and persecution, as even the final synthesis of Acts (governed by 1:8) brings out clearly. Moreover, their idea was not to spread the law of Moses (cf. Acts 15:21), but to proclaim an event, and beginning with the Jews. On the other hand, it is easy to foresee how, during a phase of reflection following the unplanned beginnings, Philo could be of help in interpreting the development of Christianity.[94]

Josephus, in the preface to the *Antiquities* (1 §3), explains that it is necessary to publish certain important facts which are useful to know, such as those recorded in "the sacred library." What that contains is not mythology, even though it goes back much earlier in time than the Greek historians (1 §22 f.). Josephus faces a twofold problem. First, he takes the greatest care to justify his enterprise of divulging the national traditions before strangers; to this end he invokes, by way of the *Letter of Aristeas*, the precedent of the Septuagint, which enjoyed the patronage of the high priest of Jerusalem (1 §9 f.). Next, he tries to clarify the status of the Mosaic law. As it turns out, his ideas are simply borrowed from the Stoics:[95] the world has been going downhill since Creation, thanks to the misdeeds of the descendants of Cain, who invented the city, weights and measures,

92. On the model of Greek colonization (ἀποικία), cf. *In Flaccum* §242 f. This is an expansion of a theme in Hecataeus of Abdera which will be taken up by FJ (cf. *Ag.Ap.* 1 §187, *Ant.* 11 §347, etc.), where he celebrates the benefits of the emigration *to Egypt*.

93. There is a comparable idea in the rab. trad. (*BPes* 87b): the exile took place solely so that Israel could spread monotheism among the nations; here, however, it is a question not of the law of Moses but of the Noachide precepts, cf. chap. V, §II.2.

94. Whence a somewhat dualistic apologetics (Origen, Eusebius), cf. chap. V, §VI.

95. At the moment when he declares that he has chosen to conduct himself according to the Pharisee tendency (*Life* §12), FJ explains that the latter is close to the Stoic school (known as that "of the Porch," αἵρεσις στοική). Cf. also chap. III, §IV.

and all sorts of harmful arts. But the law of Moses does not date from the beginnings, since it came on the scene at a rather late point in history. Josephus cannot hide this fact in his biblical paraphrase, but he adds a speech of Moses in which the ancient figures, from Adam to Jacob, serve to link Creation and Sinai (3 §83). In the prologue, he tries hard to get round the difficulty in several ways. First, he invokes the antiquity of Moses, "born two thousand years ago, at a time so remote that the poets have not even dared to put back that far the birth of the gods, let alone the deeds of men and their laws" (*Ant.* 1 §16). After this side-step, which brings Moses close to the beginnings and places him before the known civilizations, he explains that in fact the Law and the political constitution which flows from it are the fruit of Moses' meditation on the nature of God and His works.

By this move, Josephus puts the origins of the Law extremely early, but at the same time he trivializes revelation, since anyone can meditate deeply on nature like Moses. As civilizations have declined since the Golden Age, the unchanging depths of nature have become less perceptible, except for certain seers (the prophets); so it is logical to put the best of contemplatives as early as possible in time. It is thus apparent that the divine law is subordinated to nature, which fits in well with a rigorous monotheism, but leaves little room for anything specific to Israel. So there is a contradiction, which Josephus cannot escape: if God has expressed Himself entirely in Creation, then notions of Covenant, promise, election, which are nothing if not historical, become problematic, and Josephus quietly drops them,[96] not to speak of his efforts to show how the Law harmonizes with nature.[97] As a result, in contrast to Philo, he has no

96. Cf. Étienne Nodet, "Flavius Josèphe: Création et histoire," *RB* 100 (1993), p. 4–40.

97. He mentions several examples (candelabra 3 §146; temple and high priestly vestments 3 §179 f., etc.), but without any overall view; in fact, he had the idea of writing a *Treatise on the Causes*, but it never saw the light of day (despite giving a plan *Ant.* 20 §268). He ignores allegorical exegesis, which might suggest that he was not acquainted with the works of Philo, cf. Samuel Sandmel, *Philo of Alexandria; An Introduction*, New York, 1979, p. 23 f. Sandmel, after considering the opinions of I. Heinemann, S. Belkin, L. Feldman and others, denies any direct link between Philo and FJ (even *Ag.Ap.* 2), for Philo's allegory is all of a piece, and goes well beyond the undeniable but sporadic contacts which commentators have noted. This conclusion is broadly correct, but needs to be nuanced: in *Ant.* 1 §34, FJ has a sentence remarkably similar to that of Philo, *Op. mundi*, §134. Moreover, his prologue ventures into philosophy (*Ant.* 1 §25) and has so many affinities with that of Philo's work on origins as to lead one to think that he had at least consulted it. Perhaps he intended his projected *Treatise on the Causes* to make a name for himself in the same field. Finally, though he never cites Philo as an author, he knows him as a famous philosopher (*Ant.* 18 §259 f.).

clear teaching about spreading the Law throughout the world and is somewhat bothered by the fact that the best of political constitutions, divinely inspired, is not that of Rome, the best of empires.[98] His intention is fundamentally *political*.[99] This can be seen in the way he explains the essential character of the sacred writings when presenting the testament of Moses (*Ant.* 4 §194): everything is ordered to the life of the city, which is to be rational; the observance of laws is opposed to empty cults as also to mythological ravings. Accordingly, Josephus judges that Plato, who banned the poets from the city because of the danger of the irrational (*Rep.* 3.398a), drew inspiration from Moses.[100] In *Against Apion*, writing with greater commitment, he briskly paints a broad outline of the Jewish law, striving to justify it by showing the suitability of its various points, and arguing that it is orientated towards philanthropy, justice, resistance to adversity, and contempt for death (*Ag.Ap.* 2 §145), contrary to the calumnies of its detractors. He insists on the extreme severity of its punishments, which, according to him, shows that the customs can really be observed.[101] Above all, he avoids any suggestion of particularism: for example, circumcision and abstinence from pork are reasonable, since the priests of Egypt, the wisest and most pious, are circumcised and abstain from pork (*Ag.Ap.* 2 §137), etc.

Josephus has a number of contacts with the NT: census of Quirinius, differences between Pharisees and Sadducees, uprisings of Judas the Galilean and Theudas, Felix, Festus, Agrippa, Drusilla, Berenice, etc. These contacts raise the question of some sort of dependence or common source, but do not conceal the fact that his perspective is profoundly different, since he sets aside any notion of historical revelation and systematically discredits anything to do with Messianism.

98. Cf. Christiane Saulnier, "Flavius Josèphe et la propagande flavienne," *RB* 96 (1989), p. 545–562, who compares *J.W.* 6 §288–315 and Tacitus, *Histories*, 5.13.2–7; both argue that the victories of Vespasian and Titus in the Orient conferred legitimacy on their dynasty, and both narrate certain facts which could lead up to an *evocatio*: the god of Jerusalem, tiring of his own people, is ready to be invited to the Roman Capitol.

99. For an evaluation of FJ as an historian, cf. discussion and bibliography in Robert L. Webb, *John the Baptizer and Prophet. A Socio-Historical History* (JSNT, SS 62), Sheffield, JSOT Press, 1991, p. 41 f.

100. *Ag.Ap.* 2 §242 f.; the same rumor was already attested by Aristobulus (presumably the one mentioned in 2 Macc 1:10), cf. below.

101. He refers especially to daily life and avoids general principles (he makes no mention of the Ten Commandments, whose ethical part is not very original). Several laws and penalties which he mentions have, as commentators have remarked, an Essene ring; Porphyry, *De abstinentia* 4.11, who knew FJ's works, thought that he was an Essene. It is not at all unlikely that FJ, in an ethical perspective, chose the Essene ideal as a point of reference (he shows the same preference in *J.W.* 2 §119 f.), but takes care not to associate any ritual or social particularity with it.

In respect of oral teaching, both Philo and Josephus insist on the teaching and study of the Law.[102] Josephus points out several times that one of the characteristics of the Pharisees is the observance of "ancestral customs," which are not derived from Scripture, and he states that he himself is attached to this party. But when he expounds the Law, the sole authority that he indicates is the Bible. To be exact, he mentions many non-biblical usages, some of which are to be found in the rabbinic tradition, but he never suggests that he has any source other than the written instruction. One reason for this attitude may be a desire to show that the Jewish law is really ancient, but at the same time transparent and accessible to all, with no esoteric domain (cf. *Ant.* 3 §318). For his part, Philo first remarks that the patriarchs before Moses are incarnations of the Law:[103] the true sage is the one who knows how to govern without relying on any written text,[104] that is, without any external precept. Moses is at once king, priest and prophet, or even a "living law endowed with speech." So there is inspiration, but as a permanent quality *(habitus)*, and not something dictated by an oracle. In other words, for Philo the "unwritten law," universal and in conformity with nature, does not come from outside by way of tradition. This conception is the opposite of the central importance given to the oral tradition by the Pharisees or rabbis, which is not only positive, but also inaccessible outside the relationship of master and disciple. In *Spec. leg* 4 §150, Philo declares that someone who obeys the written laws is not to be congratulated, for he does so by constraint and out of fear of punishment, whereas the observance of the unwritten laws deserves praise, for it proceeds from virtue (cf. also Rom 2:14 f.). A comparison has been suggested with the rabbinic axiom that "the words of the scribes are more important than those of the [written] Torah" (*YSanh* 11:6, p. 30a). In this case it is still, however, a question of another positive element, whereas Philo, although speaking of unwritten customs established by the "men of old," is thinking above all of

102. They underline the importance of study and the weekly synagogue reading (Philo, *Op. mundi* §128; *Ant.* 16 §43, *Ag.Ap.* 2 §175, cf. Luke 4:17, Acts 13:15 and 15:21).

103. *Decal.* §1 f. has a paradoxical formula: νόμους ἀγράφους αἱ ἱεραὶ βίβλοι δηλοῦσιν "the sacred books show unwritten laws."

104. As in Plato, *Polit.*, §202 f. According to *Vita Mosis* 1 §162 and 2 §4, the king is in law a νόμος ἔμψυχος, cf. André Myre, "Les caractéristiques de la loi mosaïque selon Philon d'Alexandrie," *Science et Esprit* 27 (1975), p. 35–69. According to *Spec. leg.* 4 §149, one who observes the unwritten law is praiseworthy, for "the virtue that he shows is freely willed," cf. Isaak Heinemann, "Die Lehre vom ungeschriebenen Gesetz im jüdischen Schrifttum," *HUCA* 4 (1927), p. 155, and Ephraim E. Urbach, *The Sages; Their Concepts and Beliefs*, Jerusalem, 1973, p. 291 and nn. 22–24.

education, especially within the family.[105] It is not that he has no place for instruction, but for him the potential universality of the Law implies its transparency.

5. Conclusions: the arcanum

By way of the criteria of publication and publicity, these brief sketches show a very clear difference between Philo and Josephus on the one hand, and Essenes and Tannaites on the other. It is really a difference of *nature*, more important than any agreements or disagreements in respect of content. In fact, behind the question of oral teaching or publication lies another: in the Bible, Creation is fundamentally a work of separation and organization,[106] and the maintenance of clear boundaries is essential for the notions of election and Covenant. Even to translate the Bible posed a serious problem.[107] From this point of view, the work of Philo and Josephus belongs to a new kind of literature, apologetic, whether philosophical or historical; they address whoever wishes to read them, with the very clear idea that the law of Moses, being the best of all, should be known and should inspire every lawgiver. By contrast, the Essenes and the rabbis, taken together, with their oral teaching, are more traditional, since they accentuate the relationship between master and pupil (supported by repetition in the course of worship, where the *Shemaᶜ Israel* already sets out the program). Their characteristic feature is to take oral teaching to an absolute limit, in which the only instruction that exists is oral, not to be divulged to outside circles. That means there is a certain secret, which is not, however, to be confused with systems of initiation into the mystery religions.

105. Cf. references and discussion of André Mosès in *PhA* 25, p. 296, n. 1 and p. 360 f. (exc. 7).

106. Cf. Paul Beauchamp, *Création et séparation; étude exégétique du premier chapitre de la Genèse* (Bibl. de Sciences Religieuses), Paris, Seuil, 1969, p. 57–65.

107. The *Letter of Aristeas* (§314) refers to attempts at translation before the Septuagint, but stresses the danger: since the translators violated a prohibition, they were punished. Aristobulus, Hebrew philosopher and adviser to Ptolemy VI Philometor (181–146), writes to the king that since Plato various fragments had been put into Greek (cited by Eusebius, *Prep. ev.* 13.12.1 f., but the authenticity of the information is doubtful, cf. *Search,* p. 182–188. These rumors are complex, for they seek on the one hand to affirm the antiquity of the biblical text, despite such late translations, whence the emphasis on the prohibition; and at the same time they go in the opposite direction by trying to show that Plato's rational monotheism is derived from the Bible (the common place of the "Greek larceny," cf. Chap VI, §I.1), rather than the other way round, whence the need to have had at least partial translations in circulation at the time of Plato, or even earlier. Cf. also Arthur J. Droge, *Homer or Moses?* (Hermeneutische Untersuchungen zur Theologie, 26), Tübingen, J. B. C. Mohr, 1989, p. 12 f.

In which category should the NT be placed? Once the canon is established, it becomes a book, as public in legal standing as in content, with a message for all. Part of its content consists of legislation, which presupposes a society (the Kingdom) with well-defined boundaries within which, "Whatever you bind will be bound, whatever you loose will be loosed." On the other hand, in Luke's prologue, Theophilus is not just any reader, but a member of the community who has heard the preaching; so what is put before the public is a literature which was originally internal. In the final phase of development, it is appropriate to make a certain comparison with Philo and Josephus, since the Gnostic problem supposes the independence of the written text. However, in the first generations (at least until Irenaeus), the oral aspect was predominant: not only did Jesus write nothing, but his biography remained subordinate to the preaching. Even more, at the beginning, there was no question of a mission to the Gentiles.[108] It is noteworthy that the first Romans visited by Peter, then Paul, Cornelius and Justus, are Godfearers, "close to the synagogue" (Acts 18:7). These visits do, however, cross important boundaries, since the initial mission was a renewal within Judaism, as Jesus himself had said (cf. Matt 10:6); in the final construction of Acts, the way is prepared by the episodes with the Samaritans and with an Ethiopian adherent. At the earliest stage, the more obvious comparison would be with the reforming drive of the Essenes, or even with the zealots, although we are not well informed about their methods of proselytizing. It is less easy to make a comparison with the Tannaitic movement, which consisted, under conditions apparently quite different, of a network of brotherhoods and schools traceable in Judaea after the war of 70, then in Galilee after the war of 135. Their origins and identity will be examined further on (chap. V, §I).

The oral aspect of Christianity lasted after the movement opened up to the Gentiles, but that does not imply that it was secret.[109] Even if there was not yet an official biography of Jesus, Christians wrote on their own

108. This fundamental aspect is developed in chap. VI, §I.3.

109. There was certainly a development, as can be seen from the word μυστήριον (which becomes in Latin *sacramentum*, but analogous to סוד in the documents from the Judaean desert, which implies the idea of foundation, cf. Dan 2:18 f.): there is no doubt that it comes from the mystery religions. In Wis 2:22 etc. it concerns the knowledge of God, with a suggestion of a revelation to the privileged; similarly in Matt 13:11 par. Jesus (the Teacher) distinguishes between the disciples, who have the knowledge of the *mystery* of the Kingdom, and the others, who do not; finally, Paul uses the term to express revelation, e.g. Rom 16:25: "The proclamation (κήρυγμα) of Jesus Christ, revelation of a *mystery* kept secret throughout the ages, but today made manifest," cf. 1 Cor 11:26 and chap. II, §II.5.

responsibility, and their writings, not only the NT epistles but many other texts, were distributed, apparently without limitation. Justin, in his *Apology*, even addresses the emperor Antoninus, the Senate and the whole Roman people. Teaching was both public and oral, with some precautions in time of persecution. There was certainly no Christian *arcanum* comparable with the secret cult of the mysteries; it was not until the 3rd century that the organization of the catechumenate entailed a difference of publicity in preaching and worship, with only the initiates being admitted to knowledge of the customs.[110] On the other hand, a distinction should be made between preaching to all and the activities proper to the community, since it is clear that, from the beginning, access to the rites was protected, as we shall see later.[111]

Finally, it is worth pointing out that the NT as we have it, and especially the gospels, is entirely dependent on that branch of Jesus' disciples, gathered around Peter (and Paul), which is centered on the kerygma of the resurrection. Acts has preserved a few traces of other groups: Apollos and the disciples at Ephesus, who know only the baptism of John, represent at least one other current, which must have lived on with its own teaching; a similar observation could be made on the subject of James, to whom even Peter gives an account of himself. Little is known about the Jewish-Christians, but their biography of Jesus (the "Gospel of the Hebrews"), which was apparently not published, would have presented a rather different picture from the one we know, even if the facts related were more or less the same.[112] Traces there certainly are in the NT, but they have been almost obliterated by a final redaction which has a different orientation. Similar traces are to be found also in the Eastern Churches, which regard themselves as the heirs of Jude, Thomas, etc., although nothing in the NT would lead us to suspect that.[113]

By way of an appendix, we need to say something about the *Writings* (or Hagiographa). This third part of the OT varies to some extent in size: the Hebrew canon has the shortest list,[114] whereas the various Chris-

110. Cf. the historical dossier established by Pierre Batiffol, "Arcane," in: E. Mangenot, *Dictionnaire de théologie catholique* I (1903), col. 1743 f.

111. This conclusion agrees with that reached by Guy Stroumsa, *Hidden Wisdom. Esoteric Traditions and the Roots of Christian Mysticism* (Studies in the History of Religions, 70), Leiden, Brill, 1996, p. 27–45. When Celsus, around 170, accuses the Christian communities of being secret and so illegal, Origen, *Contra Celsum* 1.1, replies that it is lawful to rise up against unjust laws, then states that there is no secret regarding Christian dogmas; decoded, he implicitly acknowledges that the ritual was secret.

112. Cf. chap. V, §V.2 on the migration and transformation of these biographies.

113. Cf. for instance the narrative of the origins of the Church of Edessa given by Eusebius, *Hist. eccl*, 1.13.1–22, and the *Doctrine of Addai*, a later Syriac work.

114. But it includes Dan, whom FJ and the LXX regard as a prophet, cf. chap. V, §II.3.

tian canons are longer, especially when the apocrypha (pseudepigrapha) are included. The part that can vary is made up of a collection of books of different origins, having in common the fact that they do not contain legislation, with the notable exception of *Jubilees*, known to the Ethiopians as *Book of the Division of the Times*. How these works came to be deposited, then published, is not known. Here we can observe that the methods of oral publication described above concern only teaching *to be observed*, and not legends or homiletic material, which were regarded as having only an exhortative or ornamental value. This distinction, however, breaks down in Christianity, where the central kerygma is homiletic in type (this could explain the later mistrust of the rabbis towards written targums and Messianic interpretations of Scripture). The Christians, however, have things to do, the point of the question put by Peter's listeners after hearing the inaugural sermon of Acts 2:14-36. His reply ("Be converted and be baptized [. . .]") is remarkable in that it introduces a rite. Now the NT, by and large, gives no information about how to perform any rites, despite numerous allusions to them. Even more: in the gospels Jesus institutes nothing.[115] In other words, many things *to be observed* remained unpublished.[116]

II — Two Intriguing Episodes

From what has been seen in the previous section, it is clear that the gospels are not the best place to look for the origins of Christianity, that is to say, for what happened immediately after Jesus left the scene. Two reasons for this have emerged: the delay in *publishing* the biography of Jesus (perhaps because it was thought dangerous to do so),[117] and the almost total silence regarding rites. In Acts, however, we find two episodes which get round these pitfalls and enable us to glimpse the environment revealed by the first steps of the apostles.

1. Peter and Cornelius

This famous scene is certainly important, given its length and repetitions, whereas the few other episodes in the mission of Peter are reported only briefly. This narrative tells of a visit to a Gentile, something

115. The case of Luke 22:19b-20 (institution of the eucharist), already raised in §2 above, will be discussed further (chap. II, §II.5).

116. For the particular case of the (written) decrees of the assembly at Jerusalem in Acts 15:13 f.), cf. chap. V, §II.1.

117. On the abortive attempt represented by the *Diatessaron*, cf. also chap. IV, §II.2, on the appearance of Greek texts in Judaea around 120.

new and risky, since Peter has afterwards to justify himself and cannot appeal to a tradition going back to Jesus. This simple observation raises the hope that the event will throw light both on the environment of the first community *and* on Jesus' own horizon.

Following the analyses of M.-É. Boismard,[118] at the source of the passage is an earlier and simpler narrative belonging to the "Acts of Peter" (P Doc), in which the Gentile of Caesarea is not yet Cornelius the centurion, and in which the debate at the assembly of Jerusalem follows on immediately:

> (9:43) *Now it happened that Peter stayed many days with a certain Simon, a tanner.*[119] (10:9b) *He went up to the upper room to pray.* (19b) *The Spirit said to him: "Here are three men who are looking for you.* (20) *But rise, go with them without hesitation, for it is I who sent them."* (23b) *Then, rising up he left with them, and certain of the brethren of Joppe came with him.* (24a) *The next day, he entered Caesarea.* (25b) *Coming to meet him, a man, falling at his feet, prostrated himself.* (26) *But Peter lifted him up saying: "Rise. I too am a man."* (27) *And going in he found many people.* (28a) *He declared to them: "You know that a Jew is forbidden to frequent or approach a foreigner.* (29b) *So I ask: For what reason have you made me come?"* (30) *(The man) declared: "I was in my house and behold a man stood before me in shining garments.* (31a) *And he declared:* (32) *'Send people to Joppe and summon Simon who is surnamed Peter, who will speak to you when he arrives.'"* (34) *Opening his mouth Peter said: "In truth, I understand that God does not differentiate between persons,* (35) *but in every nation the one who fears God and practices justice is pleasing to Him."* (44) *While Peter was still speaking these words, the Holy Spirit fell on those who were listening. Then Peter declared:* (47) *"Can anyone refuse the water of baptism to those who have received the Spirit as we have?"* (48) *And he ordered them to be baptized in the name of Jesus. Then they asked him to stay some days.*[120]

118. Cf. *Les Actes* II:61 f. The essential point of the following argument concerning the baptism of Cornelius, does not depend on these analyses. They have been adopted here (with some modifications) since, although based solely on literary considerations, they are often of great assistance in understanding the historical context.

119. (βυρσεύς), trade close to rural life, cf. *BKetub* 77a (בורסי, בורסיקי) and below.

120. In *Les Actes* III:158 f., v. 47–48 have been suppressed in the reconstruction of the primitive P Doc, but the reasons given are narrative, rather than literary: 1. baptism is not mentioned by Peter in his report (11:15,17); 2. the stay with the Gentiles is bound up with the problem of eating with them, which is absent from the primitive narrative, where it is a question only of the prohibition of frequenting Gentiles. These reasons are not entirely convincing, as other narrative elements need to be taken into account: 1. the Gentiles here have not only been visited, but have entered into the community, whence the objection of the Pharisees; so, as well as Peter's transgression, there is an *observable* act of in-

(11,2) *Peter, after much time, wanted to go to Jerusalem and, calling the brethren to him and strengthening them, he left, speaking much throughout the countrysides. He arrived, and announced [to the brethren] the grace of God.*[121] *But they argued against him,* (3) *saying: "Why have you gone into the house of uncircumcised men and eaten with them?"* (4) *But Peter began to expound the matter to them saying:* (5a) *"I was in Joppe, the city,* (11) *and behold three men presented themselves at the house where I was, sent from Caesarea to me.* (12) *Now the Spirit told me to go with them. There came with me also these six brethren and we went into the man's house.* (13) *And he announced how he saw an angel standing in his house and saying: "Send people to Joppe and bring Simon who is surnamed Peter.* (14a) *He will speak to you."* (15) *Now as I was beginning to speak, the Holy Spirit fell on them just as on us at the beginning.* (17b) *Was I someone who could prevent God from giving them the Holy Spirit?"* (18a) *Hearing these words, they calmed down and glorified God.*

(15:5) *Now there arose certain of the party of the Pharisees, who had become believers, saying that it was necessary to circumcise them and observe the law of Moses.* (7a) *Now, since a great discussion was taking place,* (13b) *James rose up and said: "Men, my brethren, listen to me.* (14) *Simeon has told how at first God has taken care to take from among the Gentiles a people to His name.* (19) *That is why I am of the opinion not to make things difficult for Gentiles who convert to God,* (20) *but to prescribe to them to abstain from the pollution of idols and from unchastity and from blood."* (22) *Then it seemed good to all the Church to send men whom they had chosen: Jude, called Barsabbas,*

---

duction, which can only be the baptism mentioned in the text; 2. staying with the pagans certainly supposes eating with them, and the mention of the "six brethren" appears to be an allusion to the Seven (minus Stephen) who were set over the service of tables (cf. *Les Actes* V:44); this service is clearly not just a secondary detail, since it involves community meals (cf. chap. VII, §IV.2); 3. Peter's vision, telling him to eat everything (10:10-16), is an addition which deforms the primitive narrative by introducing—in order to abolish—the distinction between clean and unclean animals; but this addition has to be understood as grafted on to an important detail of the narrative, which speaks of "eating with" the Gentiles (cf. 11:4 f.), that is, of eating a food (even permitted) as an expression of communion, which constitutes a transgression of a quite different nature. For these reasons, we restore to the primitive P Doc the question "and eaten with them" (11:3). According to *Les Actes* I:40 f., baptism appears only at the level of the Lucan redaction (Acts II); previously (P Doc) entry into the community is made only by faith in response to preaching and is sealed by the reception of the Spirit. Whatever the force of this argument, or the accuracy of the analyses on which it is based, it is still necessary, for this entry to be *durable* and recognized, that there be an identifiable sign expressing adoption by the community; this could be the laying on of hands, cf. chap. VII, §IV.1; the notion of "baptism," implying the idea of immersion, is not clear at this stage, cf. below.

121. This beginning of v. 2 comes from the WT. It was later replaced by v. 1, which generalizes.

> *and Simon, men of authority among the brethren.* (30) *So they, being sent on their way, went down to [Caesarea],* (32) *And since they too were prophets, with much speaking they exhorted the brethren and fortified them.* (33) *Having spent some time, they were sent on their way by the brethren to those who had sent them.*

This narrative contains a number of remarkable features:

1. From an historical point of view, this is the first case in Acts where contact with Gentiles is not the consequence, direct or indirect, of a rejection by the Jews, but the effect of a simple movement of the Spirit, firm but gentle. Now, by comparing various chronologies, we can see that Peter left Jerusalem only around 43 or 44,[122] whereas the events which took place at Antioch, Corinth and Ephesus are earlier (perhaps as early as 39), in particular the scene in which Paul goes to stay with a Gentile Godfearer at Corinth.[123] In other words, Peter was not the first to visit Gentiles, and the principal function of the narrative is to establish his authority, by showing him as the first to do such a thing, and above all as able to maintain communion with James, which is not self-evident (cf. *Les Actes* V:46 f.).[124]

2. The redactional development of the Gentile of Caesarea into "Cornelius, centurion of the Italic cohort, pious and fearing God, as all his household, giving generous alms to the Jewish people" (10:1-2) is of interest, in that it shows an important person of the best category, as close as possible to Judaism,[125] yet who is separated by a barrier which cannot be crossed. At least since the beginning of the Empire, the Jews had been dispensed from army service, for reasons to do with the Sabbath (cf. *Ant.* 14 §227 f.), and certainly also with the regimental standards. So it is highly significant—and stretching the bounds of probability—to put on center stage an officer of the army of occupation, who as such professes an emperor worship incompatible with Judaism (cf. Matt 8:8 par.), and to have him pass directly to Christianity without first entering Judaism through circumcision. The objection of the Pharisees (15:5 f.), which im-

122. The death of Agrippa I is generally dated to 44, but Daniel R. Schwartz, *Agrippa I, The Last King of Judaea* (TSAJ, 23), Tübingen, J. C. B. Mohr (P. Siebeck), 1990, p. 107–111, finds that it took place in September or October 43.

123. Acts 18:7, cf. chap. VI, §II.2.

124. According to P Doc, but this narrative already smoothes out what must have been a serious controversy, cf. chap. V, §II on the Noachide precepts and the successors of James.

125. The Godfearer is recognizable not by his opinions or by an observance (to which he is not obliged), but typically by the alms (ἐλεημοσύνας πολλάς) which he gives to the Jews; that is a practice distinct from that of the so–called Noachide precepts, cf. chap. V, §II.2.

mediately follows the episode in the first redaction (cf. chap. V, §II), thus bears on an extreme case.

3. The Spirit is shown openly at the beginning and end of the narrative: at Peter's departure for Caesarea, and in the house of his hosts. As Peter later says to the brethren (11:15), he recognizes that the same thing has happened to them as to "us at the beginning." So there is a communion. In the P Doc, the apostles receive the Spirit while they are gathered together (4:31), but without any identifiable chronological link with Pentecost (cf. chap. VI, §III.2); on that occasion they are given an assurance which enables them to testify with power to the resurrection of Jesus. This resurrection amounts to a very serious tampering with boundaries, since the necessary separation between life and death, represented respectively by the pure and the impure, is thus compromised. It is comparable to the violation involved in Peter's communion with Gentiles (impure), and is even its model, since it is provoked by the same Spirit. Later redaction develops the manifestation of the Spirit as glossolalia, which can represent either the overthrow of the rules of language (nonsense, drunkenness, cf. Acts 2:13 f.), or communication beyond linguistic barriers (extreme sense).[126] Indeed, the earthquake of Acts 4:31 introduces a cosmic dimension, and the whole problem is to know if these transgressions are a return to primitive chaos before Creation, itself an act of separation and organization, or if they can be compared to a new creation (cf. Gen 1:2, "And the spirit of God brooded over the waters"). At a later stage of redaction, Peter's vision of *all* the animals proceeds from a similar idea: Creation in its diversity, but without separation between clean and unclean.

4. Peter's reaction, to have the Gentiles baptized, is instructive from several points of view. At first sight it seems to be simply an order to go to the ritual bath *(miqveh)*. But then, what could such a gesture signify? They already have the Spirit, so are deemed to be pure, and Peter stays and eats with them. When he asks "Can anyone refuse?" he is implicitly replying to the objection that baptism is *a priori* unthinkable for such folk. Apparently, this is because they are not Jewish (circumcised),[127]

126. The account of Pentecost (Acts 2) will be discussed when we come to the identification of the primitive community, cf. chap. VII, §III.

127. The problem of the circumcision of adults is complex. According to Gen 17:14 MT, "the one who is not circumcised will be cut off from his people, for he has broken my Covenant"; Sam and LXX have "the one who is not circumcised *on the eighth day* . . . ," which seems to exclude adult proselytes, but not their offspring, which leads to a strange situation. FJ declares (*Ant.* 1 §192) that it is a matter of preserving the nation (γένος, not ἔθνος), but he is writing of Rome, where it is obviously a question of separation from the Graeco-Roman world (as at the time of Antiochus Epiphanes, cf. 1 Macc

since the convert Pharisees will demand that these Gentiles be circumcised, so as to be able to observe the Law (themselves),[128] the question being whether the legal observance concerns all frequentation of Gentiles or only eating with them. From this it is clear, that the newcomers to the group to whom Peter is accustomed, namely Jews, get baptized.

The end of Peter's remark ("those who have received the Spirit as we have") raises the question whether the apostles were themselves baptized. This is not clearly implied by our narrative, but other factors need to be considered: some of Jesus' disciples had been disciples of John the Baptist, and in his address (10:36-43), added at a later stage of redaction, Peter recalls the model of Jesus, beginning with the baptism proclaimed by John and the anointing of the Spirit.

In the incident at Caesarea, baptism is "in the name[129] of Jesus,"

1:41-50), for in the Orient, the question has a quite different aspect: Herodotus 2.104 could already say that Egyptians, Nubians, Phoenicians, and Syrians of Palestine practice circumcision, and later on, Hadrian's decree abolishing circumcision (as a *barbarous* custom) was not aimed at the Jews in particular. That the practice was really quite ordinary can be seen from the fact that both Abraham *and Ishmael* were circumcised well after their birth (Gen 17:25); the particular mark of the Covenant, expressed in the case of Isaac, was circumcision on the eighth day. Precisely on the subject of proselytes, the Alexandrian Philo insists on circumcision of the heart rather than of the flesh (*De monarchia* §51–53, *De sacrif.* §304 f.), which shows that for him there is nothing special about circumcision, whereas the Roman Tacitus emphasizes it (*Hist.* 5.5). In fact, circumcision is so common in the Middle East that the Koran does not even bother to prescribe it. When the reformers Ezra and Nehemiah inveigh against "foreign" wives, who come, however, from *near by*, the question of circumcision does not arise; similarly, Lev 12:3 mentions circumcision only in passing, on the occasion of other precepts which are themselves expressly formulated. However, the forced circumcision of the Idumaeans by John Hyrcanus, then of the Ituraeans by Aristobulus, so of adults, raises a special question, since later on there were some who did not recognize Herod as a Jew (cf. *Ant.* 14 §403), which in turn involves the problem of ancestry, and so of race. Perhaps the obligation that Essenes should be Ἰουδαῖοι τὸ γένος simply means that they should be circumcised (but cf. chap. VII, §IV.1), a sign which could be observed during immersions, since the sect intended, by definition, a reform of Israel and not of the whole world, a project which was founded on individuals, therefore, rather than on families. For proselytes, the rabbinic tradition insists on immersion (i.e. baptism) even more than on circumcision (cf. *BYeb* 46a f.), in other words, it has adults in mind (cf. MT above); on this double rite, in relation with the Covenant, cf. below chap. V, §I.3.

128. WT περιτέμνειν αὐτοὺς καὶ τηρεῖν τὸν νόμον; the AT adds παραγγέλλειν before τηρεῖν, which totally changes the sense, by introducing the theme of the salvation *of the Gentiles* by the Law, that is to say, the entirely different (and recurrent) problem of the "Judaizers": "[. . .] circumcise them and charge them to observe the law of Moses," cf. *Les Actes* V:204, correcting II:65 and chap. V, §II.1. The necessity of circumcision may be linked to access to the Passover meal (Exod 12:48), cf. chap. V, §I.3 and VII, §I.3.

129. With ἐν and not εἰς, cf. chap. II, §I.1. That this precision is a later gloss emerges from comparison with 19:6 and (implicitly) 2:38, where baptism in the name of Jesus necessarily precedes the gift of the Holy Spirit; whereas here, they already have the Spirit.

which implies that the gesture of immersion is capable of more than one meaning. But, if what is referred to here is just an isolated act of immersion with no mention of an officiant, it is not easy to see in what sense it can be performed "in the name of Jesus."

The underlying question is really much wider. We need to see if the term baptism used here does not in fact refer to a whole procedure, with a certain number of steps and rites, in which case Peter's order would amount to the admission of the household as candidates to follow this course (and not just sending them off to a *miqveh*). In any case, what Peter has to say invites us to give close attention to the nature of John's baptism, all the more as Jesus himself was a baptizer, as were at least some of his disciples (cf. John 3:22). And is there a connection between the baptism received and conferred by Jesus and his disciples and baptism "in the name of Jesus"?

5. The sole biblical category into which baptism (immersion) can be placed is purification. For the rabbinic tradition there is an impurity inherent in Gentiles,[130] of the same force as the impurity of one who has a seminal discharge;[131] it is spread by contact, and what the person touches is contaminated as well.[132] That means it is serious, and of a kind which is invariable and does not depend on any particular contamination, such as that of a corpse (cf. *TOhol* 1:4). The tradition is aware that this impurity is not in origin biblical, but only rabbinic (*TNida* 9:14).[133] It is important to note that the same principle is found among the Essenes (1 QM 9:8 f.) and in Matt 18:16, where, after formal warnings have gone unheeded, the stubborn offender is excluded from the community: to be regarded "as a Gentile or a publican" means to be impure, so that all contact becomes impossible.[134] These notions are in complete contrast with the views of Philo and Josephus, who never mention any impurity attaching to Gentiles. Indeed, Philo hardly mentions the theme of purification. When, bound by his biblical sources, he has to concede (*Spec. leg.*

130. *BShab* 14b, which indicates it among eighteen decrees made in the 1st century (see Ḥananya b. Ḥizqya).

131. Cf. Lev 15:1 f. (זב) and chap. VII, §IV.1.

132. According to Lev 11:24 (etc.), there are three phases of purification: washing of clothes, bathing, then sunset, which gives effect to the purifications properly so-called. These three phases coexist or not according to the cases of impurity, but the rab. trad., as also the Qumran texts, tend to systematize them, though rather differently, cf. chap. V, §II.5.

133. One of the aspects of "proselyte baptism" is to lift this impurity, cf. Gedaliah Alon, *Jews, Judaism and the Classical World. Studies in Jewish History in the Times of the Second Temple and Talmud*. Jerusalem, Magnes Press, 1977, p. 174, with references. On this point, cf. also chap. V, §I.3.

134. On the position of the Gentiles and the "people of the land," cf. chap. V, §I.1.

3 §63) that even conjugal union necessitates ablution (Lev 15:18), he takes care to give a purely ethical reason, and in *Spec. leg.* 3 §205, he explains the impurity attached to a corpse as an expression of the obligation to keep well away from murder. Then, a little later, he gives himself away by declaring (3 §208 f.) that Scripture envisages the soul behind the body: only the unjust and the impious are properly speaking impure. On the subject of the Therapeutae, he makes no mention at all of ablutions.[135] Josephus has even less to say: he briefly mentions the biblical cases of impurity (*Ant.* 3 §261) and describes the rite of the red heifer (*Ant.* 4 §79–81) in terms which Roman readers would find familiar.

6. As for going into a Gentile's house, even without touching anything, *MOhol* 18:7 explains that it is forbidden,[136] because it is to be presumed that fetuses have been buried under the floor or in the walls,[137] and, under a roof, the impurity of a corpse spreads by convection, even without contact (generalizing Num 19:14-15). This may also explain why Peter went up to the upper room[138] to pray (Acts 10:9). He is living with Simon, a tanner; this trade was low on the social scale,[139] on the edge of city life, but above all it meant handling skins, which, before tanning, are nothing but fragments of corpses.[140] For his prayer, Peter separates himself by (at least) a roof from a zone tainted with impurity, and in any case rather smelly.

7. From the P Doc to the final text, there is a clear evolution which deliberately develops certain details of the primitive narrative: the anonymous citizen becomes the centurion Cornelius, a public figure and not someone on the fringes; the problem of table fellowship has been transformed by a vision in which all food is pronounced clean, in a way which evokes a new creation. As for ideas, we can note that the baptism of the

135. Of the Essenes, described briefly in *Quod omnis probus liber sit* §75 f., Philo says only that they prove their love of God by being constantly pure (ἐπάλληλον ἁγνείαν).

136. This is the point of the declaration of the centurion of Capharnaum (Matt 8:8 par.): "Lord, I am not worthy (οὐκ εἰμὶ ἱκανός) that you should enter my house."

137. In *Ag.Ap.* 2 §202, FJ condemns voluntary abortion as infanticide, so liable to the death penalty, since it destroys a soul and weakens the race; similarly the *Letter to Diognetus* 5.4, as well as the rab. trad. (*BṬebY* 62b, cf. *MSanh* 9:2), which extends the prohibition to the entire human race (Noachide precept, *BSanh* 57b).

138. According to the WT (εἰς τὸ ὑπερῷον), the same term which is used for the upper room of Acts 20:8; the AT speaks of the flat roof (ἐπὶ τὸ δῶμα), perhaps to fit in with the vision of the object which comes down from heaven (10:11, cf. *Les Actes* III:150), but in any case breaking any connection with a room for meeting and/or prayer (cf. Acts 1:13).

139. Cf. C. K. Barrett, *The Acts of the Apostles* (ICC), Edinburgh, T. & T. Clark, 1994, I:486 f., with references.

140. According to *MShab* 1:2 it is forbidden to go to a tanner's (בורסקי) at the time of prayer.

new brethren, linked to the Spirit, is later developed in a speech by Peter (Acts 10:37-43),[141] who proclaims the kerygma, starting with Jesus' beginnings in Galilee, the baptism of John and the anointing of the Spirit. It is only then, in the present narrative, that the neophytes are baptized; so baptism and the Spirit are closely related, following the example of Jesus and in his name. This is not an isolated instance. At the moment of Matthias' election to replace Judas, the disciples have to find someone who "has been with us all the time that the Lord Jesus 'came in and went out' at our head, since John's baptism" (Acts 1:22), and in Luke 5:10 f., Jesus, who was baptized after John's arrest, only then began to recruit disciples. There is a clear claim to continuity with John's baptism, an institution which does not, however, require his physical presence, but its significance has somewhat changed.

From all this it emerges that the original environment of Peter and the brethren had no idea at all of proselytism among the Gentiles:[142] it took the impetus of the Spirit to break down the barriers. As for conversion to Judaism, the Pharisees (in our narrative) allow it, since they demand the circumcision of those Gentiles who have become Christian (perhaps as the lesser of two evils); but it is not certain that Peter and his companions would have spontaneously allowed it, which would explain why their reaction was not to circumcise the newcomers.

Finally, to come back to the two historical oddities mentioned above: the visit to the Gentiles is not the result of a refusal on the part of the Jews, and the episode appears to be later than the first attempts by Paul; further, Peter is known as the apostle of the Jews and not of the Gentiles. Perhaps we should wonder if the narrative of the P Doc is not the reworking, furnished with biblical allusions, of an even earlier text (closer to the historical reality) which had a different bearing. We recall that Peter is a Galilean, a fact which does not go unnoticed in town (Mark 14:70 par.), and Acts mentions (11:2) that on his return he preaches energetically *in the countrysides*, although he did not go on with any evangelization in Caesarea. So he normally addressed Jews in the countryside or villages.[143] Finally, if we set aside the Pharisees' objection, the whole affair takes for granted a rather traditional environment, in which purification and table fellowship play a notable role. By contrast, Caesarea is

141. Attributed to Act II, cf. *Les Actes* III:156.

142. On Jewish proselytism, and on the fact that in the account in the P Doc there is no reference to Jesus, cf. chap. VI, §I.1.

143. Cf. chap. IV, §II.4 on the exclusion of cities from the "land of Israel," in a Galilean perspective: townsfolk are not in a position to keep the precepts connected with the land.

the big pagan city, whose Jewish inhabitants are townsfolk, perhaps largely Hellenized.[144] Could the underlying event have been a visit by Peter to some *Jews* at Caesarea? That would still be a major event if they were of another brand, and so regarded as impure.[145] In particular, it would explain why they knew how to recognize an angel (10:30).

2. The Night at Troas

In connection with the table fellowship just mentioned, the question arises as to the meaning of the "breaking of the bread," which recurs periodically in Acts as a regular activity of the community. Nowhere is this rite described, but one passage supplies some important details: the night-long vigil at Troas (Acts 20:7-12), on the occasion of which Paul restores the young Eutychus who has fallen from the second story (third level). This scene has been attached to Paul's third missionary journey, and has certain parallels with Acts 16:12b-13, concerning various stages around Troas of Paul's second journey. According to *Les Actes* III:246 f., it is a composition of Acts II in the style of the Travel Journal ("we"), but of independent origin. The following is a literal translation, showing, where they diverge, the AT (left hand column) and the restored WT (right hand column)

> (20:6) *As for us, we set sail from Philippi after the days of Unleavened Bread, and came to Troas in five days, and stayed for seven days.* (7) *The first day of the week, while we had come together to break the bread, Paul was debating with them, before leaving the next day; he prolonged his speech until the middle of the night.* (8) *There were many*
>
> | | |
> |---|---|
> | *lamps* (λαμπάδες) | *lights* (ὑπολαμπάδες) |
>
> *in the upper room where we had met.* (9) *A young man by name Eutychus, seated on the window ledge, being overcome by a heavy sleep while Paul was speaking, fell down from the third level and was taken up dead.* (10) *Paul went down, threw himself on him and taking him in his arms said: "Do not be troubled, his soul is in him."*

144. This episode takes place at the time of Agrippa I, when Caesarea and its games had a reputation (probably earlier) for impurity, cf. *Ant.* 19 §332 f.

145. In Acts 11:20, Cypriots and Cyrenaeans, on mission to Antioch, speak to the (Gentiles) "Hellenes" according to the WT (Ἕλληνας), but to the (Jewish) "Hellenists" according to the AT (Ἑλληνιστάς); in any case they are townsfolk, and this interesting hesitation in the text may originate in reservations entertained by the brethren with regard to both; cf. chap. VI, §I.3. For an interpretation of the like difficulty involved in reaching Gentiles and Jews outside the brotherhood, cf. chap. V, §I.3. It is even possible that the category of "Godfearer" is imprecise, and designates both Gentiles who are near and Jews who are far removed from the group, cf. chap. VI, §I.1.

(11) *Having gone up again and broken the bread and eaten and talked a good while until dawn, thus he departed.*	(11) (features in WT, but not in the first redaction, cf. *Les Actes* II:369)
(12)	(12) *While they were greeting one another*
They took the child alive and they were consoled beyond measure.	*he took the young man alive, and they were consoled beyond measure.*

Several aspects of this narrative call for commentary:

1. Just as Peter had raised up Tabitha, the woman disciple of Joppe (Acts 9:36-42), so Paul takes up Eutychus, with many biblical overtones (cf. *Les Actes* II:317). As with the approach to the Gentiles, the two apostles are thus on equal footing. All commentators associate this resurrection—quite reasonably—with the breaking of the bread on the first day of the week, commemorating the resurrection of Jesus; the rite is thus shown to be effective in reality. However, the comparison does not hold good when placed in relation with the narratives of the Last Supper. The setting there is Passover, Jesus announces his death (emphasized in 1 Cor 11:26), and, at first sight, there is no connection with the resurrection on the first day of the week. The only common element is the breaking of the bread, and the problem is to see how this gesture could have been derived from the annual Passover meal, even supposing that the bread in question is unleavened. As the other occurrences of the "breaking of the bread" give no further clarification, the problem will have to be looked at from the angle of the Last Supper (cf. chap. II, §II).

2. The episode takes place on the night of the first day of the week, *i.e.* between Saturday and Sunday. We might expect that, in a Jewish setting, the day (as a unit) is to be counted from evening to evening, but the chronology of the burial of Jesus shows otherwise. Mark 15:42 explains: "Evening had come, and since it was the Preparation,[146] that is the eve of the Sabbath, Joseph of Arimathaea went [. . .]"; there follows a whole procedure of authorization and burial, which may well have been hasty, but which is incompatible with the beginning of the Sabbath at sundown. Furthermore, the women come to embalm the body on the morning of the first day (Sunday), not on Saturday evening. The details given by Matt go in the same direction, particularly in 28:1, "After the Sabbath, at the moment when the first day was beginning to *shine* [. . .]"; for him too, the

146. On the meaning of this expression, cf. chap. II, §II.4.

Sabbath ends on Sunday morning.[147] There is a clear difference in Luke 23:44 f. There the precise detail that Jesus died at the ninth hour is omitted, and the phrase "the Sabbath was beginning to shine"[148] is placed after the burial and everything that has gone before. In other words, according to this version, everything takes place before the beginning of the Sabbath on Friday evening. Similarly, in the Troas account, the first day begins on Saturday evening, and not on Sunday morning. Such a reckoning is, then, typical of Luke-Acts, but, judging from the chronology of Jesus' burial, it represents a marked difference from the reckoning found in Matt and Mark. The detail is not insignificant, for counting the day from evening to evening, an oriental way of reckoning, was a mark of the Pharisees, whose influence was dominant at Rome (where Luke-Acts comes from); thus Augustus dispensed the Jews from appearing before the tribunal after the 9th hour on Friday, because of the approach of the Sabbath (*Ant.* 16 §163). On the other hand, counting from morning to morning agrees with the biblical (sacerdotal) reckoning,[149] and occurs in

147. The Vulg., influenced by the rabbinic custom of lighting lamps on Friday evening renders: "on the evening of the Sabbath" (cf. *MBer* 1:1, where the evening *Shema*ʿ has to be said "at the time when the stars appear" צאת הכוכבים). Cf. following note.

148. ἐπέφωσκεν; The WT (D) has ἦν δὲ ἡ ἡμέρα πρὸ σαββάτου, which does not imply that the Sabbath is about to begin; this is apparently a trace of a previous redaction, closer to Matt and Mark. The verb ἐπέφωσκεν designates very naturally in Matt 28:21 the first light of dawn (שחר, before sunrise), cf. Ep 5:14 and *TWNT* IX:304, despite the vigorous opposition of Reinhart Staats, "Die Sonntagnachtgottesdienst der christlichen Frühzeit," *ZNW* 66 (1975), p. 242–263. The meaning in Luke, according to which the Sabbath begins in the evening, is certainly secondary. On the other hand, M.-É. Boismard, *Synopse des quatre Évangiles en français. – II. Commentaire*, Paris, Cerf, 1972, p. 433, holds that Matt in its final form depends on Luke, or rather on his source (Doc. A) for the account of the burial; the line of reasoning and its result can, however, be upheld, by introducing a subsidiary argument connected with problems concerning the calendar. Replying to certain colleagues, F. C. Burkitt, "ΕΠΙΦΩΣΚΕΙΝ," *JThS* 14 (1913), p. 538–546, concluded that the expression refers to the appearance of the morning or evening star, but he based his argument above all on the elasticity of rab. expressions (אורתא נְגהי) which normally refer to the dawn, but, in the context of Passover, mean the evening (*BPes* 2a–4a); we shall see that this distortion does not proceed from any ambiguity in the terms, but from a change of calendar: originally, the reference was to the morning or at least the day, cf. chap. III, §II.2. In the *Gospel of Peter*, §9, the expression πρωίας δὲ ἐπιφώσκοντος τοῦ σαββάτου, indicating the beginning of the Sabbath at dawn, is perfectly correct.

149. Thus, the literal meaning of Gen 1:5 "Evening came, morning came: one day" is that, after a day of creation there was a night (Rashbam); taken together, they make up the "first day," cf. also Roland de Vaux, *Les Institutions de l'Ancien Testament*, Paris, Cerf, 1989[5], I:275. Similarly, the Passover lamb must be immolated on the day of 14 Nisan and eaten that evening, which is the night of the 14 when the Israelites went out of Egypt (Exod 12); so the 14th runs until the following morning. Equally, communion sacrifices have to be eaten "the same day," without leaving anything over for the morning, *i.e.* the next day (Lev 22:30). Further, the Day of Atonement, on 10 Tishri, should begin "the evening of the

Jubilees, and more generally among the Essenes[150] (cf. chap. II, §II). That opens up some interesting perspectives.

3. The final text of the night at Troas mentions the presence of many "lamps" (v. 8), an odd, isolated detail, when nothing else is said concerning the arrangement of the room or about any rite. The WT speaks instead of "lights" (in the sense of high windows or skylights), which has some connection with the narrative, since Eutychus falls from a window. Why the change, which only makes the account less coherent? In fact, lamps on a Saturday evening do have a well-attested meaning in a Jewish context. Latin satirists (Seneca, Persius Flaccus) rail against idleness and smoking lamps on the Sabbath.[151] They cannot have meant the lighting of

9th," which would mean—if the days are counted from evening to evening—that 9 Tishri is also a fast day, which *BYoma* 81b would find most surprising, whereas it is a question only of including the preceding night in the fast. Cf. Jacob Z. Lauterbach, *Rabbinic Essays*, Cincinnati, HUC Press, 1951, p. 446 f. and *Institutions* I:275 f. Other examples are given by Julian Morgenstern, "The Sources of the Creation Story," *American Journal of Semitic Languages and Literature* 36 (1919), p. 176. The question is, however, complex, for according to Gen 2:2 the Sabbath begins on the evening of the sixth day for the MT, but not for the LXX; the counting of the seven days of Unleavened Bread (Exod 12:18) goes from evening to evening (cf. chap. V, §II), etc. The custom of counting days from morning to morning was certainly maintained in the Temple for sacrifices, as in *BḤul* 83a. The scriptural proof advanced by *TTaan* 2:5 to show that the night precedes the day is Esth 4:16 (fast night and day), *i.e.* an Oriental narrative which belongs to the Pharisee current (cf. chap. III, §II.1). *BBer* 26a replies to the same question by invoking, as often since, Gen 1:5, but in reality it is because of the completion of the work on the seventh day (2:2 MT), which makes sense only if the seventh day begins on the evening of the sixth and so is its continuation. On the other hand, LXX, Sam, Syr (etc.), *Jubilees* 2:6, Philo, *Op. mundi* §89, Josephus, *Ant.* 1 §33, as well as the list of variants sent to Alexandria for translation (*BMeg* 9b), all place the completion of the work on the sixth day; that is precisely the definition of the calendar of *Jubilees*, which is to be found in the customs of Qumran, cf. Étienne Nodet, "La loi à Qumrân et Schiffman," *RB* 102 (1995), p. 57–85. However, before concluding that the MT is a simple reworking to agree with Babylonian customs, it should be noted that FJ mentions in passing (*J.W.* 4 §582, confirmed by *MSuk* 4:11) an ambo where a priest stood to sound a trumpet marking the beginning (and the end) of the Sabbath *in the evening*; so the MT is at least in agreement with the customs of the Temple. From this point of view, the weekly Sabbath introduces a certain cross-breeding into the calendar, cf. *Search*, p. 94–102.

150. Cf. Shemaryahu Talmon, *King, Cult and Calendar in Ancient Israel*, Jerusalem, Magnes, 1986.

151. Cf. *Greek and Latin* I:432–437, with references and discussions. FJ (*Ag.Ap.* 2 §282) affirms that the whole world knows the custom of weekly rest, fasts, lamp lighting, food laws, but the mention of fasts between the Sabbath and the lamps weakens the association. However, he may have in mind a connection between the Sabbath and fasting, since the Day of Atonement, a fast day, is defined by Lev 23:32 as a "great Sabbath" שבת שבתון. Among the Romans, there was a current view that the Sabbath was a fast day, cf. *Greek and Latin* II:110 (commenting Suetonius, *Divus Augustus*, 76.2). Josephus, *Ant.* 14 §66 f. (citing Strabo) says that Jerusalem was taken on the Fast Day (understood as Atone-

lamps on Friday evening,[152] since the Romans counted the day from midnight to midnight, and in any case, the Jews could only light lamps before the Sabbath began,[153] without being able to trim them later. So there was nothing special about having their houses lit up on Friday evening—perhaps even for a shorter time than usual. On the contrary, to account for the ire of Roman critics, they must have been able to observe that Jewish houses were lit up more and longer than usual—with or without smoke—on Saturday evening. In other words, the many lamps at Troas, according to the final version, in a context of a prolonged vigil, coincide with what could be seen at Rome. So the change in the account can, after all, be explained.

4. But what about the high windows or skylights of the earlier version? There is no point in mentioning them in a story which takes place at night, unless, perhaps, the group was waiting for the dawn. But the episode we are dealing with is precisely a night-long vigil, for Paul does not leave until the morning, and it is not as if he is pressed for time, since it is at the end of a week's stay. The Therapeutae practiced similar vigils, and at the moment of sunrise, they would turn towards the east and address a prayer to heaven;[154] Josephus' Essenes address their first prayer of

---

ment); similarly, *Ant.* 14 §487 states that Pompey took Jerusalem on a fast day, while Dio Cassius, 37.16.4 has a Sabbath. However, *Jub* 50:9 f. prescribes eating one's fill and forbids fasting, and *BShab* 117b lays down three or four meals; these prescriptions show that it is not all that clear, so there was an underlying controversy.

152. The rab. custom of lighting lamps on Friday evening contains two major anomalies: first, it is a duty (חובה) and not a precept (מצוה), without an associated blessing (*BShab* 23b f.); secondly, it is carried out by a woman, contrary to the usual principle that women are dispensed from obligations linked to a fixed time (*MShab* 2:6). This custom is explained in two ways: according to Isa 58:13-14 the Sabbath should be a delight, which it could not be if it were held in total darkness; alternatively, it was necessary to protest visibly against the Samaritans and, perhaps, the Sadducees-Zadokites (and later the Qaraites), who forbade any lamp on the Sabbath, even one lit beforehand, following the literal meaning of Exod 35:3, cf. J. Z. Lauterbach, *op. cit.*, p. 457 f. The rab. trad. retains a precept of lighting lamps on Saturday evening: the Tannaitic blessing on taking leave of the Sabbath, (הבדלה) is made over wine, spices and light (*MBer* 8:5); one or more lamps are then lit, without any limit of time or of trimming. The reference, mentioned in the blessing, is evidently the first day of Creation (Gen 1:3). In this case it is a true blessing, made by the master of the household in obedience to an explicit precept.

153. In order to respect the absolute prohibition of fire in Exod 35:3, cf. *MShab* 2:7.

154. Cf. Philo, *Vita contempl.* §64–90. This vigil is held every forty-ninth day, but the text does not say on which day of the week, nor from which point the fifty day periods are counted. However, the Therapeutae are very close to the Essenes, and since the latter had a series of fifty day periods, beginning with Pentecost and always falling on a Sunday, it is not unreasonable to suppose that the vigils of which Philo speaks are always on the night of Saturday-Sunday. That being said, the vigil at Troas is weekly, only six weeks after Pentecost, and so outside the fifty-day rhythm.

the day to the rising sun (*J.W.* 2 §128 and 148), which has intrigued the commentators. Waiting for the sun, especially on the morning of the first day of the week (day of the creation of light), recalls the prophecy of Zechariah to John the Baptist, whose task would be to proclaim "the visit of the rising sun from on high" (Luke 1:78):[155] a remarkable image, which carefully avoids any suggestion of veneration of the sun itself.[156] All these points of contact may not be of great significance in themselves, but it could be that their disappearance from the final redaction allows us to glimpse the trace of a discussion going on among the Christians of Rome about the meaning to be attached to the night watch.[157]

5. After the death of Jesus, on Friday 14 Nisan,[158] the following Sunday (first day of the week), day of the resurrection, was also that of the presentation of the first sheaf of the barley harvest, which, according to Lev 23:11, is made on "the day after the Sabbath."[159] Paul, who has occasion to use the metaphor of the first-fruits, explains that the night is far advanced and the day is close (Rom 8:1). These metaphors are not used by chance. All the same, in our episode, the symbolism of the first day, repeated every week, exercises a stronger power of attraction than the symbolic meanings of the annual Passover, and we are back to the same question which we have already seen regarding the breaking of the bread. As it happens, the first day of the week in our narrative falls somewhere between Passover and Pentecost (20:16), and has no special character. It is, however, precisely placed: Paul has arrived seven days earlier, *i.e.* on the previous Sunday, after a voyage of five days; so he left Philippi the previous Wednesday, which was at the end of the week of Unleavened Bread, that is 22 Nisan (Exod 12:18). It follows that the Passover meal, if it was in fact held at Troas,[160] was on the evening of *Tuesday*, 14 Nisan.

155. Cf. below chap. II, §I.2, in connection with the symbolism of Luke 1.

156. The problem of avoiding anything that could suggest sun worship had long been a major issue, cf. chap. V, §II.5.

157. In this regard, the Younger Pliny, writing to the emperor Trajan in 112 (*Ep.* 10.96), provides a brief but significant piece of evidence when he writes that the sole crime which the *christiani* admit is to meet for prayer on fixed days before the dawn.

158. The chronological difficulties in the last week of Jesus' life will be examined in chap. II, §II.4.

159. Whether the "Sabbath" means the day of rest on 15 Nisan or the Saturday which falls at some point during the seven days of Unleavened Bread, it is the same day here. The uncertainty over the position of this "Sabbath" corresponds to the twofold sense of the term, full moon, or Saturday (cf. *Search,* p. 75); it affects the day of presenting the first sheaf and also the determination of Pentecost, seven weeks after, cf. chap. VII, §III.1.

160. The fact that the Unleavened Bread is mentioned and not the Passover is not necessarily without significance; we shall see, with regard to the Quartodecimans (chap. VII, §I.2), that in the 2nd century, a number of churches, including Rome, had no tradition of

In the lunar calendar, which is independent of the weekly rhythm, 14 Nisan falls on a Tuesday roughly once every seven years if there are no other factors; on the other hand, in the calendar of *Jubilees* (and the Essenes), 1 Nisan is always a Wednesday, and so 14th always a Tuesday (cf. above §I.2). If there were no other indication, it would be difficult to choose between the two possibilities, but the insistence and the precision of the chronological information given, as well as the remarks made earlier, suggest that the calendar of the apostles at the beginning may well have been that of *Jubilees*, traces of which still remain.

Now that we have cleared the ground, let us return to the episode. It certainly has some strange aspects: Eutychus falls down in the middle of the night, yet is only restored alive to his friends and relations at dawn, when Paul departs. No attempt is made to hide this improbability, which should be related to the rite celebrated during the vigil. That consisted of two principal phases: the breaking of the bread during the night, then later on, the arrival of the dawn. On to this rite are superimposed: Eutychus' fall, Paul's word announcing that he is alive, then *later on*, his return at dawn. So the story of Eutychus ("Lucky") is a sort of eucharistic tale:[161] an action expressing death (breaking of the bread, parallel to Eutychus' fall) coupled with a proclamation of life (word over the bread and over Eutychus), then the rising sun (resurrection, Eutychus' return, joy despite Paul's disappearance). This structure is very close to what Paul has to say in 1 Cor 11:26 "Each time you eat this bread [. . .] you proclaim the death of the Lord until he comes." So there is a delay between the death, proclaimed by a ritual act performed at night, and the return, marked by the light of a new day.[162] This delay may be very long, like the return of the Messiah in an undefined future, or very brief, like the resurrection at dawn, which is about to break on the first day of the week, as befits a rite. This observation gives importance to the windows or sky-

---

celebrating Easter, which shows that the Jewish communities in which they originated had no corresponding tradition of celebrating Passover (cf. chap. III, §II.1).

161. The combination of the meaning of the rite (breaking of the bread) and a miracle which illustrates it is comparable to the proclamation of the resurrection illustrated by the raising up of the lame man at the Beautiful Gate (Acts 3:7, 15), cf. chap. VI, §III.2.

162. This model with two terms may form the substratum of the hymn in Eph 5:14 ("Rise from the dead, and Christ will shine on you"), which expresses the expectation of a new light and leads, after several exhortations, to an invitation to "give thanks" (εὐχαριστεῖν) in all circumstances, which may refer to the eucharistic rite, cf. Heinz Schürmann, *Ursprung und Gestalt. Erörterungen und Besinnungen zum N. T.*, Düsseldorf, 1970, p. 88. Similarly, Heb 6:4 and 10:32 speak of illumination, in relation to sharing in the Spirit, whence a possible connection with baptism, which is expressly mentioned in Heb 6:2.

lights of the first redaction, but not to the lamps. These latter suppose a change in the symbolism of the breaking of the bread: they burn in the midst of the night, and so the rite expresses at once death *and* resurrection. This is very close to the final statement of the disciples of Emmaus (Luke 24:35, "They had recognized him at the breaking of the bread"). The problem to be examined is, then, the evolving meaning of the breaking of the bread.

3. Conclusions

The Caesarea story allows us to see that baptism has a prehistory, tied to a particular environment, especially if it is not necessarily "in the name of Jesus." We should note that the P Doc, speaking of the conversion of Gentiles, emphasizes the continuity between Jesus and the apostles (*Les Actes* II:26); but such continuity is not really so obvious, since the mission to the nations is linked to the Spirit and to the Risen One, rather than to the Teacher, who hardly, if ever, speaks of it.

The narrative of Troas, with its very realistic setting in which cosmic and human elements are combined, deals with the meaning of the "breaking of the bread." The link with the resurrection is clear, even if the point of reference changes; there is also a link with death, and so—but somewhat loosely—with Passover. Jesus is absent from the narrative and not even named, but is replaced by the young Eutychus who dies and rises again. The rite, therefore, does not seem to be dependent on the person of Jesus, and so again there is a prehistory which we need to research.

The first narrative gave glimpses of a rather closed environment, in which baptism features; the second, though belonging to a later stage of redaction, contains several points of contact with the Essenes. What we now have to do, is examine the two essential institutions highlighted by these narratives. Up till now, no clear link between them has been apparent, apart from a few allusions to John the Baptist. Therefore, we need to begin with him.

Chapter II

The Central Institutions

The NT draws attention to a number of Jewish institutions, but without ever describing their mechanism. They are supposed to be known to the reader. The institutions that characterized the first Christian groups are mentioned in passing, and even sometimes give structural form to the narratives, but they are never clearly defined. We do not know, for instance, how a wedding or a funeral was performed. What should we make of that? Were such institutions of only secondary importance, arising more or less haphazard, whereas the essential thing for the first Christians was to proclaim the end time, a superior ethic, or the exceptional qualities displayed by Jesus? Or rather, did the communities regard these institutions as of fundamental importance, but, perhaps for that very reason, did not publish an account of how they worked? The former explanation is the one more usually adopted. Yet the previous chapter has brought out two facts: these institutions were apparently important, and marginal Jewish groups preferred oral transmission and did not publish the laws proper to themselves. It is just these laws, however, which show through in the narratives. Starting from the hypothesis that baptism and the eucharist are major institutions (even if it is not clear that Jesus established them exactly as we see them in use among the first Christians), we will pursue in this chapter a sort of detective inquiry, hunting for clues that may lead us to these cultural realities and enable us to understand them.

I – Baptism

John the Baptist is such a familiar figure to readers of the gospels, that it seems obvious that he is part of the picture. In reality, his position, so strongly emphasized in the prologue of the Fourth Gospel, is quite surprising. Just why is it necessary that John should prepare the way for

Jesus? The method adopted here is to examine gestures and customs, and so we will not study John's biography as such, but only what is relevant to the baptism which he preached. Then we shall look at Jesus and baptism, and finally at Christian baptism in the NT.[1]

Modern research on the historical Jesus, most often based on the "two-source theory,"[2] agrees that Jesus was baptized by John,[3] and that his mission properly speaking began from that moment,[4] when he became John's successor, though he eventually made some adjustments to his message and adopted a somewhat different style (Mark 6:14; 8:28). In fact, things appear to have been rather more complex, for the gospels also retain traces of another way of looking at Jesus and John, namely as par-

1. Although it reaches different conclusions, this section owes much to the study of Simon Légasse, *Naissance du baptême* (Lectio divina, 153), Paris, Cerf, 1993. This author begins by establishing an instructive distinction between the position of the believer, who affirms that baptism is indeed agreeable to the will of Jesus, and that of the historian, who does not start with this certitude. In fact, according to Matt 28:19 and Mark 16:15-16 (even if it is a later addition), it is not the Jesus of the ministry but the Risen One who sends the apostles on mission into the world, with the command to baptize new disciples. Luke 24:47 speaks at the end only in terms of the remission of sins, without referring to baptism, which comes into play only on the occasion of Pentecost, in Acts 2:38 f. So a later custom, bound up with the life of the first Christians, is placed under the authority of Jesus in a somewhat elastic fashion. During his lifetime, Jesus forbade any mission among the Gentiles (Matt 10:5), which is implied in Peter's hesitations about going to the house of Cornelius (chap. I §II.1). The problem of how far the deeds and acts of the first Christians and the later Church have been in agreement with the intentions of Jesus is vast; obviously, it involves a doctrine of the Spirit, who brings about or authorizes new things, rather than fidelity to the *ipsissima verba* of Jesus.

2. Mark and the Q *(Quelle)* document as sources of what is common to Matt and Luke. The baptism of Jesus by John is explicit in Mark 1:9, but, according to Q, as usually reconstructed, Jesus is not baptized, John's baptism is mentioned only by the way (Luke 3:7a, 16a), and there is no Jordan; for Q, John is first of all a prophet, who has disciples (Luke 7:18), and who proclaims an imminent judgment cf. Robert L. Webb, *John the Baptizer and Prophet. A Socio-Historical History* (JSNT, SS 62), Sheffield, JSOT Press, 1991, p. 40 f. The opposite "two gospel" theory (earlier forms of Matt and Luke were used to compose a "proto-Mark," cf. chap. V, §V.2) merits consideration, cf. M.-Émile Boismard, *L'évangile de Marc. Sa préhistoire* (EB, N. S. 26), Paris, Gabalda, 1994; it has two consequences which are useful here: 1. the tradition of a direct link between Jesus and John at the moment of the baptism is represented only by Matt's construction (which is comparable to John's); 2. the restored "proto-Mark" is a brief, fast-moving narrative, which goes from Jesus' baptism to the Last Supper, *i.e.* which traces an itinerary from one institution to the other. In what follows, no argument will be based on either theory, because of the constant risk of arguing in a circle.

3. Ragnar Leivestad, *Jesus in His Own Perspective*, Minneapolis, Augsburg, 1987, p. 32; Ed P. Sanders, *Jesus and Judaism*, London, SCM Press, 1985, p. 91–93; Richard T. France, "Jesus the Baptist?" in: Joel B. Green & Max Turner, *Jesus of Nazareth, Lord and Christ*, Carlisle (UK), The Paternoster Press, 1994, p. 94–111.

4. Cf. Joachim Jeremias, *New Testament Theology*, London, SCM Press, 1971, p. 42 f.

allel figures. Matt 3:2 (and 4:17) underline the continuity between them: they make the same proclamation, and all the expressions used by John are later echoed in the words of Jesus, which suggests a development along the same lines. But there is also symmetry: Jesus and John are both among those who are not listened to, apparently for the same reason (Matt 11:16-19). According to Mark 6:14 and 8:28, Herod Antipas and the people think that Jesus is John returned from the dead; in Mark 9:11-13, the destiny of John, recognized as Elijah, is modeled on that of Jesus, Son of Man and Suffering Servant;[5] in Mark 11:27 f. Jesus defends his authority in terms of that of John, or more exactly of his baptism. According to Luke 11:1-4, Jesus' disciples pray or wish to pray like John's. The strongest parallel between the two is in John 3:22 f., where both are baptizing at the same time. However, the differences between them are sufficiently clear as to lead many to conclude that Jesus later parted company with John's practices, in particular his baptism. This conclusion would even be practically certain, if it were not for the unmistakable fact that the first Christians, both Jews and Gentiles, were baptized (Acts 2:38, etc.). So the question that arises is simple, although commentators are divided over the answer: Is there continuity between this baptism and John's, or is a creation, or perhaps a restoration, due to the first communities?

1. John's Baptism

At the outset of a study of "John's baptism," it may be of some use to look first at the vocabulary. The verb *baptizein* is an intensive form of *baptein*; the general sense is to "plunge," often with a nuance of "drown, sink," or even "cause to perish" (*J.W.* 4 §137). Whether used metaphorically or literally, the negative meaning predominates, even in Philo and Josephus, and is attested in the NT (Mark 10:38-39; Luke 12:50). There is no need *a priori* to eliminate the negative or painful connotations of the term *baptizein*: since it is a rite of exchange (remission of sins), it must in some way be costly, like all biblical rituals.

The LXX uses the term, introducing the sense of ritual immersion (Sir 34:25; Jdt 12:7; cf. 2 Kgs 5:14) as distinct from the idea of "washing."[6] Following this distinction and the normal meaning of the terms, "baptism"[7] should designate a total immersion, but it does not necessarily

5. Cf. Justin Taylor, "The Coming of Elijah, Mt 17,10–30 and Mk 9,11–13. The Development of the Texts," *RB* 98 (1991), p. 107–119.

6. In the MT, טבל corresponds to "plunge, immerse," and רחץ to "wash."

7. The term βάπτισμα is proper to the NT, whether it designates John's baptism or the Christian rite; FJ, in his notice on John the Baptist (*Ant.* 18 §116), uses the terms

mean that everywhere in the NT.[8] On the other hand, the verb is used 71 times in the NT, mostly in the active or passive, rather than the middle voice, which would imply that someone officiates. However, the title of "baptist" can in itself mean either one who baptizes another, or one who practices ablutions; thus Justin, *Dial.* 80.4, speaks of a Jewish sect of "baptists." In order to avoid confusion, other early Christian writings speak of "hemerobaptist" sects, a term which suggests daily ablutions;[9] interestingly enough, it is sometimes applied to John the Baptist himself.[10]

Behind the ambiguous terminology lie two questions. Is John's baptism a single act to be performed once for all, as at first sight it seems to be, or are there further ablutions from time to time, as suggested by the fact that John settled in places with an abundant supply of water (Jordan; Aenon near Salim, John 3:23)[11]? And what exactly was the role of the officiant? On the one hand, John appears to carry out a rite which is proper to himself and so linked with him personally, but, according to Luke 3:21, Jesus is baptized after John has been arrested, so by another.[12] It is usually said that this is a secondary redactional feature aimed at separating to the maximum Jesus' ministry from John's. But such a reply is not fully satisfactory, not only because of the continuity indicated above, but especially because, according to Acts 18:25 (WT) and 19:3, John's baptism is found at Alexandria and Ephesus among the disciples of Jesus, well

---

βάπτισις and βαπτισμός (the latter occurs in the NT in the sense of ablution, cf. Mark 7:4, Heb 9:10), without any appreciable distinction. His own expression, συνιέναι βαπτισμῷ, should mean "join oneself to baptism," in the sense of a party or structured movement (cf. *J.W.* 2 §129, 4 §132 f.; *Ant.* 18 §315), which would tend to justify Herod's fears, but FJ (or a collaborator) deliberately affects an elaborate and imprecise style, and the meaning may be much more vague, cf. H. St. J. Thackeray, *Josephus* . . . , p. 110 f.

8. In theory the prepositions used should decide: βαπτίζειν εἰς τὸν Ἰορδάνην (Mark 1:9) appears to imply an immersion (connotation of motion), but the employment near by (1:5) of the same expression with ἐν (without connotation of motion) would suggest rather a rite with water but without total immersion. No firm conclusion can be drawn, but ἐν is used in most cases, and other instances show that what is being indicated is the element which is used, and not the form of the rite: ἐν ὕδατι, ἐν πνεύματι ἁγίῳ και πυρί (Matt 3:11, etc.). In Ezek 36:25, the eschatological purification is expressed by the action of throwing water, but this verse is never cited in the NT in relation to baptism, although it is in the background of a sacrificial interpretation of Jesus' death (blood and water), cf. below.

9. *TYad* 2:20 mentions among sectaries of all sorts (מינים) "baptists of the dawn" (טובלי שחרית), cf. chap. IV, §III.2.

10. Cf. *Ps.-Clementine Homilies* 2.23.1.

11. Cf. M.-É. Boismard, "Aenon, près de Salem (Jean III, 23)," *RB* 80 (1973), p. 218–229.

12. According to Luke 3:7 WT, the crowds are baptized in the presence (ἐνώπιον) of John, and not by him.

after both have left the scene. The conclusion is that this baptism existed independently of whether or not John was there in person, and it could also be connected with Jesus. So it is not a gesture of *personal* affiliation with either John or Jesus, but a rite of entry into a group, which still needs to be defined. Of course, there is no reason why, within this context, John could not have had personal disciples, as in fact we find he did.

In later Christian baptism, too, the identity of the officiant is not of primary importance. We have seen this in the case of Cornelius, where Peter simply orders him to be baptized; again, in Acts 22:16, Ananias tells Paul to "see that he gets baptized" (middle voice). So it appears that the role of an officiant is essentially that of a guarantor, who invites or receives the newcomer.

To return to the origins of John's baptism. For the NT, especially for the synoptic gospels, John is the forerunner of Jesus.[13] However, the question which John, from his prison, puts to Jesus (Matt 11:2-19 par.) shows that he is not sure whether Jesus is "the one who is to come"; besides, Jesus does not give a direct reply, or rather, he declares that the judgment has arrived in reality, under the form of cures and "remission," as we shall see in further detail. John's hesitation is natural, for he had announced the coming of "one greater than himself," in a context of imminent judgment, and it was not obvious that Jesus was that one. The proclaimed "baptism in spirit and fire" is a metaphor, with a suggestion of cataclysm.[14] In fact, John announced the coming, not of a Messiah, but of the Lord, as implied by the allusions to Mal 3:1 f. The little dialogue in Matt 3:13-15, in which John asks Jesus to baptize him, is no doubt redactional, but it is instructive. Jesus replies that it is fitting to accomplish all justice, which is often understood as an echo of Isa 53:11, where the servant of the Lord, though personally innocent, takes on himself the sins of others in order to obtain their justification.[15] Such an allusion is not impossible, but is not proved

13. There are not sufficient data to place John's activity in a more general category of "baptist movements." Charles Perrot, *Jésus et l'histoire* (Coll. "Jésus et Jésus-Christ," 11), Paris, Cerf, 1979, p. 111 f., proposes to define a "baptist movement" as the appearance of groups of "religious revival, especially in a popular setting, which proclaim the imminence of the eschatological judgment and call already to salvation through conversion of heart and a rite of immersion in living waters, in view of the forgiveness of sins." This definition is modeled on the way John the Baptist is presented in the NT (and FJ), and does not correspond to any external witness, especially as it ignores the Law and the Covenant.

14. Likewise, 1 QS 4:20-22 announces fire and Spirit (of truth), in an eschatological context, cf. Robert P. Menzies, *The Development of Early Christian Pneumatology, With Special Reference to Luke-Acts* (JNST, SS 54), Sheffield, JSOT Press, 1991, p. 78 f.; John A. T. Robinson, *The Priority of John*, London, SCM Press, 1985, p. 175 f.

15. Cf. Oscar Cullman, *Baptism in the New Testament*, London, SCM Press, 1950, p. 15 f.

beyond doubt. To take only the elements in the narrative, first, Jesus refuses to let John become his disciple, thus answering a question which necessarily arises if the two really met, namely why John did not follow Jesus, since at least some of his disciples did so.[16] Next, it implies that, even for Matt, Jesus was a baptizer. Finally, Matt 3:2 does not speak of "baptism for the remission of sins," but only of conversion. In other words, baptism seals a relationship to God, whether the one baptized has been a sinner or not,[17] for the important point is entry into the people whom John is gathering by baptism in view of the end time.[18] A similar remark can be made about the identification of Jesus by John as "lamb of God" (John 1:29 f.): it is a synthesis,[19] with immediate reference to the Passover. There too, some of John's disciples follow Jesus, though not John himself. Yet Jesus professes a great admiration for John, whom he identifies without hesitation; there is no question of regarding John as a deviant or an unbeliever.[20]

Mark 1:4 says that John was "proclaiming a baptism of conversion for the remission of sins." If John's mission was distinct from that of

16. John appears to reply to this question, though in different fashion, in John 1:30 and 3:30.

17. According to the *Gospel of the Nazarenes* §2 (quoted by Jerome, *C. Pelagium* 3.2), Jesus refused to be baptized by John, because he was free from sin: this moralizing development is certainly a secondary development, but it reflects fairly well the views of Jesus' family, which was opposed to his mission, and whose posterity (James) was precisely "Nazorean," cf. chap. V, §V.2.

18. Cf. Joachim Jeremias, *Theology of the New Testament*, 1968, p. 49.

19. This synthesis may also include a play on words, if one supposes an Aramaic substratum טליא, signifying either "child, servant" (with a possible reference to the "servant" of Isa 53), or "lamb," cf. Joachim Jeremias, ἀμνός, *TWNT* I:343.

20. However, FJ totally separates the two, placing John after Jesus and in another location; Origen, *C. Cels.* 1.41 f., who regards him as an independent witness, deduces that this was the general opinion among the Jews. In fact, the notice of FJ on John (*Ant.* 18 §116–119) is certainly authentic, if only from the unanimous attestation of the mss. and the style, but he appears to have his information from Christians at Rome, and so is not an independent witness: 1. he speaks of him only late in the piece; it is not till after he has made his sketch of Book 18 (and of the entire work) on the model of the parallel narrative in the *War*, that he makes an important change in his initial plan in order to bring in both the notices on Jesus and on John the Baptist; so he only heard speak of him at Rome, about 90 (cf. above §II.1); 2. the links which he establishes with Herod end in unlikely chronologies, cf. Christiane Saulnier, "Hérode Antipas et Jean-Baptiste," *RB* 91 (1984), p. 362–376. FJ is also responsible for certain redactional effects: 1. by a system of doublets, he suggests that John is later than Jesus, but he leaves traces of his sources, which indicate the contrary; 2. he reformulates the action of John after the categories which he knows, and which are close to his earlier description of the Essenes (in *J.W.* 2 §118 f.), but he cuts all possible link with them by the important changes which he makes in his new, very brief description of the Essenes, in *Ant.* 18 §18 f., in which he omits in particular all questions of purification.

Jesus, this definition is not so easy to interpret, as Jesus too proclaimed the remission of sins. Many attempts have been made to provide a theological definition of this mission,[21] such as the following:[22] "As a gesture of purification performed by another and as a procedure inspired by conversion, baptism guarantees to the baptized pardon of his faults, in the perspective of a judgment which is close at hand and on condition of persevering in repentance. Thus understood, in the urgency of the last hour, baptism is necessarily a unique, unrepeatable act, just as the judgment which it is regarded as anticipating is unique and definitive." This definition seems rather heavy, but above all it overlooks several aspects which are obvious. First, baptism is *proclaimed*[23] by John, and not only administered; this proclamation has to do with the coming of the kingdom, since Luke 3:18 goes so far as to say that he "preached the Gospel," which underlies his kinship with Jesus, as we shall see in further detail. Furthermore, between proclamation and baptism there is certainly an element of instruction and training, since according to Luke 3:8 (cf. Matt 3:8), John first demands fruits worthy of repentance (or conversion), which suggests a certain process to be followed. That happens to be the aspect especially emphasized by Josephus: "Baptism appears agreeable to God if it is not used for the pardon of certain faults, but for the purification of the body, *after* the soul has previously been entirely purified by justice."[24] What is in question here is not a philosophical distinction between matter and spirit, but the distance between intention and performance (cf. Heb 10:22), as illustrated by Jesus' interpretation of the Ten Commandments (Matt 5:21 f.).[25] In other words, baptism marks success in perseverance, contrary to the definition given above. Further, it involves entry into a group.

21. Cf. Jürgen Becker, *Johannes der Täufer und Jesus von Nazareth* (Biblische Studien, 63), Neukirchen, Vluyn, 1972, p. 39 f.

22. S. Légasse, *Naissance du baptême*, p. 34.

23. The verb used, κηρύσσω, is also characteristic of Christian preaching, cf. Johann Ernst, *Johannes der Täufer. Interpretation—Geschichte—Wirkungsgeschichte*, Walter de Gruyter, Berlin & New York, 1989, p. 9, and above chap. I, §I.1.

24. Contrary to his normal habit, FJ here employs terms which are particularly precise: τῆς ψυχῆς δικαιοσύνῃ προεκκεκαθαρμένης (*Ant.* 18 §117); he knows the procedure from the Essenes (and perhaps from his own experience with Bannus, cf. *Life* §11), and is careful not to attribute any magic power to the rite.

25. Cf. Barbara E. Thiering, "Inner and Outer Cleansing at Qumran As a Background to New Testament Baptism," *NTS* 26 (1980), p. 266–277; this distinction can be compared with John 3:5 f., "No one can enter the kingdom of God, unless born from water and the Spirit." On the identification of reception of the Spirit and entry into the community, cf. chap. VI, §II.3.

This group clearly regards itself as the true Israel, worthy to face the last times. Despite expressions which would have it that "the whole country of Judaea and all the inhabitants of Jerusalem" came to John to be baptized in the Jordan (Mark 1:5 par.), there can have been no question of all the Jewish people, or even of an important proportion, and for a very simple reason: everything takes place without reference to the Temple, and in particular to the annual Day of Atonement (10 Tishri). This was a popular observance, to the point of providing a subsequent frame of interpretation for the redemptive work of Jesus: Heb 5:1 f. explicitly understands Jesus as a high priest, with precise allusions to the ritual in Lev 16:6 f. It already offered an obvious setting in which to place a call to conversion. So, implicitly for John,[26] then explicitly with Jesus and later Stephen, there is a polemic against the Temple and its function.[27]

This important aspect allows us to make a comparison with the Essenes, as they are defined by the Qumran *Community Rule* (cf. above §I.3). We have noted their insistence on separation from perverse folk and on departure for the desert "when these (things)[28] happen in Israel," with a view to recovering the practice of the "first ordinances"; time is not indefinite, but shaped by a sense of urgency. The observance prescribed is defined in terms of the law of Moses and "what the prophets have revealed by the Holy Spirit." The community—and it alone—has the inspired interpretation; it alone is the Covenant (5:8, 20; 6:15), so the true Israel. This kinship on a central aspect between John and the Essenes enables us to give a sense to similarities in details. Thus, according to 1 QS 2:25–3:12, the return[29] of the sinner can be brought about only through a

26. In his notice, FJ explains that Herod had John put to death in order to forestall a sedition, because of the importance of his followers and their blind confidence in him (*Ant.* 18 §118). Whatever his real source (probably closer to Luke, who says nothing about the death of John, than to Mark 6:17-29, cf. below), his interpretation comes from precise knowledge of the Judaean environment, and from a clear perception of the probable impact (religious and social) of someone like John.

27. This effect is weakened in Luke 1:5 f., where John is the son of a priest serving in the Temple and of a mother descended from Aaron. On priests and Elders, cf. chap. VI, §IV.3.

28. Rather than "when these (persons) exist in Israel," *i.e.* the fifteen perfect men of 8:1, which would suggest that the community project was established even before there were real candidates, cf. the discussion by J. Pouilly, *op. cit.*, p. 25.

29. It has been noticed for a long time that the μετανοία to which John invites is practically equivalent to the term תשובה (לשוב) in 1 QS 5:1; similarly in the Targums (תיובתא) and the rab. trad., where repentance (mourning, change of conduct) *brings about* redemption, cf. discussions and references in Etan Levine, *The Aramaic Version of the Bible. Content and Context* (BZAW, 174), Berlin & New York, Walter de Gruyter, 1988, p. 124 f. In English, the term "conversion" is used, but "reversion" would be even more suitable, in the sense of return to the Covenant, and so observance of its charter, the Law.

process of conversion duly certified, and not by a simple ritual of purification; but when the conditions have been fulfilled, baptism expresses the remission of sins (3:6-9). Similarly, 1 QS 5:13 stipulates: "Let the impious not enter into the water, in order to touch the 'purity' of the holy men"; baptism as a simple immersion has no automatic effect. This last passage introduces a new element, to which only baptism in the sense indicated gives access: the "purity," *i.e.* the eschatological meal of the community, whose symbolic elements are bread and/or wine. This meal is notoriously absent in the case of John, since it is even said explicitly that he "does not eat bread or drink wine" (Luke 7:33). We shall have occasion, however, to speak about it again with regard to the eucharist (cf. §II.5).

2. *John, Elijah, Samuel, David, Melchizedek, Jesus and Messianism*

According to the synoptics, John proclaimed and administered this baptism not far from the place where Elijah had disappeared, near the Jordan (cf. 2 Kgs 2:4-11), which passes through the Judaean desert (Matt 3:1). However, the identification of John with Elijah is questionable. The denials of John 1:21, and the absence from the fourth gospel of any reference to the Jordan, suggest an underlying debate. Matt (17:9 f.) formally identifies John with Elijah and adds an allusion—altogether novel—to Elijah as Suffering Servant, which also expresses a certain parallel between John and Jesus.[30] In Mark 9:9 f., the identification is only suggested, but John's fate is expressed by a term which evokes Ps 118:22 ("The stone rejected by the builders").[31] In both gospels, John baptizes at the Jordan.

On the contrary, according to Luke 3:15, the question is whether John is not the Messiah (which also he denies in John 1:20), and there is

30. Malcolm Lowe, "From the Parable of the Vineyard to a Pre-Synoptic Source," *NTS* 28 (1982), p. 257–263, shows that the parable of the wicked vinedressers (Luke 20:9-19), coming so soon after Jesus' question on the origin of John's baptism, is probably derived from a form where it was applied to John the Baptist, rather than to Jesus. In Matt 21:28-32, this same parable is preceded by that of the two sons, which expressly mentions John, and is followed by that of the wedding breakfast, which also fits John very well. So there are traces of a transfer to Jesus of narratives concerning John, and especially his rejection.

31. In Mark 9:12, the proclamation of the despised Son of Man is applied to John, with the term ἐξουδενηθῇ and the indication "as it is written of him." The reference is to Ps 118:22, according to a translation other than the LXX, cited explicitly in Acts 4:11 (speaking of the rejection of Jesus). Here, John is put in parallel with Jesus, who in Mark 8:31 announces that the Son of Man is going "to be rejected," with the term ἀποδοκιμασθῆναι, corresponding this time to Ps 118:22 in the usual LXX, cf. J. Taylor, "The Coming of Elijah. . . ."

no allusion to Elijah. Further, it is said that John was at work in the desert, in the area of the Jordan (Luke 3:3), but there is no sign of baptism in the Jordan.[32] These two indications go together[33] and point to a reservation. It is true that in Luke 7:27 Jesus quotes, in regard to John, Mal 3:1, "Behold I am sending my messenger," but precisely without mentioning Elijah, and saying explicitly that John is "more than a prophet." This reservation can be connected with the question about the Messiah, which is touched on as early as the infancy narratives. They are relevant here, especially because of their very particular way of connecting Jesus and John. According to Luke 3:21 they do not know one another, since Jesus' baptism takes place after John has been arrested, but according to Luke 1:36 they are cousins, and of roughly the same age. These features seem to contradict one another, but what they have in common is the effect of ruling out the possibility that Jesus could have been a personal disciple of John.

Luke 1–2	**1 Sam 1–3** LXX
Zechariah of priestly family; periodic service in the sanctuary (Jerusalem); wife old and barren (Elizabeth); consecration of John *(nazir)*; canticle of Elizabeth *(Magnificat)*; John filled with the Holy Spirit; mission recognized for whole people; announcement of a "power of salvation in the house of David," then baptism and anointing of the Spirit.	Elkanah of Levitical family; periodic service in the sanctuary (Shilo); first wife barren (Hannah); consecration of Samuel *(nazir)*; canticle of Hannah; Samuel prophesies; mission recognized for all Israel; Samuel anoints David (1 Sam 16).

32. For identification of the places, cf. Jerome Murphy-O'Connor, "John the Baptist and Jesus: History and Hypotheses," *NTS* 36 (1990), p. 359–374, who gives useful details of topography, history and economics.

33. Aside from his proclamation, the only items which permit the recognition of John as Elijah are the Jordan and persecution by a powerful queen married to a weak king: in 1 Kgs 19:2 f. Jezebel begins to persecute Elijah, and Achab has hardly any authority beside her (cf. 1 Kgs 21:7 f.). The parallel with Herod and Herodias is rather distant, unless we suppose that John and his following had already acquired a notable social and religious weight, and so constituted a political threat (cf. above). In any case, it is remarkable that Luke 3:19-20 entirely omits the episode, thus further weakening the identification with Elijah.

Two principal biblical representations of John come together in the infancy narratives:[34] Samuel announcing David, and the herald announcing Melchizedek. Besides these, allusions to Elijah can also be discerned. The first representation, which we can follow in detail step by step, is incontestably Messianic:

Obviously the way in which John's origins are represented has been structured according to the same pattern of divine intervention which is found in the case of Samuel.[35] As for the Messiah, the anointed one is enthroned by another who himself is properly qualified as a prophet. The content of the message is at once political and eschatological, since deliverance from the enemy yoke is an expression of the mercy of God

34. As well as subordination, there is also parallelism between John and Jesus, cf. Augustin George, "Le parallèle entre Jean-Baptiste et Jésus en Lc 1-2," in: *Mélanges bibliques en hommage au R. P. Béda Rigaux*, Gembloux, Duculot, 1970, p. 147–171.

35. The comparison is not very visible in the present MT, which may be by design (cf. chap. IV, §I.3), but is very clear according to the other witnesses. 1. According to 1 Sam 1:1, Elkanah is a man of Ephraim, but *Ant.* 5 §342 makes him a Levite, which corresponds to 1 Chr 6:12-13 & 18-27 (Kohathite, but there are Kohathite towns in Ephraim according to Josh 21:5); Exod 6:24 also places an Elkanah among the sons of Korah (Kohathites). Further on (§346), FJ says (like 1 Sam 1:21 LXX Vulg, cf. the custom of bringing to the Temple the *first* tithe, attested in Jdt 11:13) that Elkanah collected the contributions of the Levites (cf. Num 18:21 f.); in other words, he makes him a Levite bringing a tithe; taking into account his contacts with texts of Qumran (cf. below), it is even simpler to suppose that this item featured in his source. 2. Zechariah, father of John the Baptist, is a priest, not a Levite, but there is some confusion between the two because of the tithe: rab. trad. cites a decree attributed to Ezra (תקנת עזרא, *BYeb* 86b) according to which the tithe would no longer be given to the Levites, since they no longer came to Jerusalem (cf. Ezra 8:15), but directly to the priests (cf. Jdt 11:13). This new custom is still attested after 70, but it was already current at the time of John Hyrcanus (*BSoṭa* 47b, *MMaasSh* 5:15), when the tithe was charged by the functionaries of the Temple; FJ himself (*Ant.* 20 §181 and *Life* §63 & 80) gives to understand that the tithe was collected directly by the priests. Philo gives two contradictory interpretations: in *Spec. leg.* 1 §156, the tithe goes to the Levites, who cannot use it until they have separated a tenth part for the priests (which is in agreement with Scripture), but according to *Virt.* §95, the tithe goes directly to the priests (which is close to the custom cited). 3. The vow of Hannah (1 Sam 1:11 LXX, also *Ant.* 5 §347) is: "I will give him to YHWH until the day of his death (MT 'all the days of his life'), *he shall not drink wine or fermented drink* (MT omits; cf. Judg 13:4, on Samson), and the razor (מורה; Aq. φόβος "fear," from מורא; similarly TYon מרות אנש "domination of another, fear of another," by play on words) shall not pass over his head." TYon and Aq., who mention neither drink nor razor, cut all link with the condition of the *nazir*. *BNaz* 66a has, however, a controversy on this point, and in the background, one may guess, is a textual debate which is not expressed, since legally there is no such thing as permanent nazirate. The identification of perpetual *nazir* and prophet is made by FJ (for Samuel as for Samson, cf. *Ant.* 5 §278 & 347), and Sir 46:13 Heb. (A) says also that Samuel was "consecrated to YHWH in the prophetic function" (cf. 1 Sam 11 MT); like the rab. trad., FJ knows only the temporary *nazir*. Finally, in 4 QSam (which often agrees with the LXX) there is a significant addition to 1 Sam 1:22, where Hannah adds: "I will make of him a *nazir* for ever."

(faithful to the Covenant).[36] It is noteworthy that in Paul's speech at Antioch of Pisidia (Acts 13:17-30), biblical persons are mentioned in only two places, and they are Samuel and David, then John and Jesus; the Messianic model is in operation, and Paul is speaking in a synagogue on the Sabbath (v. 15).

If we look now at the *Benedictus*, it is composed of two parts of unequal length: v. 68-75 ("Blessed be the Lord") and 76-79 ("And you, little child"). This second part, to which reference has already been made in connection with the night vigil at Troas (cf. chap. I, § II.2), was originally independent.[37] V. 76 ("For you shall go before the Lord [. . .]") refers directly to Isa 40:3 and Mal 3:1; Elijah is not named, but is not far away, since it is a question of the coming of the Lord, and not of a Messiah or prophet. The designation of God as "the Most High" is rare in the Bible, but is found four times in the short passage on Melchizedek in Gen 14:18-22, which suggests that there may be a deliberate allusion. In v. 78, the "rising sun which comes from on high" alludes to the successful outcome of the night watch and can easily be interpreted through several Qumran texts as the rising star (cf. Num 24:17 LXX) or the messianic shoot.[38] As we have seen, the metaphor is grounded in a rite which involves waiting for the dawn.

In v. 77, there is a remarkable expression, the "remission of sins." The formula is strange, for in the LXX "remission" has to do with the Sabbatical Year or, even more, with the Jubilee Year.[39] The use of this expression for the forgiveness of sins is not self-evident,[40] but some Qumran texts provide a path: in 11 QMelch,[41] the final end is presented as a

36. In the same spirit, the angel's announcement to Mary (Luke 1:32-33) is inspired by Nathan's prophecy to David (2 Sam 7:9-16), especially in the form cited by 4 QFlor 10-13, cf. Joseph A. Fitzmyer, *The Gospel According to Luke (I–IX)* (AB, 28), Garden City (N. Y.), Doubleday, 1981, p. 338 f.

37. Cf. references and discussion in John Nolland, *Luke 1–9:20* (Word Biblical Commentary, 35A), Dallas, Word Books, 1989, p. 83 f.

38. Cf. references in Daniel R. Schwartz, "On Quirinius, John the Baptist, The Benedictus, Melchizedek, Qumran and Ephesus," *RQ* 13 (1988), p. 635–646, cf. n. 16. This aspect is further developed in connection with the Nazoreans, in chap. V, §V.2.

39. The expression ἄφεσις ἁμαρτιῶν does not correspond to "forgiveness" (סליחה), but to the "remission" of the Sabbatical Year (שמטה) or of the Jubilee (יובל ; דרור "liberation," cf. Lev 25:10). Strictly speaking, it is a question of the cancelling of a debt, and it is worth noting that this is precisely the term which figures in the Lord's Prayer in Matt 6:12, whereas Luke 11:4 speaks directly of sin. The comparison between Luke 1:77 and the figure of Melchizedek is proposed by D. R. Schwartz, *op. cit.*

40. There is a discreet hint in Lev 25:9, since the sounding of the *shofar* announcing the Jubilee is made on the Day of Atonement (10 Tishri); regarding Isa, cf. below.

41. Cf. Jean Carmignac, "Le document de Qumrân sur Melchisédeq," *RQ* 7 (1971), p. 343–378.

year of Jubilee,[42] when Melchizedek will proclaim the "remission of sins" (or: "liberation"),[43] with quotation from Deut 15:1-2 ("Remission will be made to every debtor") and allusion to Lev 25:10 ("You will proclaim the liberation of all the inhabitants of the land").

The contact between these texts is not only verbal but also structural. Both speak of the forgiveness of sins at the end of time, and both announce a forerunner, in the one case John as prophet of the Most High, in the other the herald of Isa 52:7 (anointed by the Spirit, cf. Isa 61:1) who proclaims the reign of Melchizedek, *i.e.* proclaims salvation. This expression of Isa 52:7 enables us to understand another oddity in Luke 1:77, "to give to the people knowledge of salvation." As we have stressed before, the dimension of proclamation, or kerygma, is essential to John as it is later to Jesus and his disciples. Finally, the figure of Melchizedek is explicitly[44] developed by Heb 7:1 f., which applies it to Christ and then proceeds to develop the idea of the new Covenant announced in Jer 31:31-34. The connection is natural, since Abraham, with whom the Covenant of circumcision was made, rendered homage to Melchizedek, a theme developed also in CD 8:21 and 19:33.

The figure of Elijah is not entirely absent, since in Luke 1:17 the angel announces that John will have "the spirit and power of Elijah," and quotes Mal 3:23-24. Still, it is only in the background of other motifs which are more Messianic and which oscillate between John and Jesus: David (political) and Melchizedek (priesthood, mediation), with descent from Aaron explicit for John and implicit for Jesus (Mary is Elizabeth's cousin). This doubling of the role of Messiah occurs also in Zech 3:3-14 (Zerubbabel and Joshua), and again at the eschatological banquet of 1 QSa 2:11-22, presided over by the priest Messiah (descended from Aaron) and the king Messiah (descended from David).

42. The tenth (11 QMelch 2:7 and 3:14), but the starting point of the count, which does not appear to be linked with *Jubilees*, is not indicated, cf. Émile Puech, "Notes sur le manuscrit de 11QMelchîsédek," *RQ* 12 (1987), p. 483–513.

43. וקרא דרור. There is some confusion between the year of remission in Deut 15:1-2 (the seventh year) and the Jubilee, which is the remission *par excellence*. In the LXX, the same term (ἄφεσις) often designates both.

44. It remains implicit in Luke 1:76 f., perhaps because Melchizedek is not an Israelite, while Zechariah comes from a priestly lineage. For Luke, the perspective is continuity, whereas Heb underlines a discontinuity in the priesthood (similarly, Justin, *Dial.* §19, observes and emphasizes that Abraham paid the tithe to one uncircumcised). The fact that Melchizedek, called king and אלהים (god, or judge) by 11 QMelch, is external to the Levitical priesthood, creates no difficulty for the Essene environment, where the condition of priest is a duty (and/or a dignity), and not an hereditary state: 1. nowhere are priests identified as such at the moment of admission of new members; 2. *Ant.* 18 §20 explains that the Essenes choose good men "*as* priests" (mss [A]MW; the *epitome* E corrects "*and*

What conclusion should we draw about the identification of John with Elijah? It is certain that Elijah is a figure whose coming is awaited at the end time, but it is not less clear that the identification of John with Elijah stumbles on a major difficulty, namely baptism. In the Bible, the entry into the Promised Land across the Jordan was made dry shod (cf. Josh 3:15 f.), as was the crossing of the Red Sea.[45] In other words, baptism as such, which was certainly not just a secondary element in the mission of John, fulfills no prophetic type.[46] The only possible biblical reference is purification, which is a gesture of priestly character, although we have seen that it has to be combined with the idea of setting the seal on a lasting conversion. This reference provides a simple link with the Essenes, and so with their Messianic views, but not with Elijah. If we look only at all the mentions of John and his baptism in the NT, apart from any outside reference, two completely different interpretations are possible. One way is to see John in terms of a rather closed group, in which he is an apostle rather than a founder, and which has baptism as a typical institution. The other way is to regard John as a prophetic figure at the center of an unstructured popular movement, who has devised baptism as a symbol of response to his message. John can be identified with Elijah, in the perspective of an imminent end, only on the second model, which completely personalizes John and his action. On this model, it is obvious that Jesus has to be baptized by John, but then, why did John not follow Jesus? and how could "John's baptism" show up at Alexandria or Ephesus? On the contrary, the Messianic dimension of John is more easily

---

priests"), to receive the produce of the earth (Levitical contributions) and to prepare the food in purity; 3. as for Zadok and the Zadokites (who should perhaps be linked with Melchizedek), it is clear that Zadok himself, high priest at the time of Solomon (1 Kgs 2:35), was descended from Aaron and Eleazar only according to 1 Chr 6:35-37; 4. similarly, the Master of Justice was supposed to be (or to become) high priest and son of Zadok, even if his identification remains uncertain, cf. Jerome Murphy-O'Connor, "The Judean Desert," in: Robert A. Kraft & George W. E. Nickelsburg, *Early Judaism and Its Modern Interpreters*, Philadelphia (Penn.), 1986, p. 119–156, and discussion p. 140. This question is developed in chap. VII, §IV.3.

45. This is precisely the significance of the claim made by Theudas (under Fadus, around 45, cf. *Ant.* 20 §97–98); he said that he was a prophet (perhaps Moses, or Elijah), gathered many partisans on the other side of the Jordan, and stated that at his bidding the river would part to let a new people enter dry shod. This Theudas is mentioned by Gamaliel in Acts 5:36.

46. Contrary to a widespread opinion, which could be described as "Bultmanian," cf. Hermann Lichtenberger, "The Dead Sea Scrolls and John the Baptist: Reflections on Josephus' Account of John the Baptist," in: Devorah Dimant & Uriel Rappaport (ed.), *The Dead Sea Scrolls. Forty Years of Research*, Leiden, Brill (etc.), 1992, who rejects any link with the Essene culture and holds that John created a new, prophetic type of baptism.

understandable on the first model, which includes the project of restoring the true Israel. Further, the points of comparison with the Essenes make no sense apart from the first model. As a result, there is a strong presumption that identification with Elijah is secondary (whence the controversies), and so too that the baptism of Jesus by John in person is also secondary, contrary to what is usually inferred from the gospels on the basis of the two-source hypothesis. In the last analysis, the identification of John with Elijah, precisely as forerunner of Jesus, supposes that Jesus has been recognized as Lord, having accomplished the definitive judgment, but that is hardly likely before the resurrection. On the contrary, the identification of Jesus with Elijah may have been more spontaneous.[47]

3. John, Jesus and Their Disciples

The position of John as Forerunner has two facets: he announces Jesus under various forms, as we have seen in the previous section, and he is the model for Jesus, an aspect which we still need to examine. We have already pointed out a general parallel between John and Jesus, seen most clearly in the fact that they baptized at the same time (John 3:22 f.). The gospels contain other points of similarity: according to Matt 4:17, Jesus first proclaims, like John, "Be converted, for the Kingdom of Heaven is very close"; according to Luke 3:18, John "preaches the Gospel"; according to Mark 6:14 par., Jesus is taken for John the Baptist risen from the dead, etc. Some interesting nuances are provided by the speech of Jesus at Nazareth according to Luke 4:17 f. The scene is deliberately placed as a frontispiece for the mission of Jesus, before the recruitment of disciples, and even before the narrative of events at Capharnaum, which are recalled in v. 23. In a setting which is depicted very precisely, Jesus reads Isa 61:1-2, by which he declares himself anointed by the Spirit, proclaims Good News for the poor and announces a year of grace. This passage figures also in 11 QMelch, along with the herald of good news anointed by the Spirit of Isa 52:7; so the themes of the year of "remission" and Melchizedek are at hand, though not expressed. Jesus, however, is rejected, whence the proverb "no one is a prophet in his own country," which is developed here (v. 25-30) with the help of biblical allusions to Elijah and Elisha, one sent to a widow of Zarephath, the other to Naaman the Syrian, so to foreigners. Finally,

47. This identification is already presupposed in the pre-Lucan document which is at the basis of Acts ("Acts I"); cf. *Les Actes*, II:73 f., where it is held to represent an attribution to Jesus of features characteristic of *Elias redivivus*, previously attributed to John the Baptist by his disciples.

despite the threat of stoning by his fellow citizens, Jesus "passed through their midst and went on his way." In other words, the Jubilee proclamation, as in the case of John, leads to rejection of Jesus by his own people, but he passes through them and ends by going on mission to the Gentiles.[48] This inaugural scene at Nazareth covers, therefore, the entire project of Luke-Acts. There is no trace of Messianism, but the shadow of Melchizedek, which can be picked out, suggests a point of anchorage earlier than Abraham, so a renewal of the Covenant and its redirection towards the Gentiles.[49]

John, for his part, does not survive his arrest (he is not raised from the dead), but throughout Luke-Acts he leaves a lasting trace by reason of his baptism. This difference of scope occurs again in John's proclamation, where he announces another baptism, in the Spirit (and fire, according to Matt and Luke). This same Spirit features in the baptism and temptation of Jesus, but that too is an emblematic scene, for the Spirit is in fact manifested only later, at the occasion of baptism "in the name of Jesus" (Acts 2:38; 10:47; 19:6). Thus, by a different way, we return to the same conclusion which we reached earlier, that the real difference between John and Jesus is to be sought not in what they did, but in what they left behind.

Thus, to evaluate the difference between John and Jesus we need to look at their respective disciples. John's preaching is addressed to all and contains no special doctrine, except an exhortation to conversion (return to the Law), by way of proclaiming an imminent judgment. He has a wide influence and a reputation which makes him an object of fear on the part of the authorities.[50] In truth, these features are largely common to both

48. Cf. J. Nolland, *Luke 1–9:20*, p. 195 f.

49. This development, which supposes a certain distancing from Moses, is certainly not part of the original Essene project of renewal of the Covenant. It must be connected with a properly Christian reinterpretation, stripped of any truly Messianic feature, cf. chap. VI, §IV.

50. According to Luke 3:15, people asked if John were not the Messiah; so there is no difficulty in thinking that John's disciples (or, at any rate, some of them) could have passed for zealots, at least potentially. In this sense, it is understandable that John addressed "all Israel," even if few in fact followed him: proclaiming the imminence of the kingdom of God calls for a reform of the whole people (or the elimination of evil, which cannot but awaken the suspicion of the authorities). The Essenes said exactly the same thing: 1 QS 1:1-5 seeks, in defining the community, to establish a rule for all Israel at the end. The figure of the Messiah remains imprecise, but he is always first and foremost a liberator or restorer, as we see also with the disciples from Emmaus (and Pilate's notice of condemnation), even if it is not necessary to say exactly whether he is son of Aaron or son of David. The model liberator is Judas Maccabaeus, as in 1 Macc, which recounts the decisive battle of Emmaus according to the rules of the holy war (1 Macc 4:3 f., cf. Deut 20); it is Judas whom *MSoṭa* 7:1 f. identifies implicitly as "Messiah of war" (*i.e.* anointed *by*

Jesus and John. In the latter case, however, the gospels never show him organizing a group of disciples, or even calling them personally. Some have concluded that John, as a charismatic leader, did not have disciples in the proper sense of the word, and that only after his death did some groups claim to belong to him, in order to distinguish themselves from the people, or to resist the disciples of Jesus.[51] This conclusion is closely bound up with the identification of John as a prophet at the Jordan, his baptism being a sort of extra piece of ornamentation. But it runs counter to a number of texts. Those cases already mentioned where "John's baptism" occurs in the absence of John himself, and without reference to his prophetic role, would indicate rather that baptism played an essential part, and that there were disciples qualified to propagate it. In the synoptics, John's disciples have a well-defined profile, distinct from the people in general: they fast (Mark 2:18-20 par.), bury their master (Mark 6:29 par.), some follow Jesus, and, according to Luke 11:1, John taught them how to pray. But above all, it is very difficult to see how disciples could have emerged after John's death, if there had been none during his lifetime. This last is another form of the argument of Gamaliel (cf. Acts 5:36 f.), namely that a vague movement surrounding a strong personality disappears with its founder, if there is no successor or identifying structure to take over.

Was Jesus, then, John's designated successor? That will not really do, since, as we have seen, John was not sure of his identity. The fourth gospel speaks clearly of John's disciples and relates those of Jesus to them according to two models. In John 1:37 they form a subdivision, since two of John's disciples follow Jesus, but in John 3:26 f. they are a parallel enterprise, or even in competition. The only possible conclusion is that Jesus and John administered a baptism which had the same structure, as we shall see in connection with the disciples at Ephesus (cf. chap. VI, §II.3), and so their respective disciples had the same structure. The name "baptism of John" comes in part from the fact that John was earlier on the scene, but it also marks it off from the newly defined "baptism in the name of Jesus" which appears later with the Spirit (Acts 2:37 f.).

---

war, and not "for"), whereas he himself is neither a priest nor of royal lineage, cf. 2 Macc 5:27 f. and *Search,* p. 76–84. On the contrary, the Qumran texts (1 QS, 1 QM) feature two canonical Messiahs, as we have seen, but in a strictly eschatological perspective (cf. below §IV.5). That the term "Messiah" later became somewhat imprecise, is indicated again by John 4:25, where the Samaritan woman gives this name to the "new Moses" announced in Deut 18:18-22. Cf. also Richard A. Horsley, "Popular Messianic Movements Around the Time of Jesus," *CBQ* 46 (1984), p. 471–495.

51. Cf. S. Légasse, *Naissance du baptême*, p. 45 f.

Once again, the difference between the disciples is to be sought in what John and Jesus respectively left behind.[52] As for indications that considerable crowds received baptism, they are only an exaggeration linked to the interpretation of Jesus, like John, as a prophet. This point will emerge more clearly when we come to see "baptism" as a process, and not as an isolated ritual act (cf. chap. VII, §IV).

4. The Baptism of Jesus and Christian Baptism

To get a more precise idea of the place occupied by John, we need now to see if there is a link between the baptism received by Jesus and Christian baptism. At the beginning of the 2nd century, Ignatius of Antioch (*Ad Eph.* 18), and many after him, explained that Jesus was baptized in order to purify the water by his passion.[53] Thus the water of baptism becomes a symbol of the redemptive death of Jesus, and in this way Jesus' baptism is related to Christian initiation. The theophany which follows the baptism demonstrates that Jesus is Son of God according to the Spirit,[54] and so casts the light of post-Easter faith upon the Jesus of the ministry. The question arises, however, whether it is the voice from heaven (Mark 1:11, "You are my beloved son, in you I have been well pleased") that provides the way to understand the person of Jesus, or

52. Attempts have been made to uphold the existence of a baptist sect which developed in parallel to the first Christians, with a rival Christology, cf. Rudolf Bultmann, *The Gospel of John. A Commentary*, Oxford, Blackwell, p. 17–18 & 48–50; Walter Wink, *John the Baptist in the Gospel Tradition* (SNTS, Mon. Ser. 7), Cambridge University Press, 1968, p. 98 f. In that case, it would have been more logical to remove John from the NT, whereas he is glorified there as the greatest of the prophets. Of course, that does not exclude tensions within the same environment, for it is never said that John's disciples in general followed Jesus (more precisely, that is not the inference to be drawn from Matt 14:2, where it is said only that John's disciples came to inform Jesus of his death).

53. Cf. Dominique A. Bertrand, *Le Baptême de Jésus. Histoire de l'exégèse aux deux premiers siècles* (BGBE, 14), Tübingen, 1973, p. 26 f.

54. With the manifestation of a dove, the meaning of which is not very clear. One possible (Heb.) meaning of the expression "Bar Yona" (cf. Matt 16:17) is "son of a dove," but the reference is ambiguous. The dove is associated with the worship of Aphrodite or Astarte, cf. art. περιστερά, *TWNT* 6 (1959), p. 64 f; the Samaritans are reputed to have had an image of a dove at Garizim (*YAbZ* 5:4, p. 44d), cf. Saul Lieberman, "The Halakhic Inscription of the Bet-Shean Valley," *Tarbiz* 45 (1976), p. 54–63, n. 26; this reputation comes from the second temple on Garizim (to Aphrodite). The dove is also associated with "heavenly voices" and the Spirit (cf. *BBer* 3a, *BḤul* 139b), or even with Christian baptism (Matt 3:16 par.), since the Spirit takes the form of a dove which "hovers," cf. Gen 1:2 and M.-Émile Boismard, *Le Diatessaron: de Tatien à Justin* (EB, N.S. 15), Paris, Gabalda, 1992, p. 140 f. According to *MSanh* 3:3 those who lay bets and those who "cause doves to fly" (מפריחי יונים), among others, are not suitable to testify, but the commentators hesitate on the meaning of the second case, which seems to be identical to the first (laying bets on pigeons); there may be an allusion to Galilean "brigands," that is to zealots, cf. chap. III, §III.

rather his baptism. According to John 1:32, the Baptist attests that he has seen "the Spirit coming down like a dove," but Jesus' baptism is not expressly mentioned. Bringing together these parallel passages, one might conclude that it is the Spirit who singles out Jesus, and not the rite performed by John.[55] However, Jesus (who is later himself a baptist) comes to John, who declares: "There is one coming after me who takes rank ahead of me, because he was before me, and I did not know him; but it was that he might be manifested to Israel that I have come baptizing in water." (1:30-31). So John the Baptist here attests that Jesus has become his successor, and that his baptism in water has enabled him to be manifested, although he himself did not know him; in other words, there would have been no theophany without the baptism. Further, when John declares, "Behold the lamb of God who takes away the sin of the world," he proclaims both Passover *and* resurrection together, in a way which is difficult not to compare with the coupling of baptism *and* manifestation of the Spirit.

If by being baptized Jesus has become a disciple of John, then the theophany which follows indicates a major transformation in what it means to be a disciple. For, insofar as the theophany expresses Jesus' resurrection, then the baptism which precedes it expresses his death. Now, if we follow what John actually proclaims, this baptism is meant for sinners, to bring them back to fidelity to the Covenant, which is something apparently quite different. The link between the two meanings is provided by the costly side of baptism, which is a test (whether by water, fire, or the Spirit). Here we note that, according to Mark 1:5 par., those who come to John receive baptism "while confessing their sins": baptism, at the end of a process of conversion, is also, therefore, an identifying mark of sin, or of the sinner. The new meaning introduced by the baptism of Jesus takes this reality of sin to its ultimate significance: the sinner is likened to a dead person. In this way, the water of baptism takes on a new range of meanings: from being the essential element in purification (which supposes impurity and sin), it becomes the sign of death, which is possible only because there is something that follows, namely resurrection and the Spirit. The symbolism of water, which we cannot go

55. Thus, with others, S. Légasse, *Naissance du baptême*, p. 59 f., who concludes that the heavenly voice is meant to correct the "disconcerting humiliation" of the baptism, by which Jesus has placed himself in the ranks of sinners. His perspective is not the sequence humiliation-exaltation (cf. Phil 2:6 f.), which enhanced the value of the baptism, in the manner of Ignatius, but the quasi uselessness of baptism for someone like Jesus, in the manner of the *Gospel of the Nazarenes*, cited above (§1). In reality, this position results from the conviction that John made no disciples, and so for Jesus baptism ultimately had no sense.

into here,[56] can, therefore, include all mortal perils, the Deluge,[57] the Red Sea, the storm on the lake, Jesus walking on the waters, the water and blood flowing from his side, etc. These remarks bring out the depth of meaning in Jesus' reply to John according to Matt 3:15 ("Thus it is fitting for us to fulfill all justice"): by asking for baptism, Jesus enters into his mission. To sum up, the pair formed by Jesus' baptism and the theophany expresses the Christian kerygma (Jesus died and has been raised up), and at the same time recalls the mission entrusted to his disciples by the risen Christ.

Thus Paul's explanations find their natural place, *e.g.* Rom 6:3-4, "Baptized into Christ Jesus, it is into his death that we have all been baptized; we have been buried with him into death[58] [. . .]." A further meaning can be seen in Jesus' baptism, quite distinct from the Trinitarian revelation which follows. He enters into the Law, since it is the restoration of the Law that John proclaims; then, this entry is transformed into victory over death. This dimension enables us to understand the symbolism of baptism *at the Jordan*:[59] it is entry into the Promised Land, *i.e.* into eternal life.

56. Cf. 2 Sam 22:5; Ps 32:6; 40:3; 42:8; 66:12; 69:2; 88:18; 130:1; Isa 8:7; 30:28; Job 22:11; 27:20; etc.

57. The cataclysm by water is matched by that by fire. FJ cites (*Ant.* 1 §90) a legend according to which all human knowledge acquired before the flood was written on two tablets, one of stone (which withstands water), the other of sun-dried brick (which hardens in fire), in order to cope with both types of deluge. This is a classic theme, cf. Plato, *Timaeus* 22c, Ovid, *Metam.* 1.253 f., known also to Ps.-Philo 3.9 and the *Latin Life of Adam*, §49-50 (in which Eve, after Adam's death, passes on to Seth and his brothers and sisters the revelations of the angel Michael, then announces, among other things, a future punishment, first by water, then by fire, and finally recommends that everything should be written down on tablets of stone and clay). The cataclysm has been foretold, since Gen 6:17 announces the arrival of *the* catastrophe (המבול, with definite art., *hapax* attached to בלל and to Babel, cf. Gen 11:9; LXX τὸν κατακλυσμόν). Philo, *Abrah.* §1, identifies the two catastrophes with the biblical Deluge and the destruction of Sodom by fire; *TTaan* 3:1 says that the deluge of water (מבול המים) is in the past but the deluge of fire (מבול האש) may still come, as at Sodom. *GenR* 26:3, p. 257, underlines the symmetry of the destructions; according to *BSanh* 108b, the waters of the Deluge have passed through the Gehenna of fire. Cf. Louis H. Feldman, "Josephus' *Jewish Antiquities* and Pseudo-Philo's *Biblical Antiquities*," in: Louis H. Feldman & Gohei Hata (Ed.), *Josephus, the Bible, and History*, Detroit, 1989, p. 62 f. These twin destructions are cited as a past event in Luke 17:26-30 (Matt 24:37-39). On the contrary, 2 Pet 3:5 f. establishes the symmetry between the past deluge of water and the deluge of fire to come, with a judgment in both cases.

58. Entry into the Covenant is a passage through death; for the rab. trad. (school of Hillel), circumcision (Covenant) is likened to an exit from the tomb (new birth), cf. chap. V, §I.3.

59. According to John 1:28, "this took place at Bethany *beyond the Jordan*." This place is not to be found in terms of known geography (Bethany is close to Jerusalem, cf. John 11:18), and the expression may have a symbolic meaning. Cf. also Norbert Krieger,

We can begin to see clearly a certain number of elements which all hang together. In the first place, John's baptism, which has no intrinsic link with the Jordan, plays an essential role in the way Jesus fulfills the law and the Prophets. The prophetic figures which he fulfills are numerous, as we have seen, but those in the Law are no less so, since Jesus is above all a prophet *like Moses*; Matt insists on this dimension in the Sermon on the Mount.[60] Luke 2:21 f. has the same intention in detailing the circumcision and presentation in the Temple, "in conformity with the Law." Secondly, it is possible now to understand in what sense John the Baptist can be celebrated as the greatest of the *prophets*, even though he did not become a disciple of Jesus. This, by the way, confirms the presumption, already expressed, that in historical fact, John hardly knew Jesus, or at least had difficulty in identifying him. Thirdly, it becomes easier to place the recurrent problem of controversy between the disciples of the two. In their lifetime, there are a few signs of rivalries in baptist circles (John 3:22 f.), or even of zealot-type agitations (cf. Matt 11:12 "the violent take the kingdom by storm," also Barabbas and the "brigands"[61] of Luke 23:39 f.). Later on, any controversies which arise are part of the wider picture of conflicts aroused within Judaism by early Christian preaching, and also by the way Jesus' disciples developed.

So the baptism of Jesus has been broadly reinterpreted in terms of a later Christian perspective. From this conclusion, we can retrace our steps through the tradition, in order to get an idea of Jesus' activity as a

"Fiktive Ort der Johannes-Taufe," *ZNW* 45 (1953), p. 121 f. It is also possible that Bethany should be corrected to Batanaea (corresponding to the biblical Bashan), *i.e.* the region of the Golan (east of the Jordan), and so of the colony of Bathyra, cf. chap. III, §II.1.

60. Jesus insists on the least commandments of the Law, and is careful about the tiniest details of the text, down to the letters which are optional for the meaning (metaphor for commandments which may appear secondary). According to Matt 5:18, no detail of the Law will pass away, not ἰῶτα ἓν ἢ μία κεραία; it is an adaptation to Greek of "not an י nor a ו," where ἰῶτα is equivalent to י, et κεραία is a *translation* of וו (hook), since the *letter* ו cannot be transcribed (the *digamma* no longer existing in classical Greek, except as a number). The same is true for τοῦ νόμου μίαν κεραίαν "one ו from the Law" in Luke 16:17 (observing by the way that the ו is the smallest letter in palaeo-Hebrew script, while in the square Aramaic alphabet, it is the י), cf. Günther Schwarz, "ἰῶτα ἓν ἢ μία κεραία (Matthäus 5 18)," *ZNW* 66 (1975), p. 268–269. These details of spelling suppose a text which is directly *read*, and not only heard; in fact, tradition has it that authorized copies of the Bible should be made from direct reading, and not from dictation, cf. chap. I, §I.3. On the trinitarian structure of this narrative, cf. chap. VII, §IV.1.

61. Who are of the same nature as the "brigands" (λῃσταί) of FJ (cf. chap. III, §I.2). According to *J.W.* 2 §142, those joining the Essenes must, among other things, bind themselves to "abstain from brigandage," that is decoded, from all zealot activism. This precision, carefully noted by FJ, is certainly not superfluous, cf. chap. VI, §I.3; the same problem, linked to Messianic agitation, occurs in the entourage of John and Jesus.

baptizer. According to John 3:22–4:2, it was parallel to that of John, but with more success. The history of the composition of these passages is fairly complex.[62] For the sake of coherence with John 1:19-34, certain harmonizations have been added: "the one to whom you gave testimony" (v. 26), and v. 28 by which John declares that he is not the Messiah. The indication, "John had not yet been put in prison," is also an addition made in the interests of correcting the chronology of the synoptics. On the other hand, the precision in 4:2 that Jesus did not baptize, but only his disciples, represents a later attempt to differentiate Jesus more clearly from John, and also, perhaps, to emphasize that baptism does not depend on the person of the baptizer. What remains situates Jesus very clearly as a baptist, including topographical details, and we must conclude, for reasons of vocabulary as well as of content, that we are dealing with a pre-Johannine tradition[63] which is to be taken seriously, despite the silence of the synoptics.

Some authors conclude that Jesus at first adhered to John's enterprise,[64] then, since there is no further mention of baptism, was subsequently moved by the abandoned state of the populace to branch out on his own and proclaim mercy and free pardon, without necessity of previous conversion.[65] This sort of hypothesis detaches Jesus from his culture and calls for some comments. The two conclusions of John's gospel emphasize that the acts and deeds of Jesus which are there recorded are only a small selection, so it is reasonable to presume that, since nothing is said of his life prior to his meeting with John, that meeting was fundamental for his mission as a whole. Likewise the indication that Jesus baptized cannot have been included just by chance, but for a purpose. In fact, even

62. Cf. M.-Émile Boismard & Arnaud Lamouille, *Synopse. III—L'évangile de Jean*, Paris, Cerf, 1977, p. 25–39.

63. Cf. Charles H. Dodd, *Historical Tradition in the Fourth Gospel*, Cambridge, Cambridge University Press, 1963, p. 236 & 285 f.

64. At this point, S. Légasse, *Naissance du baptême*, p. 85 f. judges it necessary to look for a difference between the two baptists. He observes that John demands conversion to avoid judgment, whereas Jesus proclaims salvation, and then summons to conversion. This leads him to a major difficulty, since that makes Jesus' baptism fairly close to later Christian baptism, but any direct link appears doubtful, since neither the NT nor the early Christian writers speak of it, and the texts suggest rather discontinuity between Jesus' baptism and the Christian rite. The problem really comes from the fact that for the author John's baptism has hardly any significance in itself (since John is entirely identified with Elijah at the Jordan), and so any continuity of rite can have only an accidental significance.

65. Cf. Paul W. Hollenback, "The Conversion of Jesus: From Jesus the Baptizer to Jesus the Healer," *ANRW* II.25/1 (1982), p. 209 f., who supposes that Jesus suddenly discovered his powers of exorcism and recognized their divine origin. This opinion does not really enable us to understand how the movement issued from him has survived, except by invoking an impressive series of miracles (supernatural fundamentalism).

without engaging in close literary analysis, several facts emerge, if the following pericopes are looked at from the angle of baptism. As part of the complex narrative of the wedding at Cana, John 2:6 f. insists on the purification jars, in which the water is changed into wine, and stresses the difference between those who know where the wine came from and those who do not. Jesus himself relates his "hour" to the filling of the jars, that is to say, he relates his death to purificatory (baptismal) water. The result is a wine superior to that served earlier, so the test of the "hour" is passed with flying colors. Next (John 2:13 f.), Jesus neutralizes the commercial system of sacrifices at the Temple, and so the whole *expiatory* cult, with an allusion to the resurrection (the scene is situated near Passover, and so corresponds to John's declaration on "the lamb of God who takes away the sin of the world"); it is still a question, *via* baptism (water and death), of an enterprise in competition with the Temple. Jesus declares to Nicodemus (John 3:5), "no one can enter the Kingdom of God, unless by being born of water and Spirit." John 3:25 reports a discussion which John's disciples have with a Jew on the subject of purification, then they tell John that Jesus is having more success; the discussion is evidently on the meaning of baptism. Finally, during the episode of the Samaritan woman, Jesus speaks of "living water," which is the technical term for the water of purification (as opposed to water that is stagnant or has been handled).

As many have already pointed out, all these references form a homogeneous whole.[66] Baptism as such is not mentioned in any of these passages, but it underlies them all, in the sense of providing a structure of meaning which brings very varied narrative elements together.[67] Further,

66. Cf. Xavier Léon-Dufour, "'Et là, Jésus baptisait' (Jn 3,22)," in: *Mélanges Tisserant*, Vatican City, 1964, I:295-309.

67. Geography also seems to play a strongly symbolic role: Cana in Galilee (north), the Temple in Judaea (south), then Samaria (center, navel of the world, cf. Judg 9:37), with John at Aenon, Sychar, Jacob's well, and the Samaritans' profession of faith (John 4:42: "We know that he is truly the saviour of the world"). In this itinerary, we note that Jesus declares to the Samaritan woman: "Neither on this mountain, nor at Jerusalem" (John 4:21). Both these cults can pass for reformed (one represented by Deut, the other by Chr); moreover, the documents of the Judaean desert, which are often centered on the restoration of a true worship according to Lev and Num, have ties with the Samaritans as well as with the Jews, cf. chap. V, §I.1. So there is room for wondering (but not for fully discussing here) whether John the Baptist and Jesus (or Johannine circles) may have been involved in the debate between Jews and Samaritans, which appears to have begun only fairly late (during the Maccabaean crisis). 2 Macc 5:22 f. admits that the nation has two sanctuaries, on Garizim and at Jerusalem; then come controversies at Alexandria around 150 on the place of worship which suddenly has to be only one, cf. *Ant.* 13 §74 f. Finally, Judaean expansionism leads to the conquests of John Hyrcanus and the destruction of the Garizim Temple, but not of its cult, around 128, or even 112, cf. *Ant.* 13 §254 f. and chap. III, §I.1.

Jesus' activity as a baptist is recalled at the heart of the sequence. On the one hand, his baptism is similar in structure to John's, combining an act of initiation with daily ablutions (abundant waters). But two new dimensions are added, one ritual (drinking) the other real (the Spirit, announced by John, cf. 1:32 f.). It is difficult not to see in this latter aspect, which agrees with the testimony of John at the beginning, allusions to the resurrection of Jesus, and so to the properly Christian meaning of baptism. The feature which the wine of Cana and the living water of the Samaritan woman have in common, is that both result from water of purification changed into something to drink. So a further level of meaning is suggested, namely a progression from the water of baptism to a banquet.

Thus there emerges a continuity of rite together with a change of meaning, but the latter is connected with the resurrection, and not with any special features of Jesus as baptizer or healer. In the long run, it is impossible, without introducing theological elements which would be anachronistic, to make out a clear identity for the baptism administered by Jesus which is neither the baptism of John nor later Christian baptism. In other words, whatever difference there may be between John's baptism and later Christian baptisms does not come from anything created by Jesus, who invented nothing and entered into a rite administered by another, but from a new meaning which is of later date; the texts discreetly reveal a continuity which is not in dispute. The gospels reveal something similar in the case of the eucharist, where also, materially speaking, Jesus invented nothing new but entered into an existing rite to which, however, a new meaning is given.

5. The First Christian Baptisms

From a very different starting point, M. Hengel concludes that the primitive community had placed at the very center of its preaching the problem of forgiveness of sins, which was fundamental for Jesus as for John. In this respect, therefore, the community should be regarded as inheriting and bringing to fulfilment the revival movement begun by John,[68] which would explain why Christian baptism is obligatory. This statement is incontestable, but it may be misleading to speak in terms of inheritance, at least if that implies some sort of constituted authority ensuring the succession. That is certainly not the spirit of the NT, where unfore-

68. Cf. Martin Hengel, *La Crucifixion dans l'Antiquité et la folie du message de la croix* (Lectio Divina, 105), Paris, 1981, p. 196 f.; the passage cited does not occur either in the German original (1976) or in the Eng. tr. (1977), but corresponds to the author's published lecture "The Expiatory Sacrifice of Christ," *Bulletin of the John Rylands University Library of Manchester* 62 (1979–80), p. 454–475, at p. 473.

seen events jostle against one another. It is much more in agreement with the texts, more socially consistent, and finally just simpler to suppose an institutional continuity, giving a setting, but also creating a tension. In this setting, Jesus, "accredited by signs and wonders," introduces new meanings which are fulfilled by his resurrection. This continuity would form a path, on the level both of history and of ritual, leading from the baptism of John to the gift of the Spirit, as in the summary of Acts 1:22, which culminates in Pentecost. What is more, the forgiveness of sins requires not that they vanish, which would rob history of its reality, but that they be identified; so the Law has not disappeared. This point will be considered later (cf. chap. VII, §V.2).

The NT contains many allusions to the first Christian baptisms.[69] The symbolism of purification is fairly obvious (cf. Eph 5:26, Christ has sanctified the Church "purifying her by the bath of water accompanied by the word"), and the effect of baptism is certainly the remission of sins (cf. Acts 22:16; Titus 3:5; 1 Pet 3:20-21). Paul puts it very clearly in Rom 6:1-11 ("baptized into Christ Jesus, we have been baptized into his death," cf. Col 2:12-13). The statement "but you have been washed, . . . sanctified, . . . justified" (1 Cor 6:11) alludes to baptism. It is true that the idea of baptism has here taken on meanings which are metaphorical, but metaphor can be recognized only if it is based on a gesture or other reality which is already known and has a meaning.

The gift of the Spirit differentiates Christian baptism from John's baptism, but there is room for discussion. The prophecy of Ezek 36:25-27 ("I will sprinkle clean water upon you, and you shall be purified. [. . .] I will give you a new heart. [. . .] I will put my Spirit within you, [. . .] so that you may keep and practice my customs. [. . .] You will be my people and I will be your God") is never quoted in relation to baptism, which implies that the link is not firm, or else that water has a different symbolism.[70] However 1 Cor 12:13 ("You have been baptized into a

69. Baptism is certainly not a novelty introduced specially for the Gentiles, since those converted at Pentecost and Paul have already been baptized; the rite is first linked with the mission to the Jews, as Peter explicitly recalls (Acts 10:47).

70. But there is an interesting connection with 1 John 4:19-24 (observed by M.-Émile Boismard in an oral communication): there it is a question of our "heart" restored (v. 19-21), then of "keeping the commandments and practicing them" (v. 22), and of the gift of the Spirit. Commentators allow that the formula "whoever [. . .] abides in God and God in him" (v. 24) is an echo of "you will be my people [. . .], and I will be your God." However, there is no connection with purification by water. But note that 1 John 1:7 f. declares that purification is brought about by the blood of Christ "so that it may take away our sins and purify us from all iniquity." Now, Ezek 36:25 MT has "And you will be purified from all your impurities and from all your filth (LXX adds 'and') I will purify you," with the same

single Spirit so as to form only one body, Jews and Greeks [. . .]") speaks clearly of the baptism of all in one and the same Spirit (cf. Gal 3:27-28). But even Paul appears to hesitate, since according to Gal 3:2, the gift of the Spirit is linked to welcoming the preaching, and not, strictly speaking, to baptism.[71] Light is thrown on this hesitation by a psalm from Qumran (1 QH 16:11 f.): "I appeased your face thanks to the Spirit, . . . purifying me by your Holy Spirit,"[72] which is certainly about the remission of sins, while the psalmist (or at least the one who made use of the psalm) was no stranger to the system of purification. However, the emphasis falls on the ethical reality, and not on the outward and visible sign, even repeated; that is precisely what John the Baptist demanded, as Josephus explains. The same is true of the cases referred to in the NT, where the rite is in no way magical, but comes along to certify a conversion marked by a radical disruption (Acts 2:37) and more or less linked with preaching. So the reception of the Spirit has a dimension in reality

---

parallel meaning and the same verbal rhythm; further, 1 John 5:6 makes clear that "He is the one who has come by water and blood, Jesus Christ, not in water only, but in water and blood." It is possible to conclude: 1. 1 John insists on the fact that the blood, a new and supplementary element, is connected with the water, and so we find in the background the schema of Ezek; 2. there is no link with immersion, because for Ezek 36:25 (וזרקתי, LXX καὶ ῥανῶ) the water is sprinkled, or even thrown, and the terminology is rather that of sacrifice (cf. Exod 24:6; 29:16; Lev 1:5, etc.: "dash blood against the altar"); 3. the connection between this water and the blood which purifies is natural and is found once more at the death of Jesus, John 19:34 "There came out blood and water" (according to *MPes* 5:6, the blood of the Passover lamb was also thrown against the altar); 4. the baptismal symbolism of this water does not appear among the Fathers until the 3rd century, which shows its secondary character; 5. originally, if the observable sign that gave rise to the interpretation of 1 John is not baptism, it must be because the latter is a true immersion, and not simply a pouring or sprinkling of water. The sign of reference in question is to be sought in a custom familiar to the author and/or the readers. There are some indications that, duly reinterpreted, it is wine mixed with water, that is *drinkable* wine (cf. *BMen* 87a, discussing Prov 23:31: so as not to be too red, wine has to be watered or recent; cf. also 2 Macc 15:39!): 1. water and wine together cannot (or can no longer) be the new wine connected with a pentecost (cf. Acts 2:13 f.), but an older wine which is available for a rite throughout the year (in particular for Passover, cf. *Jub* 49:6); 2. watered wine is attested for the eucharist as early as Justin (cf. below §II.5); 3. by way of the eucharist, water is not linked with purification, but with sacrifice, that is to blood, well expressed by wine. Similarities between 1 John and Essene texts (making use of Ezek 36) have been recognized for a long time, cf. M.-Émile Boismard, "The First Epistle of John and the Writings of Qumran," in: James H. Charlesworth, *John and Qumran*, London, G. Chapman, 1972, who shows an analogy between the יחד of 1 QS and the κοινωνία of 1 John, and also a parallel dualism (darkness and light, truth and injustice, etc.).

71. Cf. Max-Alain Chevallier, "Baptême et don de l'Esprit Saint d'après le Nouveau Testament," in: *L'Expérience de Dieu et le Saint-Esprit* (Le Point Théologique, 44), Paris, Cerf, p. 83–117 f.

72. Cf. André Dupont-Sommer, *Hymnes*, in: *Intertestament*, p. 282.

(individual and so imperceptible) and also in ritual;[73] this latter has obvious social effects, since it is expressed in communion, and so is regulated by obedience, as Paul insists.

Another way of expressing what is new about Christian baptism is to say that it is given "in the name of Jesus." The witness of the NT is unambiguous. The meaning of the expression is, however, less precise.[74] In all probability, this expression did not originally belong to the rite itself, but served at first to distinguish this baptism from John's, and then developed in the direction of a fuller adherence to the person of Jesus Christ. Paul, in his theology, insists on participation in the death of Christ and associates it with baptism. In this way, he takes over the traditional views on the remission of sins, while insisting on the power of the Law to provoke sin and to condemn it. In Rom 7:1, Paul is speaking to people who know the Law, which obliges only during one's lifetime, so that sharing in Christ's death sets free from the condemnation of the Law. For Paul, of course, sharing in Christ's death is clearly linked with faith in the resurrection. So baptism, which expresses this passage through death to another life, is indeed ordained to the remission of sins.

In what way this is so, is made clear in other passages. In 1 Cor 1:13 f. Paul asks: "Was Paul crucified for you? Were you baptized in the name of Paul?" So baptism "in the name of Jesus" is baptism in the name of the One crucified and raised from the dead, and not in the name of a teacher or miracle worker. We can thus follow the evolution of the term "kerygma." The starting point, as we have seen, is the proclamation of the remission of debts (Jubilee), at least for those who are in the Covenant; this is the restoration of John the Baptist. Later, the proclamation of the forgiveness of sins in the name of Jesus is no longer, strictly speaking, a remission,[75] but the transfer to Jesus of a debt,[76] offered gratui-

73. In certain cases (Acts 8:17 f.; 9:17; 19:6), the gift of the Spirit is connected with the laying on of hands, cf. chap. VII, §IV.1.

74. As for baptism *in* or *into* (water, spirit, etc.) there is an alternation ἐν (or ἐπί)/εἰς; according to Michel Quesnel, *Baptisés dans l'Esprit. Baptême et Esprit Saint dans les Actes des Apôtres* (Lectio Divina, 120), Paris, Cerf, 1985, p. 118 f., in the former case (complement in the dative) the baptized person relies on Christ dead and risen, in the latter on the Lord; however, from the angle of forgiveness of sins, the difference between the two formulations looks infinitesimal. In any case, the formulae in the accusative, indicating a goal, suggest, rather than a single act, a procedure leading to a term, cf. chap. VI, §II.3. For the trinitarian dimension of baptism, cf. chap. VII, §IV.1.

75. The question still to be answered is whether the reception of baptism is or is not an entry into the Covenant, since according to the Jerusalem assembly (Acts 15), circumcision appears to have ceased being the characteristic sign of the Covenant. This point will be examined in the context of Pentecost, cf. below §IV.5.

76. Wilhelm Heitmüller, *"Im Namen Jesu": eine sprach- und religionsgeschichtliche Untersuchung zum Neuen Testament, speziell zur altchristlichen Taufe* (FRLANT, 1-2),

tously.[77] This still operates as a sacrifice of exchange, and the debt is evidently cleared only if Jesus is risen, otherwise faith is in vain, as Paul is at pains to emphasize. This is the irreducible difference from the baptism of John[78] or any conceivable "baptism of Paul."

In John's vocabulary, the same idea is expressed by his "Behold the lamb of God, who takes away the sin of the world." Here too we find the successful outcome of the cross, and it is stated by John the Baptist, who is the only one that can sum up the whole process in this way. Jesus' own baptism, we have seen, is not mentioned in John, where, however, it is clear that he moved in baptist circles. Further, if baptism has changed its meaning, the same is obviously true for conversion. With John it consisted in obliging oneself to carry out a moral effort of observance (return to the Covenant) and was not a question of faith (cf. Luke 3:10 f.). Later it is a matter of accepting the proclamation of a salvation which is free, a gift of the Spirit (faith), though not excluding a certain period of instruction, as Paul's letters prove.

At this point we need to say a word about the absence of daily ablutions from Christian baptism, which is (or at least ends up as) a single, unrepeatable rite, apparently for two convergent reasons which are bound up with new meanings. Putting together baptism and the Spirit sets up a correspondence with the death and resurrection of Jesus, and even an identification, since Christians form the body of Christ (cf. Acts 9:4 f.). That is a single, definitive act which brings about the transfer mentioned above. Transposed into the cultic language of Heb, it is a single sacrifice, as opposed to the never-ending, fragile cycle of sacrifices carried out by the high priest at the Temple. The other reason is that purification, in the proper sense of the word, has lost its object. In the pair pure/impure, the second term, which alone has power to contaminate, represents disorder,

---

Göttingen, 1903, basing his argument on economic papyri, judged that the expression "in the name of" belonged to the banking technique of transfer of debt; in this case, the initiative and the charge belong to Jesus (by way of the proclamation of the apostles). On the other hand, Hans Bietenhard, art. "ὄνομα," *TWNT* 5 (1956), p. 274 f., holds that the term expresses belonging, so the consecration of the believer to Jesus; in that case, it would be the response to the previous initiative (disruption, acceptance, cf. Acts 2:37 f.). Baptism includes both movements, but the former dominates, whereas John's baptism puts the seal on "return" to the Covenant.

77. The prototype is expressed in Peter's speech to the Jews: "You claimed the pardon of a murderer, while you had the prince of life put to death; but God has raised him from the dead" (Acts 3:15 f.; cf. 4:10 WT). Likewise 1 Cor 2:12-14, with the characteristic terminology of "wiping out a *debt*."

78. According to Matt 14:2 par., there were some rumors about a possible resurrection of John the Baptist, but Matt 14:12 par. is careful to say that after his execution by Herod his disciples buried him, and his history stops there.

evil, death, whereas the first, representing order, good, life, is weak and has to be protected.[79] To affirm the resurrection of the dead and the Spirit is a complete reversal: life has vanquished death (cf. 1 Cor 15:12 f.), and the power to contaminate is now on the side of life.[80] The parables of the Kingdom illustrate this point of view. It is typical that Matt 13:33 par. reverses the metaphor of leaven. This is the contaminating element *par excellence*, which has to be got rid of at the feast of Unleavened Bread as an image of evil (used as such in 1 Cor 5:6 f.). It now becomes the symbol of the growth of the kingdom as something which contaminates. This reversal is placed under the sign of the Spirit and is expressed in Acts by the transgressions which overthrow all the systems which have been put in place to protect from impurity: going to Gentiles, meeting a eunuch. Previously, Jesus had given signs of such transgressions, which characterize his way of acting: he enters into contact with the impure, whether Gentiles or sinners, and the illnesses which he cures are always metaphors of sin (paralysis, weakness, blindness). These actions take on their full meaning only because he has entered into the Law (by baptism), so as to work these transformations from within the Covenant.

From these remarks on later Christian baptism we can now come back to John's baptism, which certainly does not have all these meanings: it concerns only the restoration of the Covenant, with nothing to suggest a new Creation to follow the cataclysm which is announced. The synoptic narratives give the impression of a single, unrepeatable baptism, even for John. This is very surprising, given that his call to conversion and return to the Law is only too likely to yield results which are fragile and unstable. John 3:23 suggests the opposite, when it explains that John was baptizing at Aenon, a place well out of the way, but possessing abundant

79. Cf. Jacob Milgrom, *Leviticus—I. Chapters 1–16* (Anchor Bible, 3), Garden City (N.Y.), Doubleday, 1991, p. 986 f. This aspect belongs to a question of general anthropology. In her famous study, Mary Douglas, *Purity and Danger. An Analysis of the Concepts of Pollution and Taboos*, London, Routledge & Kegan Paul, 1966, identifies the perception of impurity in disorder, in interference with boundaries, etc.; Jean Soler, "Sémiotique de la nourriture dans la Bible," *Annales Économies, Sociétés, Civilisations* 28/4 (1973), p. 943–955, adds a notion of threat to integrity; Bruce J. Malina, *The New Testament World. Insights from Cultural Anthropology*, Atlanta, John Knox Press, 1981, systematizes the conceptual and legal organization which Jesus opposes (cf. next note).

80. On this theme is grafted that of the new Creation, which is not based on separation (and on the oppositions pure/impure and sacred/profane), cf. chap. I, §II.1, in the context of Peter's vision before going to the house of Cornelius; but it may also be a regression to chaos and confusion (cf. Acts 2:13, "They are full of new wine"), since every law has the role of organizing an ethical and/or ritual rationality, with a view to holding back the threat of chaos (or of nonsense).

springs. Since he can hardly have settled there with the intention of attracting large crowds, we might surmise that he and his companions practiced frequent ablutions. It is of interest that Heb 6:2 mentions among the articles which are fundamental "repentance from dead works, faith in God, instruction on the baptism*s* (pl.)"; these articles form a foundation on the basis of which it is possible to speak of other things, such as enlightenment and the gift of the Spirit. This clearly implies that the culture of reference contains a baptism with multiple ablutions. Other evidence, already cited, confirms this. Justin speaks of a Jewish movement of "baptists" practicing frequent ablutions, although he does not appear to have been aware of any connection with John the Baptist. Later on, Epiphanius mentions among Christian sects, the "hemerobaptists," *i.e.* with daily ablutions, whom it is difficult not to see as distant heirs of John. These indications may be small, but then we would have to presume that John's baptism, as it is presented in the synoptics, has been largely Christianized. This result converges with what has already been said on the interpretation of John as Elijah, bound up with the recognition of Jesus as Lord.

6. *Conclusions*

In the foregoing discussion, the position of John and his baptism has been clarified by references to the Essenes. That John has something to do with the Essenes and the Qumran texts has long been taken for granted.[81] The point needs, however, to be re-examined, for the comparison is not self-evident. We have seen that the person of John has been largely Christianized, but that contacts with Essene traditions have persisted. Furthermore, these contacts have been put to use in the process of Christianization, in particular through employing the figures of Elijah and Melchizedek.

Various explanations of these contacts have been offered,[82] along two main lines. For some writers, features common to Essenes and Chris-

81. Cf. Stevan L. Davies, "John the Baptist and Essene Kashruth," *NTS* 29 (1983), p. 560 f.

82. Thus D. R. Schwartz, "On Quirinius . . . ," p. 645, that the Christianization of John the Baptist by means of traditions attested at Qumran must be the work of former disciples of John who have joined Christianity, like the disciples at Ephesus in Acts 19:1 f.; but we shall see that these latter are disciples of Jesus who know only the baptism of John (cf. chap. VI, §II.3). For his part, Rainer Riesner, "Essener und Urkirche in Jerusalem," in: Bernhard Mayer (ed.), *Christen und Christlichen in Qumran?* (Eichstätter Studien, NF 32), Regensburg, F. Pustet, 1992, p. 139–157, holds that Essenes had become Christians, whence the introduction of a certain characteristic style, and so the use of the same OT quotations at Qumran, in Acts 1–15, and in pre-Pauline Christianity. But there are also

tians are due to the influence of people who have crossed over from one camp to the other and have left a lasting mark. Others regard such contacts simply as common elements in contemporary mainstream Judaism, and therefore as not significant. This second type of explanation is based also on the numerous contacts observable between the Essenes and rabbinic Judaism, itself regarded as the more or less direct heir of the majority Pharisee current. However, the writings of Philo and Josephus formally contradict this point of view. The first explanation, however, is based on an illogicality. If the environment of Jesus' disciples, then of the apostles, was profoundly different from that of the Essenes, itself a very closed world, then how would renegades, who are *ex hypothesi* marginal on both sides, have been able to exercise such an influence, strong enough to give rise to comparisons between the two schools? Either those who came over were few, and their influence then inexplicable, or they were many, and in that case there were major Essene influences from the beginning, from the time of John's baptism right up to Pauline Christianity. In these conditions, to postulate discontinuity from beginning to end amounts to detaching the public life of Jesus from its entire context. One hesitates to take such an option, which would, among other things, empty baptism of all direct significance.

But to stay with the texts, anyone who reads the first description which Josephus gives of the Essenes (*J.W.* 2 §119-161) cannot help but be struck by the points of resemblance with the first Christian community, as it is described in Acts 2:42 f.: network of town communities, sharing of goods, brotherhood, charity, breaking of bread, even a severe justice (cf. Acts 5:1 f.). To these could be added the personal status of women, not mentioned by Josephus, but defined in 1 QSa 1:9-10. The closeness of environment and customs is evident, and we shall return to it (chap. VII, §IV). The only important element that has prevented

---

various contacts in properly Pauline Christianity, and it would be surprising if mere renegades would have left such lasting marks on Christian compositions. Similarly Otto Betz, *Kontakte zwischen Christen und Essenern*, in: id., p. 157–175, judges that John may have been at Qumran, and that he was an "outsider Essene," whence the contacts between Essene traditions and the acts and deeds of Jesus (Lazarus and his sisters may also have been Essenes). In this case, Jesus must indeed have been a disciple of John. In the first years after the discoveries at Qumran, there was a widespread "contingent pan-Essenism," popularized by, among others, Jean Daniélou, *Les Manuscrits de la mer Morte et les origines du christianisme*, Paris, Éd. de l'Orante, 1974[2] (1957[1]). According to this view, John the Baptist emerges from an Essene background, then numerous Christian writings, both canonical and otherwise, show that influential Essenes have become Christians, while the person of Jesus remains strangely untouched, despite major Essene influences both before and after him. The oddity of this comes from concentrating on doctrines and omitting to look carefully at the significance of rites.

commentators from pressing the comparison is the system of purity, conspicuous among the Essenes but formally abandoned in the NT. The objection disappears in the light of what we have been seeing about baptism, where the observable differences, taken as a whole, result from the disruption caused to baptism by the Christian kerygma. The comparison with Josephus is all the more interesting for bringing a number of things together and for owing nothing to the discoveries in the Judaean wilderness.

Finally, these considerations have arisen from the fact that John the Baptist, although venerated and classed as a witness, did not himself become a disciple of Jesus, and so the link between the two must be a common environment with characteristic institutions. Baptism is one of these, and not the least, for it marks the return to the Covenant, the restoration of the true Israel. For the moment, this result is no more than an hypothesis, for, if it does justice to a certain number of NT texts, it leaves many others to one side. In particular, if we have been able to establish a connection between the two ends of the chain, John's baptism and Christian baptism, we still do not have all the links, not only for the ministry of Jesus, but also for the first steps taken by his heirs. The episode of Peter and Cornelius shows that the beginnings were quite unplanned. But before starting on this historical investigation, we have to examine the other characteristic institution, the breaking of the bread, which, by contrast, cannot be associated with John the Baptist.[83]

II – The Last Supper

The "breaking of the bread" is mentioned in Luke-Acts as a well-known custom, but at no stage is its origin clearly stated; the term "breaking" does, however, occur in all the accounts of the multiplication of the loaves.[84] In the synoptic narratives of the Last Supper it is said, among other things, that Jesus broke bread. As a reference point, that is very meagre. There are two reasons for this. First, the gesture is not in any way emphasized, and so it could be regarded as due simply to the material need to distribute the bread among several persons at table together. The

83. The question of the relationship between John's baptism and proselyte baptism in the rab. trad. has worried many commentators. The difficulty comes from this, that there are interesting analogies between the two rites, but the second appears clearly in the sources only after the beginning of Christianity, where, of course, there can be no question of dependence. This point will be taken up in chap. V, §I.3, where it will be shown that, though neither depends on the other, both baptisms have a common origin.

84. Cf. Matt 14:20; 15:37; Mark 6:43; 8:8.19.20; Luke 9:17; John 12:13. The term κλάσμα, in the sense of "fragment, morsel," is found in the *Didachê* 9:3.

second, and more important reason, is that Jesus does not suggest that he is performing a rite which is to be repeated.[85]

1. The Problem of Chronology

After these general remarks, let us study the Last Supper in detail. The method followed is to take as our guide the extremely thorough, and now classic, study of J. Jeremias, which is centered on an essential question: Was the Last Supper a Passover meal? His reply is affirmative (and, of course, he is not alone in this view), and he tries to solve the various difficulties which arise from this thesis.[86] The central problem can be stated very simply. All the gospel narratives agree in placing Jesus' death on a Friday, with a final meal on the previous Thursday evening. The synoptics call this a Passover meal, so celebrated on the evening of 14 Nisan (cf. Exod 12:6); according to this chronology, Jesus dies on the 15th. But for John, Jesus dies just before the beginning of Passover,[87] so the 14th; furthermore, John does not in any way suggest that the Last Supper was a Passover meal. So there is a contradiction, or at least a lack of consistency.

85. Thus Matt and Mark, not to speak of John, who says nothing about the nature of Jesus' last meal. Luke 22:19b-20, in which Jesus gives the command to repeat the gesture then blesses the cup, is absent from the WT and appears to have been imported from 1 Cor 11:24-25 (practically identical), as even Jeremias admits, p. 145 f. (cf. next n.); however, while allowing liturgical influence on the formulation, he rejects the short text, whereas it is very probable that, for Luke as for Acts, the WT is simply the trace of a first edition, cf. chap. I, §I.2b. Thus, the frequent mentions of the "breaking of the bread" (Luke 24:35; Acts 2:42, etc.) correspond better to Jesus' act.

86. Joachim Jeremias, *The Eucharistic Words of Jesus*, Philadelphia, Fortress Press, 1977 (revised translation of *Die Abendsmahlworte Jesu*, 1964[2]).

87. Similarly in the *Gospel of Peter* 2:5. Also according to a rabbinic witness (*BSanh* 43a), which Jeremias cites under the form "Jesus was hanged on the eve of Passover" and interprets according to Gustav Dalman, *Jesus-Jeshua*, London & New York, 1922, p. 89, who supposes that it concerns another, a disciple of Yehoshua b. Peraḥiah (cf. *BSanh* 107b). However, in the uncensored editions (cf. ed. Steinsalz *a. l.*), it is clearly Jesus: 1. the exact text is "On the eve of Passover, Jesus of Nazareth (or rather: "the Nazorean," ישו הנוצרי; cf. chap. V, §V.2) was hanged," which is unambiguous; 2. it is said that the (Roman) authorities sought to defend him; 3. in any case it is made clear that he was crucified (lit. "hanged" תלאוהו), whereas according to Jewish law he should have been stoned then exposed ("hanged," cf. Deut 21:22; cf. also *Ant.* 4 §206 and chap. V, §I.1); 4. immediately after there is a *baraita* referring to the disciples, who in reality are only five. The first is Matthew (מתי), and so they may be meant to be evangelists, but that supposes a knowledge of texts which were probably unknown at the time in Judaea (among Jewish-Christians); cf. what has been said above on the distribution of the NT. A better hypothesis would be to see them as "bishops," *i.e.* in charge of brotherhoods, cf. chap. V, §III.1. In any case, the information provided by the Tannaites is of Christian (or, more exactly, Jewish-Christian) origin.

Three types of solution have tried to solve the difficulty. The first, adopted by the church of Rome (which uses unleavened bread in the liturgy), essentially follows the synoptics. What John has to say is then harmonized with them. For example, even after the Passover meal, the Jews might still have feared becoming impure if they entered the praetorium and so would be unable to "eat the Passover" (John 18:28), because throughout the whole period of Unleavened Bread they had to eat communion sacrifices (cf. *MḤag* 1:1 f. and Deut 16:2). It must be said, however, that, if it were not for the synoptics, no one would ever have imagined that that was what John had in mind. The second solution, adopted by the Greek church (which uses leavened bread in the liturgy), is to follow John, and so to suppose that Jesus put forward the Passover meal, knowing that he would be dead before the exact date on the following day. But that seems to be a rather odd thing to do, and in any case could not be guessed from the texts.[88]

Alongside these traditional answers (which may even be earlier than the publication of the gospels), there is a third type of solution, which is more elaborate and looks for a way of combining both the others, namely by suggesting that there were two Passover celebrations. The simplest is to suppose that because of the great number of pilgrims, the immolation of victims took place over two days, starting on 13 Nisan, especially for those from Galilee. However, there is no evidence for such a practice, which would have involved all sorts of difficulties concerning leaven both for the Temple precincts and for the priests.[89] In that case, it is tempting to imagine a controversy between Pharisees and Sadducees. According to Exod 12:6, the lamb has to be immolated as night falls, but that is not fitting if it is the evening before Sabbath, as in our case. So, when Passover

88. Jeremias says that such an anticipation is impossible, on the basis of the rab. trad. (*MZeb* 1:3, *TPes* 3:8), which demands that the lamb be immolated at the Temple (cf. 2 Chr 35:7 f.; cf. *J.W.* 6 §423); but in reality, the customs allowed greater diversity, cf. below chap. VII, §II.3.

89. The author of this theory, Josef Pickl, *Messiaskönig Jesus*, München, 1935, argues precisely from the fact that the *seven* days laid down for Unleavened Bread (15–22 Nisan, cf. Num 28:17; cf. Philo, *Spec. leg.* 2 §150 f. and *Ant.* 3 §249, speaking of sacrifices) are extended by FJ to *eight* (*Ant.* 2 §317), whereas he is speaking of the custom of the Passover lamb at Rome, and so includes 14 Nisan; according to *MPes* 4:5, the Galileans, but not the Judaeans, took the whole of the 14th as a holiday, which may suggest that they began Passover earlier. Jeremias rejects this theory, as for him, FJ's eighth day is the day added to all feasts in the Diaspora, so here 22 Nisan; but the objection is invalid, since this additional day is simply a Tannaitic precept (originating in the need to take into account the uncertainty arising from observation of the new moon). We will show later (cf. chap. VII, §II) that the eighth day is in fact 14 Nisan, but that the uncertainty is due to a calendar difference, depending on whether the day begins in the morning or the evening.

fell on a Sabbath, the lambs were immolated a day earlier, that is on Thursday, whence the controversy: according to some, the Passover meal should then be taken immediately, so on Thursday evening, while others waited until Friday evening. This solution is purely mechanical and in any case runs counter to Philo, Josephus, and the *Mishnah*, who all agree in stating explicitly that in fact the immolation took place in the afternoon, and not the evening, so the problem disappears. In any case, the proposed scenario does not take account of Exod 12:10, which expressly forbids leaving any remains of the immolated animal until the next day. A more subtle hypothesis would be to suppose disagreement about fixing the beginning of Nisan in that particular year, since it depends on witnessing the appearance of the new moon. Since a lunar month cannot have fewer than 29 days or more than 30, the uncertainty cannot be over more than one day, and for the year in question, there may have been a double reckoning.[90] However, Pharisees and Sadducees all went to the same Temple, so it is not easy to see how two lots of public sacrifices would have been carried out, even if the priests had agreed to the duplication. In any case, there is no evidence of two official calculations existing side by side.

The most recent attempt to justify two celebrations of Passover is that of A. Jaubert, who calls on the solar calendar known from *Jubilees*, which was in use in circles connected with Qumran (cf. chap. I, §I.2b). According to this calendar, 1 Nisan is always a Wednesday, so the 14th a Tuesday; on this basis she reconstructs the last days of Jesus, arrested in the night of Tuesday–Wednesday, etc. This would be the calendar

90. Although for different reasons, that was the case in 1995, when 14 Nisan fell on a Thursday for the Samaritans, but on the following day for the Jews. According to calculations made long ago, the sole possibility for this uncertainty (14 Nisan Thursday or Friday) between the years 27 and 35 is in 30 (6 or 7 April); the other cases which can be used in this period are Thursday 26 April 31 in favor of the synoptics (uncertainty over Wednesday or Thursday), and Friday 3 April 33 in favor of John (uncertainty over Friday or Saturday). However, the probability of glimpsing the new moon in a clear sky just after sunset is not the same each month, since the lunar cycle takes a little more than 29.5 days; not only is there a variation from one month to the next, but a change every two months, since the number of days is not in fact quite whole (a little more than 59 days). It is also necessary to take into account the possibility, when the beginning of Nisan falls very close to the equinox, of the introduction of an intercalary month (Second Adar), which brings back Nisan to the following moon. In brief, the possibilities indicated above are not all equally probable. By combining all these elements with astronomical calculations and observations on the ground in spring, the most probable dates are 7 April 30 or 3 April 33, both a Friday, so clearly in favor of John, cf. experiments and calculations of Karl Schoch, "Christi Kreuzigung am 14. Nissan," *Biblica* 9 (1928), p. 48 f., and discussion of Jeremias, p. 38 f.

followed by the synoptics, while John stuck to the official calendar of the Temple. She shows that certain early Christian writings support this thesis. Jeremias rejects it and attacks what he sees as its weakest point, namely the patristic evidence. On the other hand, he does not give enough weight to the fact that the calendar in question is above all *biblical*, and that a number of other indications in the NT show that the hypothesis is very plausible. It will be discussed and, in part, adopted in what follows.[91]

2. The Nature of the Last Supper

Jeremias decides that discussions concerning the incidents of the calendar will get nowhere and comes at the question from another angle, that of the nature of the Last Supper. He first surveys a range of opinions. Perhaps it was not a Passover meal but a "*qiddush* meal"? In fact, as he points out, there is no such kind of meal, for, according to Tannaitic tradition, the *qiddush* is simply a blessing pronounced over a cup, to mark the beginning of the Sabbath or feast day; it has no intrinsic link with a meal,[92] all the more since in those days, it seems, the main meal took place *before* the evening,[93] as in the multiplication of the loaves (Matt 14:15 f. "The evening, [. . .] the meal time was already passed"). This blessing is not said outside these fixed times. Similarly, some authors have held that the Last Supper was modeled on the rite of entering into the Sabbath, since, besides the blessing of the wine, there is also the blessing and sharing of bread, which marks the beginning of the meal. However, it was only quite late that the custom was introduced (from

91. Counting days from morning to morning is one of its characteristics, as we have seen in connection with the night at Troas (cf. chap. I, §II.2).

92. In fact, there is a double blessing, on the wine *and* on the festive day beginning (*MBer* 8:1, and for Passover *MPes* 10:2). This duplication suggests that the rite has evolved, and in fact, according to the earliest witness, before 70 (R. Eleazar b. Sadoq, cf. *TBer* 3:7), the blessing of the day can be made without wine, to the point that *Tosefta kifshuṭah* 1:35 supposes that it is a question of the blessing said for the Day of Atonement, when there is no wine. It is important to observe that wine is not an intrinsic component of *qiddush* (according to *BPes* 10a, the same is true for the *great qiddush* on Saturday morning, a secondary blessing with or without wine but whose name hints that it was once more important). On the Romans' confusion of Sabbath and Day of Atonement, cf. chap. I, §II.2.

93. A *baraita* (*BBer* 48b) shows that formerly (before 70) the *qiddush* for the opening of Sabbath was combined with the blessing closing the meal; *TBer* 5:2 has a controversy on this point, but it is obscured by the later custom of the meal after the beginning of Sabbath (cf. below), recalled immediately before (5:1); *Tosefta kifshuṭah* 1:73 does not pronounce on the meaning of this controversy. The same is true for the blessing concluding the meal on Saturday afternoon (the custom of which is kept), combined with the blessing for ending Sabbath *(habdala)*.

Babylonia) of holding a synagogue service at the entry of the Sabbath, and so of putting the meal back until after Sabbath begins. In other words, the order of blessings, first of wine, then of bread, still in force today, brings together elements of originally different meaning. Further, the gospel narratives cannot support the hypothesis of a meal on the Friday evening. Finally—a detail whose importance we will show—they put the bread before the wine. Other commentators have sought a comparison with the rabbinic notion of a "meal of precept" *(ḥaburat miṣwa)*, which is to be held on feast days and various occasions. But the only context provided as an occasion is Passover, and so this explanation will not work here.[94]

The Messianic meals of the Essenes, in which the blessings of bread and wine are emphasized (1 QS 6:4 f.), have often been suggested since the discoveries at Qumran. Among more moderate versions of these views is that of K. G. Kuhn,[95] according to which the cultic meal of the Essenes influenced the eucharist in two related ways, by determining the form of early Christian meals as well as that of the gospel accounts of Matt and Mark, which bring together the rite of the bread and the wine (whereas Luke and 1 Cor put the wine at the end of the meal). Jeremias concedes that there are striking resemblances, but has some objections. First, although at Jerusalem (Acts) as at Qumran, the community comes together each day for a common meal, with parallel blessings over the bread and the wine, there is a clear difference, since women take part in the Christian meal; so it is simply a question of continuing the daily usage practiced with Jesus. Secondly, the resemblance to the gospel narrative is only superficial, for the ancient sources show that the rite was placed at the end of the meal, and not at the beginning; any way, blessing bread and wine is a general Jewish usage. Thirdly, even if Essene influence on the

94. In particular this is the judgment of Adolf Büchler, *Der galiläische 'Am ha'Areṣ des zweiten Jahrhunderts*, Wien, 1906, p. 208. However, the origin of these prescribed meals, at which it is obligatory to wash the hands only if there is bread (*BBer* 50b), poses yet another curious question, for they appear connected with the customs of the *ḥaberim*, and in addition the table is assimilated to the altar (*BBer* 54b-55a), cf. chap. V, §I.1; we shall see later that the comparison holds good. For the Sabbath, the prescribed meals have another name (סצודה), and are connected with Exod 16:12 (cf. *BYoma* 75b).

95. Karl Georg Kuhn, "The Lord's Supper and the Communal Meal at Qumran," in: Krister Stendhal (ed.), *The Scrolls and the New Testament*, New York, Harper, 1957, p. 65 f. One of his arguments is the connection with the Therapeutae of the narrative of *Joseph and Asenath*, in which there are five references to the "bread of life" and the "cup of blessing" (8:5.9, 15:5, 16:16, 19:5). Jeremias contests the comparison, as in three of these passages there is also mention of the "oil of incorruptibility," whereas the Essenes refrained from anointings (*J.W.* 2 §123). We will show later that, on the contrary, the presence of oil is a very strong argument in favor of the comparison (cf. chap. VII, §V.1).

rite cannot be demonstrated, there may have been such influence on Jesus himself, since he gives a Messianic dimension to the bread and the wine. But there too, no precise relation can be proved, since this Messianic dimension may simply have been inspired by the *Hallel*, recited by Jews all together at the end of the Passover meal, and especially by its final section (Ps 118:25-29).

Jeremias concludes that Essene usages have nothing useful to offer for understanding the rite instituted by Jesus. However, besides discussions of detail (for instance, women were full members of the community among the Therapeutae), two objections as to method can be made. Jeremias tends to confuse the Essenes with the quasi monastic group at Qumran, whereas Josephus speaks clearly of networks of town-based groups. Further, he is obviously influenced by the massive rabbinic commentary on the NT by Strack-Billerbeck, which leads to the view that Mishnaic Judaism represents the generality of Jewish usages of Jesus' time; that is quite inexact, as we hope to show later (cf. chap. V, §I). Kuhn's opinion, which allows for Essene influence on the early Christian communities but not on Jesus, is as surprising as all the other hypotheses reviewed earlier which posit Essene influence on the formulation of *Christian* baptism: what imaginable channel could have permitted communication between such closed circles? It is rather like wondering what *positive* influence Catholicism could have had on Protestantism *after* the Reformation.

3. Last Supper and Passover

Jeremias next develops his thesis, that the Last Supper was a Passover meal, arguing not so much from the explicit indications in Matt 26:17 par. ("It was the first day of Unleavened Bread"), but rather from peripheral details which have no major significance for the rite itself but, for that very reason, are less likely to have been altered.[96] They are here given and discussed in the order in which they occur in the narratives.

1. All the gospels agree that the Supper took place in Jerusalem, whereas Jesus was living at the time at Bethany, returning there each evening (Mark 11:11 par.). The significant points here are that Bethany was outside the city limits, and that Jesus chose to eat a particular meal in Jerusalem itself at a time when it was overflowing with pilgrims—surely for some special reason. At this period, it was no longer possible to hold the Passover meal at the Temple, but it still had to be eaten within the city limits, (*MPes* 5:10, *Ant.* 17 §211), so the inference is that this meal which Jesus deliberately chose to eat in town was indeed the Passover.

96. Jacob Mann, "Rabbinic Studies in the Synoptic Gospels," *HUCA* 1 (1924), p. 339 f., had already made many very acute observations in the same direction.

There is, however, some room for discussion, starting from the fact that the disciples seem to have been in some doubt about what to do: they ask Jesus where they should prepare the Passover, but he is the one who sends them "into town." More precisely, for Luke 22:8, Jesus himself takes the initiative in organizing preparation for Passover for the *whole* group, and the disciples only ask where to hold it. For Mark 14:12, they think of it first, with a suggestion of moving to another place ("Where do you wish us to *go* to prepare?"). In Matt 26:17, it is again the disciples who ask, but this time without any necessary idea of movement ("Where do you wish us to prepare?"); further, for Matt and Mark, they appear to envisage a Passover only for Jesus ("for *you* to eat the Passover").[97] So three questions remain apparently in suspense, for which general remarks concerning Jewish usages will not suffice. First, there is the question of place (Jerusalem or not?), which is the object of a very detailed narrative. Secondly, it is not clear that Jesus moves in the same circles as his disciples, since he has places where he is known, or at least he has made a booking at an inn ("Where is *my* dining room?"), whereas the disciples are not familiar with Jerusalem and hear about this for the first time. Finally, the disciples do not ask for a Passover for themselves, but Jesus explicitly invites them to take part, so we may well ask whether they have the same customs, associated with Jerusalem or not.[98]

2. The room at the inn is freely available, in accordance with the principle formulated in *TMaasSh* 1:12 and elsewhere, that Jerusalem was given not to the tribes, but to the whole people. In practice, it was possible to stay free of charge[99] with an inhabitant when coming to fulfill a precept which required at least one night; the custom, according to some, was to leave some payment in kind, such as the skins of animals offered in sacrifice, especially where domestic furniture (beds, cushions, etc.) had been used. Jeremias agrees that the texts should not be pressed too far, but they certainly speak of a room set up for a celebration (Matt 26:15; Luke 22:12).

97. A small sign indicates the same in Luke, where, according to an addition in the WT, the disciples ask: "Where do you wish us to prepare *for you* (σοί)?" Mark has a comparable variant.

98. This hesitation on the part of the disciples, who do not know Jerusalem well, as to their own participation in the Passover meal may have two different origins (which are not mutually exclusive): either because they belong to a Galilean tradition which does not celebrate Passover (cf. the case of Hillel, chap. III, §II.1), or because the narrative has been altered by later redactions at a time when Christians did not celebrate it (as we shall see, that was the ancient Roman custom; chap. VII, §I.3). Thus we can understand that Jesus announces an interruption of Passover (cf. §5 below).

99. The same is true for the involuntary homicide in Levitical cities of refuge, since the Levites who reside there are not the proprietors, cf. *Tosefta kifshuṭah* 2:723.

3. The meal is held in the evening (cf. 1 Cor 11:23; John 13:30), and not in the afternoon. This, it is argued, is itself out of the ordinary, since the main meal usually took place in the afternoon, even on Friday and Saturday, as we have seen. Now the Passover lamb had to be eaten at night, *i.e.* after sunset (Exod 12:8, cf. *MZeb* 5:8);[100] so the Passover meal took place at an hour which was unusual, at least for the time and place of the NT.[101]

A question, however, arises. The custom of eating in the afternoon is attested in the NT and among the Essenes (*J.W.* 2 §131 f.), and is in the background of the rabbinic tradition. But does that mean it was in general use among Jews?[102] The fact that Josephus mentions it in connection with the Essenes, would imply rather that it was a custom peculiar to them.

4. The meal is taken by Jesus and the Twelve (Mark 14:17 par.), and is the only case where the limited group is shown by itself at table. It would be going too far to conclude from this alone that the women mentioned in Mark 15:40 par. were absent, but Jesus is normally seen eating in wider company, or as a guest, etc. He even passes for a glutton and a drunkard, a friend of sinners (Matt 11:29). Now precisely, the Passover meal was eaten in a small group, at least ten but rarely more, except in case of necessity (*J.W.* 6 §423 f.; *TPes* 4:15), the number of diners suitable for a one-year-old lamb. So we have to conclude that there was no room for the women or others.

We can agree that the women are absent from *the narrative*, as opposed to other scenes, especially the anointing at Bethany. However, Jeremias' argument is not decisive, since it needs to be seriously modified. In fact, *MPes* 8:3 says that to eat the Passover, there should be for each lamb a group of such a size that everyone can have a piece at least as large as an olive, in which case it may contain anything up to several dozens. The problem does not really arise from economic, but from practical, con-

100. Hence the need to see to it that children remain awake, cf. *TPes* 10:9 and the developments of *Tosefta kifshuṭah* 4:653.

101. This may provide a context for the "tenth hour" as the time when Jesus allows John's two disciples to "stay" with him (John 1:39), a term implying at least that they took a meal with him. We have already seen (§II.1), in connection with Peter's visit to Cornelius, that he is criticized for having *eaten with* Gentiles (Acts 11:3), whereas the preceding narrative says that he *stayed with* them.

102. According to *MPes* 10:4, in explaining to children the unusual elements in the feast, no mention is made of the late hour: "What makes this night different from other nights? The other *nights* we eat all the vegetables, but this night only bitter herbs, etc." On the other hand, these formulae concentrate on the specific elements of Passover, and not on secondary details, cf. below §13.

siderations: the crowd in the Temple was enormous, corresponding to the number of possible sacrifices.[103] We should, however, note that, in the case of Jesus' meal, there is no hint of anything to do with the Temple, and, unlike other scenes, there is no mention of a crowd, either at the time of preparation, or later at Gethsemane. What the texts portray as a quiet Passover meal shared among a small group, is best explained if it takes place outside the official sphere, whether in another place or at another time.

5. According to Luke 22:12, the upper room is furnished with cushions. In fact, all the accounts (Mark 14:18 par., John 12:13 f.) indicate that Jesus and the disciples were reclining at table, in accordance with the Graeco-Roman custom for free citizens (despite the protests of Amos 3:12). This usage was limited solely to feasts or banquets, whereas other meals were taken standing, sitting or squatting, according to the circumstances. The present case is not a banquet, but a feast celebrated with a few companions, so it is hard to see it as other than a Passover meal, since, according to *MPes* 10:1, it is of obligation, even for the poorest, to recline for the Passover meal. This seems at first sight to be a common Jewish custom,[104] but we shall see that it was of Greek origin (chap. VII, §II.3).

6. According to John 13:10 ("One who has bathed [. . .]"), the guests at Jesus' last meal were in a state of Levitical purity, which, for Jeremias, was necessary for the Passover lamb, since it belonged to the class of holy things of lower rank.[105]

103. FJ goes as far as the figure of 250,000 lambs, and says that often the groups were of more than twenty persons, which implies an enormous crush and also difficult logistical problems at the Temple, cf. *Tosefta kifshuṭah* 4:569.

104. However, according to *MBer* 6:6, when several eat sitting down (יושבים), each one should say the blessing for himself, whereas if the guests are reclining (מסובים), one says it for all; in other words, the true meal (group gathered as such) is taken reclining. By contrast, at Qumran, all the (community) meals were taken seated (1 QS 6:4-5).

105. He also supposes that the washing of feet is a necessary supplement, but this view is not well founded and not very logical. According to Exod 30:17-21 and 38:8, a basin (כיור) is to be provided in the sanctuary "so that Aaron and his sons may wash their hands and feet"; this is a priestly rite of entering into contact with holy things (cf. similarly *MShab* 15:1), which has nothing to do with purification. In any case, hands and feet cannot be impure in isolation, and purification properly so called must be of the whole body (cf. *MEdu* 5:6). In Jesus' discussion with the Pharisees on purification before meals, this same controversy is in the background: in Luke 11:38, they want total immersion, so a purification, but in Mark 7:3, they want washing of the hands up to the elbow, which is then a gesture of sanctification implying that the table is regarded as a substitute for the altar (cf. chap. V, §I.1 and VII, §IV.1). In other words, whether a partial (hands and/or feet) or a total ablution is required before a meal signifies a major difference of perception, cf. sources and discussion H. Albeck, *Mishnah*, 6:606. In the case of John 13:8, Jesus says to Peter, "If I do not wash you [your feet], you will have no part with me." Besides the obvious idea of service (cf. Gen 18:4), the gesture implies that Jesus makes Peter enter into

In reality, there is no literary evidence that a special purification was necessary.[106] Josephus' explanations make no reference to such a practice for all, and it would certainly have been difficult to observe for the enormous crowds which he describes. In Num 9:6-13, provision is made for a second Passover for those in a state of lasting impurity, but *MPes* 9:1 f. makes allowance for some impurities, and even if the whole people is impure from contact with corpses, Passover is still celebrated. According to John 18:28 the emissaries of the high priest do not enter Pilate's praetorium "so as not to pollute themselves, in order to be able to eat the Passover"; but this is because of the presumption that Gentile dwellings were impure, since fetuses were likely to have been buried in them (*MOhol* 18:7). In any case, we are dealing here with members of the priestly class, which is not the case of the apostles, and the impurity in question disqualifies both from the Passover meal and from the communion sacrifices which normally follow.

These remarks serve to show that the ablution presupposed by John 13:10 is not associated with any particular impurity, but is part of the normal ritual for this meal, which the fourth gospel never explicitly identifies as paschal. Furthermore, Jesus says that the one who is going to hand him over is not pure (13:11), so the ablution, which is effective only for

sanctification (or glorification, in Johannine terminology), which discreetly changes the meaning of the meal, although Jesus points out that this will be understood only later. Peter's response, asking that Jesus wash also his hands and his head, adopts something of the same logic: thus *TBer* 4:1 requires that a person use face, hands and feet only for the glory of the Creator (cf. Prov 16:4 MT: "YHWH has made everything in view of Himself"), which is understood as necessitating an ablution (every day, or only on Sabbath, according to the particular tradition, cf. *Tosefta kifshuṭah* 1:56). Ephraim E. Urbach, *The Halakha, Its Sources and Development*, Tel Aviv, 1984, p. 17, offers another explanation for the apparently hybrid rite of hand washing: it is certainly not a purification, and it is significant that according to *BErub* 21b, Solomon was the one who decreed it (but for *BShab* 14b, it is one of the 18 decrees taken from Ḥananya b. Ḥizqya). Solomon was a king, and *TBer* 4:8 explains the ceremonial of princely banquets, which includes the washing of hands (with a ewer, comparable to the basin already mentioned). So it would simply be a custom of aristocratic, rather than hygienic, origin, which was afterwards generalized. This secular explanation, without any connection with purification, appears weaker with respect to Jewish customs, but illustrates the remarkable parallel between the patrician banquet and the Jewish festive meal in the Tannaitic period, cf. chap. VII, §II.3, in the context of the Passover *Seder*.

106. Philo, *Spec. leg.* 2 §145 explains that for Passover the whole nation officiates lawfully with pure hands. This is a declaration of (priestly) purity, and not a special purification to perform. In the Johannine foot washing, Peter's reaction also supposes the appearance of a new dimension: in Isa 52:7 the "feet of the messenger" (LXX πόδες εὐαγγελιζομένου) are an essential feature, cf. Acts 10:36, Rom 10:15. Suitability for evangelization, which Peter cannot yet understand, has for metaphor a "purification"; this is akin to the transformation of baptism as access to the Spirit (cf. John 1:26 f.).

ritual impurity, has no effect on impurity due to sin (whether intended or already carried out). This restriction enables us to make a very close comparison with the baptism of John, which gives remission of sins only if there is a moral change (conversion) accompanied by confession (Mark 1:5 par., cf. above §III.1).

7. In Mark 14:22 and Matt 26:26, Jesus breaks the bread and pronounces the blessing *during* the meal. Even if this feature is redactional (it is not in Luke 22:19 or 1 Cor 11:23), the gesture is an act distinct from the blessing of the meal itself, assuming that the meal is one of precept, and so requiring a preliminary blessing. According to Mark 14:20 par., at least one course has already been served, which corresponds to the Passover rite, where, by way of exception the (unleavened) bread does not appear until after the first course (*YPes* 10:4, p. 37d top). Jeremias emphasizes the contrast with an ordinary meal, which normally begins with the blessing of the bread.

In reality, however, this daily usage is not general, as Jeremias supposes, but is a peculiarity of the rabbinic tradition. In fact, in Deut 8:10 the only blessing prescribed is after having eaten and being filled, so at the end of the meal. However, in the name of the general rule forbidding enjoyment of any good thing of this world without first blessing the Creator, *TBer* 4:1 prescribes a blessing before tasting anything at all, and *MBer* 6:1 f. gives various formulae for this purpose, according to different kinds of natural produce (fruit, vegetables, cereals, etc.; meat, fish, dairy products, etc.). But from this emerges the exceptional position of bread and wine: they are produced by human work, and not simply by nature, and each has a special blessing attached to it, as distinct from wheat and grapes, which are included in the general categories of produce of the soil and fruit. We should also note that washing the hands is obligatory only if the meal includes bread or wine (*BBer* 50b). This singular character of bread and wine is noteworthy, since, in the Essene meal, these two items are the only ones over which a blessing is said. Hand washing itself is a rite of access to holy things (cf. Exod 30:17-21), which makes bread and wine even more exceptional.

8. Jesus and his disciples drink wine during the meal, which is usual only on special (particularly family) occasions and for feasts. The use of wine for the *qiddush* has been pointed out, but here the meal takes place after nightfall, and so does not correspond to the moment for the *qiddush*. On the other hand, there is an obvious comparison with the precept of drinking four cups of wine for Passover (cf. *MPes* 10:1).

The Essenes, however, used wine daily (1 QS 6:4-6; 1 QSa 2:17 f.), or rather, what they termed *tirosh*, a word whose meaning is not certain:

TNed 4:3 explains that in the Bible (Deut 11:14, etc.) the meaning is "wine," but that later the term designates a sweet, unfermented drink. From that Jeremias concludes that it is impossible to affirm that the Essenes really drank wine. However, according to 11 QT 43:7-9 (which was unknown to him), there is no possible doubt that it is new wine, the first fruits of which were presented at the second Pentecost, and which kept this name until the following vintage; besides, wine was the sign of every rejoicing (feast). This is explicitly wine and not fruit juice, but at the first it may have been only very lightly fermented,[107] which could explain the change in meaning. According to *J.W.* 2 §133, the Essenes are sober, like the Therapeutae, who drink only water, but this comes from their status as *nazirs.*[108] Grape juice could represent a compromise between wine and water,[109] but Num 6:3 has it that the *nazir* is to abstain from any produce of the grape. All the same, this has to do with the temporary nazirate, which one should, perhaps, distinguish from the permanent state of Samson (Judg 13:4), Samuel (1 Sam 1:11 LXX) and John the Baptist (Luke 1:15),[110] of whom it is said only that they are not to take wine or fermented drink, with nothing about grape juice or new wine. In any case, it is certainly legitimate to distinguish several categories of Essenes, following whether or not they took wine. There was at least one category of Essenes that took wine every day: is this significant for the Last Supper?

It is of interest that the institution narrative of 1 Cor 11:23 says that Jesus took wine "the night before he was handed over," without any definite link with a feast, which would imply that Paul does not spontaneously attach the wine to any special occasion, Passover or other. Similarly, in Luke 7:33, Jesus is contrasted with John the Baptist, who "does not eat bread or drink wine," so that the use of wine appears to have been habitual for Jesus and his entourage.

107. Joseph-T. Milik, *Ten Years of Discoveries in the Wilderness of Judaea*, p. 105, insists rightly on a light fermentation. More fermented wine (יין) is decried by CD 8:9-10, but the important thing is that it is no longer wine of the year, so no longer has any direct link in meaning with the first-fruits.

108. However, water has continued to play a not unimportant role in the eucharist, but for other reasons, cf. above §I.5.

109. According to Jerome, *Ad Jovinianum* 2.14, the Essenes drink grape juice, but he probably gets his information from FJ (or from Hippolytus). Joseph M. Baumgarten, *Studies in Qumran Law* (SJLA, 24), Leiden, Brill, 1977, p. 96, n. 42, also holds that it is only fruit juice, since wine is very difficult to keep ritually pure.

110. For the Messianic analogy between Samuel/David and John/Jesus, cf. above §III.2.

As for wine in the rabbinic tradition, there is a Tannaitic saying (*BPes* 109a)[111] according to which the rejoicing prescribed for feasts was to be done with meat at the time of the Temple,[112] but since the destruction wine is necessary (cf. Judg 9:13). This would mean that, at the time of the Passover lamb, wine was not a constitutive element in the feast, in which case Jesus' Passover meal could have been held without wine, and so the fact that there was wine would be all the more interesting.[113] Although the Samaritans have kept the custom of celebrating Passover without wine, no firm conclusion can, however, be drawn, as this saying, which makes wine a substitute for meat, may veil the fact that both customs were contemporary (and opposed), and so mask the real origin of the use of wine.

We can recall here three points already seen: the blessing of wine is special; the cup of wine was not originally a necessary constituent of the *qiddush;*[114] according to *MPes* 10:1, *each person* is to drink four cups, which goes well with the idea of rejoicing. By contrast Jesus blesses *one* single cup, which is then passed round, and so the amount drunk is strictly symbolic. In other words, if the Last Supper is placed within the setting of Passover, there is a serious discord: wine does not clearly play an intrinsic role in the Passover, whereas Jesus attaches major importance to it, even though only a small quantity is consumed.

9. According to John 13:29, when Jesus sends Judas out, some think that he is getting him to make some last minute purchases for the feast. Such urgency would make less sense if Passover was not until the following evening. Further, there was no problem about last-minute shopping even after nightfall,[115] since the law of rest obliged only the next day,

111. Attributed to Yehuda b. Bathyra, who belongs to the colony of Bathyra in Galilee (on which, cf. chap. III, §II.1.

112. With communion sacrifices, cf. Deut 12:18; 14:26.

113. Cf. also chap. VII, §II.3.

114. Jeremias adds here that the wine of the Last Supper was red, as the comparison with blood would indicate; wine could be white, red or black, but red wine was required for Passover. However, this argument is weak: 1. the text referred to (*TPes* 10:1) says only that it should have the appearance and taste of wine, even if water has been added, cf. *Tosefta kifshuṭah* 4:648; 2. Prov 23:31 asks that wine should not be drunk too reddened, which implies that it should be sufficiently light, so watered or recent (cf. Rashi on *BMen* 87a); 3. calling wine the "blood of the vine" is biblical (cf. Deut 32:14) and supposes a red color, whether lighter or darker; 4. the previous considerations throw serious doubt on the place and even on the use of wine in the Passover meal.

115. According to *MShab* 23:1, there is difficulty only if Passover falls on a Sabbath, but even then it is possible to borrow wine, oil or bread from a merchant, leaving some object as a pledge and settling the account on Sunday (for Passover supplants Sabbath, cf. chap. III, §II.1).

especially in Judaea. This agrees with Exod 12–13, which explains that the Passover lamb is to be immolated on the day of 14 Nisan and eaten that evening, and that on the night of the 14th the Israelites went out of Egypt. So the 15th, the prescribed day of rest ("Sabbath") begins only in the morning.[116] The argument holds good, but John does not expressly say that it was a meal which was supposed to begin after sunset, although that may be implied by the events which follow.

10. In John 13:29, some of those present think that Judas, who keeps the purse, is going to give something to the poor. If the meal is really at night, this action must have been a custom. What is in question is not directly almsgiving in general, but giving the poor the means to celebrate Passover, according to *MPes* 10:1 (and *MPea* 8:7).[117] Besides, in the rabbinic Passover ritual, the father of the family invites the poor in the street to come and share the Passover (cf. *MPes* 9:11). Josephus (*Ant.* 17 §29 f.) mentions that the gates of the Temple were open from midnight on Passover, and no doubt there were plenty of poor people about.

Jeremias is no doubt right to see in the disciples' reaction the trace of a custom, but it is not well defined, and we should not lose sight of the fact that John denies (or conceals) that the Supper was a Passover meal. In any case, there is no sign of an invitation to come and share the meal, which is eaten in an intimate group.

11. At the end of the meal, Mark 14:26 and Matt 26:30 mention by the way that hymns were sung, a sign of a feast. This must be the blessing which closes the meal, and it is difficult not to see here all or part of the *Hallel*[118] (Ps 113–118), which concludes the Passover meal (*MPes* 10:7).

12. After the meal, Jesus does not return to Bethany, but bivouacs in a garden on the Mount of Olives, east of the Kidron (John 18:2), for only the rich could afford a warm, comfortable shelter (cf. John 18:18). That corresponds to the rule of spending the night within the legal boundaries of Jerusalem (the chosen place, cf. Deut 16:7), not in the strict sense of being within the walls, but within a perimeter which was apparently enlarged to the distance of a Sabbath walk (about 1 km.); in this way, it was possible to come and go during the feast day within the zone thus defined, which included the Mount of Olives (cf. Acts 1:12). Bethany, on the other hand, is 15 stadia from Jerusalem (John 11:18), or nearly 3 km, and so outside this perimeter.

116. This point, already seen in the context of the death of Jesus (chap. I, §II.2), will be developed later in connection with Passover and Sabbath (chap. III, §II.2).

117. But this custom was not uniform, cf. chap. VII, §II.3.

118. Sometimes called הימנון, transcription of ὕμνος (cf. StrB IV:76). Philo, *Spec. leg.* 2 §148, also says that Passover is celebrated with prayers *and hymns*.

13. For Jeremias, the major argument for a Passover meal is the fact that Jesus announces his passion in words which he pronounces over the bread and the wine. For one of the characteristics of the paschal celebration is the obligation of interpreting certain parts of the meal, as suggested in Exod 12:26 f., where the children question their parents about its unusual aspects. According to *MPes* 10:4, these explanations come after the presentation of the bitter herbs, at the moment of the second cup; in particular, it is laid down that the three principal elements to comment on are the bitter herbs, the unleavened bread and the paschal lamb.[119] Thus, the unleavened bread is interpreted as a sign of leaving Egypt (redemption) in haste (cf. Exod 12:34 f.), but also as "bread of affliction" (cf. Deut 16:3), expressing that they were refugees at this moment;[120] for others it speaks of future abundance in the Promised Land. Further, 1 Cor 5:7 f. also gives an eschatological interpretation of the unleavened bread, as representing the purity of the new world; at the same time the Passover (lamb) is identified with Jesus. Later (3rd century), the four cups were interpreted by the rabbinic tradition as four aspects of redemption, by combining the memory of the past and the Messianic future.

Jeremias is certainly right to claim that Jesus entered into a convenient interpretative context,[121] but here the reference to the Passover meal sits less easily. It is important not to blanket everything in an eschatological mist, but to look carefully at what is done and said. If it was in

119. The saying is attributed to R. Gamaliel, and Jeremias supposes that this is Gamaliel I, before the downfall of the Temple, since he speaks of the lamb, whereas Gamaliel II began his career around 90 (at Yavneh). The argument is weak, since the same Gamaliel II continued to eat the lamb after the destruction of the Temple (*MPes* 7:2), cf. chap. VII, §I.1.

120. The first explanation is given by Philo, *Spec. leg.* 2 §158, who adds others; the second is found in *Ant.* 2 §316.

121. Jesus did not create signs but reinterpreted signs which already existed. This was the conclusion, reached *more geometrico*, by Albert Schweitzer, *The Problem of the Lord's Supper According to the Scholarly Research of the Nineteenth Century and the Historical Accounts. I—The Lord's Supper in Relation to the Life of Jesus and the History of the Early Church*, edited with an introduction by John Reumann, Macon (Ga.), Mercer University Press, 1982, who concludes that Mark's account is the most authentic, as not being influenced by later customs (joyful feast of the primitive communities): 1. Jesus speaks while distributing, and makes no request to repeat the gesture; 2. so he makes use of a pre-existing custom, in which bread and wine already feature; 3. the rendezvous given to the apostles is purely eschatological; similarly with the commentary in 1 Cor 11:26, which recalls the death, then gives a rendezvous in the future; 4. in conclusion, Jesus at this meal acts as the Messiah, who is to come. The problem of the Last Supper is therefore that of how we should understand the life of Jesus. We will come back to these judicious remarks (§II.5). Ernest Renan, *Vie de Jésus*, (1860) republished by Jean Gaumier (Coll. Folio), Paris, Gallimard, 1974, p. 466, already supposed that there was a pre-existing rite of breaking of the bread.

fact a Passover meal, then it is surprising that the elements chosen by Jesus to comment on, do not appear to be the most appropriate signs. Why not speak of the bitter herbs, on the eve of his passion?[122] Why does he identify himself with the bread, and not with the paschal lamb, as in 1 Cor 5:7 f. and John 1:29 etc.? Why comment on the wine, which is a secondary element? And, if the bread is important, the comparison with the manna (John 6:26 f.) is much clearer and has a richer meaning than the unleavened bread. In other words, in the pre-existing rite (or setting), bread and wine already have a sufficiently strong identity to require that they be taken as the signs conveying the meaning of Jesus' death; that is not so obvious in the Passover meal. Once again, the bread and the wine stand out.

Jeremias' conclusion is that Passover gives the narrative not only its context but also its point. He notes also that the rite of the first communities is not paschal, either in its content or in its rhythm (daily or weekly, rather than annual), and concludes that the primitive community cannot have invented the paschal setting of the Last Supper, which does not correspond to its practice.

This argument, which strongly resembles the criterion of discontinuity used to discover the *ipsissima gesta* of Jesus,[123] is not really satisfactory here. First of all, a doubt remains about the place of the central elements of the Last Supper, namely bread and wine, in the Passover rite. Secondly, even if this doubt were removed, it would still be necessary to explain the origin of a division among the early Christians between those who maintained a rite on the day of Passover (Quartodecimans, cf. chap. VII, § I.2), and those who created another rhythm. Thirdly, Luke-Acts, at least in the Western Text, shows that the discontinuity is rather questionable, since Jesus only performs the breaking of the bread without asking that it be repeated, and later that sign becomes characteristic.

However, despite certain difficulties of method regarding the use of rabbinic sources, it remains true that Passover provides the general context of the narrative, as also its content, at least for Luke 22:15 f. Besides problems with the chronology, the main disharmonies occur with the bread and the wine. For these reasons, there are those who contest the paschal character of the Last Supper, but Jeremias has taken the trouble to reply to most objections. These discussions are worth going over, as they throw light on other aspects and clarify the issues.

122. Cf. J. Mann, "Rabbinic Studies . . . ," p. 349 f.

123. Cf. John P. Meier, *A Marginal Jew. Rethinking the Historical Jesus. Volume One: The Roots of the Problem and the Person* (ABRL), New York, Doubleday, 1991, p. 171 f., with references.

4. *Objections to Passover as Setting of the Last Supper*

Various objections have been made against regarding the Last Supper as a Passover meal. To start with the simplest. First, the gospels speak of "bread" and not "unleavened bread." In fact, although the oriental custom of celebrating the eucharist with leavened bread would still have to be explained, there is no real objection from the side of philology, since, for example, the loaves set out in the sanctuary (Exod 25:30), although unleavened, are called "bread" by all the witnesses (LXX, targ., Philo, Josephus, rab. trad.); so "bread" can be leavened or unleavened. Next, the first Christians celebrated their rite frequently, daily or weekly, and not once a year as for Passover. Jeremias replies that the Christian rite is not the repetition of Jesus' last meal, but the continuation of the community meals which the disciples took every day with him; however, the Last Supper increasingly exercised an influence on the rite, giving rise to corresponding redactional activity, which explains incidentally why the Passover meal is described only partially, without lamb or bitter herbs. This reply, which we shall return to, meets the objection only if these ordinary meals had a meaning other than purely utilitarian which was sufficiently strong to last and especially to escape the gravitational pull of the annual Passover.[124]

Another difficulty comes from Mark 14:2 par., where the chief priests and scribes decide two days before Passover to arrest Jesus by cunning, "but not during the feast, in order to avoid unrest among the people"; but in fact he was arrested during the feast, at least according to the synoptic chronology. Jeremias originally replied that the decision was taken before Judas made his approach (Mark 14:10 par.), but then the authorities wanted to seize the favorable occasion, although they had intended to wait until after the feast. Later, realizing that this interpretation of "not during the feast" was unlikely, because of the risk that Jesus would disappear before the end of the seven days of Unleavened Bread, Jeremias concluded that the "cunning" was going to consist in arresting him without provoking disturbances, and so the expression "not during the feast" was not a reference to the time, but meant "not among the crowd celebrating the feast" (cf. Luke 22:6, "when no crowd was present").

Other objections are more difficult to answer. First, Pilate's custom of releasing a prisoner at each feast (Mark 15:6 par.) can be understood

124. Jeremias argues from the fact that when *MPes* 10 describes the (current) Tannaitic Passover meal the lamb is hardly even mentioned, whereas at the time of the Temple, it was the essential constituent of the precept: the corresponding rite had been described at length a little before (*MPes* 5 f.). However, the later rite without lamb is not directly linked to the disappearance of the sanctuary, since other origins can be discerned (cf. chap. VII, §II.3).

properly only if it is done so that the one set free can celebrate the feast, thus adding to the mood of rejoicing, which could be turned to political advantage; so *MPes* 8:6 requires that the Passover be prepared also for the one whose liberation has been promised. But, according to the synoptic chronology, Barabbas is set free *after* the Passover meal. Jeremias tries to neutralize the difficulty by supposing that *MPes* 8:6 speaks of liberation by a *Jewish* authority, which has nothing to do with a Roman amnesty. This *ad hoc* distinction is at the least artificial (*MPes* is not speaking of a decision by the Sanhedrin), and the argument is undoubtedly in favor of the Johannine chronology, according to which Barabbas can eat the Passover that same evening.

In 1 Cor 5:7b, Christ is called "our Passover which has been immolated," which suggests that he was crucified at the moment when the Passover lamb was immolated, in agreement with John. Jeremias holds that the comparison comes not from the real chronology, but from Jesus' words at his last meal. Independently of the fact that this view could be regarded as "historicizing," its obvious weakness is that Jesus' words were spoken over the bread and not over the lamb, without any hint that they are metaphorically equivalent. Further, Paul's expression, which is close to the "lamb of God" in John 1:29 and the "lamb that was slain" in Rev 5:6, presupposes a significance in the actual moment of Jesus' death which was simple and clear enough to withstand the atmosphere of confusion following Jesus' last meal.

Similarly, in 1 Cor 15:20 Christ is called "first fruits of those who have fallen asleep." Now the sheaf of first fruits was offered on "the day following the Sabbath" (Lev 23:11), *i.e.* the 16 Nisan,[125] and the comparison supposes that this day coincides with the Sunday of the resurrection, and so that 14 Nisan is the previous Friday. Jeremias simply affirms that the term *aparchê* has lost its original meaning of "first fruits" to become merely "first." This argument is somewhat gratuitous, and a better defense would have been to say that Paul refers to Pentecost, day of the first fruits of bread, which also better suits the words of Jesus, as we will show later (chap. VII, §II.4).

Another difficulty is that the Passion narrative implies many infringements of the rest prescribed for the feast, if 15 Nisan is the Friday,

125. According to the majority custom (at the Temple) which is attested by FJ (*Ant.* 3 §250), where the "Sabbath" of Passover designates the middle of the month (full moon), first day of the feast of Unleavened Bread. According to a famous controversy, reported in *MḤag* 2:4, the Sadducees (understand "Zadokites," cf. chap. I, §I.3) and other "sectaries" identified it with the Saturday following 14 Nisan. In any case, both definitions coincide when 14 Nisan falls on a Friday.

always supposing that this rest is comparable to that of a Sabbath (according to *MBeṣa* 5:2, the sole difference is the possibility of preparing food on a feast day): people move about armed, including certain disciples, Jews call on Pilate in his praetorium, Simon of Cyrene is returning from the fields, Joseph of Arimathaea buys a shroud, etc. With the aid of rabbinic sources, Jeremias succeeds in smoothing over these difficulties, taking care to treat each one separately, so as to avoid the impression of a mass. One, however, is not easily disposed of. It is not normal for the Sanhedrin to meet on the night of a feast, especially to pronounce sentence; in fact, according to *MBeṣa* 5:2, judgment may not be given on a feast day (because something might have to be written down).[126] Besides, according to *MSanh* 6:1, sentence in a criminal case has to be given on the same day as the deliberation, and all steps in the procedure have to be taken by day and not by night, including execution of the sentence on the same day before sunset. (It is true, of course, that Mark 15:1 par. indicates a second session of the Sanhedrin on Friday morning, and, in any case, it was Pilate who wielded the secular arm.) Jeremias, like others, estimates that the legislation in the *Mishnah* did not exist in this form at the time of Jesus, but above all he insists that, according to Deut 17:13 the whole people must "hear and see" the execution of serious criminals, especially false prophets: according to *TSanh* 11:7, these cases, after being judged locally, are then to be transferred to Jerusalem, and execution is put off till the next pilgrimage feast so that the whole people may be present and draw salutary conclusions. For Jeremias, this custom justifies a rather hasty procedure, on the very day of the feast, whereas the texts imply that the trial should take place *before*; the precedent which he cites (*BSanh* 43a) concerns precisely an agitator who was hanged (or crucified, around 100 B.C.) on 14 Nisan, so the *eve* of Passover. These features work rather in favor of John's chronology, in which, in any case, there is a simple appearance before Annas, then Caiphas,[127] to draw up an accusation before

126. On Sabbath and feast days, according to *BSanh* 88b, the Great Sanhedrin met as an academy (חיל, a particular place in the fortifications of the Temple), and not as a tribunal.

127. Jeremias, following Bultmann, holds that the trial before the Sanhedrin is implied in John 18:24, and so that it is as impossible as for the synoptics, since according to *MSanh* 4:1 it is forbidden to begin a trial on the eve of a feast; but the reason is that sentence would have to be passed on the following day and executed immediately, that is on the feast day itself, which is excluded. In that case it is just possible that, since the Sanhedrin did not wield the secular arm, the trial, begun urgently on Thursday evening, was concluded on Friday morning (even without real juridical effect), before being transferred to Pilate.

Pilate; the meeting of the Sanhedrin, which does not have the formal character of a real trial, had already taken place (John 11:47).

But the chief difficulty is obviously the fourth gospel, for which the eve of Passover is the Friday (John 18:28). The expression "it was the day of preparation of Passover, about the sixth hour" (John 19:14) suggests the same, but Jeremias appeals to Aramaic in order to maintain that "preparation" (*paraskeuê*) is the equivalent of "eve," and that its normal meaning is "Sabbath eve."[128] He also holds that "Passover" can designate the seven feast days taken as a whole, so that the expression can be understood in the sense of "Friday of Passover week." This is not impossible, but the obvious sense cannot be set aside, referring to the considerable activity required for preparation of the Passover meal for a great number of people.

Conversely, Jeremias emphasizes that John's account of Jesus' last meal includes several features which show that it is indeed the same meal as that described by the synoptics: same arrangement, with a common dish (John 13:18 f. and Mark 14:17 par.), and same excursion afterwards to Gethsemane. Certain details recall clearly enough the Passover meal properly so called (13:5 f.): small group, continuation into the night, guests reclining, urgent purchases, etc. Their survival in a narrative in which the meal cannot be the Passover gives the impression that the evangelist was recasting his source in order to avoid any idea of a Christian celebration of Passover (on 14 Nisan).

Finally, it is important to note that the argument relating to the "preparation" can be turned right around if we look at the synoptics. Matt 27:62 speaks of the "day following the preparation," and not of the Sabbath, which would imply that the term, taken absolutely, does not designate Friday as eve of the Sabbath. On the contrary, there are two ways of looking at the entire festal week. Viewed from a distance, it is Passover, the name of the principal moment (cf. John 2:13; 11:55; Acts 12:4), but during the feast itself, there is no difficulty in thinking that there were names for the successive days. In fact, there is the "first day of Unleavened Bread" (Matt 26:17 par.), then "preparation" (day of feverish activity culminating in the Passover meal), next "day after preparation" (day of solemn calm), etc. The gloss in Mark 15:42, explaining that the "preparation" is the eve of the Sabbath, is supposed to be intended for uninformed readers. If Mark, including the gloss, is taken to be the source of the parallels in Matt and Luke, it would be enough to recall that the principal day of the feast, 15 Nisan, is explicitly defined as a "Sabbath"

128. In patristic Greek, παρασκευή is the name for Friday, and μεγάλη παρασκευή is Good Friday; this usage is derived from the NT (especially Mark 15:42).

(Lev 23:15), with precise consequences for fixing the date of Pentecost. Still, this explanation is rather forced and suffers from the same defect with which we have been taxing Jeremias. The alternative is to regard this passage in Mark as dependent on Matt and Luke,[129] or simply to accept that the gloss is a later addition. In either case, it is possible to think that the final redactor, ignorant of the Jewish calendar and especially of Passover,[130] and perhaps influenced by the custom of a weekly commemoration of Jesus' death, gave what seemed to him to be the likeliest explanation.

In the last analysis, it is fairly natural to think that 14 Nisan had a special name. It comes round only once a year, disturbing the rhythm of the week, and there is an enormous amount of activity laid down (elimination of leaven, Passover lamb, ritual meal). By contrast, preparation of the Sabbath (food) is not of the same nature, recurring every week and not being the object of any special precept; above all, it is by nature private. These remarks suggest a novel aspect of the synoptics. By employing the term "preparation," they have kept a discreet trace of the Johannine chronology, so of the official calendar; subsequently, confusion arose from the fact that in that year, 15 Nisan fell on a Saturday, so the two "Sabbaths" coincided (John 19:31).

5. Looking for a Meaning

Each of these two camps can marshal solid arguments in favor of its own position but has difficulty in neutralizing those put forward by the other. Jeremias has brought out those features which make the synoptics' Last Supper a Passover meal, but he does not really succeed in removing those aspects which count against this presentation, namely those which work in favor of John's chronology, with Passover on Friday evening. At first sight it would seem that all the difficulties would disappear if it were accepted that there was a duplication of the calendar, with one Passover for the people as a whole at the Temple, falling that year on the Sabbath, and another private Passover celebrated only by Jesus and his disciples, traces of which can be seen even in John. As stated, this hypothesis seems to be rather arbitrary. On the other hand, the form in which it is put forward by A. Jaubert is at least well documented: according to her, the Last Supper was indeed a Passover meal, but according to a marginal rite, following the biblical calendar of *Jubilees*, so on the Tuesday evening. The

129. According to the so-called "two gospel" hypothesis (we shall see some further arguments pointing to this solution, in chap. V, §V.2). In both views, the publication of Mark is to be linked with Rome.

130. In particular, Easter was unknown to the Christians of Rome until about 160, as we shall see in connection with the Quartodeciman crisis (chap. VII, §I.2).

texts themselves give certain indications in favor of this solution, notably the anointing at Bethany, which John 12:1 places six days before Passover, which for him is on Friday at the Temple, whereas in Matt 26:2 par. this scene takes place two days before Passover, which would imply a different calendar. However, although this hypothesis would clearly resolve many inconsistencies of detail, two major difficulties still remain. First, the actual chronology of the synoptic narratives leaves no doubt that the Last Supper takes place on Thursday evening. Further, in the way the meal is described, the insistence on the bread and the wine does not fit easily into a Passover setting, in which the bitter herbs would more naturally express the passion and the lamb would more obviously represent the body of Jesus given to be eaten. In both cases, to appeal to an unspecified liturgical influence is to beg the question, since the characteristic of a rite which is clear is stability.

In order to get any further, we need to go back to the texts and analyze them, concentrating on the various stages of the meal itself. To lighten the presentation, we shall omit the first part of the meal, concerning the betrayal (or the "handing over"), introduced in Matt 26:21 and Mark 14:18 by the expression "while they were eating," which is picked up again at the beginning of the passage cited here (Luke has a different organization, cf. chap. I, §I.2):

Matt 26	Mark 14	Luke 22 WT	1 Cor 11—Cont'd
Cf. v. 29	Cf. v. 25	(15) And he said to them: I have desired with a (great) desire to eat this Passover with you before suffering. (16) For I tell you that I will not eat it again until it is fulfilled in the kingdom of God.	
Cf. v. 29	Cf. v. 25	(17) Then taking a cup, he gave thanks and said: Take and share (it) among you. (18) For I tell you, I will not drink henceforth of the produce of the vine until the kingdom of God has come.	
			(23) The Lord Jesus, the night he was betrayed,
(26) Now, while they were eating, Jesus, taking bread and blessing	(22) And while they were eating, taking bread, blessing,	(19) And taking bread, he gave thanks,	took bread, (24) and, giving thanks

Matt 26	Mark 14	Luke 22 WT	1 Cor 11
broke (it)	he broke (it)	he broke (it)	broke (it)
and giving (it) to his disciples, said:	and gave (it) to them and said:	and gave (it) to them, saying:	and said:
Take, eat,	Take,		
this is my body	this is my body.	This is my body, given for you.	This is my body, for you.
		Do this in memory of me.	Do this in memory of me.
(27) And taking a cup	(23) And taking a cup,	(20) And the cup likewise	(25) And likewise the cup
and giving thanks	giving thanks	after the meal,	after the meal,
he gave (it) to them, saying:	he gave (it) to them, and they all drank it.	*[Added by AT]*	
Drink of it all,	(24) And he said:	saying:	saying:
(28) For this is my *Covenant blood,*	This is my *Covenant blood*	This cup (is) *the new Covenant* in my blood,	This cup is *the new Covenant* in my blood.
which is shed for many, in remission of sins.	which is shed for many.	which is shed for you.	
			This, do it, each time that you drink, in memory of me. (26) For, each time that you eat this bread and that you drink this cup, you will announce the death of the Lord,
(29) Now I tell you, from now on I will not drink of this produce of the vine until the day when I drink it with you, new, in the kingdom of my Father.	(25) Amen I tell you that I will no longer drink of this produce of the vine until the day when I drink it with you, new, in the kingdom of God.	Cf. v. 18.	until he has come.

Comparison of the texts calls for several remarks, first general, then more detailed, but without losing sight of the context, which cannot be regarded as secondary:

1. Whatever the complexities of the calendar, the literary context is that of Passover. This feast traditionally has two dimensions: the commemoration of the deliverance from Egypt (Exod 12–13) and the celebration of the entry into the Promised Land (at Gilgal, Josh 6:10 f.). This second Passover has a notable feature: it corresponds to the cessation of the manna, as the Israelites then begin to eat the produce of the land, beginning with unleavened bread. In the gospel accounts of the Last Supper, there are no allusions to the exodus, but there are very clear references to the Promised Land, expressed in terms of the kingdom of God. Jesus announces a future celebration in the kingdom. This is particularly clear

in Luke 22:15-18, with explicit references to the lamb and the wine. The same distance between the present and an undefined future is indicated also in Matt 26:29 and Mark 14:25, but only in regard to "the produce of the vine." The episode takes place not simply in Judaea, but in Jerusalem, where Jesus has insisted on coming. However, this is not a true arrival, but a departure (a failed arrival). There is a Messianic dimension, seen clearly in the tradition that the Messiah will return one night of Passover.[131] *Jub* 49:15-22 fixes a Passover rendezvous "until the House has been constructed."

2. Allusions to the Covenant and to blood (Matt 26:29 par.) strike a note which does not appear to be directly related to Passover, since there is no connection with the lamb, not even with the blood rite of Exod 12:22 f. On the other hand, it has been noted for a long time now that the "Covenant blood" of Matt and Mark alludes to the sacrifice that seals the revelation at Sinai (Exod 24:8), and that the "new Covenant" of 1 Cor (and Luke AT) refers to Jer 31:31. According to *BPes* 68b, Pentecost commemorates the gift of the Law, and there are appropriate synagogue readings.[132] Further, what we have already seen about the calendars allows us to make a comparison with sectarian documents which provide a more precise context: for *Jub* 29:7, the feast of the Covenant is Pente-

131. *TYer* of Exod 12:12; this aspect is developed in chap. VII, §II.2. *BRSh* 10b reports an interesting controversy: R. Yehoshua places the Creation of the world, the birth and death of the patriarchs, the first and second liberations (exodus from Egypt, Messianic era) in Nisan; but R. Eliezer puts the Creation of the world (because of the reckoning of the years), the birth and death of the Patriarchs, and the definitive liberation by the Messiah in Tishri; the reference point here is no longer the exodus from Egypt and Passover, but solely the (renewed) Creation.

132. Henry St. John Thackeray, *The Septuagint and Jewish Worship*, p. 46–60. The Decalogue (Exod 20) is read on this day, although there are controversies, cf. chap. VII, §III.1. This is not the place to examine the poorly documented question of the triennial cycle of synagogue readings in Palestine, of which *BMeg* 29b speaks, and which begin 1 Nisan. Note, however, that the massora gives 154 divisions (סדרים) of the Pentateuch, and that the second year begins with Exod 12, which fits Passover, with the Decalogue (Exod 20) at Pentecost, cf. Adolph Büchler, "The reading of the Law and Prophets in a Triennial Cycle," *JQR* 5 (1893), p. 420–468, who remarks that the discourse on the manna in John 6:59 is placed between Passover (6:4) and Pentecost (7:2), which may correspond to the reading of Exod 16 (the manna and the quails) between Exod 12 and Exod 20. He supports his hypothesis by arguing that the four New Year days indicated by *MRSh* 1:1 originally designated the dates on which, in the triennial cycle, each of the books of the Pentateuch began (Gen on 1 Nisan, Exod and Num on 15 Shebaṭ, Lev on 1 Tishri and Deut on 1 Elul; *i.e.* Gen then Exod were begun in the first year, Lev and Num in the second, Deut in the third). These conclusions are judged severely by Jacob Mann, *The Bible as Read and Preached in the Old Synagogue*, Prolegomenon by Ben Zion Wacholder, New York, Ktav, 1971[2], p. LII, who observes that the *seder* of the Covenant with Noah (Gen 8:15–9:17) is the sixth or seventh, which will not work, since Saturday 14/III is the eleventh Sabbath of

cost,[133] which always falls on Sunday 15 of the third month; it is also the feast of the first-fruits.[134] The Covenant as such is not attached to Moses. It begins with Noah (*Jub* 6:17), for whom the Covenant seals the deliverance from the Deluge. It continues with Abraham (the division of the animals, *Jub* 14:1 f., cf. Gen 15:7 f.), who is promised land and posterity. With Moses, therefore, there is a renewal of the *same* Covenant, with a real people (cf. 1 QS 3:4bis). Running through all this is the typology of the Deluge: a new world is due to appear after the downfall and disappearance of the old world.[135] The watchword is: "If they turn to Him in justice, He will forgive all their transgression." This statement, together with a climate of apocalyptic urgency, is very close to the message proclaimed by John the Baptist.

3. As a result of these observations, we can bring together the two expressions "blood of the Covenant" and "new Covenant."[136] In both cases, it is the same Covenant being renewed, without abandoning an earlier one, first by Moses, then by all who commit themselves to returning to his Law. There is even a sort of cycle: the people is fickle, but there is always a faithful remnant led by divinely inspired guides, whom CD 2:11-12 calls the "anointed of His Holy Spirit." So the sect, which is none other than the "remnant," regards itself as the true Israel, that is, as the concrete expression of the Covenant, and to enter the community is to enter the Covenant, as we shall see. So Pentecost, as feast of the Covenant, has a twofold dimension: admission of newcomers and liturgical renewal of the Covenant, with appropriate ablutions. Obviously, this perspective gives a meaning which is both very simple and very central to the Pentecost of Acts 2, which concludes with numerous baptisms.

4. In this perspective of Pentecost, we can give a meaning to the characteristic elements of bread and wine. We have seen that they do not

---

the year (Gen 8:14 says that the earth is dry on 27/II, a Wednesday, but that is after the eighth Sabbath). However, the *seder* of the Decalogue at Sinai (Exod 19:6–20:26) comes fifty-two places later, so one year after, which may be based on a superimposition of Sinai with the Covenant with Noah, cf. below. The fact remains that there are many indications of a triennial Palestinian cycle earlier than the annual Babylonian cycle, but they are too slight and touch on calendar problems as yet too little worked out to enable any reconstruction or solidly based argument.

133. Or "feast of Weeks," which is also, by play of words on שבועות, the "feast of Oaths" (*e.g.*: Jacob and Laban, *Jub* 29:3).

134. Cf. *Jub* 6:21; 15:1; 16:13; 22:1; 44:4. For Num 28:26 LXX, it is the day of the new produce (τῶν νέων, MT הבכורים).

135. Cf. Jean Daniélou, *Sacramentum futuri. Étude sur les origines de la typologie biblique* (ETH), Paris, Beauchesne, 1950, p. 59 f.

136. The context of Jer 31:31 supposes a renewal of the same Covenant, with the same Law, but in a new way (v. 33: "I will place my Law in the depth of their being").

fit well into the setting of Passover. By contrast, Pentecost is also the feast of first-fruits, and according to Lev 23:17, those to be presented first are none other than the first-fruits of ordinary (*leavened*) bread. It is to be noted that this is not the produce of the earth in a raw state, such as wheat, but a prepared food.[137] Besides this basic feature of the feast properly so called, other Essene texts (mentioned in chap. I, §I.2) indicate a rhythm of fifty day periods, so little pentecosts always falling on a Sunday, when new wine (must) then oil—once again, prepared produce—are offered. Thus the *first-fruits* of bread and wine are related to the cycle of Pentecost, with an echatological significance which is central: eating the fruits of the new year, which represent the new world, new creation, etc. But the link with Pentecost and the Covenant is not limited to the dates imposed by the solar calendar, since the *gesture* of offering and eating first-fruits can be made at any time, as we see in the *Appendix* to the *Rule*: the Messianic meal described in 1 QSa 2:11-22, with the two Messiahs (son of Aaron and son of David) and the rest of the people in tribes, shows the priest (Messiah son of Aaron) opening the meal with a blessing of the first-fruits of bread and wine.[138] More interesting still, this rite is already to be observed even now in a minor form at every meal where there are at least ten present, as in 1 QS 6:4-5; Josephus *J.W.* 2 §133 f. says simply twice a day, with purification, the principal difference being that the blessing is said over bread *or* wine.

Comparison with the Last Supper of Jesus becomes easy when one recalls that there the rite concerns a single cup, and not all the wine available (the jug, or the cups of all those present). It is a question then of only a small, but venerated part of the foodstuff, which aptly expresses a setting apart of first-fruits. As for the bread, the gesture is one of "breaking," which has sufficient significance for it to have given its name to the rite.[139] This is not simply the material act necessary to distribute the bread, but

137. In Luke 6:1 WT, during the "second-first" Sabbath, which we have attached (chap. I, §I.2b) to the week following the first Pentecost, it is said that the disciples gather wheat *and crush it* so as to eat it. This detail sketches an elementary preparation (grinding the wheat before cooking), and suggests a gesture of consuming first-fruits.

138. ראשית הלחם והתירוש, where the term ראשית is characteristic of the first-fruits, cf. Exod 23:19; 34:26; Lev 23:10; Num 15:20 f., and above all Num 18:12, which mentions the first-fruits (best part) of bread, must and oil; "first" may refer to time or to quality.

139. Christian tradition has always regarded the gesture of the breaking of the bread as a major liturgical action, to be performed by the president; according to Hippolytus, *Apost. Trad.* 23.5 and 24.1, it is done by the bishop, who is helped by deacons only for practical reasons, if there are many present, cf. Gregory Dix, *The Shape of the Liturgy*, London, Dacre Press, 1945², p. 131 f.

once again a setting apart of first-fruits.[140] Later Christian tradition knows two types of ritual meals: the *agapê*, or Lord's Supper, where each person eats normally, and the *eucharist*, with a characteristic Thanksgiving and only symbolic consumption. According to the sources, these two forms were originally combined but later separated.[141] The witness of 1 Cor 11 and the accounts of the Last Supper attest the earlier state: symbolic meal *and* ordinary meal, the symbolic part being a sign of first-fruits. In this way, it is easy to see how the Last Supper is told in a way that suggests an *habitual* meal taken by Jesus and his disciples, distinct from Passover, without the need to appeal to the hypotheses criticized by Jeremias. On the contrary, we return to his conclusion already mentioned on the disciples' community meals (§4).

5. However, in the present state of the texts, everything has been inserted into a setting which is Paschal and so Messianic. Once again the Essene texts referred to give us a way of approaching this. The solemn renewal of the Covenant has a priestly dimension (1 QSb 3:26, cf. Sir 45:25); the meal described, taken as it is in the present time, is presided over by a priest, who makes an eschatological sign of first-fruits. But the ultimate reality hoped for is described by Isa 11:1 f.; it is the son of David who will intervene at the end, when Israel will be saved and the impious slain (1 QSb 5:20 f., 4 QPB 3-4, 4 QFl 1:11-13). This is a post-priestly Messianism, whose imagery is warlike, but which has no particular political relevance. We can thus make a clear distinction, at least in theory, between zealots and Essenes. The former propose immediate political action, in anticipation of the last times; but it is not a true Messianism, for the simple reason that the leaders who emerge have no claim to Davidic descent (cf. above §I.3). By contrast, the Essenes have in view two phases which are quite distinct: the present time, with a priestly ideal and an eschatological ritual, and the future time, in a reality which lies beyond any rite. Typically, according to *J.W.* 2 §142, when newcomers are admitted, they must undertake to abstain from zealot activism.

6. These aspects of Messianism throw light on the Last Supper. In fact the reference to Passover is twofold: the Passover of today, corresponding to the death of Jesus, and a future Passover, corresponding to

140. That is still the spontaneous understanding of Irenaeus, born in the East but living in the West: "Telling his disciples to offer to God the *first-fruits* of his own Creation, [. . .] he took this bread issuing from creation, and gave thanks, saying, etc." (*Adv. haer.* 4.17.4); it is possible that he means to emphasize a point against the Gnostics, but in any case he bases his argument on a tradition distinct from the written NT. Further, he is aware that the custom of celebrating Easter is recent, at least in the West (cf. chap. VII, §I.3), so he is not bound to any meaning in the Eucharist that is both paschal and traditional.

141. Cf. G. Dix, *op. cit.*, p. 82 f. and 96 f.

the coming of the Kingdom; in other words, the failure of a more or less overt Messianism ending in Jerusalem, and the announcement of a final Messianism, duly transformed. Between the two, the rite of bread and wine, with its connotations of Pentecost, is an eschatological sign in the present time (which other NT passages express as a symbolic participation in a heavenly liturgy). Pentecost and its associated signs, along with the Spirit, correspond to the keeping of the Covenant, that is to the time of the Church. We are dealing with a rite, with an act which is in some way incomplete, since it needs to be repeated, corresponding to an eschatology which is in the course of being realized. The final reality is, however, represented by Passover. This interpretation enables us to understand the gospel accounts as resulting from the insertion of two items into the actual Passover of Jesus: the eschatological sign of the bread and wine, and a comment on the Messianic rendezvous to come. This is particularly clear in Matt and Mark; in Luke, the two insertions are closer together, as the present and future Passovers come at the beginning, and the breaking of the bread only afterwards.[142] Similarly, the parallel should be underlined between Mark 14:12-16, the dispatch of disciples to prepare Passover, and Mark 11:1-6, the dispatch to look for the Messianic foal;[143] these elements converge to produce a Passover

142. We take this opportunity to discuss the analysis of Jean-Marie Van Cangh, "Le déroulement primitif de la cène (*Mc* 14,18-26 et par.)," *RB* 102 (1995), p. 193–225, who takes his inspiration from Jeremias and Schürmann. He regards Mark as primitive, but Luke as clearer for purposes of analysis (which poses at least a problem of method). There is a first stage originating in the Passover (v. 15-18), including two eschatological *logia* (on the lamb and the wine), then two further stages originating in the liturgy, with bread and wine (v. 19-20 AT); the two cups of wine are opposed. Reverting to Mark, he observes that the word over the wine, coming after they have drunk, is artificial. By suppressing it, v. 23, 24a, 25 gain in coherence and explain Luke 22:17-18, which depend on them; besides, the insertion of Mark 14:24b ("This is my blood of the Covenant") is clumsy, and furthermore inconceivable in a Jewish milieu, which suggests a Greek origin. Finally, the wine comes from the Passover cups according to the Tannaitic *seder*, whereas the bread comes from ordinary Jewish meals. In other words, eucharistic customs have been inserted into an eschatological tradition of a farewell meal. Despite the author's judicious comments on the blessings, some objections of method can be made to this presentation, without appealing to questions of textual criticism: 1. since it is a question of reconstructing the primitive Supper, with precise references to Passover, what about the calendar and the chronology of John? 2. appealing to "liturgical customs" only postpones the problem: where do they come from, since they are strong enough to remain independent of Passover itself? 3. technically, the result of the analysis leads to assigning a very complex origin to the texts, without precise relation to customs or coherent systems of meaning: for example, it appears strange that the scandalous word on the blood should not be of Jewish origin, since it recalls the Covenant at Sinai; or again, the reconstruction of the parallel between Matt and Mark is difficult, since the "he said's" do not correspond well.

143. The model of this construction is 1 Sam 10:1-10 LXX, where Samuel announces the Messianic signs.

scene which is properly eschatological, inaugurated by a triumphal arrival in Jerusalem.

7. The words over the bread and wine, which Jesus identifies with his body and blood, are parallel and pronounced in both cases with a delay, after the distribution, when the body has already been eaten and the blood drunk.[144] So he is reinterpreting an habitual gesture, as has long been noticed, but in terms which are very terse and even scandalous. The surprising thing is that the apostles raise no query.[145] But the reason becomes clear when one notes that the meal narrative taken as a whole includes another phase, the "handing over."[146] The formula of Mark 14:18b ("and while they were eating") is picked up in v. 23, which creates a parallel, even a sort of duplication, between the handing over and the rite of bread and wine.[147] When Jesus announces that one of the apostles is going to hand him over, each asks: "Is it I?" Judas is not named, but only "the one who puts his hand with me into the dish." So the brotherhood, represented by table fellowship, is broken, in the name of another imperative which is no longer of the moral order—a rupture motivated by the Covenant.

The Essene parallels once again offer a precise setting, founded on Lev 19:17-18 ("You shall not hate your brother in your heart; you should correct your neighbor and not encourage sin because of him. You shall not take vengeance; you shall not keep rancour against the sons of your people, but you shall love your neighbor as yourself," cf. Sir 28:1-6), developed by CD 6:20, 9:2-8. For the Covenant is also the redeemed people; as we have said, to enter the community is to enter the Covenant,[148] and there is no entry into the Covenant except through the

144. On those who benefit from the blood shed ("for many" Matt, Mark; "for you" Luke AT), cf. chap. VI, §III.2. The final redaction of Luke emphasizes (more than 1 Cor 11) the symmetry of the bread (body "given for you") and the wine (blood "shed for you").

145. It occurs in John 6:53 f.: after the declaration "Whoever eats my flesh and drinks my blood has eternal life [. . .]," the disciples, as Jesus observes, are scandalized. So it is a violent gesture.

146. The verb παραδίδωμι has in reality the wider sense of "hand over, transmit," with a connotation of execution of a commission or a contract (cf. Matt 26:24 par.); so there is also a parallel between "handing over to enemies" (Judas) and "handing over to disciples" (bread and wine). The idea of transmission or tradition is equally close, as is shown by a sort of play on words in 1 Cor 11:23: ὃ καὶ παρέδωκα ὑμῖν . . . ἐν τῇ νυκτὶ ᾗ παρεδίδοτο "what I handed over to you . . . the night when he was handed over." This double signification is even clearer in the Hebrew מסר, cf. chap. V, §IV.2, on delators.

147. Rudolf Bultmann, *History of the Synoptic Tradition* (Eng. tr. of 2nd German ed. 1931), Oxford, Basil Blackwell, 2nd ed. with corrections and additions, p. 264, followed by others, judges with good reason that the episode is constructed on Ps 41:10, not without reminiscences of the suffering servant.

148. Cf. 1 QS 1:7 f., 5:20-21; CD 6:11. Cf. chap. VII, §IV.1.

community.[149] Further, to share the same food or cup are simple and obvious signs of communion.[150] Betrayal is then a major crisis in the Covenant. On this occasion, however, the result is not excommunication, but, on the contrary, renewal of the same Covenant by means of a gesture which has every appearance of a crime. For "eating blood" is the symbol of all crimes;[151] "not eating blood" is akin to "not shedding blood."[152] Narratively, there are two movements which are superimposed: the betrayal, virtual or real, ends in the death of Jesus, but Jesus himself takes the initiative by handing himself over freely by means of a rite, through which his death provides food for his murderers. In this way it is natural[153] that the words over the bread and wine come *after* they have been distributed, as they comment on the representation of a real action. Furthermore, the historical context is blurred: the different actors in Jesus' trial disappear, and attention is concentrated on the disciples' sin and redemption ("my blood shed for you").

8. These remarks allow us to put forward an hypothesis on how the scene of the Last Supper was put together. The special elements of bread and wine, which have their own origin linked to the very simple eschatological meaning of first-fruits,[154] have been inserted into the *unique* and unrepeatable drama of the death of Jesus, for which the Passover setting announces the failure of one Messianism and the promise of another. The failure is due to two causes which converge: political impossibility or defeat, combined with the weakness of the disciples, who either betray Jesus or are scandalized by the cross. But this failure is presented as necessary, and sin leads not to condemnation but to redemption. This is Covenant renewal of a new kind, implying also the idea of a transfer of

149. Cf. 1 QS 6:14-15. The sharing of all things has an essential dimension (cf. 1 QS 6:2-3); whence also the importance of fraternal correction (CD 20:17-18), with אהבת חסד "love of benevolence" (1 QS 5:25), and even excommunication, cf. chap. VI, §III.3 and VII, §IV.2. This dimension is absent from the teaching of the Tannaites, cf. Moore I:152, presumably because the point of reference is no longer the limited community (brotherhood) but the entire people, cf. chap. V, §I.2.

150. Cf. Ps 16:5; 1 Cor 10:20.

151. Cf. *Jub* 6:7-14; 7:23-33; 11:2; 21:6 f.

152. Cf. *Jub* 7:29-31; 21:18-19, cf. Gen 9:4 f.; Lev 17:13; Ezek 24:7-8.

153. Contrary to the opinion of many commentators, cf. S. Dockx, *Chronologies néotestamentaires et vie de l'Église primitive*, Paris-Gembloux, Duculot, 1976, p. 202; Jacques Schlosser, *Le Règne de Dieu dans les dits de Jésus* (EB), Paris, Gabalda, 1980, p. 374.

154. The *Didache* 9–10 gives formulae of eucharistic prayers (of the 1st cent.) in which Jesus' death is not recalled, which brings out the fact that the rite is autonomous and prior to the NT, cf. chap. V, §V.2 at the end.

debt (cf. §I.5). So there is an obvious sacrificial dimension[155] superimposed on the rite of bread and wine, which in itself has nothing of the nature of an expiatory sacrifice (especially because of the presence of wine).[156] In other words, by being inserted into the unique Passover, the rite of bread and wine gains a new dimension. The same meaning can be found—without any need to disturb the texts—in Paul's testimony on the eucharist (1 Cor 11). He says "the night when he was handed over," but without allusion to any Passover ritual. This shows that he does not know the actual narrative in the synoptics, but, by another means, he indicates a real connection with the Passover of Jesus, who died at the very moment of the immolation of the lamb. "Do this in memory of me" simply means to continue the rite of the bread and wine,[157] but with a new meaning. By contrast, it becomes perfectly clear that Jesus gives no command to repeat in the setting of the Last Supper, as it would in that case imply the repetition of *Passover*, which is unknown in the tradition.[158] Finally, the explanation "each time that you eat [. . .] you will proclaim the death of the Lord" clarifies the meaning, rather as with the disciples' betrayal in the gospels; this is a familiar theme in Paul, who wants to know only the scandal of the cross.

9. So behind the account of the Last Supper there is indeed a liturgical tradition which is independent of Passover. It is none other than a sort of community meal in which the significant elements are bread and/or wine. This is not a feast, but only the first stage of a complete meal (which may or may not be festive), since the share which each receives is minimal and would not normally be sufficient as food. The central

155. Cf. Lev 17:11 on the blood poured out for the expiation of sins, so also Heb 9:7 and 21 f.

156. Lev 10:9 prescribes clearly for the priests: "When you come to the Tent of Meeting, you and your sons with you, drink neither wine nor other fermented drink (שכר) . . ." (cf. also Ezek 44:21). *Ag. Ap.* 1 §199 picks up this prohibition, and *Ant.* 3 §279 says explicitly that the priests do not drink wine while they are wearing the priestly vestments. However, *BKer* 13b, playing on the word שכר, understands the verse as "do not get drunk" (כדי שכרות); so some drink may be tolerated. On different degrees of fermentation, cf. above §3.

157. Which is characteristic of the community in the limited sense. The Last Supper took place in a small group, contrary to other meals where Jesus sits at table with sinners, cf. Xavier Léon-Dufour, *Le partage du pain eucharistique selon le Nouveau Testament* (Parole de Dieu, 21), Paris, Seuil, 1982, p. 51.

158. Even the Quartodecimans of Asia Minor, who celebrated a Passover on 14 Nisan, appear not to have kept the rite of the lamb, but the fast which precedes the festive vigil after midnight, seems to be the trace of an *absence* of the paschal lamb outside the land of Israel, cf. chap. VII, §I.2. This conclusion gives additional support to the presumption that the account in Luke WT is earlier than that in the AT, since it does not contain the command to repeat from 1 Cor 11.

meaning which it symbolizes is connected with Pentecost,[159] signifying both the renewal of the Covenant (Sinai) and an anticipation of the Kingdom (first-fruits). It has a weekly expression, linked to the night between Sabbath and the first day of the week (watching for the dawn). It may also have a daily expression, to judge from the episode of the pilgrims from Emmaus, from the tradition in 1 Cor 11, where the eve of Jesus' death could be any day at all, and even from the fact that the foodstuffs taken are extremely common.

This layout, which is in general agreement with Essene customs, is found in the whole of later Christian tradition with remarkable regularity. However, the traditional schema is even simpler than that of the Last Supper:[160]

The most obvious difference between the two schemas is that in the Last Supper the same sequence is repeated twice, whereas in the liturgy everything is integrated in a single sequence (although it is important to note that it is intended for the "Lord's day," that is, for a weekly rhythm). This single sequence is found in Luke WT, *i.e.* in the "breaking of the bread" properly so called. Thus we arrive at an important conclusion. The gospel narratives were not used as a model in the development of the primitive liturgy;[161] the influence was rather the other way round, which

Last Supper		**Liturgical Tradition**
Jesus takes bread,	he takes a cup,	Bread and wine presented *together*,
he blesses it;	he blesses it;	with a blessing;
he breaks it;		
he distributes it,	he distributes it,	
he says a word;	he says a word.	solemn thanksgiving,
		breaking of the bread,
		bread and wine distributed *together*.

159. As can be seen also with the Therapeutae, cf. chap. VII, §III.2.

160. The following table takes its inspiration from the presentation by G. Dix, *The Shape of the Liturgy*, p. 48 f., but this author does not isolate the words of Jesus over the bread and over the wine (Last Supper), and does not distinguish the blessing over the bread and wine from the thanksgiving (liturgy); he also finishes up with schemas in seven and nine stages respectively. However, there is reason to distinguish this blessing (offertory) from the thanksgiving (memorial).

161. At least before the establishment of a canon; later, they serve as a reference in case of crisis, as we shall see in regard to the Sunday Easter (chap. V, §I.3).

corresponds better to the way we have seen the gospels evolved (cf. chap. I, §I.1). From the remarks already made about the insertion of bread and wine into a Passover context, we should conclude that this integration was made in two stages, separately for the bread and for the wine, and with different meanings; 1 Cor 11 preserves a trace of this, since there the command to repeat is given twice, before Paul's own commentary putting it all together (v. 24).

Here we draw attention to the fact that Jesus' word over the bread speaks of his *body*, and not of his *flesh*; the latter term does not imply blood as well, whereas the former already expresses a totality.[162] In other words, "breaking of the bread" by itself sufficiently expresses the paschal significance, as Luke-Acts attest. In fact, the word over the wine expresses another dimension, the Covenant, more clearly attached to Pentecost and to the sacrificial aspect of Jesus' death. It follows that the bread comes from the daily rite, as attested by the Essenes, while the wine comes from a festive occasion, *a priori* one of the Pentecosts (a Sunday).[163] In all likelihood wine entered the normal celebration through its weekly use in a rite marking the end of Sabbath, for which Tannaitic tradition has a blessing[164] over wine, light and spices, accompanied by a prayer for the coming of Elijah. It is also likely that the original daily rite dropped out of use because it was found to be insufficiently festive or different from an ordinary meal,[165] or even impractical for large gatherings, but there is not enough documentary evidence.[166]

162. As can be seen in John 6:51; the body (σῶμα, aram. גופא) includes the flesh and the blood (בשרא ודמא).

163. The matter of the new wine in Acts 2:13 f. seems to imply that the apostles are going to drink it on this day of Pentecost. There is good reason to attach this gesture to the second Pentecost, at the moment when the grapes ripen (cf. chap. I, §I.1b and VI, §III.2).

164. It is a true precept (*MBer* 8:5), in contrast to the lamps on Friday evening, cf. chap. I, §II.2.

165. This rite may be connected with the classic problem of the fourth petition of the Lord's Prayer (Matt 6:11): "Give us today our ἐπιούσιον bread." The term left untranslated is difficult. Jerome argued against the translation *quotidianum* ("daily") in force at his time; even though he drew attention to the equivalent מחר "of tomorrow" in the *Gospel of the Hebrews*, he proposed a superlative, which can be rendered as "the bread *par excellence*," cf. M.-Émile Boismard, "Notre pain quotidien (Mt 6,11), *RB* 102 (1995), p. 371–378.

166. The daily rite, with bread alone, did, however, survive in certain places in the early Church, though no longer in the eucharist. A solemn breaking of the bread at the beginning of each meal is prescribed for the virgin in ΛΟΓΟΣ ΣΩΤΗΡΙΑΣ (*De Virginitate*), 13 (ed. by Ed. Freiherr von der Goltz, in: Texte und Untersuchungen 29 [N.F. 14], Leipzig, J.C. Hinrichs'sche Buchhandlung, 1905, p. 47; this treatise is generally attributed to St. Athanasius). Also prescribed, to accompany the gesture, is a prayer which closely resembles that for the "Thanksgiving over the Fragment (κλάσμα)" in *Did.* 9:3-4. The *Did.*

The extreme conciseness of Jesus' words over the bread and wine, which is comparable to that of the final commissioning of the apostles (Matt 28:19 f.), suggests that they have been abridged in the course of liturgical formalization. But it does not follow that he said nothing of the kind about the meaning of these signs in relation to his death. In Luke 24:31 f., the disciples from Emmaus, after a journey through the Bible, recognize Jesus at the breaking of the bread, which implies that for them the gesture is identified with the person. In John 6:48 f., the comparison which Jesus makes between the manna and his flesh depends on bread as a middle term, and from that he develops the theme of "eating his flesh and drinking his blood." In both cases, there is a lack of symmetry between the bread and the wine, which can be understood in the light of previous remarks about the two phases of institution.

Even at the end of this section, a number of problems remain unresolved. 1. The Covenant is renewed during the Last Supper, in a context of crisis, but later, in Acts 15:5 f., the convert Gentiles are dispensed from circumcision, which, since Abraham, is the characteristic sign of the Covenant. In the background is the question of the "little remnant" and the identity of the true Israel, and whether one belongs to it by heredity or by choice. 2. Jesus son of David, born at Bethlehem, is manifestly presented by the synoptic gospels as the Messiah; similarly, the Last Supper is built along Messianic lines. But there is a major transformation, for one Messianism fails and another is announced. So the interpretation of Jesus as Messiah is going to have to be looked at carefully, since it undergoes a change.[167] By contrast, John ignores both Jesus' Davidic descent and the paschal setting of the Last Supper, and therefore this form of Messianism,

---

has a "Thanksgiving over the Cup," but its position before that over the broken bread suggests that it is a later element introduced into an already established rite; cf. §II.2 above, on the place of the wine in the *qiddush*. The *Ap. Trad.* of Hippolytus, 26.1 (ed. Dix-Chadwick, p. 45) allows for a sort of private *agapê*, when individuals bring an "offering," at which the bishop "having broken <the bread> shall always taste of it, and eat with such of the faithful as are present." The rest of this section of *Ap. Trad.* (26.2-31) describes the elaborate order of the community *agapê*; this is called "the Lord's Supper," and catechumens (*i.e.* the non-baptized) are not allowed to take part (5). At the beginning, each takes from the bishop a piece of "blessed <bread>," which is explicitly said not to be the "eucharist as is the Body of the Lord" (2). No words or prayers are prescribed for the blessing and distribution of the bread. Then (3) each takes a cup and gives thanks and drinks; here it is clear that each person drinks from his or her own cup, after pronouncing an individual thanksgiving, instead of drinking from one cup which has been passed around beginning from the bishop, which would again indicate an addition to a ceremony originally conceived only with bread in mind.

167. Of which the episode of the disciples from Emmaus is the best narrative illustration (failure on the journey out, success on return), cf. chap. IV, §II.1.

as both are connected. 3. The rite of bread and wine, reinterpreted in the setting of Passover, has an aspect of mediation, and thus a priestly dimension, although it is not in itself a sacrifice. So there is a redefinition of traditional elements. 4. The problem of the calendar has not been fully cleared up: even if allowance is made for a duplication of Passover through use of the calendar of *Jubilees*, which is the least difficult hypothesis, that still does not explain why this duplication has been veiled, since the Last Supper is situated on a Thursday, and not on a Tuesday evening. 5. Finally, we need to clarify the meaning of the festal calendar, for what has been said about conversion, Covenant, expiation and redemption, is centered on Passover and Pentecost, without a recognizable link (except in Heb) with the Day of Atonement, which is, however, very biblical.

III – Conclusions: The Path Ahead

Christianity was born in a well-defined environment which was socially and politically marginal. When Jesus passed through this environment it was certainly an event of the first importance, but always within the setting and the values of this environment, as we are beginning to see clearly. So we can understand that, whether he was accepted or rejected, it was as an *internal* phenomenon, and not as something exotic. Furthermore, reinterpretations came about through disruptions. John announced a cataclysm, and a cataclysm did indeed occur, but not in the way expected. The gospels typically show the death of Jesus, then the first manifestations of the Spirit, as cosmic disturbances. In parallel to this, the apostles are shown as totally unable to cope, in the act of betrayal, denial or flight; it is indeed a cataclysm, a sort of return to primaeval chaos. Thus it is understandable that when the disciples start off again, they hold on to the elements which had formed their identity and their companionship with Jesus, namely the ritual gestures to which they were accustomed "since the baptism of John" (Acts 1:22).

The two scenes which served to get us under way, Peter's visit to Cornelius and the night at Troas, featured baptism and the breaking of the bread. Further study of baptism in the NT and the Last Supper has been greatly helped by parallel texts of Essene origin. We are obviously dealing with the same sort of Jewish culture, which is very different from the kind of Judaism that Philo and Josephus set out to present in published form.

All the same, we have to take due account of a major difference. The Essenes constitute a very traditional reform movement, strictly internal to Judaism and condemning all those who do not belong to it. On the other hand, among the Christians there appears, at a particular moment, an opening up to the Gentiles. Jesus himself took on the yoke of the Law through the baptism of John and did not look beyond the "lost sheep of the house of Israel."

Connected with these questions is an important problem concerning the rabbinic sources, or more exactly those called "Tannaitic," after the teachers who are at the origin of these writings (before c. 220). They present, in more or less coded form, a very great number of facts and customs, as well as significant controversies, which should be able to shed light on the NT. The question is precisely how to make use of them. The task is necessary, as is shown by the voluminous work of Strack-Billerbeck, which brings together so many interesting points of comparison between rabbinic Judaism and nascent Christianity; but at the same time it is unsatisfying, for, though very conservative, these sources are the product of later redaction. Above all, it is necessary to determine what form of Judaism they are heirs to, and what transformations they have undergone in the meantime.

For these reasons, we will proceed by the following stages:

1. In order to pinpoint the original environment of Jesus and his disciples, we need to take a bearing on the history and geography of Jewish Galilee. Many modern studies on Christian origins start from the more or less explicit idea that, since Galilee was distant from Jerusalem, it was easier there to be free of the Law and the oversight of the Temple. This thesis needs to be carefully examined, for it is in formal contradiction with what we have been seeing until now, according to which the environment of reference was highly traditional.

2. The rabbinic traditions took shape in Galilee in the second half of the 2nd century, as a consequence of the expulsion of the Jews from Judaea after the failure of the Bar-Kokhba revolt; later, while remaining esoteric, they spread to Babylonia, but not to the Graeco-Roman world. It may be only a chance coincidence that Galilee is one of the things which the Tannaites and the first Christians have in common; but there is at least one similar institution practiced by both which is unlikely to arise from chance, since it is totally unknown to other branches of official Judaism of that time, namely proselyte baptism.

3. Since Pauline Christianity and rabbinic Judaism are so very different, any common features can only be regarded as accidental or insignificant unless we can identify a setting in which comparison of the two makes sense of the *differences* between them. Since there is much important common ground between rabbinic Judaism and the Essenes,

and between certain central aspects of Christianity and these same Essenes, the Essene movement emerges as a useful middle term of comparison between the other two. So we need to go back to these inquiries, bringing in also what can be known about the Jewish-Christians, whom we can think of as the heirs of James the brother of the Lord. Conflicts and the ways they were resolved will enable us to make clearer distinctions among the groups.

4. Once these various currents have been identified, above all by studying their customs and the way these evolved in the course of controversies, we will be in a position to look at particular incidents. The Book of Acts is governed in its general outlook by the scene of Pentecost. It does all the same give a certain amount of information concerning some episodes which show the various forms taken by the heritage left by Jesus. These developments are closely linked with different crises due to the general situation of the important Jewish minority in the Roman world, and especially to internal agitations within the Jewish communities, in the reigns of Tiberius, Caligula and Claudius.

5. All these events opened up new horizons for the disciples. The major fact was the mission to the Gentiles, a matter of very great controversy, as we have seen from studying the episode of Peter and Cornelius. Even so, that did not affect the polemical conviction of the first communities that they were the true Israel and represented the fulfilment of the Scriptures. This central affirmation is more than just a theological view. It is expressed by customs and rites continuing the practices of marginal Jewish sects which presented themselves as restorers of the true Israel. We shall see these continuities when we take up the examination of Passover, Pentecost and the ritual of initiation.

These five points will be developed in the five chapters that follow. In the conclusion we will draw attention to different aspects which we do not develop in this book.

Chapter III

Galilee from the Exile to Jesus

Galilee does not play any appreciable role in the Old Testament. In the NT, the Galilee in which Jesus moves is rural, without any mention of Sepphoris or Tiberias, but reflecting a high degree of religious motivation: expectations, debates and conflicts within groups of various tendencies. Since the later development of Christianity, as seen in Acts, is eminently urban (Caesarea, Antioch, Corinth, Ephesus, Rome), these rural beginnings are unlikely to have been a pure creation of the first communities. So we are dealing here with a fact. What were the nature and origin of this Jewish environment without obvious roots in the Bible, distant from the big cities, and, what is more, separated from Jerusalem by hostile Samaria?

Josephus, anxious to establish his right to speak in the name of his people, drew up, around 90, an autobiography which provides a somewhat flattering self-portrait. The curious thing is that he devotes the greater part of this work to going once again over his old campaigns in Galilee during the uprising of 66. He is obviously pleading a case, but, contrary to his first account in the *War*, he entirely omits from this second version any direct engagement of importance against the Romans, and concentrates almost entirely on divisions among the Jews. No doubt, something of this is due to his position as an imperial freedman defending imperial policy, but the result is that, viewed from Rome, the events which he retells seem to be of strictly local interest in terms of their political and social consequences. Around the same time, when describing the main "philosophies" within Judaism, he has to add to the famous triad of Pharisees-Sadducees-Essenes, a fourth tendency, that of the Galilean zealots, whose origins can be traced back to the beginning of the Roman occupation. What made him dignify this movement in such a way, since just before he has fiercely criticized the zealots as responsible for the conflicts which brought about the downfall of Jerusalem? There seem to have been some strictly Jewish reasons which obliged him even at Rome to give serious attention to far-off Galilee and the Galileans, more than twenty years after the events.

In a quite different context, the *Mishnah*, the fundamental collection of rabbinic Judaism, also comes from Galilee. It was edited about 200, and, despite numerous reminiscences of Jerusalem and the Temple, its general atmosphere is rural. Shortly afterwards (about 219), the *Mishnah* was transferred to Babylonia, where it was adopted, but it did not at this time spread into the Mediterranean basin, even though the contemporary Severan dynasty at Rome was rather favorable to the Jews, and Caracalla had granted Roman citizenship to all free subjects of the Empire, including the Jews (212). Later generations of commentators produced two collections, known as the *Jerusalem Talmud* (originating in fact in Galilee) and the *Babylonian Talmud*, which are culturally twins. However, the *Mishnah* presents itself as the work not of Jews who have migrated from Babylonia to Galilee, but of schools founded by refugees from Judaea, after the defeat of Bar Kokhba, the Romanization of Jerusalem (Aelia) and the expulsion of the Jews from Judaea. What were the nature and origin of this later Galilean Judaism? and why did it turn in the direction of Babylonia? In any case, the entire phenomenon is quite marginal to the Roman world.

So we need to define the typical features of Jewish Galilee. Since direct information is rather scarce, we will begin by examining together Josephus and the rabbinic literature. We have already seen that these two blocks are quite different in time and in type, but they can be compared, with all due care, if we allow that the authors of the *Mishnah* are heirs of the Pharisees and that Josephus, who was both a courtier and close to the Pharisees, has not left out anything that could count socially. The first result of this combined study will be to show some interesting points of agreement for the period extending from Herod the Great to the school of Yavneh-Jamnia. We will draw some conclusions about the Galilee that Jesus knew and the different realities covered by the label "Pharisee." In the next chapter, we will try to delineate the Tannaitic documents, with a view to clarifying their relation to the Pharisaic current.[1]

1. An earlier version of the material in these two chapters has appeared under the title "Galilée juive, de Jésus à la *Mishna*," in: François Blanchetière & Moshe D. Herr (ed.), *Aux origines juives du christianisme*, Paris-Louvain, Peeters, 1993, p. 15–63.

I – Galilee before Herod

Galilee corresponds approximately to the territory assigned in the Bible to the four tribes of Asher, Issachar, Naphtali and Zebulun. It is a small, though fertile, rural province, which plays almost no role in the Bible, apart from the conquest of Hazor (Josh 11) and various exploits at the time of the Judges. These tribes formed part of the post-Solomonic kingdom of Israel, with the exception of the coast (Akko), at least according to most of the texts. According to 2 Chr 30:11-12, people from Asher, Zebulun and Manasseh (central Samaria) humbled themselves and came to Jerusalem at the time of Hezekiah. This information reflects the period of the Chronicler, but in any case it shows that the attachment of these folk to Jerusalem is a remarkable exception. The famous expression "Galilee of the nations (or of the Gentiles)" comes from Isa 8:23 (in the LXX), quoted by Matt 4:15. In the finale of Matt 28:16 f., the risen Christ summons his disciples to Galilee to send them out to all nations, so that Galilee appears to be the gateway to the Gentiles. This is, however, a play on words, since the original meaning of Isa is simply "ring of the nations," with an overtone of enemy encirclement:[2] this little region was exposed and lacking in fortified towns.

Josephus knew Galilee well, having fought there, but makes no precise link with the biblical tribes when he speaks of the division of lands under Joshua (cf. *Ant.* 5 §63 f.). For him (*J.W.* 3 §35–40), it extended from Carmel to the Golan, went north as far as Tyre and south as far as the city of Samaria-Sebaste. He is really speaking of "two Galilees," Upper and Lower (*J.W.* 2 §568); the extension which he gives to this region, east of the Jordan and south of the plain of Esdraelon, comes from the shape of Herod's kingdom. Geographically, the term, meaning "rolls" or "waves," is less extensive and designates the region of rolling hills north of the plain of Esdraelon and west of the Jordan, that is practically Upper Galilee.

1. After the Exile

According to Ezra-Neh, those who returned from Babylon were interested only in Jerusalem and Judaea, which extended northwards no further than Benjamin. Later, during the Maccabaean crisis, the reconquest, strictly speaking, concerned once again only Judaea, bounded by

2. In 1 Macc 5:15 (the original of which is Hebrew), the "Galilee of the foreigners" is a ring of enemies, which FJ understands as "the foreigners of Galilee" (*Ant.* 12 §331). In the expression גליל הגוים, גליל can mean either "ring, circle" (cf. גלגל, Deut 11:30; Josh 4:19, etc.), or "rolls, waves" (cf. גלול, Lev 26:30; Ezek 6:4, etc.).

Emmaus in the west (on the edge of the hill country) and by Beth-Zur in the south (half way between Bethlehem and Hebron). However, there were Jews in Galilee, for under persecution they appealed for help to Judas and his brothers, declaring that they were the victims of a coalition bringing together Ptolemais, Tyre, Sidon and all Galilee (which corresponds well to the "ring of the nations"). This event took place between 167 and 160 B.C. It was a question, at most, of a thinly spread minority, without a stronghold of their own, in contrast to other regions. Simon, sent to their aid, did not seek to organize the security of the Jews on the spot, but preferred to bring them to Judaea (1 Macc 5:14 f.). These scattered folk were certainly not migrants from Judaea, and it is arbitrary to regard them as direct descendants of ancient Israelites, whose natural ties would in that case have been with Samaria.[3]

The only notable event to which this precarious settlement of Jews in Galilee can be attached is the charter granted to Jerusalem by Antiochus III around 200.[4] The circumstances were as follows. After a century of domination of Coele-Syria (Palestine and Phoenicia) by the Ptolemies of Egypt, Antiochus had some difficulty in integrating these regions into his own kingdom, but the inhabitants of Judaea (*Ant.* 12 §133 f.) and the Jews in general were on his side.[5] As a reward he granted a charter which recognized the status of Jerusalem. But it also allowed "all those who form part of the Jewish people" to live according to their own national laws.[6] This latter provision obviously applied to more than just Judaea. In

3. Seán Freyne, *Galilee from Alexander to Hadrian: A Study of Second Temple Judaism*, Wilmington (Del.), Glazier, 1980, p. 1–44, is not the only one to hold that the loyalty of Galilee to Jerusalem, from which it was separated by Samaria, came from the success of the "deuteronomistic" reform of Josiah, along with the small scale of deportations at the time of the fall of the kingdom of Israel, at least according to Assyrian sources. However, this view is too "Judaean" and gives rise to more problems than it solves: 1. the historical substance of this reform is far from clear, since 2 Macc 6:1 f. shows that even at the time of redaction of this book, the existence of two temples for a single nation posed no major problem; 2. according to 2 Kgs 15:29, Galilee and the surrounding cities were taken and their inhabitants deported by Tiglath-Phalassar more than ten years before the capture of Samaria by Sargon; even if the information is exaggerated, it implies that the social (and religious) coherence of the region was destroyed. More recently, Richard A. Horsley, *Galilee. History, Politics, People*, Valley Forge (Penn.), Trinity Press International, 1995, tries a more nuanced approach to Jewish Galilee, but does not succeed in giving a good explanation of the bases of its traditional culture.

4. Its authenticity has been established by Elias J. Bickerman, "La Charte séleucide de Jérusalem," in: *Studies in Jewish and Christian History II*, Leiden, 1980, p. 44–85.

5. FJ has as his source a lost passage of Polybius, who mentions "those of the Jews who live around Jerusalem," which supposes that there were others, but FJ in his paraphrase identifies Jews and Judaeans, cf. *Search,* p. 216–225.

6. Which thus became the official laws of the Jewish *ethnos*; the Seleucids, as heirs of Alexander, meant to form an empire. This disposition is similar to that mentioned in

fact there had long been a large Jewish population throughout Mesopotamia and the Seleucid empire. In addition, Antiochus, perhaps continuing a policy traditional since the Persians, did not hesitate to use Jews as *civilian* colonists in distant parts of his empire,[7] to stabilize disputed border areas (for Asia Minor, cf. *Ant.* 12 §148 f.). In fact, if they were faithful to their ancestral laws, these settlers could not enlist in any army because of the Sabbath, but would peacefully occupy the land and so ensure a maximum of security. The king had, therefore, every interest in making sure of the loyalty of the Jews, by granting their *ethnos* a statutory center and supporting their traditions and Temple.

The charter takes the form of a letter to one Ptolemy, son of Thraseas. The latter, a former general under the Ptolemies, had gone over to the service of the Seleucids as governor of Coele-Syria.[8] We do not know what was the capital of this province, but Jerusalem was obviously not at its center, and we ought to look rather on the Phoenician coast or on the road to Syria. We can be a little more precise. An inscription recently discovered at Beth-Shean (Scythopolis) shows that this Ptolemy was also high priest, that is administrator general of religious cults on behalf of the king, and that he personally owned a large part of Palestine.[9] Polybius (*Hist.* 5.70.5) indicates that Scythopolis and Philoteria (*Kh. Kerak*, south of the sea of Galilee) gave themselves up to Antiochus III in 218. Such information supposes that these towns, which had good communications both with the coast and with Damascus, enjoyed a certain importance, and it is plausible that one or other formed the center of gravity of the region as it was progressively conquered.

In any case, it is logical to suppose that as a consequence of the charter Jewish settlers from various parts of the Seleucid empire, whether sent expressly or coming as volunteers, arrived in fertile Galilee and its urban centers. It is also reasonable to suppose that the traffic entailed by pilgrimages and the dispatch of offerings for the Temple led to the creation of halts on the land route from Mesopotamia, which passed through Damascus and Scythopolis. These suppositions get some support from

---

Ezra 8:25 f., by which Artaxerxes gives a mandate to Ezra to establish with authority the "law of his God" for "all the people of Transeuphratene," an expression which corresponds exactly to the Jewish *ethnos* of Syria, cf. *Search,* p. 368–370.

7. Quite distinct from the military colonies of Egypt, cf. *Search*, p. 216–225.

8. From an inscription from Cilicia, cf. G. Radet & P. Paris, "Inscription relative à Ptolémée fils de Thraséas," *BCH* 14 (1890), p. 587–589, or *CIG* n° 1229.

9. Cf. Yoḥanan H. Landau, "A Greek Inscription Found Near Hefzibah," *IEJ* 16 (1966), p. 55–70, to be supplemented by the remarks of Louis & Jeanne Robert, "Bulletin épigraphique," *REG* 83 (1970), n° 627, p. 469–473.

the results of archaeological surveys in Galilee. These show, for the Hellenistic period, a small population before the 2nd century,[10] and then a large scale rural settlement, but scattered and without much in the way of towns. It is a sign that Antiochus III's policy was working.

During the Maccabaean crisis (167–164) and for some years afterwards, Judaea remained a Seleucid province under direct royal administration. Politically, it only began to obtain some independence when Jonathan son of Mattathias became high priest in 152, at a time of disturbance. There was effectively no civil government, and the high priesthood was still a concession granted by the Seleucid authorities, but Jonathan, heir to a family which had rebelled against Antiochus IV, obtained it, thanks to a civil war between Demetrius I and Alexander Balas (1 Macc 10:17 f.), by taking sides at the right moment. Later, after 150, he successfully asked for the concession of taxes due to Demetrius II (1 Macc 11:28) against an annual payment of 300 talents. The Jerusalem high priesthood grew in strength as Seleucid power waned and at its expense. About the same time, Jonathan also obtained the assignment to Judaea of three nomes in the district of Lydda (Lod) (1 Macc 10:30; 11:34), previously attached to a region called Samaria-Galilee, which implies that the jurisdiction of Judaea did not include Samaria, much less Galilee.

Subsequently John Hyrcanus (135–104), who succeeded his father Simon, brother of Jonathan, conducted an energetic policy of territorial expansion. Josephus reports the conquest of Sichem and the Judaization of Idumaea, around 128 (*Ant.* 13 §255 f.); later, between 111 and 107, the cities of Samaria and Scythopolis were taken (13:275 f.).[11] Even if Scythopolis had been the regional capital, which we have seen is possible but not certain, that would not necessarily mean that the whole of Galilee was conquered at the same time. After Hyrcanus' death in 105, his son Aristobulus succeeded in turbulent circumstances. About 104 he annexed a part of Ituraean territory and circumcised the inhabitants by force (*Ant.* 13 §319). Josephus has no direct source for this and has to cite Strabo (*Geog.* §753–756),[12] but his way of presenting it suggests that this "part

10. E. Meyers, J. Strange & D. Groh, "The Meiron Excavation Project: Archaeological Survey in Galilee and the Golan," 1976, *BASOR* 230 (1978), p. 1–24; E. Meyers, "Galilean Regionalism: A Reappraisal," in: W. Scott Green (ed.), *Approaches to Ancient Judaism. Vol. 5: Studies in Judaism and its Greco-Roman Context* (Brown Judaica Series, 32), Atlanta, 1985, p. 115–131.

11. Facts commemorated also by *Meg. Taan* (15 Sivan and 25 Marḥeshvan).

12. The confused succession, between 106 and 104, from the high priest John Hyrcanus to the king Alexander Jannaeus (whose priestly legitimacy was contested), with the brief interval of Aristobulus, appear to mask a break in the dynasty, cf. Étienne Nodet, "Mattathias, Samaritains et Asmonéens," *Trans* 7 (1994), p. 93–106.

of Ituraea" is none other than Galilee.[13] In other words, he is insinuating that the Galileans had been Judaized by force and so were only second-class Israelites, without pedigree, of more recent extraction even than the Idumaeans. These Ituraeans are known elsewhere as mountain folk, and sometimes described as Syrians or Arabs, and they are supposed to have originated in the mountains of Lebanon. But Luke 3:1 makes a distinction between Herod (Antipas) tetrarch of Galilee and his brother Philip tetrarch of Ituraea and Trachonitis, the Jordan apparently forming the boundary between the two principalities. Luke's geographical information is not necessarily exact, but it does at least show that Ituraea is not just another name for Galilee. Further, Josephus, sheltering behind Strabo, appears not to know where this territory was to be found, otherwise he would have clearly designated it as Galilee, and he also has difficulty in situating the event in the brief and contradictory career of Aristobulus. He limits himself to implying—very effectively, but inaccurately—that the Galileans were forced converts, which changes completely the meaning of their later conflicts with Herod.

At the same time Josephus himself gives us the means of evaluating what he has to say. He explains that, before the reign of his elder son Aristobulus, Hyrcanus had had his younger son Alexander Jannaeus brought up in Galilee, so as to keep him away from power (*Ant.* 13 §322). From that we can conclude that Galilee was at that stage outside Judaea and remote from the court, but also that it provided a provincial Jewish environment. There is no difficulty in supposing that, as before, the Jewish *ethnos* had a territorial extension wider than simply Judaea, which, even after the conquests of Hyrcanus, was still only modest in size. In fact, *Ant.* 13 §337–338 mentions for Galilee the Jewish localities of Sepphoris and Asochis, but at the time when Ptolemy Latyrus was blocking the expansionist ambitions of Alexander Jannaeus, in particular at Ptolemais (Akko) and in the Jordan valley. So, even at the beginning of Jannaeus' reign, Galilee was still not attached to Judaea, which makes the business about the Ituraeans even more inconsistent. Above all, it explains why Josephus relied on the authority of Strabo to introduce an element which fits uneasily into his own documentation,[14] but which

13. This is the common opinion, cf. Schürer-Vermes I:141 and 562, II:8 f., but without real proof.

14. It is possible that Strabo (or a later copyist), aware of a matter of forced circumcision, mistakenly confused Ituraeans (Ιτουραῖοι) and Idumaeans (Ἰδουμαῖοι). Aristobulus, the successor of Hyrcanus, may also be confused with another Aristobulus, the very active and better-known "successor" of the weak Hyrcanus II (cf. below).

supports his own theses: he is seeking, discreetly but effectively, to discredit the Galileans with his readers. But why?

In 63, Jerusalem fell to Pompey (*Ant.* 14 §48–76), because of a civil war: Antipater, Herod's father and apparently governor of Idumaea, supported the weak Hyrcanus II, the legitimate heir, against the claims of Aristobulus, who had made himself king in 67. The Romans at first supported the latter, but then changed sides and laid siege to Jerusalem. The victorious Pompey made a triumphal entry. Hyrcanus, finding himself the winner, kept the titles of ethnarch and high priest, but not that of king. Judaea was severely trimmed of a series of cities with their dependent territories: in the west, south of Mt. Carmel, the coastal towns from Raphia to Dora; in the center, Samaria and Scythopolis; east of the Jordan, several cities including Pella, Hippos and Gadara. All these cities and their territories were included directly in the newly created Roman province of Syria. In this way, the Romans had immediate control of all the roads leading to Galilee, which certainly no longer formed part of Judaea (if it ever had), although we do not know if the region or any of its cities was included at this point in Syria. No change is recorded even for the Jewish town of Sepphoris, the future local capital. The clear implication is that, unlike large areas east of the Jordan (Peraea), Galilee had not belonged to the enlarged Judaea of Hyrcanus and Jannaeus.

In 57, Gabinius, the new governor of Syria, put down a Jewish revolt at the moment when Alexander, son of Aristobulus, was trying to regain power (*Ant.* 14 §82–97). Gabinius divided Palestine, or more exactly "the people," into five districts governed by as many *synedria* ("sanhedrins")[15] or "synods," and Sepphoris became the capital of Galilee. In fact, it was a reorganization of the people, and not of Judaea. This is evident in the case of Peraea, with its two districts of Amathontis and Jericho: Jews were numerous there, but since Pompey the region had in practice no longer been part of Judaea. The same is true for Galilee, al-

15. This institution with a Greek name, which the rabbinic sources depict as permanent (cf. chap. IV, §I.3), is really not well known. J. S. McLaren, *Power and Politics in Palestine. The Jews and the Governing of Their Land 100 B.C.–A.D. 70* (JSNTS, 63), Sheffield, 1991, holds that the *synedrion*, which was probably intended originally to be a permanent body with definite powers, rapidly became (especially in Jerusalem) a sort of conference of notables (of different tendencies) called together as a consultative council for certain important decisions or as a tribunal to judge certain categories of crimes. In favor of this thesis: 1. it is not, strictly speaking, a permanent council of Elders, a normal institution in any society (senate, γερουσία); 2. the term was known in Greece, where it designated *temporary* alliances of cities concluded for a precise purpose (and could be translated "common session"). A modern equivalent would be "conference" or "round table."

though Josephus does not say so expressly. Seen from Syria, the effect was to give the Jews of the region a territorial organization without according too much importance to Jerusalem, and above all by carefully ignoring any notion of a kingdom of Judaea. So there was indeed a Jewish Galilee, now with Sepphoris as its capital.[16]

To sum up, a Jewish Galilee is visible from the time of Antiochus III, but, until the arrangements made by Gabinius, the social and political attachment of Galilee to Judaea remains very vague,[17] and the affair of the Ituraeans may be intended to fill a gap, though more likely to dissemble the real origins of the Galileans. It is more than probable that no effective political link with Judaea existed before Hyrcanus II: on his return to favor in 47, his royal title was restored, and on that occasion Galilee was expressly attached to Judaea, but, it seems, for the first time. In other words, the Romans, more concerned about clear administration than religion, were the first to make Galilee just one more Jewish district among others in Palestine. The later kings of Judaea, at least those who were Roman vassals, only inherited this new situation.

For our purpose, what stands out from all this is the exceptional position of the Jews of Galilee. They have no identifiable connection with the ancient northern kingdom (Israel) or with the Samaritans, they do not belong to the political entity of Judaea, they are not simply the Jewish *ethnos* diffused throughout Syria and Mesopotamia, and they are not the result of the forced circumcision of local tribes. We shall see, however, that they have a cultural identity which is very marked.

2. Around Herod the Great

After Pompey's death in 47, Caesar re-established Hyrcanus as ethnarch as a reward for his loyalty (*Ant.* 14 §137–144), in which he had been more than encouraged by the ever-active Antipater, who was himself rewarded by being dispensed from taxes, granted Roman citizenship and appointed (or confirmed) as procurator of Idumaea. His situation was sufficiently secure for him to be able to provide for his sons.

Herod, the most outstanding among them, was put "in charge" of Galilee, in somewhat obscure circumstances. Among other feats which

16. According to *MQid* 4:5, the earlier government (called ἀρχή in transcription) of Sepphoris was strictly Jewish; this was the situation until the city was razed during the troubles which followed the death of Herod, cf. Schürer-Vermes II:174, n. 484.

17. The statement in *Ant.* 13 §154, that the Galileans depended on Judas Maccabaeus, should be considered as a slip by FJ, or else as information contrary to the spirit of 1 Macc but in agreement with that of 2 Macc, in which Judas is more interested in defending the Jews wherever they may be than in winning power by conquest at Jerusalem.

he accomplished there, he crushed a certain Ezekias and his band, who were at large on the Syrian border (14 §159 f.). But a lawsuit followed, which was tried before the Sanhedrin at Jerusalem. The way this episode is reported is instructive. First Herod, whose precise commission is not made clear, is said to be only fifteen years old; historians conjecture that there has been a copyist's error for "twenty-five," which would fit the chronology of his reign (he turned fifteen between Pompey and Gabinius, which is certainly too early for these activities). Josephus insists, however, on Herod's youth and precocity, which is not really apt for a man of twenty-five, since the point of reference is always Alexander the Great, who died at thirty. Then the trial comes as a surprise; if it had been only a question of putting robbers out of action, there would hardly have been cause for a lawsuit.[18] Finally this Ezekias is not just an ordinary bandit, since he is regarded as the ancestor of the Galilean movement (*J.W.* 2 §56). So there is something more at stake, which is both political[19] and religious. Politically, Herod's victims cannot be associated with the partisans of Aristobulus, the adversary of Rome in Pompey's time, since their sorrowing mothers laid their griefs before Hyrcanus, who was entirely a vassal of the Romans. It could be argued that Herod was trying to carve out a fief in opposition to Hyrcanus, and so earned the jealousy of the court, but his actions won the favor of the governor Sextus Caesar, who would certainly not have put himself against Hyrcanus, a protégé of Julius Caesar, and was even less likely to look kindly on a sedition compromising the *pax romana*. In the end, Herod was appointed by Sextus as governor of Coele-Syria and Samaria, thus already giving proof of that exceptional flair for politics which he was to show throughout his career.

18. The parallel account in *J.W.* 1 §209 says simply that the plotters forced Hyrcanus to summon Herod, the rising star, to answer charges of acting in despite of the "Jewish law" and the "national customs," by putting many people to death without trial. This formulation, which avoids saying that the plotters were partisans of Ezekias, draws attention to the monopoly of the Jerusalem tribunal and away from the brigands. This faction was clearly seeking to make political capital out of their demand for legality. The conclusion reached by Peter Schäfer, *Geschichte der Juden in der Antike. Die Juden Palëstinas von Alexander dem Großen bis zur arabischen Eroberung*, Stuttgart, 1983, p. 98, that the issue at stake was a monopoly of the death penalty for the Jerusalem Sanhedrin, in which the Pharisees were influential (only according to *Ant.*), goes well beyond the texts, by attributing to the Sanhedrin more substance than it can be shown to have had, and by giving insufficient attention to the nature of the "brigands."

19. Cf. Seán Freyne, "Bandits in Galilee: A Contribution to the Study of Social Conditions in First-Century Palestine," in: Jacob Neusner & *al.* (ed.), *The Social World of Formative Christianity and Judaism*, Philadelphia, Fortress Press, 1988, p. 50–68, who insists on the socio-political situation. Helmut Schwier, *Tempel und Tempelzerstörung* (Novum Testamentum und Orbis Antiquus, 11), Fribourg/Göttingen, 1989, p. 145 f. discusses various opinions about these bandits.

Only one conclusion is possible: these "brigands" were anti-Roman Jews. The lawsuit was brought against Herod by Jews who were defending the Law without the slightest thought for Roman allegiance; at the trial, the Pharisee Sameas played a notable part by his frankness of speech. The difficult or legendary elements[20] in Josephus' account cannot completely hide a fact which is important for our purpose, namely that there was a Galilean Judaism to which the Pharisees were favorable. Perhaps this Judaism gave signs of being an independence movement, but in any case it would have been totally opposed to Herod the Idumaean, who was even called a "half-Jew" (*Ant* 14 §403); so there was a principle at stake, whatever the political consequences might be. Herod reciprocated the antipathy. One of the first things he did on coming to power was to annihilate the Jerusalem Sanhedrin, and he was always in strife with the Pharisees and feared their influence with the people. Here we have one of the causes of Josephus' difficulties: on the one hand, he admired Herod and did not hesitate to regard him as God's elect (*Ant.* 14 §455 etc.), but, at least later on, he wanted to pass for a Pharisee (cf. *Life* §12), for reasons which we shall have to investigate. In any case, Herod's Galilean opponents were certainly not "maranos," forced converts, Ituraeans or what have you: Ezekias was defending a form of Judaism. Always the politician, Herod the Idumaean was cunning and mistrustful. In fact, we see that he did place confidence in an Ituraean (*Ant.* 15 §185), but not in a Galilean; perhaps this showed a fellow feeling between Ituraeans and Idumaeans, based on the forced conversion of both, but the Galileans' claim to be regarded as Jews was certainly well founded.

In 40, Herod had himself appointed king of Judaea by the Roman senate (*Ant.* 14 §381 f.), but he only obtained this promotion thanks to a war in which Rome needed local allies: Antigonus, the last Hasmonaean king, had just obtained the throne with the help of the Parthians, who pushed the Romans out of Syria and captured Hyrcanus. In 39, Herod, with the support of the Romans who were still fighting against the Parthians, landed at Ptolemais in order to reconquer Judaea. Josephus affirms that the whole of Galilee rapidly rallied to him "with some exceptions" (§395), and that he made his way to Jerusalem with ever-growing forces. The situation was complicated by the venality of the Roman general Silo, who tried to profit from both camps, and Herod was forced to consolidate his conquests. In particular, he had to go back to Galilee, where Antigonus

20. In particular it is hard to know if this trial at Jerusalem for acts done in Galilee implies the disappearance of other provincial sanhedrins. The trial is reported in *BSan* 19a-b, with other names (Jannaeus instead of Hyrcanus, etc.), and insisting on the independence of the Pharisees.

still had some strongholds. He entered Sepphoris without striking a blow, but was soon obliged to commit considerable forces in a difficult struggle against "brigands living in caves." In other words, the resistance put up by Antigonus' partisans was negligeable, but once again, Herod was up against "brigands," who formed a distinct party and were strong enough to cause him trouble.

Josephus tells how, after the main force of the enemy had been defeated, an assault was made on the caves where the last refugees held out. They were in the cliffs of Arbela, above Magdala on the shore of the Lake (*Ant.* 14 §421 f.). A notable incident: on the point of being captured, one old man (or "elder") refused to give himself up and preferred to kill his wife and seven children and throw himself over the edge. Herod was on the spot and held out his hand in sign of pardon, but the other, before jumping off, took time to shout abuse at him because of his origins. So these were not brigands who pillaged for gain, and the episode resembles those, a century later, of the prisoners at Jotapata and even the collective suicides at Gamala and Massada. Josephus probably could not afford to make the comparison, but it is difficult not to conclude that these brigands were akin to the Ezekias who had been vanquished by Herod ten years previously. Herod's outstretched hand expresses the hope of winning not only victory, but also recognition. In any case, it is noteworthy that Herod sought the backing of Galileans, as Josephus himself was to do in somewhat similar circumstances (chap. IV, §I.1).

A little later, Herod departed from Galilee, leaving a governor behind, but there were renewed uprisings, still without any link with Antigonus, and he had to return in order to put them down and impose fines on the towns. The following year, Herod went to find Mark Antony, then campaigning at Samosata, and complained about the defection of the Roman support troops which he had received. During his absence, his brother Joseph was beaten by Antigonus at Jericho; seeing the Herodian party thus weakened, the Galileans once more revolted, but Josephus again refrains from suggesting that this was in the cause of Antigonus (§450). In 37, Herod at last arrived before Jerusalem and laid siege with Roman help (§465).

Josephus tells later (*Ant.* 17 §23 f.) how, at a period which is not well defined, but probably soon after the beginning of his reign,[21] Herod

21. FJ places the call of Zamaris after he had been installed at Daphne, near Antioch, by Saturninus, governor of Syria at the end of Herod's reign (9–6 B.C.), so at the time when the latter was already mired in domestic difficulties, cf. Schürer-Vermes I:257. That is improbable. It is better to look to the period when he was consolidating his own authority (37–25). There was a governor Calpurnius in 34–33: the date is better, and the names could have been confused. This error on the part of FJ, who often seeks to cover the traces, may not be accidental.

wanted protection from raiders operating out of Trachonitis. This time they appear to have been Arab or Nabataean Bedouins who have always conducted periodic razzias on the produce of the peasants, but they could once again have been Jewish "brigands." In order to set up a buffer zone in Batanaea (Golan), the king created a peaceful Jewish settlement which could protect the pilgrimage route as well as the district. He installed a group of Babylonian Jews who were already in Syria and well regarded by the Romans. He gave them lands to break in and exempted them from taxes. Their leader, called Zamaris, built a town, Bathyra, and several strongholds. He summoned from everywhere "people faithful to the Jewish customs"; tax-free status and a remote situation were very attractive, especially for folk who had a high degree of religious motivation but were not interested in furthering political ambition. Herod's choice of Babylonian Jews who were not interested in politics was certainly clever, especially in view of the nearby Galileans on the other shore of the Lake who had resisted him; they had also come from Babylon, though at an earlier period. In fact, Herod never revoked the tax exemption, and it was west of the Lake (Sepphoris) that revolt broke out on his death. So it looks as if his policy was successful.

When Herod died, in 4 B.C., the situation once again became confused, with succession disputes around Archelaus, abuse of power by the Roman army, and various uprisings, especially on the occasion of the pilgrimages to Jerusalem at Passover and Pentecost. The religious factor counted for much in these revolts: at Jerusalem, there were demands that the new ethnarch purify the Temple worship, and vengeance was sought for the Pharisee teachers who had been put to death by Herod for wanting to remove a golden eagle from the Temple (*Ant.* 17 §206 f.). The troubles were put down by Varus, governor of Syria, who had come to the rescue with an army. He showed clemency towards Jerusalem, but was pitiless with regard to the brigands.

In Galilee, Sepphoris was at the center of a rebellion led by Judas of Gamala, who sought to profit from the weakness of Jerusalem and take over the government. The revolt was put down and the town destroyed by Varus' son (17 §289). This Judas is none other than Judas the Galilean, the founder *together with a Pharisee* of the "madness" which Josephus is constrained to call a "fourth party" (18 §4 f.).[22] Judas is represented as the "son of Ezekias," who was, of course, the one whom Herod had beaten more than 40 years previously. Obviously, Judas was his successor rather

22. Cf. Martin Hengel, *The Zealots. Investigations into the Jewish Freedom Movement in the Period from Herod I until 70 A.D.* (Eng. tr. of *Die Zeloten*, 2nd ed., 1976), Edinburgh, T. & T. Clark, 1985, p. 62–66 and 331.

than his own son;[23] the dates are too far apart, and no genealogy is given, so the meaning here has to be that they are of the same "breed." At the time of the fiscal census under Quirinius, in A.D. 6, Judas was sufficiently influential to incite widespread resistance to Roman power (and taxes) throughout Judaea—whence the label "the Galilean," which was certainly given by others and supposes appreciable influence outside Galilee itself.[24] Such influence did not come about overnight, and it was against this deeply anti-Roman party that Varus moved most severely.[25] So Jewish Galilee was strengthened under Herod, to the point of taking on a national importance which will only grow subsequently. Along with this we need to place the fact that the Pharisees never wanted to give their allegiance to Herod, who feared and persecuted them (cf. *Ant.* 17 §41 f.).

Even though it was only a rural province without great economic or strategic importance, Herod's maneuvres and the social instability after his death show both the difficulty and the importance of being in control of Galilee. Josephus himself, quite apart from the ambiguities of his own role during the action in 66, is systematically confused about the history of Jewish Galilee: he would like to see only brigands or forced converts without pedigree. When these labels are inapplicable, he gives himself away. For example, when Galilean Jews were rescued from persecution by Antiochus Epiphanes, 1 Macc 5:23 tells how Simon brought the captives with their families and goods to Judaea "amid overflowing joy";[26] it is significant that Josephus, who has no other source, omits the overflowing joy from his version of the episode, even though he is never shy of

23. Similarly, about 65, there appears "a certain" Menaḥem, "son" of Judas the Galilean (*J.W.* 2 §433); here too, it is a question of a successor rather than of a son, not only because of the distance between the dates, which makes direct sonship unlikely, but also because of the contradiction between "a certain," which suppose the lack of a known genealogy, and the "son of," which expresses the contrary. Cf. Étienne Nodet, "Jésus et Jean-Baptiste selon Josèphe," *RB* 92 (1985), p. 504 f., who follows others in showing that the duplication between Judas the bandit and Judas the founder is created by a system of doublets, in which the same episodes, after Herod's death, are told twice over and combined according to two different perspectives.

24. Attested by Luke 13:1-3 (Galileans killed by Pilate), which shows that Luke recognizes in that term the extended meaning of "brigands."

25. The *Seder Olam Rabba* (ed. Ratner, p. 145) has preserved the memory of a war of Varus in Galilee, to which it gives as much importance as that of Vespasian, whereas it ignores the civil war and arrival of Pompey, which was an event concerning Judaea.

26. This passage of 1 Macc is certainly the source of FJ, but it contains its own difficulties. There is a notable lack of symmetry between Judas' actions in Gilead and those of Simon, at the same time, in Galilee: the former are described in detail, whereas the latter are told in a sort of deuteronomistic style and contain the names only of Arbatta (not far from Strato's Tower, later Caesarea) and Ptolemais, cf. Félix-Marie Abel, *Les livres des Maccabées* (Études Bibliques, 38), Paris, 1949, p. 95.

wordy paraphrases when there are no underlying political difficulties (*Ant.* 12 §334). It is understandable that he should mistrust a John of Gischala or a Justus of Tiberias, who were his own enemies, but it is remarkable that he takes his lack of sympathy for the Jews of Galilee so far back in time. In reality he did at one time make common cause with them, as we shall see (chap. IV, §I.1), but he never succeeded in making them "reasonable," since they preferred, sometimes to the point of insurrection, loyalty to ancestral (Babylonian) traditions rather than submission to the powers that be, whether Hasmonaean or Roman. Finally, Josephus has to deprive them of any "Pharisaic" legitimacy, since he can see no future for Judaism except in obedience to the civil power of Rome.

II – Hillel and Galilee

The previous section, showing Herod's behavior with regard to Galilee and the Pharisees, provides a setting for the appearance of Hillel the Elder and a means of evaluating the rabbinic sources which mention him. Hillel is one of the great founding figures of normative Judaism (*MAb* 1:12), and the first to whom tradition accords the title of patriarch.[27] It is also with him that rabbinic tradition begins to notice controversies, which has puzzled later commentators; so he brings together several distinct currents. Hillel came from Babylonia and lived at the time of Herod, but little more can be said with certitude about him.

1. A Distant Enthronement

Josephus, who has eyes only for what counts socially, ignores Hillel, but mentions Shemaya and Abtalion, who immediately precede Hillel and Shammai in the list of transmitters of the tradition given in *MAb* 1:10 f. The narrative of Hillel's installation as patriarch is provided only by the rabbinic sources, and its main interest lies in the evidence it provides of a major discontinuity between him and his immediate predecessors. The event is reported in several similar forms, but we will comment here on the longest and best documented version (*YPes* 6:1 p. 33a),[28] omitting some extra developments which are clearly later.

27. Or נשיא; the title is certainly anachronistic, as it does not correspond to anything that can be identified socially before 70; at most it would be equivalent to "recognized teacher." The institution of patriarch, properly so called, is not attested before Bar Kokhba, and then without link with the Tannaites; from Judah the Prince, it was certainly reflected back on earlier generations, cf. Aharon Oppenheimer, *Galilee in the Mishnaic Period*, Jerusalem, Zalman Shazar Center, 1991, p. 51 f. We shall see later on the reasons for this retrojection (chap. V, §I.2).

28. The other two versions are in *TPas* 4:13-14 and *BPes* 66a. The former (*Tosefta*) differs more from that which is presented here: shorter, omitting the names of Shemaya,

This law was not known to the Elders of Bathyra. (It is a matter of infringements of the Sabbath which are permitted in order to prepare the paschal lamb, as they are set out in *MPes* 6:1 f.).

1. *It happened one day that 14 Nisan fell on a Sabbath, and they did not know if the Passover sacrifice* (פסח) *took precedence over the Sabbath or not. They said: "There is here a certain Babylonian whose name is Hillel, who has studied with* (שמש) *Shemaya and Abtalion. He will know if the Passover sacrifice takes precedence over the Sabbath"—"Can he be of any use!?"*[29] *They sent for him. They said to him: "Have you ever heard if, when 14 Nisan falls on a Sabbath, it takes precedence over it or not?"*

Hillel tries to prove the point by various arguments based above all on the Bible and using his rules of interpretation, but the others refuse his reasons or disprove them, then conclude: *"There is nothing to get from this Babylonian!"*

Although he had stayed to give them explanations all day long, they did not accept him until he said to them: "Woe is me! That is what I received from Shemaya and Abtalion." When they heard that, they rose and designated him as patriarch.

2. When they had proclaimed him patriarch, he began to criticize them, saying: *"What urged you to have need of this Babylonian? So you did not make use of the two great ones of this world, Shemaya and Abtalion, who were seated among you?" While he was criticizing them, he forgot the* halakha.

3. *They said: "What shall we do for people who have forgotten their knife?" He answered them: "I have heard the reply, but I have forgotten. But let Israel be. If they are not prophets, they are sons of proph-*

Abtalion and Bathyra, it takes place at the Temple, in front of all the people, and Hillel is installed at the end of the narrative (when he shows that he knows the *Mishnah*), but leaving out any connection between him and the priests or Sanhedrin; that is hardly realistic, except on the supposition that Hillel is entirely marginal with regard to these authorities, which is in contradiction with the presence of the whole people. Although it is the oldest, this version cannot be preferred, not only because it contains too many oddities in the way it presents the facts, but especially because it reworks the scene in view of later *halakha*, according to which the immolation of the paschal lamb can take place only at the Temple, cf. *Search*, p. 290–306 and chap. VII, §II.3. The second version *(BT)* represents an intermediate form between the other two: it speaks of "people of Bathyra" (בני בתירה) and of the Temple. Strictly speaking, even the version regarded here as primitive does not say explicitly that the scene is Bathyra (later, "people of Bathyra" are mentioned with Yoḥanan b. Zakkai at Yavneh); it could also have taken place at Jerusalem or nearby, during a pilgrimage, but the whole point of the story presupposes an isolated environment. Jacob Neusner, *Judaism in the Beginning of Christianity*, Philadelphia, Fortress, 1984, p. 110 f., proposes a different analysis, cutting any link between FJ and the rab. trad., which is certainly simple, but *a priori* arbitrary. Cf. also id., *The Tosefta. Second Division, Moed*, New York, 1981, p. 136 f.

29. Or, less probably: "Perhaps he is of some use" (without irony).

> *ets."*[30] *Immediately, those whose Passover was a lamb hid [the knife] in its wool; those who had a kid tied the knife between its horns. Thus their victims were found to bring their knives with them. When he saw what they were doing, he remembered the* halakha. *He said to them: "Woe is me if that is not what I heard*[31] *from Shemaya and Abtalion!"*

Each of the three parts of this narrative ends with the mention of Shemaya and Abtalion, the absent predecessors of Hillel (and Shammai). The part in the middle serves to link the two others, which are parallel: the first part is a general question which shows ignorance of the *Mishnah*; the last is a very particular question, which supposes knowledge of the *Mishnah* and is set more or less clearly in the Temple, in accordance with the tradition that the Passover victim is immolated in the sanctuary and eaten in the Temple precincts, or at least in Jerusalem (*TPes* 8:16 f.). We show elsewhere (chap. VII, §II.3) that this Mishnaic opinion conceals other and more ancient usages: at least in certain circles, the paschal lamb was sacrificed and eaten outside the Temple, before as well as after the destruction. So the account being studied is composite and integrates a Mishnaic perspective into customs of different origin. Here we will look only at these latter customs which underlie the first part, that is the enthronement of Hillel.

The examination that Hillel undergoes is remarkable on more than one score:

a. The entity that questions Hillel has the power to appoint him as "patriarch," at least in the sense of head of a school. It is in no way said that this entity is a sanhedrin: it is only the "Elders of Bathyra," who are hardly mentioned elsewhere,[32] but who have strong ties with Babylonia.[33]

30. The parallel in the *Tosefta* says here that they have the Holy Spirit: through inspiration, the prophets recalled the Law; similarly, the sons of the prophets can actualize it, and they are here identified as the people as a whole. This constant principle, characteristic of the Essenes, can be stated thus: it is by the Spirit that Scripture (Laws, Prophets) speak to the present. The same structure recurs in the Sermon on the Mount, cf. chap. VII, §IV.1.

31. Reading from the Geniza (Schechter: יבוא עליי אם לא שמעתי), cf. Saul Lieberman, *Hayerushalmi kiphshuṭo*, Jerusalem, 1934, p. 466.

32. In *BRSh* 29b, they appear in regard to a similar question: one year, New Year's day (1 Tishri) fell on a Sabbath, and Yoḥanan b. Zakkai (the last disciple of Hillel, according to tradition, founder of the school of Yavneh) asked the "people of Bathyra" (בני בתירה) if the *shofar* should be sounded or not (cf. Lev 23:23 f.), *i.e.* if this feast prevailed over the Sabbath or not; they wanted to discuss it, but he succeeded in having the trumpet sounded thus avoiding any debate. On the implications of this story, cf. chap. IV, §I.2.

33. One Yehuda b. Bathyra is known, at the end of the 1st century, as head of the academy of Nisibis in Babylonia, cf. *BPes* 3b; that supposes movements between Babylonia and the Babylonian colony of Bathyra, which is not at all surprising. Cf. Yavneh, chap. IV,

b. The masters who are mentioned, Shemaya and Abtalion, are the authorities recognized by all, but they are absent and have not been replaced. *BPes* 66a states that they were respectively patriarch and president of the Sanhedrin. That information is not confirmed by Josephus (cf. below) and can be regarded as doubtful, but these persons at least occupied a notable social rank, in their own day or at least according to a widespread tradition, since Josephus speaks of them. Whatever the truth of that, other passages also indicate a break in continuity between them and their successors (cf. *MEdu* 1:3); their authority is intact, but they are out of reach. So they must be dead, perhaps killed, and in any case unable to establish a succession recognized by the colony of Bathyra.

c. The profile of the candidate who is sought is quite particular: a Babylonian who has frequented Pharisee masters in Judaea. However, in the account in question, some challenge the Babylonian as such. So there is a problem of unifying different currents.

d. The context of the question asked is not academic, but indicates a concrete emergency which cannot be met either by a firm tradition or by an authority on the spot capable of giving a decision. The *Mishnah*, at least in the form in which it was edited two centuries later, is unknown, but there is no tribunal or teacher vested with the necessary authority, because of the break in continuity.

e. The question itself is odd, for, according to the normal lunar calendar, Passover falls on a Sabbath on average every seven years. With a very particular point, as in the third part, it would be understandable that the collective memory might not be clear and that a discussion could ensue, but that is not in fact what happens: the whole people are declared to be "sons of prophets,"[34] and they remember the detail they need to know. In the first part, the question is general, then in his argumentation Hillel looks for a global solution, and the final response is not given clearly. It is somewhat improbable that the entire assembly capable of promoting Hillel, even if it obtained recognition only later, should have forgotten a point of custom so general and so simple; that is precisely the point of Hillel's anger in the link paragraph (second part).

---

§I.2. 1 Esdr 5:17 mentions 3 005 υἱοὶ Βαιτηρους, corresponding to the sons of Hashum and the sons of Gibar of Ezra 2:19-20, or the sons of Gibeon of Neh 7:25; these details suggest the restoration beneath Βαιτηρους of Bet-Horon (near Gibeon, cf. Josh 10:10 f.), rather than Bathyra.

34. To say that *all the people* have an *inspired* interpretation is in fact a polemical statement, which is opposed to the Essenes (and brotherhoods) as well as to Christianity, since both these present themselves as small inspired groups; it corresponds to the development of the Tannaite movement from the brotherhood model to that of a school which is responsible for the entire people (cf. chap. V, §I.2).

The way this episode is put together presents a thick bundle of problems. To begin with the masters, Josephus gives a few points which are not particularly coherent but provide a perspective. According to *Ant.* 15 §3, "the Pharisee Pollion and his disciple Sameas" were held in honor by Herod, for they had advised the inhabitants of Jerusalem to open the gates to him when he finally arrived as king in 37. If Pollion is a (Latin) equivalent for Abtalion,[35] the transcription "Sameas" is ambiguous: it may come from his colleague Shemaya, or else from Shammai, his disciple and the inseparable opponent of Hillel, which looks more likely here. However, *Ant.* 14 §172 reports that a certain Sameas, a member of the Sanhedrin, "a just man and therefore above all fear," reproached the court and king Hyrcanus for their cowardice in face of Herod's crimes, during his trial, already mentioned, for the murder of Ezekias. Later, Josephus attributes this intervention to Pollion (15 §4), who recommended to the Sanhedrin to get rid of Herod. So he mixes them up, which would rather suggest that they belonged to the same generation, *i.e.* that Sameas was really Shemaya. Josephus' information appears imprecise, and his carelessness is proverbial, but in any case the question is largely artificial, for Shemaya and Shammai are two forms of the same name, which can both be transcribed as "Sameas."[36] Besides, we can easily guess that Josephus is ill at ease with his sources: Herod represses the Pharisees, who were not afraid to oppose the king (17 §41 f.), but, whereas he puts the entire Sanhedrin to death, he spares Sameas, the only one who dared to speak up. Josephus later tries to find an explanation (14 §176), but in reality it applies to Pollion (15 §370), and not to Sameas.

So confusion reigns, but the speech which Josephus places on the lips of Sameas during Herod's trial gives a clue. Addressing Herod, he does not charge him with acting illegally, but attacks only the sanhedrists and king Hyrcanus II for not daring to resist him, and predicts that when Herod becomes king he will kill them all. And so he did, continues Josephus, when he came to power ten years later, in 37, but Sameas and/or Pollion were spared. Sameas' speech is clever, but purely that of a courtier and impossible on the lips of an incorruptible judge: he brings off

35. Cf. Louis H. Feldman, "The Identity of Pollion, the Pharisee, in Josephus," *JQR* 49 (1958), p. 53–62.

36. שמאי being an abbreviation of שמעיה, as Yanni/Jannaeus (ינאי) is of Yoḥanan/John (יחנן), etc.; cf. discussion and examples in Joseph N. Dérenbourg, *Essai sur l'histoire et la géographie de la Palestine*, Paris, Impr. Impériale, 1867, p. 95, n. 1. It is even possible that Shammai is a duplication of Shemaya-Sameas, deliberately put at the time of Hillel, cf. Jacob Neusner, *The Rabbinic Traditions about the Pharisees Before 70*, Leiden, 1971, I:158–159, who prefers to remain critical of the rabbinic sources, rather than to look for an historical context.

the remarkable feat of flaunting his freedom of speech while at the same time attracting the favor of Herod, to which he later owed his survival. In fact, it is not Sameas speaking, but Josephus, trying to reconcile his admiration for Herod with his pro-Pharisee choice,[37] whereas in reality the two camps were at war. Furthermore, Hillel's enthronement has shown a break in continuity between Shemaya and Abtalion and their successors, in an atmosphere of crisis, and we must suspect that these teachers were eliminated along with the rest of the Sanhedrin by Herod. Josephus is very hard to pin down on the question whether Herod acted against the Sanhedrin as soon as he came to power. His maneuverings do, however, give us one piece of useful information: he has difficulty in placing Shemaya and Abtalion in an historical context, and does not speak of them in the *War*. He knows, however, or rather he has learned, that they are remembered as important by the Pharisees; so, even though they disappeared under Herod, their reputation in certain circles has earned them a lasting influence. He employed the same method in the case of Jesus: discovering (at Rome) that he left behind a movement which could not be ignored, Josephus made an effort to fit him into his account of events under Pilate. Here, he simply attempts to free Herod from blame by suggesting that his purges took place *before* Shemaya and Abtalion left the scene.

It is possible, however, to explain the discontinuity before Hillel in another way, while accepting, for want of better, the information given by Josephus: the succession from Shemaya and Abtalion to Hillel (and Shammai) may be nothing more than a simple literary device. In the second part of the account given above, Hillel gets angry and states that the whole assembly has heard the teaching of Shemaya and Abtalion. In the first part, by contrast, no one has heard them, but no one says that they are dead. In this case, Hillel's installation with an anachronistic title would simply be a literary composition, combining an origin in Babylonia, represented by the colony at Bathyra and Hillel, with the teaching of Pharisees at Jerusalem, represented by Shemaya and Abtalion. This twofold source would then correspond, as we will show (chap. IV, §I.2), to the two founders of the school of Yavneh: Yoḥanan b. Zakkai, Galilean disciple of Hillel, and Gamaliel II, important Pharisee of Jerusalem.

We still have to explain the emergence of the Elders of Bathyra, who are in no way a permanent body. There again, Josephus gives himself

37. Which he declares (tardily) in *Life* §10. On the relations of FJ with the Pharisees, cf. §III.2 below. The introduction of Pollion and Sameas into the second redaction of the narrative *(Ant.)* is a bit clumsy, but it has to be seen in the context of the development of FJ, who began by praising the Essenes, cf. chap. I, §I.1.

away: he says that many had come to settle in the colony founded by Zamaris *for they felt secure there*. Herod persecuted the Pharisees, but did not touch the status of this colony, for very clear reasons of general policy regarding the Babylonians and the Parthians, who were always potentially and sometimes actually enemies of Rome, and had invaded Judaea in 40 B.C. So it was a refuge, problematic perhaps at times of high drama, but in any case precious for all those who could not hope for protection from priestly circles, which were under Herod's sway. In circumstances which are far from clear, an informal and not necessarily permanent coalition was made with the Babylonian Hillel, which certain circles *afterwards* regarded as being in succession to the Sanhedrin. No doubt at first a simple brotherhood (i.e. without professional teachers), this group was later understood as a school, and finally as the principal academy, parallel to the development of the Tannaite movement to be described below (chap. IV, §II.3). The title of patriarch is obviously anachronistic, and it is not surprising that Josephus does not mention events so marginal, of which he may have been ignorant in all good faith. Perhaps he was aware of *several* concurrent successions to these masters, while seeking more or less to put himself forward as a candidate, and in any case placing himself above all parties. We shall see later some indications that he regarded the enterprise of Yavneh as being in competition with his own project for the future of Judaism (chap. IV, §I.1).

2. An Essential Question about Passover

The question put to Hillel provides further information. As we have seen, it is hard to imagine that everyone should have forgotten a precept which applies on average every seven years in the lunar calendar. On the other hand, the question makes no sense in terms of the calendar of *Jubilees*, which is independent of the moon and divides the year into four trimesters of sixteen weeks, or 364 days; each trimester begins on a Wednesday (fourth day of the week), and so 14 Nisan must always fall on a Tuesday and can never coincide with a Sabbath.

But we need to be a little more precise about the significance of the question about "the Passover." According to a literal reading of the biblical texts, there should not really have been a problem: for one thing, the date is 14 Nisan, which should, we have seen, be counted from morning to morning, and, according to all the texts of the Pentateuch, the Passover has to be "done" in the evening.[38] Here the expression used is the same as

38. Exod 12:6; Lev 23:5; Num 9:3, 5, 11 בין הערבים "between the two evenings." The LXX transposes ἀνὰ μέσον τῶν ἑσπερινῶν, or translates πρὸς ἑσπέραν.

for the perpetual sacrifice of Aaron,[39] as opposed to the morning in Exod 16:12 (for the manna), 29:39 and Num 28:4 (daily holocausts). That is the natural interpretation given by the Samaritans and the Qaraites. If, however, the Sabbath is counted from evening to evening, as is constant in the rabbinic tradition, it is apparent that the domestic Passover can take place after the Sabbath, and so the problem disappears. However, this same tradition unanimously understands that the Passover is to be offered "from midday," not without certain lexical difficulties,[40] alleging in support that at the Passover of Josiah the priests were occupied in sacrificing right until nightfall (2 Chr 35:14), and so they must have begun early in the afternoon.[41] This unanimous opinion comes from a tradition foreign to the Pentateuch, but it is attested by Philo (*Spec. leg.* 2 §154) and Josephus (*J.W.* 6 §423); it is strictly a question of the immolation of the Passover at the Temple.[42]

This cannot be concretely the problem at Bathyra. According to the last part of the text quoted, there is a problem which can be connected to the preparation of the Passover at the sanctuary, but the question at the beginning is more general: it supposes that the 14 Nisan entirely coincides with the Sabbath, that is, that both are counted from morning to morning. So the calendar of reference is that of *Jubilees*[43] (cf. chap. I, §II.2).

39. Exod 30:8, LXX ὀψέ.

40. Between מועד צאתן, כבוא השמש, בין הערבים, cf. *YPes* 5:1, p. 31d, *MekhRI*, boʾ §5, cf. S. Lieberman, *Hayerushalmi . . .* , p. 450.

41. 2 Chr 35:12, for assigning a portion of the Passover to the families, ends with the expression וכן לבקר "and the same for larger animals," which is not very clear (and may refer to communion sacrifices); in the background may be a controversy, as the LXX and 1 Esdr 1:14 translate "and thus until morning," from לבֹּקר.

42. In fact the rab. trad. distinguished two rites: the "Passover of the deliverance from Egypt," and the "Passover of the generations" (*MPes* 9:5). This distinction corresponds to the difference between the family rite in the evening from Exod 12:1 f., which no longer exists, since it has been supplanted by the law of Sinai, and the rite centralized in the Temple, which according to 2 Chr (or FJ) requires a complete sanctuary. In other words, the reference to 2 Chr *justifies* for the rab. trad. the disappearance of any rite of the paschal lamb, at Jerusalem or elsewhere, cf. chap. VII, §II.3. That also explains why the parallel accounts of the event at Bathyra place the question concerning Passover and the enthronement of Hillel in the sanctuary.

43. The rab. trad. has preserved a trace of a calculation which makes the 14 Nisan begin in the morning; *MPes* 1:1 indicates that the check to see that fermented products (בדיקת החמץ) have been eliminated should be made "at light on the 14 Nisan" (אור לי"ד), with a lamp but not by light of sun, moon or stars; the traditional meaning of אור here is "evening," with the result that the check is made the evening before, and throughout the whole day of the 14th everything is without leaven, as prescribed in Exod 12:18 (cf. *Tosefta kifshuṭah* 4:471 f.). However, this text says to begin eating without leaven on the 14th *in the evening*, and, with a calculation of days from morning to morning, that would

That only makes the question put to Hillel even more strange, since according to this calendar, as we have just seen, 14 Nisan is always a Tuesday. There is, however, one situation in which the question has a simple and concrete meaning: if the calendar has just been changed to adopt the lunar system, the concurrence of Passover and Sabbath is going to be a new problem which one day will inevitably arise. If various groups under pressure of persecution had come together at Bathyra—which is perfectly plausible under Herod—it is understandable that in an atmosphere of crisis they should have tried to federate, at least for the time being, but apparently there was no master of recognized authority. In this regard, the choice of Hillel, a Babylonian who had also been a disciple of Jerusalem Pharisees, is in perfect agreement with the spirit of the rabbinic tradition; it is not necessary to be suspicious of the account, but rather to note that the Tannaites were the heirs of Hillel. But the twofold origin, Judaea and Babylonia, may also have another meaning, namely Essene influence, as the problem of the calendar indicates: Josephus' description of the pious Essenes is well suited to country folk living well away, we may easily imagine, from Judaea. This point will be examined in due course, when we look at the origins of the Tannaites (cf. chap. V, §I).

In the first part, Hillel's final response is not directly formulated: perhaps he is chosen precisely because he is prepared to accept differences, or perhaps those who have escaped from Judaea will only accept a Babylonian if the others abandon their "sectarian" calendar. Whatever the value of these conjectures, the fact remains that it is with Hillel that the rabbinic tradition begins to note *internal* debates, implying subtle differences between diverse traditions: Shammai is inseparable from Hillel, and their "schools" outlasted them. Finally we see how the argument from Scripture is discredited, and what importance is accorded to oral tradition; this is particularly visible in a situation of quasi discontinuity and crisis.

There is a further aspect of the celebration of Passover (which so curiously is not well known): Hillel begins by biblical arguments and brings forward no Babylonian custom (indeed, none was asked for). There are two ways of interpreting this absence of reference to Babylonia. Passover, as we saw in connection with the Last Supper (chap. I, §IV.5), has two meanings: the commemoration of the deliverance from Egypt, which corresponds more to the domestic Passover, and the feast of arrival in the Land, corresponding to Joshua's Passover and the celebrations at the

mean eliminating fermented foodstuffs during the day of the 14th; in this case, the precept of the lamp simply means that natural lighting alone does not suffice.

Temple. Among the texts found in caves near Qumran about 800,[44] there is one which mentions the calendar of 364 days (that of *Jubilees*) and specifies that the Passover is to be done only "for those who live in the land of Israel," which corresponds very well to the case of Joshua celebrating the Passover at Gilgal. According to this Essene perspective, it is natural not to have any concrete knowledge of Passover outside the land of Israel.[45] We can also note that Exod 12:25 specifies that the rite of the lamb is to be observed "when you have entered into the land which YHWH will give you as He has said." This can mean either that the rite is linked to physical presence in the Promised Land, or that the rite is to be observed always and everywhere once the land has been reached, which still corresponds to Joshua's Passover.[46] Finally, these arrangements appear contrary to the express stipulations of Deut 16:1 f., demanding that the lamb be eaten at the "place which YHWH will choose"; however, this unique place is not named, which may well suit a sectarian outlook.[47]

Following a second line of interpretation, there are traces of a Babylonian tradition which ignores Passover even though it is eminently biblical:

1. The book of Esth is the foundation narrative of a feast commemorating, after persecution, the liberation of Jews *on the spot*, in "Babylonia," whereas in Exod, the liberation of the Israelites is linked to a migration from Egypt towards a Promised Land. At the moment of the oppression, Esther has a three-day fast proclaimed on 13 Nisan (Esth 3:12 f.), which is totally incompatible with the precept of eating the Passover on the 14th. Of course, it is possible to maintain that the coincidence is only by chance, or even, taking into account the lack of certainty about the calendar, that there is no problem;[48] however, we may suspect a con-

44. Cf. sources chap. VII, §I.2, in connection with the Quartodecimans.

45. The question whether Bathyra (Batanaea, the Golan) belongs to the land of Israel will be considered later, cf. chap. IV, §IV.1.2.

46. As Philo appears to understand. However, it should not be taken for granted that Passover was regularly celebrated outside Palestine at the time of Jesus, which has consequences for the later Christian Easter cf. chap. VII, §I.3.

47. Cf. chap. VII, §II.3 for a further singularity of Passover customs perhaps connected with Deut (last-minute invitation in Aramaic).

48. N. L. Collins, "Did Esther Fast on the 15th Nisan?" *RB* 100 (1993), p. 504 f. tries to show that the festal calendar governing Passover was slightly out of line with the civil calendar in use at court, and so the three-day fast beginning 13 Nisan could have ended just before Passover. This solution underlines, rather than solves, the problem, for the fast is commemorated in the rabbinic festal calendar, but, in order to avoid the concurrence, it has been put forward a month (13 Adar), and thus falls just before the feast of Purim itself.

troversy, and it is obvious that the standpoint of the narrative is completely different from that implied in the celebration of Passover.[49]

2. The treatise of the *Mishnah* on the proclamation of the Scripture (*Megila*, "the Scroll") deals first with the scroll of Esther and details the way in which it is to be written, read, and translated; only afterwards does it deal with the Pentateuch, by analogy. This remarkable order is the trace of great importance given, at a certain moment, to the feast of Purim; it is called "Day of Mardochai" in 2 Macc 15:36, which is of Pharisee-Babylonian inspiration, in contrast to 1 Macc, which is centered on the establishment of the priestly dynasty at Jerusalem and ignores this feast in the parallel passage.[50]

3. *MMeg* 1:1 explains that if the feast of Purim falls on a Sabbath, it is put back to the following day; an associated Talmudic discussion tries to explain this pre-eminence of the Sabbath, that is the circumstances in which the feast lost its rank (*BMeg* 2a). In fact, fixed as it is on 14 Adar (or the 15th in certain cities), it falls on a Sabbath once every seven years on average in the lunar calendar, and the foundation text makes no provision for putting off the celebration. Tradition has it that the narrative was published by the *Men of the Great Assembly*, who are identified with those who signed the commitment to observe the Law in Neh 10:1 f., and it is difficult to see what later authority could have felt able to demote it. On the contrary, the question put to Hillel supposes a context in which Passover has been promoted to be more important than the Sabbath. It is interesting that it is precisely the Sabbath which acts as the reference point in both cases and underlines their symmetry (or lack of it).

4. Taking into account the LXX and especially the "Lucianic recension," there are reasons for thinking that the MT of Esth, which is short and secularized, corresponds to a rabbinic demotion, whereas Josephus, who attests a long *Hebrew* text[51] (with prayers), dissociates himself from

49. This opposition is underestimated by Jan van Goudoever, *Fêtes et calendriers bibliques* (Théologie historique, 7), Paris, Beauchesne, 1967[3], p. 139, who makes of the book a sort of Passover narrative. It is true that the prayers of Mardochai and Esther contain allusions to the exodus from Egypt (13:6; 14:5), and that the Syriac version connects *pur* ("the lot") with *pasḥa*, but these are secondary developments, due to the accumulation on to Passover of all the deliverances, cf. chap. VII, §II.2.

50. Cf. *Search*, p. 204–206.

51. Several examples show that FJ, for Esth (apparently as for the rest of the Bible), translates from Hebrew, without using the LXX: in *Ant.* 11 §187, the "feasts during seven days" correspond to Esth 1:5 MT and the Luc. rec.; §207, Bagathoos and Theodestes are unknown to Esth 2:21 LXX, but the MT has בגתן and תרש (read as תדש and Hellenized); §209, "Haman, son of Hamadathes, an Amalekite by race," unknown to Esth 3:1 LXX Αμαν Ἀμαδάθου Βουγαῖον ("boaster"), whereas the MT specifies המן בן המדתא האגגי,

this feast which has so little to do with Judaea: he says that it is celebrated by "the Jews" (*Ant.* 11 §295), rather than by "us," as he says for other solemnities. In the background of a technical debate on the promotion of Passover against Purim, there is obviously an essential problem about the importance to be attached to immigration to the land of Israel, or even to pilgrimages. It is not at all unlikely that the Babylonians preferred Purim *at home*, and had little to say on Passover,[52] especially since the Pharisaic oral tradition does not derive from the Pentateuch.[53] By the same token, it is remarkable, but in the end very natural, that Esth is the only book of the Hebrew Bible of which there is no trace in the manuscripts of the Judaean desert.[54]

The break in continuity which is resolved by Hillel's promotion is not the first of its kind. A similar crisis is indicated in *BQid* 66a: some sixty years previously, when Alexander Jannaeus had massacred all the teachers, the oral tradition had disappeared, until Simeon b. Shetaḥ (or Shaṭṭaḥ), the predecesor of Shemaya and Abtalion according *MAb* 1:8, "restored the Torah in its primitive state." To this event the rabbinic tradition attaches the forgetting of the Torah, then the appearance of controversies at the moment of its restoration. Josephus knows this episode (*Ant.* 13 §293 f.), but he puts it erroneously under John Hyrcanus.[55]

Finally, it is clear that whereas the inflows from Babylonia are permanent, and the spread and popularity of the Pharisee movement is certain, especially in the Diaspora, as Josephus emphasizes, the establishment of a Pharisaic continuity *in Judaea* is always very fragile and runs up against both civil and priestly power. The conclusion that is useful here is that the precarious situation of the Pharisees in Judaea contrasts with a presence in Galilee which is more stable, though more discreet, and

---

where "Agagite" refers to Agag the Amalekite (cf. 1 Sam 15); §245, the wife of Haman is Zarasa, transcribed from זרש (Esth 5:10 f.) and not from Σωσαρα LXX, etc.

52. According to Exod 12:25, Passover is to be observed only "when you have arrived in the land that YHWH will give you," cf. VII, §II.1.

53. This point is developed in *Search*, p. 188–194, where reasons are given for making the comparison with the Pentateuch of the Samaritans, that is of the local Israelites.

54. The texts studied by Joseph-T. Milik, "Les Modèles araméens du livre d'*Esther* dans la grotte 4 de Qumrân," *RQ* 15 (1992), p. 321–399, emphasize the oriental origin of the book; the author concludes, with a very different argumentation, based on the versions, that the MT is a later *translation*. This result is interesting, but it is curiously associated with the idea of a *promotion* of the feast of Purim after 70 (but where?).

55. Cf. Emmanuelle Main, "Les Sadducéens selon Josèphe," *RB* 97 (1990), p. 193 f. Once again, FJ's mistake is not entirely innocent, since it has the effect of reducing the dynastic break mentioned earlier between John Hyrcanus and Alexander Jannaeus, cf. above §I.1.

which we will develop later (chap. IV). The rabbinic tradition obscures this fact, just as it glosses over the marginal and precarious reality of Hillel's situation, in order to make good its claim to be heir to the entire body of legitimate Jewish institutions from before the ruin of the Temple.

Before and after Herod, the Judaism of Galilee, created by numerous immigrations from Babylonia, was full of life and variety, and was strongly rooted in the countryside. The movement properly called "Galilean," in the strict sense of zealot, represents only part of that variety, though a significant part: it is the clear trace, continually renewed through pilgrimages, of a political drive linked to the persistent dream of Jerusalem and the Temple, and opposed to the authorities in place in Judaea. It could be called the heritage of Zerubbabel. It is noteworthy that 2 Macc, which issues from this spirit, portrays a Temple of high symbolic significance, where God's presence is very active, but deals hardly at all with those responsible for the Temple, after the failure and disappearance of Onias, who was, however, the best of the high priests.[56] At the time of Herod, who made many efforts to acquire a Jewish legitimacy (especially in Galilee), there was the exceptional enterprise of Bathyra, also the crisis from which Hillel emerged.

III – The Galilee that Jesus Knew

Before going on with the history of Galilee and the emergence of rabbinic Judaism, we need to pause. We have already seen enough to be able to form an idea of the Galilean environment in which Jesus recruited his first disciples. This environment was rural, intense and very different on either side of the Lake, which provides a setting for a number of details in the gospels.[57] Conversely, these details can throw some light on certain decisive points in the history of Judaism on the fringes of Judaea, since both Christianity and the rabbinic tradition grew out of the same soil. On the other hand, there are notable differences to be taken into account. Here we limit ourselves to putting forward a short list of characteristic features which clarify the original environment of Jesus and the disciples:

1. Broadly speaking, we have identified an opposition between zealot circles to the west of the Lake of Tiberias and others to the east which were more submissive. This lake plays an important part in Jesus'

56. Cf. Robert Doran, *Temple Propaganda: The Purpose and Character of 2 Maccabees*, 1981, p. 84, who remarks that the plea for the Temple is somewhat tragic, since the means for it to function are practically lacking; it becomes a sort of totem.

57. Cf. Simon Applebaum, "Judea as a Roman Province. The Countryside as a Political and Economic Factor," *ANRW* II.8 (1977), p. 355–396.

journeyings, not only from the point of view of geography, but also for the symbolism of water and fishing. Besides the theme of crossing the lake, the many references to "the other side" now stand out in relief (cf. John 6:1 etc.); the symmetrical cursing of Bethsaida and Chorazin (Matt 11:21 par.) includes both sides; the first multiplication of the loaves takes place on the western shore with twelve baskets (Matt 14:13-34 par.), the second on the eastern shore with seven (Matt 15:32-39 par.). These communications between the two shores were not originally meant to build a bridge between the Gentile Decapolis and Jewish Galilee,[58] but rather between two opposite tendencies within the same culture. The culture itself was very closed, and Jesus had come only "for the lost sheep of the house of Israel." The usual interpretation, which associates the twelve baskets with Israel (twelve tribes), and the seven with the Gentiles (*i.e.* Gentile Christians, from the "seven nations" of Canaan), is more in the spirit of a later redaction.[59]

2. Regarding the town where Jesus "was brought up," Eusebius cites an instructive legend (*Hist. eccl.* 1.7.14): according to a letter of Julius Africanus, the "family of Jesus" came from the Jewish villages of Nazara and Kokhaba, the latter being in Batanaea. The first thing to note is that this duplication of place corresponds to the duplication (west and east of the Lake) organized by Herod. We shall see that this family is in fact nothing else than the posterity of James, whose entourage formed the Jewish-Christians properly so called, or "Nazoreans" (the *noṣrim* of the rabbinic sources). It is natural to relate this term to Nazareth (Nazara), and then to wonder whether a similar reference is implied in the name of the other village. Kokhaba is just as unknown as Nazareth,[60] but the name means "star," and it is difficult not to see here a symbolic meaning inspired by the star of Jacob in Num 24:17, thus making Jesus a "Bar Kokhba," like the rest of his family.[61] So it is distinctly possible that Nazareth originated as a village of Nazoreans, a Messianizing group whether or not related by blood ties. Julius Africanus came from Emmaus-Nicopolis, in Judaea, a center, both real and symbolic, of active "Messianism" since Judas Maccabaeus (cf. chap. IV, §II.1), where vari-

58. Cf. the bibliography put together by Anne Hennessy, *The Galilee of Jesus*, Rome, Editrice Pontificia Università Gregoriana, 1994.

59. But not necessarily the final redaction, for there remains, on this view, a separation between Jews and non-Jews, which is close to James (cf. chap. V, §II.1), or more generally to a Jewish-Christian eschatology, but is not yet the final form of the NT.

60. On the ground, four sites with this name have been identified, two west of the Jordan and two to the east, but it is difficult to trace them back further than the Byzantine period.

61. Further discussion of the Nazoreans in chap. V, §V.2.

ous Jewish-Christian memories and legends may have developed without any connection with the NT. Besides, Jesus' own town was rather Capernaum, on the Lake, not far from Tiberias (Mark 2:1; 3:20; 9:33), where archaeological excavations have clearly shown that a fishing village existed before Herod; it was familiar to Jesus, and there he recruited disciples who were experienced fishermen and sailors.

3. The environment of reference is rural and religiously highly motivated, with different tendencies engaged in debate or even conflict. The last question put to Jesus by the disciples (Acts 1:6) concerns the restoration of the kingship in *"Israel."* The scene takes place in Jerusalem, and this terminology, similar to that of certain rabbinic sources,[62] takes no account at all of the real Judaea or of Herod's successors. It is rather the trace of a typically zealot dream of independence, also to be found in the third temptation (Matt 4:8 f.), in the disappointment of the two disciples who leave Jerusalem for Emmaus, and in the choice of Barabbas, who was a "brigand," that is, not a common law robber, but a Galilean of the purest sort according to Josephus' terminology. Jesus resisted political activism and transformed Messianism, or, more exactly, redefined it in properly biblical terms. While moving about and recruiting in Galilee, he stayed well away from Sepphoris[63] or Tiberias,[64] the only two cities of note in Galilee: they were effectively under Roman control, by way of the Herodian dynasty. To judge from Josephus' vain attempt, during the revolt, to unify Galilee by overcoming the conflicts between these cities and the intransigent Galileans in the neighboring country districts, it is clear that the environment of Jesus and the disciples is to be found among the "Galileans." This label had very marked connotations both religious and political (cf. chap. IV, §I.1), even if Jesus kept his independence.

4. The group which followed Jesus was really very diverse. It contained Matthew the tax-collector and Simon the zealot[65] (two who were

62. But on the strictly Zealot coins of the war of 66–70, we find חרות ציון ("Liberation of Zion"), and also לגאלת ציון ("Redemption of Zion"), cf. Yigael Yadin, "The Excavations of Masada—1963–64; Preliminary Report," *IEJ* 15 (1965), p. 1–120.

63. Jewish city where the first Roman governor of Syria had installed a sanhedrin (or "synod"), c. 56 B.C. After its destruction following the revolts which broke out on the death of Herod (*Ant.* 17 §289), it was faithful to Rome, and no doubt had a mixed population, as the current excavations suggest. It served as Herod Antipas' capital (*Ant.* 18 §27), before the foundation of Tiberias.

64. FJ states (*Ant.* 18 §37) that the city was founded by Herod Antipas in honor of Tiberius; coins found there suggest a date between 17 and 20 (cf. Schürer-Vermes II:179). But it was built over a cemetery, in violation of Jewish law, which was counted against its inhabitants (many of whom had been relegated there), cf. chap. IV, §II.4.

65. The epithet "Bar Jonas," conferred on Peter (Matt 16:17), may also have a connotation of "Galilean" ("brigand"), in the sense of one who refuses any compromise with

thus in principle opposed, and corresponded to the two shores of the Lake), also Joanna, wife of the bailiff of Herod Antipas, representing a third opposed focus, connected with the governing classes of the towns, particularly the new—and shameful—capital Tiberias. Disciples of John the Baptist left him to follow Jesus. In Jerusalem, Jesus had the use of a room for the Last Supper which the disciples did not know about, for they were only there on pilgrimage: so he had other contacts. Partisans from among the Pharisees warned him of danger from Herod, but he opposed the Pharisees by maintaining the primacy of Scripture over oral tradition. Some scribes accepted Jesus, while others rejected him; all upheld the Scriptures and were opponents of the Pharisees. All these tendencies make up a spectrum of the Judaism of Galilee, in which hardly any Sadducees or priests are to be found. Jesus crossed all these barriers, while still remaining within Judaism. He even kept company with "sinners," lepers or prostitutes, but his contacts with Gentiles did not go beyond a few symbolic gestures,[66] which were certainly the maximum that his environment could tolerate. These gestures were always performed in front of Jewish onlookers; that is the significance of the "sign of Jonah," which was meant for Israelites (even the worst of prophets is capable of converting a Gentile capital, whereas Israel remains stubborn). To this list of transgressions can be added the visit to the Samaritans, who followed the written text and awaited a new Moses, and whose recognition of Jesus was one of the most solemn. All these crossings of boundaries taken together signify that Jesus was not afraid of incurring impurity; fundamentally, he was not afraid of *others*.

5. Just as John the Baptist was surrounded by disciples, so Jesus, besides these casual encounters, recruited and formed a group. Within it he was acknowledged as the Teacher ("rabbi"),[67] but it was not a school in the proper sense of the word: the apostles were afterwards regarded as folk "without education or culture" (cf. Acts 4:13), which does not neces-

---

the Romans, cf. the בריוני of *BGiṭ* 56a-b (opponents of Yoḥanan b. Zakkai, cf. chap. IV, §I.2, in regard to Emmaus); in this case the (Aram.) term is derived from בר "outside, wild," cf. Jastrow *s. v.* and Martin Hengel, *The Zealots*, p. 53 f. (who, following John 1:42, prefers to regard "Yona" as an abbreviation of "Yoḥanan"); cf. Daniel R. Schwartz, *Agrippa I, The Last King of Judaea* (TSAJ, 23), Tübingen, J. C. B. Mohr (P. Siebeck), 1990, p. 123.

66. Cf. Jean-François Baudoz, *Les miettes de la table* (EB, N.S. 27), Paris, Gabalda, 1995, who discusses in particular the position of Joachim Jeremias, *Jésus et les païens* (Cahiers Théologiques, 39), Neuchâtel, 1957 (French tr. of *Jesu Verheissung für die Völker*, Stuttgart, 1953), who tries to find the mission to the Gentiles in the *ipsissima verba* of Jesus, which poses difficult methodological problems.

67. On this title, cf. chap. VI, §III.4.

sarily mean that they were ignoramuses, only that they did not fit into any recognized system of doctrinal competence. The group lived a common life, somewhat apart, following its own customs, as illustrated perfectly by the Last Supper (cf. chap. II, §II.3). So it was really a brotherhood, more or less itinerant, with its own organization, which at the same time undertook to make known to all that the kingdom was close at hand (cf. chap. V, §I). The Galilean environment was favorable to political ambiguities, as appears even from the written charge fixed to Jesus' cross.

6. Jesus went several times to Jerusalem, alone or in a group: although critical of the Temple, he never ceased to see in it the center of the promises. At the decisive moment, he insisted on confronting the authorities, despite the advice of the disciples (cf. Matt 16:22 par.; according to John 7:8 f. he hesitated). It is entirely possible that some of these had never even made the pilgrimage before, since, though grown ups, they gazed in wonder at the architecture. There is some parallel between Jesus and Judas the Galilean, who was conceived in Galilee, then came to Judaea where he flourished, and laid claim to the Temple (cf. *Ant.* 18 §3 f.; cf. Luke 3:1 f.). Gamaliel makes the same comparison (Acts 5:37),[68] and Josephus explains that Judas' movement is very close in doctrine to the Pharisees. Jesus' confrontation with the civil and priestly authorities, followed by a break in continuity and difficulties over the succession, resemble similar confrontations and breaks in continuity on the part of the Pharisees (in Josephus' sense) in Jerusalem under Alexander Jannaeus and Herod, and perhaps already at the time of the Maccabaean crisis. On his way from Judaea through Samaria he foretells the passing of both places of worship, at Jerusalem and on Garizim (John 4:21 f.), and goes on his way to Galilee: the horizon is once more the Judaism of Galilee, but with some glimpses of broader perspectives.[69]

7. The extreme importance of pilgrimages, which are occasions of encounter and conflict, is emphasized especially by Luke. A remarkable case is that of the young Jesus' meeting with the doctors at Jerusalem, and their approbation; Josephus tells a similar story about himself (*Life* §9), with the same implication of the need to have their guarantee. It was again at the Temple that Jesus took his somewhat polemical stand on the true Shepherd (John 10:22 f.); significantly, the scene is the portico of

68. It is possible that Luke-Acts makes use of the documentation in FJ, cf. some preliminary remarks in Étienne Nodet, "Jésus et Jean-Baptiste selon Josèphe," *RB* 92 (1985), p. 317 f.

69. Jesus' word to the Samaritan woman, "Salvation comes from the Jews" (John 4:22) need not be seen as a later addition, at a time of "re-judaization" (Bultmann), cf. chap. V, §V.2.

Solomon, during the feast of Dedication, and, as with the disciples from Emmaus, there is an underlying debate on political Messianism, to which the priestly and civil powers of the day were irrelevant (cf. chap. V, §II.1). So there was discussion over the true Messiah, the Temple, and, more generally, Jerusalem. The debate surely did not leave out the status of Scripture and its "power": how do the Law and the prophets speak to the present?

8. Numerous controversies are reported between Jesus and the Jews about the Sabbath, purity, the authority of the oral tradition, etc. However, at his trial, no faulty observance was brought forward as matter for accusation,[70] but solely a charge concerning the Temple, and so pilgrimages. That is significant. Like many others before him, Jesus and his companions had views about the Temple and what it should be, and these views, insofar as they attracted support, were perceived as a threat by the authorities, whether high priest or Roman governor; the fact that they could compare Jesus to Judas the Galilean or Theudas (Acts 5:35 f.) shows where the problem lay. However, it was not just a question of movements of Galilean zealots, which, after all were limited, but more generally of claims on the Temple by the Pharisees, who enjoyed widespread support in broad sectors of the Diaspora. Here we need only recall the high profile given to the Temple in 2 Macc, while its official staff remain shadowy figures in the background (cf. above §II.2). This Greek book has as its single hero Judas Maccabaeus, who has no priestly connections and is faithfully observant of the tradition (Sabbath, food purity, etc.); his famous occupation of the Temple on 25 Kislev 164 is portrayed as an exceptional pilgrimage and in any case momentary and without immediate consequences. Such rejection of priestly power obviously goes well beyond the Hasmonaean dynasty.

The sources studied have brought out a number of symbolic and religious factors, which, we shall see, explain Josephus' fixation on Galilee (chap. IV, §I). Socio-economic circumstances, famines, political oppression, all clearly played a part, but those studies of Galilee in this period which regard these material factors as decisive have not been able to come up with any coherent synthesis of the specific features of the local culture, even if they bring into play notions such as "people of the land"[71] or the "poor." They end up by making the historical Jesus a somewhat unreal figure who just happens to turn up in Galilee, but without any traditional roots there.[72]

70. Cf. David Flusser, *Jésus*, Paris, Seuil, 1970, p. 49–68.

71. On this notion, which is defined in relation to the brotherhoods and attached to the opponents of Ezra and Nehemiah (Ezra 4:4; Neh 7:6, etc.), cf. chap. V, §I.1.

72. Seán Freyne, *Galilee, Jesus and the Gospels. Literary Approaches and Historical Investigations*, Dublin, 1988, who continues earlier discussions, is typical of this current,

IV – Jesus and the "Philosophies" of Josephus

Three times Josephus gives a definition of the three famous parties, Pharisees, Sadducees and Essenes. On the last occasion (*Ant.* 18 §18 f.), he reluctantly adds a fourth, the zealots (or "Galileans"), heirs of Judas the Galilean. If we stick to these classifications, it is difficult at first sight to situate Jesus. He was certainly not a Sadducee, since there were none in Galilee and they denied the resurrection and divine Providence. Nor was he a Pharisee, since he extolled Scripture in opposition to the ancestral customs. And he was not an Essene, despite his advocacy of baptism and Scripture, since he insisted on coming to Jerusalem and accepted the Temple as it was. Finally, he was not really a zealot, even though his movement caused the politicians some anxieties.

However, for all its apparent clarity, Josephus' terminology is not really precise and only corresponds approximately to other sources. This is particularly so in the case of the Essenes. According to his very long first definition, they seem to form a network of town-based communities (*J.W.* 2 §119 f.), but in his last notice, which is very short and makes no reference to ritual, their communities are rural; despite some points of doctrine in common, it may well be a question of different tendencies.

The case of the Sadducees is even more paradoxical. For Josephus they are an aristocratic party close to the Temple and the priesthood, who are attached to Scripture and refuse the ancestral traditions of the Pharisees. On the other hand, the rabbinic sources, presumably Pharisee in inspiration, occasionally report controversies with *ṣeduqim*, an expression which is usually and very naturally identified with the Sadducees of Josephus and the NT. However, certain documents from Qumran feature opinions and customs identical with those of these *ṣeduqim*; in other words, they are to be identified as Essenes,[73] or at least as the branch which the *Damascus Document* calls "Zadokites" (cf. CD 5:2-5). So the claim to the inheritance of Zadok, the model of priesthood laid down by Ezek 44:15, can take more than one form;[74] it is not necessary to suppose

which goes back to 19th century liberal German thought, according to which Jesus promoted emancipation from the Law. The thesis of Walter Grundmann, *Jesus der Galiläer und das Judentum*, Leipzig, 1940, p. 82 f., that Jesus was an Aryan, is an extreme example (and unintentional caricature) of the tendency to remove Jesus from his Jewish context, cf. also Walter Bauer, "Jesus der Galiläer," in: *Festgabe für Adolf Jülicher*, Tübingen, 1927, p. 16–34.

73. Cf. Yaakov Sussman, "The History of *Halakha* and the Dead Sea Scrolls—Preliminary Observations on *Miqšat Maᶜaṣeh ha-Torah* (4 QMMT)," *Tarbiz* 49 (1989), p. 11–76, who asks how extremists came to be confused with notables (cf. DJD 10, p. 200).

74. The Sadducees, to whom FJ was certainly close, appear to constitute, from the reign of Alexander Jannaeus, a legitimist party loyal to the direct line of Mattathias, from

that the various heirs directly depended on one another, except by way of conflict.[75]

It is still more difficult to get a precise idea of the Pharisees. In his second literary period, Josephus declared himself a Pharisee (*Life* §12), but in reality his adherence came only late in the piece and proceeded from prudence. Possibly what he means is that he began to engage in public life by following the school of the Pharisees; in other words, he conformed to what, according to him,[76] the Sadducees did—unwillingly, because of the Pharisees' popularity (*Ant.* 18 §17), but all along he really stayed close to Sadducee circles, only following their own evolution with regret. Whatever the truth of that, his presentation of the Law at this stage *(Ant., Ag. Ap.)* is careful not to show any particularism (cf. chap. I, §I.4), yet it needed somehow to be acceptable to the Pharisees, who certainly constituted the dominant tendency outside Judaea and especially at Rome at the end of the 1st century;[77] but their very name meant "separate," as the rabbinic sources themselves prove.[78]

Josephus' way of writing shows the rise in the Pharisees' social position, as well as his changing attitude towards them, since his own preference was originally for the Essenes. In *J.W.* 1 §110, the Pharisees become visible for the first time when queen Alexandra Salome finds a place in her government for this "Jewish sect which passes for the most pious of all" (around 70 B.C.); they are powerful opponents of Herod (*J.W.* 1 §571); under Agrippa, after 66, they are among those who speak out against the zealots' move to prevent the sacrifices of foreigners (*J.W.*

Jonathan to John Hyrcanus, since the priestly class of Yoyarib, to which Mattathias belonged (cf. 1 Macc 2:1) can be regarded as Zaddokite according to 1 Chr 24:3 f.; on the confusion surrounding the succession after John Hyrcanus, cf. above §I.1.

75. There is reason for thinking that the Essenes "left for the desert"(cf. 1 QS 8:1 f. and 9:3 f.) in opposition to the Hasmonaean high priests (Jonathan, Simon, John), cf. Joseph-T. Milik, *Dix ans de découvertes dans le désert de Judah*, Paris, Cerf, 1957, p. 65 f. (id., *Ten Years of Discoveries etc*., p. 88 f.); Émile Puech, *La croyance des Esséniens en la résurrection des morts: immortalité, résurrection, vie éternelle* (EB, N. S. 22), Paris, Gabalda, 1993, I:65 f.; so conflicts over legitimacy are very plausible.

76. This is the judicious interpretation of Steve Mason, *Flavius Josephus on the Pharisees*, Leiden, Brill, 1991, p. 353 f.

77. Morton Smith, "Palestinian Judaism in the First Century," in: Moshe Davis (ed.), *Israel: Its Role in Civilization*, New York, Harper, 1956, p. 67–81, was the first to notice the evolution of FJ's perception of the Pharisees, and concluded that at the time of the war (and *a fortiori* before) they did not set the tone for the people as a whole.

78. *BQid* 66a. The Gk form comes from the Aram. פרישיא, corresponding to the Heb. פרושים. The "holy nation" of Exod 19:6 is understood as "separate" (תהיו פרושים), and not as priestly *(MekhRI a. l.)*; similarly "be holy as I am holy" becomes "be separate as I am separate" (*Sifra* on Lev 19:2 and 20:6). On changes in the meaning of "Pharisees," cf. also chap. V, §V.1.

2 §411). Later, when he takes up these episodes again in the *Antiquities*, Josephus introduces a series of incidents from John Hyrcanus to Alexandra (*Ant.* 13 §288 f., developing *J.W.* 1 §110); later, Josephus speaks once more of Herod's persecution of the Pharisees (*Ant.* 17 §40 f.), but tells us that the king respected two notables among them, Shemaya and Abtalion, who have already been mentioned in connection with Hillel.

Careful examination of these second stage narratives shows some manipulations on the part of Josephus. He suggests that John Hyrcanus, who had been educated by Pharisee masters, was originally much loved by them, before conflicts made him pass over into the Sadducee camp;[79] in other words, that the Pharisees enjoyed the favor of Simon, the first Hasmonaean high priest to have descendants, father of John and son of Mattathias of Modein. Josephus seeks to show that Pharisee influence over the people was general and that the movement originated in the distant past.[80] In so doing, he is simply following one of his constant principles, that only what is old is respectable; revolutionaries are "innovators," an expression almost equivalent to "brigands." However, when he allows himself to express his true feeling about the Pharisees, he can be sharp (17 §41 f.): "There was a sect [or: a party] of Jews who boasted of observing very strictly the law of their fathers and affected a great zeal for the Deity [. . .], people capable of standing up to kings, farseeing, emboldening themselves openly to combat and harm them." The context is Herod's period.[81] At the same time, it must be admitted that if Josephus, ever attentive to the ruling circles, made a late approach to the Pharisees, they too had changed: they had once been a party of reformers; they now represented the majority.

79. Cf. Emmanuelle Main, "Les Sadducéens selon Josèphe," *RB* 97 (1990), p. 48 f.

80. It is probably the reason why, in *Ant.* 13 §171 f., he puts the notices on Pharisees, Essenes and Sadducees during the youth of John Hyrcanus, under the pontificate of Jonathan; he thus gives to understand that already at the end of the Maccabaean crisis, the parties were well in place. However, these notices are based on those in *J.W.* 2 §119 f., which are placed at the time of the disturbances following the death of Herod, cf. *Search*, p. 39.

81. It is possible to hold, with Daniel R. Schwartz, "Josephus and Nicolaus on the Pharisees," *JSJ* 14 (1983), p. 157–171, that Josephus here passively follows his source ("sans réflexion," judges Reinach), here Nicolaus of Damascus who was certainly not pro-Pharisee, and which he transcribed (or had copied) without comment. However, in other places, and especially in the parallel developments of *J.W.* and *Ant.* (in particular the parallel to this one, *J.W.* 1 §571) Josephus is to be seen constantly reworking his sources, so, in the absence of proof to the contrary, he is to be held responsible for the result here as well; his tardy move towards the Pharisees was certainly tactical, as we have said. Besides, several phases can be distinguished between the initial sketch and the final redaction of the work; the author evolved, and he often has difficulty in rereading what he had written earlier.

In the following century, the fixed form of the rabbinic tradition passes for being the heritage of the Pharisees. That is true for belief in the resurrection and the importance of ancestral oral traditions, but not for the general style which Josephus recommends, without separatism and submissive to the Romans; furthermore, it runs up against the fact that the rabbinic tradition did not at this time spread towards the west. So it is certainly not correct to regard the Tannaites as representing the Pharisaic Judaism which Josephus saw and portrayed as the majority tendency practically everywhere.

Jesus is commonly thought of as close to the Pharisees, because of their belief in resurrection; we might add that in the gospels, Jesus never rejects the oral traditions as such, but only their use in order to "nullify Scripture" (cf. Luke 11:42). Among the first disciples were Pharisees (Acts 15:5), including Paul himself (Phil 3:5, cf. Acts 23:6). However, these Pharisees have a very particular profile, as can be seen from one example. According to Mark 7:3 f., they perform an immersion when they come back from the market place, and they blame *certain* disciples of Jesus for eating without washing their hands; in Luke 11:38, they even want a total immersion before the meal. The demand expressed by these Pharisees supposes that it is a question of the same, or a similar environment. Further, the implied difference of tradition reflects different meanings given to the meal: the washing of hands (and feet) is a priestly gesture oriented towards sanctification,[82] as we have said in discussing the Last Supper in John, whereas immersion is a gesture of purification. The Tannaitic sources prescribe washing the hands, but they also give as model the "companion [or: fellow]" (*ḥaber*, separated from the "people of the land"), who eats even profane food in a state of ritual purity,[83] which supposes complete immersion from time to time; so these sources know both traditions. It even happens that the *ḥaber* is called a "Pharisee," at least in the sense of "separated" (*MḤag* 2:7). So it is not difficult to conclude that the ideal of the *ḥaber* is thus very close to the Pharisees of the NT. However, it is marginal, since Judah the Patriarch himself, the venerated editor of the *Mishnah,* did not achieve it. Further, this ideal is obviously very close to that of the Essenes, since at the summit of community life is the "purity," namely the meal taken in conditions of total Levitical purity.

So the terminology has been altered,[84] apparently owing to certain

82. Cf. chap. II, §II. 2 (in the context of the foot washing, John 13:4 f.).

83. *BBer* 47b, cf. chap. V, §I.1.

84. With important consequences; for example, Ḥannah K. Harrington, *The Impurity Systems of Qumran and the Rabbis. Biblical Foundations* (SBL Dissertation Series, 143), Atlanta (Georgia), Scholars Press, 1993, App. II, tries to show, by putting together data

developments.[85] In the discussions and comparisons above, the Essenes, or at any rate their teachings, have turned up in various situations where they were hardly expected. This confusion provides two useful reference markers with regard to the Pharisees. First, we saw in the previous chapter many points of contact between the NT and the Essenes, but the puzzling thing is that the term does not occur anywhere in the NT, which, on the other hand, is full of Pharisees, scribes, etc. The foregoing observations give rise to the question whether the Pharisees of the NT, at least when they are not being directly opposed to the Sadducees,[86] are not simply Josephus' Essenes, or something very like them. Secondly, the Pharisaic origins of the rabbinic tradition need to be looked at again from the same angle, since we have glimpsed some important contacts with the Essenes in connection with events at Bathyra and with the "companions." This point will be examined later (chap. V, §1).

In this regard, we can note also that the term "Galilean" is fairly elastic, since according to *MYad* 4:8, a Galilean blames the Pharisees for profaning the name of Moses, by writing it on official documents along with that of the Gentile authority; according to *J.W.* 2 §145, the Essenes hold the name of Moses as sacred, something never done in rabbinic Judaism. So, in this passage, the Galileans are close to the Essenes and venerate the Scriptures, whereas the Pharisees, paying greater attention to oral traditions, had perhaps fewer reasons for doing so. Such an extreme veneration for Moses also gives a context for the reinterpretation of Jesus as a "new Moses," especially in Samaritan circles.[87]

---

from the NT, the Qumran texts, rabbinic sources and FJ, that the 1st century Pharisees in general ate in a state of Levitical purity, which thus constituted the norm for the whole people. This conclusion contradicts the formal testimony of FJ and Philo, cf. chap. I, §I.4.

85. Perhaps the labels "Pharisee" and "Essene" originated as descriptive terms applied by outsiders to groups of reformers (who may have differed from one another). The second is usually explained as the transcription of the Aram. equivalent חסין (or חסיא) of חסידים "pious," which is in the first place an adjective (but cf. the following notes). Philo's explanation, *Quod omnis probus liber sit* §75 f. (καλοῦνται Ἐσσαῖοι παρὰ τὴν ὁσιότητα "they are called Essenes because of their piety"), is at best allegorical, involving a play on words.

86. This distinction enables us to understand in particular the situation of Paul: in Phil 3:5, he describes himself as "circumcised on the eighth day, of the race of Israel, of the tribe of Benjamin, Hebrew son of Hebrews, *Pharisee as to the law*"; so it is a question of a personal adherence or choice, rather than of a heritage. By contrast, in Acts 23:6, a literary construction in which Pharisees and Sadducees are opposed with regard to the resurrection, Paul declares that he is a "Pharisee son of Pharisees"; this way of seeing the Pharisees as a stable and hereditary movement, defined by certain teachings, is at once opposed to that of Paul in Phil and strictly in accordance with FJ's presentation, to the point of suggesting that he may be its source, cf. *Les Actes* VI:150 f.

87. Cf. M.-Émile Boismard, *Moses or Jesus: An Essay in Johannine Christology*,

Jesus was neither the first nor the last "Pharisee" or "Galilean" reformer to get into trouble with the Jerusalem authorities. His profile can be associated with two known religious types, which are sometimes opposed: the teacher whose word counts ("rabbi"), as distinct from the scribe, and the *Ḥassid*, that is the "charismatic," well attested in rabbinic sources, whose behavior is sometimes paradoxical and who keeps his distance from learned circles—all those whose origin is known, come from Galilee.[88] It is important to note that these "spirituals," who bear the same name as the Hasideans at the time of the Maccabees, have to be regarded as antecedents both of the Pharisees[89] and of the Essenes.[90] Before designating different groups, the adjectives had a similar meaning.

Leuven, Peeters/Leuven University Press, 1993 (Eng. tr. of *Moïse ou Jésus. Essai de Christologie Johannique* [BETL, 84], Leuven University Press, 1988), cf. also chap. VII, §IV.1.

88. Cf. Shmuel Safrai, "The Pious *(Ḥasidim)* and the Men of Deeds," *Zion* 50 (1985), p. 134–137; Geza Vermes, "Ḥanina ben Dosa," *JJS* 23 (1972), p. 28–50; 24 (1973), p. 51–64, and discussion by David Rokeaḥ, "Am Haaretz, The Early Pietists (Ḥasidim), Jesus and the Christians," in: François Blanchetière & Moshe D. Herr (ed.), *Aux origines juives du christianisme*, Peeters, Paris-Louvain, 1993, p. 159–173.

89. In 1 Macc 2:42; 7:12 and 2 Macc 14:6, the term חסידים is *transcribed* Ἀσιδαῖοι, and not translated, which appears to indicate a definite group; but even so, it is not possible to conclude that the term is *reserved* exclusively to a single group. John Kampen, *The Hasideans and the Origin of Pharisaism. A Study in 1 and 2 Maccabees* (SBL, Septuagint and Cognate Studies, 24), Atlanta (Virg.), Scholars Press, 1988, has shown that these "Hasideans" should be compared to later Pharisees, which implies the mobility of the adjectives.

90. Cf. É. Puech, *La croyance . . .*, p. 21 f., who shows, following others, that FJ's Gk terms transcribe an Aram. plural, determinate חסיא (Ἐσσαῖοι) or indeterminate חסין (Ἐσσηνοί), exact equivalent of Heb. חסידים, "Hasideans." The classic objection to this explanation is that the word is not attested in western Aramaic, but Michael Stone has announced that he has read it on fragments 2 and 3 of 4 QLevi (Greenfield allotment; communication forthcoming).

Chapter IV

Galilee from the Jewish War to the *Mishnah*

The rabbinic sources are generally taken as representing the heritage of the Pharisees. We have seen in the previous chapter that this latter term cannot be restricted to the definitions of Josephus, which reflect a situation later than the downfall of Jerusalem. In particular, the Essenes, the "charismatics" of Galilee and the Pharisees of the NT have a number of points in common. So, to further our inquiry, we need to continue our study of the broad outlines of the history of Jewish Galilee.[1] We are hoping for a twofold outcome: first, to get a better idea of the enterprise begun at Bathyra by seeing what resulted from it, and, more generally, to have a more precise notion of the cultural environment of Galilee at the time of Jesus; secondly, to find out what the rabbinic sources have to tell us about the state of affairs before 70. In fact, both conservative and innovative forces were at work, and we want to identify the lines of demarcation between them.

This chapter will bring out aspects showing continuity in Galilee. The next will deal rather with innovations and conflicts.

1. In a well-researched study, Shmuel Safrai, "The Jewish Cultural Nature of Galilee in the First Century," *Immanuel* 24/25 (1990), p. 147–186, shows that the rab. trad. fully recognizes the Jewish (Pharisaic) character of Galilee in the 1st century, before and after the downfall of Jerusalem; he even concludes that Judaism, in the sense of the said tradition, was perhaps better implanted there than in Judaea. He thus completes the study of Aharon Oppenheimer, *Galilee in the Mishnaic Period*, Jerusalem, Zalman Shazar Center, 1991, who recalls, with all the useful references, that works on Jewish Galilee before the destruction of the Temple, and especially in the time of Jesus, have often been marred by apologetic prejudices. For some (cf. Schürer-Vermes, cited above), it was a marginal region in relation to Judaea, whose Judaism was more "liberal," *i.e.* more given to free itself

I – Before and After the Downfall of Jerusalem

The difficulties of interpreting the war in Galilee in 66 are well known. Josephus played an important part in it, but the two accounts which he gives, some twenty years apart (*J.W.* 2 §430 f. and *Life* §20 f.), are so inconsistent that no firm reconstitution of the facts appears possible. However, since he always seeks to show himself in a favorable light, it could be that the accounts are inconsistent precisely because, in the mean time, their author's assumptions and system of self-justification have undergone development. This point merits examination here, because of the very singular importance which Galilee has for him. Later, when Josephus himself has no more to say, following the downfall of Jerusalem and its immediate aftermath, the rabbinic sources provide some indications which allow us to describe the link between Galilee and the Tannaites, and in particular the school of Yavneh-Jamnia.

1. Josephus and Galilee

Towards the end of 66, following a long series of disturbances arising from various causes, Cestius Gallus, governor of the province of Syria, arrived from Antioch with an army to take Jerusalem. But he did not realize that the "brigands" were no longer in charge and that the people were ready to open the gates to him; instead of pressing his advantage and immediately conquering the city, which, according to Josephus, would have avoided the later wars, he withdrew. This only encouraged the insurgents to come after him and inflict a severe defeat between Beth-Horon and Antipatris (*J.W.* 2 §540–555). Their tactical victory was a strategic disaster, for it obliged the Romans to launch reprisals, or else appear weak. So preparations were made for war, and it was then that Josephus found himself in Galilee, charged with a mission.

At this point the second account begins (*Life* §17 f.), but with a very different way of presenting the facts. According to this, Josephus, only just returned from a mission to Rome and seeing the preparations for insurrection, remained close to the leading Pharisees, and tried in vain to prevent confrontation with the Romans. After the rout of Cestius, these notables sent him with two other priests to Galilee, which was not yet in

---

from the Law; for others (in particular A. Büchler), the two regions were culturally homogeneous, although they developed differently. Oppenheimer himself belongs in the second category, cf. *RB* 100 (1993), p. 145 f. Already, W. D. Davies, *The Setting of the Sermon on the Mount*, Cambridge, 1964, p. 450–451, had perceived in a brief appendix certain subtle differences between Judaea and Jewish Galilee, but underestimated the observance of the Law in Galilee.

full revolt against Rome. There he tried to calm the "brigands," and to gather up their arms so that they would be available to the notables if the Romans attacked, and only in that case. There follows a long inventory of the divisions among the Jews and of struggles (often armed) between the different factions (§30–70). While recounting various attempts at appeasement, he mentions several times that his mission was on behalf of the Jerusalem Sanhedrin, and even states that, in order to ensure the loyalty of the people, he cultivated the friendship of the seventy-two elders who governed the country.

In his first account (*J.W.* 2 §562–584), Josephus tells how the war party, after their victory over Cestius, eventually got the upper hand over those who favored peace with the Romans and took power in Jerusalem, with the clear intention of preparing for war; Josephus gives the reader to understand that his own rise, in opposition to the pacifists, was due only to popular pressure. Different governors were then sent to the provinces, and Josephus himself was put in charge of the two Galilees and Gamala. Next follows a summary of his action in two phases. First he sought to gain the affection of the inhabitants and instituted a civic organization, with a sanhedrin of seventy-two elders chosen "from the entire nation" and a college of seven magistrates in each town. Next, he busied himself with external security and fortified the best-situated places, with two interesting exceptions: he states that Sepphoris had seen to its defenses at its own expense, and that John of Gischala had similarly fortified his own town. At the same time, he sought to train a disciplined army in the Roman manner.

However, on careful examination, this summary turns out to have been made up by Josephus.[2] For one thing, Sepphoris had not long before welcomed the Romans with open arms (*J.W.* 2 §511) and John of Gischala was his rival from the beginning (2 §585); Josephus is thus putting a good face on the two exceptions and claiming that he supervised what in fact lay outside his control. Furthermore, the attitude which he attributes to the people of Jerusalem is inconsistent: at first ready to give themselves up to Cestius, they backed the faction which beat him and precipitated a war which could not be won. The list of governors sent to the provinces does not mention in the key posts any of those responsible for the defeat of Cestius, which is a further inconsistency. Similarly, the notables appointed to the government of Jerusalem belonged to the

2. Cf. Giorgio Jossa, "Josephus' Action in Galilee during the Jewish War," in: Fausto Parente & Joseph Sievers (Eds.), *Josephus and the History of the Greco-Roman Period. Essays in Memory of Morton Smith* (Studia Post-Biblica, 41), Leiden, Brill, 1994, p. 265–278, with references.

moderate aristocracy, and, according to Josephus, it was only popular pressure which put forward an extremist, Eleazar, who had captured the spoils of the Romans. Josephus writes vaguely, and in reality it is not Eleazar who sends out the governors. Our author himself is placed at a strategic point, since a Roman invasion would inevitably begin from Galilee; on the other hand, he has just come back from Rome and is certainly not a revolutionary.

In this light the two accounts become compatible: Josephus tried to take in hand the *civil* authority, at the same time staying on the lookout for any threat from the Romans. In his first and more warlike account, he underlines his effort at civic organization, even giving the impression that he was rebuilding the *nation* from Galilee, which gives an insight into the importance which this region had for him. Thus he appears as essentially loyal to his own people. That is also the line he takes in justifying himself in the eyes of the Romans: he did not immediately hasten to join the winning side, but on the contrary was faithful to his trust until the end. A little before, he puts in the mouth of Herod an exemplary speech on the same theme (*J.W.* 1 §387 f.): he was the friend of Antony, but after the battle of Actium (in 31), he presented himself before the victorious Octavian, and explained with dignity his faultless loyalty to his benefactor, even in defeat; thanks to this brilliant, if risky, defense, his kingship was confirmed. In the same way, Josephus emphasizes the loyalty of the high priest Yaddua to his oath to Darius III, king of Persia, even after the latter's defeat at the hands of Alexander; then, when the victor arrived at Jerusalem, he was won over by the high priest and by the cult which he represented (*Ant.* 11 §317 f.).

Josephus' mission can be defined more precisely by looking at his opponents. First, in both accounts, he deals at great length with the misdeeds and treachery of John of Gischala; there was open rivalry, but the key to Josephus' hatred is to be found in what follows. Having put down Galilee, Vespasian marched on Judaea with the idea of isolating then conquering Jerusalem. But on the death of Nero in 68, the situation in Italy became very confused, and he interrupted his campaign. At this point two rival groups took over Jerusalem: inside, John of Gischala and his Galileans entrenched themselves in the Temple; outside were Simon b. Giora and his *Sicarii*. The description which Josephus gives of these Galileans, a mixture of decadence and violence, is particularly edifying (*J.W.* 4 §558–563). But his exaggerated language is revealing: John had taken and transformed the position which he hoped for himself. In Galilee, John's principal enemies were not the Romans but unfaithful Jews, more or less Hellenized, and in particular king Agrippa, the Roman vassal reigning in the unlawful city of Tiberias.[3] Josephus had made every effort to overcome these divisions and unify Galilee, but in vain. He was denounced by John to the Pharisees of Jerusalem, who sent a delegation—of religious, rather than military cast—to depose him. His sole resource then was to plunge ahead and prepare for war, in the hope that the threat from outside would bring about unity: under pressure from the Galileans, he took Sepphoris, then saved Tiberias from the wrath of those same Galileans, etc. Finally, he was driven into war against Vespasian (or leaped into it, trying to shore up his power in the hour of danger), but changed sides after the first serious engagement, at the siege of Jotapata, and predicted to Vespasian that he would be emperor. This episode is told only in *J.W.* 3 §141 f., but there too, Josephus takes care to emphasize his loyalty to his own people, then the ultimate necessity of admitting the supremacy of Rome (§136 f.). In his *Life* §411 f., he leaves out the whole of Vespasian's campaign in Galilee: to the end he remains the one who tried to overcome the divisions among the Jews.

In the second account *(Life)*, another enemy appears, Justus of Tiberias, who accuses Josephus of raising his city against Rome. In *J.W.* 2 §645 f., our author had admitted that Tiberias, like Sepphoris, wanted to side with the Romans, but that he had mastered the city, though only for a short time. In *Life* §373 f., he explains that Sepphoris and Tiberias, fearing the Galileans, sought Roman protection, the former by appealing directly to Cestius, the latter by asking the client king Agrippa to take possession of his capital (cf. *J.W.* 2 §252). Josephus, who claims to have had some influence with the Galileans, succeeded in calming them. It is easy to see that the same reality lies behind both presentations, namely conflict between the chief towns and the Galileans, which existed independently of the serious events taking place in Jerusalem. In the first account, he poses as the *political* unifier against the Romans; in the second, he is rather the *national* unifier. This difference allows us to situate the attacks made on him by Justus. In *Life* §391 f., Josephus explains that Justus wanted to raise Tiberias against the Romans, in the hope of "taking power over Galilee and over his native city"; in other words, he accuses him of what he himself wanted to do, at least according to his first account. But the accusation is unjustified, since he says immediately afterwards that, at the beginning of the war, Justus took refuge with Agrippa at Beirut. Next Josephus tells how, when Agrippa's troops came to the aid of Tiberias, he himself attacked them with the aid of Galileans. Only one conclusion is possible: Josephus tried to rely to the maximum degree on

3. Because built over a cemetery, cf. §II.4.

the Galileans of the countryside, even to the extent of fighting Agrippa, whose position made all conciliation impossible.

In short, it is evident that Josephus had two adversaries of quite different type. In the Galilean camp, he had a rival, John of Gischala, who tried to get him recalled by the *religious* authorities of Jerusalem. In the province at large, he had another rival, Justus, who was also seeking to overcome the divisions among the people with a more political agenda; the difference between them was that Josephus tried to do it on the basis of the Galileans of the countryside, while Justus made his bid from Tiberias. However, the real action undertaken by Justus on the ground could have been little more than symbolic, since Josephus has nothing to say about it. He is a literary opponent. His work has been lost, but it apparently dealt with the history of the monarchy.[4] To counter this perspective, Josephus explains at length that Agrippa got rid of Justus (*Life* §356 f.), whereas his own works were in their time appreciated by the same Agrippa. Josephus seeks to discredit Justus, and at the same time not to show any inclination for Agrippa: he fought against his troops, as he makes no attempt to conceal in his second account, thus implying that Agrippa was not very effective as a king in overcoming divisions among Jews. In the background there is an obvious issue. Will the future of the Jewish *ethnos* in the Roman empire lie with a vassal monarchy or a priestly aristocracy? Josephus' own preference is clearly for the latter option, as his later writings show *(Ant., Life, Ag. Ap.)*, and he emphasizes its claims to a central position. However, one fact remains unexplained. Why did the criticisms made by Justus over past local conflicts and a second-rate puppet monarchy, perhaps by then extinct, require such a lengthy reply, more than twenty years after the events?

One last point will enable us to define clearly what was the real mission of Josephus in Galilee, and why it was still of importance so much later in Rome. In action, he relies on the Galileans, which explains his rivalries with John of Gischala. Later, however, he treats them with disdain: he suggests that their Jewishness is very recent, that the movement of Judas the Galilean was madness, etc.[5] So he was disappointed, and we

4. The title *(Chronicle of the Jewish Kings Set Out in Family Trees)* is given by Photius, *Bibliotheca*, Cod. n° 33; his brief summary is the sole extant evidence as to its contents. Characteristically, he reproaches Justus for not mentioning Jesus, which suggests that Justus did not simply give genealogical lists but went into contemporary history in some detail, even perhaps, since he was a monarchist, with indications of Davidic descendants.

5. Shaye J. D. Cohen, *Josephus in Galilee and Rome: His* Vita *and Development as a Historian* (Columbia Studies in the Classical Tradition, VIII), Leiden, Brill, 1979, has

can see why. Convinced of the supremacy of Rome, he thought in terms of restoring in Galilee a nation which was unified and would accept a reasonable subordination; so he set about reconciling the countrysides (the Galileans) with the towns, which were already subject to Rome. This policy may not have been too clever, since he was suspected of trying to carve out a fief for himself. In any case, he failed, principally because of the intransigence of the Galileans, impermeable to political compromise; that is the origin of his vendetta against John of Gischala, the incorruptible representative of this movement, first in Galilee and later in Jerusalem. These Galileans clearly had a very strong identity, social, cultural and religious, just as in the time of the young Herod, who absolutely needed their recognition to establish his legitimacy. Let us note too the relationship of John with the notable Pharisees of Jerusalem, in particular Simon b. Gamaliel (§190 f.), father of Gamaliel II, the second founder of Yavneh: although not zealots, they were akin in views, and perhaps in origin, to traditional Jewish Galilee, which ties in with the observations already made above.

Josephus is not afraid to show himself in opposition to Simon, while at the same time affirming that he is close to the Pharisee current. There seems to be a contradiction. On the one hand he is a priest, and expresses his readiness to accept the dispersion of Jews throughout the Empire, provided Jerusalem remains accessible to pilgrims. On the other hand, surely a more pressing reason, there was certainly rivalry between him and the house of Simon in putting forward, under "Pharisaic" auspices, a future for Judaism, as we shall see later (§2–3). John and Simon had other options, in the name of another conception of Judaism and even of the Pharisaic spirit, for which residence in the land of Israel was a major value, a dimension which we shall see again with the Tannaites (chap. V, §III.1). From Josephus' precautions, we can deduce that these other options had serious backers in Rome, whose censure he had to elude; we shall see a rivalry over Passover which illustrates this point (chap. VII, §I.3).

The conclusion is that the second account, despite having no further documentation behind it, is closer to the truth:[6] on his return from Rome, Josephus' mission was first of all religious and national, undertaken at the request or at least with the approval of the moderate authorities in Jerusalem. In other words, he went to Galilee, not because it was an outpost

---

shown (cf. synthesis p. 242) that one key for understanding the *Life* is the care taken by Josephus to prove that he is an observant Pharisee, and so to decry systematically the religious loyalty of the Galileans.

6. Cf. Uriel Rappaport, "Where Was Josephus Lying—In His *Life* or in the *War*?" in: *Essays in Memory of Morton Smith*, p. 279–289.

of the military defense of Jerusalem (patrolling the coast would have been more to the point), but because it was a region with a strong tradition, though divided, perhaps the only one *outside Judaea* from which a national restoration could conceivably come. Galilee remained a permanent religious reference point,[7] as other indications will confirm. The second conclusion is that Josephus, after failing in his attempt to join forces with the Galilean movement or even to take it over, entertained the greatest mistrust (or jealousy) of this moral primacy and sought afterwards to discredit it, even though he was eventually forced to concede the existence of a Galilean "fourth philosophy." A probable inference is that in the mean time he got wind of the rise in influence of Yavneh after its second foundation, under the patronage of Gamaliel II son of Simon (cf. §2).

From all this it appears that Josephus' politico-military activities and their failure, although they are to the forefront of the *War*, are secondary and certainly exaggerated: they arose on the ground, and even more in his narrative, from his decision to take up arms, after the failure of his mission of conciliation in which he hoped to pose as a savior. At bottom, this mission was not really different from that which he accepted or which he assigned himself later as a writer. While remaining loyal to Rome, he tried to put himself above all the various tendencies, in the hope of fixing for Judaism a stable position in the Roman world, and in some way or other to stay in charge. In other words, Josephus is addressing fellow-Jews; that is less evident in the case of the Greek edition of the *War*, but quite certain for the *Life*. These minor events in far-off Galilee could not have meant very much to Roman readers, but they are obviously so important to Josephus that they must have been essential for establishing his credibility in Jewish circles.

One final question: did Josephus know of the importance of Galilee for the origins of Christianity? There is no clear sign, other than the fairly tenuous account of how John the Baptist was feared, then put to death, by Herod Antipas, tetrarch of Galilee, but the action takes place rather in Peraea (fortress of Machaerus), and Joseph gives no hint of any link between John and Jesus. More significant perhaps is the whole dynamic of the *Life*. Josephus introduces himself with a good pedigree (priestly, not

7. Tessa Rajak, *Josephus. The Historian and His Society*, London, Duckworth, 1983, p. 152, also concludes, by a different route, that FJ composed the *Life* for his own circles, unlike *Ant.*, which was destined for the cultivated non-Jewish public. On the other hand, the *Life* is expressly defined as a continuation of *Ant.* However, the latter work is also directed towards a Jewish public, perhaps even in the first place, since FJ insists on his competence concerning *doctrines* (*Ant.* 20 §263 f.), which is not the same thing as being an historian.

Davidic), shows precocious brilliance before the learned of Jerusalem, was an assiduous follower of the baptist Bannus before spreading his wings, and finally speaks at length of his desire to rebuild the nation on the basis of the Galileans. There is to some extent a parallel with Jesus. No firm conclusion is possible, except that in the eyes of Josephus these Galileans were, unfortunately, unusable, but they formed an uncontestable reference point.

In fact Josephus unwittingly draws attention to what he seeks to play down: the Galileans had strong traditions. This fact also gives a context to the gospel narratives. The first Christian writers, who address townspeople and concentrate on the kerygma, are not interested in rural Galilee; the region only appears in the biography of Jesus and his first disciples as an indication of their roots. We shall see that these biographies circulated first in very traditional Jewish-Christian circles (chap. V, §V.2).

2. The Foundation of Yavneh

In his *Life*, written some twenty-five years after the events in Galilee, Josephus really gives no details which explain the change in his point of view, which became more pro-Pharisee while remaining distinct from the tendency represented by John of Gischala and Simon b. Gamaliel. Even though he does not mention it, this period corresponds to the birth and development of the academy of Yavneh which lies at the foundation of the Tannaite tradition.

Two outstanding personalities are at the origin of this institution: the founder Yoḥanan b. Zakkai, and his immediate successor Gamaliel II, son of that same Simon b. Gamaliel. The town of Yavneh-Jamnia, situated between Jaffa and Ashqelon, lay 10 km from the coast, but was linked by a canal to a sea port. The town and its adjacent territory had been given by Herod to his sister Salome as her personal property (*J.W.* 2 §98). On her death, it passed to the empress Livia and then seems to have become the private property of her son Tiberius. Its exact legal status at this time is not entirely clear, but we can at least say that, juridically, it did not form part of Judaea. Philo informs us, however, that the majority of the population was Jewish (*Legatio*, §200–203).[8] He was obliged to speak of this city because it played a part in the affair of Caligula's statue, which had

8. The non-Jews were resident aliens (metics), which would suggest that the Jews had a civic status, as in an imperial city; however, the town was administered by a procurator. According to Strabo, *Geographus*, 16.2.28, the region of Jamnia (which he describes in Herod's time as a village and not as a *polis*) could arm 40,000 men, which is considerable.

so many repercussions. The whole business began when some pagans set up a brick altar there and inaugurated a cult. This action was probably illegal in view of the law in force in the territory, and in any case it was regarded as provocative and set off a violent reaction among the Jews of the place, who destroyed the altar.[9] In a general climate of tension between Romans and Jews, what began as a local incident grew out of all proportion and finally brought down the wrath of Caligula, who refused to allow that Jews should impose their law on his lands. In response he decided to have a statue of himself set up in the Temple at Jerusalem. He compounded this blunder by stubbornness in the face of the widespread reactions to his project, even before it was put into effect, around the whole Mediterranean basin. Philo himself went to Rome to try to calm things down. The affair dragged on in a climate of extreme tension until Caligula's death in 41 put an end to it, but the Messianist agitations which it had provoked were to have remarkable consequences (cf. chap. VI, §I.3).

In 68, when the war in Galilee was being extended into Judaea, Vespasian brought with him "numerous citizens who had surrendered to him in return for certain rights," and installed garrisons at Yavneh and Ashdod (*J.W.* 4 §130). Later, in circumstances about which Josephus has nothing to say, he put down seditions, in particular at Lod and Yavneh and "settled there as inhabitants a sufficient number of Jews who had rallied to him" (*J.W.* 4 §444). The connection between the events is uneven, but behind them we can discern an intelligent policy at a moment when disorder was threatening the close of Nero's reign: just as Herod had done with the colony at Bathyra, Vespasian installed Jews who were loyal to him in well-chosen places. They were probably living in fixed residence, or at least under surveillance, but the notable fact is that these Jews came from Galilee.

Vespasian's son Titus directed the war in Judaea in 70. He attempted a similar policy, but apparently without the success he had counted on. During the siege, the high priests and other notables surrendered to the Roman commander and were assigned to fixed residence at Gophna, in Judaea. A little later, rumors went around Jerusalem that their disappearance meant that they had been killed, and Titus had them exhibited to the besieged in order to persuade them to give themselves up, but they could not win over the rebels (*J.W.* 6 §114 f).[10] These priests under Roman sur-

9. According to *AbRN* B, p. 66, Yoḥanan b. Zakkai, the first founder of the school of Yavneh, who was politically submissive to the Romans, was against breaking altars, cf. below.

10. The priests' attitude here gives rise to the question of a possible restoration of the Temple worship at Jerusalem after the war, cf. below §I.4.

veillance were in a situation so similar to that of Josephus himself that we may suspect him of arranging his narrative just a little. Furthermore, among the rebel leaders under siege who refused any compromise were Galileans, precisely the elements whom he had not been able to win over to moderation.

This is the context in which we can interpret the very fragmentary rabbinic data on the foundation made by Yoḥanan b. Zakkai. There are two versions of the story. According to one, he gave himself up to Vespasian, foretold that he would become emperor, and obtained permission to settle at Yavneh with some teachers. The other tells how, having tried in vain, in Jerusalem under siege, to persuade his fellow citizens to give up a hopeless war, he fled the city hidden in a coffin in order to give himself up to Vespasian and obtain concessions.[11] These accounts, which recall what Josephus writes about himself, have long been subjected to analysis because of the difficulty of reconciling them. The escape from Jerusalem is comprehensible under Titus but not under Vespasian, whereas the prediction can only fit Vespasian and not Titus. Modern historians mostly discuss the question, under which of the two generals to place this episode, even if it means interpreting it as an act of treason, but it is always taken for granted that Yoḥanan b. Zakkai came from Jerusalem. However, this all-important point is questionable.[12] First, Josephus, who never fails to mention anything or anyone of social consequence, does not speak of Yoḥanan, whereas he knows Simon b. Gamaliel, a notable Pharisee of Jerusalem and father of Gamaliel II. Secondly, Yoḥanan's active life before Yavneh, known only from rabbinic sources, consists in having kept a school for twenty years at Arab, near Sepphoris, so in Galilee proper (not Batanaea), but with only moderate success (*YShab* 16:8, p. 15d). Further, a curious Christian legend tells how, still in Galilee, his father (Zakkai-Zachaeus) had to bow before the knowledge of the child Jesus (*G. of Thomas* §6–8).[13] So, even beyond Tannaite

11. Cf. *Abot RN* A,4; these accounts have been transmitted in several versions, presented with commentary by Jacob Neusner, *A Life of Yohanan ben Zakkai, Ca. 1–80 C. E.* (Studia Post-Biblica, 6), Leiden, 1970², p. 152 f. We adopt different conclusions, except for the date of Yoḥanan's arrival at Yavneh.

12. Despite legends in which he witnesses the burning of the Temple (*Abot RN* B, §7). In order to console a colleague, he declares that there is a mode of expiation which is just as effective as the cult, *i.e.* charity (*op. cit.,* A, 4), but that is really a way of *bypassing* the Temple, for this precept already existed well before the destruction, cf. *MAb* 1:2, which attributes it to Simon the Just.

13. This legend went around, as it is known to Irenaeus, *Adv. haereses* 1.20.1. There are also some features in common between Jesus' parables (of the kingdom) and those of Yoḥanan b. Zakkai, cf. Matt 22:1-14 par. and *BShab* 153a.

circles there was talk of the Galilean background of Yoḥanan b. Zakkai, perhaps in certain Jewish-Christian groups in Galilee.[14] Finally, he is given as the last disciple of Hillel the Elder (*BMeg* 13a). As we have seen, the latter, a Babylonian, had rather narrowly succeeded in being promoted by "the elders of Bathyra" (chap. III, §II.1), an event which is to be situated in Galilee, taken in a broad sense to include Batanaea.

There is no indication that either Hillel or Yoḥanan b. Zakkai ever settled permanently at Jerusalem, but that does not, of course, mean that they never went there on pilgrimage; they may even have taught on such occasions and had disciples there.[15] On the other hand, they have clear associations with Galilee, against a background of Babylonian Judaism. They are also politically somewhat unsophisticated, in a way which recalls that of the Hassidaeans mentioned in 1 Macc 7:13 f., whose authority was, nonetheless, feared by the high priest.[16] In these conditions, the foundation of the school of Yavneh can be explained by a very simple hypothesis, in the setting of the campaign in 68: Yoḥanan, a person from the provinces, unknown or little known in Jerusalem, was one of the submissive (or non-political) Galileans settled by Vespasian at Yavneh, a Judaean town not subject to the jurisdiction of Jerusalem.[17] His prediction to Vespasian took place in Galilee, like that of Josephus at Jotapata (*J.W.* 3 §401), in circumstances so similar that we may well ask whether they

14. Cf. the discussion by J. Neusner, *Yohanan ben Zakkai . . .*, p. 53–56.

15. According to *BPes* 26a, he used to teach in the Temple precincts. *THag* 2:11 testifies to Hillel's presence in Jerusalem, but it was precisely on the occasion of a pilgrimage. *Mid Tan* 26:13 (p. 175 f.) reports that, on a legal question, Simon b. Gamaliel and Yoḥanan b. Zakkai were seen together in Jerusalem (in the vicinity of the Dung Gate) writing officially to the people of Upper and Lower Galilee and to those of the "South," Upper and Lower. However, the effect of symmetry is fictitious, as the "South" designates not Idumaea but Judaea, Upper and Lower, to the west of Jerusalem (cf. *BZeb* 22b), *i.e.* to the south of Galilee; so the redaction has been made from a Galilean perspective. The account is important from two points of view: 1. it indicates a harmony (at least momentary) between the Galilean Yoḥanan and the Jerusalemite Simon; a notable fact, this same Simon was in touch with John of Gischala, another witness to rural Galilee, although politically more active (cf. chap. IV, §I.1); 2. the episode of these common letters is nothing out of the ordinary in the case of regular authorities, and the fact that it was noted shows that it was exceptional; without going into the nature of this non-sacerdotal authority, we can at least conclude that Jerusalem was not Yoḥanan's usual home.

16. Cf. John Kampen, *The Hasideans and the Origin of Pharisaism. A Study in 1 and 2 Maccabees* (SBL, Septuagint and Cognate Studies, 24), Atlanta (Ga.), Scholars Press, 1988, p. 85 f.

17. In *BRSh* 29b, "people of Bathyra" (בני בתירא) are also to be found at Yavneh from the beginning, with a notable rank, but cf. below; later, a Judah b. Bathyra was a contemporary of Aqiba (*MKel* 2:4), but left to found (or resume) a school at Nisibis in Mesopotamia (*SifDt* §80).

were really two different events; the account featuring Yoḥanan might even be secondary, with the underlying idea of showing that he, and not Josephus, is the real savior of Judaism.[18] On our hypothesis, the first version of Yoḥanan's story is the more reliable.

The second version, *i.e.* Yoḥanan's escape from a Jerusalem famished *under Vespasian*, would then have resulted from a fusion of two themes: Yoḥanan's escape under Vespasian from an unknown place which was besieged, and the escape of unknown persons from Jerusalem under Titus. This latter theme could itself be a deliberate reinterpretation of the deportation of priests to Gophna by Titus, so as to show that the school of Yavneh, though independent of properly sacerdotal influence, was nevertheless heir to traditions relating to the Temple; various testimonies show precisely that there were tensions between Yoḥanan b. Zakkai, who was always opposed to the Sadducees, and certain priests.[19]

This conclusion, which assigns to the school at Yavneh a modest beginning *before* the downfall of Jerusalem, throws light on other points. First, Yoḥanan never cites his master Hillel (or any other), but numerous decisions are attributed to him concerning the calendar[20] or rites, sometimes involving discussions with "the people of Bathyra," that is to say with the circles of Babylonian origin which had promoted Hillel.[21] So he

18. On probable contacts between FJ and circles around Gamaliel, cf. below, §II.

19. *MEdu* 8:3, *MSheq* 1:4, etc., cf. Alexander Guttman, "The End of the Jewish Sacrificial Cult," *HUCA* 38 (1967), p. 137–148, who, although maintaining traditional views on the patriarchal authority at Jerusalem of the Hillelites (Gamaliel, Simon, etc.), insists, with support of sources, on the opposition of Yoḥanan to war against the Romans, also to the Sadducees, the priests and the temple worship. It has also been noted that of the fourteen doctors who report memories of the Temple in the Talmud, only one (Yehoshua b. Ḥanania) was a disciple of Yoḥanan b. Zakkai, cf. Adolf Büchler, *Die Priester und der Cultus*, Wien, 1895, p. 16 f. In another order of ideas, the rab. trad. shows little interest in the twenty-four priestly courses who assured the service of the Temple, cf. Dalia Trifon, "Did the Priestly Courses Transfer in Galilee?" *Tarbiz* 59 (1989), p. 77–93; *TTaan* 3:9 f. explains that each destruction of the Temple took place when the course of Yoyarib was on duty (that of Mattathias and his sons, high priests after the Maccabean crisis); it was indeed the first of the courses, but afterwards lost its rank, cf. below §II.1 and *Tosefta kifshuṭah* 5:1075, l. 5.

20. Fixing the authority to establish the calendar, it is noteworthy that he defines a place to receive testimony of the new moon (בית הועד), even if the one in charge of this place (president of the tribunal, patriarch) is absent (*MRSh* 4:4); *MEdu* 7:7 recounts a fact indicating that such was the custom at Yavneh (Gamaliel being absent). *MRSh* 3:1 even says that a tribunal of three suffices, whence later controversies on the role of the Jerusalem Sanhedrin when it existed (cf. Maimonides, *Sefer haMiṣvot, ʿaśeh* 153), for another saying affirms that it alone had power to intercalate a month (*MekhRI boʾ* §2). Is this a case of succession or of competition?

21. As we have seen, these "people of Bathyra" are situated at Yavneh (*BRSh* 29b). Their controversy with Yoḥanan, already mentioned (chap. III, §II.1), concerned the

was not principally a transmitter but, in circumstances which required it, an organizer, who encountered a certain amount of opposition. Perhaps his school was originally a brotherhood, without statutory authority over others. Eventually, he had notable disciples (*MAb* 2:8), among whom was a priest, also Eliezer and Yehoshua who praised Aquila's translation of the Bible (cf. chap. V, §II.2). Finally, we can note that he was aware of the growing authority of Scriptural reference.[22]

3. Gamaliel II

Yoḥanan's successor, Gamaliel II (fl. 90) was of a quite different caliber. His grandfather Gamaliel I, St. Paul's teacher according to Acts, and his father Simon, mentioned by Josephus, were leading Pharisees who were known in Jerusalem. However, tradition has it that Gamaliel I was the son, or perhaps the grandson, of Hillel, himself descended from king David. This statement is, however, questionable, since it belongs to the later legitimation of the patriarchal dynasty, and especially of Judah the Prince. *MAb* 1:16 presents Gamaliel I, in the chain of transmitters, immediately after Hillel (and Shammai), but without indicating any family tie[23] or special master-pupil relationship; indeed it attributes to him the direc-

relative importance of New Year and the Sabbath. This narrative is at the origin of the decree attributed to Yoḥanan b. Zakkai, after the downfall of the Temple (*MRSh* 4:1), to sound the *shofar* even outside the sanctuary if New Year fell on a Sabbath. However, the rest of this decree (4:2) explains that Jerusalem (including the sanctuary) is more important than Yavneh in terms which suppose the two cities and their institutions to be contemporaneous, as Epstein concludes, p. 652, on the basis of *YRSh* 4:2, p. 49b (cf. the discussion of *Tosefta kifshuṭah* 5:1048). In other words, if the episode really took place *before* the downfall (but after the foundation of Yavneh), the final normative decision appears to have been reworked by adding the words "after the downfall of the Temple" (משחרב בה"מ); in that case it was a question originally of an *ad hoc* decision taken locally and proper to the school (or brotherhood) of Yoḥanan. In the last analysis, it cannot be excluded that, as in the case of a Passover on the Sabbath, the concurrence of New Year and the Sabbath was a new phenomenon, since in the calendar of the *Jubilees* New Year 1 Tishri (like 1 Nisan) is always a Wednesday, and we have seen this calendar problem arising in connection with the Passover at Bathyra, in the time of Hillel. Finally, it cannot be excluded either, that the *ad hoc* decision in question, then the decree in its normative form, was made *after* 70, if some cult had been restored (cf. §4); in this case, the words "after the downfall of the Temple" can be taken as being originally a chronological indication.

22. According to *MSoṭa* 5:2, he forecasts that in the future the category of third degree impurity will be abolished, for want of scriptural basis, but Aqiba eventually finds one, based on a detail of the Hebrew text; for Yoḥanan, therefore, the laws on impurity are traditional, but the problem of their being abolished for want of a scriptural basis is *new*.

23. According to *YKetub* 12:3, p. 35a, Judah the Patriarch is expressly presented as a descendant of Hillel, and he expresses his admiration for the Elders of Bathyra. It must be admitted that real descent cannot be entirely excluded.

tive to "choose a master for oneself," which may well reflect his own situation (or, less probably, a certain liberalism). In this text, there is an even greater break in continuity than that which separates Hillel from his predecessors, and Yoḥanan b. Zakkai and not Gamaliel is named as the heir of Hillel and Shammai (2:8). But any discontinuity is only hinted at: both Yoḥanan and Gamaliel are considered to have inherited the authority of Hillel, who combined, as we have seen, a Babylonian origin (or culture) with the teaching of the Pharisees of Judaea, and is thus presented as their common ancestor. So several tendencies have been fused together.

All these details are important, for they help us to characterize Gamaliel II. He reinforced the prestige of Yavneh, got good teachers and students to come there, kept in touch with the Roman authorities, and visited Jewish communities, particularly in Galilee and Rome. His authority allowed other schools, such as Lod, to develop, and attracted to Yavneh a spectrum of people of various opinions, as several signs suggest, notably the famous Benediction against the "sectaries," which was adopted only with difficulty (*BBer* 28b). Whether or not it was from the first directed specifically against the Christians, which appears unlikely, the difficulty with which it passed is evidence of a struggle between a normalizing Pharisaic tendency, perhaps Yoḥanan's party, and another which was more liberal, or at least more concerned with the people as a whole and admitted several parties (perhaps to keep them under control, for Gamaliel was authoritarian). In addition, a number of rabbinical sayings, which it would take too long to analyze here, can be associated with the parties described by Josephus, or at least presuppose them. We can add a further indication: we saw earlier that Josephus, who had written about three traditional parties, Pharisees, Sadducees and Essenes, later introduced a fourth, the successors of Judas the Galilean (*Ant.* 18 §23 f.). His point of reference is always post-war realities (cf. chap. III, §IV). In all likelihood, he had heard of the growing moral authority of the school of Yavneh, even perhaps of some legal status conferred by the Romans (cf. *MEdu* 7:7). In point of fact, immediately after the war, the Jews of Judaea had been deprived of their own jurisdiction (as *dediticii*),[24] and many had chosen, like Josephus, to adopt a Roman status. However, it was not self-evident that the school of Yavneh, even with a Gamaliel who sought understanding with the Romans and was open to Greek culture, would be universally recognized as sole heir to all the institutions of Jerusalem, especially since it lacked any sacerdotal authority. One can well imagine a Josephus treating it with respect and at the same time bypassing it.

24. But freedom to practice their religion was maintained (except for the *fiscus iudaicus*), cf. Schürer-Vermes, III:122 f. and below §4.

Gamaliel was a Pharisee, but of a tendency less strict than many Galileans. Several anecdotes[25] show that he or his sons submitted without protest, when in Galilee, to local customs which were more restrictive, but at the same time, at Yavneh, he insisted on greater openness (the tendency called "Beth Hillel"). He was, however, motivated rather by concern for unity than by liberalism, as a number of details show: he was keen to control licenses to teach (*BNida* 24b) and practical decisions, and could at times be rigid; he had to have the last word on fixing the calendar, even though not claiming to be the greatest expert (*MRSh* 2:8 f.); Yoḥanan b. Zakkai, who ended his days at Bror Ḥail, appears to have been expelled; Eliezer b. Hyrcanus his disciple, known for his fidelity to received teachings, was banished for not submitting to the majority (*BBabaM* 59a–b). At least in these last two cases, Galilean traditions were at stake.

Gamaliel's authority as head of the school was, however, insecure. At one point he was deposed (*BBer* 27b), and none of his sons succeeded him directly at his death, but here the Roman authorities could have played a part, since he died about the time of the revolts under Trajan. Other elements enable us to define a little better his profile and his teaching. It is said that, after these revolts (the "war of Quietus"), the decision was taken to ban the study of Greek, but that the house of Gamaliel was excused from observing it because it was close to the Roman authorities; so nationalist pressure brought about a split in the power structure. Further, Simon II, Gamaliel's son, was later to express pride in his father's school but was not well up in oral tradition and had difficulty in imposing his authority on the school of Usha (*BHor* 13b). He, however, had his own tendency, as we will show later: he was more aware of a need to be faithful to explicitly *biblical* precepts.[26] These slight indications show that Gamaliel and his successors, Pharisees with better connections in Jerusalem, were of a tendency rather more open than the surrounding culture, but above all more biblical than the persons and customs associated with Galilee, which were entirely centered on the oral tradition. One difficulty remains: how to understand here the term "Pharisee"? Gamaliel II seems to have been of the same kind as John of Gischala and Simon b. Gamaliel,

25. Translation and commentary by S. Safrai, "The Jewish Natural Culture of Galilee," p. 178 f.

26. Later tradition credits Yoḥanan with a lively interest in the Bible (*BSof* 16:8), in particular for homiletic, cf. Wilhelm Bacher, *Die Agada der Tannaiten*, Straßburg, 1903,[2] I:26 f.; similarly, the Aramaic translation of the Prophets (except for Dan, cf. *BMegila* 6a), is attributed to the first disciple of Hillel, Yonatan b. Uzziel; once again later syntheses have been retrojected into the past.

combining oral tradition and Scripture, whereas Yoḥanan b. Zakkai, heir to the Babylonian Hillel, admitted only the ancestral traditions. Both can be described as "Pharisees," but the clearest feature they have in common is to be "separate."

Finally, as well as doctrinal differences, we need to emphasize an even more important difference in nature between Yoḥanan's foundation and Gamaliel's enterprise. The former founded only a restricted group, originally of the same dimensions as that of Bathyra; we will show later that it was essentially a brotherhood, similar to the Essenes and not much concerned about the people as a whole (cf. chap. V, §I). Gamaliel, by contrast, sought to take responsibility for the reorganization of the people under Domitian and later. This move had several important consequences: the federation of diverse currents,[27] the respect for Galilee, and the insistence on schools rather than on brotherhoods;[28] perhaps, too, a certain influence on Josephus, obliging him to admit the fourth philosophy; and finally, the problem of the Jewish-Christians *(minim)*, which we are going to see reappear at several points.[29] Official Jewish opposition to Christianity thus takes a new form. Until this point, it was above all conducted by the Jerusalem authorities; now it will proceed from circles much closer to the Jewish-Christians, but intending to speak for the

27. This aspect of federation may explain not only the multiplicity of controversies, so characteristic of the rab. trad., but also the use and then the maintenance of the term *sanhedrin* to designate the highest authority, both academic and judicial: the Greek term suggests a loose federation, with only consensual authority, cf. chap. III, §I,1.

28. Gamaliel travelled about, even to Rome. A rather later rab. trad. (*Derek Ereṣ Rabba* §3, a "minor tractate" of the Talmud) reports that he came with several companions (including Aqiba) in the time of Domitian to prevent a persecution of the Jews, and there met a "philosopher." Now Josephus, freedman of the Flavians, frequented the imperial court and had pretensions to be a philosopher (cf. *Ant.* 1 §13 f.); further, the term "philosopher" when written in Hebrew (פילספוס) is close to the Hebrew form of "Fl. Iosefus" (פליספוס), and it is tempting to conclude that it was he whom Gamaliel met, even though that "philosopher" is represented as a Gentile, cf. Louis H. Feldman, *Josephus and Modern Scholarship (1937–1980)*, Berlin-New York, W. de Gruyter, 1984, p. 78 f. Two further observations speak in favor of the identification: 1. in the perspective of the brotherhoods, it is not unlikely that Josephus would have been described as a Gentile (*i.e.* having the same degree of impurity), at least by later traditions (cf. below chap. V, §I); 2. the projects of Josephus and Gamaliel, to reorganize the people after the disaster of 70, are obviously different but also incontestably alike, beginning with the "Pharisaic" perspective (cf. chap. III introd.); on this, we can point out again that in *Life* §190 f. he tries to discredit Simon, father of Gamaliel, by emphasizing his collusion with his then rival, John of Gischala. On any hypothesis, it is natural to suppose that conflicts of this order left some traces in the literature, more or less veiled since each camp maintains that it is the only one. In connection with Passover, we shall see a further indication that Josephus was familiar with circles close to Yavneh (cf. chap. VII, §I.3).

29. Cf. in particular chap. V, §III.2.

whole of Judaism. In this way we can understand how, when the gospels were reworked to produce the current texts, polemics with Judaism mixed together earlier memories from the time of Jesus and contemporary quarrels with opponents who were *close* and who were taken as representing the people as a whole (*e.g.* “the Jews” in John’s gospel). We will deal with these aspects in the following chapter (V, §V).

4. The Jerusalem Temple after 70

It is usually taken for granted that the Jerusalem Temple was entirely destroyed during the war of 70, and that no cult was ever restored there. In support of this view, the rabbinic tradition indicates that the daily sacrifices ceased during the siege of Jerusalem on 17 Tammuz (*MTaan* 4:6), and that the half-*sheqel* poll tax and the offering of first fruits have been suspended, since they are due only if the Temple exists (*MSheq* 8:8). So the source for financing the public sacrifices has dried up. Josephus confirms the date when the sacrifices stopped as 17 Panemos (August) 70,[30] and mentions that after the triumph of Titus the poll tax was taken over by the Romans and paid into the Capitol (*J.W.* 7 §218).[31]

These texts clearly show that there was an interruption, but what happened afterwards? The rabbinic sources mention some significant decisions. For example, a new convert had to offer a dove in sacrifice, or put aside the corresponding amount until the day when the Temple should be restored, but Yoḥanan b. Zakkai abolished the obligation to keep this money unused (*BRSh* 31b). This rite,[32] which completes circumcision and immersion, is the propitiation which opens the way to participating in sacrificial meals, in particular the Passover (*TSheq* 3:20). So its abrogation is to be understood as the abandonment of hope for a swift restoration of worship and thus suppresses any link, real or virtual, with the

30. In *J.W.* 6 §94, FJ explains that the sacrifice was not offered on that day, “for want of men” (ἀνδρῶν ἀπορίᾳ; the corr. ἀρνῶν “for want of lambs,” suggested by Loeb, is rightly rejected by Reinach), that is probably for want of suitable personnel for the cult.

31. On the *fiscus iudaicus*, cf. Schürer-Vermes III:122. This measure, which FJ presents without unfavorable comment, is consistent with his speech on God’s weariness with Jerusalem and his desire to reply to the imperial invitation to go to Rome *(evocatio)*, cf. Christiane Saulnier, “Flavius Josèphe et la propagande flavienne,” *RB* 96 (1989), p. 545–562. There is no known trace of an authorized cult, at Rome, of the God of Jerusalem, but the insistence in Acts on showing how Paul came to Rome may be a kind of response to the imperial invitation: in Luke 2:1 f., it is really thanks to an imperial census that Jesus is born in Bethlehem, David’s city.

32. Not biblical, but the proselyte is regarded as newly born (cf. *BYeb* 48b), which may explain a sacrifice analogous to that prescribed for the firstborn (Lev 12:1-8), cf. below §III.2.

Temple.[33] Similarly, it is reported that, in the days of the Temple, witnesses of the new moon could break the Sabbath in order to present their testimony, so that the sacrifice of the new month could be made on time (*BRSh* 21b); after the downfall, Yoḥanan b. Zakkai had to declare that there were no more sacrifices (as if that was not obvious), and the possibility of breaking the Sabbath was restricted to Nisan and Tishri, since these months begin the liturgical and civil year respectively and contain the principal feasts. There too, there is no reason to suppose that these decisions were taken only in view of prevailing circumstances. Yoḥanan was opposed to the priests, as we have seen, and made no move to prepare for a restoration of the Temple cult. His effort was given to a reorganization, without official cult, of Judaism (or at least of his own school), conceived not as a continuation of the ruined Temple, but in opposition to it.[34] This feature relates him to the dissident Essenes and the brotherhoods,[35] as we shall see (chap. V, §I). Furthermore, there is no trace of customs "in memory of the Temple" in Galilee or originating there between 70 and 135. The feature in common to all these pieces of evidence is not the expectation that the Temple worship would be restored, but rather the setting up of an independent organization. Further, the occasional reminder that the Temple cult no longer exists does not look like a simple statement of fact so much as a statement of position: there is no longer a *valid* cult. It is not necessarily a very polemical statement, since, seen from Jerusalem, the enterprise of Yoḥanan b. Zakkai was at best a marginal current, no doubt hardly perceptible. So it is not possible to conclude firmly that no cultic custom was maintained, or that it was not restored after the war by other groups, especially under priestly influence.

33. Whence a rite of substitution, expounded in *BYeb* 47a–b.

34. There is even some uncertainty on the date of the downfall: according to *MTaan* 4:6, the annual fast of 9 Ab commemorates first the condemnation of the Israelites in the desert not to enter the Promised Land (Deut 1:35; Num 14:29, cf. 1 Cor 10:5; Heb 3:17), then the destruction of both Temples and finally the defeat of Bar Kokhba at Betar in 135 as well as the destruction of Jerusalem (become Aelia). But Josephus indicates (*J.W.* 6 §250) that the two Temples were destroyed on 10 Ab (Loos), which corresponds well to the fifth month of Jer 52:12 (the parallel in 2 Kgs 25:8 gives the 7th of the month). The change from the 10th to the 9th cannot be due to a disagreement on the lunar month (preceding month short or long), because of the biblical precedent. The date of 9 Ab comes rather from a concentration of disasters on a single point: the most serious is the last (access to Jerusalem cut off), and is in line with the first (access to the Promised Land cut off). In other words, Yoḥanan's descendants did not at first keep a very lively memory of the downfall of the Temple, but that memory was restored after the downfall of Jerusalem in 135.

35. Contrary to the conclusions of Shaye J. D. Cohen, "The Significance of Yavneh: Pharisees, Rabbis, and the End of Jewish Sectarianism," *HUCA* 55 (1984), p. 27–53.

In fact, there are positive indications that some sort of worship was restored, even if the Temple poll tax continued to be confiscated by the Romans at least until Domitian.[36] Well after 70, Josephus speaks of the laws concerning the marriage of priests, which require a study of genealogies in order to avoid any mismatch (*Ag. Ap.* 1 §31); he explains that a copy of all documents concerning personal status drawn up in the Diaspora is sent to the archives at Jerusalem, which have been restored after each war (of Antiochus, Pompey, Varus, *and recently*, that is to say after the war of 70). So this administration was functioning at the time he was writing, very probably still during the reign of Domitian (about 95). Again, when Josephus describes the organization of the cult, he writes systematically in the present (*Ant.* 3 §224 f.); in *Ag. Ap.* 2 §193 f., he recalls, still in the present, that there is one sole Temple for one sole God, and that the priests are constantly occupied in its service, and he even mentions the daily sacrifices offered by the Jews for the emperors and the Roman people (2 §77 f.).[37] In this perspective, the reservation of priests at Gophna by Titus, to prepare, just in case, for a future cult under Roman control, can be understood as a wise measure.[38] It is also worth noting that

36. Suetonius, *Domitian*, §12; cf. Schürer-Vermes I:528.

37. According to Philo, *Legatio* §157, these sacrifices had been instituted by Caesar at his own expense, but a change of custom after 70 is likely, since the poll tax was confiscated, which implies the Roman authority's control of the cult as of the rest of the administration. Previously, the half-*sheqel* served also for maintenance of the city, aquaducts, etc. cf. *MSheq* 4:2 and Gedaliah Alon, *The Jews in their Land in the Talmudic Age (70–640 C. E.)*, Jerusalem, I:46 f. (the sums in question could have been considerable, cf. *Ant.* 18 §313). Until Domitian's death (96), there appear not to have been any major conflicts, which would tend to show that a *modus vivendi* was found, at least for the time being. It is also not impossible that the place where this cult was restored, at least for a time, was the temple of Onias, cf. below.

38. FJ affirms that when Jerusalem was taken, Titus held a council in the course of which it was decided to spare the Temple, but that afterwards he could not check his troops, who wrecked and pillaged (*J.W.* 6 §243 f.). Sulpicius Severus, *Chron.* 2. 30. 6 f., reports this same council of war, but affirms on the contrary that Titus, despite the advice given by certain generals, intended to "destroy the Temple first, so as the better to eliminate *the* religion of the Jews and Christians; although opposed, these religions had the same founders; the Christians were descended from the Jews, and, once the root was torn up, the branch would perish." Josephus is suspect of being tendentious in order to stay on side with his protectors, but Sulpicius Severus, who appears to depend on a lost passage of the *Histories* of Tacitus, has, perhaps, reworked his source, particularly on the subject of the Christians, cf. Loeb, II:XXIV f. (notice by Thackeray); Charles Saumagne, "Les incendiaires de Rome," *Revue Historique* 227 (1962), p. 337–360, and discussion in Schürer-Vermes I:506, n. 115. On any hypothesis, Titus had resolved to conquer the sanctuary, occupied by the Jews (*J.W.* 6 §249). Further, according to *J.W.* 6 §322, after the destruction of the sanctuary he put to death the priests who had remained. Despite FJ's certain bias, Titus' two acts towards the priests are not contradictory: one corresponds to

Josephus begins his account of the *War* with the Maccabean crisis, that is by a cessation of the cult (the daily sacrifice) followed by its restoration at the end of three and a half years (half a "week of years," to borrow the terminology of Dan), which suggests that he was already envisaging something similar after 70, even if he does not say so expressly, or even perhaps that things were already moving in this direction.

Various Christian authors, writing after 70, speak of the Temple in the present.[39] Moreover, Justin, *Dial.* 46.2, reminds Tryphon, about 150, that it is since the Bar Kokhba war, and not since that of 70, that the sacrifices are no longer possible in Jerusalem. He could, strictly speaking, be taken to mean that they were only *possible* and not really practiced between 70 and 135, but that is not the most natural sense, and in this particular case Justin's argumentation would be pointless. Passages in the rabbinic tradition suggest that in the period 70–135 the Temple cult was not so much materially impossible, but rather was rejected, especially because of the misdeeds of the Herodian Temple.[40] One teacher (Yehoshua, at the end of the 1st century) is reported as wanting still to permit the sacrifices and the consumption of the most holy foods, even if there were no longer an altar or curtains, since the holiness of the *place* is permanent since Solomon (*MEdu* 8:6). *BNed* 23a mentions pilgrimages after the downfall (and before the Bar Kokhba war).[41] It is clear that the "place"

---

the military action of reducing a revolt in Judaea (including priests still in the sanctuary, presumably in revolt or under the influence of the rebels), the other, more political, corresponds to the desire to look to the future (with submissive priests), even if the local gods had decided to quit Jerusalem. For the Roman authority, and especially for Titus, son of the emperor, the Jewish *ethnos* constituted a recognized *religio*; it was certainly not a negligible portion (about one tenth, cf. chap. VI, §I.1) of the population of the Empire, where it was widely diffused, and also in the territories of the enemy Parthians, which required some precautions.

39. Cf. Kenneth W. Clark, "Worship in the Jerusalem Temple after A.D. 70," *NTS* 6 (1960), p. 269–280. In particular, arguments concerning the cult in Heb are always couched in the present tense, which supposes the existence of the Temple (always σκηνή, never ἱερόν or ναός); for this reason, John A. T. Robinson, *The Priority of John*, London, SCM Press, 1985, p. 17, holds, as others have done, that this text should be dated before 70, but his argument is not entirely convincing.

40. Cf. A. Guttman, "The End of the Jewish Sacrificial Cult," p. 137–148, and above §2.

41. Another, less certain, sign: there is a discussion (*TSoṭa* 15:9 f.) about the mourning to observe because of the impossibility of the cult; that could go back to the destruction of 70, called the "war of Vespasian," but the context has already mentioned this war, then that of Quietus, under Trajan (with the prohibition of whitewashed walls, cf. chap. V, §IV.2), and the discussion referred to is introduced by "after the ruin of the last Dwelling." So the way the passage is constructed suggests mourning for the service of the sanctuary after the Bar Kokhba war, either because it has become finally impossible, or because

can survive the Temple installations, as the persistence of the Samaritan customs demonstrates. On the most basic level, for sacrifices only an altar is necessary, and it can be erected quickly and inexpensively, as at the time of Zerubbabel (Ezra 3:2 f.) or Judas Maccabaeus (1 Macc 4:44 f.).[42]

All these hints of the possible remains of a cult at Jerusalem between 70 and 135 do not, of course, amount to formal proof, but they do con-

---

some cult still existed until the outbreak of this war, but not because Bar Kokhba restored an altar which was then destroyed. This passage is, however, complex, for the discussion on mourning is led by Yehoshua, apparently Yehoshua b. Ḥanania, disciple of Yoḥanan b. Zakkai (*MAb* 2:8), and, as a Levite, a witness to the customs of the Temple (*BSuk* 53a); his remarks may have been made after 70, but it has not been proved (and is not probable) that he lived after 135, cf. *Tosefta kifshuṭah*, 8:772 f. (n. 58 f.). It seems then to be a literary composition defining a usage after 135, but making use of earlier elements.

42. This question is distinct from that of possible dissident sanctuaries. It is also a good question, why the sacrifices did not continue elsewhere. *MZeb* 14:4-8 explains that before the Dwelling was set up in the desert, the high places were allowed, and the cult was performed by the firstborn (patriarchs); when it was set up, the high places were forbidden, and the cult restricted to the priests; when they arrived at Gilgal, the high places were allowed (Joshua); when they arrived at Shilo, the high places were again forbidden (Elijah); when they arrived at Nob and Gibeon, the high places were once more allowed (Samuel, David); finally, when they arrived at Jerusalem, the high places were definitively forbidden (Solomon). This series of decisions does no more than follow the biblical narratives, with some simplifications. Another passage indicates that the holiness of Shilo was extinguished when its temple was destroyed, but that the holiness of Jerusalem is indelible, as also its monopoly of the cult (*MMeg* 1:11). A dissident opinion denies that the holiness of Jerusalem survived its downfall, and states that sacrifices then took place in the temple of Onias (*BMeg* 10a). The prophecy of Isa 19:21 announced that "in those days, Egypt will know YHWH; there will be sacrifices and offerings; vows will be made and fulfilled." Commenting implicitly on this passage, *MMen* 13:10 declares that vows and sacrifices can be fulfilled in the temple of Onias (בית חוניו, distinguished here from the Temple of Jerusalem [מקדש] by a term which leaves out the idea of holiness [קדושה]), but that the priests who officiated there will no longer be able to serve in Jerusalem. This disqualification contradicts Deut 18:6 f., which allows any Levite, from anywhere, to come and serve in the "place chosen," but it is based on 1 Kgs 23:9 where, in the course of the reform of Josiah, the priests of the high places "could not sacrifice at the altar of YHWH in Jerusalem; they could only eat unleavened bread with their brethren" (כי אם אכלו, lit. "but they ate"; the LXX has ὅτι εἰ μὴ ἔφαγον ἄζυμα [כי אם לא אכלו], meaning "unless having eaten," which is a more positive view of the high places, so also of the temple of Onias: they did not automatically disqualify those who served them). The contradiction disappears, however, when one notices that the "priests of the high places" are not represented as Levites, let alone as sons of Aaron, which entirely fits the line of Onias, of Egyptian origin, cf. *Search*, p. 255–263; this is discreetly suggested by TYon לא סלקין כהניא כומרי במתא, which glosses with a word designating pagan priests. *TMen* 13:14 f. discreetly removes the contradiction, by restricting the principle of Deut: it applies only when the high places are authorized, which was no longer the case in the time of Josiah (cf. *MZeb* 14:8, cited above). *SifDt* p. 268, is even more restrictive, by considering that this rule applies only to the 24 priestly courses, who can effectively reside anywhere outside Jerusalem. To sum up, the rab. trad. holds that the temple of Onias had a certain reason for existing, but that it could

stitute a very likely presumption. What is certain is that the rabbinic tradition, in discussing *halakha*, always presupposes the non-existence of the Temple worship. It gives no procedure for appointing the high priest, and at no point does it mention concrete means to be taken in order to restore the sanctuary and its operation.[43] This cannot be simply by chance, owing to a mere historical contingency making these things materially impossible after 135. It is a deliberate attitude and springs directly from a pre-war tradition.

II – Migration into Galilee after 135

Not much is known about the history of the schools which came out of Yavneh at the end of the 1st and the beginning of the 2nd centuries. A few facts suggest that there was wide diversity accompanied by lively debates. Gamaliel II, we have seen, wanted to introduce into the prayer of the *Eighteen Benedictions* an extra blessing directed against the "sectaries," but had difficulty in getting his way, which indicates either that the assembly was not as homogeneous as it was said to be, or that there were some dissidents.[44] There are other signs of persistent diversity of

not become a substitute for Jerusalem, and that its priests were disqualified. FJ always uses the present tense when speaking of cultic prescriptions, and adopts a prudent position; he has a strange way of understanding the precept of the three annual pilgrimages (of Exod 23:14 f.): "Let them assemble in the town where they will have *declared* that the Temple is to be found" (*Ant.* 4 §203); so there is room for flexibility. With regard to the temple of Onias, he only indicates that, after the war, it was closed by the Romans because of local troubles, but not destroyed (*J.W.* 7 §421 f.). In particular, it cannot be entirely excluded that the cult which he mentions after the war (*Ag. Ap.* 2 §73 f. & 193 f.) was in Egypt: 1. he is arguing against Apion, an Egyptian of Alexandria (or so it is claimed, cf. *Ag. Ap.* 2 §34); 2. it is not a question here of the construction of the sanctuary, or a place chosen by God (Deut 12:5), to which FJ has referred a little before (*Ag. Ap.* 2 §200), but apparently of something which comes later.

43. Except a ritual vow of speedy rebuilding, but by the gift of heaven, cf. *BSuk* 41a, etc.

44. Cf. *BBer* 28b. It has been thought that this Benediction (ברכת המינים), which is directed against various adversaries, was aimed primarily at crypto-Christians; its exact form is somewhat fluid, and the allusion to Christians is undeniable according to later witnesses (Epiphanius, *Panarion* 29.9; Jerome, *In Esaiam* 5.18 f., 49.7, 52.4, attest a form with נצרים, as later discovered in the Cairo *geniza*, cf. Wilhelm Bacher, "Le mot 'Minim' désigne-t-il quelquefois des chrétiens?" *REJ* 38 [1899], p. 37-45). Originally, it was a question more generally of apostates or dissidents, cf. Schürer-Vermes II:463. However, the question can be reopened with some new considerations: 1. the term מינים alternates often in the sources with צדוקים; this term, usually understood as "Sadducees," is taken to be a sort of self censorship, but if it is understood as "Zadokites," which is more likely (cf. chap. I, §I.3), it is then a question of a category of (adverse) Essenes who refuse a central authority; one passage even calls all the dissidents, including the מינים, by the term פרושין (cf. chap. V,

schools and customs.[45] Some time after 100, the proselyte Aquila translated the Torah into Greek in front of Eliezer b. Hyrcanus and Yehoshua, who praised him, which points to a crisis on another front (cf. chap. V, §II.3). About 115 there was a Jewish revolt, first in Egypt, then in Cyrenaica. The disturbances were energetically repressed by the Romans, but broke out in Cyprus and reached Mesopotamia, where they were put down with violence by Lucius Quietus, who later became governor of Judaea, almost at the time of Hadrian's accession in 117.[46] There may have been some disturbances in Palestine, for rabbinic tradition has kept the memory of a "war of Quietus."[47] After the repression of the revolts under Trajan, the use of Greek was banned about 120,[48] and various measures of mourning were imposed. It was at this time too that Aqiba, the master who tried to attach the oral traditions to the written word, developed hermeneutical rules which work only for details of the *Hebrew* text, whereas his colleague Ishmael b. Elisha, a more classical figure in the line of Yehoshua and Eliezer, recommended formulae for daily life intended to be practiced by the people as a whole[49] and stuck to rules of interpretation which were also valid for the Greek text.[50] The world of the schools was taking measures to prevent its own breakup.

There were also cases of exclusion due to diversity of opinions. Gamaliel II, in his attempt to unify the tradition, expelled Eliezer, even though he was his brother-in-law, because he refused to accept a majority decision of the academy in order to stick strictly to the teaching that

---

§V.1); 2. according to *BBer* 12b, the Decalogue was suppressed from public recitation in the Tannaite period because of the "trick of the *minim*"; it is a question of circles which deny the autonomy of the oral tradition, in particular the same Zadokites (cf. chap. V, §IV.4); 3. the present study tends to bring the beginnings of Christianity very close to Essene circles, and we will show later that there were fractures within certain brotherhoods (chap. VI, §II.2); 4. the most singular fact is the late appearance of this Christian problem, around 90 or 100, giving the impression that there was no tension before; this point will be discussed later (chap. V, §V).

45. Cf. *BYeb* 14a, with a significant verbal play on לא תתגדדו from Deut 14:1 "you will not gash yourselves (for a dead person)," understood as "you will not form clans" (אגודות), *i.e.* rival schools or tribunals.

46. Cf. Schürer-Vermes I:529 f.

47. Cf. *SOR*, p. 66, *MSoṭa* 9:14 פולמוס של קיטוס; the mss hesitate between קיטוס (Quietus) and טיטוס (Titus) but according to the context this war is later than that of Vespasian and earlier than the "last" (Bar Kokhba), cf. *Tosefta ki-fshuṭah*, 8:767.

48. On changes in attitude towards Greek, cf. chap. V, §II.2.

49. As emerges from a debate with Simon b. Yoḥaï, cf. *BBer* 35b and chap. V, §IV.2.

50. Or for any other language, since "the Torah has spoken the language of men," *SifNb* on Num 15:31, cf. Dominique Barthélemy, *Les devanciers d'Aquila. Première publication intégrale, etc.* (VTSup, 10), Leiden, Brill, 1963, p. 4 f.

he had received (*BBabaM* 59b). Gamaliel himself was dismissed from office, then restored, but he had to co-exist with his successor Eleazar b. Azaria (*BBer* 27b), which indicates that syntheses were made only with difficulty. On his death (about 115), his son Simon II did not immediately take his place, but only much later, in Galilee, where he had difficulty in getting himself accepted.

Without trying to characterize these tendencies *a priori*, we shall simply look at two important moments which will throw light on them: the Bar Kokhba adventure, then the resettlement in Galilee.

1. A Messianic Endeavor

The immediate causes of the Bar Kokhba revolt (132–135) are not very clear.[51] The most obvious factors include Hadrian's general policy of prohibiting circumcision to all the peoples of the Empire who practiced it and of founding or rebuilding cities, of which Jerusalem was only one.[52] What he intended was a renewal of the policy of Hellenism, to eliminate everything barbarous in favor of civilization. There were also local causes. The *Midrash GenR* (64:8, p. 710) implies that Hadrian, who had taken part in putting down the Jewish revolts under Trajan (115–117), had promised to rebuild the Jerusalem Temple, but had yielded to opposition from the Samaritans who suggested putting a temple elsewhere. Such a policy is not very likely on the part of Hadrian himself,[53] but it is not impossible that the Roman administration, then as on other occasions, had refused to pronounce in favor either of the Jewish or of the Samaritan temple. In any case, a temple of Zeus (or Serapis) was later built on Garizim. It could also be that the revolt was unleashed by the transformation of Jerusalem under a new name, and in particular by the disappearance of the site of the Temple, where certain cultic acts were still possible, as on Garizim after the destruction of the sanctuary. However, if some official worship still continued (§I.4), and so also veneration of the place and access to it, it is simpler to suppose that what set the match

51. Cf. Saul Lieberman, "Persecution of the Jewish Religion," in: *Festschrift Salo Baron*, Jerusalem, 1979, III:214; Moshe D. Herr, "Causes of the Bar Kokhba Revolt," *Zion* 43 (1978), p. 6, with bibliography.

52. According to Dio Cassius, *Roman History*, 69. 12. 1 f., cf. discussion in Schürer-Vermes I:537.

53. As shown by Gedaliah Alon, *The Jews in Their Land in the Talmudic Age (70–640 C. E.)*, Jerusalem, 1984, II:435 f., rejecting modern Jewish historiography since Graetz, which sees the abandonment of the policy as a cause of the revolt, cf. Schürer-Vermes I:535. However, the question can be put the other way round, whether this legend does not disguise an attempt by Hadrian to get rid of the remnant of the cult at Jerusalem (and Garizim).

to the powder keg was imperial suppression of an existing cult, as in the time of Antiochus IV.

The leader of the revolt was called Simon b. Kosiba, as shown by discoveries in the Judaean desert[54] meaning "son of (the) Shepherd." Christian authors, beginning with his contemporary Justin,[55] call him Bar Kokhba, that is "son of (the) Star," in allusion to Num 24:17, which speaks of the rising of "the star of Jacob,"[56] traditionally interpreted in a Messianic sense.[57] Obviously this name corresponds to a reputation.[58] However, the rabbinic sources make a different verbal play and systematically put Bar Koziba, "son of (the) Lie," which indicates a total opposition to his bid. Indeed, Bar Kokhba is sometimes represented as an impious man, who corrupted the Israelites.[59] This rejection goes hand in hand with a decision made about the Hebrew book of 1 Macc, which tells the reconquest of Jerusalem as a holy war, with the Messianic battle of

54. בר כוסבא, which is connected by metathesis with the biblical term כבש "sheep." Cf. Naḥman Avigad *& al.*, "The Expedition to the Judean Desert, 1960," *IEJ* 11 (1961), p. 41–50.

55. Justin, *Apol. I* 31.6 Βαρχωχέβας; the name is correctly explained by Eusebius, *Hist. eccl.* 6.6.2 (ἀστήρ "star").

56. The meaning is clearer in the LXX (ἀνατελεῖ "a star will rise") than in the MT (דרך "will tread"), but the targums (and Rashi) understand it as in the LXX (יקום); this reading is attested also in CD 7:19, 4 QTestim 9-13, 1 QM 11:6-7. Cf. below §III.3c.

57. As he was proclaimed by Aqiba b. Joseph (cf. *YTaan* 4:7, p. 68d), who has, however, remained a teacher of reference in the rab. trad. This error was pardoned because he died as a martyr (*BBer* 61b); it was later interpreted as a transgression of the prohibition to enter Paradise (*i.e.* the Messianic era), cf. chap. V, §II.1.

58. "Son of (the) Shepherd" could also be a Messianic title ("son of David"); a simple vowel change (כשבה) could also make him "son of (the) Ewe Lamb," as Melito of Sardis designates Jesus (Easter Homily, No. 71, SC 123, p. 98). Without further data, and especially in view of the fact that Bar Kokhba's movement did not survive him, it is impossible to say how far the comparison with Jesus could be pressed. The principal difference seems to be that Jesus refused the kingship (John 6), yet he was put to death as "King of the Jews." As we shall see later (chap. V, §V.2) both must have been "Nazoreans," and we have already seen a tradition which associates Jesus with Kokhaba (cf. chap. III, §III). In any case, it is remarkable that early Christian writers, in particular Justin, should have known him by his Messianic title; that implies some contacts, and may explain why Christians regarded "Nazoreans" as heretics only after 135. Similarly, there are strange confusions in the rab. sources: *BSanh* 93b makes the curious statement that B. Kokhba claimed to be the Messiah after a reign of two and a half years, but that he was put to death *by the sages*, for incompetence; Jesus is not named, but such a declaration would apply better to him than to B. Kokhba.

59. Cf. *YTaan* 4:7, p. 68d and the review by Adele Reinhartz, "Rabbinic Perceptions of Simeon bar Kosiba," *JSJ* 20 (1989), p. 171–194. Jesus and his disciples are treated in the same way in the rab. trad., cf. chap. V, §IV.1. The idea that the defense or reconquest of the Temple could be presented as an act of impiety recalls the case of Stephen, cf. chap. VI, §IV.

Emmaus as its most characteristic action.[60] There is reason to think that this book was later set aside as a dangerous charter of Messianic war, because Origen, who gives a list of the books of the Hebrew Bible with their names, mentions only one apocryphal work, the *Book of the House of the Rebels of God;*[61] this is none other than 1 Macc, and as it is the only one mentioned "outside" the canon, it must have been only recently rejected.

Whatever its immediate causes, the war was very harsh and lasted three and a half years, until the battle of Betar, where the Romans had to mobilize reinforcements; there Bar Kokhba fell.[62] Jerusalem was then rebuilt under the imperial name of Aelia and forbidden to Jews and consequently also to Jewish-Christians.[63] Circumcision remained illegal throughout the Empire. Rabbinic tradition has it that judicial autonomy was abolished (*BSanh* 14a) and study of the Torah proscribed in Judaea (*MekhRI* 20:6). After Hadrian's death in 138, Antoninus Pius reallowed

60. With the name of Emmaus are associated of course the two disciples of Luke 24:13 f., who had dreamed of political Messianism (cf. chap. III, §III). It is said (*AbRN* A,14 et B,29, p. 59) that in the days of Yoḥanan b. Zakkai the teachers who came to Yavneh increased their wisdom, but that those who came to Emmaus (B מאום העיר, A מאוס or דמסית, derived from δημόσιον, cf. below) lost it, beginning with the best of Yoḥanan's disciples, Eliezer b. Arakh (who had spoken about the end times, cf. chap. VII, §III.1). In a troubled period of reconstruction, Emmaus may have symbolized the place from which to lead a reconquest by force, in the manner of 1 Macc. This Eliezer b. Arakh was particularly prized by Aqiba, who believed for a time in the Messianism of Bar Kokhba (cf. below, chap. V, §IV.1). There is also mention of "rules of Emmaus," reputed to be dissident (*YShebi* 8:4, p. 38, with a play of words עימעום "obscurely" for עימעוס "Emmaus"). According to *MArak.* 2:4, the trumpets were sounded on feast days in the Temple by the families of Emmaus (who were not priests or Levites), perhaps in memory of the victorious trumpets of the decisive battle of Emmaus in 1 Macc 4:13. According to Yoḥanan b. Zakkai (*YShebi* 9:2), Emmaus was situated where the plain meets the mountains; in Greek it was called Nicopolis, and corresponds to the village of *Amwās*, which was destroyed in the war of 1967. The name Emmaus (Εμμαυς) is already a Greek transcription of חמות or חמאות, meaning hot springs or baths (in Greek δημόσιον, whence the transcription already mentioned); ancient sources speak of abundant waters and healing mud (*BShab* 147b).

61. It gives the remarkable name σαρβηϑσαρβανεελ (cited by Eusebius, *Hist. eccl.* 6.252), which is to be understood as ספר בית סרבני אל (restoring at the beginning σφαρ- for σαρ-): it is a question first of rebels *in the name of* God (resisting Greek persecutions), but later, the flexible construction allows it to be understood as "rebels *against* God," cf. *YTaan* 4:5, p. 68d. Mikhael Avi-Yonah, "The Caesarean Inscription of the 24 Priestly Courses," *Eretz Israel* 7 (1964), p. 24–28, has also shown that the addition of מסרבי מרום "refusing heaven," to the name of Yehoyarib, on the priestly lists found in Palestine, is very pejorative, or at least is so interpreted by the rab. trad., cf. below §I.2; it is precisely to the class of Yoyarib that Mattathias and the Hasmonaean high priests belonged, circles from which the Pharisees kept their distance, cf. chap. III §I.1 and *Search*, p. 276–288.

62. Cf. Schürer-Vermes I:551 f.

63. Whence in particular the disappearance of the Jewish-Christians and their "bishops," cf. chap. V, §III.1.

circumcision for Jews, perhaps as a measure of appeasement on the occasion of the revolt mentioned in the *Historia Augusta*.

This war had no historian comparable to Josephus; it is known only by a few external documents, but that should not lead to the conclusion that it was less serious than the first. In any case, the remarkable fact is that the rabbinic sources speak of it as little as they do of the war of 70, just as they have nothing to say about Judas Maccabaeus, who is not one of the national heroes for them, or about Antiochus IV Epiphanes, who does not figure among the accursed Gentiles of *MSanh* 11:1 f. All that remains is the fast of 9 Ab, which commemorates all the destructions and their victims, but does not give any special place to warrior heroes as such.

2. After the Failure of Bar Kokhba

After this war refugees from Judaea emigrated to Galilee, in particular the disciples of Aqiba, who had believed in Bar Kokhba and was put to death cruelly by the Romans. Sanhedrin and patriarchate had ceased long before the war, at least according to rabbinic tradition, although the discoveries in the Judaean desert show that Bar Kokhba had the title of patriarch,[64] and a certain Batnia b. Mesah, not known to the classical sources, is designated in several documents by a term normally reserved to the patriarch.[65] That would suggest that between the revolt under Trajan and Bar Kokhba the central Jewish authority *in Judaea* was outside the tendency recognized as normative by later tradition, which had its roots in Galilee, as we shall see.

According to *YḤag* 3:1 p. 78c, an assembly of Aqiba's disciples was held without a patriarch in the plain of Beth Rimmon in order to fix the calendar. That constituted an act of major authority, which established the rhythm of the feasts;[66] the absence of Aqiba supposes that the event took

64. נשיא, according to coins dated according to the era of the "liberation of Israel," cf. references in Schürer-Vermes I:544, n. 133. The rab. trad., which has condemned the memory of Bar Kokhba, leaves a gap between the patriarchates of Gamaliel II and Simon II his son, which corresponds roughly to the reign of Hadrian, but it implies that the family was established at Betar (*BSoṭa* 48b, *YTaan* 4:5 p. 69a), and suffered sorely there; this information, which places Betar in the direction of *Beth Jimal* (*Gamala*, in the Gk sources), is questionable from the point of view of geography (but not of literature, cf. Adolphe Neubauer, *La géographie du Talmud*, Paris, M. Lévy, 1868, p. 103 f.), but it underlines the solidarity of the patriarchal family with the victims; in any case the dynasty can hardly be suspected of favoring zealot currents.

65. רבנו, in the letters from the Naḥal Ḥever, cf. N. Avigad, "The Expedition . . ., 1960," p. 3–72, and Pierre Benoit, Joseph T. Milik & Roland de Vaux, *Les grottes de Murabbaʿat* (DJD, 2), Oxford, 1961, p. 124 f.

66. Until the war, the Jewish calendar apparently served as reference for the Christians, at least for Passover, cf. chap. V, §I.2.

place after the war. Beth Rimmon is the name given in 2 Kgs 5:18 to the temple where Naaman the Syrian worshipped; according to Neh 11:29, there was an Ein Rimmon in Judaea. Here the plain of Beth Rimmon must be in Judaea, since the earlier discussion with Hadrian about the Temple was supposed to have taken place there, but the name may have only a symbolic value.

The same group also assembled at an unknown date at Usha,[67] not far from Haifa, with, in particular, Judah b. Ilai, who came from there. He had been a disciple of Aqiba at Bene-Beraq (near Lod), and like him was a virtuoso of the *midrash halakha*, that is to say, the attachment of oral traditions to Scripture (*BSanh* 86a). He had also frequented the school of Tarfon at Lod (*TMeg* 2:8). The latter, a former disciple of Gamaliel II and Yoḥanan b. Zakkai (*TḤag* 3:36), was alive before the war; he too is designated several times by terms normally reserved to the patriarch,[68] and it is said that he used to speak first in the "vineyard of Yavneh" (*MYadaim* 4:3). Gamaliel II was probably dead before Hadrian's reign, and Tarfon may have filled in before the war, at least for the teaching,[69] which would mean that he was the leading figure in the tendency opposed to the Bar Kokhba movement. He was someone of the first rank, and there is reason to identify him with the Tryphon of Justin's *Dialogue*. That does not mean that the dialogue, in its present form, really took place, the less so as the historical Tarfon was an altogether more pugnacious character than Justin's Tryphon. It is enough to allow that the writer wanted, for his apologetic purposes, to bring on stage a learned Jew who was both well known and also not implicated in the rebellion, so that his defeat, or at least his weakness in debate, would be especially significant; in particular, Tryphon declares that he had fled the war.[70]

This assembly of Usha, without a patriarch, invited the Elders of Galilee to come and study with them (*CantR* 2:16, on Cant 2:5); they came from the east, from a distance of 10 to 40 miles, which corresponds to a region extending from Sepphoris to the eastern shore of the Lake. Another version situates the event in the "vineyard of Yavneh" (*BBer* 63b–64a), but the context implies that Judah is really at home, at Usha, and he is presented as "the first to speak." So he is the successor of Tarfon, and with a comparable dignity. The transfer from Yavneh symbolizes

67. Identified with *Hūša*, at the foot of Carmel (co-ord. 163/244); at a distance of two Sabbath walks from Shefarʿam according to *BAbZ* 8b.

68. "R. Tarfon and the Elders," רבן של ישראל, etc., *YYoma* 1:1 p. 38d, *YYeb* 4:12 p. 6b, cf. Gedalyah Alon, *Jews, Judaism and the Classical World*, p. 231 f.

69. As suggested by G. Alon, *The Jews* . . . , II:465, who discusses other hypotheses.

70. Cf. Schürer-Vermes II:378.

a shift of the center of authority and associated institutions. That means that there was an interim arrangement of sorts after the war, but it may have been in opposition. In fact, there is a tradition of migrations of the "Sanhedrin," let us say the patriarchal academy, after the downfall of Jerusalem: Yavneh, Usha, Shefarʿam, Beth-Sheʿarim, Sepphoris, Tiberias (*GenR* §97 on Gen 49:13, p. 1220). There is a longer version of this list in *BRSh* 31a-b, which gives two stages in Jerusalem and a doublet "Yavneh, Usha, Yavneh, Usha." This repetition is not simply an accident in copying, as the whole list gives ten stages, and the context requires this number. Nor does it represent a real shift back and forth of the central institution, which would in that case have had two migrations to Galilee, one before and the other after the war, as some have held.[71] Rather, it is evidence of a long-standing hesitation about the center of moral authority. This does not exclude the possibility that there was already a school at Usha, in fact quite the contrary, since Judah b. Ilai himself studied there with his father (*BMen* 18a), so in this school, and, according to *BBabaB* 28b, among those who visited it was Ishmael b. Elisha, who died before the war and was the renowned head of an exegetical school descended from Hillel and opposed to that of Aqiba.

There are several different signs implying such hesitation between Galilee and Judaea, which have political connotations. One is the apparently long vacancy in the patriarchate in Judaea, and the "interim" authority of Tarfon and Judah b. Ilai, with Galilean associations. Then there is the lack of unanimity concerning Bar Kokhba, regarded by tradition as a renegade (cf. *YTaan* 4:7, p. 68d), which implies a very deep conflict, so that it is all the more remarkable that Aqiba's authority emerged unscathed. Finally, a famous passage of the Passover *Haggada*[72] tells how five masters, including Aqiba and Tarfon, passed one Passover night in hiding at Bene-Beraq, without their families or disciples, discussing the "liberation from Egypt." The scene, which has clear political significance, is to be placed under Hadrian, and there are two notable absentees: Ishmael, who was not in favor of martyrdom,[73] and Gamaliel II. Their absence could be by chance, but in the case of the latter, there is a comparable but *opposite* episode (*TPasḥa* 10:12): the patriarch Gamaliel passed an entire Passover

71. Since then Heinrich H. Graetz, *Geschichte*, IV:131, followed by W. Bacher, *Die Agada der Tannaiten*, p. 233 f.

72. The narrative accompanying the rabbinic Passover ritual, discussed in chap. VII, §I.2 and §II.3.

73. Because it is written to observe the laws "so that you may live" (Deut 30:16), and not to die; so observance is to be suspended if it involves danger of death, cf. *Sifra aḥaré mot* 13:14.

night at Lod studying with the Elders the *halakha* of Passover, that is to say the precepts strictly bound up with the celebration of the feast; in the context of this narrative, such study is an exclusive obligation.[74]

The hesitations which we have glimpsed mask oppositions: first Yoḥanan against Gamaliel, that is, two different forms of submission to Rome; then Gamaliel against Aqiba, diverging on the revolt against Rome. It is not *a priori* surprising that conflicts more or less disguised should break out at a time of crisis. Zealots and Pharisees may have been violently opposed on the ground, but Josephus noted that they were very close in fundamental ideas and customs (*Ant.* 18 §23). This remains true if the meaning of "Pharisee" is widened, since according to *J.W.* 2 §142 the Essenes had to commit themselves to renouncing all politico-military action; such an oath, even if given heightened significance by Josephus, was certainly not superfluous. Politically speaking, two main currents can be distinguished. The adherents of the first, from Judas the Galilean to Bar Kokhba, were intransigent nationalists, opposed to the Romans and even more to Roman influence ("Hellenization"). Those in the second camp, from Hillel to the assembly of Usha, including also Yoḥanan b. Zakkai and the dynasty of Gamaliel, were just as nationalistic, especially in comparison with Josephus, but, despite major doctrinal differences, they were non-political, in the sense of not seeking independence at all costs but only a tranquil vassalage. Thus, after the revolt under Trajan, the house of Gamaliel was permitted to continue teaching Greek *because it was close to the Roman authorities* (*TSoṭa* 15:8-9); that is the precise moment when that dynasty went into eclipse, while the Bar Kokhba party was rising to power.

3. Developments in Galilee

Another episode at Usha gives us an even more precise idea of the issues at stake within the body which rejected the war. According to an account in *BHor* 13b–14a, Simon II son of Gamaliel II was patriarch, Nathan president of the academy (or the tribunal) and Meir master (or

74. It is certainly possible to see how studying the *halakha* and discussing the deliverance from Egypt, even in the sense of immediate political problems *(agada)*, are two complementary private activities, associating rite and meaning; so judge later commentators, cf. *Tosefta kifshuṭah* 4:655 f., and Daniel Goldschmidt, *The Passover Haggadah. Its Sources and History*, Jerusalem, 1977[3], p. 70 f. However, the separation of the participants into two groups suggests rather a controversy, even a conflict; further, according to an opinion attributed to Gamaliel, the Messiah would arise only from total ruin (*BSanh* 97b), which is incompatible with the activism of Bar Kokhba and Aqiba. On the importance of the deliverance from Egypt in the Passover ritual, cf. chap. VII, §II.2 and 3. The feature

expert). One day there was a quarrel over precedence, and the last two, reckoning that they had been humiliated by the patriarch, decided to ridicule him on the following day by revealing in public his ignorance of a whole tractate of oral tradition, so that he would be deposed and they themselves promoted respectively to the posts of patriarch and president of the court. The plot was foiled, and they were expelled. Standing outside the door, they communicated with the interior of the hall by throwing notes inside, until those within exclaimed: "Here we are inside, and the Torah is outside." The conflict was finally resolved, but things must have been difficult, since, among the "decrees of Usha" there is a prohibition against excommunicating an Elder (*YMoedQ* 3:1 p. 81d).[75]

Beneath the picturesque exterior of this narrative, which puts everything on the level of personalities, lies a major event. In fact, Simon was an outsider to the academy: he was ignorant of the Torah, and there was already a president. The conflict shows that he was attempting to take charge of the institution by strengthening his own position. Other passages show that very often he quotes other sages[76] and that his decisions are always in line with the debates in his court.[77] One inference which has been made is that he was exceptionally humble, which is actually said by his son Judah the Prince (*BBabaM* 84b). However, those whom he quotes are always contemporaries, and never his masters or the Elders, whereas he emphasizes with great respect the importance of the school led by his father, Gamaliel II (*BSoṭa* 49b). Finally, in comparison with Simon b. Yoḥai, another major disciple of Aqiba, he is "like a fox faced with a lion," which is a sign of ignorance (cf. *MAb* 4:15 and *YShab* 10:7, p. 12c). To be more exact, Simon b. Gamaliel was weak in the *oral tradition*: the plot mentioned earlier was meant to show his ignorance of the tractate *Uqṣin*, which deals with the purity of inedible parts of food items, a subject both subtle and lacking any scriptural basis, and apparently unknown also in his father's school.

Obviously, that does not mean that he was ignorant in all fields, as other facts show. According to *MShab* 1:3, one should not read by the light of an oil lamp on the Sabbath (Friday evening), so as not to be

common to both tendencies is that the whole night is occupied, which has the effect of excluding other festivities, cf. the *afikoman*, chap. VII, §I.2.

75. *YBik* 3:3, p. 65c, gives a different account, which also shows resistance to the installation of Simon b. Gamaliel.

76. *MBer* 6:9, *MBabaM* 8:8; the witness of the *Tosefta* is significant by reason of its frequency: *TBer* 5:2, *TMaasSh* 3:18, *TSuk* 2:2, *TYeb* 10:16, *TKetub* 6:10, *TKel-BQ* 4:2, 5:4.

77. *YBabaB* 10:2, p. 17d.

tempted to bend down to soak the wick once more in the oil and reactivate the flame. However, according to *TShab* 1:12, Simon b. Gamaliel permitted the children (of his school) to do so, in order to prepare the scripture readings for the next day, and apparently he had this custom from his father's school (cf. *BShab* 13a); later justifications of this different custom try to prove that it is reasonable,[78] which makes it hard to understand why it has since disappeared. Here too, the issue is the primacy of the written word, or even perhaps an environment in which the Sabbath strictly speaking did not begin until the morning, which would be a further point in common with the Essenes. Likewise, in a controversy over the use of unleavened bread prepared by Samaritans, he said that "for every precept *(miṣwa)* which the Samaritans observe, they are more careful than Israel" (*TPes* 1:15), which is another way of saying that he appreciated their *biblical* exactness. In another context (*TTer* 4:12), he said that the Samaritans are "like Israel," whereas Judah the Prince would later say that they are "like the Gentiles." The change of opinion regarding the Samaritans may not be entirely unconnected with the crisis over the accession of the emperor Septimius Severus, but it could mask a difference of criterion: for Simon, Israel is defined in terms of obedience to the Bible, for Judah, in terms of oral tradition alone. These slight indications suggest that Gamaliel and his successors, who came from Jerusalem, tended to be more biblical than the strictly Galilean circles, and that this was a cause of friction.

The other actors in the episode at Usha came from different horizons. Meir was regarded as Aqiba's most faithful disciple (*BSanh* 86a), the first of the five "southern masters" (*BYeb* 62b); so it is significant that in the assembly he was the academic authority. Nathan, president of the court, was the son of the exilarch of Babylonia, which is noteworthy. Before the war he had studied with Tarfon and Ishmael b. Elisha (*TZeb* 10:13), and later he opposed the fixing of the calendar by the authorities in the Diaspora, as proposed by Ḥanania, who mistrusted the patriarchate and regarded it as compromised with the Romans (*YNed* 6:8, p. 39b). Eventually, once Simon b. Gamaliel was in a stronger position, he carried on the struggle against the exilarch in order to maintain the privilege of the land of Israel (*BBer* 63a). In different circumstances, Gamaliel II had also demanded that the patriarch be the final authority in the matter, even if others were more expert in matters of astronomy (*MRSh* 2:7 f.).[79] For

78. Cf. *Tosefta kifshuṭah* 3:10.

79. According to a *baraita* (*BRSh* 22a), he had been discredited over an affair similar to sighting the new moon.

obvious reasons, the fixing of the monthly calendar or the introduction of an intercalated month has always been a delicate problem, since it involves a central authority: in earlier times, when the monthly signals were sent out from Jerusalem, there was a conflict over competence between priests and Pharisees (*MRSh* 1:7).

The assembly of Usha therefore represents a crossroads, immediately after the difficult period under Hadrian, with a certain competition for power. Aqiba's successors, to whom the *Mishnah* and related sources are favorable, at first joined forces with the Galileans, then with a branch of a Babylonian patriarchate. On the other hand, it was proving more difficult to integrate the traditional patriarchate descended from Yavneh, all the more as it had been suspended for a score or more of years. It is reported that Simon b. Gamaliel[80] had had to spend a long time in hiding from the Romans. He himself says (*BSoṭa* 49b) that of the thousand boys who used to study in his father's house[81] there remained only himself and a cousin who had fled; however, as we have been able to see, that was not the only cause of the "vacancy," since his father Gamaliel II had previously had difficulties at Yavneh, linked to the rise to power of the activist party.

Behind these personal conflicts, there was opposition on several levels; the political aspect is certainly the easiest to see, but it was not necessarily the most important. The question of the primacy of the oral tradition also played a role; we have seen the patriarch in difficulties on this point. One of Aqiba's great specialties had been to show, with the help of very subtle hermeneutical rules, that the written and the oral Torah were one, despite apparent differences;[82] he even wanted to reform certain non-biblical usages in force, such as the direct payment of the tithe to the priests (*BYeb* 86b, *baraita*; cf. Deut 26:13). Josephus had already said that Pharisees and Galileans (the fourth party) had the same ideas, especially with regard to the primacy of the ancestral traditions. In fact, Aqiba's disciples who had got away from the war joined forces with the Elders of Galilee, apparently without major problems, which implies a fundamental similarity. Even if Bar Kokhba was a distant successor of Judas the Galilean or even of John of Gischala, he had been disavowed

80. *BTaan* 29a, which bears the name of "Gamaliel," so his father, but the context requires the correction, cf. discussion in G. Alon, *The Jews . . .* , II:667.

81. "There were 1000 boys, 500 studying the Torah, 500 studying the Greek wisdom"; no doubt to be understood, according to the context and parallels, as meaning that they were studying the Greek language and literature, cf. Lieberman II:102, n. 18.

82. Thus he was reducing the difference between Scripture and oral tradition. In *BZeb* 13a, in connection with a certain custom, Tarfon observes that he has received it as tradition, without explanation, but that Aqiba has found it by examining a (biblical) verse.

by the refugees and presumably not followed by the Galileans who stayed put. The latter were certainly not ignoramuses: the school of Usha was in existence at the time of Yavneh. It is also said that Jose ha-Gelili, one of the great figures of his generation, born and trained in Galilee, succeeded in stumping Aqiba and Tarfon in argument, when he came to study at Yavneh around 120 (*BZeb* 57a). It is interesting to note that he was very close to Aqiba, but did not allow scriptural arguments, in which he showed that he was faithful to his origins.

To sum up, Jewish Galilee had its own culture, which can already be identified in the days of the young Herod and which persisted long afterwards. It was Babylonian in origin, by virtue of continual immigrations. Josephus gives more attention to its activist fringe, which was, all the same, rooted in fertile soil. This was the cradle of rabbinic Judaism, but two other elements which contributed to its growth came rather from Judaea. One was a considerable effort to combine the written text and oral tradition, that is to say, in fact, to make possible the fusion of several groups at a time of crisis; the *Mishnah* as it was eventually edited contains relatively few direct citations of Scripture, but shows a discreet dependence on the Bible. The other element is the care taken to gather and preserve memories of the Temple and especially of Jerusalem. The rabbinic sources on the whole do not express much sympathy for Herod's Temple and show no interest in any resumption of the cult after the war of 70. These memories only became important after Bar Kokhba's failure, at the moment when Jerusalem had become inaccessible. It was the sign of a major development, as we shall see (chap. V, §IV.1).

4. Rural Galilee and Babylonia

For defining the characteristic features of the rural Jewish environment of the Galilean Tannaites the most important document is the mosaic inscription discovered in 1974 in a synagogue near Reḥob, in the Jordan valley, some 10 km south of Beth-Shean. It dates from the 6th or 7th century and contains 29 lines of text. It consists of several passages not attested elsewhere and also large extracts from the *Talmud* (*YDem* 2:1, p. 22c), which was compiled only two centuries earlier, so that this very well-preserved inscription is by far its oldest and surest witness.[83] According to these texts, Jewish Galilee is surrounded by zones (around Caesarea Maritima, Sebaste, Beth-Shean, Hippos, Nawa, Paneas and

83. Publication and detailed discussion by Yaaqob Sussman, "A Halakhic Inscription from the Beth-Shean Valley," *Tarbiz* 43 (1973), p. 88–158 and id., "The Boundaries of Eretz-Israel," *Tarbiz* 45 (1976), p. 213–257.

Tyre) which are not strictly Jewish for the purposes of precepts connected with the land (tithes, Levitical contributions, etc.). But not all cases are alike: the zones of Caesarea and Beth-Shean had been dispensed from precepts tied to the land by Judah the Prince (*YDem ibid.*), so around 200, then some obligations later returned; Sebaste, a Samaritan territory, is mentioned only in the inscription. The four other zones mentioned are, on the contrary, external to Galilee proper and even to Palestine, but the presence of Jews there caused some precepts to be reintroduced, which was equivalent to regarding them as belonging, at least in some respects, to the land of Israel, a term which therefore has a degree of elasticity.

A more general setting is, however, defined in terms of a "domain of those who have come up from Babylon."[84] This notion defines a wide perimeter, by reference to Ashqelon, Akko, Paneas,[85] Reqem in Trachonitis (near Bostra), and Reqem of the Torrent (Petra, with the *W. Mūsa*). Such a domain does not coincide with the territory of the repatriated exiles in Neh 11:21-36, which comprises only Judah and Benjamin, and even less with the Judaea of the Maccabean reconquest, which was bounded on the west by Emmaus and on the south by Beth-Zur and Idumaea (1 Macc 4:1-35). However, if we look at the many-sided activity of Judas Maccabaeus and his companions, besides the actual restoration of the Temple and of Judaea proper, we see that it extended over the whole of Palestine and large sectors of Transjordania (1 Macc 5, etc.), which is more like the "domain" of the inscription. The Maccabees' activity centered on the defense of Jewish communities spread over this territory, particularly in the Hellenistic cities (Ptolemais-Akko, Scythopolis-Beth-Shean, etc.). Our text confirms that, throughout this area, the Jewish communities consisted of returnees from Babylonia and not of refugees from Judaea. The size that it assigns to this domain, which can be taken to be the *practical* extent of the "land of Israel," is linked to the possibility of observing the precepts tied to the land, particularly the tithe, which, as we shall see, has a high symbolic value. If Babylonia is then taken as a metaphor for the Seleucid and Parthian kingdoms, we are back with what was said earlier about the circumstances in which Antiochus III issued his famous charter. So these migrations are to be regarded as a permanent and widespread flow of *civilian* settlers, who, ever since the Persian period, had been establishing themselves in zones of cultivation.

The text of our inscription describing the "domain" of these migrants cannot, however, be very old, for it uses Roman terminology. Fur-

84. עולי בבל.
85. And/or קסריון "little Caesarea," *i.e.* Caesarea Philippi.

ther, it defines this domain as the land of *Israel*. The use of this term is significant, for, even if the domain is geographically comparable to Herod's kingdom, it makes no reference to it: for one thing, Herod is execrated, and in any case, there is no trace of the name of his kingdom, Judaea. The perimeter of reference is really that of Joshua's conquest,[86] that is, of "those who came up from Egypt."[87] However, the rabbinic redefinition of the zones where the precepts connected with the land are in force, is expressed in terms not of conquest, as in Joshua's day, but of acquisition: for those who have come back from Babylonia, the lands which have been *bought* have thereby become "holy," a long, slow process. There is even an associated controversy, whether a piece of land thus promoted loses its holiness if it is resold to a Gentile (*TDem* 5:21). For obvious commercial reasons, and also because of the variety of produce of the soil, this debate was not purely theoretical, but its solution depended on the place,[88] which implies some slight differences of tradition, probably corresponding to different waves of immigrants.

Geographically, rabbinic Galilee comprises Upper and Lower Galilee, the boundary passing through Kfar Ḥanania (northwest of Safed), and also the "ring of Tiberias" (*MShebi* 9:2). It thus appears bounded on the east by the line of the Jordan, which also corresponds to the biblical borders of Naphthali and Issachar. Because of this biblical background, the territory east of the Jordan (including Paneas, Hippos, Nawa) has a slightly more questionable status, since Num 35:10 states: "When you have crossed the Jordan. . . ." These are, however, artificial effects of relating the immigration from Babylon to Joshua's conquest. If they are omitted as secondary considerations, the perspective becomes simpler. With regard to a strict geographical definition, Jewish Galilee goes north to Paneas and east as far as the Golan, called "Jewish Syria," cf. *TShebi* 4:11; it is thus very similar to Josephus' Galilee (*J.W.* 3 §35 f.). However, in the south it does not include the territory of Sebaste, which would tend to show that Samaria never received Babylonian immigrants and that it was regarded as a Gentile land, which is worthy of note.

86. In particular, it comprises only part of Upper Galilee and so is notably smaller than the territory sketched in Num 34:7-12 and Deut 1:6-7, which goes as far as the Euphrates. Since it is derived from the Pentateuch, this latter is strictly speaking the domain of those who have come up from Egypt (in reality the Transeuphratene of the exiles), whereas for the rab. trad. (*TMaasSh* 2:16; *TBabaQ* 8:19) Joshua's conquests constitute the "domain of the Land of Israel according to the Writings (שבכתובין)."

87. עולי מצרים, cf. *MShebi* 6:1.

88. Cf. Saul Lieberman, "The Halakhic Inscription from the Beth-Shean Valley," *Tarbiz* 45 (1975), p. 54–63.

This way of regarding Samaria has no historical basis, despite Josephus' efforts to place the Samaritan schism as early as possible, for, according to 2 Macc 5:22 f., as we have seen, the Samaritans of Garizim and the Jews still formed a single nation at the time of the Maccabean crisis. In other words, the inscription reflects a situation well after the schism. As mentioned above, the Pharisee Simon b. Gamaliel appreciated the biblical observance of the Samaritans, whereas the Galilean tradition proper regarded it as negligible. Viewed in this light, the inscription, which concerns only those who have returned from Babylonia, is strictly Galilean.

From these considerations we can draw the following conclusions. First, the Samaritans are absent, and the text deals with the land of Israel in the sense of stable oral traditions of Babylonian origin; so the older problem of the relation between Jews and Samaritans concerned Jerusalem. Secondly, the extreme importance of Galilee and the Golan, with some 200 localities, shows the large number of rural settlements, in which slight differences of customs were due to various waves of immigrants, corresponding to "those who came up from Babylonia." Thirdly, the important Hellenistic cities (Ptolemais, Scythopolis, Hippos, Sepphoris, Caesarea) contained Jewish urban minorities, but these were less tied to the land and so more like exiles.[89]

III – Final Remarks. Geography

When the *Mishnah* was published, Jewish Galilee had certainly had a Babylonian culture for four hundred years. It persisted for a further two hundred years until the 4th century, when the local Talmud, originating in Tiberias and Caesarea,[90] shows the same spirit as the Babylonian Talmud, both differing profoundly from anything in Hellenistic Jewish literature.

89. That may throw light on the fact that Peter the Galilean was a foreigner in Caesarea, cf. chap. I, §II.1.

90. Saul Lieberman, *The Talmud of Caesarea. Jerushalmi Tractate Nezikin* (Tarbiz Suppl.), Jerusalem, 1931, has shown that a part of the *Yerushalmi* comes from an important school at Caesarea Maritima, to be distinguished from Caesarea Philippi. This latter ("Little Caesarea") is normally identified as Paneas, following *Ant.* 18 §28; but in the talmudic sources, the two names are found side by side (cf. A. Neubauer, *Géographie*, p. 238), and they may have been two neighboring places. A school can change localities but keep its name (cf. *supra* the "vineyard of Yavneh"). Recent excavations at the ruined village of *Qaṣrin*, on the Golan, have uncovered the remains of a synagogue and associated school. The name of *Qaṣrin* is significant: it does not come from the local Arabic (*Qaṣrēn* could mean "two castles," but that does not correspond to anything in the area); on the other hand, it would suit a talmudic *Qaisarin* (= Caesarea); a near by valley has kept the name of *Yahudiyeh* ("the Jews").

It was true earlier, as shown in the person of Nathan, the Babylonian whom we saw as president of the academy of Usha in the Tannaite period, and who bears a marked resemblance in type to Hillel. In the first two centuries of our era, there were reciprocal influences with Judaea, but over all it was an environment in which oral traditions were dominant. The prototype is the Nehemiah of the second expedition (Neh 13): he too came "from Babylonia," with very precise views on the Sabbath and separation from foreigners, as well as a keenness to rebuild Jerusalem on a model of separation. The influences do not exclude tensions. Yoḥanan b. Zakkai, as we have seen, spent eighteen years as a young man not far from Sepphoris, around the time when Herod Antipas restored the city and granted it self-government (*Ant.* 18 §27). He had a disciple, Ḥanina b. Dosa, who stayed there, but it is said that during all his time as a teacher, he was asked only about two very particular points relating to the Sabbath, and a later tradition states that he lamented the contempt which the Galileans had for the Torah.[91] Clearly, like Josephus, he had little liking for the zealot spirit, but the meaning of this saying is that the Galilean movement proper (political) was only an unfortunate offshoot, and that Galilee could do better.

A few remarks on geography to conclude this overview. The stages of the migration of the Sanhedrin to Galilee have a certain significance (*BRSh* 31a–b). At the beginning, Usha, Shefarʿam, Beth-Sheʿarim and Sepphoris are rather to the west; these movements correspond to the Tannaitic period, when there were links with the Roman world. The final stage, Tiberias, the most southerly point of the itinerary (Isa 26:5 and 29:4 are cited), corresponds to the later Talmudic period, after Judah the Prince. This city is more central for the region around the Lake, comprising the Golan, Upper Galilee and the eastern part of the plain of Esdraelon. This is the region where abundant remains of synagogues from the Roman and Byzantine periods have been found. The region also corresponds to the zone, east and north of Sepphoris, from which the Elders of Galilee came in response to the invitation of Judah b. Ilai. It corresponds further to the areas in revolt which Josephus had to deal with and to Herod's operations against the "brigands." It is indeed what we could call the heart of Jewish Galilee, open to Babylonian influence, on both sides of the Lake of Tiberias. It is rural and in the Promised Land, whence the extreme importance of the precepts tied to the land (tithes, sabbatical year, etc.), with which, incidentally, the *Mishnah* begins. Its main line of

91. שנאת התורה, *YShab* 16:8 p. 15d; on the difficulties of this passage, cf. Jacob Neusner, *A Life of Yohanan ben Zakkai, Ca. 1–80 C. E.* (Studia Post-Biblica, 6), Leiden, 1970[2], p. 47–53.

communication is not towards Ptolemais or Phoenicia, but towards Damascus (and the Fertile Crescent), which is appropriate. This Jewish Galilee is clearly also that of Jesus (chap. III, §III),[92] with the exception of Tiberias, which did not previously belong to it.

This city had a strange history. Despite his reconstruction and embellishment of Sepphoris, the former capital, Herod Antipas founded Tiberias around 17–20,[93] over a cemetery, in contradiction with Jewish law, and apparently settled there a mixed population, which included Jews forbidden to emigrate, gave them tax advantages, and made it his capital (*Ant.* 18 §37). Later rabbinic tradition mentions a synagogue and visits by Gamaliel II. Josephus might, however, be tendentious, since he mentions the tombs only in *J.W.* 2 §168, and in the *Antiquities* and the *Life* he seeks to discredit the Galilean rebels as bad Jews. But not all was of his invention, since around the middle of the 2nd century Simon b. Yoḥai, attracted by the thermal baths of nearby Ḥama, proceeded to purify the place, against some opposition. The narrative (*YShebi* 9:1, p. 38d) shows however that it was not a cemetery that he purified but the scattered remains of former burial places. So Josephus exaggerated his information: when Tiberias was founded, there was no cemetery belonging to a large center of population but just some tombs, and any house might be suspected of being built over one. A century later, the reawakening of the suspicion and its resolution by Simon b. Yoḥai presuppose a development of construction on new terrain. Certain passages (*YMeg* 1:1 p. 70a) keep for Tiberias the biblical name of Raqat (Josh 19:35, between Ḥamat and Kinneret). Besides its warm springs, the place was very attractive, though not necessarily for a city. In all likelihood, Antipas created Tiberias as an act of local politics, by settling in a place both central for the Galileans and also symbolic, if the graves were those of heroes. In fact, he already had a newly rebuilt capital, so he must have been trying to place in the heart of traditional rural Galilee an outpost of Roman obedience flaunted inappropriately and aggressively, emphasized by the name of Caesar as well as by its emplacement over the graves. That could explain the insuperable opposition between the town and the neighboring countryside which defeated Josephus even as he sought the support of the Galileans. In the next century, after many revolutions, less ambitious sages succeeded where he had failed.

92. But Nazareth, near Sepphoris, poses a particular literary problem.

93. According to coins of Trajan's time, whereas *Ant.* 18 §26–28 speaks of it only after the arrival of Pilate in 26.

Chapter V

Nazoreans and Jews in Palestine

In our survey of the Galilee that Jesus knew (chap. III, §III), we have already suggested some comparisons between the native environment of the first Christians, the Essenes, and the rabbinic sources. It is time now to discuss them more systematically by looking at certain institutions. In the last chapter we saw that the Tannaites of Galilee formed a network of little groups, deeply rooted in the countryside and in very ancient local traditions. The next step is to analyze the characteristic features of their religious culture, which, as we saw with regard to Hillel, was originally quite marginal; it also had a close kinship with that of the Essenes. After that, we shall see how the Tannaites and their successors took steps to distance themselves from the Christians, or more precisely the Jewish-Christians. Finally, we shall see that the type of Christianity in question was only indirectly linked with the environment that produced the NT, namely by way of the successors of James.

I – The Environment in which the *Mishnah* Arose

Although strongly rooted in tradition, the Tannaitic environment that produced the *Mishnah* underwent some notable developments around the turn of the first and second centuries. In this section we shall try to trace them and to seek their causes. To this end, we shall develop further the analogies with the Essenes which have so far been only hinted at. Their true significance comes into focus over the whole matter of purity. In particular we shall look at two institutions which are especially well defined: the brotherhoods and proselyte baptism.

1. The Ideal of the Brotherhoods (ḥabura)

Rabbinic tradition speaks of an organization of brotherhoods with exceptionally strict religious requirements. This organization is revered as an ideal, which has left many traces in Mishnaic legislation, but it is not recommended, since by its sectarian structure it introduces an element of selection into the heart of the people. We will show here that these brotherhoods were originally of Essene type, but that they came to be regarded rather as schools or academies. This development, whose precise stages are not always clear, is itself the sign of a change of outlook: from a sectarian model of renewal, to the direction of a whole people.

We begin by looking at a few texts which immediately introduce some precise distinctions. According to *MḤag* 2:7, the clothes of the "people of the land" contaminate a "Pharisee" with an impurity like that of the Gentiles.[1] The "Pharisee" here is one who is separate from "the people of the land." These terms define two quite distinct categories of Jews, and it is clear that these "Pharisees" are rather different from those whom Josephus describes and to whom he says he belongs.[2] In the rabbinic context, they are really to be identified with a particular type called *ḥaber*,[3] that is a member of a special kind of brotherhood *(ḥabura)*,[4] on

1. These clothes are regarded as if "polluted by someone who has a seminal flow" (זב, cf. Lev 15:1 f.), which is a serious impurity (אב טומאה, cf. *MZab* 5:1). On the other hand, *BShab* 14b indicates, among eighteen decrees issued in the 1st cent. (*apud* Ḥananya b. Ḥizqya), that the Gentiles have the same impurity as one who has a seminal flow (this impurity not being linked, however, to any particular contamination, even from a corpse, cf. *TOhol* 1:4). So, in a certain respect, the impurity of the "people of the land" is of the same degree as that of the Gentile.

2. He implies that it is a question of the majority of the people, cf. chap. III, §IV. According to *BPes* 49b, a man who marries the daughter of a "people of the land" is cursed (with reference to Deut 27:21 on bestiality); the curse falls on anyone at all, but the context shows that it is a question of "disciples of sages" (תלמידי חכמים), who are thus closely related to *ḥaberim*. The same passage indicates that the "peoples of the land" detest them even more than the nations detest Israel, which is meant to be a superlative. On the other hand, no text compares the "peoples of the land" to *minim* ("sectaries," Christians), cf. below §2.

3. In Arabic, the term *ḥabr*, meaning "non-Islamic religious authorities" (particularly the priests of the Bible), has probably come in by way of Judaizing channels. The expression "people of the land" (עם הארץ, usually understood by deriving עם from the root *ʿmm*) is in reality rather strange (why "people"?), but, still in Arabic, the word *ʿām* (distinct from *ʿamm* "paternal uncle") designates the layperson, as such lacking competence in religious matters. In Hebrew, the transcription would also be עם; perhaps there is a homonym in the background.

4. Hannah K. Harrington, "Did the Pharisees Eat Ordinary Food in a State of Ritual Purity?" *JSJ* 26 (1995), p. 42–54, follows and clarifies Gedalya Alon, *Jews, Judaism and the Classical World: Studies in Jewish History in the Time of the Second Temple and Talmud*, Jerusalem, Magnes, 1977, p. 219, and Jacob Neusner, *From Politics to Piety: The Emergence of Pharisaic Judaism*, Hoboken, Ktav, 1979, p. 47 f., who conclude that the 1st century Pharisees ate as if they were priests ("pure food club"; but the argument, centered on rabbinic sources, really has to do with the brotherhoods and not with the Pharisees in the sense of FJ; Ed Parish Sanders, *Jewish Law from Jesus to the Mishna*, Philadelphia,

which the sources provide a few scattered details.[5] The most characteristic passage is *TDem* 2:2 f., which divides the people into three classes:[6] 1. the "people of the land," who observe the Sabbatical year and the food prohibitions, but do not regularly give tithes and do not observe Levitical purity; 2. the one worthy of confidence *(ne'eman)*, who is scrupulous about tithes;[7] 3. the *ḥaber*, who goes even further and eats in a state of Levitical purity, even if he is not a priest. This gradation shows that the *ḥaberim* constitute a sort of élite, who go beyond what the Law demands of all; however—and this is important—it is in reference to them that the norms are determined. These three categories eat separately, although it is theoretically enough, for the strictest, to make sure that the tithe has been properly separated or even to begin the operation again, which can be done while the meal continues.[8] In other words, a very high value is placed upon table fellowship (cf. chap. VII, §IV.2).

In order to enter one of the two higher classes, the candidate had to pronounce a solemn vow before a *ḥabura*, a tribunal of three qualified persons or a recognized master.[9] As the second class had no organization of its own, it seems to have been only a preparatory phase for the state of *ḥaber*, a sort of novitiate lasting a certain time, in which the candidate no longer belonged to the "people of the land" but had not yet become integrated into the brotherhood. This period, devoted to study, began with an initial vow, or declaration of intent, and concluded with the final admission. The texts acquired their present form long after the institution had disappeared and they are far from perfectly clear, but this process of admission seems to have consisted of two phases: first, access to a certain

---

Trinity Press International, 1990, p. 209, raises some objections, but without asking about the nature of these sources. In particular, he states (p. 174 f.), relying also on the NT, that the extension of the principles of purity to the profane world did not come from the Tannaites or their predecessors, but results directly from the Bible (Lev 11:2, etc.). That is true, but a distinction has to be made between marginal reforming groups (including those that lie behind the NT) and the national law of Judaea.

5. Cf. Ephraim E. Urbach, *The Sages; Their Concepts and Beliefs*, Jerusalem, 1973, p. 583 f.

6. Cf. Chaim Rabin, *Qumran Studies* (Scripta Judaica, 2), Oxford University Press, 1957, p. 16 f. The three classes are called עם הארץ, נאמן, חבר.

7. The passage summarized here comes from a tractate of the *Mishnah* entirely devoted to cases of doubtful tithes *(Demai)*, which shows their importance, especially since there is no tractate on circumcision (nor on Pentecost, cf. chap. VII, §III.1).

8. The central character of the meal for the *ḥaber* gives a very precise meaning to the rather vague rabbinic notion of "*ḥabura* meal," discussed in connection with the eucharist, chap. II, §II.2.

9. Cf. *Tosefta kifshuṭah* 1:210 f.

garment (called "wings")[10] and to pure solid foods, then access to another garment and to liquids. This gradation corresponds to the fact that only liquid foods are liable to impurity (cf. Lev 11:38), and so are more difficult to consume in a state of Levitical purity; thus it is logical that the probation period before being allowed access to them was longer. Each of these phases lasts a year in principle, at least according to the opinion of Beth Hillel. Every Israelite can be a candidate, provided true signs of piety are shown. Conversely, grave faults can entail exclusion, or at least return to one or other phase of the novitiate. Certain occupations are incompatible with candidature, in particular that of tax collector.[11]

These arrangements are on the whole remarkably similar to the system described by Josephus for admission among the Essenes (chap. VII, §IV.). They are similar also to the stipulations of the Qumran *Community Rule* 1 QS 6:13-23: period of probation, oaths before the community,[12] and access by stages—first solid foods, then liquids—to the community

10. Probable allusion to Num 15:38 f., in respect of the fringes (ציצית) put on the hems of garments (כנפי בגדיכם) as a reminder of the commandments.

11. Perhaps because he handles images (effigies), or because he is really a collaborator with the occupying power; both aspects are present in the question on the tribute due to Caesar (Matt 22:15-22). According to Matt 18:16, the tax collector is classed with the Gentile, as is apparent also in many other passages.

12. Represented by the רבים "many," which Jean Carmignac, "HRBYM: Les "Nombreux" ou les "Notables"?" *RQ* 7 (1971), p. 575–586, prefers to understand qualitatively ("rabbis, notables") rather than quantitatively ("nombreux"), cf. chap. VI, §III.4 on the possible origins of the title "rabbi." For the rabbinic sources, we are following Saul Lieberman, "The Discipline in the So-Called Dead Sea Manual of Discipline," *JBL* 71 (1952), p. 199–206, who draws particular attention to a passage in which רבים is equivalent to חברים, and draws the general conclusion that חבורה is practically identical with the יחד of 1 QS, allowing for a few controversies which suppose a certain variety of more or less rival groups. Laurence H. Schiffman, *Reclaiming the Dead Sea Scrolls*, Philadelphia & Jerusalem, The Jewish Publication Society, 1994, p. 81 f. and 104 f., curiously ignores Lieberman's study (which is important, though little known), and concentrates on differences of customs in order to isolate each group (Essenes, Qumran community, *ḥaberim*), but without giving a clear definition of what he understands by "Judaism," which makes it impossible to interpret the classic problem of internal controversies (and *a fortiori* of excommunications) in the rab. trad., which assume the fusion of different brotherhoods (cf. chap. III, §II.1). For his part, Ellis Rivkin, "Defining the Pharisees: The Tannaitic Sources," *HUCA* 40 (1969), p. 205–249, observes the similarities between these *ḥaberim* and the Pharisees before 70 (or more precisely the פרושים of the rabbinic sources, very different from the Pharisees of FJ, cf. chap. III, §IV), and concludes that it is these latter who fixed the rules for individual pietists *(ḥasidim)* who wanted to become *ḥaberim*, but that they were not themselves members of the brotherhoods; the distinction is rather artificial and becomes untenable when the whole picture is put side by side with the Essenes. Cf. also Geza Vermes, *Discovery in the Judean Desert*, New York/Tournai/Paris/Rome, 1956, p. 52, and Chaim Rabin, *Qumran Studies*, Oxford, 1957.

meal, named precisely "purity."[13] The slight differences which occur are no greater than those involved in the controversies which fill rabbinic tradition.[14] We note, however, that the profane foods of the brotherhoods are not specified, whereas we have seen the importance of bread and wine for the Essenes (chap. II, §II.2). Still, there are traces of a similar importance in the rabbinic system as well, since the blessings over bread and wine are special (they are not made over wheat or grapes), and it is obligatory to wash the hands before a meal in which bread will be served (*BBer* 50b).

On the other hand, the purification rituals of the *ḥaber* are not clearly mentioned as such. It is not difficult to imagine that "eating in a state of Levitical purity" implies a purification before each meal, but it is not stated that it has to be a total immersion. Hand washing is expressly mentioned in *MErub* 1:10, but entirely unconnected with the situation of the *ḥaber*, although it is prescribed even for profane foods.[15] Baptisms in the proper sense, marking the stages of admission to the brotherhood, are not directly mentioned, but a passage, also not connected in context with the *ḥaber*, shows that there were steps in the admission to various degrees of sacred things, and a general principle is stated: "Whoever performs an immersion without having been admitted [to a given degree], is as if he had not done it."[16] Here, then, is a trace of a system of baptisms, in which the rite marks a candidate's formally recognized status.[17]

13. Jacob Licht, *Megilat ha-Serakhim*, Jerusalem, Bialik, 1965, p. 122, has explained the three phases of admission set down in the *Community Rule* before the final examination as corresponding to the ways one is freed from decreasing degrees of impurity. These three degrees agree exactly with their rabbinic equivalents: at the beginning, אב טומאה (corresponding to the impurity of the Gentiles, cf. *BShab* 14b, and below §2), then ראשון, then שני.

14. This intrinsic kinship between the brotherhoods and the Essenes also justifies (in retrospect) the comparison of their esoteric teaching (without written publication) envisaged in chap. I, §I.3.

15. By reason of presumptions of impurity, cf. *MYad* 3:1-2.

16. *MḤag* 2:6 טבל ולא הוחזק כאלו לא טבל; this principle results in a list of cases whose formulation contains a significant textual ambiguity. In fact, the first case states הטובל לחלין והוחזק לחלין "Whoever performs an immersion in order to take profane foods, *and who is qualified for it*, [. . .]," so the immersion is a daily act; but a small variant gives a very different meaning: הטובל לחלין הוחזק לחלין "Whoever performs an immersion in order to take profane foods, *then becomes qualified for it*, [. . .]"; in this case it is a question of an inaugural immersion for admission, so a baptism properly so called. For the following cases, cf. VII, §IV.1.

17. More generally, Hannah K. Harrington, *The Impurity Systems of Qumran and the Rabbis. Biblical Foundations* (SBL Dissertation Series, 143), Atlanta (Ga.), Scholars Press, 1993, shows that an early level of the rab. trad., especially in the area of purity, is comparable to the precepts of Qumran, but she concludes from this evidence of convergence that such was the practice of the Pharisees as presented by FJ, even before their separation from the Essenes. Cf. review and discussion in *RB* 102 (1995), p. 116–128.

Several peculiarities in comparison with later rabbinic Judaism deserve to be noted, since they are to be found also among the Essenes. First the extreme severity of the *ḥaberim* with regard to the "people of the land," that is to those who have not been initiated: *BPes* 49b says that someone of the "people of the land" is capable of murder, that his children are not his own, etc.; Simon b. Yoḥai, mentioned in connection with the purification of Tiberias and supposed ancestor of the Kabbalah, says that one of the "people of the land" is accursed, even if he is pious, holy and honest. Certain cases of excommunication, going as far as stoning the coffin of one who has been expelled and dies without having made amends, are contrary to later practice, according to which membership of the people cannot be lost,[18] as opposed to the status of *ḥaber*. According to *BBer* 47b, even Samaritans can be regarded as *ḥaberim*, since their observance is very meticulous; that was precisely the opinion, as we have seen, of Simon b. Gamaliel, who had difficulty in being accepted into the academy of Usha. Finally, a woman can be "worthy of confidence" even if her husband is not, or has lost that status, but apparently she cannot become independently a full member of the brotherhood (*BBek* 30b); here there may be a trace of a position for a woman, obscured by the later obligation to marry (cf. chap. VI, §III.4).

The properly Essene parallels to these stipulations are undeniable; they will be presented in detail later (chap. VII, §IV), since they also agree with certain traits of primitive Christianity. Let us just draw attention here to the admission of Samaritans as *ḥaberim*, something which is remarkable for Jews,[19] and important under two aspects. First, the biblical fragments from the Judaean desert have numerous points in common with the Samaritan texts,[20] and some are written in Palaeo-Hebraic script, which has been preserved by the Samaritans; moreover, certain texts make explicit references to them.[21] Then, in the NT, Jesus is careful not to oppose the Samaritans (cf. Luke 9:54 f.). To the Samaritan woman, he

18. Cf. *MEdu* 5:6 f., with cases from the time of the foundation of Yavneh. What is at stake is obedience to a new majority, resulting from the fusion of several tendencies: a member may thus find himself excluded because he remains faithful to the teaching that he has received.

19. And to which FJ is certainly opposed (*J.W.* 2 §119), cf. chap. VII, §IV.1.

20. Cf. the synthesis of Maurice Baillet, "Le texte samaritain de l'Exode dans les manuscrits de Qumrân," in: André Caquot & Marc Philonenko (ed.), *Hommages à André Dupont-Sommer*, Paris, 1971, p. 363–381.

21. A papyrus fragment in 1st century Hebrew script was found at Massada which includes the place name הרגריזים "Mount Garizim" as a single word, corresponding to the Samaritan usage, cf. discussions by R. Pummer, "ΑΡΓΑΡΙΖΙΜ: A Criterion for Samaritan Provenance," *JSJ* 18 (1987), p. 18–25, and Hanan Eshel, "The Prayer of Joseph. A Papyrus from Masada and the Samaritan Temple on ΑΡΓΑΡΙΖΙΜ," *Zion* 56 (1991), p. 125–136.

replies "neither on this mountain [*i.e.* Garizim], nor at Jerusalem" (John 4:21). In the spirit of this reply, brotherhoods which happen to include both Jews and Samaritans are to be seen as opposed to *both* cults, or to both priesthoods.[22]

2. *Towards a System of Schools*

Independently of the brotherhoods, the sources often have to do with "people of the land." An anthology of opinions is collected in *BBer* 47b :

> *It has been taught* [baraita]: *Who is "people of the land?" Whoever does not eat profane food in a state of Levitical purity; such is the opinion of R. Meir. But the sages say: Whoever does not pay the tithe correctly.*
>
> *The masters teach* [baraita]: *Who is "people of the land?" Whoever does not recite the* Shema^c Israel *morning and evening; such is the opinion of R. Eliezer. R. Yehoshua^c says: Whoever does not put on phylacteries. Ben Azzai says: Whoever does not put fringes on his garment. R. Nathan says: Whoever does not put a* mezuza *at his door. R. Yonatan b. Joseph says: Whoever has sons and does not educate them to study the Torah. Others say: Whoever has studied the Scripture and the* Mishnah, *but has not frequented the masters, is regarded as "people of the land."*

Several small variants[23] in the passages parallel to this text show that it results not from a debate, but from the compilation of opinions expressed in different circumstances. These definitions fall into two categories: "people of the land in respect of the commandments," where it is a question of not observing *biblical* precepts bearing on the life of the individual, and "people of the land in respect of the Torah,"[24] where it is a question of not frequenting the masters, so of the *oral tradition*. In any case, these definitions are very demanding, but they all belong to the period between the foundations of Yavneh and of Usha.[25] Later, in the days

22. Even with an idea of replacing the hereditary priesthood: *BSanh* 90b indicates that a priest *ʿam haʾareṣ*, that is outside the *ḥabura*, cannot receive the tithe, but that a *talmid ḥakham* can receive it in certain cases even if he is not a priest; however, if a priest is a *ḥaber*, so are his sons. Cf. chap. VII, §IV.

23. Cf. E. E. Urbach, *The Sages . . .*, p. 633, n. 55–57.

24. Respectively עם הארץ למצוות and עם הארץ לתורה, cf. Aaron Oppenheimer, *The ʿAm ha ʾAretz. A Study in the Social History of the Jewish People in the Hellenistic-Roman Period* (ALGHJ, 8), Leiden, Brill, 1977, p. 67 p.

25. A word needs to be said here on an idea which has been widely held for over a century, according to which Christianity was born from the "people of the land," *i.e.* in an environment which was poorly educated and scattered throughout rural Galilee, and which was in more or less silent conflict with the Pharisees who, as educated town dwellers, had

of Judah the Prince, so at the time of publication of the *Mishnah* (around 200), there is a development which takes two directions. First, the veneration reserved until now for the *ḥaber* passes to the sage, so the ideal passes from the closed "brotherhood" to the more open school (*BBabaB* 75a). At the same time, there is a greater tolerance for the "people of the land" (*BErub* 32b). In fact, this evolution had already begun under Gamaliel II (cf. §I.3), but it had met with resistance and perhaps retreated, since Gamaliel had no immediate successor and the severe judgments on the "people of the land" are later than his death. We have seen that Simon b. Gamaliel had difficulty in picking up again, after 135, what his father had attempted.

Still, taken all in all, this change is of the first importance. Whereas, like the Essenes, the brotherhood is opposed to the rest of the people regarded as perverse, the school sees itself on the contrary as representing the whole people. That explains also why the *Mishnah* is so accommodating and preserves all sorts of traditions which are foreign to its native environment, in particular concerning Jerusalem, the Temple and the priesthood. Thus too the title of "patriarch" at last acquires a clear meaning. We have seen that, precisely within the rabbinic tradition, it has real substance only with Judah the Prince. Before that, it could be used plausibly for Gamaliel and his son Simon b. Gamaliel, but hardly for Yoḥanan b. Zakkai or for Hillel, and not *a fortiori* for previous generations. It is an anachronism answering to the need to show that the "schools," which at the time were only marginal brotherhoods of Essene type, were already the real guides of the whole people. The foundation of Bathyra, bringing together several currents at a time of crisis, but without recognized scholars, was really only a brotherhood, and certainly not a school recognized as competent. This is expressed in the following synthesis: "Hillel and Menaḥem were in agreement. Menaḥem left, Shammai arrived," and they

---

a monopoly of religious authority; the "people of the land" saw a chance to be free of the yoke of the Pharisees, not without some zest for class struggle, cf. references in A. Oppenheimer, *op. cit.*, p. 2 f. (who disputes this thesis, even though he regards rabbinic Judaism as the direct descendant of FJ's Pharisees). In fact, this theory, popularized by the views of M. Weber on social conflicts, is hardly compatible with the available sources, but it has taken root thanks to the convergence of two apologetic outlooks. For Christian authors, it was important to see the environment of the first disciples as rural and poor, as far away as possible from the oversight of the Law (Jerusalem, Pharisees), and so ready to cut a tie which was heavy and sterile (cf. Schürer, *Geschichte* II:454 f., largely modified in Schürer-Vermes II:399 f.). For Jewish historians (in particular Büchler, Zeitlin, Baron), the preoccupation was to show that rabbinic Judaism was descended from leading circles in Jerusalem and at the Temple, and so that Galilee was really Jewish only after Bar Kokhba (but not at the time of Jesus). For these reasons, FJ's rhetoric seeking to discredit the Jewish culture of Galilee has often been taken at its face value (cf. chap. III, §I.1).

disagreed;[26] this Menaḥem was an Essene of the time of Herod,[27] to whom he foretold the future even before he became king (*Ant.* 15 §373 f.).

This development from shadowy existence on the fringes to responsibility for a whole people can be seen later in the rabbinical axiom: "Only what the *majority* of the people can follow should be decreed" (cf. *BBabaB* 60b). It can be seen also in the emergence of a very strange institution known as "proselyte baptism," which we need to examine.

3. Proselyte Baptism

The question has long been asked if there was a connection between John's baptism and the baptism of proselytes described by rabbinic tradition, because of the obvious similarities (cf. chap. II, §I.6). A difficulty arises over dates, since, apart from a few texts which may perhaps allude to some practice of this rite before 70,[28] it is attested neither by the Bible nor by the classical authors Philo and Josephus. With regard to the forced Judaization of the Idumaeans and then of the Ituraeans, Josephus mentions only circumcision. Similarly he speaks only of the circumcision of

26. *MḤag* 2:2; the object of the controversy (reduced to a single word, לסמוך "lean on") is interpreted in the immediate context (2:3) as whether or not it was possible for a priest to lay hands on a sacrificial victim on a feast day: the gesture is prescribed in Lev 1:4 etc., but it is forbidden to draw profit from an animal on a feast day (*MBeṣa* 5:2), so in particular to "lean on" it (implying imposition of hands). According to this interpretation (which is suggested by *TḤag* 2:8-10), the controversy is strictly speaking infinitesimal. According to the text, it had gone on for generations before Hillel, so in the days of the Temple (where there must have been a well-defined usage, and not simply a school debate), and we must suspect that the *Mishnah* conceals what was really at stake. A better hypothesis on the underlying debate is that of Solomon Zeitlin, "The Semikah Controversy Between the Zugot" *JQR* NS 7 (1917), p. 499–517, who links the term at the center of the controversy with a previous passage (1:8), in which "lean on" means "find a Scriptural basis for an oral tradition"; so it is a matter of discussions about the relations between the oral and the written Torah, which were precisely at stake in the accounts of the enthronement of Hillel, who sought first to find Scriptural arguments (chap. III, §II.1). According to an even better, and already older, hypothesis, it concerns the laying on of hands for the authority and title of *rabbi*, cf. A. Sidon, "Die Controverse der Sunedrialhäupter," in: M. Braun & F. Rosenthal, *Gedenkbuch an David Kaufmann*, Breslau, 1900, p. 355 f., and Leopold Löw, *Gesammelte Schriften*, Szegedin, 1900, 5:82 f. If so, the case could be widened to include admission to a brotherhood (cf. chap. VII, §V.1). Here, Hillel and Menaḥem are in agreement to "lean on," whatever the exact meaning of the expression.

27. And not the zealot Menaḥem, of the same type as Judah the Galilean, who carried the rebellion to Jerusalem shortly before the intervention of Cestius in 66 and was killed (cf. *J.W.* 2 §433 f.), and whom an ancient *midrash* wrongly shows as a colleague of Hillel before he separated in order to devote himself to action, cf. Lieberman I, p. 180 f.; this error does, however, have a motive, for it draws attention to the fact that Hillel and his descendants (Y. b. Zakkai) did not follow the zealots.

28. *MPes* 8:8, *Or. Sib.* 4.162 f., *T. Levi* 14:6.

Izates king of Adiabene, then of Azizus king of Emesa, without any allusion to an immersion (*Ant.* 20 §34 f. and 139 f.). The most radical solution of this problem is that of Jeremias, who decides the question with a simple logic: since proselyte baptism cannot have been borrowed from the Christians, it must have existed previously as a Jewish institution.[29] He justifies his reasoning by explaining that the Gentiles were held to be impure, whence the need for an immersion. This, however, is to argue in a circle, for, apart from the Essenes, the impurity of Gentiles is mentioned only by the rabbinic sources. This brings us back to the question of how far these sources are to be regarded as representative of early Judaism taken as a whole; what we have been seeing up till now casts serious doubts on their claim. Besides, it is methodologically unwise to suppose that such or such a rite has only a secondary significance or has been introduced without a precise reason.

Proselyte baptism is described at length in *BYeb* 47a–b. The ritual presents three remarkable peculiarities. The first is that the baptism takes place *after* circumcision, and not the other way around; in other words, the neophyte has already become part of the people before he is baptized. That forms an interesting contrast with the discussion in Acts 15:5, where the Pharisees demand unsuccessfully that the newly baptized converts be circumcised,[30] so that they may become part of the people.[31] The second peculiarity is that circumcision and baptism form a sort of doublet: each is preceded by a similar preliminary teaching, imparting some grave precepts and some light. There is therefore some sort of twofold entry into the Covenant, by circumcision then by baptism. L. Schiffman has made an interesting comparison with the entry ritual of 1 QS 6:21 f., with its associated series of grave and light precepts, which apparently constitute the minimum to be known.[32] The third peculiarity is that there have to be three "witnesses" to the baptism (*BYeb* 46b), contrary to the universal rabbinic principle that two joint witnesses (who are seen by one another) suffice to establish a fact. Among the Essenes, serious matters have to be

29. Joachim Jeremias, *Infant Baptism in the First Four Centuries*, London, SCM Press, 1960, p. 24–37.

30. Cf. chap. I, §II.1. The meaning of James's reply is discussed in chap. V, §II.1.

31. At least in principle, but the expression used suggests that the Gentiles should be circumcised *after* becoming believers, so apparently after baptism. However: 1. the Pharisees here are demanding a *sanatio in radice*, in order to re-establish an order which has been overturned; 2. the "baptism" in question here is a process, and not an isolated act, and nothing suggests that these new converts have completed it; 3. the Pharisees' demand is very similar to Josephus' requirement, that the Essenes be "Jews by race (τὸ γένος)" (cf. chap. VII, §IV.1); in both cases, that cannot be taken for granted.

32. Cf. Étienne Nodet, "La loi à Qumrân et Schiffman," *RB* 102 (1995), p. 38–71.

attested by three witnesses (cf. CD 9:16-23), but they are not necessarily joint witnesses. More significant is the fact, which we have seen, that the admission of a candidate into the *ḥabura* requires the presence of three qualified members, which suggests rather a basic tribunal (cf. *MSanh* 1:1). So the "witnesses" of baptism constitute a formal court pronouncing admission.

A B C

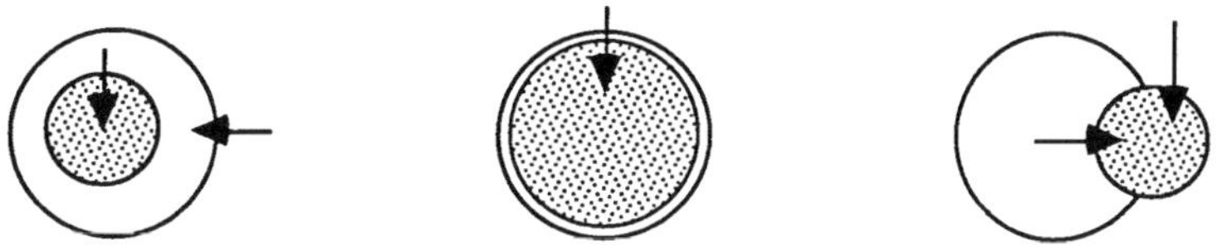

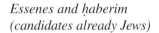

Essenes and ḥaberim (candidates already Jews) — *Rabbinic Judaism (Gentile proselytes)* — *Christianity (Jews and Greeks)*

(The large white circle represents the people, defined by circumcision; the dotted disk, the group that keeps the Covenant, defined by baptism)

By combining these observations with the conclusions put forward above on the remarkable kinship between the Essenes and the brotherhoods of *ḥaberim*, it is possible to formulate a very simple hypothesis on the origin of proselyte baptism. The brotherhood was originally a reforming sect intent on the renewal of the Covenant for Jews (and perhaps Samaritans), with initiation and baptisms, but not related in any way to entry into the people by circumcision, presumed to have been acquired previously; that is what is represented by fig. A in the diagram above. This configuration later develops in two different ways. In rabbinic Judaism (fig. B), the brotherhood has taken over responsibility for the whole people, after the failure of Bar Kokhba; so, for the proselyte, entry into the people (circumcision) is superimposed on entry into the enlarged brotherhood (baptism),[33] a practice whose origins are later retrojected into a distant past, before Hillel.[34] By contrast, in Christianity (fig. C), access to the brotherhood, identified uniquely by baptism, has become independent of whether the candidate has or has not become part of the people by circumcision (cf. Acts 15 in its present redaction, and below §II).

33. Certain passages show precisely that the people as a whole have the Spirit (are "sons of prophets"), and not only the brotherhoods, cf. chap. III, §II.1 (*TPes* 4:14).

34. Just as the later title of patriarch has been retrojected back to Hillel, so he (or at least a current emanating from him) has been credited with an opinion favorable to the ways the brotherhoods developed at the end of the 2nd century.

A much quoted passage (*MPes* 8:8) contains a controversy whose meaning becomes very clear in this perspective: if someone is converted on the eve of Passover, the school of Shammai says that he is then baptized and can take part in the Passover meal the next evening, but the school of Hillel judges that "one who is parted from his foreskin is as if he were coming out of a tomb,"[35] so he cannot eat the Passover, since the required ablution takes place later (the third and the seventh days, cf. Num 19:18 f.). Now, Exod 12:43 f. stipulates that the uncircumcised cannot share in the Passover. It seems, therefore, that for the school of Shammai the proselyte strictly speaking is one who enters into the brotherhood of the *ḥaberim*, so has been circumcised long before, whereas for the school of Hillel he first becomes part of the people, so is circumcised on the eve of Passover, and hence is impure for seven days. In other words, for the school of Hillel, which has fixed the norm, the reception of the proselyte comprises both circumcision *and* (later) baptism, the latter act being more or less assimilated to a purification after contact with death, *i.e.* reduced to a lower status. This school represents well the extension of the model of the brotherhood to the people as a whole.

For diagrams A and C (Essene and Christian), the true (renewed) Covenant, very important for both groups, as we have seen, implies entry into the small circle; in both cases, too, there is a polemical attitude with regard to the rest of the people.[36] Furthermore, writing about the Essenes, Josephus explains that "if an elder happens to touch a newcomer [novice], he has to purify himself as after contact with a foreigner" (*J.W.* 2 §150); in other words, since the novice is certainly Jewish,[37] those who do not belong to the community, whether Jews or Gentiles, all have the same degree of impurity. Similarly, a passage in the *Mishnah* cited above explains that for the *ḥaber* the "people of the land" has the same impurity as a Gentile (*MḤag* 2:7).

If this opinion is projected on to the first Christians, it means that the mission to the Gentiles, like that to the Jews, presupposes the abolition of the *same* ritual barrier. This remark may throw light on the development

35. So entry into the Covenant is a new birth. Rom 6:3 f. ("it is into his death that we have been baptized") expresses the same idea, but by way of baptism and not of circumcision; the opinion of the school of Hillel may have a polemical note.

36. This arrangement may help to understand Paul's baptismal theology. It borrows its fundamental elements from circumcision (prototype of the Covenant), cf. Geza Vermes, "Baptism and Jewish Exegesis: New Light from Ancient Sources," NTS 4 (1958), p. 308–319; its form is, however, the same as that of "proselyte baptism," which is also a reaffirmation of the Covenant. Cf. also following n.

37. Which has many implications, cf. chap. VII, §IV.1.

glimpsed in the account of Peter's visit to Cornelius, which may originally have told of a visit to Jews counted as impure (cf. chap. I, §II.1).

Rabbinic Judaism, on the contrary, expressly includes circumcision in the Covenant:[38] "As your fathers entered into the Covenant by circumcision, immersion and the casting of blood, so too the proselytes" (*BKer* 9a). Again, it is said that the two principal signs of the Covenant are the Sabbath and circumcision, but the latter is more important, since one may break the Sabbath in order to circumcise on the eighth day.[39] Already, according to 1 Macc 1:5, circumcision was being identified with the Covenant. The fact that it is a rite performed on a newborn child shows the importance of physical descent, and consequently of the people. Further, according to *MBik* 1:4, every child belongs to the people automatically through the mother, even if not circumcised. However, the *Mishnah* contains an anomaly in this regard: there is no tractate on circumcision, even though there are many on questions of purification, and even on "circumcision of the earth," which is the prohibition of eating the fruit of a tree in its first three years (cf. Lev 19:23). This gap is the trace of an earlier situation, centered on the brotherhoods: candidates are presumed to be already circumcised, just like the "people of the land."

Our concern here has not been to write the history of the Tannaites, but only to describe more exactly the nature of the rabbinic sources, and in particular their way of being at once very traditional and very late. Their traditional dimension is to be found both among the brotherhoods, which are only a kind of Essene groups, and in oral traditions of Babylonian origin, allowing also for the fusion of various small groups. The new element, which is probably later than the failure of Bar Kokhba, can be defined as the opening up of the system of brotherhoods to an entire people. In this sense, an act of major significance was the transfer of the *Mishnah* to Babylonia, about 219, followed by the opening of schools. At first marginal with regard to the exilarch, the schools later became normative for all, without any note of exclusiveness, and in particular without expulsion: "A Jew, whatever his sin, remains a Jew." This confirms, by the way, the cultural ties between Galilee and certain circles in Babylonia,[40] and may help to explain why the *Mishnah* did not in this period spread to the West.

38. The Covenant implies a sign (σφραγίς); on the hesitation between circumcision and the sign of the Spirit (cross) which confirms baptism, cf. chap. VII, §I,1.

39. *MekhRI* and *MekhRS* on Exod 19:5. Cf. Moore II:16 f. In John 7:23, Jesus too admits the superiority of circumcision (which is a law *of Moses*) over the Sabbath.

40. And with the Aramaic language, despite the episode related below (§III.3b).

All that appears quite foreign to the NT as we have it, that is to the heritage of Peter and Paul. The missing link is not well documented, but it turns around James and his "Davidic" successors in Judaea, the Jewish-Christians. This modern term happens to be regarded at the moment as unsuitable,[41] but is retained for its usefulness, and we shall see that it corresponds to a precise reality.[42] After the unplanned and uncertain beginnings, a distinction opens up between a main branch which is properly Jewish, or at least Jewish-centered, and awaits the return of Jesus as Messiah, and a branch which emerges as a new and unforeseeable phenomenon. This latter, coming forth with much hesitation from Messianism properly so called ("neither Jews nor Greeks"), recognizes Jesus as Lord. Despite their internal subdivisions, these branches entertained very different attitudes towards the Law; either might at any moment receive new members, whether Jewish or Gentile in origin, but that does not affect the definition.

II – James at Jerusalem

What was James's position? Contradictions between various NT texts have long been discussed: according to Gal 2:11 f., Peter at Antioch was afraid of emissaries from James, who did not allow table fellowship with the uncircumcised. On the contrary, according to Acts 15:12 f., James seems to reply officially to Paul and Barnabas, who have come from Antioch, and to Peter on his return from Caesarea, that circumcision is not necessary.[43] Curiously enough, Paul, long afterwards, shows no knowledge of these decisions in his letters, which suggests that we should look more closely at these texts. This examination will show that at the beginning James allowed the conversion of Gentiles, but kept them at a distance by *excluding* their circumcision. Such a position is in keeping with the Messianic views which we shall find in his successors.

1. The Jerusalem Decrees. Moses and Noah

The account of the Jerusalem assembly (Acts 15:12-22) already referred to in chap. I, §II.1), includes some significant details. They are

41. Cf. Simon Mimouni, "Pour une définition nouvelle du judéo-christianisme," *NYS* 38 (1992), p. 161–191.

42. We follow closely the definition, centered on observance, given by Marcel Simon, *Verus Israel. Étude sur les relations entre chrétiens et juifs dans l'Empire romain (135–425)*, Paris, 1948, 1964². Given the origin of the name "Christian"« (cf. chap. VI, §I.3), the term "Nazorean" would be more exact, but it is somewhat ambiguous (chap. VI, §V.2).

43. Jerome Murphy-O'Connor, *Paul. A Critical Life*, Oxford, Clarendon Press, 1996, p. 138 f., asks why James and Paul were in agreement on the question of circumcision, and looks for a political explanation.

given here, in literal translation, indicating the chief variants of the WT (on the righthand side):

(15:5) *Now there arose certain of the party of the Pharisees, who had become believers, saying that it was necessary to circumcise them and bid them observe the law of Moses.*	(15:5) *Now there arose certain of the party of the Pharisees, who had become believers, saying that it was necessary to circumcise them and*[44] *observe the law of Moses.*
(7a) *Now, a great discussion having come about,*	(7a) *Now, a great discussion having come about,*
(12a)	(12a) *The elders giving their assent to what Peter had said,*
All the assembly kept silent.	*the assembly kept silent.*

(13b) *Rising up, James said: "Brethren, hear me.* (14) *Simeon has expounded how first God has visited in order to take from among the nations a people to His name.* (15) *The words of the prophets agree with that, since it is written:* (16) *"After that I will come and I will raise again the fallen tent of David. I will raise up its ruins and restore it,* (17) *so that the rest of humanity may seek the Lord (*WT *God), as well as all the nations which have been consecrated to my name, says the Lord who*

makes this (18) *since always known.*	*makes this.* (18) *Since always is known the Lord's work as His.*

(19) *That is why I myself decide that it is not necessary to harass*[45] *those of the Gentiles who turn to God.* (20) *Let us send to tell them to abstain*

from what has been polluted by idols,	*from what has been polluted by idols,*
from unchastity	*from unchastity*
from strangled meats	
and from blood.[46]	*and from blood.*

(21) *Moses indeed from ancient times has*

in each city	

people who proclaim him in the synagogues, for he is read each Sabbath.

44. The AT adds παραγγέλλειν, with a very different meaning, cf. chap. I, §II.1.

45. The verb used, παρενοχλέω, is a hapax in the Bible; it is related to ὄχλος "crowd" (with the idea of disturbance, cf. Lat. *turba*) and to ἐνοχλέω "to be sick, troubled by an illness" (cf. Luke 6:18; Heb 12:15; MT חלה). The underlying idea is to impose a burden, a yoke (cf. Acts 15:10, and also *MBer* 2:2, the yoke of the Kingdom, then of the precepts).

46. These prescriptions are repeated by WT and AT in v. 29, with some modifications: 1. the last two are given in the reverse order; the "pollutions of idols" (ἀλίσγημα, hapax) become εἰδωλόθυτα "idolothytes, meats consecrated to idols," a plausible development

The way the text is presented above essentially follows the reconstruction of the P Doc as proposed in *Les Actes* III:195: James is replying to Peter, not to Paul. Two changes have, however, been made: v. 15-18 and 21 are maintained (that is to say the quotation from Amos 9:11-12, and the proclamation of Moses in the synagogues), which had been relegated by Boismard and Lamouille to a later stage of redaction (Acts II, which bring Paul into the discussion). For one thing, the quotation agrees exactly with the themes expounded by James, and is their model rather than their illustration. Then, since v. 21 appears embarrassing, insisting as it does on the law of Moses, it is not easy to see why it has been added to the narrative at the same time as Paul.

On the contrary, if we include these elements, they give a very precise meaning to James's speech. For him, it is a question of Gentiles who are converted *to God*, without any definite relationship with Jesus Christ; it is the fulfilment of an eschatological prophecy. This latter introduces a certain link with the reappearance of the posterity of David. However, Moses is proclaimed each Sabbath in the synagogues. In other words, the Law and the Prophets, far from being abolished, speak to the present; it could be said in this regard that James is "powerful in the Scriptures."[47] The legal question to which James replies is therefore simple: Should the nations which recognize God—a new fact—be integrated into Israel or not, that is concretely, subjected to the law of Moses or not? The response, drawn from Amos, is: Clearly not; there is no question of circumcising them, so of integrating them into the people. This response, with a Scriptural basis, reinforces the reproach made to Peter on his return from seeing Cornelius, that he went into his house and ate with him (Acts 11:3), in other words, that he had abolished an essential barrier.

In his speech James gives the impression that what is in question is the conversion of Gentiles to a form of Judaism, or at least to God as He is attested by the Jews. But this is not an isolated case. In the episode of Peter at Caesarea, as told by the P Doc, it is a question of God, the Spirit and baptism, but with no allusion to Jesus. In other words, the observable elements are fairly close to John the Baptist and his baptism, but with a new dimension, which is attributed to the Spirit no longer announced but

---

since the attested uses of the associated verb ἀλισγέω concern food; this prohibition is found also in early Christian texts, cf. *Les Actes* V:211 f.; 2. the WT (alone) adds the Golden Rule in its negative form ("do not do to others what you do not want done to yourself," cf. Tob 4:15 and *J.W.* 2 §139); the same addition occurs in v. 20 in certain witnesses of the WT, but as a later harmonization. Finally, the list of v. 29, with the same difference between WT and AT, is repeated in 21:25, in the scene between James and Paul.

47. Like Apollos (Acts 18:24 f.), cf. chap. VI, §II.1.

now manifested. But in James's speech it is precisely the Spirit who actualizes the Scriptures (cf. v. 28) and makes it possible to issue decrees based on tradition.

So, our text tells us, it is decided to transmit certain precepts to these Gentiles. Before we look at these precepts and try to see what is new in them, we need to notice that in the redaction of the P Doc, whether or not the two passages discussed above are included, the obvious meaning seems to be that James raises no direct objection to Peter's action: he is ready to accept table fellowship with uncircumcised folk on the condition that they observe the said precepts. But that is only an impression given by the redactor, for in reality James says nothing of the sort. Several conclusions follow. First, there is no longer any contradiction with Paul's statement of the situation in Gal 2:11 f., according to which James refuses table fellowship with uncircumcised Gentiles, even if they have become believers. At the time of writing, Paul does not forget that he was once in communion with James (cf. 2:9), but he has come a long way since then, as we shall see (chap. VI, §IV). Peter, for his part, has stayed in a more pragmatic position somewhere in between Paul and James. Finally, the P Doc, although much earlier than the final redaction, represents an attempt to synthesize which is already at some distance removed from the origins. James is of the family of Jesus, and through him can be discerned a Jewish-Christian profile which can tell us a little more about the original environment. This remark is confirmed by another meeting between Paul and James at Jerusalem (Acts 21:19 f.). Paul has reported all that God has accomplished among the Gentiles, and is told in turn that thousands of believers who observe the law of Moses declare[48] that he is pushing Jews who live among Gentiles to abandon the Law; then he is asked to show publicly that he himself has remained observant. Paul's difficulties come uniquely from the fact that he has brought Jews and Gentiles together, but without making the Gentiles enter Judaism.

Here we can add a remark on the vocabulary used for the assembly over which James presides, which has two different names. In v. 12, in the P Doc, it is called the "great number"; in v. 22, whose substratum belongs to the same document, it is called "church." This latter term (Gr. *ekklêsia*) has the precise sense of an assembly convoked according to law by the proclamation of a herald (literally, a "kerygma"); in the immediate context (v. 21), it corresponds well to the assembly convoked by the proclamation of Moses. The question then is to decide whether the parallel term

48. WT (κατήχησαν); the AT puts it in the passive (κατηχήϑησαν), which neutralizes the conflict: these believers have heard it said that Paul, etc.

"great number," which is often understood simply as "crowd," is also a precise technical term, as we shall show (chap. VI, §III.4). Other small differences between WT and AT also concern community structures: first, the approbation of the elders disappears in the AT (v. 12, later than the P Doc, but printed above in smaller characters); also, the AT adds the detail (v. 21) that the synagogues where Moses is proclaimed are *in each city*. These two alterations may look minor, but we shall see that they are the trace of important developments (chap. VII, §IV.3).

As for the precepts determined by James, the first question to ask is whether they have an ethical, or only a ritual dimension. If they are moral commandments, it is possible to see in them, though indirectly, the prohibitions of adultery and murder fixed by the Decalogue, but in that case, we should expect theft to be mentioned, but it is absent. The ritual meaning, which does not require any distortion of the text, is therefore the more probable. That is also implied by the WT's addition to v. 29 of the Golden Rule, which is eminently ethical: the author of the gloss seems to have felt that otherwise this dimension would be missing.

After these preliminaries, we need, in order to find a setting for these precepts, to go a little out of our way to see the position of Gentiles who come close to Judaism at this period. This question is not the same as that of proselytism properly so called, in the sense of a deliberate activity, which we shall look at later (chap. VI, §I.1).

2. *Godfearers and Children of Noah*

Attitudes towards the Gentiles varied greatly in the different branches of Judaism. At one extreme was the openness of Philo and Josephus; at the other, the barriers put up by the Essenes and the *ḥaberim*, who recommend limiting as much as possible all contact with the impure, whether they be "people of the land" or Gentiles (cf. above, §I).[49] In between, are the Godfearers of the NT, and later on rabbinic tradition defines "seven precepts of the children of Noah," which are valid for every human being.

How does the NT express the fact that Cornelius is "Godfearing,"[50] as also his household? We are not told what he thinks or believes, but that he gives generous alms to the Jewish people (Acts 10:1). Similarly, in

49. According to *MḤul* 2:7 "every foreigner is presumed to be thinking of idolatry" (Eliezer b. Hyrcanus, who approved of the translation of Aquila); similarly, *CD* 12:8 forbids the sale of clean animals to Gentiles, because of the risk of sacrifice to idols.

50. The expression employed φοβούμενος τὸν θεόν (Acts 10:2 and 22; 13:16 and 26; cf. Rev 14:7) is characteristic of Sir 1:13 f. (with κύριον); regarded here as analogous to εὐσεβής "pious" (Acts 10:2, etc.) or θεοσεβής "worshipping God" (John 9:31).

Luke 7:5, the centurion of Capharnaum has helped to build the synagogue (a detail not given by the parallels in Matt, Mark, John). Perhaps these touches are proper to Luke-Acts,[51] but they indicate a characteristic attitude, which is attested also by the inscriptions from the synagogue at Aphrodisias:[52] from a Jewish point of view, to worship the one God in the abstract meant nothing if there were no visible acts implying some sort of commitment. The Gentiles, it is true, are not *a priori* subject to the precepts of the Law, since the Mosaic Covenant is not for them. The two examples quoted demonstrate a sort of delegated observance: these Romans worship God by helping the Jews to observe the divine law. In other words, the chosen people is implicitly recognized as having a mediating or priestly role in the world as a whole. This is defined in Exod 19:5-6: "All the earth is mine; I will take you for a kingdom of priests, a holy nation." This theme, with many variations, is constantly expressed by the Prophets, often with an eschatological coloring: for Isa 2:1 f., it will come to pass that all the nations will come to the mountain of the house of YHWH, established above the hills; for Zech 14:16 f., the survivors from all the nations will come up to Jerusalem to prostrate themselves before the king YHWH-Sabaoth and celebrate the feast of Tabernacles. In the same way, Messianic allusions in the Scriptures are always focused: "It is I [YHWH] who have consecrated my king on Sion, my holy mountain," says Ps 2:6 (cf. chap. VII, §V.2). This perspective can be related to the general movement of Luke-Acts, in which the Christians are, in the last analysis, the true Pharisees, and also mediators charged with a universal mission (cf. below §V.2).

51. Conclusion of A. T. Kraabel, "The Disappearance of the God-Fearers," *Numen* 28 (1981), p. 113–126.

52. In Asia Minor; these inscriptions, discovered in 1976 and dated to the 3rd century, have been published by Joyce Reynolds & Robert Tannenbaum, *Jews and Godfearers at Aphrodisias. Greek Inscriptions with Commentary. Texts from the Excavations at Aphrodisias Conducted by Kenan T. Erim* (Cambridge Philological Society, Suppl. Vol. 12), Cambridge Philological Society, 1987; cf. also Schürer-Vermes III/1:25. Jerome Murphy-O'Connor, "Lots of God-Fearers? *Theosebeis* in the Aphrodisias Inscription," *RB* 99 (1992), p. 418–424, surveys the often confused discussions which followed the first announcements of the discovery, and concludes that the lists of non-Jewish benefactors given by these inscriptions show that the notion of "Godfearing" (θεοσεβής) is ambiguous, since it embraces two distinct categories: two names correspond to Gentiles who, although not proselytes, have been admitted to prayer or study meetings of the Jewish community; fifty-four others are only identified as external benefactors, without any further indication of their motivation or their status. However, the notion of "Godfearer" is simplified if the criterion is that of having given something, and not of having taken part in this or that activity; indeed, such participation cannot amount to the same thing as observance for someone who is outside the Covenant. It is, of course, impossible to say how far one may general-

The rabbinic sources have developed another approach which is more consistent with their origins. In their earliest layers, debates are internal to Judaism, which we saw to be characteristic in the question of the "people of the land." Later, when the horizon has been expanded to take in the whole of the Jewish people, and Messianic hopes have been put off to an undetermined future, no missionary outlook is developed. On the contrary, the boundaries are made clear, and the intermediate category of "Godfearers" disappears, a development which may not be totally unconnected with the emergence of Christianity.[53] All the same, in order to maintain a strictly monotheistic (and peaceable) perspective, the nations as a whole have to be given a place, without, however, engaging in properly missionary activity. This is the object of the "precepts of the children of Noah."

These precepts are given in various similar forms. The best known is in *TAbZ* 8:4: "Seven commandments have been prescribed for the children of Noah; [they concern] judgments, blasphemy, idolatry, uncovering nakedness [forbidden unions], bloodshed, theft and living flesh [torn from a live animal]." The passage occurs in other collections, in particular in *BSanh* 56a–b, where it is followed by a discussion among Tannaites (datable to 100–150), who propose the addition or suppression of certain articles; Scriptural arguments are also added to justify this or that point.[54] The most notable feature of this list is that its global content, especially the five articles in the middle, form a sort of semi-Decalogue,[55] but that

ize on the basis of the synagogue at Aphrodisias, as there is no discernible link with Tannaitic circles; further, the imprecision of the NT evidence suggests that caution is needed.

53. This was probably a major factor in the eclipse of the book of Ben Sira, Hebrew fragments of which have been found in the *geniza* of Cairo and at Qumran. In the 1st cent. B.C., it is cited as an authority by Simon b. Shetaḥ (*YBer* 4:1, p. 11b), one of the masters of the rab. trad. (cf. *MAbot* 1:3); then, in the Tannaitic period, it becomes "heretical" (or "exterior," *YSanh* 10:1, p. 28a and *BSanh* 100b); but later, it becomes once again a quasi-Scriptural authority (*BBabaQ* 92b). At first sight, this book contains nothing really scandalous that would explain its rejection. However, from the start it celebrates wisdom, piety and "fear of God" (φόβος and derivatives), then it identifies the Law with wisdom, with a cosmopolitan attitude which is fairly close to Philo, and finally celebrates the chief persons of biblical history beginning with Enoch and Noah; the perspective is at once focused and open, obviously hospitable to "Godfearers" of Gentile origin. These are precisely the points emphasized by the translator, who, it is interesting to note, declares in his prologue, that he discovered the Hebrew original of the book in Egypt (even though he presents himself as the grandson of the author).

54. Cf. the sources assembled and discussed by Markus Bockmuehl, "The Noachide Commandments and New Testament Ethics, With Special Reference to Acts 15 and Pauline Halakha," *RB* 102 (1995), p. 72–101.

55. In the episode of the rich young man (Matt 19:16-22 par.), Jesus reminds him of the commandments in the form of a semi-Decalogue (only ethical; the part on God is re-

nothing in their formulation refers them expressly to the Decalogue strictly so called.[56] This remark will be developed below (§IV.4) in connection with the "trick of the *minim*," which entailed the suppression of the Decalogue in daily prayer. But we note here that the reference to these seven precepts is not the particular Covenant with Israel (Abraham) or its renewal (Sinai), or even Creation (implied in observance of the Sabbath),[57] but Noah,[58] that is to say, a very general covenant between God and humanity as a whole.[59] The difference is capital, because in this form,

---

placed by a question about money): the immediate context suggests that this man is Jewish, but the formulation could just as well be addressed to a Gentile.

56. Even for theft: the Decalogue has לא תגנב, whereas the list here has גזל; according to the constant tradition (*YSanh* 8:3, p. 26b, *BBabaQ* 57a, etc.), the former term indicates theft by stealth (with or without witnesses, but out of sight of the owner), while the latter term indicates seizure by main force (in front of the owner and against his will). It is not too much to think that the formulation of the Noachide precept is not a semantic subtlety distinguishing between these two cases, but that it seeks only an expression different from that of the Decalogue to designate the same field.

57. Later, it was thought that these commandments had been revealed to Adam at his creation (Maimonides, *melakhim* 9:1).

58. The idea of Noachide precepts developing Gen 9:4 f. (which gives only the prohibition of animal blood and murder) is not necessarily an innovation on the part of the Tannaites. In the book of *Jubilees* (Essene, *i.e.* close to the original environment of the *ḥaberim*), Noah gives fairly detailed instructions (but without fixing their number) to "his children's children": to do justice, cover their nakedness, bless their creator, honor their parents, love their neighbor, avoid fornication, pollution and all injustice (7:20); not to shed blood (7:23); not to eat animal blood, and to offer first fruits (7:28 f.). Later in the book it is stated that the nations (children of Noah) have not observed these precepts, whence the need to choose a particular people, with the Covenant and the law of Moses in the desert; so it is not at first a question of positively assigning a *present* position for the nations, but of explaining the singularity of Israel in a monotheistic perspective. *MekhRI, yitro* §5, develops a similar idea: after the failure of the covenant with Noah, in which the penalties were ill defined, the Law was proposed in the desert (*i.e.* outside any particular nation) and in seventy languages; only Israel accepted it with the corresponding sanctions (responsibility). Philo, with similar elements, had a different outlook, cf. chap. I, §I.4. On the other hand, in the formulation of *Jubilees,* the *direct* influence of the Decalogue is obvious, as well as allusions to the Creation (references to the Creator and to the precepts that can be drawn from Gen 1–7), which marks a clear difference from the rabbinic list. However, among its seven precepts, the first is really the same as in *Jubilees* (which suggests some derivation), and the last comes directly from Gen 9:4, *i.e.* from the biblical covenant with Noah; in other words, the five middle precepts still make up a semi-Decalogue, carefully distinguished from the Decalogue in Exod. Finally, the sequence "nakedness, murder, theft" in the list does not correspond to the order in the MT (murder, fornication, theft), but to that attested by Deut LXX (B), Philo, *Decal.* §51, the Nash papyrus and Luke 18:20; a further (small) sign of the antiquity of developments on the Noachide precepts.

59. A connected question is whether these laws are natural or revealed. In general, any idea of natural philosophy is foreign to the rab. trad., but certain sayings make a connection between it and the precepts of the Noachide list (and also of the Decalogue): in *BYoma*

there can no longer be any rivalry between Israel and the nations.[60]

The reference to Noah is especially clear in the seventh article, forbidding the eating of living flesh, which does not appear to be on the same level as the rest and has constantly been interpreted as having a pedagogical purpose: one who infringes it will do worse things.[61] In fact, it is drawn directly from Gen 9:4 f., and its inclusion is necessary to make the reference to Noah clear. The first, very concise, article can be understood as "rules" or "judgments,"[62] so jurisprudence (interpretation of general laws) or settlement of disputes; in both cases, as the tradition has understood, appropriate institutions, tribunals or schools are needed.[63] From this results a complete independence of jurisdiction: the tribunals of the nations are autonomous.[64] Thus, a "Godfearer" like Cornelius, close to the synagogue, no longer has a definite position, or, more exactly, is sent back to his own nation.

67b, it is stated that idolatry, immorality, murder and theft would have had to be prohibited by a law if they had not been by the Torah; similarly, a saying in *BErub* 100b states that laws could have been drawn from observing nature: decency prescribed by seeing the behavior of the cat, theft prohibited by watching the ant, etc., cf. Alan F. Segal, *Paul the Convert. The Apostolate and Apostasy of Paul the Pharisee*, New Haven-London, Yale University Press, 1990, p. 195. However, according to this very characteristic outlook, the function of the "natural" law is to correct nature.

60. This observation suggests why the notion of Noachide precepts is totally foreign to Philo and FJ (who recommend a diffusion of the law *of Moses*), but it does not exclude, quite the contrary, a certain parallel between these precepts and the *ius gentium* of the Romans, cf. Boaz Cohen, *Jewish and Roman Law: A Comparative Study*, New York, Jewish Theological Seminary, 1966, p. 26 f.; in both cases, it is a question of stipulations of a sort of implicit peace treaty between one nation (and its own law) and the peoples outside its jurisdiction.

61. Similarly, with regard to the prohibition of mating animals of different species (Lev 19:19), Philo, *Spec. leg.* 3 §46 and FJ, *Ant.* 4 §229 explain that the observance of insignificant prohibitions prevents more serious (bestiality).

62. דין, well attested in the Bible (Deut 17:8, etc.), and normally rendered κρίσις in the LXX (which is also the most frequent equivalent of משפט "sentence"). In the rab. trad. this meaning is preserved, but often in the more specific context of litigation and sanctions (cf. *MḤag* 1:8, *MSanh* 1:1, etc.).

63. Maimonides, *melakhim* 9:14 (cf. *BSanh* 59a). At any rate, a constant principle has it that to every commandment must be assigned an appropriate penalty (cf. *BYeb* 3b). Similarly, Philo, *Decal.* §176, remarks that the great singularity of the Decalogue comes from the absence of associated penalties; so it has to be made specific by particular laws which do have associated sanctions. Certain rabbinic sayings sought to assign precise penalties to the Noachide precepts (capital punishment, cf. *BSanh* 57a). This corresponds to the fact that the chief articles of the list (idolatry, forbidden unions, murder) are the most serious in the rab. trad., as not only are they associated with the death penalty, but also their transgression is never permitted, even under threat of death (*BSanh* 74a).

64. The separation of the jurisdictions is a theme dear to Paul, cf. 1 Cor 5:12 f.

These considerations bring us back directly to the Jerusalem assembly and the decrees of James, which the P Doc places just after Peter's return from Cornelius. This is the moment to return to the question put by the Pharisees, before James's speech. The problem raised, which fittingly follows Peter's stay with these folk in Caesarea (assumed to be Gentiles), is that of "our observance," concretely, contacts with Gentile converts. The response deals with Gentiles converted to God in general, without giving any very clear idea of what is meant by conversion; in fact, the response could equally well have applied to Cornelius *before* Peter's visit, since he had already begun to turn towards God. The real problem implied in all this is not in the first place contacts with these converts, but their status.[65]

We can now look at the content of James's speech. His opening statement uses a vocabulary characteristic of divine intervention (cf. Luke 1:68 "Blessed be the Lord, [. . .] for He has visited"),[66] which governs the Covenant in general. In Exod 3:16, YHWH has Moses tell the people: "I have visited you, I have seen what is being done to you in Egypt." Then, at the moment of the revelation on Sinai, YHWH defines the Covenant (Exod 19:5): "If you hear my voice and keep my Covenant, you will be for me a people (MT omits) chosen among all the nations, for all the earth belongs to me." The stipulations of the Covenant are given in the Decalogue and the body of legislation connected with Sinai. It is noteworthy that circumcision does not occur: it is mentioned as required only for the Passover (Ex 12:44 f.),[67] which is outside the gift of the Law properly so called, which in turn is celebrated at Pentecost (chap. VII, §III).

The question raised about circumcision concerns the Covenant, or at any rate can be interpreted in that way. That is really what James does, and we need to find what form of the Covenant he is referring to. The allusion to the effective choice of a people among the nations (now), and not to the posterity of a family (future), steers us in the direction of Moses and Sinai, as suggested, rather than towards Abraham. In this sense, it is logical for him to ignore circumcision. However, James makes no allusion to the Decalogue. In fact, the last prescription which he gives, to abstain from blood,[68] refers directly to the Covenant with Noah (cf. Gen

65. Thus rightly M. Bockmuehl, "The Noachide Commandments . . . ," p. 93, contrary to numerous commentators.

66. The technical term ἐπισκέπτω corresponds to the פקד of the MT; on the associated nouns ἐπίσκοπος, פקיד (מבקר) "inspector," cf. chap. VII, §IV.3.

67. It is mentioned in passing in Lev 12:3, which deals with the purification of the woman after childbirth.

68. A prescription which has worried the commentators, and perhaps also the final redactors, for it appeared to be fairly slight. The last precision "all that has been strangled"

9:4 f., which prohibits both eating the blood of animals[69] and shedding human blood). The prohibition of unchastity is also present in the story of Noah. According to Gen 10:22, Cham has *uncovered* to his brothers the nakedness of their father, which earns him a curse. So there is implicitly a prohibition, which can be developed into a complete body of laws governing sexual relations, since the expression "uncover the nakedness" precisely designates all the sexual prohibitions of Lev 18:5 f. Finally, the prohibition of the pollution of idols is simply a practical expression of monotheism, avoiding pagan feasts and rites,[70] whereas Noah built an altar to God. From a Jewish point of view, monotheism is not a matter of opinions, but of acts, performed or avoided.

These remarks contain the answer to the question already raised about James's prescriptions: Why did he not forbid theft, or murder (expressly), or the abandonment of children, or covetousness, etc.? Why is there no positive precept about baptism, for example, or feasts to observe? It is hardly likely that he was advocating moral laxity. Rather we must conclude that in all these areas he was referring the addressees back to civil legislation, Roman or other, and so to the sanctions assigned there. From this angle, he is close to the first of the Noachide precepts in the rabbinic list: the nations must have their own laws and judicial institutions. In other words, there is no need to be in contact with them, which would certainly imply circumsion, as required by the Pharisees.[71]

(AT) gives a little more substance to the precept (taken in a limited sense), by attaching it to Lev 17:15-16, which defines the meats permitted to Israelites *and to "proselytes."* Cf. *Les Actes* V:211.

69. This prohibition, foreign to the Decalogue, is found also in early Christian literature, cf. *Les Actes* V:213.

70. In Rev 2:14, permission to eat "meat consecrated to idols" is the quintessence of the traps set by idolatry (perverse doctrine of Balaam).

71. In the final redaction of Acts, James's precepts are expressly reported and then become the object of a letter sent to Antioch; in this sense, they are *published* (cf. chap. I, §I.5), that is made available to anyone. This anomaly can be explained by the fact that these prescriptions remained in force among Christians of various sorts. However, in the P Doc, they are only *pronounced*. This is also the way to take v. 21 ("For Moses since ancient times has in each city people who proclaim him [κερύσσοντας αὐτόν]"), which there is no reason to separate from the P Doc: the prescriptions, which come from Moses, will all be spread orally in every place. It was to Moses that the whole of ancient history was revealed, including the covenants with Noah and Abraham, cf. *Jubilees* 2:26. The formulation "Moses is proclaimed" proceeds from an extreme personalization of Moses regarded as living by virtue of being proclaimed. Two comparisons can be made: 1. Paul uses the same model for the Christian kerygma (Jesus Christ living by being preached, cf. chap. I, §I.1); in this formal sense, Jesus is another Moses, and it is all the more remarkable that James makes no allusion to him here; 2. FJ (*J.W.* 2 §145) reports that the Essenes had an extreme veneration for Moses (prohibition of blaspheming his name), cf. chap. VII, §IV.1.

To sum up, James associates Gentile converts neither with Abraham nor with Moses, but with Noah. In so doing, he bases himself on an immemorial tradition, which has no link with Jesus, except by way of the restoration of the house of David, with an eschatological touch. Gently but firmly, he keeps them at a distance from the Mosaic Covenant, whose charter is precisely the Decalogue. Thus he is very close to the outlook of the rabbinic tradition on the Noachide laws, even if the position of the Decalogue had by then become more complex. Finally, in later redactions of Acts, all these arrangements have simply been understood as facilitating relations between converts of different origins :[72] they have only to be reinterpreted as if addressed to people converted *to Jesus Christ*, with the new significance of baptism and the Spirit. For example, with the final formulation of the AT, in which the Pharisees want the Gentiles to observe the law of Moses (v. 5), the reader will inevitably understand that James in his speech eases for them the law *of Moses*; in this way the covenant with Noah fades out of the picture, or that with Moses is broadened, which amounts to the same thing.

James does not lay down anything about rites. Not only is circumcision missing, but there is no mention of baptism, the breaking of the bread, or any other positive prescription relating to worship. Baptism is, however, in the background, not only in the case of Cornelius but also of the "Gentiles who have become believers" whom the Pharisees want to circumcise, and whose faith is certainly expressed by visible acts, whether the process has yet been fully carried out or not. For them, these newcomers have in fact entered into the Covenant, and the question of circumcision then arises with a certain urgency. Confronted with this new reality, James says nothing; the final meaning of the discussion is that he accepts it, but the original meaning is on the contrary that he rejects it. An undeniable divorce, foreseeable in its source, is thus concealed, and it is important to find out why.

In order to do this, we must examine the posterity left by James in Judaea.

72. For example, the introduction of the Golden Rule puts the stress on a universal ethical dimension and blurs the problem of external jurisdictions. There has been much discussion about whether James's prescriptions were ritual or ethical (surveyed in *Les Actes* V:210). The way they are formulated does not allow any firm conclusion, perhaps because the question implies categories that are not strictly relevant. The important point is that they are stipulations of a covenant with God; to observe them is to honor God, and not another.

III – The Jewish Bishops of Jerusalem

What do we know about the Christians of Judaea between James and the Bar Kokhba war? According to Eusebius,[73] the Jewish-Christian church of Jerusalem emigrated to Pella after 70, but some came back to Judaea and remained there until the time of Trajan and Hadrian;[74] perhaps some never left, since until 132–135 all the bishops of Jerusalem were "Hebrews of ancient stock" (*Hist. eccl.* 4.5.2-4), descended, like James, from the family of Jesus. After 135 and the expulsion of the Jews from Judaea, the Christians of Jerusalem, now Aelia, were attached to the diocese of Caesarea, which was of western obedience.[75] Previously, they had remained close to local Jewish customs, but little is known about them, since they were distant from the circles that produced the NT.

The principal item in the dossier is a list of fifteen bishops, which Eusebius gives twice. He states that he obtained his information from Hegesippus, a Jewish-Christian writer contemporary with Trajan and Hadrian, but makes clear that his source contained no chronological data. Other authors later on give various additional details, especially dates.

These items of information have been under discussion for a long time, since they appear suspect,[76] especially because of their apparent contradiction with the decrees of James in Acts. Different opinions have been expressed as to their authenticity, of which we shall mention only one: for Harnack, the list in Eusebius is not a succession of bishops, but

73. *Hist. eccl.*, 3.5.3. According to Jozef Verheyden, *De vlucht van de christenen naar Pella. Onderzoek van het getuigenis van Eusebius en Epiphanius* (Verh. Koning. Acad. België, Jaar. 50, 127), Brussel, 1988 (summary in Eng. p. 241–244), Eusebius wanted to show that, unlike the Jews, the Christians experienced a return, which obviously presupposes a flight. That is not impossible.

74. Cf. Adolf Schlatter, *Die Kirche Jerusalem von 70–130*, Gütersloh, 1898.

75. There is no precise information about Christianity at Caesarea before 132. The *Apostolic Constitutions*, 7.46.2 mention, after only three bishops of Jerusalem (James, Simeon son of Cleophas and Judas son of James), three bishops of Caesarea in the first century, who are none other than "Zachaeus, a former publican, then Cornelius, and finally Theophilus." The *Clementine Homilies* also give Zachaeus as the first bishop of Caesarea. All these may be regarded as Lucan characters: Luke 19:2 is the only mention of Zachaeus, the publican of Jericho; Cornelius is the centurion of Acts 10:1 f.; Theophilus is the real or supposed person to whom the Lucan double-work is dedicated (Luke 1:4; Acts 1:1). An effort is clearly being made to show that the church of Caesarea enjoys an apostolic origin and authority not less than Jerusalem.

76. Cf. the data brought together by Frédéric Manns, "La liste des premiers évêques de Jérusalem," in: François Blanchetière & Moshe D. Herr (ed.), *Aux origines juives du christianisme*, Peeters, Paris-Louvain, 1993, p. 133–158.

a list of bishop-presbyters who existed more or less at the same time, and it probably includes members of Jesus' family *(desposunoi)*.[77] Taking into account what we have seen of the position originally adopted by James, our object now is to take up this opinion of Harnack and give it greater precision, which will allow us to see what exactly these "bishops" were.

1. The Bishops Lists

The list of the Jewish bishops of Jerusalem has come down to us in several parallel forms. The principal witnesses are:

—Eusebius, *Historia ecclesiastica*, 4.5.3. On the subject of this list he writes: "I have not found any written statement of the dates of the bishops of Jerusalem, for tradition says that they were extremely short-lived."[78] In 4.22.1-8, he makes it clear that his source is Hegesippus, who would have known a great number of the bishops.

—Previously, Eusebius had compiled a *Chronicle* in two parts, now lost. The first part, a sort of summary of world history, has been preserved only in an Armenian translation (hereafter *Chron. arm.*);[79] the second part, consisting of chronological tables, has been preserved only in Jerome's Latin translation (hereafter *Chron. lat.*).[80] Both give the list of bishops, but cut it up into several blocks around isolated dates.

—Epiphanius of Salamis, *Panarion,* 66.20 (*PG* 42.59–62), gives a list of twenty-seven "bishops of the Jerusalemites," of which the first fifteen correspond to those of Eusebius.

77. Cf. Adolf von Harnack, *Die Mission und Ausbreitung des Christentums, in den drei ersten Jahrhunderten*, Leipzig, Hinrichs, 1924^4, p. 631.

78. Translation Kirsopp Lake, *Eusebius. The Ecclesiastical History. Vol. I (Bks I–V* (The Loeb Classical Library), Cambridge, Mass. & London, Harvard Univ. Press & William Heinemann, 1949.

79. Joseph Karst, *Eusebius. V—Armenische Chronik* (Die Griechischen Christlichen Schriftsteller der ersten drei Jahrhunderte, 20), Leipzig, Hinrichs, 1911.

80. Rudolf Helm, *Eusebius. VII—Die Chronik des Hieronymus. 1. Teil : Text ; 2. Teil : Kritischer Apparat* (Die Griechischen Christlichen Schriftsteller der ersten drei Jahrhunderte, 24 & 34), Leipzig, Hinrichs, 1913–1926.

	Eusebius *Hist. eccl.*	*Chron. arm.*	*Chron. lat.*	Epiphanius
1	James, brother of the Lord		=, from Tiberius 18 (32), to Nero 7 (61/62)	=, martyred under Nero
2	Simeon	Crucified under Trajan (107)	=, to Trajan 10 (107)	=, son of Cleophas, crucified under Trajan
3	Justus	=	=, to Trajan 14 (111)	Judas
4	Zachaeus	=	=	Zechariah
5	Tobias	=	=	=
6	Benjamin	=	=	=
7	John	=	=	=, to Trajan 19
8	Ma(tha)thias	=	=	Mathias
9	Philip	=	=, to Hadrian 7 (123)	
10	(S)eneca	=	=	=
11	Justus	=	=	=, to Hadrian
12	Levi	=	=	=
13	Ephres	=	=	Ouaphris
14	Joseph, Josê	=	=	=
15	Juda(s)	=	=, to Hadrian 19 (135)	=, to Antoninus 11

The Principal Witnesses of the List of Jewish Bishops of Jerusalem
(*Legend:* Tiberius 18 = 18th year of Tiberius)

These lists agree, allowing for small variants in transmission. So they depend on a single source. The appearance of the chronological data only after Eusebius makes that aspect of the information suspect. However, there is a major chronological problem: after James and Simeon, all the dates given begin in 107. So there is a gap before that date, but then follows a succession of thirteen names in less than thirty years. This difficulty was seen by a Latin copyist of Jerome, who tried to identify Simeon with Peter, who died under Nero according to tradition. What Epiphanius has to say about James is the trace of a similar gloss, but it can be attached to the information given by Josephus, that the Sadducee high priest Ananias had him stoned to death in 62, that is under Nero (*Ant.* 20 §200). These corrections or hesitations do not get rid of the problem, but rather emphasize it.[81] In other words, we must conclude that the chronological elements have not been invented to fill out a succession of bishops of Jerusalem, but come from a form of the list which did not convey the idea of a regular succession since James.

81. Later witnesses to the same list assign a period of office to each bishop, but they are very short: for George Syncellus, they add up to 46 years, which approximates to the period between Trajan 10 (107) and Antoninus 11 (149), if one follows Epiphanius; for Nicephorus of Constantinople, the total is 37 years, cf. F. Manns, "Liste," p. 144.

That brings us back to Hegesippus, who, as Eusebius himself declares, had known many bishops, precisely at the time of Hadrian and before (Trajan). Epiphanius also depends on Hegesippus, as both add the detail that Simeon was the son of Cleophas (*Hist. eccl.* 4.22.4). Eusebius' omission of the dates can be explained very simply. He is preoccupied by heresies and other dissension, and his concern is explicitly "the succession from the holy apostles" (1.1.1), which alone can guarantee the maintenance of orthodoxy; consequently, he takes the greatest care to specify the dates of the bishops of Rome. The list of Hegesippus, comprising mostly Semitic names, suits perfectly the same interest in the case of Jerusalem, provided the dates are left aside. Eusebius even admits this indirectly, when, in the passage already quoted, he writes that these bishops reigned only for a short time, which does not fit the chronological references in his *Chronicle* and in Epiphanius; in the *Chronicle*, he had already explained the omission of detailed dates by the fact that he had not found *complete* information.[82] Furthermore, in his *Church History* he has inserted his bishops list for Jerusalem in the time of Xystus, bishop of Rome (119–129) that is under Hadrian.

So he has no real document to hand which he could attach to earlier periods. Elsewhere he cites Hegesippus (3.32.3), who explains that James's successor Simeon was the son of Cleophas, brother of Joseph; so he was a first cousin of Jesus, and was martyred under Trajan as a descendant of David and a Christian, at the age of 120. This account is legendary. For one thing, the motif of persecution of the descendants of David is recurrent (3.20.1), and in any case, the relationship to Jesus comes only from John 19:25, which *can* be understood grammatically to mean that Mary, the wife of Cleophas, is the sister of Mary, the mother of Jesus; that is hardly likely to mean that the two Marys were full sisters with the same name, but could mean that they were sisters-in-law. The only possible conclusion to draw from Hegesippus is that, before Eusebius, he had already tried to reconstruct a succession of bishops of Jerusalem from lists which in reality had to do only with the periods of Trajan and Hadrian.

Thus it seems that the absence of the dates in Eusebius does not mean they were invented later, but that he deliberately left them out, whereas they were present in Hegesippus and his sources. Consequently,

82. In fact he mentions that Hegesippus belonged "to the first generation from the apostles" (*Hist. eccl.* 2.23.4). The Latin translation of Rufinus, understanding that Hegesippus belonged to the 2nd cent. (Eusebius elsewhere, cf. above), more prudently writes "to the first generation*s* from the apostles." Cf. W. Telfert, "Was Hegesippus a Jew?" *HTR* 48 (1960), p. 143–153.

there is no reason to think that the dates which Eusebius himself gives in his *Chronicle* are glosses added by later copyists. For one thing, they are attested by two distinct traditions, Latin and Armenian, which both give the same grouping of names under Trajan and Hadrian, and for another, they agree with Hegesippus and Epiphanius.

To sum up, the list of Eusebius (or Hegesippus) does speak of bishops under Trajan and Hadrian, but without a very clear link with James. The names given fall into four blocks: two isolated individuals over a long period, then two groups of six. Harnack's judgment is confirmed: it is not a question of a succession, or at least not only that, but of multiple bishops, more or less contemporary, and in the same spirit as James. The notion of "diocese" of Jerusalem is not really suitable, although that is precisely the fiction which Eusebius tries to introduce. Furthermore, we have no knowledge of multiple dioceses in Judaea. In any case, it is certainly anachronistic to think in terms of territorial jurisdictions; it is better to ask what a "bishop" might be, and whether there could be more than one in the same region.[83] We shall return to this question later (chap. VII, §IV.3); suffice it to say here that they were very similar to *peqidim* and other *mebaqerim*, supervisors of Essene groups qualified to pronounce on the admission or expulsion of members of the community. But before that, we need to look more closely at what Eusebius has to say and the context which it presupposes.

2. James's Eclipse and Return to Favor. The minim

In two places, Eusebius mentions that the Christians of Judaea were circumcised: once, when he records the accession of Justus (*Hist. eccl.*

83. A passage in the Babylonian Talmud (*Sanh* 43a), missing from the usual editions (but mentioned by Raphael Rabbinovicz, *Variae lectiones. IX – Sanhedrin*, Magenza, Bril, 1878, p. 125 f.), gives a list of the disciples of Jesus: "Jesus the Nazorean had five disciples: Mathai, Naqi, Neṣer, Buni and Toda." To them are assigned five parallel Scriptural polemics, based on these properly Semitic names, which are also biblical words. The attempt has been made, but in vain, to see in these names the evangelists, or to understand them as labelling Jesus, cf. Joseph Klausner, *Jesus of Nazareth* (Eng. tr. by W.F. Stinespring), New York, 1925, p. 28 f., but no explanation covers the whole of the list, which also has the anomaly of not naming James, even though he is well known in the rabbinic sources as having worked in the name of Jesus close to Tannaitic circles (*THul* 2:22-24; *BAbZ* 17a). However, Yoḥanan Lederman, "Les évêques juifs de Jérusalem," *RB* 1997, p. 211–222, shows that these names refer in code to five disciples: Mathias, Zechariah (Zachaeus), Ephres, Benjamin and Judah, that is to five in the two groups of six "bishops" of Jerusalem under Trajan and Hadrian; furthermore, the polemic is double edged, as it attacks both the disciples and through them Jesus, a superimposition which is to be found also in the gospels (§V.2). In sum, this tradition points to polemics at a well-determined period (which coincides with the appearance of the problem of the *minim*, cf. below), in a context of persecutions.

3.35); later, when he gives the list just discussed, he adds that the church of Jerusalem as a whole was formed of *believing* Hebrews (4.5.2). This detail is instructive. Not only were these Christians of Jewish origin, but even more they were circumcised and observant. In other words, the information given by Eusebius, that the Judaean group associated with James was formed of observant Jews, is perfectly consistent. Furthermore, the continuing rumor that James and his successors were of David's stock is a Messianic symptom which is strictly Jewish.[84]

In that case, the difficulty of establishing a clear succession from James raises two problems which are connected: Why is there no significant information about the immediate successors of James? and, at the same time, Why is Eusebius so careful to report what Hegesippus has to say and to emphasize the legitimacy of the Church of Jerusalem, despite what seems to have been something of an eclipse? The question becomes all the more acute in the light of Eusebius' extreme mistrust of any kind of heresy, and *a fortiori* of Judaism; he does not deal kindly with the Ebionites (*Hist. eccl.* 3.27), who are only Jewish-Christians who have no known link with James. We might go so far as to allow that for him the successors of James constituted an extinct branch, and were not a problem for his own time.

A first sign is provided by Eusebius himself, quoting Hegesippus (*Hist. eccl.* 3.20.1-6), who reports that the grandsons of Jude, brother of the Lord (Matt 13:55), had been arrested as descendants of David on the order of Domitian, who feared the coming of a Messiah from the east. Brought before the emperor, they showed that they were simple folk who worked with their hands and had only a small amount of landed property; they were released as posing no danger, and returned to "govern the churches." This narrative certainly includes some legendary elements, in particular the appearance before the emperor in Rome, but three facts stand out. First, these were country folk, small farmers or manual workers, which fits into the original Galilean environment, far from towns. Next, that they were related to the Lord qualified them to be heads of

84. It is impossible without begging the question to draw from this an argument in favor of the historicity of Joseph's descent from David (Matt 1:16, Luke 3:23 f.); it is an attribute linked to the title of "Nazorean." On the other hand, the fact that James and "the brothers of Jesus" in general were sons of Joseph, but not of Mary, is much more solid, as they could be the issue of a previous marriage; further, Jesus is the firstborn of Mary (Luke 2:23), but is not said to be Joseph's eldest son. Again, the fact that Joseph was legally married to Mary (Matt 1:19; Luke 1:27) assures that all his sons had the same legal status. Finally, Mary's reply to the angel's announcement that she will conceive and bear a son, that she "knows not man," seems to imply that this will continue to be true, even though she is married to Joseph, and so some sort of intention to remain a virgin, cf. chap. VII, §III.4.

communities, as with James; although their function is not named, it corresponds well to that of "bishops." Finally, there are several communities, and there is no definite link with Jerusalem. Eusebius is always aware of dynastic legitimacy, so it is not hard to guess his interest in such information. It is a question of the family of Jesus, which he cannot suspect of doctrinal deviation, since the account of the Jerusalem assembly in Acts 15, of apostolic authority, emphasizes the communion between Peter, Paul and James. As for Jewish customs practiced by these folk, he either neglected to omit them when quoting his sources, or, more likely, regarded them as of no importance, since the only things that mattered for him were doctrines.

One problem, however, remains. It is understandable that there should not have been much information available about James and his immediate successors and their followers: the problems with the Judaizers at Antioch or Corinth were enough to explain why groups of a Pauline type (dominant in the publication of the NT) kept their distance, since contact was impossible. We can even understand perfectly well why such groups delayed a long time before giving final form to the gospels, *i.e.* to biographies of Jesus, precisely because of the danger presented by Jewish-Christians.[85] But then, why this newfound interest in the bishops of Jerusalem at the time of Trajan and Hadrian? It seems to imply some contact at a later stage, on the occasion of events which were sufficiently important to relegate ancient quarrels to the past.

Different convergent facts enable us to form an hypothesis. First, under Trajan and Hadrian, there was a climate of persecution, both of Jews and of Christians.[86] Then, remarkably, the rabbinic sources begin to concern themselves with Christians, called "sectaries" *(minim)*, only in the time of Gamaliel II, that is after 90, which brings us close to Trajan and Hadrian, and also to Hegesippus' "bishops"; in other words, at a certain moment, the Jewish-Christians were regarded as having changed sides. The simplest conclusion is that up till then, the successors of James were hardly distinguishable from the proto-rabbinical groups, whom we classed before in the general category of Essenes. This category certainly contained many currents, some of them more or less Messianic. Thus we arrive, with a little more precision, at the same results as those we already obtained from looking at proselyte baptism (§I.3 above).

The event which brought Jewish-Christians and other Christians together could well have been persecution. But more is needed to explain a

85. Doubtless combined with a censure on the publication of the rites, cf. chap. I, §I.1.

86. Cf. Pliny the Younger, *Ep. ad Trajanum*, 10. 96 and the Christian apologists of the 2nd century.

rejection by other Jews, culminating in Bar Kokhba's persecution of Christians during the war (Justin, *Apol. I* 31.6).[87] Further, after the war, Gentile Christians joined those who had remained in Judaea and at Aelia Capitolina, which was garrisoned by a legion, though administratively dependent on Caesarea, and which was forbidden to the circumcised.[88] Communication had become possible, at least for one sector of the Jewish-Christians.

We will show, from various aspects of the rabbinic sources, that the simplest hypothesis, in order to explain the change on the Jewish side, is to suppose the arrival in Judaea of western Christian texts *in Greek*, perhaps even a biography of Jesus in a form related to the gospel *harmony* attested by Justin, which precisely continued to exist in Syriac.

IV – Tannaites and Christians

The different patterns of the Covenant sketched above (§I.3) are a simplified way of showing diametrically opposed developments. Officially, for the pre-Constantinian Jewish sources, Christianity does not exist, that is to say, is not a significant event in the history of Judaism. This view is in agreement with a traditional outlook, according to which the *Mishnah* is supposed to issue from an environment representing the whole people, and so is the natural heir to the totality of traditions from before the two destructions of 70 and 135. The symmetrical view, with which the NT is imbued, consists in regarding the Christians as the true Israel. Underlying all this are more or less muted polemics. In fact, on the Jewish side there are various signs of positions taken with regard to Christianity at an early stage; certain questions were even sufficiently important to have played an appreciable role in the development of the rabbinic system.[89]

These elements coalesce around the term "sectarian" *(min)*, by which the rabbinic sources designate Christianity,[90] at least from

87. In fact, he persecuted the Jewish-Christians (Nazoreans) for reasons very close to those that animated Paul before his Damascus experience, cf. below §V.2.

88. Cf. Augustin Fliche & Victor Martin (ed.), *Histoire de l'Église. I—L'Église primitive*, Paris, 1934, p. 392, following Eusebius, who organizes everything in terms of the development of the Greek-speaking Church, and is not interested in Jerusalem as such or in holy places, cf. P. W. L. Walker, *Holy City, Holy Places?* Oxford, Oxford University Press, 1990.

89. The first two headings represent a revised form of Étienne Nodet, "Miettes messianiques," in: *Messiah and Christos. Studies in the Jewish Origins of Christianity, Presented to David Flusser* (TSAJ, 32), Tübingen, J. B. C. Mohr (Paul Siebeck), 1992, p. 119–141.

90. The term מין, alternating with צדוקי ("Sadducee, Zaddokite") in certain sources, designates other deviations as well, cf. the sources assembled by Sacha Stern, *Jewish*

Gamaliel II's reorganization at Yavneh. Concentrating as it did on access to the Covenant by baptism, Christianity had little interest in the people as a whole; in this sense, it kept one of the recognizable features of a reforming sect of Essene type. From a Jewish point of view, therefore, Christianity's openness to the Gentiles appears to be only a subordinate detail.[91] However, we are going to have to define more precisely the notion of "Christianity," and in particular to trace the Jewish-Christians at a moment when they are no longer acceptable to the groups surrounding Gamaliel.

1. Second Century Messianism

The origins of Messianism in general will be considered later (chap. VI, §I.2); here we shall only point out some debates which occurred rather late in the piece. We have already seen the very firm condemnation of Bar Kokhba's Messianic adventure. In reality, there were two forms of Messianism rejected by Tannaitic circles, as we see from a famous passage which fuses episodes originally distinct. Four sages (Simon b. Zoma, Simon b. ʿAzzai, Elisha b. Abuya and R. Aqiba b. Joseph) strayed into Paradise.[92] The experience was disastrous, and their minds were deranged, except for the last, and his escape was almost a miracle;[93] the three others, although teachers (or *ḥaberim*), were all deprived of the title "rabbi." They suffered unusual fates. Elisha, born in Jerusalem before 70, apostasized: he was to be seen riding an ass on the Sabbath, he used to sing Greek hymns, and even at the rabbinic school he had "sectarian" books.[94] The other three, slightly younger, reached their maturity after the downfall. B. ʿAzzai refused to get married so as to dedicate himself to the Torah, but insisted on the necessity of marriage, which caused some astonishment.[95] B. Zoma went in for odd behavior, and had to reply to a

Identity in Early Rabbinic Writings (AGAJU, 23), Leiden, Brill, 1994, p. 109 f. It is not impossible that it is the result of self-censorship in the Byzantine period in order to cover the earlier and more precise term נוצרי ("Nazorean"), which is still found here or there, cf. chap. V, §V.2.

91. *BḤul* 13b explains that "there are no *minim* among the nations"; *BGiṭ* 45b distinguishes between *minim* and Gentiles sharing the same beliefs. Decoded, only the Jewish-Christians lay themselves open to the *halakha* and so also to the diagnosis of being *minim*.

92. נכנסו לפרדס; not (only) the earthly Paradise (גן עדן), but Heaven. Entry either real (according to Rashi, as the anachronisms of the following debate on the pregnant virgin suggest that it should be situated in Paradise), or imagined, through study of the mysteries (cf. *Arukh s. v.* פרדס).

93. *TḤag* 2:3, cf. *BḤag* 14b.

94. ספרי מינים, cf. *BḤag* 15b.

95. Cf. *BYeb* 63b.

strange question: "Can a high priest marry a pregnant virgin?" (according to Lev 21:11 f., he must marry a virgin).[96] The deviant element in Aqiba's history is that he believed that Bar Kokhba was the Messiah.[97]

Everything in this story turns around a sort of Messianism, that is the arrival of that ill-defined era which wavers between "the days of the Messiah" and the "World to come" (the latter bringing together the beginning and the end of all things, whence the synthetic term "Paradise"). To say that these four intruded into Paradise, is only another way of saying that they stepped into this Messianic era, expressed in terms of a transgression. The illusion took on a political hue for Aqiba, though only briefly;[98] he was soon martyred by the Romans. The other cases represent, with a slight shift of vocabulary, a collection of Christian elements, diverse but characteristic, which have been condensed in the form of a perilous entry into the Kingdom of Heaven: profanation of the Sabbath (especially by riding an ass),[99] Greek language (liturgical chants?), "sectarian" books, celibacy for the sake of the Word (the Torah), a virgin mother.[100] The term "Christian" does not necessarily imply here views that are in agreement with the NT, but may belong to proto-gnostic currents, or to the posterity of James, as we have seen.

The two kinds of Messianism are treated in symmetrical fashion,[101] although the term "Messiah son of David" is used expressly only by the disciples of Bar Kokhba *(YTaan* 4:7, 68d). The key persons of both movements are stigmatized in analogous terms: Bar Kokhba, nicknamed "son of the lie," corrupted Israel (cf. chap. IV, §II.1), and Jesus practiced magic

96. *BḤag* 14b בתולה שעיברה מהו [לכהן גדול], or, according to other witnesses which omit the bracketed words: "What should be said of a pregnant virgin?" cf. R. Rabbinovicz, דיקדוקי סופרים, *a. l.*, and *Tosefta kifshuṭah* 5:1290. The reply to the question is veiled by later considerations.

97. Cf. *BSanh* 93b; *YTaan* 4:7, p. 68d, who explains that he *profaned* Israel.

98. He was favorable to a celebrated teacher from Emmaus, a highly symbolic place, cf. §II.1.

99. In another passage, Elisha plucks a radish on the Sabbath to give it to a prostitute, which is a sort of parody of a long reading of Luke 6:5 WT (ears of wheat plucked on the Sabbath): "Seeing someone working on the Sabbath, [Jesus] said to him: 'Man, if you know what you are doing, you are blessed; if you do not, you are cursed and a Law breaker.'"

100. This "entry into Paradise" does not exclude a mystical experience, which unites the vision of the origins *(maaśeh bereshit)* and that of the end *(maaśeh merkaba)*; since W. Bacher, *Die Agada der Tannaiten*, 1903^2, I:333 f., this "entry" has been interpreted as purely gnostic, but Gershom Scholem, *Jewish Gnosticism, Merkabah Mysticism, and Talmudic Tradition*, New York, 1960, p. 16, makes an enlightening comparison with 2 Cor 12:2-4, "I know a man belonging to the Messiah who, [. . .] was lifted up to the third Heaven (ἕως τρίτου οὐρανοῦ)."

101. On the similarities between Jesus and Bar Kokhba, cf, chap. IV, §II.1.

and led Israel astray (*BSanh* 43a[102]). From this symmetry a useful conclusion can be drawn: Jesus and his disciples are looked at from a Jewish-Christian perspective, since the fully developed Pauline perspective, which abolishes the distinction between Jews and Gentiles,[103] cannot be regarded as a brand of Messianism; the debate on Messianism is strictly Jewish (cf. chap. VII, §V.2).

This mistrust with regard to all Messianism corresponds to the fact that rabbinic Judaism distances itself from apocalyptic and eschatological speculations on salvation, in order to concentrate on the sanctification of daily life; from this follows a very rational outlook and the great importance given to the benedictions. We will come back to this in connection with the 613 commandments.

2. Greek, Hebrew, Aramaic

We have already seen that Eliezer and Yehoshua, both renowned for their scrupulous fidelity to tradition, congratulated the proselyte Aquila on his new translation of the Pentateuch, published after 100.[104] There are good reasons for thinking that this approval was given not primarily out of a desire to see the Bible distributed in Greek, but rather in order to resist a form of translation which was reckoned to be dissident, namely the LXX.[105] At a later stage, around 200, Judah the Prince elevated Greek al-

102. Passage referred to in chap. II, §II.1 (execution on the eve of Passover).

103. Thus in Eph 2:11-22. However, a passage like Gal 3:25-29 appears to imply that this distinction continues to exist like all the others (man-woman, master-slave) with all its effects in this world, but has little significance in view of the unity acquired in Christ with the admission of the Gentiles into the inheritance of Abraham. Such a position could at the outset have been almost compatible with that of James. Paul certainly evolved, and the label "Pauline" here designates, not so much his thinking at any one moment, as the extrapolation of his options as they are manifested in the final redaction of the gospels (cf. §V.2).

104. *YMeg* 1:11, 71c; they cite Ps 45:3, "You are the most beautiful (יפיפית) of the children of men." The term used for congratulations, וקילסו אותו, comes precisely from κάλος: they declared the person (or the work) "beautiful (and good)," cf. Lieberman I:17 f. (contrary to Jastrow *s. v.*, who cannot get beyond the existence of the root קלס in the Bible, where it has the opposite sense of "derision"). According to *YQid* 1:2, p. 59a, Aquila made his translation in front of Aqiba, that is a little later; in parallel to this, Jerome, *In Isaiam* 7.14, indicates that Aquila was a disciple of Aqiba. According to Epiphanius, *Weights and Measures* §14, Aquila was a relation of Hadrian, and his translation was made in 128–129, which is a very plausible date. The tradition is all the same a little confused, as Onqelos, to whom is attributed the official (Aramaic) targum of the Pentateuch, is only a doublet of Aquila: also a proselyte, he was congratulated by the same masters for his translation (*BMeg* 3a).

105. Cf. *Search*, p. 182–188 It is hard to determine the precise reason for this opposition to the LXX, so much used by Philo; it is not impossible that it was perceived as having become the Christian Bible, cf. below.

most to the level of a sacred language, and had no wish to hear Aramaic, a "castrated" language.[106] His disciple Bar Qappara even wanted the Torah read in the language of Japhet (*i.e.* in Greek), because of Gen 9:27, "May God make space for Japhet, and let him dwell in the tents of Shem." Japhet is the ancestor of Greece (Yavan, Gen 10:2), and this text is understood as an invitation to welcome the Greek language.[107]

Between these two examples of reverence for Greek, comes an episode which goes in the opposite direction. After the "war of Quietus," who crushed the revolts of 115–117, it was decided, according to *MSoṭa* 9:14, to do away with bridal crowns, and also that "no one should teach his son Greek." Earlier, at the time of the civil war between Hyrcanus II and his brother Aristobulus (67–65 B.C., until the arrival of Pompey), a curse was pronounced, or so tradition has it, on anyone who taught his son "Greek wisdom."[108] Both traditions may in fact refer to the same episode, as there is a tendency to mix up the wars, which all feature divisions among Jews. An interesting reason is given for forbidding Greek under Trajan: it was *at the time* a measure taken provisionally for protection against "informers."[109] No other detail is provided, and the traditional explanation is that there was a risk that young Jews might become informers and, since Greek was the language of the authorities, betray the community, whether deliberately or not, especially in matters concerning taxation.[110] This is hardly satisfactory, as it is difficult to see why this would be a new problem at the time, and why it ceased to be so later;

106. לשון סורסי, *BBabaQ* 82b. The term is derived from סורי "Syrian, Syriac," by verbal play on סריס "eunuch."

107. *GenR* 36:8. The verbal play on the verse (יפת אלהים ליפת) implies also a comparison with יפה "beautiful," equivalent of κάλος used to congratulate Aquila (cf. above).

108. חכמת יוונית, *BSoṭa* 49b. Lieberman II:100 f. tries to show that what is meant is Greek wisdom in the sense of family religious and cultural tradition, and so there was no ban on personal study of Greek language or wisdom like any other profane subject or skill; it was only a question of resistance to Hellenization. But this reason is too general and does not take account of the passing nature of the measures taken. In particular, the question was once put to Yehoshua, one of those who congratulated Aquila, if it was permitted to teach Greek to one's son; he replied: "Let it be taught at a moment that is neither day nor night, as it is said (Josh 1:8), *May the book of this Law be always on your lips: murmur it* [והגית בו] *day and night* [. . .]" (*YSoṭa* 9:14, p. 24c); it appears difficult to understand these words of Yehoshua as expressing one single opinion, and simpler to imagine successive phases.

109. מפני המָסוֹרות, *YSoṭa ibid.* (noun of agent in form *paʿōl* from the verb מסר "hand over, transmit").

110. Thus Rashi (on *BRSh* 17a). Lieberman II:101, n. 13, imagines them even wanting to become *rhetores*, and it would then be a question of prohibiting a profession, but not a language as such.

Roman domination, since the arrival of Coponius (about 6) or even since the death of Herod, had not fundamentally changed its nature.

A further decree was added to the prohibition of Greek: "Let no one whitewash the walls of his house." A little later, this new decree was given a more limited bearing: "This is what the masters said (*i.e.* 'meant to say'): 'Each one paints his house with lime, but it is necessary to keep a small part (*i.e.* 'not painted'), in memory of Jerusalem.'"[111] However, this interpretation must be secondary, since the decree was made well after 70, and equally before 135, so not near the time of either of the two great destructions, and especially before the Jews were expelled from Judaea. If we try to find a link between the two decrees, forbidding Greek and the complete painting of one's house, it is enough to observe that in Greek "painted" is *christos*, a common term with several meanings (including "anointed"), as we saw in connection with the *Testimonium Flavianum* (chap. I, §I.1). In a culture which paid a lot of attention to signs, walls that were "anointed" could certainly pass for a symptom of Christianity.[112] In Hebrew and Aramaic, "whitewash" and "anoint" are different words;[113] in these languages, the identification is not made automatically as it is in Greek, and so can be easily forgotten or concealed, which is the reason why the later decree assigns a quite different reason to the gesture.[114]

111. *TSoṭa* 15:12.

112. It is difficult in that case to admit that walls that are *christos* bear "all the words" that should be written on the door posts (*mezuza*, cf. Deut 6:9), under variable forms, legible or not from the outside. In *Ant.* 4 §213, FJ associates phylacteries and *mezuza*, and says that one should inscribe a "reminder of the greatest benefits of God." Among the Samaritans, the inscription (on the lintel or at the entrance) is legible and contains the Decalogue, which is in agreement with the letter of the *Shemaᶜ* (which refers to "all these words," cf. below §II.4), at least according to a well-attested tradition, cf. Reinhard Pummer, "Samaritan Rituals and Customs," in: Alan D. Crown (ed.), *The Samaritans*, Tübingen, 1989, p. 654. Similarly, a *mezuza* on parchment, found at Qumran (4 Q149), contains only the Decalogue, cf. Roland de Vaux & Joseph-T. Milik, *Qumran Grotte 4* (DJD, 6), Oxford, 1977, II:39 and 80. According to the rab. trad., the *mezuza* is a little scroll enclosed in a container (so not legible), on which are inscribed only two passages, Deut 6:4-9 and 11:13-21, which do not include the Decalogue.

113. *TSoṭa* 15:8 לא יסוד איש את קירות ביתו; the verb טייח is also employed; משח is strictly reserved to an anointing with oil or perfume.

114. In Acts 23:2, Paul, in a passage belonging to a later level of redaction, calls the high priest Ananias a "whitewashed wall" (τοῖχε κεκονιαμένε), whom God will strike, which is received immediately as a grave insult; this could have been, by way of two translations, "painted, anointed wall," perhaps with allusion to the priestly anointing being conferred on stone (Temple which is going to be overthrown?). In Matt 23:27, when Jesus compares the Pharisees to "whitewashed tombs" (τάφοις κεκονιαμένοις), that too may have originally meant that they keep the Messiah buried (refusing to believe in his resurrection). In both cases, however, the Messianic pun, though at least possible, is not clear enough in the context and certainly escaped the final redactor (and perhaps others for a long time before).

The decree presupposes for Judaea a population, or at least a group, whose customs are homogeneous, so that it is not easy to pick out who are Christians, a problem which suddenly becomes important. If it was necessary to be able to tell one house from another, they must all have been living in close proximity. It is very likely that we are still dealing with brotherhoods (or schools), who could well have known Greek, as certain texts from Qumran and the rabbinic tradition[115] show. Indeed, that is even probable, when we recall the case of the three dissidents, who were certainly *ḥaberim*, and remember that the special benediction against the "sectaries" was meant in the first place to clarify the situation within the brotherhood itself (above, at the beginning of §II). Taking into account all that has been said about the immediate successors of James, who were not greatly different from other marginal Jewish brotherhoods, we can conclude that the Christians aimed at here were of a Jewish-Christian type, and that they were widespread, or suspected of being so.

This question of prohibited painting will come up again in the context of Passover (chap. VII §I.2). Right now, we need to find out why the Christians were regarded as dangerous at this time, whereas until then they appear to have coexisted peacefully with other Jews. In *BSoṭa* 49b, Simon, son of Gamaliel II states that there were a thousand boys in his father's house (at Betar), five hundred studying the Torah and five hundred studying Greek,[116] and that he himself and a cousin were the only ones who remained. This massive disappearance is due, at least in part, to the war, as a parallel passage speaks of the massacre at Betar of boys studying the Torah (*BGiṭ* 48a). This massacre by the Romans corresponds to the disappearance of the "five hundred studying the Torah" in the other version, but what about the equal number who were studying Greek? The saying implies that, besides the war, there was another reason for the disappearance of his father's pupils, just as serious and linked to the knowledge of Greek.

This brings us back to the "informers" mentioned above, who were corrupted by Greek. In *BRSh* 17a, there is a list of those who are vowed to eternal damnation: the "sectaries," the "informers," the "epicureans," those who have denied the Torah, those who have denied the resurrection of the dead, those who have separated themselves from the community, those who have sinned and led others to sin, like Jeroboam, etc. This list is in fact composite, comprising first, categories of sinners designated by

115. According to *MYad* 4:5, the books of Homer are permitted, but they do not have the holiness of the Bible; what is interesting is that it was necessary to say so, and that the criterion of distinction (at the time of the *Mishnah*) is not that of language.

116. With the correction proposed by Lieberman II:102, n. 18.

generic names, then a list of *the same*, but defined by what they have done. Comparing this list with that in *MSanh* 10:1-2, which gives those who have no part in the World to come (which is equivalent to eternal damnation), it is clear that the "informers" correspond to "those who have sinned and have led others to sin." The conclusion is, that it is a question of those who have gone over to Christianity *and taken others with them*, which is a new phenomenon,[117] not to be confused with the existence of "sectaries."

This new phenomenon corresponds to an active proselytism and also to a sudden fear of Greek, and can be explained by a new contact between these Jewish-Christians and Christians of another type. That is the hypothesis expressed earlier, which fits easily into what we have just been seeing. Putting together the various signs and taking into account the difference between the Jewish and Christian points of view, we can conclude that Gentile Christian missionaries began to make their appearance at the end of Trajan's or the beginning of Hadrian's reign, at the same time as the zealot spirit was on the rise once more among the Jews; they may even have contributed towards that rise. These Christians came from Rome,[118] and probably had with them some books in Greek, in more or less published form. We have seen that Justin, with his *Memoirs of the Apostles*, witnesses to a first stage in which there were authoritative texts, even if they had not yet been formally published (chap. I, §I.1).

At this point, the question of the circulation of texts must be broadened and seen as going in both directions. It may have been at this moment that the *epistles* of James and Jude, of Jewish-Christian type, were brought into the collection that was in the process of becoming the NT, which would agree with the fact that their canonicity was under discussion until the 3rd century.[119] Similarly, the question of the *Gospel ac-*

117. Perhaps the word מסור has been kept because of a possible double meaning, as the root signifies also "transmit a tradition" (cf. *MAb* 1:1, etc.), which is found also in the term "Massoretic": these "informers" are those who hand over (to the enemy), but also those who transmit (the Gospel), so missionaries, whether or not of Jewish origin. These variations in meaning can be related to those of the Greek equivalent παραδίδωμι, cf. chap. II, §II.5 (Judas, Matt 26:23 par.).

118. Palestine was now directly subject to Rome, cf. chap. VII, §I.4.

119. The Muratorian canon (end of 2nd cent., perhaps Roman) leaves out Jas (and Heb), and mentions separately Jude and "two epistles of John," apparently to include them; however, according to Th. Zahn, *Geschichte des neutestamentlichen Kanons. Das Neue Testament vor Origenes*, Leipzig, 1888–1892, II:66, a negative which has disappeared should be restored. For Eusebius, *Hist. eccl.* 3.25.1-7, Jas, Jude, 2 Pet and 2–3 John are discussed (ἀντιλεγόμενα) but well known, cf. Bruce M. Metzger, *The Canon of the New Testament. Its Origin, Development and Significance*. Oxford, Clarendon, 1987 (1988^2), p. 191 f., 305 f.

cording to the Hebrews mentioned by Eusebius (*Hist. eccl.* 3.27.4) may have some connection with a properly Jewish-Christian form of Matt.[120] These questions will be raised again later (§V.2), but in any event it is difficult to be more precise about the circumstances of these new exchanges under Trajan and Hadrian; we can only suppose that they did not happen overnight. We should also bear in mind that Greek was common to all. These exchanges of texts, which were not published but were of apostolic authority, would not have taken place without creating some tensions between those who accepted and those who rejected them. We have seen that there were doubts in Gentile-Christian circles about the epistles of James and Jude, and it is very probable that there were corresponding hesitations over the texts newly arrived in Judaea.

It is now possible to get some idea why Judah the Prince, about 200, accepted Greek with honor, but showed mistrust of Aramaic, which he called "castrated" by a contemptuous play on the name *Syriac*.[121] The center of activity is now Galilee, around the Lake. Does this give a clue to understanding why the danger from Christianity is no longer connected with Greek but with Syriac? The spread of Christianity eastwards, to eastern Syria and Mesopotamia, is not well documented, but it does not appear to come from Palestine.[122] There were certainly Jewish-Christian groups whose origins lay in Galilee and Batanaea: archaeology yields undoubted traces,[123] and the episode of Paul at Damascus implies it, at least for the earliest times (chap. VI, §II.1). But even if Christianity existed in

120. Cf. Anthony Saldarini, *Matthew's Christian-Jewish Community*, Chicago, University Press, 1994, who opens up new paths in this direction.

121. With his usual acuteness, Rashi (*BBabaQ* 83a) has seen that Syriac is the Aramaic *of the nations*; but his disciples contested it (Tos. לשון).

122. Despite the legends which attach to the Twelve the foundation of Churches in the four corners of the globe. In reality, there was always a stage of transmission in Greek. For Edessa, the legend of Abgar and Addai establishes a direct link with Jesus (the "Letter of Jesus") and with the apostle Thomas, cf. J. B. Segal, *Edessa, 'The Blessed City,'* Oxford, 1970, p. 64 f. This sort of legend probably expresses certain contacts between Jewish-Christian groups (with Thomas or others) and "Pauline" missions, and so with the NT. It is a fact that the oriental churches today, more or less attached to Antioch, still preserve clear Jewish-Christian traces, above all in liturgical usages (mourning for the Temple, etc.).

123. Cf. Claudine Dauphin, "De l'église de la circoncision à l'église de la gentilité; sur une nouvelle voie hors de l'impasse," *Liber Annus* 43 (1993), p. 223–242, who has found at several points in the Golan various architectural fragments in basalt (earlier than the 4th cent.), some ornamented with properly Jewish symbols *(menora)*, others with properly Christian symbols (cross, anchor), still others apparently with both (palm, fish, boat, grapes, cup, etc.); in certain cases, combinations of Jewish and Christian symbols seem to indicate Jewish-Christians. So there was coexistence between several groups. The regular cross is originally a Jewish symbol (cf. chap. VII, §V.2), but it is not unlikely that, from the 2nd cent., it became inseparable from Christian references.

these regions well before 200, the spread of Christian *texts*, whether the Syriac NT translated from the recently canonized Greek, or even only a gospel harmony such as the Diatessaron of Tatian (cf. chap. I, §I.1), belongs to this period.

By the end of the 2nd century, there was at Edessa in Upper Mesopotamia a sizeable Christian community which acknowledged its dependence on Antioch,[124] cradle of all the eastern churches that adopted the NT, and center from which Christianity progressively reached the interior of Syria (Damascus, Palmyra) and Persia (Seleucia-Ctesiphon). About 195, Septimius Severus divided the province of Syria into Syria Phoenice (Antioch) and Syria Coele, with Damascus as capital,[125] thus restoring importance to a city which was situated close to the Golan and Batanaea, the regions corresponding to the "Jewish Syria" of the rabbinic sources (cf. §II.4). About 200 there was a Christian community at Bostra[126] south east of Damascus (in the province of Arabia),[127] so still close to "Jewish Syria." Let us recall that Syriac, both the language and the writing, originated as that branch of eastern Aramaic proper to the region of Edessa,[128] and is very close to Talmudic Aramaic.

The conclusion is simple: the Aramaic banished by Judah was really Syriac, as the term he used implies. His intention was to protect his community against a threat coming from Damascus, which was connected with texts whose circulation was certainly due to a new missionary wave. So the episode is the first attestation of the appearance in circles of a Jewish-Christian type of Christian texts translated from Greek but originating among non-Greek Gentile-Christians (Antioch, Edessa) in the region of Damascus and Bostra. In fact, the rejection of Syriac was only temporary, since from the 3rd century Talmudic discussions were conducted in Aramaic, both in Galilee and in Babylonia, and they remained in that form; one saying even defends *Syriac* as a biblical language, referring to the Aramaic passages in Dan and Ezra-Neh (*YSoṭa* 7:3, p. 21c). Thus, the

124. Cf. William Cureton, *Ancient Syriac Documents Relative to the Establishment of Christianity*, London, 1864, p. 72; A. Fliche & V. Martin II:126.

125. On Damascus and the entourage of Ananias, cf. *Les Actes* V:17.

126. At the beginning of the 3rd cent. Bostra had a bishop, Beryllus, whose errors provoked Origen to come and put them right, cf. Maurice Sartre, *Bostra. Des origines à l'Islam* (BAH, 117), Paris, 1985, p. 99 f.

127. Probably the region to which Paul withdrew after his conversion (Gal 1:17 "Arabia").

128. Cf. Fr. Briquel-Chatonnet, "Rôle de la langue et de l'écriture syriaques dans l'affirmation de l'identité chrétienne au Proche-Orient," in: *Phoinikeia grammata. IXe colloque (déc. 1989). Documents*, Liège, 1989, p. 165–169.

measures taken with regard to Syriac and Greek are strictly parallel, and both appear to have been taken, at different times, for the same reason.

Mistrust of Greek disappeared. This implies that the Greek-speaking churches, even those nearby (Caesarea Maritima), had taken a position quite independent of Judaism (after 135), and that the missionary effort had changed direction. It is at this time that Origen had very close relations with learned Jews.[129]

To sum up, it seems that the circles that produced the *Mishnah* had to position themselves pragmatically with regard to the ways Christianity was developing. For our purposes this has a twofold importance. First, these problems concerning Jewish-Christians throw light on the original environment of Jesus' disciples, and fill out what we saw earlier. Secondly, the way to use the earliest rabbinic sources can be refined. At first, there were very clear areas of kinship with the environment of primitive Christianity; then measures were taken to keep a distance between the two; finally, these measures were hidden by later developments, at the moment when the brotherhoods broadened their horizon to include the people as a whole. The idea behind these moves was presumably to show that the appearance of Christianity was not a notable event in the history of Judaism, but only a very lateral incident, certainly unfortunate, but without any sort of effect on the *halakha*.

Other examples will confirm what is still only an hypothesis.

3. The Bible

The way in which the NT uses the OT raises a number of problems, most of which we do not need to tackle here. We shall look at just one aspect: What type of text has been used, whether or not in the form of florilegia of selected verses? Anyone can see that in many places the NT follows the LXX against the MT when these differ. The simplest explanation is to say that the NT authors, writing in Greek, naturally used the Greek Bible. The problem is more complex, however, for several reasons. First, the answer just given does not explain what form the quotations had in the underlying Aramaic or Hebrew text. Then in certain cases, the Greek translation used differs from the LXX (one instance has been pointed out in chap. II, §I.2), without any reason to think that a different form of the Hebrew text has been translated. Finally, the Qumran documents and even Josephus[130] show that the Hebrew original behind the

129. Cf. Nicolas de Lange, *Origen and the Jews. Studies in Jewish-Christian Relations in Third Century Palestine* (COP, 25), Cambridge, Cambridge University Press, 1976.

130. Cf. Étienne Nodet, *Le Pentateuque de Josèphe*, Paris, Cerf, 1996, where it is shown that FJ used a Hebrew *exemplar* with glosses, very close to the LXX, which, how-

LXX continued to exist for a long time, to such a point that it is the MT that appears singular. How, then, did the latter text come into being?

The question is vast,[131] but not purely technical, since it brings into play a number of issues which can be identified. We have already seen two significant cases, both having to do with John the Baptist in the Lucan infancy narrative. First, according to the LXX, Samuel, son of a Levite, is expressly consecrated by his mother as a perpetual *nazir*, whereas for the MT he is not a Levite and does not become a *nazir*. We have seen (chap. II, §I.1) that one of the ways of representing the relationship between John the Baptist and Jesus is to regard them as fulfilling the figures of Samuel and David, the anointing being represented by the baptism; but with the MT, the comparison becomes artificial and forced, as Samuel and John have nothing in common. These details are not negligible, since this is one of the aspects under which Jesus is "son of David," with an obvious Messianic connotation. A rabbinical controversy shows that there was an opinion affirming that Samuel was a *nazir* (*BNaz* 66a); under cover of an exercise in imaginative exegesis, it is in fact a textual debate, which presupposes that the LXX or a similar Hebrew text was not far away.

The second case is in the *Benedictus*. In Luke 1:78, the "rising sun from on high," is easily interpreted as the star in the ascendant, with a Messianic meaning attached to the dawn. The reference is Num 24:17, but according to the LXX ("A star will rise") and not according to the MT ("will tread down"), while the targums understand the expression in the same way as the LXX, as do certain texts from Qumran. The end of the verse also has two forms: MT "A scepter will arise from Israel," LXX "A man [. . .]"; only the LXX has a clearly Messianic meaning,[132] which is found also once again in the targums and in CD 7:19 f. Furthermore, this verse is the source of the nickname of Bar Kokhba "son of the Star," with

ever, he did not see until towards the end of his work. This implies that authorized copies of the LXX (deposited in a library) only arrived at Rome towards 90.

131. According to a rabbinic tradition (*SifDt* §356), there were at the Temple three copies of the Torah, which were named after their characteristic variants; it is said that a revision was made by putting together an eclectic text based on majority readings. According to *MMoedQ* 3:4 (with the variant עזרא, supported by *TKel BM* 5:8), there was a "book of Ezra," traditionally used (cf. *MSoṭa* 7:8) for the proclamation of the Law every seven years (Deut 31:10) in the forecourt of the Sanctuary (עזרה, whence the variant "book of the forecourt"). These sayings are interesting because they show: 1. that the original environment did not have its own tradition; 2. that a revision leading to the MT was made *after* the destruction of the Temple (or perhaps after that of Jerusalem).

132. Cf. Geza Vermes, *Scripture and Tradition in Judaism* (Studia Post-Biblica, 4), Leiden, Brill, 1961, p. 59 etc.

an allusion to the Messiah son of David (cf. above §II.1). It is a real question whether in the form that it has in the MT this verse could have been used in this way, as the two variants proper to it imply rather a negative evaluation of the "star": the Hebrew verb "tread down," which also has the meaning "draw a bow," expresses rather adversity and hostility, as does the scepter (a form of mace; cf. Ps 2:9).

We will add a further example which has consequences for the Messiah and for the Passover. A passage from the *Mishnah*[133] on the content of the evening recitation of the *Shema*ᶜ *Israel* contains a fixed rule, followed by the discussion in which it was established (*MBer* 1:5):

> *The departure from Egypt should be remembered in the evening. R. Eleazar b. Azarya said: Here I am at the age of seventy, and I have never succeeded in having the departure from Egypt said in the evening, until Ben Zoma drew it from Scripture, for it is said* (Deut 16:3): So that you may remember the day of your departure from Egypt all the days of your life, *[so]* the days of your life *[mean] "the mornings";* all the days of your life *[are to be understood as] "the evenings." But the Sages say:* "The days of your life *[mean] "this world"; [the repetition]* all the days of your life *is to include the days of the Messiah.*

The debate bears on the word "all" in the verse, which appears redundant, and so must add some further meaning, in the name of the principle that there is nothing superfluous in the Bible. In *TBer* 1:10, the discussion continues:

> *[Ben Zoma] said to them: And because the departure from Egypt is remembered in the days of the Messiah?! But is it not already written* (Jer 23:7 f.): See the days are coming—oracle of YHWH—when it will no longer be said: "As YHWH is living, who brought the Israelites up from the land of Egypt," but: "As YHWH is living, who brought up, and who brought back the nation of the house of Israel from the land of the North (*or*: 'from the land of the hidden sun')." *They said to him: Not that the departure from Egypt may be taken from its place, but that the departure from Egypt may be a supplement to [the victory over] the nations: this becomes the essential thing, and the departure from Egypt secondary.*

The passage cited by Ben Zoma, according to which "in the days of the Messiah" the invocation will contain a twofold reminder, one abbreviated *(who brought up)* and the second developed *(who brought back . . .)*, is ill suited to his own argument, but fits perfectly with that of his opponents, who do want a double reminder. In fact, there is another verse which is

133. This passage figures in the Passover *Seder,* cf. chap. VII, §II.3.

very similar (16:14-15), but which leaves out the first reminder: ". . . when it will no longer be said: *As YHWH is living, who brought the Israelites up from the land of Egypt*, but: *As YHWH is living, who brought the nation of the house of Israel back from the land of the North*." This verse, which has the same beginning and the same structure as the other, proves Ben Zoma's argument. So it would be enough to allow that originally only the opening words of the Scriptural verse were given, as was the custom, and that copyists made a mistake when filling in the rest of the quotation. Another version of the same debate is given in *MekhRI* ("boʾ," p. 60), where the two opposed opinions are no longer contemporary: Ben Zoma gives his argument, with the verse that suits it, then a much later contribution is cited, from Nathan (after 135; he has been mentioned in connection with the arrival of Simon b. Gamaliel at Usha).

This purely technical solution of the difficulty is however too easy, for if Ben Zoma relies on Jer 16:14, which goes in his favor, and his opponents on Jer 23:8, which goes against him, the discussion is futile, since the Scriptural argument is indecisive, as both sides must realize. In fact, Ben Zoma was famous for his talent in searching the Scriptures, to the point that at his death it was said that there was no longer a biblical commentator living (*MSoṭa* 9:14). Furthermore, the verse is quoted in its entirety, which is rare, and other parallels, though drawn up differently, also develop the same verse in the same terms (*YBer* 1:6, p. 4a, *BBer* 12a). So the copyists would have had to make the same mistake independently in several different places, which is very unlikely in the case of well-known verses. We must conclude that Jer 23:7 is really the verse at the center of the debate.

This result becomes very clear if we look at Jer 23:7-8 in the LXX: there the first reminder (departure from Egypt) is omitted, as in 16:24, where the LXX has the same content as the MT.[134] In other words, Ben Zoma argues from the LXX, or rather its Hebrew source: in the days of the Messiah, the departure from Egypt will no longer be remembered, as *both* passages express. On the contrary, his opponents rely on Jer 23:7-8 MT, which alone justifies the twofold reminder. In this way, the complete quotation of this passage in *TBer* 1:10 (above), far from being a simple copyist's error, clearly takes on a double meaning: first a statement on the right text, in a debate on textual criticism; also a discreet allusion to Ben Zoma's incompetence in Scriptural interpretation.

134. But not the same form: Ζῇ κύριος ὃς ἀνέγαγεν (brought up) τὸν οἶκον Ισραηλ supposes a Heb. אשר העלה את בית ישראל; the verb used is precisely that of Jer 23:7 MT, but to designate the departure from Egypt; in this way, the departure from Egypt is totally replaced by Messianic salvation.

Now, despite being a good exegete, he was one of those who intruded into Paradise and came out with a mind deranged, which we have interpreted as straying into Christian Messianism. The debate on whether or not the departure from Egypt will be remembered in the days of the Messiah, makes sense for the feast of Passover. The rabbinical Passover (still in force) is entirely centered on remembering the departure from Egypt, which is retold and commented on, whereas, among the Christians, where the Passover as such has been obscured, neither the NT nor later liturgy give importance to it, except as one moment among others in the history of salvation. In a word, there is a Christian problem, under the appearances of a purely technical question.

This conclusion, involving hints of Messianism, is strengthened when the context of the passage under discussion (Jer 23:5-6) is examined: "See the days are coming—oracle of YHWH—when I will raise up for David a righteous branch (MT; LXX 'a righteous branching'[135]), and he will reign as king [. . .]; in his days Judah will be saved, Israel will dwell in security, and here is his name, by which he will be called: *YHWH our justice* (MT; LXX 'by which the Lord will call him: *Yoṣedeq*'[136])." The "branching" in the LXX can also be understood, according to the most usual meaning of the term, as "rising sun," which brings the Greek close to the Messianic star that "will rise from Jacob" (Num 24:17).[137] On the other hand, the name given by the MT to this descendant of David is remarkable, and *BBabaB* 75a gives three cases where something or

135. MT צמח צדיק, LXX ἀνατολὴν δικαίαν; the only other use of ἀνατολή in Jer (38:40) corresponds to מזרח "orient." However, ἀνατέλλω regularly translates the verb צמח "to branch," and the LXX may have understood צמח here as a verbal noun ("branching"). In Zech 3:8 ("Behold I summon my servant *Branch*"), there is the same equivalence between צמח and ἀνατολή. Finally, Jesus is often called "the Righteous one" in Acts (3:14; 7:52; 22:14).

136. MT אשר יקראו יהוה צדקנו, LXX translates normally ὃ καλέσει αὐτὸν κύριος Ιωσεδεκ (from יוצדק or יהוצדק); the translation given in the text is inspired by *BBabaB* 75a quoted later, which is perhaps based on a reading יקראו. In Jer 33:16 the MT has an analogous formula for Jerusalem אשר יִקרא לה יהוה צדקנו ("which will be called *YHWH our justice*"); curiously, this passage is both missing from the LXX and ignored by *BBabaB* 75a. The form צדקנו is not to be found elsewhere.

137. The same proclamation of Messianic in-gathering, in a Christian form (the "Church," invocation of the name of Jesus), is an aspect of the breaking of the bread, cf. *Did.* 9:4; *Apost. Const.* 7.25.3. It is notable that the prayer, that the Church may be gathered like the bread which has been "scattered," is to be found in eucharistic prayers in early Egyptian and Ethiopian liturgies; texts in Anton Hänggi and Irmgard Pahl (ed.), *Prex eucharistica. Textus e variis liturgiis antiquioribus selecti* (Spicilegium Friburgense 12), Fribourg, Éditions Universitaires, 1968², p. 124 (Fragment of Dêr-Balyzeh), 130 (Anaphora [Eucologion] of Serapion of Thmuis 3.13), 158 (Anaphora of John the Son of Thunder); see also *De Virginitate* (attributed to St. Athanasius) §13.

someone receives the name of the "Holy one blessed be He": the saints according to Isa 43:7, Jerusalem in Ezek 48:35, and the Messiah here (Jer 23:5). This last statement, that the Messiah will receive the name of God (YHWH), is all the more interesting in that it cannot be made with the LXX as we have it now. Unfortunately, it is not possible to know precisely how Ben Zoma understood the entire passage, but this is a clear indication that even in a Jewish perspective, the Messiah son of David, appearing at the end of time,[138] could be called Lord. There may be a connection with the "day of the Lord" announced by the return of Elijah, and, of course, with the recognition of John the Baptist as the forerunner of the Messiah.

These examples concern simple variants of verses. What the MT readings have in common is that they make the messianic interpretation more difficult.[139] The inquiry can certainly be taken further, but in any case, many rabbinic discussions, where there hardly seems to be any ideological issue at stake, are really aimed at establishing the present Hebrew text,[140] which implies serious, systematic work; most of those who take part are 2nd-century teachers. The result, namely the present Hebrew version (MT), must then be regarded as the rabbinic edition of the Bible, contemporaneous with the *Mishnah*. It was of sufficient repute to be collated in the same period by Origen, who was hardly given to Judaizing, but was trying to put some order into the mass of Greek versions in circulation.

The cases discussed are all drawn from the Law and the Prophets, which form the undisputed basis of the sacred library. The third part of the Bible, Writings or Hagiographa, forms a sort of extra shelf, whose contents are less fixed. One received opinion has it that this part, which

138. And indeed during a Passover celebration, according to Jer 31[38]:8 LXX, which to "I will bring them back from the ends of the world" adds ἐν ἑορτῇ φασεκ "at the feast of Passover," cf. chap. VII, §II.3.

139. These debates on the right text should be compared with the famous discussion reported by Justin, *Dial.* 67.1, on the meaning of Isa 7:14 הנה העלמה הרה ("Behold the maiden is with child": Justin defends the translation παρθένος "virgin" (thus the LXX), against Tryphon's νεᾶνις "girl" (translation closer to עלמה, found also in Aquila and Theodotion). The discussion is not over the Hebrew but over existing translations which are presumed to be authorized; it is once again a debate on the right text, with a Christological issue at stake. In fact, Tryphon could have neutralized his opponent by pointing out that even after she has been raped (Gen 34:3), Dinah is still παρθένος for the LXX; but Justin does not leave him much initiative.

140. Cf. Viktor Aptowitzer, *Das Schriftwort in der rabbinischen Literatur*, with a Prolegomenon by Samuel Loewinger, New York, Ktav, 1970 (collection of articles published between 1906 and 1915). Cf. also the examples assembled by É. Nodet, *Le Pentateuque de Josèphe*, p. 22, n. 1, where the rabbinic controversies imply a confrontation between the MT and the LXX (or its Hebrew source); frequently, a strange-looking opinion is really a sort of synthesis of conflicting readings.

closes the canon, was fixed by the school of Yavneh around 90: *MYad* 3:5 gives a discussion which appears final on the retention or elimination of Cant, Qoh,[141] but the tradition that reports it is very confused. Josephus indicates a total of twenty-two books, of which thirteen are prophets and four collections of maxims and songs (*Ag. Ap.* 1 §38–41). That would seem to correspond to the twenty-two Hebrew books whose names are given by Origen, or to the twenty-four of the rabbinic tradition and the MT (which separate Ruth from Judg and Lam from Jer). But Josephus does not name his books, with the exception of the five of Moses; he appears to retain an artificial count originating in the twenty-two letters of the Hebrew alphabet. The reality must have been more fluid, since, for example, we have seen the circumstances in which the Hebrew text of 1 Macc was dropped, after 135, for reasons which can be identificd. That does not necessarily imply that it was very canonical before; only that it was read, which implies a certain authority. The only decisions relating to canons which can be traced, are eliminations, not adoptions. As we saw for the formation of the NT, books begin by being used in practice and without any particular status, until circumstances (probably urgent) require some sorting out to be done. The suppression of some books gives, by contrast, a status to those that are kept. The primary sense of the term "apocryphal," as also of its Hebrew equivalent, is "hidden, suppressed."

This is not the place to look at the whole question in itself. One instance will suffice for our theme. *BMeg* 6a reports that when Jonathan b. Uzziel was translating the prophets, he was suddenly thrown into confusion, because he was going to unveil the secrets of the end of time. The apocalyptic atmosphere of this account shows that he was starting on the book of Daniel. Decoded, it means that Dan, which appears in the MT among the Writings, was then classed as a Prophet, as Josephus and the LXX clearly show. So the book has been downgraded, doubtless on account of apocalyptic Messianism.

To sum up, the Tannaites, at the end of the 2nd century, were creative also in the biblical field. One of the mechanisms at work was clearly the desire to keep Christianity at a distance, and in the first place the Jewish-Christians, who were more aware of Messianism in the true sense. Thus it is possible to understand why the new Greek translation of Aquila, which is close to the final state of the MT, was duly celebrated about 100; by then the LXX passed for a Christian text.

141. Cf. Schürer-Vermes II:317 f. The useful data have been brought together in handy form by Sid Z. Leiman, *The Canonization of Hebrew Scripture: The Talmudic and Midrashic Evidence* (Trans. of the Conn. Acad. of Arts, 47), Hamden (Conn.), 1976.

4. The 613 Commandments and the Decalogue

A famous passage states that Moses received 613 commandments,[142] 365 prohibitions, as many as the days of the year, and 248 positive precepts, as many as the parts of the human body;[143] just as these measures are unchangeable, so too the law of Moses cannot be modified. This say-

142. The term used (מצוה) is biblical (Gen 26:5, etc.). The rab. trad. distinguishes these commandments, which are finite in number and stable in form, from the way of putting them into practice, called *halakha*; this is multiple and detailed, and can develop in view of new problems or changing circumstances.

The term *halakha* (הלכה) is traditionally attached to the Heb. הלך "to go" (cf. *Arukh, s. v.*), but it is of Aramaic origin, cf. Lieberman II:83. In Ezra 4:13 f. הלך (2 Esdr φόροι) designates a fixed tax; in certain Aramaic documents, הלכא designates a fixed tax on landed property, and the Akkadian from which it is derived (*ilku* "fixed contractual tax," cf. the Aram. emphatic הילכתא and the Heb. construct state הלכת) figures already in the code of Hammurabi. Such a tax, linked to the land register, is a fixed sum, at least if the *boundaries* are stable. It is natural to see a connection between an obligation (law) and a recurring fixed sum owed (land tax). Several texts show that the divine origin of the land register (arising from the division of the land by Joshua) is a metaphor of the (divine) authority of the Law and the customs, cf. Deut 19:14 (CD 1:16, Philo, *Spec. leg.* 4 §149 f., *Ant.* 4 §225, *MAb* 1:1); one who removes the boundary stones (which affects the taxes) is the prototype of one who breaks the Law. Origen, *Ad Afric.* §8, also uses Deut 19:14 to justify and defend the "canon" of Scriptures, that is its "boundaries" (exclusion of the apocrypha); Eusebius, *Hist. eccl.* 7.7.5 cites a case (Dionysius of Alexandria) where this verse justifies the refusal to change a received "rule" (κανών), which sets a boundary to the community (exclusion of heretics). Parallel to הלך, the term "canon," in the sense of juridical obligation (as opposed to casuistic), was also used for the annual rent of a piece of land (lease) or a land tax, which shows exactly the same conjunction of these two apparently different meanings. Similarly, νόμος "law" is related to νέμω "share," with connotations of landed property (cf. νέμος "grazing ground"). In a word, the term *halakha* denotes delimitation, obligation and permanence.

For the rab. trad., that which is not *halakha* is *agada* (אגדה), comprising chiefly homiletic. The same *Arukh* gives two definitions, one based on Heb. הגיד "to tell a story" (whence הגדה and אגדה, and the transcriptions *haggada, aggada*), the other on Aram. אגד "attract, seduce" (whence אגדה and *agada*). So the written form אגדה is ambiguous. The second explanation is nonetheless preferable: 1. it is based on Aram., like the corresponding term *halakha*; 2. the meaning is better suited to the nature of homiletic (to win over, encourage). On the other hand, the first explanation is very well suited to being the central feature in the celebration of Passover, which is the liturgical *narrative* of the departure from Egypt (called precisely *haggada*, cf. chap. VII, §II.3). W. Bacher, *Die Agada der Tannaiten*, p. 451 f., holds that originally מגיד served to clarify the precepts contained in Scripture, and so was attached to the *halakha*, the homiletic expansion coming later.

With regard to the strictly Hebrew terminology of the Qumran texts, there are certain points in common (cf. chap. I, §I.3): 1. מצוה and נגלה designate explicit commandments; 2. הלכה and נסתר, those that are hidden and transmitted orally (by the masters), which are regarded as the more important; 3. אגדה and פשר designate the rest (homiletic, prophecies, explanations, etc.).

143. *BMak* 23b. The two categories are called respectively "do" (עשה) and "do not" (לא תעשה).

ing is attributed to a brilliant preacher of the 3rd century, Simlai, who cites no earlier authority. More than a century ago, M. Bloch formed the hypothesis that these figures, which appear only late in the piece, originated in a defensive reaction against certain Jewish-Christians, in particular Paul of Samosata, bishop of Antioch, who was seeking to reunite Judaism and Christianity by emphasizing how very alike they were, with the exception of a few secondary precepts.[144] We will take up this thesis here and revise it a little.

It must be said that Bloch's thesis was challenged, and with good reason.[145] These figures (613, etc.) are cited by various later works, but are never attributed to Simlai; furthermore, a saying attributed to b. ᶜAzzaï (one of the four who strayed into Paradise) already speaks of 365 negative precepts a good century earlier (*SifDt* §76), but without mentioning the positive prescriptions. So it seems to have been a Tannaitic tradition.[146] In any case, no early text gives a detailed list of precepts, and no simple compilation of biblical texts arrives at 613.[147] Some medieval authors tried to reconstruct this list, the best known being Maimonides. Others, and not the least, judged that it was false to say that there were only 613 precepts; for them, a precise number of this sort is only homiletic in nature.

To get a clearer idea of what is at stake, let us return a moment to the brotherhoods. The *ḥaber* is defined as one who eats in a state of Levitical purity. That does not mean that he does not observe the other commandments, but only that for him they all converge on one precept which brings the rest together. The same could be said of the Essenes: to take part in the "purity," the community meal, presupposes not only the completion of the baptismal course, but also faithful observance of the whole Law, since any violation which is picked up entails a certain degree of impurity, separating the offender for a shorter or longer time from the meal (cf. chap. VII, §IV,2). The same is also true in Christianity, of all periods, with its procedures of access to the eucharist and excommunication.

On the contrary, the rabbinic tradition is vigorously opposed to any reduction of the Law to one or several principles or precepts which act as

144. Moïse Bloch, "Les 613 lois," *REJ* 1 (1880), p. 197–211.

145. Cf. B. Halper, "A Volume of the Book of Precepts by Ḥefeṣ B. Yaṣliaḥ, Edited from an Arabic MS. &c." *JQR* N.S. 4 (1915), p. 519–576.

146. The fact that the Samaritans also adopted the number of 613 laws is not an argument in favor of its antiquity, since Jewish influence on them was very strong in the Middle Ages, cf. I. R. M. Bóid, "The Samaritan Halacha," in: Alan D. Crown (ed.), *The Samaritans*, Tübingen, 1989, p. 638. It shows only that they agreed that the number corresponded to the properly Scriptural precepts.

147. Not to speak of the difficulty of distinguishing between biblical precepts and non-biblical customs (cf. *MḤag* 1:8, quoted in chap. I, §I.3).

a synthesis of the whole (cf. chap. I, §I.3). It is true that a number of sayings fix "great principles of the Torah," the best known being the Golden Rule given by Hillel to an inquirer: "Do not do to others what you would not want done to you.[148] That is the essence of the Law; the rest is only commentaries. Go and study" (*BShab* 31a). But it is not a question of a logical, or even practical reduction, only of homiletic: it is still necessary to study the rest of the Law. Jesus' statement (Matt 22:35-40 par.), that the whole Law and the Prophets are founded on these two commandments of love of God (*Shemaᶜ*) and love of the neighbor (Lev 19), is in the same vein[149] and cannot be regarded as negating the precepts. The 613 are not put in hierarchical order. All are important, and correspond to a multiplicity of benedictions, which allows the transformation of very many actions of daily life into so many acts of sanctification. On the contrary, the convergence of all the precepts on a single action, which has an eschatological dimension, indicates an orientation towards salvation, *i.e.* the Messianic expectation, more or less urgent. Furthermore, a number of precepts of this sort is much more stable than a system focused on a center, if the center comes to be disturbed.[150] That is precisely what happened with Christianity. There the central institutions (baptism and eschatological meal) were already in existence, but they changed their meaning when the Covenant was reinterpreted, which in turn entailed a general transformation of the precepts and their meaning. This is another form of the same argument.

The problem is the identity of the Covenant, whose charter is the Decalogue, and whose feast is Pentecost (commemoration of Sinai). We will show later on that in the rabbinic tradition Pentecost has become simply an appendage of Passover (chap. VII, §III.1). The Decalogue itself has suffered a long eclipse. The explanation given is that its recitation in daily prayer was abolished "because of the hostility of the *minim* ('sectaries'),

148. In this negative form the rule appears also in Acts 15:29 WT, cf. §II.1, and in *Did.* 1:2 (also Tob 4:15). It is given in its positive form ("Do to others [. . .]") in Matt 7:12. It is part of ancient international wisdom, cf. A. Dihle, *Die goldene Regel. Eine Einführung in die Geschichte der antiken und frühchristlichen Vulgärethik*, Göttingen, 1962.

149. And features almost identically in a somewhat later midrash (8th or 9th cent.), cf. Ephraim E. Urbach, *Sefer pitron ha-Torah*, Jérusalem, 1978, p. 215. These two precepts and the Golden Rule (in its negative form) are found together also in *Did.* 1:2.

150. As for the origin of the number, *BMak* 23b-24a explains that Simlai preached a homily (דרש), based on Deut 33:4 "Moses prescribed for us a law (תורה)," understood as "Moses prescribed for us תורה," where תורה is read as a number (ת=400, ו=6, ר=200, ה=5), or 611 commandments given by Moses, and two given directly by God to the people (Exod 20:2-3 "I am YHWH your God" and "You shall not have other gods before me"); a total of 613. This explanation is not the worst.

so that they could not say that only the Ten Commandments were given at Sinai." Some parallels speak of the "trick of the *minim*," implying a deliberate maneuver. This abolition has remained in force (*YBer* 1:8, p. 3c), despite various later attempts to restore the recitation of the Ten Commandments in Galilee or Babylonia (*BBer* 12b). The recurrent argument of the danger posed by the *minim* is not very clear in itself, but its permanence suggests at least that the suppression of the liturgical use of the Decalogue is not linked to the disappearance of the Temple, where its official recitation was prescribed (*MTam* 5:1), nor to the downfall of Jerusalem; in itself, it could be recited elsewhere.

Some have assumed that Christians were involved,[151] and that the recitation of the Ten Commandments was suppressed during the synod of Yavneh, at the time when a benediction against the *minim*, taken to be Christians, was introduced into the prayer of the Eighteen Benedictions.[152] The reasoning behind this, is that the Decalogue is used in the NT, but that the food laws were suppressed during the episode of Peter with Cornelius (Acts 10:9 f.), then circumcision during the Jerusalem assembly (Acts 15:19 f.), and, since these laws do not feature in the Decalogue, its recitation would tend to justify their suppression and so give comfort to the Christian cause.[153] The argument is not, however, convincing. For one thing, although the NT contains a number of antilegalist passages, it nowhere gives importance to the Ten Commandments as such.[154] Only the last five are cited, sometimes adding respect for parents, and they are said to be summed up by Lev 19:18 (love of the neighbor), in an ethical perspective; in a corresponding way, the first four commandments are absorbed by the *Shema*ᶜ ("You shall love the Lord your God with all your heart, etc."). To this should be added the breaches, or at least the tensions with the Decalogue expressed in Jesus' paradoxical attitudes towards the Sabbath or the honor due to parents.[155] A second reason is that it is at least premature to identify the Jewish-Christians with those who

151. That is the traditional Jewish opinion, cf. Rashi on *BBer* 12a (discussed above). Also Geza Vermes, "The Decalogue and the *Minim*," in: *In Memoriam P. Kahle* (BZAW, 103), Berlin, 1968, p. 65–72. On the promotion of the precepts of the "children of Noah," meant for everyone, cf. above §II.2.

152. W. D. Davies, *The Setting of the Sermon on the Mount*, Cambridge, 1964, p. 281 f.

153. Viktor Aptowitzer, "Bemerkungen zur Liturgie und Geschichte der Liturgie," *MGWJ* 74 (1930), p. 104–108.

154. Cf. Ephraim E. Urbach, "The Role of the Ten Commandments in Jewish Worship," in: Ben-Zion Segal & Gershon Levi (Eds.), *The Ten Commandments in History and Tradition*, Jerusalem, 1990, p. 170 f.

155. Cf. David Flusser, "The Ten Commandments in the New Testament," in: B. Z. Segal & G. Levi, *The Ten Commandments . . .* , 1990, p. 219–246.

were spreading the Greek NT, at least in the time of Gamaliel II at Yavneh; as we have seen, Gamaliel had no fear of Greek. Finally, it would go too far to attribute to the Jerusalem assembly any intention to suppress circumcision.

If Yavneh will not do in this form, we may still look for a later occasion on the Christian side. Several patristic witnesses from the 2nd century (Justin, Irenaeus) emphasize the Ten Commandments in opposition to other laws, explaining that they express the law of nature, and so are universal and unchangeable, whereas the others (especially the ritual laws) were given to mark Israel off from the nations or to punish the people, and so have become obsolete.[156] This conception, which is more or less inspired by Stoicism, is very close to that of Philo or Josephus (cf. chap. I, §I.4), the difference being that the particular laws no longer have for the Christians anything but an allegorical meaning, which is not to deny their divine origin, but quite the contrary to underline it.[157] In other words, from this point of view, Philo and Josephus could be regarded as *minim*[158] just as well as the Christians, since all were trying to do away with particularism. Besides the fact that Stoic ideas are foreign to the rabbinic tradition, such a result would show that the interpretation of *minim* as Christians in general still remains very confused.

E. Urbach, after reviewing various theories to explain the suppression of recitation of the Ten Commandments, proposes another explanation, linked to the prohibition of circumcision by Hadrian.[159] At the time of the Bar Kokhba war, many underwent martyrdom rather than break the commandment (*SifDt* §32; *BShab* 130a). Others disguised their circumcision, as in the days of Antiochus Epiphanes (cf. 1 Macc 1:15). A controversy is reported from the post-war period, as to whether or not it was necessary to recircumcise them (*TShab* 15:9), and one opinion suggests that the rabbinical rule in the matter is stricter than that imposed by Scripture (*BYeb* 72a). However, as circumcision is not in the Decalogue, some may have argued from that to suppress it or remove evidence of it, and so

156. Cf. the discussion by V. Aptowitzer, “בשכמל“ו. Geschichte einer liturgischen Formel,” *MGWJ* 73 (1929), p. 111 f., n. 4, citing Harnack; he concludes that this was indeed the argument of the *minim*, and, with some hesitation attributes the decision to Yavneh. Origen, *Hom. in Ex.* 4.6, establishes a kind of symmetry, for the restoration of a corrupt world, between the ten plagues of Egypt, which destroyed, and the ten commandments, which correct.

157. As even the Gnostics do, for example Ptolemy, quoted by Epiphanius, *Pan.* 33.3; likewise the *Epistle of Barnabas*, cf. Gedaliah Alon, “Halakhic Elements in the Epistle of Barnabas,” *Tarbiz* 11 (1940), p. 23–38.

158. The suggestion of Yehoshua Amir, “The Decalogue according to Philo,” in: B. Z. Segal & G. Levi, *The Ten Commandments* . . . , p. 121–160 (cf. p. 125).

159. E. E. Urbach, “The Role of the Ten Commandments . . .” p. 180 f.

the daily recitation was omitted in order to counter this reason and prevent the claim that "only the Ten Commandments were given at Sinai."

This argument is not really very satisfactory, and for several reasons. If circumcision needed to be reinforced, would it not have been more natural and effective to add to the daily recitation one of the passages of Gen prescribing it, instead of going about things in such a roundabout way? We have come across another instance of discussion about whether to add or retain a Scriptural passage which recalls something of importance (the deliverance from Egypt, cf. *MBer* 1:5). Again, how could this laxist tendency have got the name "trick of the *minim*," which implies some deliberate sectarian undertaking? Further, even if there were some particularly acute sectarian crisis under Hadrian, why was the problem so permanent that the suppression of the recitation of the Decalogue has remained in force ever since, despite attempts to restore it? Later on, tradition insists that the suppression of the Decalogue concerned *public* prayer, and not private recitation, but that does not fit in with a supposed pedagogical intention to correct deviants in the community. Finally, the coins of Bar Kokhba sometimes show, within an Ark of the Covenant installed in a temple, the design of a scroll, *i.e.* the Torah, but never the tables of the Law, in contradiction with Exod 40:20;[160] the Decalogue as such is missing right at the moment when an attempt was being made to mobilize the whole people.

This matter of circumcision steers us towards another, much simpler explanation, which takes account of the extreme importance of the Decalogue. The real problem is not that of placing all the commandments under ten headings, as Philo does, but the fact that the Decalogue is the biblical charter of the Covenant; it is, by the way, the only passage in the Bible whose reading has to be preceded by a benediction (*YMeg* 3:7, p. 74b). However, the Covenant had in a way been confiscated by the reforming groups, Essenes, brotherhoods, Christians, etc., by way of the rite of baptism, itself incompatible with the admission of the whole people, which had become the enterprise of the rabbis.

The "trick" of the *minim* was audacious and very clear. They argued from the renewal of the Covenant made at Sinai and associated with the Ten Commandments and Pentecost, in order to minimize circumcision; so the problem is permanent, without any particular connection with

160. Leo Mildenberg, *The Coinage of the Bar Kokhba War*, Frankfurt/M., 1984, Large Silver Series, n° 1–104; A. Reifenberg, *Coins of the Jews*, Jerusalem, 1948, pl. 12. Contrary to later usage, the Decalogue is completely absent from earlier iconography, cf. Gad. B. Sarfatti, "The Tablets of the Law as a Symbol of Judaism," in: Ben-Zion Segal & Gershon Levi (eds.), *The Ten Commandments* . . . , p. 383–418.

Hadrian's persecutions. Confronted with that, the Tannaitic schools which were emerging from the brotherhoods, turned things around: the Covenant is strictly circumcision. A Tannaitic saying makes the typical statement that circumcision is worth all the precepts, and that the "blood of the Covenant," in the rite of Exod 24:8 which follows the reception of the Decalogue, is none other than the blood of circumcision (*TNed* 2:5). It is difficult not to think of another "blood of the Covenant," associated with Pentecost, feast of the Covenant, by way of one particular Passover.

So these *minim* can be interpreted after all as Jewish-Christians. The suppression of the recitation of the Decalogue may even go back to the school of Yavneh. We can now see a further reason why the schools departed from the system of brotherhoods, which gave greater opportunity for Christian preaching. Also why Josephus, who had praised the Essenes, that is the brotherhoods, in the *War*, distanced himself from them at the precise moment when he began to be aware of Christianity (cf. chap. III, §II.1).

In short, upholding a large number of precepts of equal importance and placing less emphasis on the Ten Commandments both flow from the Rabbis' reaffirmation of circumcision as sole symbol of the Covenant. Both signify the abandonment of the Essene ideal of the *ḥaberim*, itself closely related to the pillars of Christianity: hence the disappearance of Pentecost as feast of the Covenant, and the disappearance of the "purity" as Covenant banquet and fulfilment of all the precepts by virtue of a baptismal instruction and initiation.

5. A Counter-example: the Sun

The sun plays a notable role among the Essenes, as we saw in connection with the night at Troas (chap. I, §II.2). Josephus emphasizes the extreme importance of the rising sun for them: "Before sunrise, they do not speak any profane word: they address traditional prayers to this heavenly body, as if they were begging it to appear" (*J.W.* 2 §128 and 148). The calendar of *Jubilees* is solar, and the first fruits of the produce of the earth, whose importance cannot be overestimated, are bound up with the cycle of the solar year. We have also seen the significance which the rising sun had for the Christians, especially on the first day of the week, corresponding to the creation of light (chap. II, §I.2); we might add that the orientation of churches towards the east, which is still practiced, comes from the earliest communities, who gathered before dawn and prayed facing the east.

By contrast, the customs prescribed by the rabbinic tradition keep well clear of any reference to the sun. Besides the fact of using a lunar calendar, which is not necessarily an original characteristic, we will give two further examples. The first is the feast of Dedication, which begins on 25 Kislev (ninth month of the calendar beginning at Nisan) and lasts eight days. Its founding story is 1 Macc, resumed in 2 Macc, both books missing from the MT, although the former had an original written in Hebrew, the title of which is known. The feast is clearly attested in John 10:22 f., with very precise details: "It was the time of the celebration of the feast of Dedication in Jerusalem. It was winter. Jesus was walking up and down in the Temple, under the portico of Solomon." This setting combines two types of Messianic allusions, converging on the establishment of the Temple: Solomon, as son of David and builder of the sanctuary, prefigures the Messiah, and the feast of Dedication commemorates the restoration by Judas Maccabaeus, interpreted as a Messianic adventure which succeeded, as we have already seen. It is at this moment that Jesus is asked: "If you are the Messiah, tell us clearly."

Precisely such Messianic features are missing from the rabbinic Dedication (*Ḥanukka* "Inauguration"), as it is described in *BShab* 21b, which makes only scant reference to the story of Judas Maccabaeus. The brief founding narrative gives no really historical information and says only that the Hasmonaeans vanquished the Greeks, came to the ruined sanctuary, and found a flask containing enough oil to keep the perpetual lamp alight for one day. By a miracle, this oil lasted eight days, giving time to prepare more; whence a commemoration lasting eight days. All the same, the principal rite consists of lighting in each house one lamp on the first day, two on the second, etc. (with traces of an opposite usage: eight on the first day, seven on the second, etc.), and to put these lamps *in the window*, taking care not to make use of their light. This rite corresponds only vaguely to the narrative of the ancient victory, but can be very easily understood with reference to the sun,[161] especially according to the calendar of *Jubilees*, as then the feast coincides exactly with the octave of the winter solstice (from 25/9 to 1/10, since the ninth month, corresponding to December, has 31 days). Its meaning is then very simple. It is a matter not of replacing the light of the sun by lighting these lamps, but of stimulating that light where it should appear (at the window), by accompanying the sun. Hence the eight lamps are lit either in increasing or in decreasing order, depending on whether the solstice is the starting or the finishing point (whether daily sunshine begins increasing or finishes decreasing).[162]

161. Cf. the data brought together by Julian Morgenstern, "The Chanukka Festival and the Calendar of Ancient Israel," *HUCA* 20 (1947), p. 1–136 and 21 (1948), p. 365–496.

162. To these eight lamps is added a ninth (whence the nine-branched candlestick), which serves expressly to light the others and to give some illumination; this ninth is called

This solar dimension is attested by Josephus. In telling the story of Judas Maccabaeus, he calls the commemoration of his deed not the Dedication but the "Feast of Lights"; he does not know why, and tries to imagine a reason (*Ant.* 13 §325). In other words, the replacement of the (cyclical) solar meaning by an historical commemoration was already for him a fact.[163] That obviously supposes a coincidence of date, so the use of a solar calendar, but the ancient name survived (and perhaps also the domestic rite). To sum up, the feast brings together Messianic and solar elements.[164] In the rabbinic tradition, everything is obscured,[165] first by the use of the lunar calendar, which separates the dedication from the solstice by making it a movable feast, and then by introducing a very brief founding story which puts as little emphasis as possible on the warlike aspects.

The other example is the procedure for purifying one who has become unclean. In Lev 11:24 etc., three phases are defined: the washing of clothes, ablution (immersion), and finally waiting for sunset (on the same day), as it is only at that moment that the preceding purifications take legal effect. In the different texts, these three phases are not always all mentioned, but the traditions attested have systematized them in two opposite directions.[166] The Qumran documents, "Zadokite" version (11 QT 45:9 f. and 4 QMMT), insist that the uncleanness remains in effect and *can be transmitted* until sunset on the last day of purification. On the contrary, the *Mishnah* takes an interest in the special status of the unclean person or object between the ablution and the following sunset. A whole tractate is dedicated to this subject *(Ṭebul-Yom)*,[167] which shows its im-

---

שמש, a word traditionally taken in the sense of "servant" (because it is used), but which can also be read as "sun". . . .

163. This replacement needs to be put in parallel with the major event which took place during the Maccabean crisis, namely the replacement by the sons of Mattathias of the previous priestly dynasty of the Oniads, of Egyptian origin and associated with a solar cult (*Ôn* or ʿΗλίου πόλις "City of the Sun," cf. Exod 1:11 LXX), cf. *Search*, p. 255–260. On the Temple at the time of FJ, cf. chap. IV, §I.4.

164. This mechanism of substitution is strictly parallel to the institution of the Christian feast of Christmas, an historical commemoration with symbolic meaning ("rising sun . . .") which has also been substituted for the same winter solstice.

165. The feast is residual, since there is no tractate consecrated to it. In the *Mishnah*, there are simply a recollection of the importance of the feast at the time of the Temple (*MRSh* 2:2), which is quite conceivable (cf. John 10:22), and an allusion in connection with the liturgical cycle (*MMeg* 3:2).

166. Cf. Ḥannah K. Harrington, *The Impurity Systems of Qumran and the Rabbis. Biblical Foundations* (SBL Dissertation Series, 143), Atlanta (Georgia), Scholars Press, 1993, ch. II.

167. טבול יום "immersed of the day," from טבל "to plunge, immerse, baptize," cf. chap. II, §I.1.

portance. The general principle is that the object or person ceases to be unclean after immersion; between that moment and the following sunset there is retained only the ability to transmit a lesser degree of impurity to priestly offerings.[168] In other words, the role of sunset has been reduced to the strict minimum, so that the verses which speak of it are practically emptied of legal content. There is an associated controversy over whether this arrangement is necessarily derived from the letter of Scripture, or whether it results from the interpretation of a scribe acting on his own authority;[169] in both cases, the reference is the written text, and not an independent oral tradition, but a written text reduced to the minimum.

Despite the contrast mentioned, there is no reason to think that all these arrangements aimed at limiting as far as possible the role of the sun have anything to do with the rise of Christianity. Already, the mistrust of any sign of veneration of the sun,[170] though absent from 1 Macc, is one of the characteristics of 2 Macc, which is close to Babylonian traditions,[171] themselves very attached to the lunar calendar. In particular, the second festal letter (2 Macc 1:10 f.) intends, among other things, to show that the fire on the altar comes from Moses and not from the sun. Here we can recall that Hillel, founder of the school (brotherhood) of Bathyra, was a Babylonian, and that this foundation represents the fusion of different currents, including non-biblical oral traditions.

An important methodological remark follows from this. The problem of the sun shows that a notable divergence between the Essenes and the rabbinic tradition should not automatically be attributed to a reaction against Christianity, but rather to notable diversity within the world of the brotherhoods.[172] Such diversity is implied by Josephus and proved by the innumerable controversies within the rabbinic tradition. Often these are

168. This is the least degree of impurity, *i.e.* of the power to contaminate. Further, contrary to other analogous agents of impurity, the *ṭebul-yom* does not make liquids impure (*MṬebY* 2:1-2).

169. Respectively *BShab* 14b (דאורייתא "of the Torah" and *MZab* 5:12 (מדברי סופרים). In Qumranian terms, that would amount to hesitating over whether to qualify this norm as "explicit" (נגלה) or as "hidden" (נסתר), cf. chap. I, §I.3.

170. There are also rites, connected with the Sabbath, designed to limit the symptoms of sun worship, cf. chap. VII, §III.1.

171. Cf. *Search*, p. 261–262.

172. Dealing with the liturgy of the feast of Tabernacles, *MSuk* 5:4 indicates a change of usage. When the people arrive at the eastern gate, they say (following Ezek 8:16): "Our fathers when they were here turned their back on the sanctuary of YHWH and turned towards the east, and they prostrated themselves before the rising sun. As for us, our eyes are turned towards YHWH." This is presented as a criticism of the idolatry of the ancestors, but it is really a still-active controversy against an (unnamed) opposing party deemed to be impious.

not conflicting private opinions, but more or less noisy clashes between distinct traditions, with each camp able to call on the teaching of its masters.

Finally, we observe that "proselyte baptism," which in form is common to Christianity and to rabbinic Judaism, stands out as all the more singular. The meaning given to the rite in the two religions which practice it is not, of course, the same. But the fact that it has been kept in Judaism proves how extremely important it was in the original Tannaitic environment, itself far removed from Philo and Josephus who mention only circumcision.

V – A Family Quarrel

After this chapter and the two earlier ones on Galilee, this is a good moment to pause and draw up a provisional balance sheet. The general purpose of our study has been to depict the environment in which Christianity began, by defining its characteristic institutions. Already, an examination of Christian and Jewish literary sources has led us to give great importance to events and texts of the 2nd century. By contrast, evidence from the 1st century is rarely direct and has in most cases been transmitted through successive redactions over a period of more than 100 years. These facts have two methodological consequences which justify the procedure that has been followed. First, the distinction between historical facts and customs is of the first importance. We have seen, for example, in the case of the feast of Dedication, that the founding narratives appear to have undergone various developments as they were required to speak to ever new situations. On the other hand, widely observed rites and customs associated with the feast were presumably more stable and underwent change only as the result of perceptible conflicts. Secondly, even if oral transmission was long dominant, Christians possessed collections of notes on the life of Jesus, which no doubt enjoyed apostolic authority. Thanks to the distinction which we established at the outset (chap. I, §I) between composition or redaction and publication, we can see how such collections could circulate and evolve. There is no decisive reason to suppose that formal, definitive publication took place all at once. Since the basic act of written publication is to make a copy (or translation), it is natural to imagine rather successive editions, from which in turn copies were made, with resulting contaminations, then revisions, etc. As far as the NT is concerned, the idea of a written, published canon, that is an authoritative selection, emerges in various forms between Justin and Irenaeus, but always in the West, a fact which deserves to be noticed. We do not know precisely what circumstances, that is, what conflicts of authority, led to the production of these fixed lists, but it is reasonable to think that in any case, with the passage of time, such collections must have been changed less and less, as the apostolic traditions became ever more ancient and so venerable.

In this general framework, the 2nd century saw a parallel development leading to the emergence of rabbinic Judaism on the one hand, and the formation of the NT on the other, both issuing from an original environment which was similar and had strong roots in Galilee. The result was the existence of two religions which were quite distinct, both claiming to be the true Israel, but the process which separated them was slow and marked by many conflicts. The case of the Jewish-Christians in between, gathered (let us say for simplicity's sake) around James, demonstrates the truth just outlined: they were certainly the majority Christian group at the beginning, but dwindled away to a remnant after 135. For this reason, they can act as tracers in order to recover the original environment.

From this vantage point, we can see the two central points of interest of this stage of our investigations: the formation of rabbinic Judaism, enabling us to define a way of using the Tannaitic sources, and the conflicts around the Jewish-Christians, permitting some insights into the formation of the gospels.

1. Using the Rabbinic Sources

At the risk of oversimplification, the analyses already undertaken enable us to pick out several main lines in the formation of the rabbinic tradition.

At the outset, we find marginal ("separated") brotherhoods, illustrated in particular by the episode of Hillel at Bathyra under Herod. At the moment when the *Mishnah* was published, about 200, a group of brotherhoods became an academy, which undertook to legislate for the whole people. The head of this academy, Judah the Prince, took the rank of ethnarch, a title which was then attributed to his predecessors, as if the earlier brotherhoods had also been central academies. In reality, the Hasmonaeans had already been ethnarchs, then Bar Kokhba had this title, without its being attached in any way to Tannaitic circles. The school of Yavneh-Jamnia had been founded on a very restricted scale (essentially a brotherhood) by Yoḥanan b. Zakkaï, who had come from Galilee. Then Gamaliel II was the first to try, after 90, to federate several brotherhoods in order to form a central authority in Judaea for the entire people, whence the progressive appearance of the problem of "sectaries," *i.e.* groups of the same origin who refused that authority. This first attempt did not lead to any clear results, probably because of the presence of zealot elements, but was resumed after 135.

This problem of sectaries apparently had a fairly complex history, as can be seen from the famous "malediction of the sectaries" in the *Eighteen Benedictions*, mentioned above (chap. IV, §II). One passage reports that it was imposed only with difficulty, at the time of Gamaliel II (*BBer* 28b); the deviants aimed at were in the first place those who departed from the norms, that is, did not accept Gamaliel's authority.[173] The earliest and strangest name given to these dissidents is found in a single text, which has managed to resist all sorts of corrections (*TBer* 3:25): they are "Pharisees" *(perushin*, "separated"), with whom are later associated the "sectaries." In order to avoid the usual meaning of "Pharisees," the traditional explanation is that it is a question of those who "separated themselves from the common way."[174] However, the term is only odd if the rabbinic tradition is regarded as heir to the Pharisees in the sense of Josephus, which we have seen to be inexact (chap. III, §IV). In fact, the traditional explanation of the word is correct in both cases. The first "Pharisees" were "separated" from the people and wanted to return to the sources. Those denounced by Gamaliel were also "separated," by refusing his normalization (gathering the people) and holding instead to their own brotherhoods. We can thus understand why the term "Pharisee," which is very rare in the rabbinic sources, could be compared to the *ḥaberim* and Essenes. Of course, to bring together under the same anathema both "Pharisees" and "sectaries," especially in the later sense of Christians in general, could have created some confusion. However, if we stick to the first meaning of the term *minim*, as applying to Jewish-Christians, it is easy to see how it was originally a question of parallel resistances to Gamaliel's enterprise coming precisely from the milieu that he was trying to unify.

The original Galilean brotherhoods had resulted from a fusion of several currents at a time of crisis, principally a Babylonian wave bringing non-biblical oral traditions,[175] and Essenes, reformers based on Scripture who had emigrated from Judaea; it is not impossible that they

173. Cf. Philip S. Alexander, "The Parting of the Ways, From the Perspective of Rabbinic Judaism," in: J. D. J. Dunn (ed.), *Jews and Christians: The Parting of the Ways A.D. 70 to 135* (WUNT, 66), Tübingen, J. C. B. Mohr (P. Siebeck), 1993, p. 1–25. David Flusser, "Some of the Precepts of the Torah from Qumran (4QMMT) and the Benediction Against the Heretics," *Tarbiz* 61 (1992), p. 333–374, even shows, by other means, that such a benediction existed before Christianity.

174. Cf. *Tosefta kifshuṭah* 1:54, which suggests reading here פָּרוֹשִׁין (noun of agent in *paʿōl*, cf. מסור, §IV.2) instead of the usual פְּרוּשִׁין ("Pharisees"); but this does not get us very far: 1. nouns in this form always have a plural in וֹת- and not in ין; 2. if an exception were allowed in this precise case, the same explanation would also be valid for the "Pharisees" themselves.

175. This important point is developed in *Search*, p. 286–290.

included Samaritans in their number. That left outstanding the problem of coherence between written text and oral tradition, which was dealt with only later (Aqiba).[176] In all this we have seen the extreme importance of Galilee, bridgehead between the land of Israel and the eastern Diaspora, which the Romans always suspected of colluding with the Parthians. Unlike other brotherhoods (Essenes as described by Josephus, Therapeutae, the disciples whom Paul found at Ephesus, etc.), those in Galilee were very focused upon living in the *countryside* of the land of Israel, which was the only way of observing the precepts bound to the soil, and above all the tithes,[177] a feature which is underlined also in Luke 11:43. In a more general way, the Galilean environment in which Jesus himself grew up and moved about, was rural and traditional, but with various shades of political awareness.

In the NT, the term Pharisee ("separated") has two senses. When it is opposed to "Sadducee," it has rather the meaning defined by Josephus, who was speaking *in his own day* of what was then the majority tendency among the people, and to which he himself had more or less come round. In other contexts, it designates, as in the rabbinic literature, the "separated," in the first place the members of brotherhoods.[178] The terms "Pharisee" and "Essene," before being well defined labels applied by Josephus, were names with similar bearing, corresponding to successive movements with the same objective. By this route, we find ourselves back with the usual opinion, according to which the "Hasideans" of the Maccabaean period (a Hebrew word equivalent to the Aramaic which gave rise to "Essene," but known to rabbinic literature) can be regarded as the ancestors of the Pharisees; they are also the ancestors of the Essenes.

The evolution of marginal brotherhoods into a school at the service of the entire people led finally to the *Mishnah*. It is characterized by three facts, which can be situated after the defeat of Bar Kokhba. First, the generalization for all of various precepts which were proper to the brotherhoods, and

176. Cf. *MḤag* 1:8 (cited in chap. I, §I.3), where a textual doubt points to an instructive hesitation: according to one reading, all the precepts (oral and written) are called "Torah"; according to the other, only those with a Scriptural basis are so called.

177. For the precepts bound to the soil strictly apply only in the land of Israel (*MQid* 1:9, *TKel BQ* 1:5); it is only by extension that they are to be observed elsewhere (cf. *YTer* 1:5).

178. Cf. chap. III, §IV on the "parties" of FJ. The problem then arises of distinguishing, especially in the synoptic gospels, the "Pharisees" who criticize Jesus from those involved in the controversy over the *minim*. This is a task still to be done, and there were probably contaminations between the two phases, but the criterion of violence may be useful, in the sense that the Christians of Gamaliel II's time were certainly judged to be more dangerous than Jesus and his disciples under Pilate were *for the non-zealot Pharisees*.

in particular the emergence of "proselyte baptism," but with no move to converge on a synthesizing precept, such as the "purity" of the Essenes. Next, the collection of various traditions arising from Jerusalem and the Temple, and more generally from circles which had previously been opposed to one another. Finally, the disappearance of certain singular features of the brotherhoods, such as the presence of Samaritans or the relative autonomy of women. This evolution came about under different sorts of pressure, one of them (but not the only one) certainly being Christianity, which was itself a product of Galilean brotherhoods. The reaction to Jewish-Christianity, very clear from the time of Gamaliel II, is, however, systematically camouflaged, since, from the viewpoint of schools representing the whole of Judaism, Christianity can only be a deviant marginal sect: in fact, its characteristic point is lack of interest in the Jewish people as such. As a result, wherever we might assume that there were natural points in common between Christianity, in one form or other, and rabbinical Judaism, we should expect that the latter has brought about some changes in order to maintain or create a distance from the other. These changes may bear on customs themselves or on the academic or homiletic reasons given for them; the latter case is *a priori* more likely, as customs, being popular, are by their nature more stable.

Bearing this in mind, it is possible to benefit from the wealth of the rabbinic sources. Centered above all on institutions and customs, they are by nature traditional and so very stable. Any lasting innovations must be due to profound upheavals, which, since they have been able to affect the traditions, were even more serious than persecutions inflicted by the Romans from outside. This remark enables us to overcome the perpetual question concerning the dating of the rabbinic sources, by reformulating it in terms of the dating of conflicts. We shall also be able to go back in a later chapter to the investigation of Passover and Pentecost, which we began earlier with Jeremias.

2. *The Jewish-Christians, the Nazoreans and the Gospels*

In the introductory chapter, we saw that the publication of the gospels, that is of biographies of Jesus, came about only quite late. Closely related to this is the fact that Paul's letters, the Roman Creed[179] and, more generally, a whole current of early Christian texts Jesus only as Risen, and not as Healer, Teacher or Messiah (chap. I, §I.1). The case of

179. In the sense of the Christological confession of faith attested by FJ and Acts 13, cf. chap. I, §I.1.

the Jewish-Christians,[180] with their *Gospel of the Hebrews*, allows us to press the question more closely. In the sources, they are divided into two branches, but it is hard to know at this stage if they were really distinct. In one camp are James and his successors. Until they disappear after Bar Kokhba, they are revered as "sons of David," and await the return of Jesus as Messiah. In the other are the much disparaged Jewish-Christians. They are still known by the name of "Nazoreans" by Epiphanius,[181] Eusebius and Jerome, who thus expresses the harsh judgment which had already become traditional: "Since they wish to be both Jews and Christians, they are neither one nor the other." Jerome also knows that the rabbinic tradition calls them "Mineans," that is *minim*. The other side of the coin is that these same Jewish-Christians are the first to be denounced as *minim* by the rabbinic sources, which call them also *noṣrim*.[182]

Since the canonical gospels are biographies of Jesus, it is natural to look there for traces of Jewish-Christianity and, in the background, signs of rabbinical condemnations. The first point to make is that the epithet "Nazorean" is applied several times to Jesus himself. There are two in-

180. The documentation is put together by A. Frederick Klijn & G. J. Reinink, *Patristic Evidence for Jewish Christian Sects* (NTSup., 36), Leiden, Brill, 1973.

181. Who, of course, mentions other "heresies." It is difficult to know if the term "Nazorean" refers to a number of groups taken together, or only to one group among others. In any case, it is the only one for which we have plausible information, cf. Joan E. Taylor, "The Phenomenon of Early Jewish Identity," *Vigiliae Christianae* 44 (1990), p. 313–330.

182. In passages which have not been censured, cf. Ray A. Pritz, *Nazarene Jewish Christianity From the End of the New Testament Period Until Its Disappearance in the Fourth Century*, Jerusalem-Leiden, Magnes-Brill, 1988, p. 98 f. Epiphanius, *Pan.* 29.9.2 and Jerome, *Epist.* 112.13 (and elsewhere), indicate that the *Birkat haminim* curses the Nazoreans, formula found also in the Cairo *geniza*. The term ναζωραίοι, unknown to the LXX, corresponds to נְצוֹרִים, which can easily be the equivalent of נוֹצרים: one has the form of a noun of agent, the other of an active participle (cf. likewise פורשים-פרושים above); the forms in ναζαρ- suppose rather נצרי, without appreciable difference in meaning; for simplicity we shall stick to "Nazorean." The term survives in Syriac *(naṣraya)* for "Christian," which is a trace of Jewish-Christian origins. The reference to the shoot springing from Jesse in Isa 11:1 (נצר), which suggests descent from David, is not necessarily primary, and certainly not the only one possible. More precisely, the corresponding verbal root has the sense of "observe," "watch," "keep," cf. 2 Kgs 17:9; 18:8 ("watchtower"); Jer 4:16; Ps 25:10 has the expression נצרי בריתו ועדתיו "keeping his covenant and his commandments," etc. Such a name is well suited to an observant group which keeps the Covenant and watches for an outcome. In fact, in Aram., the corresponding form is נטוֹרא "guardian," and the expression *naṭoré qarta* "guardians of the city" is known to the rab. sources, with a special sense of "guardians of the tradition," cf. *YḤag* 1:7, p. 76c; likewise ליל שמרים ("night watch") in Exod 12:42 becomes in the targums לילי נטיר, cf. chap. VII, §II.2. There may also be an allusion to the idea of "watchers," in relation to the expectation of the dawn, through attentive observation (cf. Luke 1:78, etc.). We have seen just such a night watch at Troas (cf. Acts 20:7 f.). In parallel fashion, the Samaritans call themselves "guardians" (שמרין, cf. Isa 62:6).

stances in Matt. In 2:23, the town of Nazareth, where Joseph and his family go to live, is related to a verse taken from "the prophets"[183] and applied to Jesus: "He will be called a Nazorean." In Matt 26:69, 71, two serving women in succession ask Peter if he was with Jesus the Galilean, then with Jesus the Nazorean; the two expressions evidently have much the same meaning. Equally obviously, they both have a geographical meaning, which is found also in the parallels: according to Mark 14:67, the serving woman speaks of "Jesus the Nazarene," where Matt has "Galilean," and in Mark 14:70 par. Peter's Galilean accent gives him away. However, these allusions are not limited to the territory. The term "Galileans" also designates zealots, which may not be irrelevant to Peter's own origins (cf. chap. III, §III), and the attachment of "Nazorean" to Nazareth is clearly artificial, as the false quotation of Matt 2:23 shows. In Luke, there is only one instance. In 18:37 the blind beggar at Jericho is told that "Jesus the Nazorean" is passing by, and cries out: "Jesus son of David, have pity on me." So the name is associated here with descent from David, which can have a zealot connotation, as we have seen in connection with James's succession (§III.2 above). Once more, the parallel in Mark 10:47 is limited to the place name (Nazarene). The term "Nazorean" is entirely unknown to the second gospel. Is this omission deliberate?

In Acts, to be seen here as a continuation of Luke, the term appears six times to designate Jesus:[184] in 2:22, in the second part of Peter's speech at Pentecost (WT: "Jesus the Nazorean, accredited by signs and wonders"); in 3:6, in Peter's words to the paralytic at the Beautiful Gate (WT: "In the name of Jesus [AT adds: 'Christ'] the Nazorean, walk!"), then in his speech before the authorities (4:10); in 6:14, in the false testimony laid against Stephen ("We have heard him say that Jesus the Nazorean would destroy this place"); in 22:8, in Paul's account of his vision ("I am Jesus the Nazorean, whom you are persecuting"); in 26:9, in Paul's speech (AT: "I believed I ought to do everything I could against the name of Jesus the Nazorean"). To these references should be added a mention of Jesus' disciples on the occasion of Paul's trial (Acts 24:5), where he is accused by an advocate appearing for the high priest of stirring up trouble

183. The passage is nowhere to be found as such, and the collective attribution to the prophets shows a deliberate synthesis. Jerome, *In Isaiam* 11:1 affirms that the "learned among the Hebrews" judge that Matt refers to the "shoot springing from the stock of Jesse" in Isa 11:1 (*PL* 24.148), *i.e.* that Jesus will be designated in reference to this verse; in *Ep. 57 ad Pammachium*, he directly cites Isa 11:1 in the form "the Nazorean will grow out of the root [of Jesse]."

184. In Acts 9:5 and 26:14, certain versions of the WT add "the Nazorean," a gloss inspired by the parallel Acts 22:8. The mention of the epithet in 26:9 AT is probably also a gloss inspired by the same passage.

"in our nation and in the entire world,[185] being a leader of the sect of Nazoreans." The movement is here called a "sect,"[186] like the Sadducees (Acts 5:17) or the Pharisees (15:5); it is obviously a Jewish movement.[187] Paul in reply does not say he is a Nazorean, but disputes the term "sect," and states that he is a follower of the Way, at the same time protesting his peaceful conduct. So there is something of a gap between the two views of Paul. From the Jewish side he is regarded as a Nazorean; he himself does not really deny this, but reinterprets it, while insisting on his fidelity to the Law and the Prophets. This reinterpretation, which waters down the singularity or marginality of the Nazoreans, should be compared to the insistence of the synoptics on the geographical reference (Nazareth, Galilee), which is another way of neutralizing the term. It seems to present a danger, but what, and for whom? By way of preliminary remarks, let us note that the name or title of Nazorean is applied to Jesus *and* to his disciples, which is unique: all other titles of Jesus are proper to him. What is more, it is generally given by Jews who are outside the group of disciples, except in the case of Peter, who insists on the name "Jesus the Nazorean."

That brings us to the testimony of John: the charge written by Pilate had "Jesus the Nazorean, the king of the Jews" (19:19). Afterwards, the high priests contested the second part of the inscription, but not the first: he was indeed "Jesus the Nazorean" whom they had earlier sent to find (18:5, 7). So he was known by this name, even though he never calls himself by it. In this instance, as before, the title carries overtones of kingship, or at least of power of some kind. Thus we have found several indications that the name goes back to Jesus, but we still need to find out if it is favorable or not. In the case of the charge on the cross, it may serve to identify Jesus, or to give the reason for his condemnation, made explicit as a claim to kingship. However, the Jewish-Christians known to Epiphanius and Jerome, who called themselves Nazoreans and were presumably not innovating, also the use of the title by Peter (before any meeting with Gentiles), prevent us from seeing it as a mere nickname given by opponents. It must come from the group surrounding Jesus. On the other hand, the title is clearly residual in the NT as we have it, with connotations which are rather unfavorable or at best neutral. The simplest

185. Thus the AT; the WT is more precise: "among all the Jews of the entire world."

186. In *Ant.* 13 §171; 18 §11; *Life* §10, 12, etc. FJ uses the same term (αἵρεσις) to designate the Jewish "parties"; in *J.W.* 2 §119 f., he had spoken of *philosophies*.

187. Commenting on Acts 24:5, Epiphanius, *Pan.* 29.6.3 f., is a little embarrassed that Paul allows himself to be called a "Nazorean." He has to admit that Jesus' disciples were called "Nazoreans," like their master. In order to distinguish them from the later heresy of the "Nazoreans," whom he condemns, he insists on a break of continuity after 70: it is *after* the exodus of Christians to Pella that the Nazorean heresy appeared.

hypothesis is, then, to see this disappearance as the sign of an *intention* to keep a safe distance from the Jewish-Christians, who had remained Nazoreans, at the moment of the final redaction. Here we note that in the synoptics, Pilate's charge does not have "the Nazorean." In order to identify the person condemned, one would normally expect the name, patronymic ("son of") and any nickname or alias, but not a place of origin as such, especially if the place is not well known;[188] it is therefore understandable that the synoptics should have suppressed "Nazorean," since they were unable to give it a geographical sense. Mark and Luke even omit "Jesus," which makes the inscription hardly intelligible, or rather reduces it to the reason for condemnation alone, without giving the name of the condemned.

To throw light both on the meaning of the title and the reservations shown towards it, we need only bring together Epiphanius' Nazoreans who come from Jerusalem, and James's successors, so extolled by Eusebius, who can boast Davidic descent and give rise to suspicions on the part of the Romans. From the Jewish-Christian angle, it is clear that James *and* his successors are equally descendants of David and can bear the same title, and by extension their partisans. In other words, we come back to the marked kinship usually admitted between "Nazoreans" *(noṣrim)* and the shoot *(neṣer)* springing from the stock of Jesse, father of David (Isa 11:1). The interplay already noticed between the use of this term and the apparently synonymous "Nazarene" points to ancient debates about the Davidic descent of Jesus, and especially about the meaning of that descent, in which the Nazorean element has been watered down as much as possible. There are other traces of the same debate. Matt and Luke, with their genealogies and Jesus' birth at Bethlehem, affirm his Davidic ancestry without using the term "Nazorean" in this context. John 7:42 expressly denies it, emphasizing that Jesus came from Galilee (cf. also 1:45 f.), and refuses to associate Jesus' Messianic identity in any way with descent from David: "When the Messiah comes, no one will know where he is from" (John 7:27). In Rev 5:5 and 22:16, Jesus calls himself "the root and the posterity of David," with a transparent allusion to Isa 11:10 ("the root of Jesse"), but avoiding v. 1, which has exactly the same meaning but lends itself to a more explicitly "Nazorean" coloring. These remarks have a precise consequence in relation to the Messiah son of David for the Jewish-Christians. The victorious Messiah is not identified as any of the Nazoreans already known, not even as Jesus, since he failed,

188. In that case, one would expect a clear indication of the place, as with Judas Iscariot (איש קריות).

but he is awaited from among them, in the form of the return of this same Jesus *or a successor*, who will *then* be recognized as Messiah or king. This belief is expressed unambiguously by Acts 1:6 WT, "Is it in this time that you will *be re-established* (ἀποκαταστήσῃ)? And until when the kingship of Israel?"[189] This enables us to understand how it was that Jesus and his successors bore the same title, and that descent from David was followed with such extreme attention; what Hegesippus and Eusebius have to say on this point should not be dismissed as fantasy. Another consequence is that the identification of Jesus, and of him alone, as Messiah should be regarded as a further development in the community; this fundamental aspect will be developed later (chap. VII, §V).

To sum up, then, the gospels distance themselves somewhat from symptoms of Nazoreanism, but preserve traces of it.[190] The conflicts with the Jews can now be put in perspective. Take first the Johannine commu-

189. This expression is very clear if Jesus' (royal) title depends on the effective restoration of the kingship. The AT gives a version which presupposes that the title already belongs to Jesus: "Is it in this time that you will re-establish (ἀποκαθιστάνεις) the kingship for Israel?"

190. The literary projection of the Nazoreans on to the village of Nazareth must then be regarded as secondary. This is not the moment to pronounce on whether such a place existed at the time of Herod; we note only that its Hebrew name (נצרת) has been found in Galilee on a fragment of an inscription from the 3rd or 4th cent. giving the places of refuge in Galilee of the priestly courses (a subject rather foreign to rabbinic circles), cf. Mikhael Avi-Yonah, "The Caesarean Inscription of the 24 Priestly Courses," *Eretz Israel* 7 (1964), p. 24–28, who restores the rest of the inscription from rabbinic texts which are already known, cf. Samuel Klein, "Die Barajta der vierundzwanzig Priesterabteilungen," in: *Beiträge zur Geographie und Geschichte Galileas*, Leipzig, 1909, p. 97–108. One of the interests of this witness is to confirm the traditional Hebrew way of writing the name and remove any link between the various Greek forms of "Nazorean" and *nazir* (this traditional confusion comes from Tertullian, *Adv. Marcionem* 4.8, who makes of Lam 4:7 זכו נזיריה a prophecy of Christianity). In fact, we have seen in chap. II, §II.3 that it is John the Baptist and not Jesus who is presented as a *nazir*, which is a personal choice. On the other hand, if we suppose a "community of Nazoreans" (perhaps in the form of a village, analogous to Bathyra or its satellites) beneath certain instances of Nazareth in the gospels, we obtain a richer meaning: first, Matt 2:23, with the settlement at Nazareth and the famous verse; then Luke 4:16 explaining that Jesus gave his inaugural sermon at "Nazara, where he had been *brought up*" (lit.: "nourished"; Matt and Mark put only: "in his own country"), which allows the possibility of something like a Nazorean education for Jesus, followed by a conflict after his baptism; finally, John 1:46 puts on the lips of Nathanael, the true Israelite without guile, a severe exclamation, which is, however, instructive in the light of John's objection to any Davidic descent: "Can any good come from Nazareth?" One final remark: Eusebius, *Hist. eccl.* 1.7.14, gives a tradition already mentioned (cf. chap. III, §III) affirming that the "family of the Lord" (δεσπόσυνοι) came from the villages of Nazara and Kokhaba (=כוכבא "star"), in Batanaea. This is historically very doubtful, but not absurd, if we imagine a legend that Jesus spent his youth in a group not far from Bathyra (or at least its spirit), with a more or less Messianic name derived from Num 24:17 (cf. the nickname of Bar Kokhba "son of the Star"): there may well have been rivalries later on over the

nity.[191] Recent studies of John have shown that this gospel is more Jewish than used to be thought,[192] and that it needs to be read on two levels:[193] at the same time as it tells and reinterprets the story of Jesus, it presents also the later story of the Johannine Christians. In particular, fear of the Jews and exclusion from the synagogue in John 9:22 (as well as the expulsions foretold in 16:2) do not concern Jesus' own days, but later conflicts, at a moment when "among the leaders themselves, many had come to believe in him, but, because of the Pharisees, they did not dare to confess him, for fear of being excluded from the synagogue" (12:42). It is evidently a question of Jewish-Christians, who wish not to be excluded, but their timidity is severely criticized soon afterwards (v. 43): "They preferred the glory which comes from human beings to the glory that comes from God." The gospel itself hardly provides a setting for this conflict, and it is a good question how it could appear here if it is not primitive. Then it must be remembered that the final editorial touch *is not* Jewish-Christian and is even opposed to this tendency: weakening of Nazorean and Davidic shades of meaning;[194] insistence on the resurrection, the Spirit (20:21 f.) and the non-Messianic universal mission (4:35 f., 12:19 f.). If these few aspects are omitted, the environment in which the fourth gospel originated emerges as clearly Jewish-Christian and *in conflict with the Jews*, especially the Pharisees. These Jewish adversaries belong to circles which are close and doubtless very active, and are not the people as a whole or the authorities of Jerusalem.[195] Taking into account what has already been said about the similar origins of the first Tannaites and of the

---

attachment of Jesus to one or other shore of the Lake, or more generally to different groups. It is also worth noting that in Rev 22:16 Jesus is represented both as the shoot of David (Nazorean) and as the morning star (Kokhba).

191. Cf. Martinus C. de Boer, "L'évangile de Jean et le christianisme juif (nazoréen)," in: Daniel Marguerat (ed.), *Le déchirement. Juifs et chrétiens au premier siècle* (Le Monde de la Bible, 32), Genève, Labor et Fides, 1996, p. 179–202, with numerous references.

192. Cf. The synthesis of Pierre Grelot, *Les juifs dans l'évangile selon Jean* (CRB, 34), Paris, Gabalda, 1995.

193. Cf. J. Louis Martyn, *History and Theology in the Fourth Gospel*, New York, Harper & Row, 1968; id., *The Gospel of John in Christian History*, New York-Toronto, Paulist Press, 1978; David Rensberger, *Johannine Faith and Liberating Community*, Philadelphia, 1988.

194. Add also the transfer of the image of lifting up Jesus (cf. John 3:14; 8:28, etc.) to the resurrection; in Acts 1:11, the lifting up (or taking away, as with Elijah or Enoch) is also transformed by the announcement of the Spirit and the intervention of the two "men in white," who bring the disciples back to earth. The idea of lifting up is linked to waiting passively for a more or less Messianic return; it easily gives rise to dualism (the rest of the world is wicked) and to gnosticism.

195. Still less Judaeans, as is sometimes suggested, in the name of a presumed opposition between liberal Galilee and narrow Judaea, cf. Ricardo Pietrantonio, "Los 'Ioudaioi'

disciples of Jesus, the conclusion is self-evident: this later conflict is none other than the struggle against the *minim,* attested by the rabbinic sources, after 90 and in relation with Gamaliel II's reorganization (cf. §III.2).

Two corollaries can now be set out. First, the biography of Jesus that emerged in Johannine circles arrived in the west[196] after the crisis of the *minim*, which presupposes that there were contacts at that time if not before; but the final redaction is to be placed after separation, no doubt stormy, from the branch that remained Jewish-Christian (Nazorean). It is tempting to date this final split after 135, when the Jewish-Christians attached to Judaea had to choose between the Romans and Bar Kokhba.[197] Secondly, there is no reason to suppose that all these conflicts were limited to Judaea alone: Galilee must certainly be included, and we shall see in connection with Passover some very clear links with Asia Minor (chap. VII, §I.2). Similarly Rev 3:9 speaks in the context of Philadelphia of "people of the synagogue of Satan, who call themselves Jews, but are not, for they lie"; according to Rev 2:9 there is also a synagogue of the same brand at Smyrna. In a word, there are clear signs that for Rev, which has preserved some veiled Nazorean traces, the real Jews are the Jewish-Christians.[198]

Similar remarks can be made for the other gospels. Thus the fundamental question discussed by Matt is of a sectarian type: Which is the true Israel?[199] The parables of the kingdom include menacing scenes in which the legitimate heirs are dispossessed; it is a family quarrel. There too a twofold reading has to be made. On one level the gospel tells the traditional story of Jesus, continuing that of John the Baptist and connected, as we have seen, with groups of reformers of Essene type. Superimposed on this is the growing hostility of Israel towards the disciples, a later stage

en el evangelo de Juan," *Revista Bíblica* 47 (1985), p. 27–41, with a large bibliography. Malcolm Lowe, "Who Were the ᾿Ιουδαῖοι?" *NovT* 18 (1976), p. 101–131, shows that for the period 200 B.C.–200 A.D. the term ᾿Ιουδαῖοι was taken locally meant inhabitants of Judaea in the strict sense, whereas outside Palestine it had the wider meaning of inhabitants of Herod's kingdom or of the later province of Judaea/Palestina.

196. Most likely *via* Ephesus, the traditional view, cf. Raymond E. Brown, *The Community of the Beloved Disciple*, London, Chapman, 1979, p. 39.

197. Because they were caught between Bar Kokhba and the Romans, cf. chap. IV, §II.1.

198. The extreme importance of the Samaritans for John, which is opposed to the mistrust of them shown by the synoptics, then the debate implied by Philip's mission to Samaria and its confirmation from Jerusalem (Acts 8:5-25), pose particular problems which we do not intend to deal with here.

199. Cf. Ulrich Luz, "Le problème historique et théologique de l'antijudaïsme dans l'évangile de Matthieu," in: Daniel Marguerat (ed.), *Le déchirement. Juifs et chrétiens au premier siècle* (Le Monde de la Bible, 32), Genève, Labor et Fides, 1996, p. 127–150.

which followed a calmer period represented by Matt 17–20, which is dominated by training for mission. At the end there is a *final* split. Among the Jews, it is told "until this day" that the body of Jesus was smuggled away during the night (28:12 f.). Likewise, to proclaim the resurrection would be "worse than the first imposture," say the high priests *and the Pharisees*—the association of these two groups is an anachronism, since historically they were opposed, as we have seen. The Risen Jesus sends out his disciples to all nations, and declares that he will be with them until the end of time (28:16 f.). But that is not really Messianism, since here Jesus occupies the place of the Paraclete in John or the Spirit in Acts, and all the other titles fall into second place. In other words, the eventual conflict of the community with the Pharisees, long after Jesus, is superimposed on the condemnation of Jesus by the authorities, then rebounds as a mission to the Gentiles, or more exactly to the whole world.

This ultimate conflict, expressed very aggressively, strongly resembles the crisis of the *minim*;[200] it is a properly Jewish-Christian problem, still closely bound up with a form of Messianism. On the other hand, the universal mission opens up another horizon, according to which it is precisely thanks to this conflict that such a mission could develop, by moving out of a strictly Jewish Messianism. That is the theory expressed in Rom 11:11 f. : "Thanks to their [the Jews'] stumbling, the Gentiles have access to salvation." The gospel of Matt had an earlier Hebrew form, Papias tells us, which "each one interpreted as he pleased."[201] It is hard to pin down the precise form, but the final crisis seems to have had a twofold dimension, corresponding to two phases of literary composition. First, the Jewish-Christians are rejected as *minim*, and a conjunction is brought about with groups of Pauline type. Finally, the fading out of the title "Nazorean" points to an estrangement from those Jewish-Christians who refused this conjunction. Such an outline also shows a further channel by which a biography of Jesus could have circulated, then been transformed.

200. As J. Andrew Owerman observes, *Matthew's Gospel and Formative Judaism: The Social World of the Matthean Community*, Minneapolis, Fortress Press, 1990, pointing out sectarian aspects (p. 107–113).

201. Cited by Eusebius, *Hist. eccl.* 3.39.16. Epiphanius, *Pan.* 30.13.2 f. says that he has seen an Ebionite *Gospel of Matthew*, declares it to be corrupt and mutilated, and is indignant that it should be called "Hebrew"; from the context it appears that Epiphanius saw it in Greek and that it did not contain the infancy narratives. However, in *Pan.* 29.9.3-4, he states that the "Hebrew" *Gospel of Matthew* of the Nazoreans was complete. R. A. Pritz, *Nazarene Jewish Christianity*, p. 85 f. shows that several versions of this *Gospel of the Hebrews* were in existence, which is fairly natural in the absence of formal publication (with deposit in a library).

Luke-Acts presents an analogous case.[202] In the prologue, the benediction uttered by Simeon on seeing Jesus is unambiguous (Luke 2:32), "Light to enlighten the Gentiles, and glory of Israel your people." However, as early as the inaugural sermon at Nazara/Nazareth (4:16 f.),[203] the congregation is at first enthusiastic, then rejects Jesus and wants to stone him when he cites biblical references to salvation brought to the Gentiles. Similarly, Paul's inaugural sermon at Antioch of Pisidia, also in a synagogue, at first arouses enthusiasm (Acts 13:42 f.), but on the following Sabbath, the Jews oppose him and unleash a persecution (v. 45, 50). In both cases, the rejection is modelled on the Deuteronomic figure of the rejected prophet,[204] who is striving to save Israel from itself. That is also the final scene in Acts 28:26 f., where Paul at Rome quotes Isa 6:9-10 to the Jews who are divided among themselves ("For the heart of this people has grown dull [. . .]"), but at the same time proclaims a hope. There also, two conflicts, in which the mission to the Gentiles plays a decisive role, have been superimposed: opposition to Jesus, then opposition to Paul and his companions.[205]

Putting these two distinct historical moments in parallel is, however, a deliberate literary effect, as several indications show. For one thing, the Pharisees are represented as opponents from the beginning (Luke 6:2 f.), but they are not there at the passion (Luke 22–23); then they defend the apostles (Acts 5:33 f.; 21:3; 23:1-10), and at the end Paul says he is one of them (23:6). Then the problem of Jewish-Christian opposition (James, Pharisees) to the abandoning of the Law by Jewish converts is entirely played down (cf. above §II.1). The resulting effect is twofold: on the one hand, Paul and the Jewish-Christians are represented as united, while "the Jews" are divided; on the other hand, the Christians are finally the true Pharisees, that is the true Israel. This apparently astonishing result, which is quite foreign to the outlook of John, is arrived at by superimposing two conflicts. The first is the rejection of Jesus by the Jewish authorities; the second, less definite, is once again clarified by reference to the crisis of the *minim*, and turns out to be a problem which is properly Pharisaic (in

202. Cf. Daniel Marguerat, "Juifs et chrétiens selon Luc-Actes," in: Daniel Marguerat (ed.), *Le déchirement. Juifs et chrétiens au premier siècle* (Le Monde de la Bible, 32), Genève, Labor et Fides, 1996, p. 151–178.

203. If we suppose that Nazareth stands for "Nazorean" (cf. above), we can also understand how Jesus, formed in a Nazorean environment ("guardians"), causes a commotion in his *own country* (v. 23).

204. Cf. David P. Moessner, "Paul in Acts: Preacher of Eschatological Repentance to Israel," *NTS* 34 (1988), p. 96–104.

205. According to *Les Actes* I:26 f., the immediately pre-Lucan level of Acts ("Acts I") is entirely centered on Israel, with Jesus as Messiah.

the sense of the rabbinic tradition). The unanimity around Paul, and *a fortiori* around Peter and James, guarantor of the purest Mosaic tradition, disqualifies the other Jews, but above all it emphasizes, by underlining the continuity between Peter and Paul, that it is the *same* mission which brings Jews and Gentiles together. This is a far cry from Gal 2, and the final redaction of Acts (or sub-final with the WT) is therefore to be placed after the Jewish rejection of the Jewish-Christians and their partial conjunction with Pauline groups. The title of Nazorean is weakened or reinterpreted, but there is no precise accusation against those Jewish-Christians who have not yet come round.

For these reasons it is tempting to put the WT before 135, under Trajan or Hadrian; the AT characteristically shows a hardening of attitudes towards "the Jews,"[206] which points to a date after 135, like the final stage of John. On the other hand, the credit given to the Jewish-Christian tendency (James, Peter) suggests that the chief material for Luke-Acts originated in those quarters. They have, however, been integrated into a universalist perspective which is properly Pauline. Jewish opposition to Jesus and then to the apostles is violent but systematically confuses the two stages and is always associated with internal controversies or divisions among the Jews (cf. chap. VII, §IV.1). The constant model of interpretation is the sequence death-resurrection in fulfilment of the Scriptures, always with a positive outcome: Judas was necessary so that the promises might be fulfilled; then a criminal is released, and Jesus is killed by the Jews, but it was out of ignorance, and God raised him up; the persecution at the time of Stephen resulted in the mission outside Jerusalem; conflicts in the synagogues led to the mission to the Gentiles, etc.

In Mark, the outlook is even more teleological. A dominant feature of this gospel is the disciples' lack of understanding (Mark 4:13; 6:52 etc.), associated with Jesus' concealment of his own identity (1:34 etc.). The disciples will understand only after the resurrection, *i.e.* when Jesus' identity has been manifested and his titles reinterpreted; in particular, the properly Messianic phase is entirely avoided. Also the entire narrative culminates in the passion, which has been foretold three times (8:31 f.; 9:30 f.; 10:32 f.). This forms a remarkable contrast with Matt, where the disciples already understand the Master while he is among them (Matt 13:52), which is precisely the position of the Jewish-Christians. In Mark, there is no trace of Jewish-Christians (Nazoreans) and no identifiable symptom of the crisis of the *minim*. The opposition of the Jewish author-

206. Cf. *Les Actes* I:14 f.

ities does not clearly appear to be continued by any later crisis. Unlike Matt and Luke, the expulsion from the synagogues foretold in Mark 13:9 is drowned in the mass of tribulations linked with the universal mission, while the Pharisees are violently opposed to Jesus from the beginning of his mission, but do not feature in his trial. This is therefore a biography of Jesus that *is not* of Jewish-Christian origin, which makes it stand out from the others. Papias, cited by Eusebius, attributed it to Peter, which should bring it close to Jewish-Christian traditions, since Peter was the apostle of the Jews. But the attribution suggests also, and even more, contacts with Rome. In that case, the question arises why Justin, when he uses the *Memoirs of the Apostles*, is most often close to Luke, Matt or John, but never to Mark; his gospel harmony owes nothing to Mark[207] (and so should not, strictly speaking, be called "dia*tessaron*"). In a word, it appears difficult to identify an ancient tradition leading to Mark.

This is certainly not the place to reopen the discussion of the synoptic question, since no text has been studied in detail, but the identification of an intrinsic (and natural) link between the traditional biographies of Jesus and Jewish-Christian circles would seem to argue in favor of the Griesbach hypothesis (the "two-gospel theory"). According to this view, Mark is the result of a synthesis of the two narrative traditions represented by Matt and Luke, which both preserve traces of Jewish-Christian problems. The hypothesis commonly accepted today (the "two-source theory") has it that Matt and Luke depend principally on Mark and another source (named Q) comprising essentially the passages common to Matt and Luke that are not in Mark.[208] This hypothesis has the merit of sim-

207. Cf. M.-Émile Boismard, with the collaboration of Arnaud Lamouille, *Le Diatessaron: de Tatien à Justin* (EB, N. S. 15), Paris, Gabalda, 1992, p. 71 f. The table p. 37 f. shows that in the primitive harmonies associated with Tatian (derived from that attested by Justin), taken as a whole, the contribution of Mark is infinitesimal.

208. There can be no question of citing the innumerable works which defend or presuppose the two-source theory. Let us take only the case of Gerd Theissen, *The Gospels in Context. Social and Political History in the Synoptic Tradition*, Minneapolis, Fortress Press, 1989, who bases his argument on it and on the mass of historical and archaeological data from the first centuries, but minimizes the nature and duration of conflicts with Judaism; he concludes however, somewhat in spite of himself, that Mark, whose composition he places in Syria (Antioch), is a meeting place in the history of the traditions, with numerous Pauline traces and precise memories of Palestine (p. 239 f.). On the two-gospel theory, an interesting idea is floated by Harold Riley, *The Making of Mark. An Exploration*, Macon (Ga.), Mercer University Press, 1989, based especially on narrative considerations; but he finds himself hampered by the affirmation (derived from Irenaeus, but not demonstrated) of a very early date for Mark (around 65, soon after Peter's death). The early patristic testimonies on the gospels are brought together by Bernard Orchard & Harod Riley, *The Order of the Synoptics. Why Three Synoptic Gospels*, Macon (Ga.), Mercer University Press, 1987.

plicity, but, besides detailed difficulties which require it to be refined,[209] it cannot easily explain the sudden appearance in the texts of a problem of identity over against "Pharisaic" Jewish circles. Why would this problem emerge *later* than a tradition of presenting the biography of Jesus in a manner entirely focused on the "Pauline" interpretation of the Risen One?

VI – Conclusion: A Pluriform Christianity

This chapter has been based almost entirely on Jewish and Christian documents from the 2nd century, often originating outside Palestine. We have tried to show that these texts are useful for reconstructing the realities of the days of Jesus and the first disciples. The salient factor is the similarity between the environment in which John the Baptist and Jesus arose and the brotherhoods that led eventually to the formation of rabbinic Judaism; in both cases we are dealing with a movement of Essene type, but in a traditional Galilean setting. Against this background emerge several bundles of facts, which in turn open up fresh questions.

209. Cf. Pierre Benoit and M.-Émile Boismard, *Synopse des quatre évangiles. II*, Paris, Cerf, 1972. However, at the end of long stylistic analyses, in conjunction with those of Frans Neirynck and Philippe Rolland, M.-Émile Boismard, *L'évangile de Marc. Sa préhistoire* (EB, N. S. 26), Paris, Gabalda, 1994, comes closer to the two-gospel theory, and concludes that Mark is the result of a proto-Mark massively revised in the wake of archaic forms of Matt and Luke. He reconstructs a proto-Mark which is very short and stops after the account of the Last Supper (14:25), so represents an itinerary from baptism to the eucharist (cf. chap. II, §I); in particular, the gloss of Mark 15:42 ("the 'preparation,' *i.e.* the eve of the Sabbath"), on which Matt and Luke cannot depend, no longer presents a difficulty (cf. chap. II, §II.4). This reconstructed text brings out the already known fact that it contains traces of two parallel sources (proper to Mark). Such a line of interpretation would tend to show that the final Mark is the result of substantial elaboration, whose intermediate stages may never have circulated in written form (but it is interesting to note that the *Didache* 9–10 gives eucharistic prayers, precisely in a baptismal context, without any allusion to the death of Jesus, a feature which appears quite Jewish-Christian, cf. chap. II, §II.5). In these conditions, the attribution to Peter by Papias can take on a very simple meaning, independent of the apostle's teaching or ministry: the workshop which produced Mark was in Rome, where all roads meet. The rapid style and simple theology (no argument concerning salvation history, the true Israel, etc.) suggest that it was composed for liturgical use, perhaps so as to be easily memorized; the form of the prologue ("Beginning of the gospel of Jesus Christ," followed by a twofold prophetic quotation by the redactor) also points in the same direction, since the term "gospel" refers to a proclamation. Irenaeus, *Adv. haer.* 3.1.1 (quoted by Eusebius, *Hist. eccl.* 4.8.2 f.) explains the usual order of the gospels by the chronology of their composition: Hebrew Matt in the time of Peter and Paul, then after their death Mark for Peter and Luke for Paul, and finally John. But there are nuances of vocabulary: for the first two, it is a question of being put in writing (for us), for the two others, of formal publication (βίβλος, ἐκδίδωμι). A *publication* of Matt (final Greek) and Luke after Mark may still fit in perfectly well with earlier phases of redaction in which one or other was used by the (final) redactor of Mark.

1. When disciples of Jesus turned to the Gentiles, it was from every point of view a major event. Such a development could not have been foreseen at the outset, and it entailed a long series of difficulties, since the primitive community was by nature observant and saw itself at the center of the tradition of Israel. Fairly rapidly a gap widened between Paul and James, while Peter held a pragmatic position in between. However, the starting point of it all had been a missionary effort within Judaism, which then gave rise to conflicts. This missionary effort is depicted as beginning at one particular Pentecost (Acts 2), but its characteristic features need to be determined in relation both to John the Baptist and Jesus and also to the notion of Messianism. In the background are traces of the name "Nazorean," which was oddly enough shared by both Jesus and his disciples and which was to be kept by groups that remained strictly Jewish-Christian and were regarded as heretical after 135. These groups are the successors of James. They remained fixed in the expectation of a more or less imminent fulfilment of the Scriptures, *i.e.* of a latter-day Davidic kingship, centered on Judaism but also gathering the nations, though without any fusion with Israel. In the eschatological climate of the earliest days, the Jewish-Christians saw themselves as having a mission of a sort to the Gentiles, as is evident from the words of James at the Jerusalem assembly (Acts 15) and from the Pseudo-Clementine literature.[210] On a wider scale, the way in which the titles given to Jesus evolved appears to be a more complex question. Jesus' descent from David can be attached to his being a Nazorean, but can also be detached from it and is later contested in certain circles (John). Sometimes it is combined with the idea of Messiah, but that title too is less clear than might at first appear and becomes free floating. In the primitive Roman Creed, Jesus occupies the second position, normally reserved for Scripture (Moses, the Prophets) as the embodiment of divine revelation, and is called Son of God. If to that is added the notion of "Son of Man," originating in Dan 7, it can be seen that all these titles imply points of view which are distinct and may even be in conflict. At the center is the idea of sonship, in the last analysis, therefore, Jesus' legitimacy.

2. Paul's outlook is quite different. In his realized eschatology, the last things are already here in the form of a more or less symbolic communion between Jews and Gentiles. The *final* redaction of Acts makes an effort to depict James and Paul as being in fundamental agreement and to play down their real differences. Hence the scenes of reunion (Acts 15

210. Cf. Jean-Daniel Kaestli, "Où en est le débat sur le judeo-christianisme," in: Daniel Marguerat (ed.), *Le déchirement. Juifs et chrétiens au premier siècle* (Le Monde de la Bible, 32), Genève, Labor et Fides, 1996, p. 262 f.

and 21). The rejection of the *minim* from the time of Gamaliel II offers a hint at what was going on: at a difficult moment, at least one group among the Jewish-Christians began to re-establish contacts with communities of Pauline type, whereas others remained isolated. In this setting it is easy to imagine various texts in circulation, in particular an early (Jewish-Christian) non-published version of St. Matthew's gospel, around 90–100.

3. To speak of the biographies of Jesus (gospels) as having a Jewish-Christian origin is something of a tautology, since the first missionaries came from that environment. The case of Apollos, who had learned with exactness about Jesus (Acts 18:25), and the similar case of the disciples at Ephesus (19:1) show that the deeds of Jesus and the facts of his life were widely known at an early stage, even before the missionary journeys of Paul (whose reputation went before him to Rome; cf. chap. VI, §IV). Nothing was published *ad extra*, but it is still a good question in what form these stories went around, at least as private notes.[211]

4. About 120 (or a little before), the rabbinic authorities of Judaea forbade Greek for a while, a measure which is to be related to a Christian missionary effort: the *minim* are still close, and "sectarian" books are in circulation. We suggested above that these could have been an earlier form of the *Diatessaron* attested by Justin, that is a *published* gospel, bringing together in a reworked "Pauline" form traditional texts of Jewish-Christian origin. However, this harmony makes no use of Mark; this datum, in itself of no great importance, could be used with other facts to take a new approach to the synoptic problem and to help reconstruct the original environment.

5. It has long been established that in the redaction of the gospels, later conflicts between Christians and Jews have been superimposed on opposition which Jesus himself met from fellow Jews. The intention to identify the two moments of history could be called prophetic actualization:[212] the account of events in the past always has the capacity to speak to the present. Discussion of the sources allows us to show that these later

211. A. Frederik Klijn, *Jewish-Christian Gospel Tradition* (Sup. Vig. Chr., 17), Leiden, Brill, 1992, shows that the known traces of Jewish-Christian gospels can be classed in three separate branches and appear to be later than the canonical collections. That may only be a sign of late *publication*, as the outcome of an esoteric tradition.

212. This mechanism has operated in different ways; for instance, the presence of Pontius Pilate in the (Roman) Apostles' Creed has been taken to be a simple chronological marker, but was originally a reminder of Jesus' trial (meant for persecuted Christians), showing him as the first martyr in the period of Roman persecutions, symbolized all together by a Roman official, cf. Stephen Liberty, "The Importance of Pontius Pilatus in Creed and Gospel," *JTS* 45 (1944), p. 38–56.

quarrels are not of the same kind as the first. Essentially they turn on the problem of the Jewish-Christians, symbolized by James, who find themselves in trouble on two fronts, first in respect of the "Pauline" developments which lift the barrier between Jews and Gentiles, and then, after Gamaliel II begins his work of reorganization, with regard to their own original environment ("Pharisaic" as defined above), which rejects them as sectarian *minim*.

6. Two consequences result. On the Jewish side, we need to analyze afresh the way in which the gospels (especially Matt) tend to lump together all those who oppose Jesus (Pharisees, Sadducees, priests, kings, Romans, etc.), as this all-embracing outlook erases almost entirely the internal struggles between the different camps. On the Christian side, the position of Peter, striving to promote a quasi-impossible synthesis, stands out more clearly. In this context, mention should also be made of another quite different figure, venerated by tradition, in the person of Mary. In Acts 1:14, Mary the mother of Jesus is placed[213] at the point of conjunction between the "heirs," who find themselves divided into two camps which later history shows to have been in rivalry: on the one hand "his brothers," and on the other "the apostles," all, however, "persevering in prayer with some women."[214]

From this general setting an essential question emerges: where should we situate these attempts at synthesis and protestations of unanimity among the different heirs of Jesus? This question implies another which looks at first to have more to do with chance circumstances: How did the texts circulate, in other words, what were the channels of communication among the different communities?

The principal cities of the Empire were Rome, Alexandria and Antioch, with excellent communications among them. The paths taken by Peter and Paul, in the redaction of Acts, lead to Rome, with a major halt at Antioch, where the name of Christians was given to the disciples, and where the crisis arising from the mission to the Gentiles took place, reinterpreted as having provoked the Jerusalem assembly. By contrast, Alexandria is deliberately bypassed, as if it had not been possible to bring

213. By Acts II (*Les Actes* III:40). It is significant that the AT adds to the WT πάντες and ὁμοθυμαδόν "all . . . unanimously"; there too can be seen the very clear intention in Acts to underline the unity of all the heirs of Jesus (cf. §II.1 above).

214. This synthesis poses in passing the problem of the insertion of the infancy narratives in Matt and Luke (in the latter case ignored by Marcion); although independent, they are visibly of Jewish-Christian origin, not only through numerous details of Essene type (cf. chap. II, §I.2), but also by the emphasis placed upon the Davidic descent of Jesus (not without conflicts over the kingship) and on his family (which includes even John the Baptist). Each, however, has received a final universalist touch.

that city into the harmonious outlook of Acts. Apollos is the only one who comes from Alexandria, and it was there that he had heard of Jesus, even if he had to be taken in hand later at Ephesus. Against the background of communications in the Roman world, there stands out what could be called a second axis, one end of which is in Judaea and Galilee, and the other in Asia Minor, with an extension to Achaia (Corinth). This axis is illustrated by the fourth gospel. On the one hand, John shows a precise acquaintance with the realities of Palestine, Samaritans, John the Baptist, etc., and gives a chronology for Jesus which is more realistic than those in the synoptics. On the other hand, the tradition reported by Irenaeus (*Adv. haer.* 3.1.1) places this gospel's origin at Ephesus, the most venerable city of the province of Asia, the region also indicated for the Johannine tradition by Rev. However, the appendix of John 21, Johannine in style and centered on Peter, emphasizes an undeniable link with Rome.

In these different places occurred the founding events, which we must now examine.

Chapter VI

The Mission

The scene of Peter and Cornelius makes no reference at all to any instruction given by Jesus, and appears to be unprecedented. That immediately poses the questions of how the Gentile mission was begun and how it was justified. In fact the primitive community was, as we have seen, so deeply rooted in a Jewish and Galilean environment which was close to that of the Essenes, that any opening up to the Gentiles was *a priori* unlikely. It was in very truth a cataclysm, and we need to take the measure of it. A further passage from Acts will show the beginnings of this phenomenon in the series of episodes linked with Apollos, Aquila and Paul at Ephesus and Corinth. But before we look at them, it is not out of place to underline the difficulties that commentators have had in clearly attaching the Gentile mission to Jesus, all the more since, as we shall see, the political and social context in which Christianity began was rather disturbed.

I – Jews and Gentiles

It is usually held[1] that the first Christians saw the mission to the nations as a basic constituent of their overall mission and did no more than follow the example of Jesus, the first missionary.[2] However, the exact position of Jesus on this point is not so easy to determine, as there are no clear statements, with a result that commentators are divided into two camps, depending on whether or not they attribute this mission to Jesus

1. Cf. Ed. P. Sanders, *Jesus and Judaism*, Philadelphia, Fortress Press, 1987, p. 220; Eckhard J. Schnabel, "Jesus and the Beginnings of the Mission to the Gentiles," in: Joel B. Green & Max Turner, *Jesus of Nazareth: Lord and Christ*, Grand Rapids, William B. Eerdmans, 1994, p. 37–58, with numerous references.

2. Cf. Martin Hengel, "The Origins of the Christian Mission," in: *Between Jesus and Paul: Studies in the Earliest History of Christianity*, London, SCM, 1983, p. 48–64.

himself. Some emphasize that Jesus limited himself to promoting a restoration of Israel and regarded the arrival of the nations into the Kingdom as an eschatological event, by which God would fulfill the prophecies; it was only after Jesus that the Hellenists and Paul transformed the original mission. The other attitude tries to attach this mission to Jesus' ministry, by maintaining either that he himself envisaged it, even though it is attributed to the Risen Christ, or that various isolated encounters with Gentiles and certain sayings of his opened up perspectives which were later realized by the first apostles.

So the question remains open. In order to sort out the various opinions, we first need to look at the Jewish context, then examine in detail certain elements provided by the NT.

1. Jewish Proselytism

In order to fill out what the Gospel texts leave unclear, the first step is to inquire whether there is any trace of Jewish proselytism among Gentiles, for if there is, then the first apostles simply fitted into a pre-existing custom, without any need to justify it.[3] The famous verse of Matt 23:15, on the scribes and Pharisees who cross land and sea to *make* one proselyte,[4] has been used to prove the existence of an active Jewish proselytism among the Gentiles. This isolated witness needs, however, to be interpreted.[5]

Two opposite observations have already been made on this question (cf. chap. I, §I.4). For Philo, who wished to see the spread of the Mosaic law throughout the entire world, proselytism of Gentiles appears obvious, even though he never deals with it *ex professo*; admittedly, the "conversion" of the legislators would be enough for him, without the Jews ceasing to be a distinct people.[6] Similarly, Josephus insists on the fact that the law of Moses is a *political constitution,* the most ancient and the most di-

3. For a general bibliography on proselytism, cf. Schürer-Vermes III:150 f. and Louis H. Feldman, "Jewish Proselytism," in: Harold W. Attridge & Gohei Hata, *Eusebius, Christianity & Judaism* (Studia Post-Biblica, 42), Leiden, Brill, 1992, p. 372–408 (396 f.).

4. ποιῆσαι ἕνα προσήλυτον; the targums similarly interpret Gen 12:4 (Abraham).

5. Cf. Édouard Will & Claude Orrieux, *"Prosélytisme juif"? Histoire d'une erreur* (coll. Histoire), Paris, Les Belles Lettres, 1992. However, they underestimate the oral traditions and actual customs of various groups, in particular the mechanisms of separation. Correlatively, they tend to presuppose that Judaism was more or less homogeneous: on the contrary, there are very clear traces of proselytism *within* Judaism (cf. below §2).

6. Philo, *Vita Mosis* 2 §36 f., explains that the Pentateuch was translated into Greek so that "the greater part or even the whole of humanity might benefit from it and be guided towards a better life, etc."; this is the viewpoint of a legislator who addresses *readers*, cf. chap. I, §I.4.

vine, but his position on the Jewish people is not very clear, for he totally ignores the notions of covenant and election. Presumably he is thinking in terms of the Roman empire, federating and governing the subject peoples, whether organized as provinces or as kingdoms, but each keeping its own culture. At the opposite extreme, we saw that the Galileans did not accept Herod as king because he was not Jewish by origin. Likewise, Josephus states that the Essenes have to be Jews *by nation* (*J.W.* 2 §119).[7] For these circles, then, there was no possibility of proselytism in the direction of the Gentiles (chap. III, §I.2). A similar remark has been made about Peter and his companions in the context of the episode at Caesarea (chap. I, §II.1); it was also the opinion of James, who however allowed that Gentiles might turn to God (chap. V, §II.2).

To obtain greater precision, we need first to draw a distinction between active proselytism (mission) and the acceptance of candidates who come forward on their own initiative. For one thing, no ancient source mentions professional missionaries as a regular institution, and none laments the fact that Gentiles in general are not Jews.[8] Philo and Josephus condemn blasphemy against gods worshipped by other nations,[9] which is consistent with their legislative point of view. However, during the expansion of Judaea, the Idumaeans were forcibly circumcised by John Hyrcanus, under threat of expulsion (*Ant.* 13 §257); later, Aristobulus did the same with the Ituraeans (13 §319),[10] and Alexander Jannaeus carried out the same policy in the cities that he conquered (13 §397). Marriage with a non-Jew also required the other's conversion for validity (20 §139). These "normalizations" were simply intended to unify the king-

7. This expression is discussed in chap. VII, §IV.1.

8. Cf. Martin Goodman, "Proselytizing in Rabbinic Judaism," *JJS* 40 (89), p. 175–185.

9. *Ant.* 4 §207, commenting Exod 22:27: "Thou shalt not curse (לא תקלל; LXX οὐ κακολογήσεις) God (אלהים; LXX θεούς 'the gods,' TOnq [etc.] דיינא 'the judge[s]')." According to *BSanh* 66b (followed by Rashi), this forbids blaspheming God and cursing the judge, but that is not the understanding of FJ, who has just dealt with blasphemy against God (4 §202), the LXX or Philo, *Vita Mosis* 2 §205, *Spec. leg.* 1 §53; in the latter case, the reason given is the respect due to the word "god" (thus also FJ in *Ag.Ap.* 2 §237). The meaning of the prohibition may be either respect for foreigners (and their culture, cf. *Ag.Ap. ibid.*), or the ban on invoking other gods who are actually honored by "other cities," which implies that they have a certain existence (cf. Exod 20:3-5; *MSanh* 7:6). This second case is evoked in *Ag.Ap.* 1 §167, where FJ cites Theophrastus who reports (in the 4th cent. B.C.) a Tyrian law forbidding foreign vows, among which the Jewish *qorbân* (Lev 27:2, understood as "one who dedicates himself"; cf. *Ant.* 4 §73 and *Spec. leg.* 2 §32, also Matt 15:6 par.); he concludes that biblical customs were widespread, but with the obligation to respect local cults.

10. It does not matter here whether or not this item, in which FJ cites Strabo, is a doublet of the preceding one, cf. discussion chap. III, §I,1.

dom, its laws and government, under a single jurisdiction. They do not appear to have worried Josephus, who remained a great admirer of Herod the Idumaean. All the same, the term "conversion" is not quite the proper one to apply to these cases,[11] all the more since their legitimacy was contested in certain quarters.

According to various calculations, it appears that, under the emperor Claudius, who ordered a census around 42, there were in all eight million Jews, of whom two million lived in Herodian Judaea (the Roman *Palaestinae* of later times), four in the rest of the Roman empire,[12] and so two further east, in enemy territory. This *ethnos* was fairly mobile, as Josephus states that for Passover some 250,000 lambs were sacrificed, (*J.W.* 6 §423 f.); the figure may be exaggerated, since it supposes several million adult pilgrims, but we need to bear in mind how extremely important the pilgrimages were. In order to get a true idea of this Jewish population, we need only point out that the total population of the Empire at the time was not more than seventy million. So the Jews formed an appreciable minority, widely spread, to be found especially in the cities of the diaspora, cosmopolitan and highly visible. The desires entertained by Philo and Josephus for the diffusion of the Mosaic law were far from being groundless dreams,[13] but had an impressive social basis. This healthy demography was due to two factors: natural growth[14] and the arrival of proselytes.

We are not well informed about how these latter were recruited, but several facts can be mentioned which throw light on possible motives. First of all, Philo explains that there were preachers in public places

11. The rab. trad. distinguishes the "resident foreigner" (גר תושב) from the "convert from conviction" (גר צדק, lit. "proselyte of justice"); the former stays uncircumcised and is not a proselyte, but rather a "son of Noah" subject to the corresponding commandments, cf. *BAbZ* 64b. Between these two extremes comes the "forced proselyte" (גר גרור, lit. "towed"), corresponding to the Idumaeans and others officially circumcised (*YQid* 4:1, p. 65b-c).

12. Cf. Salo W. Baron, *A Social and Religious History of the Jews*, New York, Columbia University Press, 1952^{2}, I:168 f. (and n. 7). Adolf von Harnack, *The Mission and Expansion of Christianity in the First Three Centuries*, London, Williams & Norgate, 1908, I:3 f., gives the same number for the Empire, but underestimates Judaea.

13. According to Augustine, *City of God*, 6.11, Seneca raged against this "accursed nation" spread through every place, deploring the fact that the vanquished had given *their laws* to the victors.

14. Tacitus, *Hist.* 5.5, mentions that the Jews forbid the killing of unwanted children *(ex agnatis)*, whatever the defects they may be born with; as a result the father was obliged to give legal recognition to his children. Likewise, in *Ag.Ap.* 2 §202, FJ says that the Jews are obliged to feed their children (which excludes abandoning them, *expositio*), and are forbidden to bring about abortion or prevent conception. (That these obligations needed to be recalled shows that they were not always observed, cf. *MQid* 4:2.)

(*Spec. leg.* 1 §320 f.). Their audience must have been mixed, as with the numerous synagogues open to all where there was teaching each Sabbath on virtue and on duty towards God and the neighbor; presumably, the listeners came for religious, ethical, philosophical,[15] or even social reasons.[16] This information about Alexandria can be combined with what we know of Antioch, where the Jews, numerous and prosperous since the Hasmonaean period, welcomed many proselytes and well wishers, who were integrated into the people, but there is no suggestion that this was the result of an organized mission among the Gentiles (*J.W.* 7 §45). Likewise, from Josephus we learn that at the same period there had been proselytes at Rome since the time of Augustus (cf. §2). The famous case of the royal family of Adiabene (*Ant.* 20 §49–53), converted by the Bible through contact with Jewish merchants, raises the question of possible socio-economic advantages, both on the side of the merchants and on that of the rulers: independence with regard to the two competing great powers (Romans and Parthians), commercial contacts throughout the whole of the then-known world, community solidarity, etc.[17] It is not unlikely that agitation of a zealot or Messianizing type (cf. below, §2) attracted a following who wanted to get out of paying taxes.

Josephus also relates how people from beyond the Euphrates had come at great expense to Jerusalem but did not offer sacrifice when they learned that "Moses forbade it to anyone who does not observe our laws or share our ancestral customs" (*Ant.* 3 §318); they willingly accepted this prohibition, says Josephus, out of respect for Moses. This last case brings out the existence of well wishers or Godfearers, who were prepared to make costly gestures. They are well attested by Philo (*In ex.* 2

15. The philosopher par excellence was Plato, and FJ is the first to report a rumor that he had borrowed his rational monotheism from the Bible (*Ag.Ap.* 2 §242 f.). Cf. chap. I, §I.5.

16. FJ (*J.W.* 2 §559) mentions that women were converted to Judaism at Damascus, and S. W. Baron, *op. cit.*, p. 191 presumes that in this way they escaped the authority of their husbands, who, in virtue of the Roman *patria potestas* (which had become generalized), had, at least in theory, the right of life or death over them.

17. Cf. S. W. Baron, *op. cit.*, p. 171, emphasized by Louis H. Feldman, "The Contribution of Professor Salo W. Baron to the Study of Ancient Jewish History: His Appraisal of Anti-Judaism and Proselytism," *AJS Review* 18 (1993), p. 1–27. Thus, Deut 23:21 forbids lending at interest only among Jews, a point taken up by FJ (*Ant.* 4 §266); likewise, in *Ag.Ap.* 2 §208, he is against the taking of interest in general, but concludes: "Such are the relations which unite *us*." In reality there are two different cases: the loan for investment (formation of income-earning capital, cf. Matt 25:27), where national solidarity plays an exclusive role, and the loan to the needy whoever they may be, even foreigners (cf. *MBabaM* 5:6). Philo, *Spec. leg.* 2 §74 f., is not aware, when it comes to helping the poor, of any distinction between compatriot or foreigner, and earlier (in connection with the Sabbatical year) he has assimilated the proselyte to the compatriot.

§2) and Josephus (*J.W.* 2 §454, 463, 7 §45), by 1st century Latin writers,[18] and even by archaeological evidence.[19] However, we have already seen the particular view of them held by James and his followers, which recurs in rabbinical Judaism: maintenance of the boundaries of Judaism, linked to the law of Moses, whereas the Gentiles were bound to certain precepts associated with Noah (chap. V, §II). Philo's idea that the law of Moses is destined to become the charter of the whole world is profoundly foreign to such views.

So from different points of view Judaism was attractive, particularly under the Empire. These remarks provide a context for certain episodes reported of the first apostles. First some figures. A dozen disciples are mentioned at Ephesus (Acts 19:7), which is very few in comparison with the crowds of Jews who presumably lived in that city (v. 8 f.); likewise, only a few proper names of converts are given in the Epistles and Acts. We are dealing with tiny numbers, and it is interesting that the redactional generalizations, which appear out of proportion (2:41 "three thousand," etc.) approach the size of the Jewish communities in important cities.[20] So two realities of quite different dimensions have been superimposed.

Let us look now at Paul's visit to Athens. Its composition is complex. In the primitive form (Acts I) it is a question only of a visit to the synagogue (v. 17a), with very moderate success (v. 34); the episode conforms to the general pattern of preaching to the Jews, provoking a division among the audience. On to this narrative is grafted a meeting with Greeks in the agora (Acts 17:15-34), which includes some instructive features: Paul's speech arouses various reactions, then, when he speaks before the Areopagus to give an official account of the "new religion,"[21] he provokes a rejection; the context shows that there was a leisured clientele to listen to preachers of novelties. The failure suggests, however, that direct access to Gentiles, although theoretically possible, was impractical.[22] So there is a contrast between the Jewish and the Gentile audience. The final redactions try, however, to reduce the distance between the two groups. The statement that "some became believers" (v. 34), which

18. In particular Juvenal, Seneca and Tacitus, who express great revulsion for the success of proselytism, cf. M. Stern, *Greek and Latin*, II:5.

19. Cf. Louis H. Feldman, "The Omnipresence of the God-Fearers," *BAR* 12/5, 1986, p. 58–69, with particular reference to the recent discoveries at Aphrodisias.

20. According to *Ant.* 18 §84, when the Jews were expelled from Rome in 19, four thousand were sent to Sardinia, and they represented only a small proportion.

21. In view of a formal approval, cf. *Les Actes* V:298 f.

22. Even if the passage (v. 18-33) is only a construction of Acts II (cf. *Les Actes* III:227), it must presumably be true to life in its general content (rejection by Greek culture) and its setting (public preachers).

comes from the discussion in the synagogue, now occurs after the session of the Areopagus, so that the new disciples appear to come from a Gentile background. Conversely, among the audience in the synagogue, the AT adds Godfearers to the Jews present.

This last detail is significant. Cornelius, whom Peter visited, is a Godfearer (cf. chap. I, §II.1); Justus, to whom Paul goes on leaving Aquila, is another Godfearer, "close to the synagogue" (Acts 18:7 WT); they are no ordinary Gentiles, but close. These two scenes are fundamental, as we will show (cf. §III). Suffice it to note here two remarkable features. They do not take place in the synagogue, still less in public, but in private homes. Secondly, they occur on the edge of the spread of a reform movement within Judaism, with more or less well accepted itinerant preachers. It emerges that internal missionary activity was nothing unusual; according to Acts 13:15, such visitors were regularly permitted to speak in the synagogue.

To sum up, it is clear that there were proselytes, but—apart from the exceptional case of Judaea under the Hasmonaeans—their existence is not due to any organized, active proselytism, but rather to an attitude of openness combined with some power of attraction. By contrast, there are clear signs of active proselytism *internal* to Judaism, taking various forms which we shall now have to examine. Let us note in passing that the invective of Matt 23:15 against the scribes and Pharisees takes on a simple meaning consistent with Jesus' general outlook; these are reforming groups who are seeking to make new recruits *within Judaism*.[23] They obviously have much in common with another reformer, namely John the Baptist. The *political* fear which he inspired in Herod Antipas (cf. *Ant.* 18 §118), no less than the charge written by Pilate attributing a political position to Jesus, invite us also to look at the spread of "Messianizing" movements in the Jewish communities of the Roman world.

2. *Reformers and Rebels*

The question of proselytism in the true sense of the word needs to be looked at from the angle of movements internal to Judaism. The

23. This thesis is ably defended by Martin Goodman, "Jewish Proselytizing in the First Century," in: Judith Lieu, John North & Tessa Rajak, *The Jews Among Pagans and Christians In the Roman Empire*, London-New York, Routledge, 1992, p. 53–78. All the same, he tends to identify without further ado the Pharisees of FJ (spread everywhere) and the rab. trad. (which has another definition of "Pharisees," cf. chap. V, §I.1), whereas the proselytism in question certainly aims at establishing, enlarging or renewing well-structured *groups*, cf. chap. III, §IV. Joseph Sievers, "Lo status socio-religioso dei proseliti e dei timorati di Dio," *Ricerche Storico-bibliche* 8 (1996), p. 183–196, is also skeptical about external proselytism aimed at Gentiles, and brings together useful information about the juridical and fiscal status of the Jews from Tiberius to Constantine.

prototype is surely the reform of Ezra and Nehemiah. Although the episode is not easy to date because of the complex way in which the two biblical books have been redacted, Ezra's proclamation of the law of Moses is presented in Neh 8:1 f. as something new; it is followed by a celebration of the feast of Tabernacles such as had never been seen since the days of Joshua son of Nun. The statement that "all the people" took part in these events has to be qualified by the fact that just a little before, the rebuilt city (or "quarter") was practically empty (7:4) and that afterwards the general commitment to observe the Law was signed by only eighty-five names (10:2 f.). Later, this group is identified with a whole founding generation.[24]

We shall limit ourselves here to pointing out two large scale reform movements which were closely related, even though their observable consequences were different: the Pharisees and the zealots.

In the earliest account given by Josephus (*War*), the Pharisees make their first appearance about 70 B.C., when queen Alexandra Salome brings into her government the "Jewish sect that passes as the most pious of all" (*J.W.* 1 §110). They are a powerful opposition under Herod (1 §571), and under Agrippa, after 66, they are among those who protest against the zealots' claim to prevent foreigners from offering sacrifices (2 §411). The notice describing the parties (Pharisees, Sadducees, Essenes) is placed at the same point as the affair of Judas the Galilean, after the death of Herod (2 §119–166). In his second account, Josephus develops several points: he mentions certain episodes from the time of John Hyrcanus, so before 106 (*Ant.* 13 §288 f., developing *J.W.* 1 §110); later on, Herod takes action against the Pharisees (*Ant.* 17 §40 f., developing *J.W.* 1 §571). However, when Herod subjugated Judaea, Josephus emphasizes that among his supporters were notable Pharisees Shemaᶜya and Abtalion (15 §3, 370).[25] In this work he gives the list of parties twice: once at the place corresponding to that in the *War*, where he also includes as a party the movement of Judas the Galilean (18 §11–22); the other is put well before, during the youth of John Hyrcanus (13 §171–173), implying that Pharisees and Sadducees were already well defined and kept schools from the time of Jonathan son of Mattathias, around 150. All these changes go in the same direction: the Pharisee party, dominant among the people, enjoys a venerable antiquity. The reason for this reworking is to be found in Josephus' *Life*, which he presents as an annexe to the *Antiquities*; here he implies that he had chosen this party from his youth, and takes the opportunity to show that his own ancestors were well known at least since

24. Called "The Men of the Great Assembly" by the rabbinic sources, cf. *Search*, p. 277–286.

25. The masters of Hillel and Shammai, cf. chap. III, §II.1.

the time of John Hyrcanus (*Life* §4 f.). In other words, at Rome, around 90, the Pharisaic tendency is dominant, or more exactly sets the tone (cf. chap. III, §IV).

Although this phenomenon had certainly been accentuated by the consequences of the war, it was not entirely new. In 139 B.C., the Jews were expelled from Rome, but they were allowed to return, and Cicero can refer in 59 to a numerous Jewish minority, emphasizing the strength it gained from its solidarity, but without any suggestion that its presence was illegal. A little later, about 40, a series of Roman decrees was promulgated in favor of the Jewish communities in the cities around the Mediterranean (*AJ* 14 §220 f.), including the authorization of Sabbath rest and dispensation from military service.[26] We can note in passing that this latter point was never the object of a claim in Judaea or Egypt,[27] which had not so far come under the influence of the Pharisees. The communities privileged by the Romans were certainly not new, but the measures indicated are in conformity with the pillars of Mesopotamian Judaism and with its oral tradition, which can be broadly called Pharisaic, at least in the primitive sense represented by Nehemiah and the Hasideans. These decrees can be put into a precise political context: the Romans were in standing conflict with the Parthians, who were seeking to control the whole of Syria and had even succeeded at one time in imposing a king, Aristobulus, in Jerusalem; this was also the moment when Herod got himself appointed king by the Senate, with the mission to reconquer his capital. There were as many Jews living east of the Roman empire as in Judaea itself, and it was from those parts that Nehemiah's successors came. So we should conclude that the Pharisaic reform, which obviously presupposes missionaries, had been a success. The strong oriental influence which that implies could not but worry the Romans, and that is enough to explain their decrees which confer a favor, and at the same time remove the beneficiaries from any future conflicts.[28]

All that does not, however, mean that, even at the time of Josephus, observant Pharisees were really in the majority. They had certainly become the reference point, the standard of orthodoxy, as it were. But it would not be the first time that a minority group had served as a standard of reference. That was the case, we have seen, with Nehemiah. Something similar is to be seen also during the Maccabaean crisis, when the

26. According to the usual Roman norms respecting conquered peoples, cf. Miriam Pucci Ben Zeev, "Caesar and Jewish Law," *RB* 102 (1995), p. 28–37.

27. Cf. *Search*, p. 134–140.

28. This policy is fairly similar to that of Antiochus III favoring at most the restoration of Jerusalem, about 200, cf. *Search*, p. 214–215.

Hasideans, though politically very naive, provided a guarantee, at least literary, for Mattathias (1 Macc 2:42) and Judas (2 Macc 14:16), whereas they did not necessarily stand for the same political options (cf. chap. III, §I.1). Much later, Josephus states very clearly that the Pharisees, influential under Alexandra Salome[29] then sent packing by Herod, once again enjoyed authority over the people as a whole at the time when he was writing (around 90), and that even the Sadducees had reluctantly to follow them. That does not, however, mean that they were in a majority.

All this is quite consistent with what was said earlier about the Pharisees according to the rabbinic tradition (chap. III, §IV), as groups which were marginal but active, and served as a reference point which was disputed. It explains very well why Gamaliel II, in his enterprise of reorganization, sought to win over and control this more or less unstable reality, as Josephus had already tried to do (cf. chap. IV, §I.3); we have seen that that would also explain the latter's obsession with Galilee (chap. IV, §I.1). When he was writing the *War*, his preference lay with the Essenes, not that he envisaged everybody joining them, which would hardly have made sense, but in order to fix a reference point for a whole people *(ethnos)*, which was juridically well defined, but whose piety was in the nature of things variable and occasional. That is very different from the beginnings of Christianity, where there was never any question of a whole people, in the sense of a nation, but of strictly limited communities affirming that they and they alone were the true Israel (and not the true Judaism).

The second wave of "reformers" to have left traces behind can be grouped under the term "zealots," understanding by that what Josephus defines as the "fourth philosophy," connected with Judas the Galilean (*Ant.* 18 §23). The definition which he gives is brief: they have the same doctrines as the Pharisees, but accept no human being as master. He has already provided an illustration by telling how Judas had risen against the imperial census under Quirinius, and had promised his followers that their possessions would be safe—an attractive offer. In *J.W.* 2 §117 f., Josephus had already spoken of the sect of Judas and of his rejection of Roman domination and taxes, but without connecting it expressly with the census, or raising it to the rank of a "philosophy."[30] This Judas was the

29. For the relations of Alexandra Salome with the Pharisees and the "multitude" (πλῆθος) after the death of Alexander Jannaeus who had expelled them (*Ant.* 13 §407 f.), cf. below §III.3.

30. There are good reasons for thinking that the Judas of Sepphoris, who according to *J.W.* 2 §56 rose in revolt after Herod's death, at the beginning of the reign of Archelaus in Judaea, and Judas the Galilean, at the end of the same reign, are one and the same person

successor of Ezekias, who had been active in Galilee and whom the young Herod put down, only to be later accused by the Pharisees; these episodes have already been dealt with (chap. III, §1.2), and we have seen that these bands of what Josephus calls "brigands," were none other than zealots close to the Pharisees, their brigandage consisting in the first place of seizing tax money, and perhaps also of pressing forced recruits into their own bands.

Whatever their precise ideals, two characteristic features of these bands constantly stand out, from the beginning of the Roman occupation. For one thing, they aroused division among the Jews, some accepting the movement, others fearing it and denouncing it to the Romans. At the same time, many who joined them were presumably attracted by the prospect of finding an identity while at the same time escaping without danger from paying taxes and from various humiliations, especially in the countrysides and in the poorer quarters of the towns. In other words, such groups would be as unstable as their members' motivation was weak, whence the occasional rivalries and attempts to outbid one another, such as we see in Jerusalem just before the war: each group defined by a chief, and sometimes by a name (sicarii, etc.). An excellent example of the ensuing troubles is provided by Josephus himself, in a complex narrative in which he was involved (*J.W.* 7 §407 f.). After the fall of Massada, sicarii who escaped to Egypt provoked sedition at Alexandria, even pursuing the Jews who resisted them; this naturally aroused a very anxious opposition among the leading members of the Jewish community, who finally handed them over to the Romans in order to restore their own reputation with the authorities. Joseph goes on to tell the story of Jonathan, who did the same thing in Cyrenaica, but despite the troubles which he caused, he managed to denounce the community leaders to the Roman governor, who even got false witnesses to testify against them; in this way many rich people were executed and their goods confiscated. Josephus explains that he himself was among the accused, but the matter reached Rome, where Vespasian whitewashed him. Josephus is certainly tendentious, but he brings out well both a mechanism of serious divisions among Jews, with physical coercion and Roman punishments, and also the eagerness of the Romans to exploit these divisions in order to strengthen their own power which does not seem to have been all that secure.

(cf. Schürer-Vermes I:381), and that the attachment of these events to Quirinius and the imperial census is only an artificial device in order to cover over a long period of disturbances and Roman repressions, cf. Étienne Nodet, "Jésus et Jean-Baptiste selon Josèphe," *RB* 92 (1995), p. 503 f.

These phenomena were not new in Josephus' time. Conflicts within Judaism were a constant reality, and can be followed from the events leading up to the Maccabaean crisis until Pompey's arrival in Jerusalem (chap. III, §I.1). There is always, in one form or another, a party faithful to the Law, and another more political, negotiating for advantages with the suzerain power, first Seleucid then Roman; the "observant" party, by nature non-political (cf. the Hasideans), always has an activist fringe that rejects the "collaborators" (cf. Mattathias and Judas). After Pompey, the Roman occupation was certainly better organized than the previous Seleucid domination which had become decadent; so the activist fringe reappeared with force. In particular, at the time of Herod, before, during and after his reign, a movement of Galilean origin can be discerned, from Ezekias to Menahem, passing through Judas the Galilean. The movement created by Jesus fell into this category, or at least was so perceived.[31] Josephus was on familiar ground in reporting the preventive execution of John the Baptist by Herod Antipas, who feared that someone with such influence over the crowds would bring about sedition (*Ant.* 18 §118). The personalization of the groups was a constant feature; when the high priest says (John 11:50), "It is better that one man die for the people rather than the entire nation perish," he judges that the initiator of a group only needs to disappear for the whole group to dissolve. Gamaliel's argument, which represents an extreme personalization of the movement begun by Judas the Galilean, is of the same nature (Acts 5:36 f.).

The problem was, however, on a much bigger scale, as is shown by the case of Jonathan in Cyrenaica, as well as the proportions taken by the unfortunate project to place Caligula's effigy in the Temple, around 40 (cf. chap. IV, §I.2). If there were so many leaders with varying success, if local problems were all the time getting out of hand, there must have been widespread tensions which drew a notable following towards the agitators.

3. Christiani *at Rome, Alexandria, Antioch . . .*

This is not the place to analyze the social tensions in the Roman world, but only to take notice of certain Jewish phenomena which keep recurring in the great cities. We shall look first at the main ones, Rome, Alexandria and Antioch, which we shall take in that order for purely practical reasons.

Rome. In A.D. 19, Tiberius banished all the Jews from Rome, states Josephus, because of the crimes committed by four of them (*Ant.* 18

31. According to Matt 26:69; Mark 14:70; Luke 22:59; 23:6, cf. chap. III, §I.2.

§84).[32] However, he gives a few details which enable us to assess the implications of this summary. A Jew, accused of misdeeds in Judaea, had escaped from condemnation and taken refuge at Rome, where he occupied himself in teaching people the true wisdom of the Mosaic law; he recruited three collaborators, who in turn persuaded Fulvia, a proselyte and wife of a high-ranking person, Saturninus, to send large gifts to the Temple in Jerusalem. But these individuals pocketed the funds and were denounced by Saturninus to Tiberius, who then banished all the Jews from Rome. The consuls exiled 4000 men to Sardinia, and punished more for having refused army service;[33] in other words, the only ones condemned were troublemakers, so a minority, who are not to be equated with "all the Jews." A major crisis seems to have been sparked off by the episode of Fulvia, which was quite minor in itself, though not lacking in interest for us. Josephus' information seems partial—in both senses of the word—,[34] but the whole affair has a strong odor of "brigandage," with all the distaste which Josephus has for this term, by which he means zealot agitation in the name of the Law, because of its very visible socio-political fall-out (army, money) which obliged the Romans to react. It is interesting to note a certain Jewish proselytism towards the Romans, dating perhaps from before the reported disturbances, as it is not said clearly that the agitators themselves won the converts. In any case, we have to distinguish carefully a kind of proselytism on the boil in troubled times, leading to repressions but creating nothing lasting, from the existence of *permanent* well-wishers and proselytes, integrated in different ways into the Jewish people, such as Josephus mentions at Antioch (cf. §1).

32. Cf. Ernest L. Abel, "Were the Jews Banished from Rome in A.D. 19?" *REJ* 127 (1968), p. 383–386.

33. According to the decrees of Caesar and his successors, reported in *Ant.* 14 §190 f., Jews who were Roman citizens were dispensed from the army. Here, either this privilege has been suspended, but evidence from Philo (cf. below) makes this unlikely, or else it is a question of provincial subjects who refuse to leave Rome.

34. For Suetonius, *Tiberius*, §36, it was a matter of prosecuting those who had adopted Jewish or Egyptian cults, by banishing the propagators of these cults and their proselytes (the latter not necessarily very numerous); those Roman citizens who refused to leave were exiled or threatened with being sold into slavery. Tacitus, *Annals* 2.85, also mentions these events, in a context in which Tiberius, towards the beginning of his reign, was seeking to prevent prostitution among women of equestrian rank. So there was a certain dangerous instability in Roman high society, perhaps related to the weakness of official worship. In fact, Josephus places the episode just after the curious and more or less edifying story of Paulina, wife of another Saturninus and follower of the cult of Isis (§65–80). Although a virtuous matron, she was deceived into sleeping with an admirer, under the belief that he was the god Anubis; once the truth was discovered, the temple and its cult were destroyed. In other words, FJ puts together an affair concerning Egyptian proselytism (with a suggestion of prostitution) and another concerning Jewish proselytism. In

Later on, Claudius,[35] according to Suetonius (*Claudius*, §25), expelled Jews[36] from Rome, who were stirring up constant tumults at the instigation of "Chrestus" *(impulsore Chresto).* Suetonius gives no date, but by combining what he has to say with other texts we can conclude that the events reported are to be placed in the first year of the emperor's reign, that is 41.[37] Before even envisaging who this "Chrestus" might be, let us first look at a highly important scene which converges with the text of Suetonius, namely the meeting between Aquila and Paul at Corinth

---

this respect, we note that he places both incidents *after* his notice on Jesus, which closes the episodes relating to Pilate, who, however, arrived in Jerusalem only in 26 (*Ant.* 18 §35). This is an important chronological distortion on the part of Josephus, who thus places these events towards the *end* of Tiberius' reign; the distortion is deliberate, since it does not occur in the earlier narrative (*War*). This manipulation, which also results in separating John the Baptist and Jesus, leads us to wonder whether the connotations for a Roman ear of the name "*Christos,*" thus discreetly placed in the *Testimonium* ahead of the various Jewish disturbances in Rome (presumably also *impulsore Chresto*, as Suetonius might say, cf. below), may not in reality be meant to guide the meaning of "*christianos*"; it is even possible to think that he is seeking to emphasize the already obvious lexical link connecting the memory of a chronic agitator *(Christos)* and a dangerous breed with a movement founded by Jesus but now quite different in nature.

35. Here and in what follows, we rely on the documentation and arguments of Justin Taylor, "Why Were the Disciples First Called 'Christians' at Antioch? (Acts 11,26)," *RB* 101 (1994), p. 75–94.

36. Or perhaps "the Jews." The sentence *Ioudaios impulsore Chresto adsidue tumultuantes Roma expulit* is just a little ambiguous, since Latin has no definite or indefinite article, but it is more natural to take the *tumultuantes* as determining *Ioudaios* ("the Jews that"); the normal way to have expressed the expulsion of all "the Jews" would be *Ioudaios quod . . . tumultuarent.* A Semitic speaker, such as FJ, could be easily confused, as he would restore an article and thus produce a different meaning, depending on whether he understood *Ioudaios* as a definite object (גרש את היהודים המורדים, "expelled the Jews, continually in revolt") or as indefinite (יהודים המורדים, "Jews continually in revolt"). It is not impossible, then, that FJ's generalization, according to which "all the Jews" were expelled under Tiberius, is the result of a Latin source misunderstood or containing the same ambiguity as Suetonius. A similar remark may apply to the expulsion of "all the Jews" in Acts 18:2 (cf. below).

37. Thanks to Dio Cassius, *Hist.* 60.6.6, who reports these events at the beginning of the reign of Claudius (41) and states that the emperor wished to expel all the Jews, but could not do so without risk, and only forbade assemblies (this rather odd explanation may be the best he could do with information which he considered improbable, namely that Claudius expelled all the Jews, cf. prec. n.). The texts are presented and discussed by Jerome Murphy-O'Connor, *St. Paul's Corinth. Texts and Archaeology* (Good News Studies, 6), Collegeville (Minn.), The Liturgical Press, 1990^2, p. 138–148. The date of 49, adopted by many commentators, is based on a rather uncertain text in Orosius, *Hist.* 7.6.15-16; it allows an apparently simple chronology for Acts 18:1-17, between Aquila's arrival in Corinth (edict of Claudius) and Paul's appearance before Gallio, proconsul of Achaia in 51–52, established by the famous Delphi inscription (cf. Murphy-O'Connor); but literary analysis shows the composite character of the passage, cf. *Les Actes* V:313 f.

(Acts 18:1 f.), in which the WT (right-hand column) and the AT (left hand) show characteristic differences:[38]

(18,1) *After leaving Athens, Paul arrived at Corinth.*

(2) *Having found a certain Jew named*	(2) *Having found*
Aquila, originally from Pontus,	*Aquila, originally from Pontus,*
who had recently arrived from Italy,	*a Jew who had recently arrived from Italy*
and Priscilla his wife,	*with Priscilla his wife,*
	he greeted them with joy.
	They had left Rome,
for Claudius had ordered all the Jews to depart from Rome,	*for Claudius Caesar had ordered all the Jews to depart from Rome;*
	they had emigrated to Achaia.
(3) he attached himself to them.	(3) Paul was known to Aquila
And, through their being of the same trade,	*through their being of the same* kind,[39]
he stayed with them, and they were working.	*and he stayed with him.*
They were tent makers.	

Between the WT and the AT, Aquila undergoes some interesting transformations. For the AT, Aquila is fairly harmless. An unremarkable sort of person, he has come from Italy, without further specification, rather than precisely from Rome. He works quietly at a trade which he and Paul have in common, and gives Paul a base and somewhere to live. That is all. We can even guess already that he will become a disciple of Paul, as the narrative goes on to imply. Things are quite different in the WT. There Paul and Aquila belong to the same *movement*, but, of the two,

38. According to *Les Actes* III:228 f., vv. 2-3 are an addition by Acts II to a narrative of Acts I comprising Paul's arrival (v. 1) and discussion in the synagogue (v. 4a), followed by an outburst (v. 6). The argument given is above all narrative (with some associated literary elements), and results indirectly in making the WT a secondary development of the AT (when Paul and Aquila separate, v. 7). However, the redactor of Acts I has already given plenty of evidence of being a Messianizing Jew (the savior of Israel is close at hand), which exactly suits Aquila, as we will show. It would be begging the question to assume that Paul and Aquila are already "Pauline" in the sense of Rom (even if the final redaction strongly suggests this, by making Paul's conversion at Damascus a total and instantaneous change, cf. §III,1).

39. The word ὁμόφυλος could be rendered "being of the same tribe" (Benjamin), but how would that be a reason for being already acquainted? In fact, φυλή means any body of persons united by a bond, whether or not of real or supposed common descent.

the more important is Aquila,[40] since the fact that Paul is known to him is significant. Aquila and Paul need not have been personally acquainted. Information must have circulated within the movement, especially among the ports around the Mediterranean basin, which were always in touch with Rome. The expression "having found" then takes on its true meaning: Paul, with a rumor going before him, was looking for Aquila in order to find support for his own action.[41] But that is not all. Aquila does indeed come from Rome. Since the WT already represents a redacted narrative (Act II), Luke's sources might have given an even more distinctive profile of Aquila. Be that as it may, Claudius' edict of expulsion enables us to be precise enough: the government was expelling trouble makers, who were creating "disturbances," and Aquila was one of them, and not the least. What was the "movement" to which Aquila and Paul both belonged? The account in Acts does not mention the name of Jesus. In other words, this is the Paul who was noted for his aggressive zeal for the Law (cf. Phil 3:6). If he spoke to Aquila about Jesus, it would have been as the Messiah of a zealot movement.

Paul does in fact call himself a "zealot" in Acts 22:3 WT[42] and states that he was educated at the feet of Gamaliel I, and belonged to "the strictest party[43] of our religion." That answers well to the Pharisees in the primitive sense (cf. chap. III, §IV). It could well be that Gamaliel, certainly very strict in matters of doctrine, was a moderate in politics, but that says nothing about his disciples: we have seen that the "zealots," or at any rate their spiritual guides, had the same strict tendencies as the Pharisees. Where did Paul come from? Jerome says in two different places that he came from Gischala, in Upper Galilee, though he tries to harmonize this tradition with the well-known passages which say that he came from Tarsus (Acts 9:11, 30; 21:39). This piece of information, whether or not it is historically founded,[44] is highly significant, as is shown by two episodes well apart in time. Gischala was in the sphere of operation of Ezekias and other "brigands" at the time of Herod (chap. III, §I.2). In 66, Gischala was a bastion of Galilean tradition opposed to Tiberias, and Josephus did not

40. The mention of Priscilla with Aquila may have been introduced (already in the WT) in order to weaken further the latter's Messianizing character, cf. below §II.1.

41. Likewise in Acts 11:26 AT, Barnabas goes to look for Saul/Paul at Tarsus and, when he finds him (εὑρών), asks his help (cf. below under *Antioch*).

42. That is ζηλωτής; the AT adds τοῦ θεοῦ, with a less markedly political meaning, "zealous for God."

43. Or more literally: "the most exact sect" (ἀκριβεστάτην αἵρεσιν); the same term features in the discussion of the exactness of Apollos' teaching, cf. below §II.1.

44. Jerome, *In epist. ad Philem.*, §23 (*PL* 26.617) and *De viris inlustr.* §5 (*PL* 23.615), takes the information very seriously, as in fact it deserves, cf. *Les Actes* VI:138 f.

succeed in winning over the famous John of Gischala, who had good relations with the leading Pharisee Simon, son of the same Gamaliel I and father of Gamaliel II (chap. IV, §I.1). Simon was in Jerusalem at the time, but that does not exclude links with Galilee and/or Babylonia, since Gamaliel I had been the disciple or successor of Hillel (cf. *MAbot* 1:16). All this points clearly to identifying the young Paul as a zealot[45] and allows us to see just how far he had come when later on he recommends his readers to respect the authorities and pay their taxes (Rom 13:1-7)!

That Aquila and Paul belonged to the same movement has a very important consequence. In fact, if Suetonius' formula *impulsore Chresto* characterizes the disturbances repressed by Claudius in 41, those troubles certainly date back much earlier, since they are described in terms of a constant agitation; we would not go far wrong in attributing them to the provocative policies of his predecessor Caligula. In that case the *Chrestus* mentioned by Suetonius, though definitely Jewish, is unlikely to be Jesus.[46] So, then, who was this person, real or imagined, who aroused revolts?[47]

The first point to make is that it is not directly a question of "Christians," but only of Chrestus (or Christus: at this time these two Greek words were pronounced identically). Later on, in 64, in the context of the

45. In the strict sense, but not an armed sicarius, cf. Justin Taylor, "Why Did Paul Persecute the Church?" in: G.N. Stanton and G.G. Stroumsa, *Tolerance and Intolerance in Early Judaism and Early Christianity*, Cambridge, Cambridge University Press, 1998, p. 99–120, who draws attention to the facts that Paul was a Pharisee and that those who opposed the disciples were priests and Sadducees, but not Pharisees (cf. chap. V, §V.2), and concludes that Paul was hostile to the pacifism of the Jesus movement, which in his eyes was ruining the Pharisees' cause *from within*. Whatever the redactional complexities of Paul's arrest by the tribune Lysias (cf. *Les Actes* III:257 f.), Acts 21:37-38 is careful to emphasize that Paul knows Greek well, that he is not the leader of an uprising of sicarii, and that he is even a Roman citizen by birth (22:27); it is not certain that Paul in his youth would have been happy with this profile!

46. Of course, Suetonius may have been mistaken. Strictly speaking, the possibility cannot be excluded that Aquila, and maybe others as well, associated his Messianizing activity at Rome with Jesus, but the way in which Acts minimizes this activity and seeks to make Aquila a disciple of Paul suggests otherwise. Cf. below his meeting with Apollos §II.1.

47. Suetonius' spelling (also Tacitus' *chrestiani*) suggests a reference to χρηστός "useful, amiable, preferable," a well-known slave name without any special Jewish connotation. As applied to the "Christians," it could have been a popular deformation, as Tacitus suggests (cf. below), since there is no trace in the known sources of anyone of that name taking up the mantle of Spartacus as leader of a slave revolt. In the NT, the term χρηστός features seven times; the two words are spelled differently but were pronounced identically (itacism), thus making certain word plays possible, cf. Matt 11:30 ("My yoke is *easy*"), 1 Cor 15:33 ("Evil company corrupts *good* morals"), etc. Later apologetic made an effort to cancel out the criminal associations of χριστιανός, by claiming that the Christian was "useful" (χρηστός) to the empire, cf. Justin, *Apol. I* 4; Clement of Alexandria, *Strom.* 2.4.

fire at Rome under Nero, the same Suetonius speaks clearly of the *christiani* and their new and harmful *superstitio* (*Nero* §16); Tacitus reports the same events in a famous passage, where he expressly distinguishes the popular name *chrestiani* from the name of the founder, Christus, put to death by Pontius Pilate. Something has happened between these two dates: the *christiani* are now the followers of a definite person, Christus. The conclusion is clear: first, Suetonius' Chrestus in 41 does indeed refer to the Hebrew Messiah; the identification of this figure with Jesus comes only later, but the Romans react in both cases in an identical way. This allows the interpretation of two literary details. Tacitus links a popular name *chrestiani* and a definite person *Christus*, but the spelling suggests that there were indeed *chrestiani*, that is Messianists, before the link with Jesus was made. For his part Suetonius speaks of instigation, or literally, "impulsion," and not of real command or leadership; in other words, the Messiah exercises an influence in his absence, which suggests that the leaders were proclaiming the imminent coming of a Messianic kingdom.

This result allows us to recognize a common character in all the similar movements which appear in turn, starting with Ezekias under Herod. Time and time again, people who are religiously highly motivated, though militarily very weak, dare to stand up to the power of Rome or its representatives, and carry with them a great number of Jews who are attracted also by the idea of avoiding oppressive taxes. Unless we assume that they are simply crazy, the only plausible explanation is that, in all cases, they are proclaiming that the end of time, or the kingdom of God, or else the Messianic era, is close, and doing so with conviction, based on a well worked out interpretation of the Law. The imminent coming of the Messiah gives a major *impulsion*, and at the same time it seriously divides the Jewish community, since those who do not accept the message see how dangerous it is.[48]

Alexandria. Shortly after he came to the throne in 41, Claudius replied to the official good wishes sent by the citizens of Alexandria.[49]

48. This is not the place to discuss the classic problem of the literary sources of Jewish Messianism (or rather Messianisms), which has been given a renewed vigor by the discoveries in the Judaean wilderness. We simply refer the reader to certain well-documented studies: Pierre Grelot, *L'Espérance juive à l'heure de Jésus.* New edition revised and enlarged (coll. "Jésus et Jésus-Christ," 62), Paris-Tournai, Mame-Desclée, 1994; John J. Collins, *The Scepter and the Star. The Messiahs of the Dead Sea Scrolls and Other Ancient Literature* (The Anchor Bible Reference Library), New York, Doubleday, 1995. For ways of representing the enemy, cf. Lambertus J. Lietaert Peerbolte, *The Antecedents of Antichrist. A Traditio-Historical Study of the Earliest Christian Views on Eschatological Opponents* (Suppl. to JSJ, 49), Leiden, Brill, 1996.

49. *PLond* 1912 (date of discovery of the papyrus), cf. *CPJ* II, n° 153, which discusses the many views put forward as to the import of this text.

Among other things he expressed his will concerning the Jews. After mentioning recent troubles amounting to war against them (or some of them), he began by confirming their privileges,[50] then announced certain measures he was taking in their regard. In particular, he forbade them to bring in Jews from Syria or Egypt, and also to send two lots of official representatives to Rome. Some commentators[51] have held that these agitators from Syria were Christians, because of the parallel with Suetonius already cited, understood as referring to Christians. This parallel is not, however, decisive, and the problem seems to be more complex, since one of the results of the troubles at Alexandria was a duplication, in fact if not in law, of the Jewish community structure there, a development which the emperor formally forbids: a single status should cover all the Jews together.[52] So the disturbances have given rise to repression and then to a visible division of the community, serious enough to worry the government at Rome, where similar troubles had recently broken out. Such a split is *a priori* quite distinct from the emergence here or there of tiny groups meeting in private, such as we see in Acts. On the contrary, the situation that we glimpse through Claudius' letter seems to be very like the episodes described by Josephus in Cyrenaica and Alexandria, as the sudden appearance of widespread and dangerous popular movements presupposes agitators with a simple political message. The conjecture that these troubles were due to the arrival of Christian missionaries would amount to supposing that they were zealots or "Galileans," and in any case not much concerned about evangelizing the nations as such. All these things need careful examination. There is no difficulty in allowing that Jewish agitators who could be called *chrestiani* came from Judaea, Galilee or even Antioch, but the question still remains of their connection, if any, with the disciples of Jesus.

For now, it is enough to note that the situation at Alexandria resembles that at Rome, in its effects and in its causes, even though the idea of "Messiah" is not expressed in the emperor's letter. In Acts, Alexandria does not feature in the itineraries of Peter or Paul, which may sufficiently explain why that city is hardly mentioned. On the other hand, it was at Alexandria that Apollos got to know "the things concerning

50. According to FJ, this was thanks to the intervention of king Agrippa I, to whom Claudius owed his throne (*Ant.* 19 §278–286).

51. Cf. Henri Grégoire, reviewing the *editio princeps* of *PLond* 1912 by H. Idris Bell, *Byzantion* 1 (1924), p. 638–647; interpretation proposed independently by Salomon Reinach, *CRAIBL* (1924), p. 313–315.

52. Cf. E. Mary Smallwood, *The Jews under Roman Rule from Pompey to Diocletian. A Study in Political Relations*, Leiden, Brill, 1981, p. 138.

Jesus," as well as the baptism of John, but without a Messianic dimension, as we shall see (§II.1). That forms a contrast with the situation glimpsed at Rome, where Messianists and the heritage of Jesus were fused some time between 41 and 64.

Antioch. It was there, according to Acts 11:26, that for the first time the disciples were called "Christians." The first thing to note is that the name *Christiani* is of Latin, not Greek, formation, and that the formulation of the sentence in Acts has an official ring about it.[53] The name may well be of popular origin,[54] but it is likely that its use here, with its juridical coloring, comes more immediately from the Roman authority. It is given (imposed) for the first time at Antioch, and it will mark its bearers as criminals;[55] perhaps it already did so before it was applied to the disciples of Jesus.

What has taken place? As we have already seen, the Jewish community of Antioch had for a long time been prosperous, peaceful and open; it welcomed Gentiles, who could be regarded as integrated into the people, even though neither they nor their children are said to have been circumcised (*J.W.* 7 §45). However, the affair of Caligula's statue had a major impact there. In the winter of 39–40, Petronius, governor of Syria, received an order from the emperor to go to Jerusalem and install his statue by force in the Temple. Philo tells us (*Leg.* §185 f.) that the Jews of Antioch were the first to get wind of the affair, then, according to Josephus, Petronius, on his way to Jerusalem, met with Jewish opposition, which was total though non-violent, at Ptolemais and Tiberias (*Ant.* 18 §261 f.). There were, however, disturbances at Antioch at the same time or even before, involving Jews and put down with severity.[56] Did these concern the same affair, or were they a Messianic agitation as at Rome, or perhaps violent reactions to preaching about Jesus?

On this last point, Acts 11:19-26, taken in three sections, preserves the trace of several missions to Antioch (the AT, on the left, is given only when it contains a different reading from the WT that is significant for the present discussion):

53. Cf. Eric Peterson, "Christianus," in: *Micellanea Giovanni Mercati* (Studi e Testi, 121), Biblioteca Apostolica Vaticana, 1946, p. 355–372, who emphasizes that the form of the term, designating "partisan of X" (e.g. "Herodians"), suggests a derivation from a proper name (real or supposed by the authorities), here *Christus/Chrestus* (personalized equivalent of Messiah).

54. As Tacitus suggests (*Ann.* 15.44), with great probability.

55. Cf. Pliny the Younger, *Epist.* 10.96, who asks Trajan whether a Christian is punishable for the mere fact of being one (*nomen*), or if he must also have committed the crimes usually associated with Christianity (*flagitia*).

56. Cf. *Les Actes* V:67 f.

A (19) *On the one hand, those who had been scattered by the storm that broke out through Stephen went as far as Phoenicia, Cyprus and Antioch, speaking to no one*

the word, but only to the Jews.	*but to the Jews.*

(20) *On the other hand, there were men from Cyprus and Cyrene, who having gone to Antioch, were speaking*

also to the Hellenists (Ἑλληνιστάς),	*to the Greeks* (Ἕλληνας),

proclaiming the Lord Jesus. (21) *The hand of the Lord was with them: a great number having become believers turned to the Lord.*

B (22) *The matter concerning them came to the ears of the "church" of Jerusalem, and they sent Barnabas to Antioch.* (23) *He, having arrived and seen the grace of God, rejoiced, and he exhorted them all to remain profoundly attached to the Lord.* (24) *He was indeed an upright man, filled with Holy Spirit and with faith. A considerable crowd joined themselves to the Lord.*

C (25)	*Having heard that Saul was*
He went to look for Saul at Tarsus.	*at Tarsus he went to look for him.*
(26) *Having found him he brought him*	*Having found him* he asked him *to*
to Antioch. It happened	*come to Antioch. Having arrived,*
that during an entire year	*during an entire year*
they joined	*they were in agitation.*[57]
themselves to the "church,"	
and instructed a considerable crowd,	
and that for the first time at Antioch	*Then for the first time the dis-*
the disciples were called Christians.	*ciples were called* Christians.

In the AT, the first section (A) gives the impression of a doublet which has been harmonized, since the idea of "speaking to the Jews and also to the Hellenists" is redundant, unless we gratuitously imagine that by "Jews" is meant those who spoke only Hebrew or Aramaic. The result is to make this mission analogous to those that will follow (Acts 13–14), which all began in a Jewish environment before turning to Gentiles. By

57. Thus ms D συνεχύθησαν (not retained as WT, but without textual justification, cf. *Texte occidental*, II:81). This verb and the associated substantive σύγχυσις are proper to Acts in the NT: in 2:6 it designates the upheaval in the *plêthos* of the disciples (cf. §III.2 below); in 9:22 Paul "puts into confusion" the Jews of Damascus; in 19:29, 32 agitation spreads in Ephesus; in 21:27, 31 the Jews of Asia stir up the crowd in Jerusalem. The LXX translates by Σύγχυσις the name of "Babel" (Gen 11:9), also the "upheaval, panic" of 1 Sam 5:11 (cf. gloss on v. 5) and 14:20.

contrast, the WT indicates two distinct movements ending at Antioch,[58] one starting in Jerusalem and addressed only to Jews, the other starting from Cyprus and Cyrene and addressed to Greeks (Gentiles). What is going on here? We may get an idea by bringing together the following points. 1. The final "proclamation" in v. 20 has all the marks of a later hand,[59] which is trying to blend the two movements together by attributing the same message to both (cf. WT). 2. In v. 21, the expression "turn to the Lord" is the same as that in James's decree (15:19), where it concerns the Gentiles; it is indeed the continuation of v. 20, but there was originally no connection with Jesus. 3. The propaganda addressed to the Greeks becomes more precise when we consider all together the great number of recruits, the fact that at Antioch the Jews had numerous Greek well wishers, and also the fact that the missionary movement originated in Cyrenaica, which recalls the disturbances in Alexandria. 4. The preachers are anonymous, and are not known from elsewhere as disciples. 5. The Roman description "Christian" is not far away.

The whole of this passage can be put into the context of the disturbances caused by Caligula's plan to place his statue in the Temple at Jerusalem. On this hypothesis, Jewish preachers came to arouse *among the Greeks,* perhaps with a note of eschatological urgency ("The Messiah is coming"), a lively reaction against this abuse of the cult of the emperor, a reaction which was probably sharpened by other abuses of Roman power. Antioch was the seat of the Roman government of Syria, and it is not difficult to imagine demonstrations against Petronius in the winter of 40. From a Roman point of view, they would have taken place *impulsore Chresto,* and from a Jewish point of view, it would all have amounted to a visible and promising act of renunciation of idols.

This hypothesis is reinforced by the mission of Barnabas (part B). It is recounted in lyrical fashion, insisting on the qualities of Barnabas, who is surely "powerful in the Scriptures."[60] Two important details, however,

58. As suggested also by the balanced construction of vv. 19-20 μέν . . . δέ.

59. Acts II, according to *Les Actes* III:167 n. 1. This ending εὐαγγελιζόμενοι can also be attached grammatically to v. 19, which in the WT ends with a verb in suspense λαλοῦντες: "(they were) speaking," without saying what. The AT adds τὸν λόγον.

60. He was called Joseph, and received from the apostles the nickname of Barnabas (Acts 4:36). This name obviously means "son of a prophet," so "inspired," which is another way of saying that he was "powerful in the Scriptures" (like Apollos, cf. below). The Greek translation given by Acts is interesting: "son of consolation" (υἱὸς παρακλήσεως, cf. Luke 2:25 "consolation of Israel") which is a qualification bestowed by the Spirit, cf. Acts 9:31 "thanks to the consolation of the holy Spirit"; perhaps the "word of consolation" for which Paul was asked in Acts 13:15 was just such an "inspired" homily on the texts of the day. The connection between the Spirit, consolation and memory (of events and of Scripture) is firmly established by John 14:16, 26, etc. (Paraclete).

stand out. It is a "matter" which comes to the knowledge of Jerusalem, which was not initiated there, and now needs to be looked into. Then Barnabas exhorts the "considerable crowd"[61] to remain faithful. In other words, the amazing success might turn out to be no more than a flash in the pan, *a priori* unlikely to prove durable, especially if there were a severe repression. What is really remarkable is the absence of any reference to Jesus, or baptism, or any union between Jews and Gentiles. On the contrary, the mission to the Jews at Antioch in v. 19 appears to be entirely independent of the other, and no co-ordination is established between them.[62] Coming also from Jerusalem, it makes up a diptych: the missions to the Jews and to the Gentiles are *distinct*, and apparently without conflict, which fits in perfectly with the position of James (cf. chap. V, §II).[63]

61. According to *Les Actes* II, 195, v. 24 is redactional: it attributes to Barnabas the qualities of Stephen ("filled with holy Spirit and with faith"), and the "large crowd" (ὄχλος ἱκανός) which joins him is the same as that which he teaches with Paul in v. 25.

62. According to *Les Actes* III:114, this verse is based, as to both content and form, on 8:4 (especially in the WT), mentioning the dispersal after Stephen's execution, and must likewise be attributed to Acts II, which seeks to establish a parallel between the mission to Antioch and the evangelization of Samaria (which also ends in the decision to send a delegation from Jerusalem). In fact, 8:1, introducing the mission to Samaria as the consequence of a persecution, is picked up in v. 4, which adds nothing new (the redundancy is more obvious in the WT than in the AT) but acts as a frame for inserting vv. 2 (the mourning of Stephen) and 3 (the misdeeds of Saul). Later, 11:19 refers back to the synthesis represented by 8:1-4. However, this solution is not entirely satisfactory, for the following reasons: 1. in fact, 8:4 is strictly redundant, whereas 11:19 gives quite precise (non-redactional) information, since people come to Phoenicia, Cyprus (so sea travel) and Antioch and address Jews; this is more than a mere redactional seam; 2. even in the P Doc, the episode of Stephen (6:8-11 and 7:58-60) and the great persecution (8:1b-2) are simply juxtaposed ("And it happened on that day"), so that a later redactor could take the whole passage as reporting one and the same crisis; 3. in that case, 11:19 links up those who were scattered as a result of this single crisis; 4. so the parallel between the episodes in Samaria and in Phoenicia-Antioch may very well have existed already at the level of the P Doc. That would mean that originally, there was a notice on a persecution in Jerusalem, followed by dispersal in various directions (from Samaria all the way to Antioch); into this setting were inserted the episodes of Stephen in Jerusalem, Philip in Samaria, and others unnamed who go as far as Antioch (addressing Jews). These last were then combined with still others unnamed who came from Cyprus and Cyrene (addressing Gentile well wishers, with political agitation). Those "scattered" are very active, and do not at all resemble refugees displaced from camp to camp: it is tempting to see them as zealots and other Messianizers, whether or not connected with Jesus' disciples. The redaction of the P Doc undoubtedly links all these movements together, although that is not necessarily the way they were originally presented.

63. In the reconstructed P Doc, the entire episode concerning Antioch occurs immediately after the Jerusalem assembly (*Les Actes* II:65-66), which is very logical. The way the present text is constructed has the effect not only of introducing Paul into this assembly, but especially of suggesting that the Pauline churches (Antioch of Pisidia, Iconium, Lystra, Derbe) have already absorbed large numbers of Gentiles, who have table fellow-

Paul's intervention (part C)[64] is essentially one of backing up and giving substance to the action taken by Barnabas, which seems to have developed beyond his original mission. For the WT, Barnabas hears of Saul by chance, looks for him at Tarsus and invites him to Antioch, even though he had no mandate to do so. In the revised version represented by the AT, it appears to be well known that Saul is at Tarsus, and Barnabas seems to be more securely in charge of his mission and keeps the initiative. In the earlier stage of redaction, Barnabas appears to be overwhelmed by the situation at Antioch.[65] The ending according to the WT refers in the clearest possible way to a year of disturbances, which was certainly enough to be noticed by the Romans and to give the movement that he was trying to manage the name of "Christian." The Jews reached by the mission mentioned in v. 19 probably found themselves also included in this category. (Decoded: Jewish disciples who were not zealot activists have been assimilated to the Messianists, that is to say, accused of subversive activities.[66]) Barnabas, "filled with Holy Spirit and with faith," but not seeing how people from Jerusalem can be of much help in the situation, thinks of Paul, with his reputation as an activist, as the most appropriate person to call in. We shall discuss later the general profile of the Jerusalem community (§III.3), but we can say here that, in view of the Jerusalem decrees and the personality of Barnabas as it appears in Acts 4:36 f., it is not really likely that he would have been the one to proclaim, and certainly not to Gentiles, that the Messiah was indeed Jesus.

This long detour through three great cities of the Roman world has brought out the picture of a Jewish Messianism whose outline can be discerned by following the Roman reactions to the disturbances that it caused, especially under Caligula. At its center was an eschatological urgency, but this was filled out by associated particular interests (such as avoidance of taxes); it gave rise to insurrection in the Jewish community and also among Gentile proselytes and well wishers, especially at Anti-

---

ship with Jewish members, and always against a background of divisions within the wider Jewish community.

64. For the sake of convenience we shall generally call Paul by his Roman name.

65. As suggested by the vocabulary employed: Barnabas and Paul join the "church" (ἐκκλησία) and teach a "large crowd" (v. 26). This "church," in the context, can only be the product of the mission in v. 19, *i.e.* those who have responded to a proclamation, and who therefore are in a parallel situation to the "church" that sent Barnabas (v. 22). On this term, cf. chap. VII, §IV.3.

66. A passage of Heb may allude to a similar situation (10:32-33): "You have endured a heavy and painful combat: in one place, exposed to public insults and persecutions, in another, identified with those who were undergoing such treatment." Certain ancient traditions attribute Heb to Barnabas.

och. Originally, this Messianism had no identifiable connection with Jesus and his successors, but later, once the link was established in the confused situation at Antioch, the criminal label of "Christian" was attached indelibly to the disciples, which presupposes some intrinsic and durable link. Two questions then arise about this Messianism, which we are going to study further by following the Jerusalem-Asia Minor axis, which is better documented than the three great cities: why did a rumor of Jesus as Messiah spread in this way? And why did Jesus' disciples make use of it, despite the scandal of a crucified Messiah?

Adjacent to these questions is the observation that the social body of the disciples develops on two tracks: alongside little groups of believers are crowds large enough to worry the Roman authorities. The connection between the two entities is still not very clear. That was already the reality surrounding Jesus in the Jewish world.

II—Ephesus and Corinth

At first sight, the way in which the apostles began their activity, according to Acts 1–2, is fairly clear. After Jesus had left the scene, there was a period of reorganization and low-level activity in Jerusalem, and then the major event of Pentecost, when the Spirit was made manifest, opened a mission in all directions, with an astonishing success in which all nations were reached. We have already seen the very great importance of the feast of Pentecost in connection with the Eucharist (chap. II, §II.5); in Acts chap. 2 it forms a sort of frontispiece which presides over the rest of the book, in which all notable actions are placed under the sign of the Spirit.

This general movement ensures the overall cohesion of an itinerary which leads from Jerusalem to Rome, and at the same time draws attention away from the discordant facts which we now need to examine more closely. The manner in which the different phases of the life of the Jerusalem community are told represents a synthesis, especially insofar as they are made to prepare the way for future developments. So it is a better strategy to begin with events that took place elsewhere. After the great cities of Rome, Alexandria and Antioch, let us now visit Ephesus and Corinth.

The narratives of Acts 18–19 appear to provide a detailed account of the evangelization of Corinth and Ephesus, in which Paul has the principal role. In reality, these chapters are a more or less coherent collection of small narrative units with different origins. Let us now try to unscramble some of them, by following first Aquila and Apollos, the main persons who are mentioned alongside Paul, apparently as his fellow workers.

1. Apollos and Correct Teaching

We have already seen Aquila's first appearance on stage (§I.3). He is a Messianizing Jew whom Paul finds at Corinth, who had been expelled from Rome under Claudius in 41; we also saw that the AT makes him a rather uninteresting person, and in any case quite harmless. We shall have occasion later to follow up his relations with Paul, but, in order to get a better idea of him, we shall first study another scene from which Paul is absent: a certain Apollos, from Alexandria, teaches at Ephesus in the presence of Aquila and his wife Priscilla, who then put him right. The text is not without its problems and has undergone a number of changes in the course of reinterpretation. As before, we place the WT on the right:

> (18:24) *A Jew called Apollos, from Alexandria* (AT adds *by nation*), *an eloquent man, had arrived at Ephesus, being powerful in the Scriptures.*[67] (25) *He had been "catechized"*

	in his own country
in the way *of the Lord*	*in the* word *of the Lord*

> *and filled* (lit. "boiling") *with the Spirit he was holding forth and teaching exactly the things concerning Jesus, knowing only the baptism of John. (26) He began to teach with assurance in the synagogue. Having listened to him,*

Priscilla and Aquila took him aside, and expounded to him more exactly the way of God.	*Aquila took him aside, and expounded to him more exactly the way.*

This brief narrative gives rise to a number of problems.

According to the AT, Aquila and Priscilla simply give greater precision to Apollos' teaching, which amounts only to a difference of degree in his knowledge of the "way of God," an expression in itself fairly banal. It is not said whether these additional items concern Jesus. For the WT, Apollos did not know "the way," but only "the things concerning Jesus." In what follows, he is instructed in "the way" (without "of the Lord" or other complement). This expression often occurs in Acts,[68] most often to designate the disciples of Jesus, and always in a context of disturbance in which Paul is involved. The notion of "way" refers essentially to preparing for the final coming of God, according to Isa 40:3; it already featured,

67. The expression δυνατὸς ὢν ἐν ταῖς γραφαῖς (discussed in chap. I, §I.1) is also very like one of the qualities required in a bishop by the *Ecclesiastical Constitution of the Apostles*, n° 16, to be capable of interpreting the Scriptures (δυνάμενος τὰς γραφὰς ἑρμηνεύειν).

68. Acts 9:2; 18:26 (and 18:25 AT); 19:9, 23; 22:4; 24:14, 22.

along with the return to the desert, in the preaching of John the Baptist (Matt 3:3 par.), and is found in the same form in the Qumran *Community Rule* (1 QS 8:12 f.).[69] This goal of preparing the way can, however, split into two very different attitudes: either rigorous observance of the Law (call to conversion, etc.), with a course of initiation, as with the Essenes; or Messianizing activism, wanting to get rid of evil by force, as with the "brigands." Apollos belongs obviously to the first type, acquainted as he is with John's baptism and with Jesus; Aquila belongs no less obviously to the second, as a member of the "movement" who has been expelled from Rome, and he is the one who speaks of the "way." What Aquila proposes to Apollos is certainly a reinterpretation of the *nature* of what he already knows about Jesus (who is not called Christ or Lord), and this development brings Apollos closer to Aquila. Already at Corinth (Acts 18:1 f.), Aquila—like Paul at Damascus and certainly under his influence—had come to acknowledge Jesus as the Messiah who is shortly to return. On the other hand, for him the important thing is the imminence of the Messiah's return and not precisely his identification as Jesus. That is the nature of his "exactness," which classes him with Paul, that is, with Paul as he knew him at Corinth. Accordingly, he instructs Apollos with a more Messianizing view of Jesus (effectively, as we shall see). Apollos knows John's baptism, but he is not a personal disciple of John; he belongs to a group for whom Jesus is a Teacher, as also do the twelve disciples of Ephesus (Acts 19:2, cf. below §3).

The "exactness" that is required and verified is a technical term normally used for checking the accuracy of a (handwritten) book.[70] In this case, Aquila is checking the accuracy of an *oral* teaching, according to a technique attested in the rabbinic tradition. Whether or not this scene comes from the source or from the redactor, it is realistically portrayed: Apollos has already been "catechized,"[71] so has received an oral teaching, and Aquila's intervention is also oral. In this context, the presence or absence of Priscilla has this precise meaning: Is a woman qualified to judge the accuracy of a teaching? If so, can she be a witness along with her husband, since at least two witnesses are required in any matter (Deut

69. Mentioning several times the "perfect in the way" (cf. 1 QS 8:10,18,21; 9:5; 11:11), not without severity towards "those who deviate from the way" (10:21).

70. Cf. Luke 1:3 and chap. I, §I.3 on written and oral publication.

71. On the term *catechumen*, cf. chap. I, §I.1. In Luke 1:4, Theophilus has received an oral instruction (κατηχήθης). Κατηχέω is unknown to the OT. Here a fairly clear distinction is made between the oral form of the instruction and its content, which is either exact or not; this is indicated by the expression ἐδίδασκεν ἀκριβῶς ("was teaching, informing exactly").

19:15)? But Priscilla[72] is absent from the WT, and Apollos seems to accept the corrections, doubtless as part of a tacit agreement with the "way." Questions concerning teaching are a serious matter (cf. Matt 5:19), but here the problem is solved in a friendly manner,[73] which, juridically, would amount at most to a warning.[74] Priscilla is introduced at this point by the AT, which gives a more peaceable image of Aquila (Acts 18:1 f.) and a less serious view of his amendments; she intervenes simply in a matter of teaching, and not of active Messianism. The position of the married woman with regard to teaching is an interesting question and crops up elsewhere. 1 Cor 14:34 and 1 Tim 3:11-12 forbid her to speak in public, but Paul recommends that her husband instruct her. According to the Qumran *Community Rule*, a married woman can take part in discussions and give witness in certain cases (1 QSa 1:9-10).[75] We shall see other passages (especially in Acts) which show that for the environment in which Christianity arose, a woman, even if not married, could have a personal status.

Apollos has acquired his knowledge of Jesus and received John's baptism at Alexandria, but John certainly never went there, and in addition, Apollos has been reached by disciples of Jesus. So "John's baptism" is indeed an institution, with procedures and rites; it is not necessarily connected with John personally, and is certainly more than a simple rite received once for all in the past. The formulation of v. 25 implies that knowledge about Jesus is linked with access to the rite. Apollos belongs, like Jesus before him, to a group of baptists. There is also some connec-

72. *Les Actes* III:233 points out that the mention of Priscilla with Aquila is surprising (she is absent from 18:21, 26 WT). She may have been added here (and in 18:1) following 1 Cor 16:9, in order to correct Aquila's overly activist profile (we know of no female zealots); Aquila and Priscilla may have got married only later. In that case, the problem of a woman being able to examine and/or correct instruction is simply put back to the time of the redactor of the AT, but the important thing is that it is still the same kind of problem.

73. But it is not hard to imagine that if Apollos (powerful in the Scriptures) had refused, Aquila would have "breathed threats of bloodshed" against him; that was the way in which the young Paul, Aquila's "disciple," had reacted (cf. Acts 9:1) towards the disciples of Jesus, *i.e.* of *this* (faulty) way.

74. The procedure is illustrated by CD 9:2-8: no one may accuse another unless he can prove that he had given a previous warning, otherwise he lays himself open to a charge of revenge (cf. Lev 19:18 also TYon and TNeof of Deut 32:35) or even of complicity in the other's crime (cf. 1 QS 5:24 f., also Ezek 33:8 and Sir 19:13 f.).

75. This question has puzzled the commentators (cf. chap. VII, §IV,2), as in the rab. trad. a woman may not testify (*BShab* 30a, and likewise in *Ant.* 4 §219), and she does not even receive much encouragement to study, since according to *MSoṭa* 3:4, whoever teaches the Torah to his daughter prepares her for frivolity (תפלות).

tion with the "Therapeutae"[76] described by Philo, who form brotherhoods living in purity and eating Covenant meals during a Saturday-to-Sunday all-night vigil, at least at intervals of fifty days (cf. chap. VII, §IV.1). Philo's sublime description has led some critics to suppose too hastily that these Therapeutae existed only in his imagination. Eusebius, who does not shrink from stating that Philo had met Peter in Rome, believed that they were proto-Christians (*Hist. eccl.* 2.17). He was wrong, but the error is instructive: certain of Philo's expressions occur also in the description of Apollos (whom Paul treats with respect), and there is a general resemblance with the summaries in Acts on the primitive community.

The entire episode is to be dated after Aquila's arrival in Corinth, which was connected with Claudius' decree of 41. That is also the period of his letter to the Alexandrians which, as we have seen, tries to restore order to Messianic agitations. All the same, if Apollos had something to do with the Therapeutae, he must be regarded as rather non-political; he is an itinerant preacher, but there is no reason to think he had been expelled, or was suspect in the eyes of the authorities. However, after his meeting with Aquila, he begins to proclaim that Jesus is the Messiah, and a few difficulties occur, as we shall see. In a word, he becomes a Messianist. That is to say, he belongs to a group capable, *in the name of tradition*, of giving a *durable* reception and propagation to a Messianizing message, exactly like the Pharisees who followed Judas the Galilean. That is very different from a flare-up, set alight by a few agitators and catching hold of some marginalized malcontents; it is also much more dangerous for the authorities. Apollos can thus be compared to Barnabas: both come from similar backgrounds, both are eloquent and powerful in the Scriptures, and both take very seriously a Messianic proclamation centering on Jesus. We can now understand why Barnabas took such an interest in Paul.

The AT hides the fact that it was in his own country, Alexandria, that Apollos (whose Jewish identity has already been played down) heard the "things concerning Jesus"; in the context, it suggests rather that everything happened in Ephesus. Why? Likewise, the way in which the AT is written makes Aquila and Priscilla disciples of Paul, as it also tries to make Apollos almost a direct disciple of Paul, who had recently passed through Ephesus (Acts 18:18 f.), had spoken in the synagogue, and left Aquila and Priscilla behind when he departed. It is not surprising then

76. One of the classical meanings of θεραπευτής (Plato, *Phaedrus*, 252c; *Laws*, 740b, etc., cf. LDJ) is "servant of a god"; the attribution of such a description presupposes "servants *par excellence*," that is, in a Jewish perspective, "observants" or "guardians" of the Law; despite a different (Greek) terminology, this is very close to "Nazoreans."

that Paul's close companions should make sure that Apollos, the brilliant beginner, knew his catechism. The reality, which can be obtained from the WT, is quite different: at Alexandria, as we shall see for Ephesus and Damascus, there were Jewish disciples of Jesus who owed nothing to the movement originating in Jerusalem, and in particular to the missions of Peter and Paul. There is no reason to suppose that these folk, certainly all Jews, had become disciples only after Jesus' death, or at any rate after Pentecost. In his own lifetime Jesus had sent out disciples to proclaim to the Jews a message similar to that of John the Baptist that the kingdom was close at hand (Matt 10:5 par.; Luke 10:1 f.).

Immediately after meeting Aquila, Apollos is seen to be a changed man, but the narrative has been much reworked in the AT:

(18:27)	*At Ephesus were residing some Corinthians. Having heard [Apollos],*
[Apollos] wishing	*they asked him*
to make the voyage	*to make the voyage with them*
to Achaia,	*to their country.*
the brethren, having approved,	*He gave his consent, and*
wrote to the disciples	*the Ephesians wrote to the disciples of Corinth that they might*
to welcome him.	*welcome him.*
He, once arrived	*He, having left for Achaia,*
was a great resource	*was a great resource*
to those believing by grace,	*in the "churches,"*

(28) *for he was refuting vigorously the Jews, in public,* (WT adds *debating*), *showing by the Scriptures that the Messiah is Jesus.*

The account in the AT is both flat and uselessly complicated: there were disciples at Corinth, as the reader of Acts has known since 18:8, then Apollos has the happy idea of going to Achaia (whose capital was Corinth),[77] where he is able to be of help in difficult public discussions. At the most one might wonder what was the exact point of the letter sent from Ephesus. The grace which surrounds Apollos makes one think of Stephen, who was also "filled with grace and power," and stood up to the Jews in debate (Acts 6:8-10). Nothing really new, then.

The WT is profoundly different. First, there were indeed disciples at Corinth, certainly Jews, and some of them were impressed by Apollos when they heard him at Ephesus. Apparently the novelty of his message consisted in showing that the Messiah is Jesus, with eloquence and texts

77. In fact, if not in law, cf. *Les Actes* V:309 f.

to make the point. But what sort of disciples were they? The business about the letter is indeed strange: the Corinthians who bring Apollos with them, need a guarantee from the Ephesians! Ephesus was, of course, a great center, with an ancient Jewish community enjoying long-established privileges,[78] whereas that at Corinth was more recent and may have been founded from Ephesus. But the real problem lies elsewhere: these Corinthians from Ephesus have grounds to fear that they will be disowned by the disciples at Corinth, that is by their own brethren. In other words, Apollos is a problem person, capable of provoking divisions at Corinth. That is to say, he has become a Messianist. The conclusion of the narrative then falls into place very easily: whether or not he really got as far as Corinth, he has shown himself to be a good advocate in the "churches" (understanding by this term, not as such communities of disciples, but Jewish assemblies holding contradictory debates, not necessarily in different places).

Once again, there is an obvious comparison with Stephen, but we can see more clearly why he provoked such violent reactions. In assemblies of this sort, opposition could come on two fronts: from Jews, whether or not they were disciples of Jesus, who did not accept Messianism or were afraid of it, as we shall see in connection with Paul, or from Messianists who did not accept the reference to Jesus. It is interesting to observe that the Corinthians who invited Apollos are not described as disciples, and that they disappear in the AT; likewise, the Ephesians who write the letter are not recognized as community leaders and become "brethren" in the AT. There is a hint of different parties among disciples of Jesus who owe nothing to Paul, and so it is understandable that the AT has shortened and watered down a narrative which gave evidence of divisions. Finally, we note that in all the discussions there is no mention of the resurrection or of missions to the Gentiles: there is no reason to think that they were among the additional points made by Aquila to Apollos.

There are later traces of divisions centering on Apollos: Paul denounced disagreements among Corinthians in 1 Cor 1:12, where some are for Paul, others for Apollos, others still for Cephas, and others again for "the Christ." Later on he says that he planted, Apollos watered, and God gave the increase, but adds that he himself is the real father (4:15). Finally, he states that he and Apollos serve as an example for the brethren

78. As attested by Philo and FJ, cf. *Les Actes* VI:10 f. Epigraphical and archaeological remains attesting a Jewish presence in Ephesus are however rare, but there was an extremely important Jewish presence in the countryside, descended from volunteers sent about 200 by Antiochus III in order to stabilize the frontier of Lydia and Phrygia by means of strong civilian colonization (2000 families, cf. *Ant.* 12 §148 f.).

not to take sides against one another and to learn the principle: "Nothing beyond what is written."[79] Paul does not say or imply that he and Apollos say the same thing, quite the contrary in fact; but, rather than underline the differences, which were surely real enough (cf. 1 Cor 16:12), he takes another point of view, which puts all preachers ("pedagogues") on the same level and makes all their quarrels futile, namely the reality of the cross of Christ. Thus the story of Apollos in the WT becomes perfectly intelligible. Even if Apollos limited himself to saying that the Messiah was Jesus, without speaking of the cross, even if there were a few Messianic agitations (some "for the Messiah"), even if Paul himself has changed, everything can be brought under the central affirmation (corresponding to "what is written") that Christ has been crucified "for you." This "spiritual" method of overcoming contradictions and conflicts,[80] which Paul uses here (and elsewhere), shows that he is no longer the same man who sought out Aquila, precisely at Corinth, a city with a tradition of agitation and division which lasted until the time of Clement of Rome! For the moment let us simply notice the fundamental change in Paul expressed by one text: he now speaks of Jesus Christ risen as Lord (1 Cor 1:2 f.).

What has happened? Just as Apollos' development could be traced by an itinerary from Ephesus to Corinth, that of Paul can be followed by going in the opposite direction.

2. Paul, from Corinth to Ephesus

The narrative of Paul's voyages between Corinth and Ephesus (Acts 18–19) is complex, as we have said, as it combines episodes from different periods.[81] We shall limit ourselves here to following Paul's relations with Aquila, and his interventions in Ephesus.

In fact, Paul parted from Aquila at Corinth, on the occasion of a crisis provoked by his preaching[82] (WT on the right):

79. This principle is sometimes regarded as incomprehensible, and many attempts have been made to amend it. It has, however, a classic rabbinical equivalent (Scripture does not depart from its literal sense, cf. *BSanh* 34a); here, it means that a commentary or development never annuls what is essential (Scriptural or not).

80. Wishing to judge not the words spoken, but the "power" (δύναμις), for the "kingdom of God is not in the word, but in the power." This is once again the power of the Spirit, who makes the Scriptures speak, cf. chap. I, §I.1, and VII, §IV.1.

81. Cf. *Les Actes* VI:32 f.

82. This passage immediately follows Aquila's arrival (v. 1-3), discussed above (§I.3). According to *Les Actes* III:230, vv. 4b-5a (Paul "persuades" Jews and Gentiles, then Silas and Timothy arrive from Macedonia, cf. 2 Cor 1:19) belong to a later redaction, which again would imply that here the AT (Acts III) is more primitive (closer to Acts I) than the

(4) *He was holding forth in the synagogue each Sabbath.*	*Entering the synagogue each Sabbath he was holding forth, introducing the name of the Lord Jesus.*
(4b) *He was persuading Jews and Greeks.*	*He was persuading not only Jews but also Greeks.*
(5b) *Paul devoted himself to the word, attesting to the Jews that the Christ is Jesus.*	
	(5b) *Many words being spoken and the Scriptures being interpreted,* certain *Jews*
(6) *These opposing and blaspheming, after tearing his garment, he said to them: "Your blood is on your own head; as for me, I am pure.*	*were opposing and blaspheming. Then Paul, after tearing his garment, said to them: "Your blood is on your own head; as for me, I am pure.*
From now on I will go *to the nations."*	Now I am going *to the nations."*
(7) *Then withdrawing from* there, *he went to one called Titius Justus, a Godfearer, whose house adjoined the synagogue.*	*Then withdrawing from* Aquila's, *he took refuge with Justus, a Godfearer. His house adjoined the synagogue.*

The AT gives a very simple account. After some interest has been shown by both Jews and Gentiles in his message, Paul devotes his efforts to the Jews. When they reject him totally, he pronounces something like a curse inspired by Ezek 33:2-9, and ends by announcing a future mission to the Gentiles, then takes himself off to a Gentile Godfearer. Such a declaration by Paul is not new in Acts: in 13:46, with Barnabas, he said the same thing at Antioch of Pisidia, but that did not prevent him from systematically visiting the synagogues wherever he went; by contrast, he had little success before the Areopagus at Athens. What is new here is that he goes to stay with a Godfearer, a point which recalls the episode of Peter and Cornelius. The theme which provoked the rejection was the *testimony* that "the Christ is Jesus." In the context of the AT it is difficult to

WT (Acts II); this is not *a priori* impossible, but would need to be established. Furthermore: 1. Paul is still a Messianist (cf. Aquila), and a total rejection by all the Jews is improbable; 2. after the episode at Antioch, in which Greeks were also involved, there is no difficulty in allowing that Greeks (whether or not Godfearers like Justus) also hear an explosive proclamation; 3. vv. 8-10, speaking of a great number of Corinthian converts (baptized), but also of the danger run by Paul, imply a background of Messianic agitation, duly transformed in parallel with the synthesis of Acts chap. 2 (cf. below §III.2). We would thus keep v. 4b in the primitive narrative (Acts I), and maintain the priority of the WT.

see in it a properly Messianic proclamation; it is rather a Pauline kerygma witnessing to the resurrection.

The WT presents a quite different image. The first and essential point is that Paul provokes a *division* among the Jews. Only two items of his message are given: there was discussion, copious and perhaps confused, about the Bible, and he "introduced the name of the Lord Jesus." This second feature, which does not contain the term "Christ," is suspect. For one thing, it strongly resembles the Gentile-Christian confession of faith (1 Cor 12:3). The *name* of Jesus looks ahead to Paul's intervention at Ephesus, after he has changed (cf. §3 below). Finally, the expression used is somewhat strange, and can only be understood properly in the perspective set out by the WT at the beginning of the passage: Paul, like Aquila, is a Messianist. This accounts for the mixture of excitement, biblical debates on the Messiah, and divisions; later, a glossator with good intentions[83] added a phrase showing that to talk of the "Messiah" Paul added "Jesus" and "Lord," that is Jesus as Lord, and not only as Messiah.

Finally, the fact that in the WT Paul declares "Now I am going," and leaves Aquila for the house of a Godfearer, looks very much like a movement of anger, accompanied perhaps by a significant transgression (entering a Gentile's house). In what follows, vv. 18-21 explain that Paul arrives in Ephesus with Aquila (and Priscilla) and leaves them there, but commentators have for a long time regarded these as redactional touches[84] which prepare for the meeting between Aquila and Apollos in this city: Aquila is under Paul's orders, and so Apollos will receive sound teaching. In reality, Paul has split up with Aquila, who never says that he will go to the Gentiles, and who certainly did not recommend Apollos to do so.[85] In the WT of v. 21, Paul leaves Ephesus expressing the hope of returning, but he absolutely has to go to Jerusalem to celebrate the coming feast;[86] it is interesting to note that he says nothing about meeting brethren there. The AT omits any allusion to Jerusalem or the feast, perhaps because the redactor is aware that it does not agree with the overall

83. The term employed in 18:4 WT for "introduce into the debate" (ἐντίθημι) does not occur elsewhere in the NT and seems to be a gloss later even than the AT.

84. Cf. *Les Actes* III:232 f. In 1 Cor 16:19 Paul mentions that Aquila and Priscilla are at Ephesus.

85. We do not have to go here into the complexities of Paul's visits to Corinth (cf. *Les Actes* V:311 f.): Paul's appearance before Gallio (Acts 18:12-17) is dated to 51, but the episodes discussed here, in which Aquila is the leading figure, have to be dated after 41 (expulsion from Rome).

86. Pentecost, according to Acts 20:16; but the route followed by Paul is very complex, according to Acts 18:22-23: Caesarea, church (probably Jerusalem), Antioch, Galatia, Phrygia, cf. below.

presentation of the mission to the Gentiles as having originated in Jerusalem.

Following back from the AT to the WT, we can make out a picture of Paul as a Messianizing activist. This scene is told after the episode at Antioch, which we have already examined, which itself follows the incident on the road to Damascus, which we have yet to see. That episode took place before 39 (cf. §III.1), while the meeting with Aquila occurred after 41. Our conclusion would be that Paul (and perhaps Aquila following him) already believed that the Messiah whose return was imminent was Jesus, but that this belief had not yet brought about any major change in him.

3. The Disciples at Ephesus

In fact we find Paul again shortly afterwards at Ephesus (we leave aside insignificant differences between WT and AT):

(19:1)	*Paul wishing of his own will to go to Jerusalem, the Spirit told him to return to Asia.*
It happened, while Apollos was at Corinth, that Paul,	
having gone through the highlands, went to Ephesus	*Having gone through the highlands, he comes to Ephesus*
and there found some disciples.	
(2) *He said to them:*	(2) *and says to the disciples:*

*"Did you receive the holy Spirit when you became believers?" But they: "But we have not heard that there is a (*AT adds *holy) Spirit."* (3) *Paul said to them: "In view of what have you been baptized?" The others said: "In view of John's baptism."* (4) *He said: "John baptized with a baptism of conversion, saying to the people 'in view of the one coming after him,' so that they might believe—that is in Jesus."* (5) *Having heard that, they were*

baptized in the name of the Lord *Jesus.*	*baptized in the name of Jesus*
	for the remission of sins.
(6) *And Paul having laid his hand*s *on them, the* holy *Spirit came on them.*	(6) *And Paul having laid his hand on them, the Spirit fell on them.*
And they were speaking in tongues,	*They were speaking in tongues,*
	and themselves interpreting them
and they were prophesying.	*and they were prophesying.*
(7) *All these men were* about *12.*	(7) *These men were 12.*

This passage has the reputation of being difficult, especially regarding the identity of the disciples.[87] But let us continue with the method employed up till now, of looking closely at the differences between AT and WT.

In the perspective of the AT, Apollos arrives in Corinth after Paul has left, which agrees with 1 Cor 3:6. At Ephesus, Paul finds *some* disciples who are totally unaware of the holy Spirit, and he brings them up to date. At best it is an untypical left-over from earlier tradition, dealing perhaps with some "disciples of John the Baptist." They can hardly be disciples of Jesus, since just before, Paul, Aquila and Priscilla have been through Ephesus and laid the foundations of a Christian community. The group is small, which brings out Luke's concern not only for large numbers but even for a dozen or so individuals. By baptism in the name of Jesus and the gift of the Spirit, they are brought into contact with Pentecost (cf. Acts 2:41), thanks to Paul. Thus, everything is in order, and the development of the Church is all of a piece.

Comparison with the WT brings out the fact that the passage has been reworked, and the interpretation just given breaks down. First, Paul has been turned aside from his plan to go to Jerusalem, with a remarkable contrast between what he himself wanted and the impulse of the Spirit making him turn back in his tracks.[88] Then, at Ephesus he speaks to *the* disciples, who number exactly twelve, and tells them about the Spirit. There is no connection with the following episode, in which for three months Paul goes to the synagogue at Ephesus. So we have here a little marginal group of disciples of Jesus, resembling Apollos, of a Jewish-Christian type, rather like James in fact. In this short narrative we get a new image of Paul. For the first time, he speaks of the Spirit; for the first time, he "knows all about Jesus"; for the first time, he addresses disciples

87. This passage (like the meeting between Aquila and Apollos) has intrigued commentators since ancient times, cf. the review by Werner Thiessen, *Christen in Ephesus. Die historische und theologische Situation in vorpaulinischer und paulinischer Zeit und zur Zeit der Apostelgeschichte und der Pastoralbriefe* (TANZ, 12), Tübingen, Francke Vlg, 1995, p. 61–70.

88. Taking 19:1 WT after 18:21 WT, in which Paul declares that he wants absolutely to go to Jerusalem, as both these passages are omitted by the AT. According to *Les Actes* III:259 f., 18:22a (departure from Ephesus) is followed by 21:26 (arrival in the Temple): for Acts I, Paul concludes his missionary journey with a visit to Jerusalem, where he is taken prisoner. The section 18:21 and 19:1 would in that case be the remains of another travel account, abruptly interrupted; 19:1 WT (with the arrival by way of the high country) goes with 16:6 f., in which Paul and his companions are turned aside *by the Spirit* from their (inland) route in Asia, and prevented from speaking; this narrative fragment could be ultimately attached to a return from Damascus (cf. Acts 9:17), which would give a better context to Paul's first arrival at Ephesus.

without Messianist language or disorderly scenes. These new features can only be connected with the Spirit who makes him turn back and indeed turns him round. It is not too much to speak of a (second) conversion: Paul's way of viewing Jesus has undergone a profound transformation.

We have described these twelve as "disciples[89] of Jesus." However, they had been baptized "in view of John's baptism," and Paul now tells them that John was proclaiming Jesus. At first sight, they seem to be rather disciples of John, but when we look more closely at the text, we see that Paul's question has to do with whether they received the Spirit when they became believers. Later (v. 4), he explains that John was proclaiming a baptism in view of the one who would come after him, so that they might believe. This successor would be the definitive Liberator, whatever the precise label attached to him, and to "believe" means to enter into baptism (or be admitted to it). Jesus as a baptist also preached that the kingdom was at hand. Thus, these disciples are in the same position as Apollos: within groups defined by John's baptism, Jesus is a Teacher, but not the definitive Liberator. In other words, there is no major difference at this stage between being a disciple of John or a disciple of Jesus (cf. John 3:23): Jesus' disciples are simply a sub-group of the same type, whatever the personal qualities of Jesus himself.[90] Similarly, baptism in the name of Jesus is "for the remission of sins," like that of John. What Paul has to say that is new, is that Jesus *is* this definitive figure; this identity can be perceived only through the Spirit (within the baptism of John). So, when these disciples say that they have not heard there was a Spirit, they are not talking about the divine Spirit in general, which would not make sense; rather, they have not received the power to recognize that Jesus is this definitive figure, that they *are* even now in his kingdom, for he lives. This is one of many ways of talking about the resurrection, different from the empty tomb ("the earth has yielded its fruit"), raising up or healing, as we shall see with Peter, but resembling the final scene in Matt: "I am with you until the end of time."

The rite that Paul proceeds to perform requires a few remarks. First, Paul himself does not confer the "second" baptism, but he lays on his hand,[91] and the effect of the Spirit is an unaccustomed language, at once glossolalia (lack of meaning) and prophecy (excess of meaning), which

89. According to the constant meaning in the NT of μαθηταί taken absolutely. The number twelve is certainly significant: it is legally a brotherhood (or at least the superior class, cf. chap. VII, §IV.3), and it also implies a possible debate about who are the real Twelve, as it is obviously a question of the same environment.

90. John could not know that it would be Jesus, cf. Matt 11:2 par. and chap. II, §I.2.

91. Or "hands (pl.)" according to the AT, cf. chap. VII, §IV,1.

shows that the Spirit is none other than that of the Prophets. There is no need to suppose that a redactor has put together two disjointed fragments: Paul's gesture puts a closure on a course leading to admission, which is precisely "baptism," reformulated in the name of Jesus. For this baptism is not an isolated rite conferred "in the name of Jesus," but "in view of the name"; to "be baptized" means therefore to "have been admitted into a baptismal course." This is exactly what we saw in connection with John's baptism (chap. II, §I.3), and in particular its relationship to Essene institutions. In this sense, the completion of baptism, with the Spirit, is the same as entry into the kingdom.

That is what was handed on by Paul once he had been turned round by the Spirit. As a Messianist, he was already focused on the kingdom (to come), *impulsore Christo*. That is exactly what he says in 2 Cor 5:16, when he implies that he had known the "Messiah according to the flesh"; he does not mean he knew the historical Jesus, but that he had been involved in socio-political Messianist agitation. The new feature which he has come to realize is that by the Spirit, the Messiah (kingdom) is already here, which involves a new way of looking at baptism. This new feature goes together with the one we have just seen when Paul declares that he is "going to the Gentiles." In this picture, Paul the ex-Messianist now addresses a tiny structured group connected with the baptism of John,[92] and does not seek a large audience or arouse dissensions. In what follows at Ephesus (Acts 19:8 f.), he will go from noisy meetings in the synagogue to long-term preaching before a little group of disciples. Thus, through a series of scenes which appear to be haphazard and isolated, but in fact are characteristic, we can see taking shape what will finally be the Pauline doctrine, deeply rooted as it is in the tradition of which Paul made so much. The AT constantly anticipates the end result, but the WT allows us to reconstruct the steps which led to it.

One link in the chain is still missing, and that is the first of all: the discovery that this Messiah is none other than Jesus. That is what happened to Paul at Damascus, as we are going to see (§III.1), but from what we have already seen, it does not seem that the details of the life of Jesus played an important part at any of the stages of Paul's evolution; that is so for the Pauline kerygma, and it remains so for the Creed. This is a

92. In Acts 9:17, Paul's reception of the Holy Spirit, foretold by Ananias, is expressed in the next sentence by his baptism, without specifying "in whose name" he was baptized. The entire narrative of Paul's conversion forms a frontispiece which anticipates the whole of his mission, but if he was able to enter the circle of the twelve disciples at Ephesus, it was because he was qualified by baptism, that is by John's baptism duly transformed.

major difference between Paul and those who know "the things concerning Jesus," Apollos as well as the twelve at Ephesus.

This brief visit to Asia Minor and Achaia has included episodes which are essential for the development of Christianity. Earlier, we looked at other scenes in other places, from Rome to Antioch, from Galilee to Athens, from Caesarea to Alexandria, passing through Jerusalem for the apostolic assembly. It is to Jerusalem that we must now turn. We have left until last a study of the inaugural events at Jerusalem, as we had good reason to regard them as a sort of frontispiece to Acts, bringing together in a single picture all the later developments, or more exactly a selection of later developments made in accordance with a very precise point of view.

III – Jerusalem and the Communities

And did everything really start in Jerusalem?

This question admits of several different answers. First there is the simple aspect of geography. The ending of Luke and beginning of Acts are centered on Jerusalem, but Matt, Mark and John end on a Galilean note, and Acts 9:31 WT mentions that the churches of Judaea, Galilee and Samaria[93] are living in peace and growing. There is also the curious fact of two Pentecosts: in Acts 4:31, when the apostles are at prayer, the house rocks, and they are filled with the Spirit and speak the word of God with confidence. Finally, the size of the inaugural community or communities seems to be variable: what are we to make of the three thousand baptized on the same Pentecost Sunday who afterwards disappear without trace?

1. Judaea, Galilee, Damascus, Tarsus

Luke-Acts taken together describes a single journey in two stages: from Galilee to Jerusalem, and from Jerusalem to Rome, with a few detours on the way. There is no return to Galilee, even understood as a metaphor for the nations. The same is true of the long ending of Mark (16:9-20),[94] and the first conclusion of John (20:21 f.), where the disciples are sent out on mission from Jerusalem. However, even Luke makes an allusion to Galilee. In 24:44, the risen Jesus says to his disciples: "These

93. In this order. This verse is a summary, in Pauline style, to be attributed to Acts II according to *Les Actes* III:189. The three regions indicated correspond, if we extend them a little, to the preceding narratives, which are situated in Jerusalem, Samaria and Damascus (regarded as belonging to Galilee in a very broad sense, cf. below).

94. But this evidence is not independent, as the passage combines elements derived from Luke and John, cf. M.-Émile Boismard, *L'évangile de Marc. Sa préhistoire* (EB, N. S. 26), Paris, Gabalda, 1994, p. 237 f.

are the words I spoke to you while I was still with you"; in 24:6, the angels tell the women and, through them, the disciples: "Remember how he spoke to you when he was still in Galilee." The content of the words is the same, as if the angels are referring to words spoken by the Risen One in Galilee.

So there was a return to Galilee. In fact, the disciples had no firm or stable connection with Judaea; not only did they come only rarely to Jerusalem (and were not well acquainted with the Temple, cf. Matt 21:1 par.), but they were even afraid to go there (cf. John 11:16). Jesus was more familiar with the places, but apparently only came as a pilgrim, which certainly does not exclude important activities around the sanctuary.

To fill out a little this Galilean base, we need to take into account not only both sides of the Lake (cf. chap. III, §III), but also the "road to Damascus," which runs close by. In Gal 1:12 f., Paul tells how he, the persecutor, had a direct revelation of Jesus Christ, then left for Arabia, and came back to Damascus. In 2 Cor 11:32, he recalls that at Damascus the ethnarch of king Aretas was guarding the city in order to arrest him. So there is a connection between persecution, revelation and Damascus, which he fled before 39, the year of Aretas IV's death. Further, he says that he did not go up to Jerusalem until three years after his return to Damascus (Gal 1:18), and only then made the acquaintance of Cephas and James; he adds that no one in Judaea knew him, but that a rumor went before him. For all that, he was very active and very visible, and if his activity was judged dangerous by the civil (non-Jewish) authorities of Damascus, it must have been because it stirred up trouble in society.

In order to work out what may have taken place, we need to consult all three narratives of Paul's conversion in Acts, which can provide details that are complementary. First, it is widely recognized that the insertion of Paul into the account of the stoning of Stephen is artificial. Then, the account of his conversion explains that there were "followers of the way" at Damascus (Acts 9:2; 22:4) and that he had obtained a commission from the high priest to arrest them and bring them to Jerusalem. These items locate Paul's activities solidly in Jerusalem,[95] but they run up against two major difficulties. First, they formally contradict Paul's own statement that he was not personally known to the disciples in Jerusalem

95. In the second account of his conversion, Paul tells of a vision in the Temple at Jerusalem, where he receives a mission to go to the nations (22:17-21). This event has a very clear symbolic meaning (similar to the mission of Heliodorus, the former persecutor, cf. 2 Macc 3:34), but is difficult to place historically, all the more as in the first account, it is Ananias at Damascus who shows Paul his mission. There may be in the background a play on words between מקדש (temple) and דמשק (Damascus), cf. similarly chap. VII, §III.2.

until three years later.[96] Secondly, according to the general plan of Acts, there was as yet no mission further afield than Samaria; indeed, according to the restored P Doc, the mission outside Jerusalem had not even begun. We are surprised, then, to learn of these disciples at Damascus, and find it hard to account for Paul's obvious interest in this city.

Acts has, however, preserved some traces of the items provided by Gal. According to Acts 9:26 f., Paul did indeed come to Jerusalem after leaving Damascus, but everyone was afraid of him. Even more interesting, it was Barnabas who introduced him to the apostles, as if he already knew him. But that is a later redactional development,[97] occasioned by the needs of the narrative: at Antioch, Barnabas hears that Saul is at Tarsus (cf. §II.3), so we are led to suppose that he knew him well and had been sent to find him. But, as we have seen from Acts 11:23 WT, it is clear that Barnabas, who may or may not have known Saul already, *learns* that he is in Tarsus and goes in search of him. Rumors circulate, and Barnabas is the one who puts Paul in touch with the mission originating in Jerusalem. In this way, Paul's activity in Damascus appears less eccentric: Antioch is midway between Damascus and Tarsus, and he himself writes of time spent in Syria and Cilicia, which fits in very well (Gal 1:21).

At Damascus, Paul met disciples and was baptized (Acts 9:18).[98] These were certainly Jewish-Christians, whether or not directly disciples of Jesus, but not Messianists. Later at Ephesus Paul will meet a similar

96. Cf. *Les Actes* V:10 f. Theodor Mommsen, "Die Rechtsverhältnisse des Apostels Paulus," in: *Gesammelte Schriften*, Berlin-Dublin-Zürich, 1962, jurist. Abt. III:431-446, was the first to throw doubt, on the basis of Gal, on the reality of Paul's persecutions at Jerusalem; others have followed, cf. Arland J. Hultgren, "Paul's Pre-Christian Persecutions of the Church: Their Purpose, Locale and Nature," *JBL* 95 (1976), p. 97–111.

97. According to *Les Actes* III:135, the entire passage 9:24-29 contains Pauline expressions, designed to harmonize with Gal, and is to be attributed to Acts II. Consequently, a brief form of v. 30, explaining Paul's departure for Tarsus (without passing through Caesarea), originally followed immediately after the episode at Damascus, when the brethren save Paul from a plot, but also get him off their hands.

98. According to the literary criticism proposed in *Les Actes* III:132 f., vv. 10-19a are judged to be later, except for v. 12 (Paul's vision; absent from the WT), which is held to be primitive, then omitted by WT and restored by AT. All the same; 1. in general, the argument of a v. lost (by WT or earlier) then found again (by AT) should not be used without a very good reason (it is invoked without real necessity in connection with Acts 15:21, cf. chap. V, §II.1); 2. this v. 12 reminds one of the parallel visions of Peter and Cornelius, which do not belong to the primitive redaction; 3. the primitive account needs a transition between 9:8-9 (Paul blind for three days) and 9:20 (immediately preaching in the synagogues), that is some entity which concerns itself with Paul and gets him started; vv. 18b (sight recovered, baptized) and 19b (several days with the disciples) provide the useful link, which can even be improved by reversing the order, which goes better with preaching "without further ado."

group of Jesus' disciples who know only John's baptism (cf. above §II.3). In any case, his new message in the synagogues is characteristic (9:20a-22c): "He was proclaiming Jesus, that he is the Christ." He had already been a Messianizing zealot, associated by one tradition with Gischala (not far from Damascus, cf. above §I.3). The fundamentally new feature is his identification of the Messiah as Jesus, giving rise to disturbances and anxieties, among both Jews (Acts) and Gentiles (2 Cor). The disciples who sent him to Tarsus no doubt saved his life, but they were also removing someone who was dangerous for the community. In Acts 9:26 there is a trace, even if reworked, of the fear which Paul inspired in the disciples. By the same token, that indicates that the disciples at Damascus formed a little group who were not in conflict with their Jewish neighbors. This peace is emphasized in Acts 9:31, that is just after both Stephen and Paul have disappeared, and Simon Magus has been neutralized—all of them linked with disorders. In conclusion, we can see the sort of problem which someone like Barnabas had at Antioch, and the risk he took in going to find someone like Paul. From much earlier in his career Paul could have been called a *christianus* by the Romans, and if he had turned up at that stage in Jerusalem, he would certainly have aroused the greatest mistrust in the authorities, beginning with the high priest himself. Finally, there is no reason to think that at Damascus Paul would have shown any interest in Gentiles as such. Quite the contrary.

Like John the Baptist, Jesus did not preach political violence or insubordination. Certainly an appreciable number of their disciples stayed far away from Jerusalem and its crises, before and after their deaths. The literary construction of Luke-Acts does not really hide the fact that Peter and the rest began by returning to Galilee, which was not originally a metaphor for "the nations." Even so, they went on to undertake major activity from Jerusalem. In order to identify it, we now need to look at some important episodes.

2. Pentecosts, the Spirit

The parallel between Pentecost and the episode described in Acts 4:31 has long been noticed. It extends even to the wider context, as shown by the following table, to which we have added the reconstruction[99] of the P Doc, which does not duplicate the scene:

99. According to *Les Actes* II:31-48.

Stages	First cycle	Second cycle	P Doc
(Ascension)	(Acts 1:1-11)		(Luke 24:50-52)
Prayer	1:12-14	4:24-30	(Luke 24:53)
New members	1:15-26 (Matthias)		
Spirit	2:1-13 (Pentecost)	4:31	
Confident proclamation	2:14-36	(4:31)	
New members	2:37-41 (and 47)		
The community	2:42-47	4:32-33	2:44
Sharing of goods	2:45	4:34–5, 11	2:45
Healings	(2:43) and 3:1-26	5:12-16	3:1-16
New members	4:4	5:14	
Arrest	4:1-3	5:17-26	4:1-2
Trial	4:5-20	5:27-39	4:7b, 8, 10-17, 21
Punishment and release	4:21	5:40-42	
(Gift of the Spirit)			(4:23, 24, 27-31, 33)
(No growth)			(5:12b-13)

Behind the similar structures are important differences. With regard to the admission of new members, the first cycle is generous: three thousand on Pentecost Sunday (2:41), again five thousand on a later occasion (4:4). By contrast, the second cycle is more sparing: admission of Barnabas (4:36 f.), brutal exclusion of Ananias and Sapphira, after which no one dares to join the apostles (5:13); this restrictive attitude is tempered by a strange and apparently unnecessary item which we shall look at later (5:14): "More and more numerous *multitudes* of men and women were joining."

The divergence on numbers between the two cycles is all the more striking because in the P Doc there is no trace of any growth in the community. This source tells a story of something on a very small scale. After a brief notice on the community, there is only the account of the paralyzed man raised up at the Beautiful Gate of the Temple by Peter and John in the "name of Jesus the Nazorean," followed by an angry scene, on the spot, featuring Sadducees and other local leaders who do not accept the resurrection of the dead and try in vain to intimidate the apostles. The gift of the Spirit follows next, as a confirmation of the power of God. The leading theme throughout is the resurrection of Jesus, proclaimed by the apostles and illustrated by the restoration of the sick man, which silences the objection of the Sadducees. The vocabulary is unambiguous: in 3:7a, Peter "raises up" the sick man,[100] just as in 3:15 and 4:10 he

100. According to *Les Actes* III:72, the whole of vv. 6-7 is the only case in the entire NT where the word of a wonder worker is not effective by itself and needs to be completed by a gesture. That is so, but insufficient to prove that v. 7a was not in the primitive account

declares that God has "raised up" Jesus from the dead. The healing is a sign expressing the reality of what is being proclaimed, which is given further confirmation by the Spirit. This combination of a miracle and a speech resembles the scene of the night at Troas, where the fall and restoration of Eutychus is an illustration of what is being celebrated by the breaking of the bread (cf. chap. I, §II.2). We note in passing that at this point in the P Doc, Jesus is indeed a Nazorean, but Peter does not declare that he is the Messiah. This is in striking contrast with the activity of Paul at Damascus and the anxieties which he arouses there. The P Doc situates the event in the forecourt of the Temple, but there is at the most a minor commotion and no arrest takes place. It is not impossible that the P Doc has transferred to Jerusalem an episode which took place elsewhere. The fact that people recognize the apostles as companions of Jesus (4:13) could suggest a scene in Galilee, but, on the other hand, there is no evidence for the presence of Sadducees there.

In the first cycle of the text as we now have it, the most obvious effect of the invasion of the Spirit is an immediate increase in the number of disciples, combined with a serious aggravation of pressure on the apostles, who are really arrested this time and appear the next day before the supreme Jewish authorities (4:3-6). This development bears all the marks of a tumult, that is to say, a Messianic agitation likely to worry the authorities. In fact, at the end of his speech to the crowd (which is not in the P Doc) Peter proclaims that "God has made Lord and Christ (Messiah), this Jesus whom you had crucified" (2:36). All the same, the turbulence is more apparent than real, since the crowd stays surprisingly quiet. Peter's listeners ask: "What are we to do?" The question could appear very dangerous, as it is just the sort of thing that authorities responsible for law and order fear from an excited crowd. But the reply, which

(P Doc): 1. the marked parallel in vocabulary between the raising up of the sick man and that of Jesus (ἤγειρεν) would then be destroyed; 2. Peter has to pronounce the name of Jesus and perform a gesture, because the action of raising up is transitive (physical, rather than persuasive), and if there were only the word, the result would be that the sick man would raise *himself*, which would once again destroy the parallel with Jesus, who did not raise himself but was raised up (he was really dead); 3. the parallel invoked with Mark 9:27, in which Jesus raises up (ἤγειρεν) a possessed boy without speaking, is not really to the point, as Jesus has already threatened the unclean spirit; in other words, the healing was performed in two stages, a word followed by a gesture. The resurrection to which the Sadducees are opposed is expressed by another term, of more general import (ἀνάστασις ἐκ νεκρῶν), alluding to the last judgment, but with no connection with the idea of immediate healing; in this sense, the discussion is somewhat artificial, or rather Peter's speech is not yet integrated into a general doctrine of resurrection, unlike the discussion with Paul in Acts 23:6 f., in which everyone speaks of ἀνάστασις.

is worthy of John the Baptist, is carefully non-political: "Be converted, and let each one be baptized."

To understand more precisely how this crowd effect has been produced, we have to look at the narrative of Pentecost. It does not belong to the P Doc, but to later redactions, where it has been much reworked, as we can see from the differences between WT and AT.[101] We give first the reconstruction of the first state of this narrative (Acts I, or its source):

Acts I[102] primitive form	Later addition (Acts II), in WT
(2:1) *And it happened, when the days of Pentecost were being fulfilled, they being in the same place* (2a) *and behold from heaven an echo like a violent gust of wind.*	
	(3) *And there appeared to them as it were a fire which rested on each one of them,* (4) *and they began to speak in tongues as the Spirit was giving them to express themselves.*
(6a) *The "great number" assembled,*	(6a) *This sound having occurred, the "great number" assembled, etc.*

(11b) *and (the people) heard them speaking in tongues the greatness of God.*

(12) *They were amazed at what had occurred, saying: "What does this mean?"*

(13) *Others mocked saying: "They are full of new wine."*

There are two things to point out in this basic narrative framework (Acts I). First, there is no mention of the Spirit, nor of Jesus, nor of resurrection or healings; so it is not really a doublet of Acts 4:31, but a quite distinct episode. Then, this episode, though recounted only briefly, is dated in a curious way: instead of simply saying "on Pentecost day," there

101. The whole setting, with pilgrims from everywhere (v. 5, 6b-11a), belongs to a later redaction; the redactional reprise ἤκουν . . . λαλοῦντων αὐτῶν . . . γλώσσαις of vv. 6b and 11b is very clear in the WT, but weakened in the AT (v. 11b ἀκούομεν . . . ταῖς ἡμετέραις γλώσσαις). In the whole of this passage, the redactional activity between WT (short) and AT (clearly longer) is intense, and we may suspect that the present WT (deriving from Acts II) has already been much reworked; in that case, not all is of redactional origin, but there is the trace of another source, modified in view of very different redactional outlooks.

102. The analysis developed in *Les Actes* III:46 f. retains in the primitive account (cf. *Les Actes* II:98) vv. 3-4 and the beginning of v. 6. In that case, the meaning is that they began to speak in tongues.

is a long circumlocution involving an idea of "fulfilment," which needs to be looked at more carefully.[103] Comparable expressions are: Luke 8:23, where the same verb indicates that the boat is in danger of being overfilled, but is not yet full; Luke 9:51, where the same expression is used for the fulfilment of the days in which Jesus is to be taken up, but it is not yet there. In this place, then, it is a question of a day close to Pentecost, and not the feast itself.[104] Furthermore, the exact expression used shows that Pentecost is not a single day, but a fulfilment; its name signifies the "fiftieth" day, which is generally regarded as the closure of Passover.[105]

A further significant detail is that the disciples are suspected of being full of new wine. In that case, the episode cannot take place in May or June, when the ordinary Pentecost falls, but after the first vintage, in August. Peter's reply (2:15 "It is only the third hour of the day") presupposes that they will in fact be drinking new wine later in the day, so the suspicion is not totally groundless. A simple solution is provided by the calendar of Jubilees, which turns up at various points in the NT:[106] there the Passover of 14 Nisan is followed by a series of fiftieth days ("pentecosts"), falling around the times when the harvests of wheat, the vine, and the olive begin, and corresponding to the first fruits of bread, wine and oil. So, the new wine is available after the first fruits of the second pentecost, and the "fulfilment of the days of Pentecost" refers to a moment during the *third* fifty-day period, before the first fruits of oil; in that case the term "Pentecost" stands for the three major cycles taken together.[107]

All this shows that originally, the event in question was on a small scale and took place one day in late summer, at Jerusalem or elsewhere, and was witnessed by a few onlookers. Two final remarks are in order. First, in the development of the narrative (WT, representing Acts II), the coming of the Spirit is linked not to the glossolalia (which follows on the violent wind), but to the intelligible speech, which each of the numerous visitors hears in his or her own language. But before the intelligible speech there is an upheaval. The term employed is the same as in Acts

103. Like those prompted by the "day after the preparation" in Mat 27:62, cf. chap. II, §II.4.

104. The AT, which smooths over the rough points throughout this passage, has the singular: "When the day of Pentecost was being fulfilled." Although the expression is heavy, the date is precise.

105. In Num 28:26, it is the feast of Weeks (שָׁבֻעוֹת); in *Ant.* 3 §252 FJ gives it the name of ἀσαρθά transcribing an Aramaic form of עצרת "closure," current in the rab. trad. (*MḤag* 2:4, etc.).

106. And described in chap. I, §I.2b.

107. The primitive narrative may have had a plur. τῶν πεντηκοστῶν "the day*s* of the pentecost*s*," changed to the sing. by the WT (as the AT has the sing. τὴν ἡμέραν "the day" instead of the WT's plur.).

11:26 (WT) for Messianic agitation leading to the name of "Christians," where the Spirit comes on the scene only later (cf. §I.3). The comparison is not accidental, since in later redactions everything is placed unambiguously under the common Pentecost (the first, fifty days after Easter), with pilgrims from all over the world, which could be the occasion of disturbances. There is a distant echo of the primitive scene with the Twelve at Ephesus, but without any crowd. The upheaval is on a small scale, and the expression of the Spirit is not only glossolalia (interpreted), but especially intelligible discourse (prophecy). There may be some influence of 1 Cor 14:1 f. Paul himself, through his conversion, has passed from violence to the Spirit.

Secondly, the introduction of the Spirit is accompanied by the presentation of the scene as a large scale demonstration which is peaceful but could be viewed as Messianic by the authorities. Through Peter's speech, the upheaval is transmitted to the listeners, who ask what they are to do: by baptism they become *christiani*, but in a new sense, "in the name of Jesus." The second half of the speech gives the clue (2:29-36): Jesus is not the Messiah who will shortly return (occasioning Messianic disturbances), but the Messiah is Jesus son of David risen from the dead; he has *already* returned, he is exalted, and he has bestowed his Spirit (occasioning communion, abolition of barriers). In other words, the Spirit and that which the Spirit brings about (conversion) are the expression of the definitive coming of the kingdom *here and now*, signified by a new language, which creates communion and blots out the distinction between Jews and Gentiles. Through the resurrection, Messianism is still a renewal of history, but it has undergone a profound transformation: its violence has been turned into speech. This is very close to the position of Paul with the twelve at Ephesus, ending also in a new language.

Whether or not they were numerous, the baptisms on Pentecost Sunday indicate a further dimension of this feast which will have to be examined, namely entry into the Covenant (chap. VII, §III). For now, let us take note only of the expression *plêthos* "the great number," which suggests the idea of a crowd in the final redaction, but originally designated the community of disciples. This is an odd expression, because its undefined quantitative element seems never to be the main characteristic of the community. So let us look at the elements which make up the community.

3. The Community, a Complex Entity

The summary of Acts 4:32 f. emphasizes the unanimity of the "great number" of those who have become believers and who place everything in common.[108] This text immediately follows the "little Pentecost" (v. 31) referred to above, which in the P Doc closes a narrative concerning Peter and centered on the resurrection. Let us now look at it (WT on the right):

> (4:31) *And while they were praying, the place where they had gathered was shaken, and they were filled*

all with the holy Spirit,	*with the Spirit,*

> *and they were speaking the word of God with assurance*

	to whoever was desiring to believe.

> (32) *The "great number" of those who had become believers was one soul and one heart,*

	and there was no separation[109] *among them,*
and no one said that any of his goods was his own, but all to them was common.	*and one did not say that any of his goods was his own, but all was common.*

> *(33) And with great power the apostles were giving testimony*

to the Lord Jesus, *and great grace was on all.*	*to the resurrection of Jesus,* *and great grace was on them.*

> *(34) Indeed, there was no one needy among them, etc.*

The first point to make is that the WT has two long readings, an anomaly which raises the question whether they have been omitted from the AT in order to gloss over a reworking of the text. In fact this series of

108. According to *Les Actes* II:44, the gift of the Spirit in Acts 4:31 ("little Pentecost") was followed in the P Doc by testimony to the resurrection (v. 33a). The section 4:34–5:11, on the sharing of goods, followed by the episodes of Barnabas and of Ananias and Sapphira, is a later insertion, and should be attached to the summary of 4:32: "the 'great number' of those who had become believers (πιστευσάντων) was one soul and one heart, . . . and everything was common." This passage owes nothing to the Spirit nor to the resurrection: on the contrary, there is the approval of Barnabas' good deed and the judgment passed on Ananias and Sapphira. One might think that the whole section should be attached to the ending of v. 31 WT: "(they were speaking with assurance) to whoever was wanting to believe (πιστεύειν)"; however, the link word "believe" strikes a discordant note (which may explain why the said ending has disappeared from the AT), as in v. 31 it is a question of believing the word spoken with assurance (without any particular action), whereas in v. 32 the aorist indicates a definite act of entry into the community. In short, this passage can be regarded as a glimpse of the community before the coming of the Spirit; it is a πλῆθος. This term has also acted as a link word facilitating a junction with v. 16, cf. what follows.

109. The word χωρισμός "separation, division," not attested elsewhere in the NT, denotes above all a departure, physical or moral (cf. χωρίζω). Certain witnesses (WT^2) give or presuppose διάκρισις *(accusatio, discrimen)*, attested only in Rom 14:1, 1 Cor 12:10 and Heb 5:14, with an idea of criticism or discernment.

reports on the effects of the Spirit is composite and mixes together two themes,[110] the proclamation of the word of God, which is associated with *believers*, and the power of testimony to the resurrection. Only the second theme belongs to the narrative of the P Doc in which Peter raises up the paralytic; it already looks ahead to the many healings and other signs and wonders recounted later, in which Peter once again plays a central role (5:15). The first theme has hardly anything to do with the previous narrative centered on resurrection and healing, but it introduces the "great number" of believers, that is the series of narratives which describe the life of the community. The summary which closes this series (5:12-16) also has a complex history (cf. below), but it still combines both themes of admission of new believers and healings. A strong link between the two themes is provided by Peter himself, who is the healer and at the same time controls entry into the community (5:1-10).

If we now separate these two themes which have been knitted together in this way, we come to the conclusion that the P Doc did not contain the development about the community (v. 32 and 34 f.).[111] Furthermore, the end of v. 31 ("They were speaking with assurance [. . .]") has been added (WT) in order to introduce this development,[112] but too hastily. In the expression "those who were desiring to believe," which is continued by "those who had become believers," the verb "believe" has the sense of "belonging to the group," through an entry procedure; it has the same meaning when Paul questions the Twelve at Ephesus. By omitting this expression, the AT brings out a more Pauline idea of faith, as response to the proclamation of the word; thus it has the appearance of a new theme, namely the growth of the community.

In that case, the "great number" is in the first instance the well-defined group of those who have entered the community. Now we can understand the other long reading of the WT, which expressly says that there were no departures ("no separation"). Two reasons may have led the redactor of the AT to leave it out. First, the following episode of Ananias and Sapphira shows a mechanism of exclusion (5:1-10), and there are traces of conflict further on (15:39). But also, and more importantly, if the expression "great number" can take on the meaning of "crowd," with the

110. Already combined in the preceding prayer: 4:29 (to speak the word with assurance) and 30 (to grant numerous healings).

111. Thus *Les Actes* III:59 f.

112. Attributed to Acts II; a literary confirmation comes from the expression μετά παρρησίας ("with assurance"), which does not occur in the other books of the NT, but features four times in Acts (WT+AT: 2:29; 4:29, 31; 28:31) and three other times in the WT alone (6:10; 9:20; 16:4), where the AT has short readings. It appears to be characteristic of Acts II.

idea of indefinite growth, the boundaries of the group have to be left fairly fluid, which goes better with many converts than with a small restricted group. In that case, there would be a reason for omitting any mention of departures, which has the effect of tightening the boundaries.

The result is that the notice on the life of the community, even if it is based on the summary of Acts 2:44-45,[113] is entirely independent of the manifestation of the Spirit and Pentecost. This was already the case in the P Doc. So we are dealing here with descriptions of the community of disciples and its structures which are independent of Jesus, above all independent of events connected with the resurrection. Thus we can understand the nature of the two episodes that follow: Joseph, called Barnabas by the apostles, is worthy of consideration because he brought them the price of his field, then Ananias and Sapphira are severely condemned for their fraud and punished by God. This way of handing out rewards and punishments is not all that typical of the NT, and there is no mention of Jesus or of his resurrection. What we have here is a window opened on a group at some time after Jesus has left the scene. Furthermore, there is no reason why the scene has to be Jerusalem. On the contrary, talk of sales of fields may indicate rather a rural setting.

The sharing of goods is certainly essential for the community, but before going into it, we need to return to the summary we have just looked at, to ask why the two different themes found there—the life of the community, and powerful testimony to the resurrection—have been fused. To arrive at an answer, let us examine the summary that closes the affair of Ananias and Sapphira:

> (5:11) *And there was great fear on all the "assembly"*[114] *and on all those who learned of these things.* (12a) *By the hands of the apostles there were (*AT adds: *numerous) signs and wonders in the people.* (12b) *And they were (*AT adds: *all) of one mind in the portico of Solomon.* (13) *And no one (*AT adds: *of the others) dared to adhere to them, but the people praised them.* (14) *And more believers were being added to the Lord, "great numbers" of men and women.* (15a) *To the point that the sick were brought out into the streets, and placed on beds and stretchers,* (15b) *so that at least the shadow of Peter passing by might fall on one of them*

113. Cf. *Les Actes* III:59 f.

114. There is no reason to translate ἐκκλησία here by "church"; it is not a question of the community itself, but of spectators supposed to have been attracted by the event or the word (like the onlookers of Acts 2:6b, 11b, cf. above), then by rumors which spread. In fact, the community is protected by a solid and impenetrable boundary, which no one dares to cross (v. 13 "adhere to them," κολλᾶσθαι, cf. Gen 2:24).

and that they might be cured of their sickness.

(16a) *The "great number" of the towns round about flocked to Jerusalem, carrying sick people and those possessed by unclean spirits.* (16b) *And all were cured.*

This passage does not flow easily, but it includes the two themes we have picked out. The community is of one mind (v. 12b) and is both admired (v. 13) and feared (v. 11). Furthermore, it is installed quietly in the portico of Solomon, which is odd for a permanent group, but very significant when we recall that this same area of the Temple precinct is mentioned in the aftermath of the scene in which Peter and John raise up the paralyzed man (Acts 3:11). Thus the two quite different themes are firmly linked in v. 12: the united community is indeed that of Peter the healer, but no one dares to join them.

In what follows, the theme of healing is strongly emphasized (15a), linked to Peter (15b) and redoubled (16). This duplication, particularly marked in the WT which mentions healing twice, is watered down in the AT, which eliminates the first mention. In reality the duplication originated as a redactional resumption: v. 16b has been added in order to anchor the insertion of v. 16a, which combines the "great number," the many cures, and the importance of Jerusalem. This reworking allows the introduction of the associated theme of the growth of the community, which returns in force in v. 14 in a twofold form: individuals and "great numbers" of men and women. In itself that has nothing to do with the cures, but the connection is made in v. 15a.[115] The result of this analysis can be expressed in three columns (following the WT):

Community of one mind	Signs and wonders	Growth
(5:11) *And there was great fear on all the "assembly" and on all those who learned of these things.*		

115. In *Les Actes* III:61 f., the analysis leads to the identification of a summary of the P Doc (12b-13), encased in another summary of Acts I (12a.15a.16b), both fused together by Acts II, who has added vv. 14, 15b, 16a. We follow this analysis, but with two modifications: 1. the transposition of the "healings" (15b and 16b), based on the fact that 16a is redactional, to bring about a synthesis; 2. more importantly for the content, the possibility that "great number" can change its meaning allows us to see that the summary of the P Doc already synthesizes the unanimous community ("great number") and the healings in the portico of Solomon.

Community of one mind	Signs and wonders	Growth—Cont'd
	(12a) *By the hands of the apostles there were signs and wonders in the people.*	
(12b) *And they were of one mind in the portico of Solomon.* (13) *And no one dared to adhere to them, but the people praised them.*		
		(14) *And more believers were being added to the Lord, "great numbers" of men and women.*
	(15) *To the point that the sick were brought out into the streets, and placed on beds and stretchers, so that at least the shadow of Peter passing by might fall on them, and that they might be cured of their sickness.*	
		(16) *The "great number" of the towns round about flocked to Jerusalem, carrying sick people and those possessed by unclean spirits. And all were cured.*

The conclusion which has to be drawn is that the summary of Acts 5:12-16, which develops that of 4:32, is a real work of art combining *three* themes: 1. healings, in relation to the resurrection; 2. the growth of the community; 3. the life, or "culture" of the community ("great number"), with unanimity and sharing of goods. By including the developments which occur between these two summaries, we can see that the Spirit features in three positions: the power of the name of Jesus (miracles, exorcisms), the power of the word (growth), and the discernment of the unworthy (restriction of the community). The fact to be noted is, however, that these three themes were sufficiently different from one another to require an elaborate literary exercise in order to combine them. At the same time, we observe that there is no direct link between healing and the growth of the community. This was so also in the life of Jesus, who did not recruit those he had healed into the group, and even refused to admit them (Mark 5:18 f.; Luke 8:38 f.).

To come back for a moment to the great inaugural scene of Pentecost, as we have it in the final redactions, we see that the dominant themes are the Spirit, the word (with Peter) and the massive increase of the community; we do not find either the "great number" or healings, which are, however, the domains where Peter is competent. However, the phenomenon is presented as gravely worrying to the authorities. There is obviously a Messianic dimension, and the shadows of Paul and Stephen are not far away.

4. The "Great Number," the Many

What is the meaning of this "great number" *(plêthos)*, which is both well defined even before Pentecost and at the same time able to turn into a crowd for later redactors? What we have already seen on baptism and the eucharist (chap. II) encourages us to look among the Essenes.[116] In the

116. The summary Acts 4:32, 34-35 picks up and develops that of Acts 2:44-45 ("And all those who were believing were in the same place and [AT: 'were believing in the same thing'] had everything in common. And all those who had goods or possessions, sold them and distributed them to those who were in need"), as shown in *Les Actes* II:160. The conclusion drawn there is that the first summary dealt with a distribution to all the poor, which was later restricted to the community, even large. However: 1. the first summary is not sufficiently explicit to be able to affirm that it is opposed to the second on this point (especially in the WT, it speaks of a limited group living together); 2. above all, the second summary describes the original environment, before Pentecost. Furthermore, the description of the Essenes by Philo, *Quod omnis probus liber sit* §85–86 is very enlightening: the house of each one is open to all, they live in communities, they have a common fund and put into it all their income, etc. Even before the discoveries at Qumran, Lucien Cerfaux, "La première communauté chrétienne à Jérusalem," *ETL* 16 (1939), p. 5–31, had shown, and others after him, that these summaries fit the model way of life prescribed by Plato for those responsible for the defense of the city: Plato, *Repub.* 3.406d says that they will possess nothing of their own and will keep nothing private and inaccessible to others, and they will be united by the same sentiments. This model, derived from the Pythagoreans, was taken up later by the Neoplatonists until the 4th cent. at least, cf. W. Tyloch, "Les thiases et la communauté de Qoumrân," in: *Fourth World Congress of Jewish Studies*, Jerusalem, 1967, I:225-228. There is an undoubted similarity, but even more with the Essenes, who regarded themselves as the guardians of the Covenant, in the name of the whole people (and often against it), in view of refounding a temple-city; the same is also true of the Nazoreans, in the sense of guardians or watchers (cf. chap. V, §V.2). Similarly, the expressions designating unanimity (ὁμοθυμαδόν four times in Acts and six extra occurrences proper to AT; ψυχὴ μία Acts 4:32, cf. 1 Chron 12:39, etc.) characterize friendship ever since the Pythagoreans and have remained classic, cf. Aristotle, *Eth. Nic.* 9.8. The increased frequency of ὁμοθυμαδόν in the AT could be a later Greek influence (Act III). However, this term, employed 36 times in the OT, corresponds in the MT to יחד (or יחדו) and is precisely the name of the community in the Qumran *Rule*, which weakens the argument (although appeal could be made to Deut 33:5, where the gathering of leaders of the people forms the יחד of the tribes of Israel). In reality, the problem of Greek influences, direct or indirect, on the NT, has to be seen in the context of the various waves of Hellenistic (Greek) influence on the whole of Judaism, beginning with the events leading up to the Maccabean crisis; the struggle against Greek contamination does not imply that these influences ceased, but on the contrary it presupposes a profound penetration, even in the most protected circles. The classic work of Edwin Hatch, *The Influence of Greek Ideas on Christianity*, London, Williams and Norgate, 1889 (re-edited by Frederick C. Grant, New York, Harper, 1957), shows all sorts of parallels, while always (implicitly) assuming that Judaism remains essentially untouched.

Qumran *Rule* (1 QS), the qualified community is precisely designated by the expression "the many" *(ha-rabbim)*, which we have also seen in connection with the brotherhoods (chap. V, §I.1).[117] One of the essential features[118] of the community structure is the sharing of goods. A nuance is necessary, however, because the arrangements indicated in Acts 4:32–5:10 concern two different kinds of goods: the sharing of chattels and incomes among all is obligatory, but the sale of landed property, or more generally of capital, remains voluntary, and so the management of such goods can stay in private hands. In the documents from the Judaean desert, certain passages presuppose private possessions (cf. 1 QS 7:5-8).[119] But at the same time, in the penal code of 1 QS 6:24 f., the first misdemeanor to be mentioned is that of having lied in respect of property, and the punishment is exclusion from the "purity" for a year, also restriction of food. Likewise, Josephus (*J.W.* 2 §124) mentions that the Essenes go from one town[120] to another without money, knowing that the community which receives them will attend to their needs; personal use of money is forbidden, and the fact that one who has been excommunicated is often reduced to dying of hunger shows that the oaths taken and the habits acquired prevent such persons from eating ordinary food (§143). In a word, no artificial effort is needed to find a general likeness between the primitive community and the Essenes.[121]

In the Greek language of the Roman empire *(koinê)*, as it is attested by inscriptions, the term *plêthos* designates a quantity of persons or things, which is large but capable of being numbered, or even a corporation.[122] In the NT, it is usually translated by "crowd," as the context ap-

117. Where "many" is to be taken in a qualitative sense ("qualified, notable members") rather than quantitative. This may be the origin of the title "rabbi" to designate a (specially) qualified member, such as Jesus or John the Baptist, cf. chap. VII, §IV,1.

118. Already emphasized in chap. II, §II.5 as a fundamental constituent of the Covenant.

119. Chaim Rabin, "Private Property in the Qumran Community," in: *Qumran Studies* (Scripta Judaica, 2), Oxford, 1956, p. 22–36. In CD 10:17-19, it is forbidden to lend on the Sabbath, as also to deal with matters of wealth or gain (11:15), in terms that recall Isa 58:13 (cf. also Neh 10:32; 1:14-22; *Jub* 50:8). Similarly *MShab* 23:3 f.

120. Cf. below, §5.

121. P. Wernberg-Moeller, *The Manual of Discipline, Translated and Annotated, With an Introduction* (STJD, 1), Leiden, Brill, 1957, p. 111, followed by others, argues against any comparison between 1 QS and Acts.

122. Cf. Moulton, *s. v.* πλῆθος. The usual term to designate collectively a crowd of indeterminate size is ὄχλος *(q. v.)*, with an idea of confusion or agitation (cf. *turba*); it occurs also in the plural (but only for human beings). In Philo's definition of the Essenes, *Quod omnis probus*, §75, he speaks of a πλῆθος ὑπερτετρακισχίλιοι "association of more than 4000 members"; it is not clear whether he has a more precise technical meaning in mind.

pears to require, which weakens the relevance of what we have been seeing. So we need to check the meaning. There is one passage from the Synoptic gospels which suggests that the word may have a special meaning in an early Christian context: Mark 3:7-8 twice employs this word for the crowds which come to Jesus from everywhere, but Luke 6:17 prefers a periphrasis—"a great quantity of people"[123]—on the first occasion and omits the second; it is as if he recoils from using the word for an ordinary crowd. The term does not recur in Mark, and Matt does not use it at all, nor do the epistles.[124] By contrast, it occurs 8 times in Luke and 16 times in Acts (AT, 17 times in WT, but absent from Acts 7–13); it looks then as if it belongs to Luke's vocabulary. The summaries already discussed show it as having both a technical meaning equivalent to community (4:32; 5:14), and also a rather more vague quantitative sense, which makes it possible to slide imperceptibly from one to the other.

The cases in Luke-Acts where *plêthos* has a precise sense are not isolated, as other examples show. At Jesus' Messianic entry into Jerusalem, Matt 21:8 and Mark 11:9 mention an imposing crowd accompanying him, but Luke 19:37 has "the great number of the disciples," making a distinction between them and the onlookers. He has in mind the community of disciples, and not just a crowd, and the later redactions have considerably inflated the scale of the demonstration. In Acts 6:2a, at the institution of the Seven, the "great number" of the disciples convokes the Twelve (according to the P Doc) or is convoked by them (Acts II, present narrative), and in both cases it is this same *plêthos* that is invited to choose seven persons for a new task.[125] The expression recurs in v. 5, to indicate the approbation of the participants. It is clearly a question of an organized body competent to act, but the final redaction tends to make it a large assembly convoked by the Twelve. In Acts 15:12, during the Jerusalem assembly, the "great number" keeps silent after Peter's speech. Here too it is the group of the disciples (described as "apostles and

123. Luke has πλῆϑος πολὺ τοῦ λαοῦ (cf. 1:10), which is redundant (to express indeterminate number), and adds an ὄχλος πολύς of disciples. In the parallel narrative, Matt 4:24 blends everything into ὄχλοι πολλοί who accompany Jesus. Cf. preced. n.

124. It occurs only in three citations from the OT: Heb 11:12 citing Gen 22:17; James 5:20 citing Prov 10:12; 1 Pet 4:8 citing the same Prov 10:12. John has two examples: in 5:3 in the connection with the great number of sick people under the five porticoes of the probatic pool; in 21:6 for the great number of fish caught miraculously. In both cases, the interpretation of the "great number" as a symbol of "community members" would give a precise and plausible meaning, but would be difficult to demonstrate; it is interesting that the normal term for "crowd" (ὄχλος) is used 20 times in John (out of 175 times in the NT, against only 49 times in the OT, where it corresponds in part to המון, more often rendered by πλῆϑος), and so the use of a different term in two places introduces a nuance.

125. This *diakonia* will be looked at later; cf. chap. VII, §IV.3.

brethren of Judaea" in 11:1). Later, the emissaries from Jerusalem arrive in Antioch, assemble the "great number" and hand over the letter (15:30). It is now a question of instructions given to the *particular* community of the disciples at Antioch. Later still, at Ephesus, Paul goes to the synagogue, but, when he is contradicted before the "great number" (Acts 19:9), he leaves, taking his disciples with him. Here the term designates the assembly in the synagogue, distinct from Paul's own disciples. This assembly, which Paul addressed over a period of three months, has a definite constitution and cannot be an undifferentiated crowd. Finally, when Paul is summoned before the Sanhedrin, what he has to say causes the division of the "great number" (Acts 23:6); it is evidently a regularly constituted assembly, consisting of Pharisees and Sadducees.

This brief investigation leads to a fairly clear result. The term *plêthos*, employed by itself, designates in the first place an organized assembly, of limited dimension. It is possible to add a nuance. In the first part of Acts, centered on Peter, it is a question of the assembly of the disciples in general, or of a particular assembly. In the second, properly Pauline, part, the word occurs less frequently, but it appears to designate a Jewish assembly of limited size, synagogue or sanhedrin, in which only one part is favorable to Paul, who provokes a division of the *plêthos*. This is in striking contrast to Acts 4:32 WT, which emphasizes that there was no division in the *plêthos* of the disciples. The distinction between the two usages appears sufficiently clear for us to attribute the term in its technical sense to one of the major independent sources of Acts, namely the P Doc. In other words, when this document was integrated into what was becoming the Book of Acts (Acts I, etc.), the term by and large lost its earlier, quasi-technical meaning, and allowed itself to be used in the wider sense of a crowd.[126]

126. The same may be true of FJ: in *Ant.* 13 §408, Alexandra Salome, who succeeded her husband Alexander Jannaeus, restored the customs of the Pharisees, and ordered the "great number" (πλῆθος) to obey them; she was loved by the "great number" (πλῆθος), as she deplored the faults of her husband, who had persecuted the Pharisees. This passage is usually understood in the light of the development of the Pharisaic tendency at the moment when FJ is writing: Alexandra ordered "all the people" to follow them. It could all the same refer to more limited groups, among whom the Pharisees were one (with the special feature of oral rather than biblical traditions). The rab. sources provide an argument for this interpretation: *BSoṭa* 47a and *Meg. Taan* 10–11 (28 Ṭebet) say that Shimon b. Shetaḥ (two generations before Hillel, according to *MAbot* 1:3) was Alexandra's brother and was *nasi*, and that he expelled the "Sadducees" from the Sanhedrin because of their ignorance, *i.e.* restored the customs of the Pharisees, as FJ says. Taking into account a retrospective exaggeration, the operation should be understood as restricted to a limited group (the Aram. of *Meg. Taan* has כנישתא, "assembly"), and the "Sadducees" taken as "Zadokites" (cf. chap. I, §I.3); in that case there has been a reworking of the sense of רבים, corresponding to FJ's πλῆθος.

If we understand the "great number" *(plêthos)* in this way as a definite community, that of Peter or another, we can interpret[127] fairly simply the passage of the summary already seen which speaks of "great numbers of men and women" who were being added to the Lord (Acts 5:14). It is a question of the—somewhat unexpected—addition of groups of men *and* groups of women. In Acts 8:3 and elsewhere, the mention of persecutions against men *and women* suggests that the latter have a juridical entity, which was not to be taken for granted in the Roman world or in ordinary Jewish culture, where, except in certain cases of widowhood, a woman was always identified in terms of her father, husband, brother or son.[128] Josephus never speaks of any consecration of women, but Philo provides a parallel case, the groups of female virgins, whom he calls "Therapeutrides." In particular, these take part equally with similar masculine groups ("Therapeutae"), though separately, in the Sabbath assemblies and celebrations every fifty days;[129] these groups of men and women are of Essene type.

Besides this mention of women, let us take note of the fact that whole groups, brotherhoods and sisterhoods we might say, join up. The style of v. 14 is noteworthy: "There were added to the Lord those who were believers (masc.), communities (neut.) of men and of women."[130] We have observed that the theme of community growth is foreign to the texts concerning Peter and belongs to later literary development; the term "Lord" for Jesus belongs there too. What may have been the circum-

127. Light is thus thrown on a further detail of vocabulary: in Acts 2:41; 4:32 and 19:2 the members of the community are defined as "having become believers" (πιστεύω in the aorist, distinct from the perfect and designating a point in the past) and not as "believing." What is meant is not a belief presently held (as in 5:14, cf. above), but a verifiable action giving entry to the group (rite).

128. The NT contains some traces of consecrated virginity: 1 Cor 7:34 makes a distinction between the unmarried woman and the virgin (ἡ γυνὴ ἡ ἄγαμος καὶ ἡ παρθένος), both marriageable, which points to a special qualification. In v. 36 f., if anyone thinks he is lacking in what is becoming (ἀσχημονεῖν recalling the LXX trans. of צרות דבר in Deut 24:1) with respect to *his* virgin, let him marry her; in this case the one concerned thinks he is lacking in chastity. In v. 37 if he has authority over his desire *and* the decision in his heart to honor it, let him abstain. Here the virgin seems to be not an orphan who has been taken into the man's home, but a woman who has a certain intention of remaining a virgin, though without any irrevocable commitment, and who lives in his house (later Christian tradition knew such women as *virgines subintroductae*). It was in some such manner that Mary lived with Joseph, cf. chap. V, §II.2.

129. Philo, *Vita contempl.* §32 f., 68 f., 83–87. On the Essenes and women, cf. chap. VII, §IV.2.

130. The break in construction is quite clear: προσετίθεντο, πιστεύοντες τῷ κυρίῳ, πλήθη ἀνδρῶν τε καὶ γυναικῶν; this phrase may have been added to show that whole πλήθη joined, as well as individuals.

stances in which these groups joined up? A simple hypothesis would be that, when the crisis over the *minim* broke out, after 90, and the loose networks of brotherhoods underwent reorganization (chap. V, §III.2), various Jewish-Christian groups owing allegiance to Jesus joined in the Pauline movement, whereas others refused. This would be the context in which James returned to favor in the environment that produced the NT, through at least part of his spiritual descendants.

Finally, we observe that strictly speaking the *rabbim*, even if they constitute a brotherhood, a "great number," are more precisely the "many."[131] Obviously, the corresponding Greek term most often has its ordinary meaning, but sometimes it has an identifiable technical sense. This is well illustrated in *J.W.* 2 §124, when Josephus explains that the Essenes reside[132] "many" in all the towns. Likewise, Paul speaks in 2 Cor 2:6 of blame inflicted by the "many," though using another term;[133] it is a question of a definite disciplinary act performed by the community, and not by a crowd, a fact which shows that here we are still in the primitive environment. A further interesting example is provided by the narrative of Jesus' Last Supper: in Matt 26:28 and Mark 14:24, he speaks of his blood "shed for the many," whereas in Luke 22:20 it is "shed for you" (like the bread "given for you" in v. 19), that is to say, for a very limited group of twelve. The term "many" means "you" first of all, but also similar groups, limited in membership if unlimited in number.

131. In the LXX, πλῆθος corresponds regularly to רב (and πολλοί to רבים), but also to המון (crowd). The Qumran *Community Rule* offers a variant which suggests that these two terms are equivalent: in 1 *QS* 5:2-3, the expression על פי רוב אנשי היחד ("according to the *plêthos* of the men of the community (who belong to the Covenant)" is rendered in two parallel fragments (B et D) על פי הרבים "according to the many," cf. James H. Charlesworth et al. (ed.), *The Dead Sea Scrolls. Hebrew, Aramaic and Greek Texts with English Translations*, Tübingen, J. C. B. Mohr, 1994, I:19–20.

132. He uses the verb μετοικέω, which is not attested in the Bible, but there μετοικεσία translates גלות "exile" (Judg 18:30; 2 Kgs 24:13). It is an allusion to a return to the desert. The "towns" are rural villages, close to cultivated land, a link which is essential, as for the *ḥaberim* and the first disciples (cf. chap. I, §II.1). According to *MMeg* 1:3, a "large town" (as opposed to a "village") is defined as a settlement where ten men not actually occupied can always be found (to constitute a *minyan* for prayer).

133. The term πλειόνες without article would designate the majority, but with the article it is a question of an entity, the "great number" in the sense of community with legal capacity (as distinct from κοινωνία "communion, union," 2 Cor 6:14; 9:13; 13:13). Similarly in 2 Cor 4:15 (ἡ χάρις πλεονάσασα διὰ τῶν πλειόνων "the grace accrued through the community"); in 2 Cor 9:2 ("your ardor has stimulated the community"); in Phil 1:14, it is possible to understand τοὺς πλείονας τῶν ἀδελφῶν as "the greater part of the brethren," but also as "the community of the brethren," as such, which fits very well with the context. The twelve disciples whom Paul meets at Ephesus may also be regarded as "many," especially with John's baptism.

5. *Final Remarks*

According to Acts 8:1, a violent persecution drove a number of believers (but not the apostles) out of Jerusalem. This was the beginning of different missions, though no program had been drawn up in advance. This statement contains both facts and a thesis. The thesis is succinct and recurs throughout the Book of Acts, *viz.* that the mission progressed only thanks to persecutions. The first, directed against Jesus, allowed the Scriptures to be fulfilled, by means of Judas and the Jewish authorities, who did not know what they were doing. The next caused the exit from Jerusalem, towards the nations and eventually Rome. Obviously, nothing would have happened had it not been for the events concerning Stephen. In this sense, Paul, even before his conversion, was already, without knowing it, helping the primitive community to develop. The facts were certainly less cut and dried than this reinterpretation suggests: a persecution at Jerusalem, large or small in scale, connected no doubt with Messianizing agitation, but not easy to date (probably at the time of a pilgrimage). This does not rule out the possibility that the group of apostles had already left Jerusalem. A return to Galilee after the pilgrimage in which Jesus died is easy to imagine: not only have we seen that certain episodes in Acts have been placed rather artificially in Jerusalem, but the convergent testimony of Matt, Mark and John implies a mission beginning in Galilee. Paul's meetings with Peter and James in Jerusalem do not change this conclusion, since they could have taken place during a pilgrimage (cf. Acts 20:16), which was certainly the best way to make sure of meeting people.

The cultural environment of reference is of Essene type, with "great numbers,"[134] and a rural note already observed when Peter visits Cor-

134. And remained so for a long time: the term πλῆθος has a remarkable continuity in ancient Christian texts. First, the *Ecclesiastical Constitution of the Apostles* (composite document, with sources dating from 140–180, but related to the Pastoral Epistles), published by Theodor Schermann, *Die allgemeine Kirchenordnung, frühchristliche Liturgien und kirchliche Überlieferung. I—Die allgemeine Kirchenordnung des zweiten Jahrhunderts*, Paderborn, Schöning, 1914, and discussed by Alexandre Faivre, "La documentation canonico-liturgique de l'église ancienne," *RSR* 54 (1980), 204–215 and 273–297; in n° 16, the πλῆθος designates a body of at least twelve members, competent to elect a bishop (ἐπίσκοπος, term discussed chap. VII, §IV.3); further on, the case is foreseen where the bishop could be confounded by the "many" (πολλοί); Adolf Harnack, *Die Quelle der sogenannten apostolischen Kirchenordnung. . .* (Texte und Untersuchungen, II/5), Leipzig, Hinbusch, 1886, p. 10, noticed the equivalence of the two terms πλῆθος and πολλοί, and also their precise technical sense (and, with his usual acuteness he would no doubt have attempted a comparison with the *rabbim* of CD and 1 QS, if he had known those texts); in n° 20, it is once again a πλῆθος that is qualified to confer community offices. Likewise, Clement of Rome, *Ad Cor.* §54, explains that whoever has provoked an uprising (στάσις; Messianic agitation?) or a division (σχίσμα) is invited to pronounce his own exclusion, de-

nelius. The persistent allusions to "John's baptism" as the absolute origin of the whole movement launched by Jesus proves it, no less than the recurrent references to the breaking of the bread (without any particular link with Jesus' death). On to this original stock, two grafts were successfully implanted,[135] represented respectively by Peter and by Paul, each acting independently, but with authority: the former bringing together the resurrection of Jesus (raised up) and healings of sick people (raised up), the latter renewing his disquieting Messianic drive under the name of Jesus, but without any clear idea from the first of a mission to the Gentiles. The fact that Paul was baptized *after* receiving the Spirit, like Cornelius, would indicate that he did not originally belong to the primitive environment, but that may be no more than a redactional effect. The growth of the community is infinitesimal in the first case, and confused in the second, but at this stage everything stays within the Jewish world.

It is becoming clearer that the development of NT Christianity occurred only gradually. The construction of Acts 1–2, which probably originated in the liturgy (with Pentecost on a Sunday), makes a synthesis which can be summed up in two phases. At the ascension the apostles' first reflex is to wait passively for the return of the Messiah, who will come to establish his kingdom and set everything to rights; this corresponds to the position of James and his successors, as we find it in the tradition, and it is certainly not oriented towards any mission (short term, "vertical" eschatology). Then the angels bring everybody back to earth in order to wait for the Spirit, which opens up the perspective of a universal mission of conversion, whose success is necessarily distant (long term, "horizontal" eschatology). James is obviously absent from this phase, but the other two are much in evidence: Peter proclaiming the resurrection, and Paul pushing ahead with the development of the community and worrying the authorities. However, it is not really a question of the sick, or of Messianism properly so called. In other words, between the primitive figures of Peter and Paul and their final position in the frontispiece of Acts,

---

claring that he will do all that the πλῆθος may order! Again, Ignatius of Antioch, *Ad Magn.* 6.1, *Ad Trall.* 8.2, uses πλῆθος to designate the community legally constituted; in *Ad Smyrn.* 8.2, he makes a notable distinction between πλῆθος and ἐκκλησία, cf. chap. VII, §IV.3.

135. Thus we can also understand that rites have been preserved, more or less reinterpreted, independently of these grafts. In fact the canonico-liturgical literature which has come down has preserved many Jewish-Christian features, as already observed by Gregory Dix, Ἀποστολικὴ παράδοσις. *The Treatise on the Apostolic Tradition of St. Hippolytus of Rome, Bishop and Martyr*, reissued with corrections, preface and bibliography by H. Chadwick, London, Alban Press, 1992 (orig. 1937), p. XL f.

there have been other transformations, both connected with the resurrection of Jesus and with the Spirit. In the one case, the healing (raising up) of the sick has become a metaphor for the forgiveness (mercy, conversion) of sin (another sickness). In the other, the expectation of Jesus Messiah has become the declaration that he has already returned (resurrection), and that the definitive kingdom has already come, as seen by the opening of all frontiers, and the abolition of the line, which could not be crossed, separating Jews from Gentiles. Because Paul sees this kingdom of the Risen Christ (of the Messiah already returned) as a new creation, he naturally calls its founder "Lord."[136] In the narratives of Acts, which attribute Pauline features to Peter (preaching, visiting Gentiles) and Petrine features to Paul (healing, cf. Acts 19:11 f.), the figures of the two apostles end up by blending together, as the author intends,[137] but without losing sight of communion with James, which is emphasized in the central episode of the Jerusalem assembly.

IV – Conclusions

The characteristic episodes in the development of the mission, as well as the position of the principal actors, can be summed up in the following table. The three main vertical columns are defined by the three fundamental ways of looking at Jesus which have emerged: as disciple of John the Baptist (which can be further subdivided), as Messiah and as Lord. To take the case of Paul, we have seen that he first identified the Messiah (Christ) as Jesus, then Jesus Christ as Lord, inaugurating a kingdom without boundaries, as expressed in Phil 2:11: "That every tongue proclaim that Jesus Christ is Lord."

Horizontally, there are three phases. One is static, tied to the memory of Jesus and earlier than Pentecost (or what Pentecost stands for). In

136. Cf. *BBabaB* 75a (chap. V, §IV.3) on the attribution of the name "which is above every name" to the Messiah *in actu*. The decisive moment for Paul the Messianist, who was never *troubled* by any biographical knowledge of Jesus, was to recognize him as risen, *i.e.* Messiah in the act (of bringing about a new creation). Of course, the mechanism of the divinization of the savior is well attested in the Graeco-Roman world (and no doubt more widely); there is a good example in Acts 14:11 f. when the crowd at Lystra, impressed by a healing, takes Barnabas and Paul for gods (Barnabas, head of the expedition, takes after Peter, the healer). There is no difficulty in allowing that Paul was influenced by the surrounding culture, but *as a Jew* (and not in any way borrowing basic elements from outside Judaism).

137. In the early Christian writings, Peter and Paul are always associated with the church of Rome, as apostles, martyrs and founders, cf. Clement, *Ad Cor.* §5; Ignatius, *Ad Rom.* 4.3; Denis bishop of Corinth (quoted by Eusebius, *Hist. eccl.* 2.25.28); Irenaeus, *Adv. haer.* 3.2; Tertullian, *De praescr. haer.* 36.3.

the second, in a climate of agitation about the right "way," Jesus is identified as the Messiah who is about to return. The third is characterized by the Spirit, and Messianism, strictly so called, has disappeared, or rather, has been transformed: the Messiah has already arrived (resurrection), and "Christ" becomes a special proper name, or a sort of surname. For the chief persons, a Roman numeral indicates the principal stages in their evolution.

	Jesus (John's baptism)			Messiah	Lord
	Nazorean	Teacher	Healer	(about to come)	(already come)
Phase I (Jesus)	James (brothers of Jesus)	Apollos	Peter I, Barnabas	Paul I, Aquila	
Phase II ("Way")		joins Aquila (Corinth)	*(christiani)*	Paul II (Damascus, Antioch)	
Phase III (Spirit)	James (Jewish-Christians, Jerusalem)		Peter II (resurrection, Cornelius)		Paul III (Ephesus; neither Jews nor Greeks)

This table is complex, but it is an extreme simplification of a great number of small facts which have never fallen into any ready-made scheme. Three points stand out. First, James, brother but not disciple of Jesus, becomes the reference point after the dispersion following the disappearance of the Master. Next, the enormous convulsion caused by Messianizing agitation, under Caligula and afterwards,[138] led to contacts with

138. Apart from the peaceful demonstrations against Petronius in Ptolemais and Tiberias, which we have mentioned (cf. above §I.3), there is no clear trace of agitation aroused by Caligula's project in Judaea, as we would expect. At this point, we might ask what was the position of Stephen, who appears untypical and does not feature in the schema given above. The violence of the reactions aroused by his speeches against the Temple raises the question whether he may have been in favor of the plan to erect the emperor's statue there, in order to precipitate the end; his death is commonly put earlier than 39 but in fact cannot be dated with any degree of certainty, and his opponents, people from Cyrene, Alexandria, Cilicia and Asia (Acts 6:9), may well have been caught up in the Messianizing movement. N. H. Taylor, "Palestinian Christianity and the Caligula Crisis. Part I—Social and Historical Reconstruction; Part II—The Markan Eschatological Discourse," *JSNT* 61 et 62 (1996), p. 101–124 and 13–41, indirectly suggests this possibility, since Jesus had foretold the destruction of the Temple as a prelude to the *parousia*, and so his disciples may not have been opposed to its profanation (but he assumes that Chris-

Gentiles, brought about by popular movements, which broke down the barriers isolating the Godfearers.[139] Finally, Peter ends up in a position midway between that represented by James, who does not change (passive expectation within the original circle), and Paul (long-term movement towards the nations).[140] Of the three, Peter alone is properly speaking a disciple of Jesus. Like James, he stays close to the original environment, characterized by the "great number." Like Paul, but rather differently, he has, under the influence of the Spirit, an active sense of the resurrection as already effective here and now.

We have seen how important the episodes at Ephesus and Corinth were for Paul. The role of Aquila is particularly instructive. He was undoubtedly a stronger personality than we are led to suppose by Acts (especially the AT), and was the mentor, in different circumstances, of Paul and of Apollos. His protégés, however, went on to follow different paths. Paul separated from Aquila, but his final outlook, in which everything came together to make manifest the risen Christ, made it possible for him not to disown Aquila or discredit Apollos' activities. Following the latter from Alexandria to Ephesus and on to Corinth, we have seen that in each place he was in touch with disciples who were not Messianists but who, like himself, knew "the things concerning Jesus"; these circles may well have possessed some form of written biography of Jesus, perhaps more than one, since John's gospel also originated in Asia Minor. Another whose role was capital, even if he is less visible on the table above, was Barnabas. Also a strong personality, he it was who went to look for Paul at Tarsus, and who introduced him to the Jerusalem apostles. Paul parted from him too (Acts 15:39), in order to blaze a new trail. James hardly changed from his original position, but it is clear that he was the pivot on which everything turned, and to whom even Peter had to give an account (Acts 12:17; cf. his first place in the triumvirate mentioned in Gal 2:9); this central role shows, by the way, to what extent Jesus' death had scattered the disciples (as, in fact, we should expect). Afterwards, the center of gravity shifted to Peter, in such a way that James and his spiritual heirs,

---

tianity had its historical beginning at the Pentecost of Acts chap. 2, which leads him into difficult hypotheses). He concludes that the eschatological discourse of Mark 13:5-27 is by and large based on the memory of this threatening crisis in the past, reinterpreted as the prediction of a final crisis still to come.

139. As we see in Acts 15:3-4 (the question about the circumcision of the Gentiles), which in the P Doc immediately follows 11:20 (Messianizing activity at Antioch, in which the word is spoken to the Greeks).

140. This point, and also the probability that a biography of Jesus circulated in the Jewish-Christian circles frequented by Apollos, have already been raised in chap. V, §VI.

the Jewish-Christians properly so called (Nazoreans, family of Jesus) became marginalized with respect to the newly created movement that became NT Christianity.[141] It is in this way that we can speak of Christianity as a "sect which burst open."

But we have not got as far as that yet. The final phase of development turns about the nature of Messianism. So far we have seen how the heritage of Jesus became Messianized, almost it seems by chance, in a fairly turbulent Roman and Jewish context, under Caligula. By way of the name *christiani*, this Jesus Messianism, even transformed, remained definitively associated with the "Christians." For this to have happened, there had to be an intrinsic link, already existing or waiting to be discovered, between the two movements, whereas the "Nazoreans" became more and more marginalized and finally disappeared. On the other hand, the Jewish-Christian environment of Jesus' disciples, immediately after their Master's failure and death, certainly had no properly Messianic drive, as we have seen with James and Peter. But what about before, while Jesus was still alive? The story of the disciples from Emmaus shows traces of a disappointed Messianic hope. Jesus' arrival in Jerusalem on a donkey, then the Last Supper, both have characteristic features of a Messianic outcome. The fear and reactions of the various authorities in Jerusalem also presuppose something of the kind.

Even if Jesus had no directly political intention, he undoubtedly set off a number of shock waves in society. The question is, however, whether the description "Messianic" was directly linked to all these facts at the time, or whether such language, though biblical, was foreign to the original environment and only imported later under the stimulus of the agitation surrounding Paul. It is well known but nonetheless remarkable, that the whole of Jesus' life, including the resurrection, was retold *after the event* as a fulfilment of the Scriptures. That does not necessarily mean that his story lent itself easily to such an interpretation. Furthermore, the confusion following Jesus' death was certainly not favorable to the fixing of precise recollections. So were such Messianic features, duly reworked, only a product of these Scriptural meditations, linked with the affirmation that the end of time was come, and the kingdom of God inaugurated in reality? In any case, the theme of fulfilment was not a program for the events of Jesus' life, but a thesis to serve as a grid for reading the facts

141. FJ recounts the execution of James (with a few companions) in a passage which has always been regarded as authentic (*Ant.* 20 §200); characteristically, he describes him as the "brother of Jesus, called Christos," but in no way treats him as a "Christian," despite the fact that he had companions.

that had been preserved, as can be seen from the selective and often approximative nature of the OT citations in the NT.

In order to examine this question, we need to return to the culture and especially the rites of the environment of reference, which always remained, despite the various developments, that of James. This is the subject of our next and final chapter.

Chapter VII

Passover, Pentecost and Covenant

The term *christiani* is of Roman origin. We saw in the previous chapter how it was grafted on to some of Jesus' disciples, from the time of the disturbances over Caligula's statue. Our search for the origins of Christianity is not yet closed, however, as we have to see why this graft "took," and therefore—following our method—find a link with rites and customs.

The original Jewish-Christian environment, represented by James, remained the trunk on to which the different grafts were implanted. The resulting synthesis is depicted by the scene of Pentecost in Acts 2, which features a quasi-Pauline Christianity under the leadership of Peter less than two months after the death of Jesus. That is extremely quick, even if one extends the time a little with the aid of other "pentecosts." In reality, literary analysis of the texts has shown two major features: the various episodes retold in Acts are worked into a connected and coherent whole by being put under the sign of the Spirit; at the same time, the whole process is started up in the setting of a Pentecost which has become the feast of the Spirit, that is, of the risen Jesus now alive and active in the world. For Pentecost to have attracted such a vast synthesis, the feast must already have had enough substance, in terms of distinctive rites with precise meanings. Our study of Jesus' Last Supper, with bread and wine (chap. II, §II), also brought out the character of Pentecost as feast of first fruits and of the Covenant, allowing for several possible cycles. At the same time, we noticed that Passover was put to one side, or rather suspended, as representing the failure of Messianism, until another Passover, when the kingdom will finally come at a moment as yet undefined, implying a long-term eschatology. In other words, Passover was effaced from the liturgical rhythm, while Pentecost was promoted as the Church's feast between the two Passovers, with the death of Jesus reinterpreted as the sacrifice suitable for renewing the Covenant.

In this chapter, we propose to take up the study of Passover and Pentecost and the connection between them, in order to arrive at some conclusions about the Covenant and the Messiah. We may then understand why NT Christianity, especially with the new horizons opened up by Paul, still felt the need to retain a polemical link with Judaism by declaring itself the "New Covenant" and transforming Messianism, instead of cutting all such ties and launching out into entirely new waters.

I – Passover and the Lamb

The chronology of Jesus' last week is difficult to establish. The paschal setting of the Last Supper in the synoptics seems very clear, Thursday evening 14 Nisan, but, as we have seen, there are two major problems. First, there is a doubt about the calendar, since in John this 14 Nisan, day of "Preparation," falls on a Friday. The other problem is that the elements emphasized in the Supper, bread and wine, are not central to the Passover ritual, whereas the lamb, which is meant to be sacrificed and eaten, would have provided a much more obvious sign of the redemptive death of Jesus, betrayed (eaten) by his own. That is precisely the symbolism emphasized by John, but the rite of the paschal lamb is unknown to Christianity, at least as determined and expressed by the NT.

In the rabbinic tradition, there is a domestic Passover rite which has two notable features. First, it is to be carried out in the same way in every place, Jerusalem and elsewhere, and is entirely focused on the commemoration of the Exodus from Egypt. Further, it contains more signs than those required by Exod 12, particularly the cups of wine which we saw in connection with the Last Supper, but the paschal lamb is missing. Officially, the absence, or rather disappearance of the paschal lamb is explained by the absence of the Temple. Rabbinic tradition states that, after its destruction, all sacrifices became impossible, including the immolation of the Passover. This reason is not good enough, however, as the Samaritans, who follow Deut, have never ceased to perform the Passover at Garizim, the "chosen place," even after the destruction of their sanctuary by John Hyrcanus. Furthermore, the precept is to eat, the immolation being required only in order to prepare the animal, and there are traces of the celebration of Passover with the lamb outside Jerusalem before the downfall of the Temple. In fact, the rabbinic celebration in every place of the deliverance from Egypt could quite well do without the lamb, on the understanding that the entry into the Promised Land had already taken place. Finally, there was obviously a problem with regard to the Christians. We shall start with this last point.

1. The Paschal Lamb

Justin Martyr gives a precise description of what the paschal lamb looked like: "When the lamb is roasted, it is arranged in such a way as to represent the cross: a spit goes right through it from the lower limbs to the head, another spit is at the shoulder, to which the paws are fastened."[1] This description, which is not drawn from the Bible, may well show the influence of Christian symbolism, but it must have been close enough to actual Jewish custom for it to have made some sense to the Jew Tryphon. He, like Justin, came from Palestine, where this custom may still have been in use until quite recently. Justin, writing after 150 (cf. 46.2), states, in accordance with Deut, that the immolation is to take place in Jerusalem (the "chosen place" for the Jews), but that it is no longer possible, since Judaea is forbidden to the Jews. He makes no reference to the Temple, but only to the "chosen place," and—it should be noted—the ritual is now impossible, not since the downfall of 70, but since the Bar Kokhba war. That is one of the signs that some cultic activity continued at Jerusalem until then, even after the sanctuary was destroyed (cf. chap. IV, §I.4). Finally, Justin makes no reference to any Christian custom corresponding in any way to the paschal lamb. He does not even say that Christians of Judaea were able to celebrate Passover in this form before the war.

The Jewish custom referred to by Justin is attested by rabbinic sources, whose interpretation requires some technical specifications. First, according to Exod 12:9, the lamb must be "neither raw nor boiled, but roasted over the fire." Further, according to *MPes* 7:1, the lamb is to be roasted on a spit of dry wood.[2] Damp wood gives off steam, with an effect similar to that of boiling, whereas a metal spit heats up in the fire, and so too would play a part in cooking the meat. The entrails pose a further problem: contained within the body, they would be cooked as in a pot, and not roasted directly over the fire. For this reason, Aqiba requires them to be fastened[3] on another branch fixed to the paws, so that they can be outside the carcass. In other words, there has to be a second, transverse

1. Justin, *Dial.* 40.3; Melito of Sardis, fr. 9, says similarly ὡς ἀμνὸς ἐσταυρώϑη "*like* a lamb he has been crucified (or: spitted)."

2. Normally from the pomegranate tree, which burns slowly, cf. discussion in *YPes* 7:1 f.

3. The term used, תלה "hang, suspend," is not clear in this context (as it does not indicate the method of attachment), but it is very suggestive, as in the LXX it is rendered normally by σταυρῶ (in particular for Haman and his sons, cf. Esth 9:13, targ. צלב), with the sense of "hang" or "crucify," depending on whether it is a question of exposition *after* execution or of crucifixion alive. Deut 21:22 fixes a general rule: "If a man, for his sin, has incurred the pain of death, and you have put him to death and hung him (TYon: "and has

spit forming a cross with the first. The specifically culinary explanation converges with Justin's overall description:[4] Jesus is very simply identified with the paschal lamb, giving an eloquent symbolism to the cross and emphasizing the wood. That also explains, by the way, why the Christian cross has four branches, whereas a gallows, normally shaped like a T, has only three. The condemned, often already fastened to the cross beam *(patibulum)*, carried it to the place of execution, where there was already an upright post in place; a notice bearing the reason for the condemnation could be pegged on to the crossbeam,[5] thus giving rise eventually to the fourth branch. Whatever the exact shape of the instrument of execution, the symbolism of the lamb on a cross is so simple and significant that it leads immediately to two related questions. What place did the rite of the paschal lamb hold in the environment from which the disciples came? And how did the Jews, especially those in circles close to the disciples, react to a symbol of even more obvious significance than whitewashed walls (cf. chap. V, §IV.2)?

The annual Passover is present in the NT, at least as a metaphor, but—apart from the Last Supper in the synoptic gospels—there is no trace of any significant celebration on 14 Nisan, whatever the calendar of reference.[6] The same is true for the earliest Christian writers already cited: there is no trace of transfer to the Sunday of any properly paschal rite (centered on the lamb),[7] whether weekly or annually. The narrative of

---

been condemned to lapidation, he will then be hung") on a wood (or: "tree"; TOnq צליבא: "gallows, cross"), his body will not pass the night on the wood"; this can be understood either as ". . . and you have put him to death by hanging" (*i.e.* by crucifixion, cf. Esth 7:10; John 18:31; Rev 11:9, and also 11 QT col. 64:6-13), or as ". . . put to death then hung. . . ," as perhaps in Philo, *Spec. leg.* 3 §151, Gal 3:13, and certainly in Esth 9:13 (Haman's sons are *already dead*, in the context), also FJ (*Ant.* 4 §202) and the rab. trad. (cf. TYon); this last rejects the first meaning as being the Roman method, cf. *BSanh* 46b.

4. He states that it is in conformity with Scripture (*Dial.* 111.3): "The Passover was Christ, as Isaiah says: *Like a sheep, he was led to the slaughter.* It was on a day of Passover that you arrested him, and it was also on a day of Passover that you crucified him, it is written" (ἐν ἡμέρᾳ τοῦ πάσχα συνελάβετε αὐτὸν καὶ ὁμοίως ἐν τῷ πάσχα ἐσταυρώσατε, γέγραπται). The last word, invoking scriptural authority, refers to the OT, and not to the "memoranda" of the apostles (cf. chap. I, §I.1.).

5. Cf. the sources collected in *Dict. Antiq.*, "crux," I:1574 f. This is the way to understand the inscription placed "above" Jesus (Matt 27:37 ἐπάνω τῆς κεφαλῆς αὐτοῦ; Luke 23:38 ἐπ᾽ αὐτῷ), indicating the reason for his condemnation (αἰτία, Matt, Mark; *titulus* John 19:19). On the various significations of the cross, cf. below §V.3.

6. The episode of the night at Troas appears well situated in relation to a week of Unleavened Bread, but does not itself provide any chronological indication, cf. chap. I, §II.2. For the significant exception of the Quartodecimans, cf. §2 below.

7. Despite numerous homiletic developments on the lamb and the blood, cf. J. Daniélou, *op. cit.*, p. 220 f.

the Last Supper suggests as much: between the death of Jesus and the final coming of the kingdom, the Passover is interrupted, or rather, replaced by a substitute rite derived, as we have seen, from Pentecost (first fruits) and linked to the weekly rhythm of the first day (cf. chap. II, §II.5). In short, the circles that produced the NT gave hardly any grounds for Jewish counter-measures on this point.

The paschal lamb has almost entirely disappeared from the Tannaitic ritual, a point to which we shall return (§II.3). However, there is a story (*MPes* 7:2) that Gamaliel II, the second founder of Yavneh, ordered his servant to roast the Passover lamb on a grid,[8] whereas just before, it is laid down that it is to be roasted on a wooden spit. The date is certainly later than 70; the place is not specified and could be Jerusalem, but would more naturally be taken to be his home, in Yavneh or Lod, though that does not affect the present argument.[9] In any case, his orders do not represent a personal fancy, especially taking into account Justin's evidence already quoted. It really does look as if he were trying to avoid the symbolism of the lamb on a cross. For this gesture to have had some point, the sign itself must have had a meaning *at that moment*, that is 14 Nisan. That in turn implies an environment in which it could be significant and also circumstances in which an urgent problem of differentiation had arisen. In order to see why Gamaliel should seek to avoid the symbol of the lamb on the cross, we have only to recall that he is associated precisely with a period of reorganization of the brotherhoods, after 90 in Judaea, giving rise to a problem of dissidents who resist this normalization, and in particular to the need to put the *minim* at a safe distance (as we have seen in chap. V, §I.2).

Approaching the question from another angle, we need to find Christians, or at least disciples of Jesus, who celebrate the Passover on 14 Nisan (with or without the lamb) and who live side by side with Jews. They existed, though we do not know much about them: they are those Jewish-Christians called Quartodecimans.[10]

8. That is a metallic object, whence a subsequent discussion on the steps to observe to make sure that the lamb is really "roasted over the fire," cf. *BPes* 75a. Various commentators have tried in vain to show that it could not be the paschal sacrifice, or else that it must have been Gamaliel I (Paul's teacher), since all sacrifices had ceased after the downfall, but this point is precisely the one in question (cf. chap. IV, §I.4). Cf. discussion by Albeck II:451.

9. It is, however, possible that it was at Jerusalem ("chosen place"), given the general policy of Gamaliel, to federate various currents; some parts of the sanctuary seem to have been restored after 70, cf. chap. IV, §I.4.

10. Term adapted from the Latin equivalent of τεσσαρεσκαιδεκατῖται.

A further problem arises from a confusion of terminology, in Latin and Greek and other languages, where Passover and Easter have the same name (though not in English, except for the adjective "paschal"). The Christian Easter, celebrating the resurrection on the night between Saturday and Sunday, does not appear to have much to do with the Jewish Passover on 14 Nisan. But it is to this latter that the Last Supper refers, even if, as we have seen, the narrative introduces foreign elements into a Passover setting, in order to reinterpret through them the unique event of Jesus' death. So, if the ancient sources give the same name ("Passover") to such different realities, a link must have been created, since the transfer of the name echoes a transfer of meaning, as we shall see (cf. §II.4).

2. *The Quartodecimans*

These communities, which the sources place in Asia Minor, have left a few traces in Christian writers, and indirectly in the rabbinic sources, but none, it seems, in the NT.

The paschal rite of the Quartodecimans can be reconstructed as follows.[11] It took place during the night of 14 to 15 Nisan, until three o'clock in the morning. During the Jewish celebration of Passover, the Quartodecimans kept a fast on behalf of their Jewish brethren who did not believe in Jesus; it was only then, around midnight, that the joyful feast began.[12] At the same time, the ritual was apparently the same, and included commentary on the Passover narrative of the deliverance from Egypt (Exod 12), insisting on the fact that the lamb designates Christ, as we find in Melito of Sardis' *Paschal Sermon*. In accordance with the Jewish expectation that the Messiah would come on the night of Passover,[13] they were hoping for the Parousia in the middle of the night, as at the Exodus.[14] The principal moment of the feast was then the *agapê* and the eucharist, which broke the fast. This synthesis does not clearly state whether these Christians did or did not observe the rite of the lamb, but closer attention to their fast "on behalf of their brethren who did not believe" gives the clue. This meaning of the fast is given by Epiphanius, *Pan.* 70.11.3, but it is not the real one. The paschal lamb was supposed to be eaten *before* midnight, which does not go with a Messianic feast *after*

11. Following the synthesis of Bernhard Lohse, *Das Passafest der Quartodecimaner* (Beiträge zur Förderung der Christlichen Theologie, 2/54), Gütersloh, Bertelsmann, 1953.
12. Cf. Epiphanius, *Pan.* 70.11.3.
13. Well attested by the *targum*, reflecting popular tradition, cf. below §II.2.
14. In *Ant.* 17 §29, FJ reports, without giving any reason, the custom at Passover of opening the Temple doors at midnight, as if to welcome some important visitor (cf. chap. II, §II,3).

midnight, and in any case, Jesus himself ordered the suspension of Passover.[15] The conclusion is simple: the fast was first and foremost an abstinence from the paschal lamb, so the suspension of the positive precept of eating; it is interesting that *MPes* 10:1 prescribes a brief fast, between the time of the evening sacrifice and the paschal meal. A possible practical reason for abstaining from the lamb is provided by Exod 12:48, which requires circumcision for sharing in the paschal lamb and sends us to the Pharisees' demand in Acts 15:5 that the Gentile converts be circumcised.[16] The final result, whether by design or not, is that the Christian Paschal Vigil on 14–15 Nisan is rather like the vigil leading to the first day of the week (cf. the episode of Troas). It was only later that this abstinence developed into a fast of major importance, *i.e.* into another positive precept.

Rabbinic traditions provide some useful information about the antiquity of the Quartodeciman rite. We have already seen (chap. V, §II.2) the prohibition of whitewashed walls, whose primary meaning (avoiding the possible reference *in Greek* to Christ or Messiah) was reinterpreted when it became a matter of leaving part of the whitewashing unfinished. Other decrees are to be found also "in memory of Jerusalem," which may well result from a similar transformation (*TSoṭa* 15:13 f.): "The man who provides what is necessary for the meal should leave a small portion, in memory of Jerusalem; the woman who adorns herself (with make-up)[17] should leave a small portion (*i.e.* not made-up), in memory of Jerusalem. For it is written (Ps 137:5-6), *If I forget Jerusalem, may my right hand be forgotten. May my tongue cleave to the roof of my mouth, if I lose thy memory* [. . .]."

To get the bearing of this measure, we have to enter once again into certain practical details. One particular opinion (Eliezer, around 100–120) has it that feminine make-up goes on the list of products which may contain yeast, and so have to be put aside at Passover time, or more exactly for the seven days of Unleavened Bread.[18] An associated explanation[19] speaks in this connection of depilatory treatment: with chalk for the poor, flour for the rich, and oil of myrrh for kings' daughters (cf. Esth

15. As various commentators allow, cf. in particular Étienne Trocmé, *The Passion as Liturgy*, London, 1983, p. 30.

16. Cf. chap. V, §II.2, on the Noachide prescriptions and the precepts formulated by James.

17. תכשיטין: it is not a question here of jewelry, but of make-up and other beauty care, cf. *Tosefta ki-fshuṭah* 8:774; in particular, *YPes* 3:1, p. 29d offers a variant with a similar meaning טפולי נשים "feminine treatments."

18. *MPes* 3:1.

19. *BPes* 42b, *baraita*.

2:12).[20] The substances mentioned are not fermented and appear naturally free from leaven; it could, however, be argued that, since flour belongs with those cereals that must be avoided during the days of Unleavened Bread, all similar beauty treatments are suspended by analogy. On the other hand, another passage shows that during the days of "lesser festivity," so here the days of Unleavened Bread after the day of Passover itself, a woman may use make-up (*MMQaṭ* 1:7). So the products in question are in fact free from leaven, as confirmed by another list of unguents for the face, fingernails and skin. In other words, the suppression of make-up and other beauty care for the day of Passover alone, and not for all the seven days of Unleavened Bread, must originally have had another motive. We note that the same term is used here, "paint," as for the whitewashed wall; if we take the comparison a little further, we realize that a made-up or painted face can also be understood in Greek as *christos* ("smeared"). There is no such ambiguity in Hebrew, and the problem obviously arises only on the day of Passover, or more exactly the day of "Preparation," the 14 Nisan. Once there is no longer a problem, the custom becomes that of leaving part of the face without make-up "in memory of Jerusalem," exactly as with the walls.

What is new here is that it is strictly a question of the day of Passover, and it is necessary to find a way of marking off Jews from Christians on a feast of major importance to both which is celebrated on 14 Nisan. The sign in dispute has to do with the hope expressed on this day: has the awaited Messiah arrived, or not? We can be sure that we have to do with Quartodecimans and their Jewish neighbors, who all understand Greek.

The text quoted above draws a parallel between the preparation of a meal and feminine make-up, with in both cases the obligation to leave the task unfinished "in memory of Jerusalem." We can go further and ask whether there may not have been a parallel transformation in the case of the meal. According to *MPes* 10:8, it is forbidden to finish the paschal meal with an *efiqoman*, deformation of a Greek expression meaning "To the revel!"[21] The clearest explanation is given in *YPes* 10:4, p. 37d: it is forbidden to go from one brotherhood *(ḥabura)*[22] to another to continue the festivities. Once this meaning had disappeared, secondary explanations arose, interpreting the *efiqoman* as dates, nuts, sweets,[23] etc.; or else,

20. This royal treatment is applied to Jesus by a woman, precisely in view of Passover and burial (death of the Messiah), at the anointing at Bethany (with myrrh, as all four evangelists agree, cf. Matt 26:7 par. and John 12:3). It is not certain that the final redactors have kept a clear perception of the Messianic reference, cf. below §V.1.

21. אפיקומן, transcription of ἐπὶ κῶμον.

22. On the brotherhoods, cf. chap. V, §I.1.

23. Cf. *TPes* 10:11, *BPes* 119b.

that at the end of the meal one must not eat things which would dissipate the taste of the lamb,[24] whence the conclusion that it is a question of an incomplete meal, without dessert. This interpretation cuts any link with the Greek and brings the custom back to the time when the lamb was actually eaten, *i.e.* before 70, according to a constant rabbinical method.

But if we come back to the first meaning of "feast," and recall that the paschal meal is to be over before midnight (*MZeb* 5:8), then the prohibition of passing from one brotherhood to another takes on the very clear meaning of not going to celebrate with those whose feast is after midnight. The usual explanation is to avoid any pagan worship, or Dionysiac orgy, but in that case, why is the prohibition strictly limited to the day of Passover and not permanent? Since the Quartodecimans began their *agapê* just after midnight, it is much simpler to see the original decree as forbidding going to the Christian feast next door. Further, the ritual contains an invitation to spend the whole night discussing the Exodus, whether from a political or strictly religious point of view (*TPes* 10:11), as we saw earlier on in connection with the five masters of Bene-Baraq and with Gamaliel II (chap. IV, §II.2); that would certainly have the effect of preventing any early departure for other brotherhoods. Finally, all these arrangements concern Judaea, and there is no question of a vicarious fast, but precisely of preventing deviants from celebrating both the properly paschal rite and the Messianic rite afterwards; this suggests that the Quartodecimans of Judaea practiced both.

Was, then, the suppression of the paschal lamb a voluntary act of abstinence, or simply the re-interpretation of a custom, current in the environment from which the disciples came, of not eating the paschal lamb? Our earlier conclusions on baptism and the eucharist (chap. II) were based on the fact that institutions and customs tend to remain stable, whereas the interpretations put on them can and do change. In connection with the Last Supper the disciples ask an odd question: "Where do you want us to prepare for *you* to eat the Passover?"[25] Then Jesus brings them to Jerusalem, where he celebrates the Passover before declaring it suspended. In this context, the Passover with the lamb appears associated with Jerusalem, but the disciples seem not to envisage it for themselves. In the gospel narrative, it is a domestic celebration, with no reference to crowds in the Temple, etc. In any case, it is a Passover in the "chosen

24. Which can be understood as a total abstinence; according to *BBabaB* 60b it is an abstinence from a certain dish of fish and flour (הרסנא), which suggests a mixture of bread and fish; for the later (present) tradition, the *efiqoman* is a piece of unleavened bread *(maṣa)*, put aside at the beginning of the meal, cf. §II.3.

25. Cf. chap. II, §II.3, with slight differences among the synoptics.

place." It does seem from these texts that the disciples had no custom of a domestic Passover *elsewhere*. From an historical point of view, it is not so easy to say definitely whether that was the usage of the disciples at the actual time of Jesus.

There are a few scattered references to the Passover outside Jerusalem. First the affair of the Elders of Bathyra (chap. III, §II.2) suggests that the Passover rite was established in a place distant from Jerusalem,[26] but that the Babylonian Hillel had no tradition of his own in the matter. Even more curious is the evidence of the Arab historian Al-Bīrūnī (11th cent.), already cited, whose sources informed him about what he calls the *Maġāriyya,*[27] or "cave dwellers." These are not troglodytes, but a Jewish sect known only from documents found in caves near Qumran about 800, and since lost.[28] Al-Bīrūnī speaks of their calendar of 364 days (that of *Jubilees*) and states, in reference to their Passover which always falls on a Wednesday that "they regard as necessary for Passover only those obligations and rites prescribed for those who live in the land of Israel." This would suggest that these people, who are of Essene type, perform the Passover rite outside the Temple,[29] which agrees well with the custom of Josephus' Essenes, who perform sacrifices,[30] but are prevented from doing so in the sanctuary, because of their own purification ritual. Such

26. Batanaea (Golan), where the colony of Bathyra was established, belongs to what the rabbinic sources call Jewish Syria, whose status is in many respects similar to that of the land of Israel, especially for the precepts tied to the land, cf. *MAbZ* 1:5 and *MShebi* 6:2.

27. Cf. Dominique Barthélemy, "Notes en marge de publications récentes sur les manuscrits de Qumrân," *RB* 59 (1952), p. 199–203.

28. Cf. Alexander Di Lella, *The Hebrew Text of Sirach. A Text-Critical and Historical Study* (Studies in Classical Literature, 1), The Hague, Mouton & Co., 1966, p. 78 f., on the relationship between certain texts of the Cairo *geniza* and those of Qumran. The chance discovery in the 8th cent. of ancient biblical texts (in particular Sir) in caves is not unrelated to the appearance of the Qaraites. In the 4th cent., Jerome had judged that similar discoveries were of no interest.

29. Besides, excavations of the site of Qumran have discovered a great quantity of unbroken bones of sheep and goats, buried in clay jars, but not burnt or simply thrown out. They cannot be from burnt offerings (holocausts), but could be left over from paschal meals, corresponding to pilgrimages made by the sectaries, cf. Jean-B. Humbert, "Espaces sacrés à Qumrân," *RB* 101 (1994), p. 161–214. On the community's worship, cf. below, §IV.1.

30. According to the mss. The Latin translation and a mediaeval *epitome* add a negative ("they do not perform sacrifices, for they are prevented, etc."), but this is a facilitating reading, cf. the discussion by Louis H. Feldman in the Loeb edition, *ad loc*. On the Therapeutae, who resemble the Essenes, Philo, *Quod omnis probus liber sit* §74, explains that their devotion does not consist in sacrifices, but in their will to sanctification; it would be wrong to conclude that they performed no sacrifices. Cf. Robert L. Webb, *John the Baptizer and Prophet. A Socio-Historical History* (JSNT, SS 62), Sheffield, JSOT Press, 1991, p. 116.

customs indicate that Passover commemorates not only the deliverance from Egypt, but also the entry into the Promised Land, provided one is actually there; that corresponds very exactly to Joshua's Passover at Gilgal (Josh 5:10 f.), when the manna ceased.[31]

From all these items of evidence, it emerges that, for the groups that interest us, the rite of the paschal lamb was not celebrated outside the land of Israel. In order to celebrate the rite within the land, however, it is not certain whether or not it was necessary to be at Jerusalem;[32] both tendencies may have existed side by side, depending on the particular group in question. Jesus' disciples, both at the beginning and later with the Jewish-Christians of Gamaliel's time, may have belonged to either camp; the Last Supper narrative would suggest that they habitually abstained outside Jerusalem, whereas the rabbinical evidence would tend to show that they ate the Passover in Judaea. In any case, the important point is that there was no question of eating the paschal lamb outside the country. Thus the "vicarious fast" of the Quartodecimans of Asia Minor takes on a precise meaning: at the moment when the Jews eat the Passover in Judaea (or celebrate a ritual without the lamb outside the country), their abstinence is not a new custom, created after Jesus' death, but the reinterpretation with a new motive of a venerable usage.

3. Passover and Easter at Rome?

The fast is a matter of prime importance. Eusebius (*Hist. eccl.* 5.23-24) reports a memorable controversy, around 191, occasioned by the paschal fast. The churches of Asia Minor had the custom of celebrating Easter on 14 Nisan, the day when the lamb was sacrificed, so they broke the fast then. But in all other churches, the fast continued until the day of the resurrection, the Sunday. The bishops in the first camp, led by Polycrates, bishop of Ephesus, defended this tradition as apostolic, with the authority of John and Philip, as well as that of Polycarp of Smyrna. The spokesman for the opposite camp, which was in the majority, was Victor, bishop of Rome, who had no argument to offer except that of authority;

31. The schema of Josh 5:10 f., with cessation of the manna in the desert, Passover and finally consumption of the produce of the land, corresponds also to the schema of John 6:49 f., with the manna, Jesus given as food (paschal lamb) and resurrection (kingdom); the eucharistic elements (consumption of the first fruits of the kingdom) complete this picture, and are still placed at the entry into the kingdom (Gilgal) and not at the final goal (Jerusalem).

32. The absence of the rite of the paschal lamb, certain outside the land of Israel, may also explain why the problem of the circumcision of Gentile converts (prescribed by Exod 12:48 for sharing in the Passover) disappeared: there was no head-on collision with an essential rite.

apparently, if Irenaeus had not intervened to calm things down, he would have excommunicated the others.[33] The Judaizing custom appears to have been solidly rooted, as we might expect, but at this time was restricted to a limited region. In any case, there can *a priori* have been no question of a paschal lamb in Asia Minor, outside the land of Israel.

However, certain complementary documents[34] give us a better idea of the origin of the other custom, represented by Victor. Paschal homilies of the time show that both Quartodecimans and Sunday observers had the same idea of the Christian Easter, as the feast of the salvation of the human race. So the difference was not ideological, or at least was no longer so. In his letter to Victor, cited in part by Eusebius, Irenaeus reminds him that at Rome, before pope Soter (167–174), "among others, the presbyters who presided over the church which you presently direct [. . .] *did not celebrate*[35] *[Easter]* and did not allow their faithful to celebrate it [. . .]. Nevertheless, they remained at peace with those who came from other churches where it was celebrated." Irenaeus also recalls that at the time of Polycarp's visit to Anicetus (around 100), they remained at peace, even though one celebrated Easter, and the other did not. Furthermore, Irenaeus' expression ("among others") shows that the usage of not celebrating Easter was in no way limited to Rome. This evidence has in-

33. Eusebius, who is favorable to oriental traditions, is doubtless tendentious, as later on he submits to the decisions of Nicaea, which fix a general usage opposed to the Quartodecimans (at least for the fast), cf. William L. Petersen, "Eusebius and the Paschal Controversy," in: Harold W. Attridge & Gohei Hata, *Eusebius, Christianity and Judaism* (SPB, 42), Leiden, Brill, 1992. Georg Kretschmar, "Christliche Passa im 2. Jahrhundert und die Ausbildung des christlichen Theologie," in: *Judéo-christianisme. Mélanges Jean Daniélou*, Paris, 1972, p. 287–323, reviews the discussions of the last 100 years.

34. Presented and commented by Marcel Richard, "La question pascale au IIe siècle," *L'Orient syrien* 6 (1961), p. 179–212.

35. The formulation is very concise, but the verb τηρεῖν here, especially without expressed complement, should be taken in a broad sense, attested among ancient Christian writers, and not in a strictly technical sense (in the manner of Acts 15:5 "observe the law of Moses"), which would be "observe the precept of the Passover" (*i.e.* on the Jewish date of 14 Nisan). In fact, a narrow sense could imply, supposing that Easter was necessarily celebrated, a Sunday usage (*i.e.* Easter on Sunday, and not on 14 Nisan), as shown by Christine Mohrmann, "Le conflit pascal au IIe s. Note philologique," *Vig. Chr.* 16 (1962), p. 154–171. If the difference of custom bore only on the date of Easter, and not on the fact of celebrating it or not, Irenaeus would have adopted a less roundabout way of speaking, or would not have mentioned it at all, since it was a question for him of convincing Victor by an argument *a fortiori* ("our venerable custom, common to us both, is in reality recent, so why do you object to another custom, different, it is true, but older?"), as shown by Karl Holl, "Ein Bruchstück aus einem bisher unbekannten Brief des Epiphanius," in: id., *Gesammelte Aufsätze für Kirchengeschichte*, Tübingen, 1928, II:204–224. Finally, for Irenaeus, the eucharistic offerings are essentially first fruits, *i.e.* remain attached to a symbolism originating in Pentecost, cf. chap. II, §II.5.

trigued commentators,[36] little inclined to allow a Christianity without Easter, but it goes perfectly well with the fact that in the synoptic gospels Jesus gives no command to repeat the *paschal* rite during the Last Supper, and even announces the contrary, the interruption of Passover with himself (cf. chap. II, §II.3). Furthermore, it is well known that Justin, who gives a very detailed picture of Christian life at Rome in his own time (around 150), never makes any kind of reference to Easter when he speaks of the eucharist and the Lord's day (*Apol. I* §65-67); in his description of the paschal lamb, during his debate with Tryphon, there is no hint of a parallel or analogous Christian custom.

The conclusion is obvious: the custom of observing Easter on the Sunday, defended by Victor, was a novelty, whereas the weekly Lord's day was universally observed and is well attested in the NT. For his part, Epiphanius, who came from Palestine and knew the country well, judged that church controversies on the date of Easter only began in 135, after the disappearance of the Jewish-Christian bishops of Jerusalem (*Pan.* 70.9 f.),[37] that is, after the disappearance of the group that kept alive the reference to the Jewish date of Passover. The Sunday Easter appeared between 135 and 167. In what circumstances, we do not know, but we have already seen that the Easter celebration of the Quartodecimans, at least after 100, had the same structure as the weekly Saturday-Sunday vigil, which could have facilitated a transfer. The process may also have been helped by the survival of a custom of keeping seven or eight days of Unleavened Bread, on which there had never been any geographical restriction.[38]

36. Cf. the references and discussions of S. G. Hall, "The Origins of Easter," in: *Studia Patristica XV, Part I* (TUGAL, 128), Berlin, Akademie-Verlag, 1984, p. 554–567; he takes up the discussion of the verb τηρεῖν, and concludes that originally at Rome as elsewhere the Quartodeciman Easter was celebrated, and that the Sunday usage only came in with Soter, who gave official approval to a controversial change of usage which was quasi-general (except in Asia Minor). There are objections to this view: 1. the explanations proposed for the introduction of the Sunday usage are complex; they might be persuasive in the case of establishment by act of authority, but not for a widespread practice which finally reached Rome; 2. to allow that τηρεῖν has here the technical sense of observing Passover in the Jewish manner implies also the rite of the paschal lamb, but we have seen that there is no trace of it among the Christians, at least outside Judaea; 3. the idea of an originally general Quartodeciman practice presupposes that the Jews everywhere celebrated the domestic Passover, both before and after the downfall of the Temple, but we have seen, both with the Last Supper (chap. II, §II.3), and with Hillel (chap. III, §II.1) that this is doubtful; we will show later that it was a controversial usage (§II.3).

37. Epiphanius appears to deform his source, the *Didascalia of the Apostles* 21.17.1, which does not speak of Jewish-Christians, but says clearly to celebrate Easter the same day as the Jews; in that case, the divisions mentioned are later than the Bar Kokhba disaster and the expulsion of the Jews from Judaea. Such a conclusion is not unlikely, given the difficulties of restoring the Jewish calendar after the disturbances of the war, cf. chap. IV, §II.2.

38. Here we can make a few remarks about the ecclesiastical traditions still in force

The total absence of any tradition regarding the paschal lamb at Rome does, however, raise a curious question, since Josephus, writing around 90 at Rome, gives two hints that the rite of the paschal lamb was still practiced. Retelling the story of the deliverance from Egypt following Exod 12:1-36, he speaks of sacrifices made by clans or groups of families,[39] of purification by blood and of a meal; he does not explicitly mention the paschal lamb, but he concludes (*Ant.* 2 §313): "Whence it comes that even today we sacrifice according to the custom." Further on (3 §248), he recalls what he has already said while explaining that these sacrifices made by clans are called "Passover," and continues to speak in the present, but without any reference to Joshua's Passover.[40] As so often, Josephus' language is imprecise, or more exactly he generally tries to place himself above all controversy; here, it is not clear whether he is speaking of the Passover at Jerusalem, in the setting of a more or less restored cult, or at Rome (or anywhere at all), which would bring him fairly close to Philo.[41]

---

regarding the eucharist. The oriental tradition is to use leavened bread *and* celebrate Easter only *after* the week of Unleavened Bread; whereas western Christians use unleavened bread *and* may celebrate Easter *during* the week of Unleavened Bread (as shown by Pope Victor; this corresponds to one possible meaning of the "day after the Sabbath" in Lev 23:11 f.). There is clearly a connection: with, or without, leavened bread. However, the oriental rite, which is to be attached to Antioch rather than to Caesarea or Jerusalem, may be secondary with respect to the calendar (why a special "Lord's Day" each year, without any significant link with Passover?). Even so, its usage regarding the eucharist must be regarded as primitive. For one thing, it is difficult to see how, if the eucharistic bread were intrinsically paschal (unleavened) in its origin, the orientals would have lost this sign, even for Easter Sunday itself. Conversely, it is easy to see how, if the bread did not originate in the Passover rite, it could have received an additional paschal symbolism in the west; since Easter Sunday is only one particular Lord's Day (commemorating the coming of the Messiah), this symbolism could be spontaneously (or at any rate naturally) extended to all eucharistic celebrations. It is significant that in his description of the eucharist, Justin, *Apol. I* §65, speaks of bread without any other specification, likewise Hippolytus, *Trad. apost.* §4. By contrast, these authors specify that the wine is mixed with water; the water, which was originally only added to make the wine more palatable, is *later* endowed with significance. In these circumstances, it is difficult to believe that a very significant paschal symbolism could have been omitted by these writers.

39. Of at least ten persons, according to *J.W.* 6 §423.

40. Which however he mentions (*Ant.* 5 §20 f.), but without any particular significance other than a simple accident of the calendar; so for him, Passover is only the commemoration of the departure from Egypt, and not the celebration of the entry into the Promised Land.

41. Philo, *Spec. leg.* 2 §146 is also imprecise, probably for similar reasons (he never refers to a legal controversy): he emphasizes (well before 70) that for the paschal sacrifice the whole people is a priest, as in the time of Moses; this could mean either "the whole people assembled," that is on pilgrimage, or each one at home, that is outside the "metropolitan area." Behind the ambiguity, there may be two concurrent customs, cf. §II.

There is a rabbinic tradition which throws light on Josephus' hesitation.[42] A certain Theodosius (or Theodore), at Rome, wanted to institute (or restore) the paschal lamb,[43] and they sent from Yavneh to tell him that, if he had been a less important person, he would have been excommunicated. As to why he was important, some say that he was a scholar, others that he possessed power which could be dangerous, so should not be too openly opposed. Both opinions suit Josephus quite well, in his position as a recognized writer and high-ranking imperial freedman, not to speak of his rivalry with the dynasty of Gamaliel.[44] The name of Theodosius ("gift of God"), is obviously not the same as Joseph, but it could be the translation of the Hebrew Mattathias (*mattat-yahu* "gift of YHWH"), which was precisely the name of Josephus' father (*Life* §3).[45] Whatever the truth of that, this initiative left no trace that can be identified, except perhaps for the rabbinic Passover *Seder*, which also focuses on the Exodus and may have been an indirect response to an initiative that was judged too hasty (cf. §II.3).

4. Easter Transferred

After a Greek hierarchy with no custom of celebrating Easter had been installed at Caesarea, the center of Roman administration since Coponius, it is at least possible that those Jewish-Christians in Judaea who joined forces with them after 135 exerted pressure to keep a tradition of paschal observance, which was then placed on the Sunday following Passover, so as not to give rise to any suspicion of Judaizing. One clear sign that this was so is the fast: its origin is connected with Passover (abstinence from the lamb), and the usage of fasting until Easter Sunday suggests a transfer of custom.[46] However, if such a novelty was able to get

42. *BPes* 53a-b. Theodosius (or Theodore) is transcribed תודוס or תודרוס.

43. A lamb roasted whole (גדי מקולס), that is with its inwards exposed to the fire, cf. *Tosefta kifshuṭah* 5:958 (on *TBeṣa* 2:15), and above §1.

44. To take in hand the restoration of the people, cf. chap. IV, §I.1.

45. The use of this sort of code is not rare in the rab. trad. (cf. the disciples of Jesus, chap. V, §III.1); the fact of giving a Greek, rather than a Hebrew name could also be significant (FJ wrote in Greek); finally, the name Mattathias lends itself to such a transfer, since it has a Greek equivalent, whereas Joseph does not.

46. Another sign that a custom has been transferred can be detected in the narrative of Peter's miraculous deliverance from prison (Acts 12:1-17), which was the original conclusion of the P Doc (*Les Actes* III:173). In the final redaction, in v. 4b, Herod (*i.e.* Agrippa I), who has imprisoned Peter, wants to put him on trial before the people after Passover; in v. 6, "when Herod was going to put him on trial, that night, Peter was sleeping between two soldiers [. . .]"; v. 12, set free by the miraculous opening of the doors, Peter goes in the middle of the night to Mary's house, where members of the community are gathered in prayer. These items clearly suggest a Messianic deliverance on Passover

established, travel as far as Rome, and maintain itself outside its original context, it must have had a natural *and traditional* meaning. In fact there was a weekly celebration of the resurrection on the first day, perhaps recalling Pentecost (itself a Sunday), as we saw in connection with the night at Troas, which fell on an ordinary Sunday (chap. I, §II.2).

These results do, however, come up against some difficulties. According to Eusebius, the Quartodecimans were only in Asia Minor, whereas the problems concerning make-up and the *efiqoman* are connected with Judaea, or perhaps Galilee. Again, during the crisis under pope Victor, both Easter customs under discussion differ only concerning the date of celebration but have the same meaning and apparently the same structure. One should notice the chronology, however: according to the passage quoted from Eusebius, the bishops of Palestine (Jerusalem-Aelia, Caesarea) followed the western custom[47] of celebrating Easter on the Sunday after 14 Nisan, but this is true only after the Bar Kokhba war,[48] at a time when the prohibitions mentioned above receive an interpretation "in memory of Jerusalem" which no longer has any connection with Chris-

---

night, and many commentators have noticed the various literary details recalling the Passover night of the Exodus (cf. *Les Actes* II:70 f.), but there is no reference to the lamb, and it does not seem to be Passover for everybody, as the king and "the Jews" are not celebrating a feast (cf. a similar disparity for the Last Supper, chap. II, §II.4). However, v. 3b situates the episode "during the days of Unleavened Bread" *before* Peter's arrest. Many explanations of this difficulty have been proposed, but it is evident that this redaction results in a vagueness of chronology, as if this night which resembles a paschal vigil were detached from the actual day of Passover (but without being clearly attached to the "Lord's Day," except indirectly insofar as there is a night watch at Mary's house); in any case, the whole episode takes place during, and not after, the week of Unleavened Bread, which agrees with the western custom noted above. A text from about 150, the *Epistle of the Apostles*, gives (§15, quoted by Raniero Cantalamessa, *La Pâque dans l'Église ancienne*, Berne, 1980, p. 31 f.), under the form of a prediction by Jesus, a very similar narrative in which Peter is set free during the night and joins the brethren in prayer, to celebrate with them the eucharist and *agapê*; it is explicitly identified as a "paschal" night (commemorating the resurrection), but without any identifiable link with the Passover itself.

47. After the war of 70, Judaea ceased to be attached to the province of Syria and was placed under more directly Roman control; in other words, Caesarea began to depend more on Rome than on Antioch. Christian influences always followed imperial organization, so it is not unlikely, especially towards the end of the 2nd cent., to find western customs in Palestine, as opposed to those coming from Antioch. The first elements of the Greek NT (of Pauline inspiration) arrived in Palestine before being absorbed by the Syriac world, cf. chap. V, §IV.2.

48. From what we have already seen, we can understand the opinion of Yehuda b. Ilai (in connection with the foundation of Usha after this same war, cf. chap. IV, §II.2), who declared around 150 that women may not use make-up during the *seven* days of Unleavened Bread (*MMQaṭ* 1:7): in fact, the Sunday following Passover can fall at any time during this week. This is a slight sign of the establishment of Easter Sunday a little after 135.

tianity or with Greek. These prohibitions, in their primitive form linked to the Greek language, are therefore earlier than this war, even if we cannot show that they go back to the beginnings of Christianity.

So there must have been several stages of development. 1. There were, certainly until 132, Quartodecimans in Judaea, culturally very close to the first Tannaites; some of them probably celebrated a Passover with the lamb, but all celebrated the Messiah after midnight. That agrees with what we have seen of the brotherhoods, both Jewish and Christian, and gives further support to Eusebius' list of the "bishops" of Jerusalem before 132, who are no more and no less than the guardians ("overseers") of brotherhoods under Trajan and Hadrian:[49] all are of Jewish origin and observant, which fills out Epiphanius' evidence. 2. The problem of differentiating clearly between Jews (belonging to brotherhoods) and Jewish-Christians (belonging to similar brotherhoods) arises after 90, at the time of the refounding of Yavneh under Gamaliel II, whence all the difficulties regarding the *minim*. 3. Later, after Gamaliel, Bar Kokhba's persecution of the (Jewish-) Christians of Judaea, mentioned by Justin, was a more vigorous prosecution of the same kind of operation as Paul's persecution of the first disciples (for holding back from militant Messianism). After the war and the banishment of Jews from Judaea, the local Christians abandoned their paschal celebration on 14 Nisan under the combined pressure of the Romans and of bishops of Greek origin, and transferred it to the following Sunday, but there was not the same pressure in Asia Minor. 4. The connection between Judaea and Asia Minor shown by the Quartodecimans throws new light on those surprising disciples at Ephesus who knew only John's baptism (Acts 19:1 f.), and on the fact that Apollos of Alexandria came precisely to Ephesus, capital of Asia Minor (cf. chap. VI, §III.1). 5. The Quartodecimans claimed the authority of John the Evangelist, and their special link with Judaea, at the time of Gamaliel II's reorganization, reinforces the suggestion already made (chap. V, §V.2), that John's vehemence against "the Jews" arises from this circumstance, that groups both close and yet hostile to Jesus' disciples were seeking to represent the people as a whole. By contrast, at the same time Josephus, solely preoccupied with imperial politics and opposed to all separatism, could be more conciliatory.

5. Conclusion on the Last Supper

This section has brought out some close contacts between Jews and Christians regarding Passover/Easter. The Jewish reorganization from the

49. The authenticity of this list is discussed in chap. V, §III.1.

time of Gamaliel II took very clear steps to keep the distance between them (in Judaea), but such steps only make sense if the Christians concerned had the same customs, and in particular if they were Quartodecimans. This, by the way, raises the question of the relation to the land of Israel: rabbinic tradition, as we have seen, attached very great importance to the precepts connected with the land, tithes, offerings, Sabbatical Year. On the Christian side, the most visible aspect of the NT is the universal expansion outwards from an empty tomb (the earth has yielded its fruit), but there are clear traces of some relationship to the land. Not only is the environment of Galilee rural, but Pentecost is the feast of first fruits of the (promised) land,[50] likewise the proclamation of the Jubilee Year is the metaphor by which Jesus proclaims the coming of the kingdom (year of remission, Luke 4:19 par).

These factors allow us to make a further remark on the synoptic narratives of the Last Supper, which owe very little to the Quartodecimans. We have seen that, whatever the calendar of reference, the Thursday of that week *was not* 14 Nisan: according to the reckoning in John, it was the evening of the 13th, and according to the calendar of *Jubilees*, in which the 14th of the first month is always a Tuesday, it was the evening of the 16th (cf. chap. II, §II.5). So there is a negation of the real celebration of Passover, which agrees with Irenaeus' evidence on the customs at Rome. Even more, beginning with Jesus' death, Passover is suppressed until the coming of the Kingdom: the rite has been supplanted by the reality. This arrangement has a territorial dimension. Jesus' Passover in Jerusalem, where all pilgrimages end, leads to his death and burial, which are expressed both by the anointing at Bethany and by the Last Supper. The Passover to come is attached to the New Jerusalem evoked by Rev 21:9 f. In the meantime, the earth has rendered its first fruits (empty tomb, resurrection), and there is an appointment to be kept in Galilee, which has become a metaphor for the nations. All this constitutes a profound revolution. Clearly, the gospel narratives, which devalue entirely any real celebration of Passover as such, represent the western tradition, and not the Quartodeciman custom, a further sign that the final redaction was late.

But all this represents a transformation of Messianic symbolism: the symbols are both forcefully affirmed, and at the same time denied. Simi-

50. According to the *Didachê*, §13, the first fruits are to be given to the prophets, since they are "our high priests" (ἀρχιερεῖς ὑμῶν). For Hippolytus, *Trad. apost.* §28, the bishop receives "the first fruits and the produce of the harvests," and there is a list of fruits to bless or not to bless. On the transfer of the biblical contributions for the priests to those in charge of the communities, cf. §IV.3.

larly, with Paul, Messianism, at first affirmed extremely energetically, changes completely from the moment when he realizes that the awaited Messiah is already here (resurrection, Spirit). This whole development can be regarded as a confiscation of Messianism, which we now need to look at from the viewpoint of Passover.

II – The Passover Ritual, Redemption and the Messiah

Passover is associated with the Exodus from Egypt and commemorates and actualizes a real liberation. The coming of the Messiah is associated with the establishment of a new realm and also has to do with a liberation, but one that is still the object of future hope. So it is not surprising that tradition has linked the Passover ritual, which remembers one successful liberation, with the hope for another. That is in any case the general pattern of prayer in the Bible, which always joins a request to God to the memory of similar benefits in the past.

Before we look at the Jewish traditions, let us take a brief look at the biblical data.

1. Passover in the Bible

The general label "Passover" in fact groups together several feasts which need to be distinguished, as we saw momentarily in connection with the Last Supper.[51] Philo makes this abundantly clear (*Spec. leg.*, 2 §145 f.). In pursuit of his idea of bringing the whole Law together under the Decalogue, he gives a list of ten feasts that develop the Sabbath precept, three of which are attached to Passover: 1. 14 Nisan, feast of the Fortunate Passage,[52] or Passover properly so called, for which the entire people is invested with the priestly dignity and offers sacrifices from midday to evening: the victims are readied for a ritual meal. 2. The feast of Unleavened Bread, which follows (15 Nisan) and lasts for seven days, the first and last being holy: during all this time the people eat unleavened

51. For a full critical discussion of the texts, cf. J. B. Segal, *The Hebrew Passover, From the Earliest Times to A.D. 70* (London Oriental Series, 12), London, Oxford University Press, 1963.

52. Τὰ διαβατήρια, elsewhere meaning sacrifices offered either to ask a god for a happy crossing, or to give thanks when it is made. In *Ant.* 1 §92, in connection with the sacrifice offered by Noah on leaving the ark (cf. Gen 8:20), FJ cites an Armenian tradition localizing the altar, which is called ἀποβατήριον; it is an attribute of Zeus, who "favors the disembarkation." Here, according to Philo's explanations, it is a question of a sacrifice at the moment of departure from Egypt, the commemoration of which is a thanksgiving. Like the LXX, he makes no link between the name of the feast of the "passage" and the "passing" of the destroying angel (Exod 12:11 f.).

bread, "a particular and unusual food," with several symbolic meanings. 3. In the course of this week-long feast falls another, the Sheaf, on the day following the first day of Unleavened Bread, so 16 Nisan: a sheaf of barley is presented as first fruits, "both of the country in which our nation has been able to live, and also of the whole earth." Josephus is less explicit (*Ant.* 3 §249), and describes the offering of the first sheaf on 16 Nisan according to the ritual prescribed for the oblation accompanying sacrifices in general (Lev 2:11 f.), in which he is followed also by the rabbinic tradition (*MMen* 10:4); the first fruits significance is thus reduced. Philo follows his source more closely, but emphasizes that the real first fruits feast is Pentecost, as we have seen (chap. II, §II.5).

These definitions are obviously inspired by the biblical data, but with some differences. Philo, although very attached to the custom of pilgrimages to Jerusalem for the feasts,[53] makes no reference to it in connection with Passover. He even says that on this occasion "each dwelling is invested with the dignity and majesty of a temple," although he has been insisting that the Temple has a monopoly of worship and that sacrifices in private houses are in general forbidden. So Passover constitutes a notable exception, when the lamb is immolated and eaten in every place. The meaning of this rite is strictly the commemoration of the deliverance from Egypt, without any echo of the entry into the Promised Land,[54] consistently with a celebration that can take place anywhere. Such a practice seems to be in disagreement with the precepts of Exod 12–13, to commemorate the deliverance from Egypt only after the entry into Canaan, corresponding exactly to Joshua's Passover.[55] For Philo, however, this entry has been accomplished once for all, since Jerusalem has been established as the metropolis, from which the nation can migrate in every direction; so it is logical to concentrate on the memorial of a departure, which he goes on to develop on the levels of history, geography and ethics.

Thus, Passover is not bound to the sanctuary. The same effect results from Lev 23:5 f. (and Num 28:16 f.), where the feasts of Passover and Unleavened Bread are clearly distinguished: "In the first month, on the

53. Cf. Philo, *Spec. leg.* 1 §68 f. In particular, pilgrimage consists in leaving one's *fatherland* in order to go to the *metropolis* (lit. "mother city"), cf. *Legat.* §281.

54. More generally, Philo entirely ignores the historical books (Josh, Judg, Sam, Kgs, Chr, Ezra-Neh), as well as the Prophets.

55. Strictly speaking, this territorial restriction applied only to the lamb, and not to eating unleavened food. Note that the chronological details regarding the night at Troas (cf. chap. I, §II.2) are given in relation to the season of Unleavened Bread, rather than to Passover itself.

14th of the month, Passover for YHWH; the 15th of this month, feast of Unleavened Bread for YHWH: for seven days you will eat without leaven." It is then specified that the first and last of these seven days (*i.e.* the 15th and 21st of the month) are special ("holy convocation"), and that sacrifices are to be offered throughout this time. According to these texts, Passover is entirely distinct from the feast of Unleavened Bread and the associated sacrifices. However, other passages establish more precise connections. First, Deut 16:1 f. indicates that the Passover is to be immolated at the "chosen place" and not elsewhere, and that "on it" unleavened bread is to be eaten for seven days. This double rite is immediately explained by the two phases of the deliverance from Egypt, the final meal, followed by a hasty departure, with only a bread "of deprivation" for food. The formulation is, however, ambiguous, and could be understood to mean either that unleavened bread must be eaten *after* Passover (as in Lev and Num above), or *with* the lamb. This second possibility corresponds to Moses' prescriptions at the moment of the Exodus, in which the seven days of Unleavened Bread are clearly associated with the Passover (Exod 12:18): "On the 14th of the month, in the evening, you will eat unleavened bread, until the 21st of the month, in the evening. During seven days [. . .]." Including both the 14th and the 21st would bring the tally to eight days, but by counting the days from evening to evening, the total comes to seven, since then the evening of the 14th is already the 15th. However, according to the same passage (v. 6), it is actually on the 14th at dusk "between the two evenings" that the lamb is to be immolated and eaten, which presupposes that the day is reckoned from morning to morning.[56]

These inconsistencies give rise to the vagueness of Josephus, according to whom the Unleavened Bread lasts seven days (*Ant.* 3 §249), or eight days (*Ant.* 2 §317). They presuppose a complex history of texts and institutions, which it is not the place to discuss.[57] Suffice it to say, that there has been a fusion of two distinct spring feasts, connected with the full moon.[58] The Passover, which requires circumcision and presupposes a pastoral life, is attached to a blood rite intended to ward off the Destroyer, whence a link with the tenth plague of Egypt (death of the firstborn). The seven days of Unleavened Bread are the rite of settled country

56. The two counts have left their traces in the NT (cf. chap. I, §II.2) and in the rab. trad. (cf. chap. III, §II.2).

57. Cf. discussions and references in John I. Durham, *Exodus* (Word Biblical Commentary, 3), p. 150.

58. That is on the "Sabbath," according to its primitive meaning, still perceptible in Deut 5:12 and 15, cf. *Search*, p. 95–100.

folk, in which the elimination of all yeast means eating the first produce of the new year without contamination from the remains of the old year, whence the idea of a very simple food,[59] associated with the memory of a hasty departure. It should be noted that the texts explicitly attach the deliverance from Egypt not to Passover but to the Unleavened Bread,[60] as we see again in the precept of the three pilgrimages in Exod 23:14 f. (Unleavened Bread, Harvest, Crops); the association with Passover is indirect and comes only from the combination of this feast with that of Unleavened Bread. This combination has some basis in the logic of biblical sacrifices. Thus Exod 23:18 prescribes, as a general rule, that no sacrifice should be offered "on" leavened loaves;[61] it is a question of the oblation associated with a sacrifice, consisting of unleavened loaves or cakes, as further developed in Lev 2:4 f. This rule holds good both for holocausts and for communion sacrifices consumed by the one making the offering; the paschal lamb and associated unleavened bread fall under this latter category.

The texts establish a link between the feasts of Passover and Unleavened Bread that is solid but at the same time flexible enough to allow for a number of variations: Passover can be celebrated everywhere (Lev, Num), or only in the Promised Land (Exod), or even only in the "chosen place" (Deut); if the details of Josiah's Passover are added (2 Chr 35:7 f.), the sanctuary and all its clergy are necessary.[62] But even in this case, Passover and the associated sacrifices commemorate only the *success* of the deliverance from Egypt, but not directly the arrival in the Promised Land, let alone in Jerusalem. The inauguration of the sanctuary is always attached to the full moon of the other equinox, the autumn feast of Tabernacles, or Tents, both in the time of Solomon (1 Kgs 8:2) and in that of Ezra (Neh 8:14);[63] in the eschatological vision of Zechariah, all the nations converge on Jerusalem in order to celebrate a feast of Tabernacles (Zech 14:16 f).

59. Cf. discussions and references in *Institutions* II:389 f.

60. Despite the difficulty of the duration of the seven days: Exod 12:15 f. clearly defines seven days without leaven, then explains the commemoration (v. 17): "For it is on *this* day that I brought your armies out of the land of Egypt." The hesitation between one day (the 14th or the 15th of the month, *i.e.* the full moon) and seven days (a week) coincides with the double signification of "Sabbath," either as the full moon or the week (from its last day); thus, commemoration of the Exodus is a Sabbath (at full moon), but also lasts a Sabbath (seven days).

61. Because of the context, it may sometimes be a question of the Passover sacrifice (TOnq), but the parallel passage of Exod 34:25 makes a clear distinction between the general principle and the particular case.

62. On the variations in interpretations of Passover, cf. chap. III, §II.2.

63. Cf. *Search*, p. 244–246.

The biblical elements which enable us to define a domestic rite fall into two categories: the meal, with paschal lamb, unleavened bread and bitter herbs (Exod 12:8), and the ritual gestures associated with the meal, which are the object of the questions that the children put to their parents. These questions do not deal with the past events themselves, but with the visible gestures and the meaning that they have for those who perform them; this is tradition, in the proper sense of the word, and not an historical inquiry. In Exod 12:21 f. blood of the slaughtered victim, gathered in a basin, is to be applied with a tuft of hyssop to the door frames and lintel;[64] the sons ask the meaning of this rite, and the reply tells of the sacrifice of the Passover and the "passage"[65] of YHWH, who "passes over" the houses so marked. Later rabbinic tradition, as we have seen, concentrates the explanations on the items of food prescribed, and not on the blood rite (cf. chap. II, §II.3). In Exod 13:5 f., the unleavened bread constitutes the memorial of the deliverance from Egypt; that is the explanation, given to the children, of this rite which is to be practiced on arrival in the Promised Land. In Exod 13:12 f., the redemption of the firstborn is laid down, without indicating a fixed occasion, and the explanation given to the son is that the deliverance from Egypt was an act of salvation, as YHWH killed all the firstborn. In these last two passages, it is said, "this will be for you a sign on your hand and a memorial between your eyes," a formula analogous to that on wearing phylacteries prescribed in Deut 6:8; the form of this sign is not very clear in the context, but by comparing it with the commentary on the blood rite of the Passover, it is easy to infer that it is a question of applying blood to the forehead and the hand, rather like an amulet.[66]

Finally, in Deut 6:21 f., when the son questions his father on the whole body of the laws and customs of Sinai, the reply bears on the totality of the liberation from Egypt and the entry into the promised land; no ritual occasion is indicated, but it seems to be a question of the Covenant, and not of Passover. In sum, to recall the Exodus from Egypt is an essential responsibility for the father, going beyond even the occasion of Passover; the dominant element in that feast is the saving blood rite, which has a fairly clear relationship with the redemption of the eldest son, who belongs to God. The underlying conclusion is that Passover

64. According to a rite still practiced by the Samaritans, cf. J. Lerner, *A Critical Investigation and Translation of the Special Liturgies of the Samaritans for their Passover*, unpublished Ph.D. dissertation of the University of Leeds, 1956.

65. There is a verbal play in Heb. between פסח "paschal lamb" and פסח "skip, omit, avoid"; the LXX renders the latter by ἐσκέπασεν "protected."

66. This is the prophylactic meaning developed in *Jub* 49:15. Cf. Ernst Bammel, *Das heilige Mahl im Glauben der Völker*, Gütersloh, 1956, p. 56. Cf. also §V.2.

celebrates in their own land the birth of Israel as the firstborn people, that is to say, it connects the memory of the origin of the people with their entry into the land.

This makes all the more remarkable the story of Esther and the feast of Purim, which renders impossible the celebration of Passover (cf. chap. III, §II.2).

2. Passover, Covenant and Blood

The traditional link between Passover and the last things is given classical expression by the poem of the four nights, attached by the targum[67] to Exod 12:42 ("It was a night of watching for YHWH"):

> *This is the night kept and fixed for deliverance in the name of YHWH when the children of Israel went out freed from the land of Egypt. Indeed, four nights have been written in the Book of Memorials.*
>
> *The first night was when YHWH revealed Himself to the world in order to create it. The world was waste and void and darkness was spread over the surface of the abyss* (Gen 1:2), *and the word of YHWH was the light and gave light* (cf. John 1:2). *It was called the first night.*
>
> *The second night was when YHWH revealed Himself to Abraham aged 100 years and Sara his wife aged 90 years* (Gen 17:17), *so that what Scripture said might be fulfilled [. . .]. And Isaac was 37 years when he was offered on the altar: the heavens came down and abased themselves* (cf. Gen 22:14) *and Isaac saw their perfections, and his eyes were darkened because of their perfections* (cf. Gen 27:1). *It was called the second night.*
>
> *The third night was when YHWH revealed Himself against the Egyptians in the middle of the night* (Exod 12:29; Wis 18:4 f.)*: His hand slew the firstborn of the Egyptians and His right hand protected the firstborn of Israel in order to fulfill what Scripture said: My firstborn son is Israel* (Exod 4:22). *It was called the third night.*
>
> *The fourth night will be when the world fulfills its end in order to be dissolved.*[68] *The yokes of iron will be broken and the generations of*

67. Translation from Roger le Déaut, *La nuit pascale. Essai sur la signification de la Pâque juive à partir du Targum d'Exode XII 42* (Analecta Biblica, 22), Rome, Pontifical Biblical Institute, 1963; in particular he insists on the fact that the Palestinian targums, being of more popular origin than the official Tannaitic collections, have often preserved more ancient traditions.

68. According to Jer 31[38]:8 LXX, the final (Messianic) gathering will take place *on the feast of Passover.*

> *impiety annihilated. And Moses will come out from the desert, and the king Messiah will come out from on high*[69] *[. . .].*
>
> *This is the night of Passover for the name of YHWH: night kept and fixed for the salvation of all the generations of Israel.*

The term "night" originates in the paschal celebration properly so called, which is recalled at the beginning and the end of the whole passage: in the midst of darkness or distress, liberation is revealed. This is the way to understand the second "night" which is not mentioned as such by the biblical texts. This night is in fact duplicated, since it comprises both Isaac's birth to childless parents and the way in which he survived the sacrifice. Behind the "night" is the recurrent idea of birth or new birth (salvation) in unforeseeable conditions. However, even with this interpretation, the second night does not appear to belong with the rest. The whole passage is really a bird's eye view of the entire history of the world, from Creation to the final salvation, when the Messiah as a second Moses will bring about a definitive deliverance from Egypt. Put like that, it would be enough to mention, between the beginning and the end, the major event of the Exodus commemorated by the Passover rite; that could symbolize everything, both the creation of the people and its salvation in all circumstances. Viewed in this way, the story of Isaac is only one particular case of salvation, exemplary no doubt, but of lesser interest for the rite.

In reality, the story of Isaac, which includes a miraculous birth and a no less miraculous rebirth, brings out another dimension of Passover, that of redemption or repurchase by a sacrifice. Certain details of the Hebrew text allow—but do not oblige—us to take it that Isaac was really sacrificed: in Gen 22:13, a textual difficulty could suggest that the ram was sacrificed *after* Isaac,[70] and in v. 19 Abraham comes back alone to the servants. This is the origin of all sorts of later explanations *(agada)* on the redemptive blood of Isaac,[71] on his carrying the wood for his sacrifice, on

69. Or "from Rome" (מרומא), that is, by a later verbal play, after Rome has been vanquished, in other words, after a definitive salvation, cf. *BSanh* 98b, interpreting Dan 7:13.

70. MT והנה איל אחר; depending on the vocalization, it may be either another ram, or a later ram, in other words, either a substitution (ram offered in place of Isaac) or a second sacrifice (Isaac immolated, then a ram offered next). The other witnesses (LXX, Sam, TYon, TNeof, etc.), which read אחד for אחר (TOnq combines the two), say unambiguously that the ram was offered in place of Isaac.

71. According to *Mid Gad Gn* 22:8, a quarter of a measure of blood was required for redemption; likewise, at Passover (cf. below §3) at least a quarter of a measure of wine is to be drunk (on the four cups, cf. *Tosefta kifshuṭah* 4:647 f). However, such a link between the wine and the redeeming blood is at most residual (cf. §3): for instance, 2 Chr 3:1 identifies Mount Moriah with the Temple, then tends to connect the sacrifice of Isaac with the Passover; similarly, according to *Jub* 17:15 f., Abraham arrives on the third day in the high

his death, on his resurrection, etc.; in any case, it is in this spirit that the targum says that Isaac saw the perfections of the heavens.[72] There is good ground for emphasizing in this way the relationship between the sacrifice of Isaac and Passover, for the feast is founded on the redemption of the firstborn: the deliverance from Egypt is the act of birth of Israel as the firstborn people. The profound difference is that in one case the people's salvation is paid for by the sacrifice of the firstborn, whereas in the other case the purchase price is an animal substituted for the firstborn (the paschal lamb).

Besides the final victory over the external forces of evil, symbolized by Egypt, this dimension of redemption introduces the reality of the people's own sin, and so their need of redemption. The Bible and associated traditions are at one in affirming that there is no expiation without blood.[73] That being so, it is not very daring to make a spontaneous comparison between Isaac and the Jesus of the gospels. At his baptism and transfiguration, Jesus is for the synoptics the "beloved son,"[74] just like Isaac; in John 1:36 he is called "lamb of God" in direct reference to Passover, thus introducing the idea of purchase by sacrifice. This is the same theme, since in this case the paschal lamb is identified with the sacrifice of the firstborn. Likewise, when Jesus says, "Abraham saw my day," the reference is certainly to redemption through Isaac's sacrifice (John 8:56). In this way Abraham, the father of the nation, is put in parallel with God, whence the importance in the Johannine context of the discussion about the true sons of Abraham. Even the rabbinic sources, despite their reservations about seeing the Passover as redemptive, may give unwitting confirmation of the comparisons just made:[75] according to *GenR* 56:3, Isaac

country (cf. Gen 22:2 LXX Γῆν ὑψηλήν), identified as Sion (18:23); on the contrary, Moriah is identified as Sinai in *BTaan* 16a, and the sacrifice of Isaac is then connected with the conclusion of the Covenant.

72. Shalom Spiegel, "Meʾagadot ha-ʿaqeda," in: *Alexander Marx Jubilee Volume*, New York, Jewish Theol. Sem. of America, 1950, p. 471–547, has made a very complete investigation into the rabbinic sources. He holds that the sacrifice of Isaac, with its dimension of sacrifice of the firstborn and its traditional links with Passover, retains traces of pre-biblical pagan cults, which nonetheless have left lasting imprints in the tradition (cf. *GenR* 55:5 on Mi 6:6 f.); similarly with developments on the redeeming blood of Isaac, with the legal minimum of a quarter of a measure, etc.

73. Cf. *BYoma* 5a, *BZeb* 6a, *BMen* 93b. Similarly the blood rites and the scapegoat on the Day of Atonement (Kippur, cf. Lev 16:15 f.), themes taken up by Heb 9:12 f.

74. Jesus is ἀλαπητός son; in the LXX, this term translates יחיד when it is an only son who has been put to death, cf. Roger le Déaut, "La présentation targumique du sacrifice d'Isaac et la sotériologie paulinienne," in: *Studiorum Paulinorum Congressus Internationalis Catholicus*, Roma, 1963, II:563–574.

75. They are weakened by the link established later between the sacrifice of Isaac and the New Year of 1 Tishri, cf. Israël Lévi, "Le sacrifice d'Isaac et la mort de Jésus," *REJ* 64 (1912), p. 161–184; cf. also Geza Vermes, *Scripture and Tradition in Judaism* (Studia

carries his cross on his shoulder (the instrument of his death, cf. Gen 22:6), a theme amply developed by the church fathers; likewise, according to *TSoṭa* 6:5, Ps 8 ("You have made him almost a god, you crown him with glory and splendor"), has Isaac's sacrifice in mind; again, *MekhRI* on Exod 12:13 explains that the blood of the paschal lamb is able to bring about redemption because it commemorates the sacrifice of Isaac, etc.[76]

It is not necessary to develop here this line of interpretation, which is simple and traditional. It is more important to ask what is the connection between Passover and the Covenant. It appears to be intrinsic, since only the circumcised (the mark of the Covenant) are allowed to eat the paschal lamb; furthermore, Jesus' Last Supper makes a clear connection between Passover and "the blood of the Covenant." However, in the fresco of the four nights there is no allusion to the Covenant, whether with Noah, with Abraham, or even with Moses.

The biblical texts make it abundantly clear that the deliverance from Egypt is the creative event from which emerges the people that becomes God's Covenant partner. The prototype of this affirmation is the prologue to the Ten Commandments: "I am YHWH your God who brought you out of the land of Egypt" (Exod 20:2). The formula used is that in which the high contracting party sets out his titles, and especially his past favors. These titles are structurally prior to the alliance about to be contracted, and serve as its motive. This enables a clear distinction to be made between the act by which the people comes to birth, the Exodus itself, and the Covenant, which presupposes an already existing partner as well as the past events that are recalled. Thus the Decalogue and the body of associated legislation correspond to a stage which is different from that of the Exodus properly speaking, namely that of the gift of the Law at Sinai. The Covenant strictly so called, whose stipulations are forthwith proclaimed, is sealed by a blood rite, which follows immediately (Exod 24:7 f.). There is thus a sort of treaty of vassalage between the people and its God; any breach of this contract is regarded as neglect of the divine benefits that are at its base, as expressed by Deut 6:12 (etc.): "Take care not to forget YHWH who brought you out of the land of Egypt."

Post-Biblica, 4), Leiden, Brill, 1961, p. 204 f., who explains also that the connection between this New Year's Day, on which the *shofar* (ram's horn) is sounded, and the ram in Gen 22 is secondary. Be that as it may, the ritual of this day invokes the merits acquired by this sacrifice, calls for God's reign, and commemorates the creation of the world; this puts together three of the four nights, which have therefore remained connected. The rabbinic paschal ritual no longer contains the commemoration of the "nights," cf. §3.

76. In the NT, the representation of Jesus as Isaac is superimposed on that of the suffering Servant of Isa 53 (Rom 4:25, etc.), cf. R. le Déaut, *La nuit pascale*, p. 204 f.

There is a formal proposition that declares the meaning of the Covenant at Sinai as it is about to be concluded (Exod 19:5 f.): "If you keep my Covenant, you will be my precious portion among all the peoples, since the whole earth belongs to me, and you will be for me a kingdom of priests." The outlook expressed is quite different from the passage about the four nights, which has nothing about the Law, Covenant, or election. The difference can be summed up in the notion of promise, emphasizing God's initiative; that is what characterizes the nights, which cover the whole of time and are commemorated by a rite. By contrast, the Covenant is a contract with legal stipulations, in which neither creation nor the last things play any appreciable role; time is real, a moment in ordinary human history, in which Israel is committed to playing a role of mediator.

Passover commemorates hope in the promise renewed in its various forms, whereas the feast *par excellence* of the Covenant is Pentecost, as we shall see (§III). The two phases are quite distinct, even though they are linked by the interweaving of the biblical texts: Passover presupposes circumcision, thus recalling the Covenant with Abraham, whose only stipulation was precisely circumcision (Gen 17:4);[77] Pentecost is connected with Passover, and indeed regarded as its close; both involve a sacrifice, with a blood rite. Finally, the same character, Moses, was both the guide that led the people out of Egypt and the one that made the Covenant on their behalf.

To carry these observations further, we need to give closer attention to the ties between Pentecost and Covenant. But before that, we have to look briefly at the rabbinic Passover, which we have mentioned several times already.

3. Passover in Rabbinic Judaism

The Passover celebration in rabbinic Judaism is a family meal during which a number of gestures are carried out according to a precise order, whence the name *Seder* ("order"). This *Seder* is entirely regulated and commented on by a narrative, or *haggada,*[78] that turns on the memory of the deliverance from Egypt. The principal elements of the rite are as follows:

a) At the beginning, the table is laid with the following items: loaves of unleavened bread *(maṣa)*, greenery (parsley, chervil or radish), salted

77. Although the precept has an associated sanction (banishment, cf. Gen 17:14), this covenant resembles rather a promise, as does that previously concluded between the divided animals (Gen 15:18).

78. The term is explicitly taken from Exod 13:8: "And you will tell (והגדת, LXX ἀναγγελεῖς) your sons on this day: 'It is because of what YHWH has done for me when I went out of Egypt.'" Cf. above §1.

water, bitter herbs, a brownish pastry (representing the bricks) and a bone served with roast meat (representing the lamb).

b) The diners, even if they are very poor, should be reclining on couches, as a sign of freedom; likewise, each should drink four cups of wine (*MPes* 10:1).

c) The ceremony begins with the *qiddush* for the day over the first cup; this is a series of blessings (over the wine and over the feast itself, with references to God's choice of His people).

d) After hands have been washed, the head of the family dips some parsley into the salted water, passes it round and eats it himself. Then he puts aside a piece of *maṣa*, called *efiqoman*, with which the meal will end, to the exclusion of any other festivity.[79] Traditionally, these two actions are meant to draw the children's attention.

e) Then follows a declaration in Aramaic about the bread of deprivation *(maṣa)*, accompanied by an invitation to anyone who is hungry, then a proclamation of the hope that next year the land of Israel will be freed (cf. below).

f) Next, the children ask why this night is different (bitter herbs, everyone reclining), and they are answered by recalling the Exodus, insisting on the fact that all generations have been under the domination of Pharaoh, but that today we celebrate liberation. Then four children, real or represented, each ask in their own way about the meaning of the rite; suitable replies are given, starting from the promises made to Abraham and continuing through various persecutions. It is recommended to speak as much as possible (and for as long as possible) on the deliverance from Egypt. The second cup covers the whole of this phase.

g) Then come blessings and rites over the unleavened bread, the bitter herbs, then over both together (in such a way as to evoke the third, missing, element, *i.e.* the lamb).

h) Next the meal properly so called is eaten, and closed by the third cup and the blessings over the food.

i) Finally, the recitation of the *Hallel* accompanies the fourth cup of wine.

From this analysis it is clear that, after the general arrangements (§a-b), the *seder* consists of two main parts, in each of which two cups of wine are taken. The first is dominated by story telling, and can be very long (§c–f), while in the other, which is more formal, small amounts of the prescribed foodstuffs are eaten, and then the festive meal. All the bib-

79. The *efiqoman* has already been interpreted (§I.2) as originally summoning to the feast in another brotherhood (perhaps Quartodeciman, after midnight).

lical passages on Passover are read, but it seems that the only phase clearly corresponding to the ritual in Exod is that of the unleavened bread and bitter herbs (§g). All the rest of the ritual is a development of a festive meal. Wine is obviously important, but its origin is purely festive, and not particularly biblical[80] or even Jewish.[81] The point has also been made long ago that the general shape of this meal, as well as a number of its detailed features, are parallel to Graeco-Roman banquets, and especially to the *symposium*, a term which, since Plato, has designated meetings of well-born people, who take a meal together then discuss serious questions over a jar of wine.[82] Naturally, the circles familiar with such customs were free, well-to-do and educated. A remarkable feature of the *Seder*, is that even the poorest are to enjoy all the marks of a banquet among free citizens (§b above); in particular, the guests are waited on by "deacons."[83] This festive banquet symbolizing freedom seems to have little in common with the paschal meal "eaten hastily, sandals on your feet, and staff in your hand" of Exod 12:11. The explanation given is that all generations were present when Israel went out from Egypt, and so every Passover is a day of liberation for the present generation.[84]

There is no paschal lamb in this *Seder*, but there are traces of it in the sketch given in the *Mishnah* (*Pes* 10:3). According to this source, the roasted lamb was brought from the Temple between the parsley dipped in salted water (§d above) and the children's questions (§f), but the declaration on the bread of deprivation and the invitation to the Passover (§e) are not mentioned. That the lamb appeared at this precise point gives a clearer understanding of the structure of the ritual, with its extension as a festive banquet. In fact, the two gestures that are supposed to arouse the

80. According to *TPes* 10:4, it is a precept (מצוה), on each pilgrimage, to give joy to the household with wine, as it is said (Ps 104:15): "And wine rejoices the heart of man." However, this definition is contested, which suggests that it is only a secondary explanation.

81. Cf. StrB 4:41 f., 1. Exkurs ("Das Passahmahl"); 4:611 f., 2. Exkurs ("Ein altjüdisches Gastmahl"). The *qiddush* properly speaking (*i.e.* the blessing for *this* feast day), is distinct from the ordinary blessing over the wine, said in first place (or in second, according to another opinion given in *MPes* 10:2, which underlines the independence of the two). Cf. also chap. II, §II.2.

82. Cf. S. Stein, "The Influence of Symposia Literature on the Literary Form of the Pesaḥ Haggadah," *JSJ* 8 (1957), p. 13–44; Plutarch, *Quaest. conviv.* 629C, 708D, explains that the *symposium* is a communion (κοινωνία) with speeches and actions; the institution is revered, since various later compilations of discussion topics and menus for these banquets refer constantly to Homer, Plato and Aristotle.

83. Or "servants," שמש, cf. *Tosefta kifshuṭah* 4:647; we have already come across this term chap. V, §IV.5; cf. also below §IV.3.

84. The same idea is expressed in *Jub* 49:13 f.: on the day of Passover, there is no tribulation for Israel.

children's attention are not primitive. The *efiqoman*, as we have seen, is introduced in order to provide a closure for the meal. The parsley dipped in salted water and passed round is a sort of appetizer at the beginning of the meal, but, by referring to the biblical ritual, we can easily make out the similar gesture which lies behind it: when the lamb was immolated, its blood was gathered in a basin, then, while it was being roasted, a tuft of hyssop was dipped in the blood which was thus applied to the door frame (Exod 12:22), and perhaps also to each guest, as we have seen, to be "a sign on the hand and a mark between the eyes" (13:16).

Whatever may be the case about this last detail, the statement in Aramaic is then in its right place, since it brings out, at the beginning of the rite, after the introductory blessing, the essential elements, namely the unleavened bread and the lamb. This declaration consists of three sentences:

1. *This is the bread of deprivation which our fathers ate in the land of Egypt.*

2. *Whoever is hungry, let him come and eat; whoever needs Passover, let him come and celebrate Passover.*

3. *This year here, next year in the land of Israel; this year slaves, next year free.*

These three propositions are independent, as is clear from the manuscript tradition, which sometimes omits one or other or changes the order. Further, the invitation to join the Passover, given at the time of the meal itself, contradicts *MZeb* 5:8, which specifies that the lamb is to be eaten only by those for whom it has been intended and immolated, which excludes last-minute invitations. Finally, the wish for return from exile is late, as it cannot have been expressed at the time when the rite of the lamb was being performed in reality in Jerusalem. The generally accepted conclusion is that the passage as a whole is composed of insertions made no earlier than the Talmudic period.[85] This may be regarded as certain for the final wish,[86] all the more so as it omits the festive dimension of Passover as a celebration of liberation. The other two statements directly introduce a simple meal of unleavened bread and lamb, without any note of festivity, even wine,[87] but after an appetizer derived from the bitter herbs. Although solemn, they are recited in Aramaic, whereas the ritual language

85. Cf. Daniel Goldschmidt, *The Passover Haggadah. Its Sources and History*, Jerusalem, Bialik Institute, 1977[3], p. 8 and 117. But this point has always been disputed, cf. Menahem Kasher, *Haggada shelema*, Jerusalem, ToraShelema, 1967, p. 110 f.

86. All the more as it is drawn up in typically Talmudic language, in which Heb and Aram are mixed: השתא הכא, לשנה הבאה בארעא דישראל. השתא עבדי, לשנה הבאה בני חורין.

87. According to *BPes* 109a, for rejoicing the wine has taken the place of the meat consumed in the sanctuary, cf. chap. II, §II.3.

of the Tannaites was Hebrew, except for what had come down from an earlier period. This confirms the conclusion that these declarations are left over from an earlier ritual that included the lamb.[88]

As for the last-minute invitation, several different cases can be distinguished. The passage quoted that makes such an invitation impossible, concerns the Passover at the sanctuary, where it would be normal to impose some order on the enormous crowd of pilgrims, especially since, for Exod 12:3 f., each lamb and those who are to eat it are to be defined on 10 Nisan. But *MPes* 4:4 underlines a diversity of customs, explaining that in the land of Israel there were places where roast meat was eaten for Passover, and others where it was not, and that these customs were not to be changed. In other words, the usage of eating the paschal lamb outside Jerusalem existed,[89] as we have seen in connection with Hillel (chap. III, §II.1). This being so, it seems that the declarations concerning the unleavened bread and the lamb were made by the head of the family addressing his household, and in particular his children, and inviting the needy right up to the last moment.[90] It may even be that the invitation to join the meal, extended to all who are hungry, had no intrinsic link with Passover or with a pilgrimage, as it is well suited to a household head keeping open table on feast days or even every day.[91]

So beneath the Passover *Seder* which has become a banquet, it is possible to reconstruct a domestic rite of a meal that is both festive (exceptional) and simple, with bitter herbs, unleavened bread and the lamb, and very probably without wine. The disappearance of the lamb from the rite can then be better envisaged in a definite context. We have already seen (§I.1) Gamaliel II ordering the lamb to be prepared without using spits in the form of a cross. Since it was he who came across the problem of the *minim* in his work of reorganization, we can conclude that the lamb was suppressed in these circumstances and replaced by a dish of cooked meat,[92] even though at the time, before 135, Jews still had access to Jeru-

88. This was already the opinion, though based on different arguments, of Leopold Zunz, *Die gottesdienstlichen Vorträge der Juden, historisch entwickelt*, Frankfurt a/M, 1832; Heb. trad. edited and commented by Hanoch Albeck, Jerusalem, 1974^3, p. 4 and 227.

89. That is contrary to the express stipulations of Deut 16:1 f., which raises interesting questions.

90. In a more sectarian outlook, such a practice may boast of a good reference, since Deut 16:2 f. specifies only that the animal (which may be either from sheep or goats or from cattle) is to be set aside in advance for a definite group, but insists on the "place that YHWH will choose."

91. Certain masters practiced this custom before every meal, with a very similar formula of invitation, cf. *BTaan* 20b.

92. Or eventually two (תבשילין), replacing both the lamb *and* the sacrifice prescribed for every pilgrimage, cf. *MPes* 10:4.

salem and some official worship had been re-established there (chap. IV, §I.4). It is thus possible to understand why the suppression has lasted until now, even when Jerusalem became accessible once more, whereas the Samaritans have never lost sight of the rite at Garizim, with or without a sanctuary.

The development of the *Seder* into a banquet of free citizens would have been the result not of a spontaneous development, but of authoritative steps taken by governing circles which were well organized and empowered to fix usages, although that does not prevent them from having preserved certain exegetical customs connected with earlier or dissident customs. Some passages of the *haggada* are certainly later than 135, but, if we had to identify a strong personality behind these innovations, the name and authority of Gamaliel II would come spontaneously to mind, at least as the initiator, since he was known to be close to the Romans and to cultivate Greek (*TSoṭa* 15:8). Perhaps even Theodosius, with his paschal lamb at Rome, may have played a part, especially if he was in fact Josephus, the distinguished Roman freedman (cf. §I.3 above). In any case, the *Seder* has lasted to the present day in its Tannaitic form, which dates essentially from between 150 and 200, or later for certain details.[93] The reference point for the rite and its commentaries has remained Galilee, even though it has spread, along with the *Mishnah*, beyond the land of Israel,[94] beginning with Babylonia. Clearly, the later spread of the rite and the absence of the paschal lamb reinforced one another. Equally clearly, this whole process is far removed from the views of Philo on voluntary migrations from the metropolis in order to spread the law of Moses.

Now that we have briefly located the ritual aspects,[95] we need to come back to their significance, especially by comparison with the passage from the targum on the four nights (§2 above). It can be seen immediately that the Messianic dimension of the *Seder* is transformed. The theme of the Exodus is central and certainly remains the model of the hoped-for liberation, as expressed by the Aramaic declaration of the wish for return to the land of Israel. It is not a question of the end of time or the last judgment, but of the re-establishment of an order on earth. Furthermore, there is only one brief Messianic allusion in the *haggada*, to

93. According to *BPes* 116a, its formulation was still discussed in Babylonia by Rab and Shmuel (first half of the 3rd cent.).

94. And the feast of Purim, which ignores the deliverance from Egypt, has not been re-elevated, cf. chap. III, §II.2.

95. The ritual associated with elimination of fermented products retains a trace of counting days from morning to morning (biblical calendar of *Jubilees*), cf. chap. III, §II.2.

suggest that even in the days of the Messiah, the deliverance from Egypt at night will be recalled. This passage has already been discussed (chap. V, §IV.3); in fact it comes from the *Mishnah*, and deals only with the reminder of the Exodus in the recitation of the *Shemaᶜ Israël* each evening, even in exile. Its introduction into the *haggada* is the only positive indication of a connection between the celebration of Passover and the coming of the Messiah during the night, perhaps also with the associated idea of celebrating the *Seder* even in exile. However, this indication is scarcely perceptible and would be almost unintelligible without the help of the texts seen earlier, all the more since the memorial of Isaac's sacrifice, the creation and the end of the world are attached in the rabbinic tradition to the first day of the year on 1 Tishri (cf. below §III.1).

It is difficult to escape the conclusion that the Tannaitic Passover has reduced to a minimum the eschatological significance, and in particular any Messianic implications.[96] Further, the hope of a return is attached to a promise,[97] and not to the Covenant properly so called.

4. Conclusion on the Last Supper

Whereas the targumic text of the four nights has shown a number of points of comparison with the NT, study of the rabbinic *Seder* and its meaning has provided hardly any. It is difficult to see how such a clear result could have come about by chance. In any case, it goes well with the complete absence, in the NT and the early Fathers, of any allusion to a properly paschal custom, outside the very special case of the Quartodecimans, certainly connected with Judaea and the crisis of the *minim*.

Study of the Messianic dimension of the night of Passover has allowed us to clarify the distinction between Passover and Covenant, with its feast at Pentecost. The former, which continues until the end of the world (cf. the fourth night), develops the symbolic dimension of salvation or redemption brought about by the sacrifice of the paschal lamb, on which the sacrifice of Isaac is superimposed. The latter, closely linked with the course of ordinary time, brings the Law into play and is concluded by a sacrifice of another sort. So there are two distinct blood rites.

In Jesus' Last Supper the two sacrifices and rites are overlaid by the death of Jesus, who himself becomes the paschal lamb, not without reference to the sacrifice of Isaac, and also presents himself as the sacrifice

96. We have already seen the parallel mistrust shown with regard to both Messianisms (chap. IV, §II.2 and V, §IV.1).

97. *YPes* 3:7, p. 21b, says that the Israelites in Egypt had only two works (laws fulfilled): the blood of the Passover and that of circumcision. So their merit was not great.

of the Covenant. But the two are not perfectly equal, as Passover is suspended, while the rite of the Covenant is promoted. In terms of the categories mentioned above, the cycle of promise has been fulfilled, which corresponds to the completion of Passover, that is to a realized eschatology: it is no longer a rite, but a reality, which has as such no further reason to be attached to the memorial of the departure from Egypt (as B. Zoma wanted, cf. chap. V, §IV.3). At the same time, the Covenant is renewed, which corresponds to the simple fact of experience that the history of the world is not over and there are things still at stake: evil is reborn in every generation, the ultimate reality still lies in the future but is anticipated by rites that are both self-contained and repeatable.

We saw earlier (chap. II, §II.5) that this renewal of the Covenant, with the signs of bread and wine in the form of first fruits, should be attached to Pentecost, which is indeed the feast of first fruits but is not intrinsically connected with the Covenant except by the calendar.[98] A simple relationship between the two can, however, be seen from an eschatological point of view. We thus come back by another way to the twofold dimension of the eucharist. As substitute for the Passover, it signifies that the ultimate kingdom has come, in the form of first fruits, with the note of new creation. But also, as after the deliverance from Egypt, the eucharist has a dimension of Covenant sacrifice, expressed in connection with the wine, but also perceptible in the gesture of "breaking" the bread. The symbolism points to an Israel renewed and fulfilled. Thus are found combined the two classic meanings of the "new Covenant." For the Essenes and their like, it was a renewal of the traditional Covenant, passing by way of Abraham and Moses. For Jer 31:31, it was something new that would appear in the last times to replace the "old Covenant." The two are fused through the eschatological dimension of Christ's resurrection.

III – Pentecost

Despite being classed with the other two pilgrimage feasts, Pentecost does not appear to have as much substance to it as Passover and Tabernacles. In his vision of the future Temple, in which the Zadokite priests are promoted at the expense of the Levites, Ezek 45:17-20 foresees a complete ritual in which, however, Pentecost does not feature. Evidently, it is not a feast with an eschatological dimension. According to the biblical data, it is dependent on Passover, as its name implies; it lasts

98. No firm conclusions can be drawn from the available data on the ancient triennial cycle of synagogue readings of the Pentateuch (known as Palestinian), which emphasizes the link between Pentecost and the Covenant, cf. chap. II, §II.5.

only one day and is not the occasion of special food laws.[99] Finally, the gift of the Law at Sinai is not closely attached to Pentecost. According to Exod 19:1, the Israelites arrived in the Wilderness of Sinai in the third month after leaving Egypt; whatever the calculation used in relation to Passover, Pentecost does indeed fall in this month (Sivan), but that does not necessarily mean that this feast coincides with Moses' ascent on to the mountain. In other words, the enormous importance of Pentecost in the Essene texts and in Acts 2 should be regarded *a priori* as an anomaly, or at least as an unexpected development. We will begin by examining the rabbinic tradition, for which Pentecost remains or has once more become a secondary feast.

1. The Rabbinic Pentecost

There is first of all a question about the date. Lev 23:15 f. defines the day of Pentecost, or feast of Weeks, from the offering of the sheaf of first fruits of barley that follows the *Sabbath* of the Passover: "You will count for yourselves, from the morrow of the *Sabbath*, that is from the day of the rite of presentation of the sheaf, seven *Sabbaths* (LXX "weeks"); they will be whole; so until the morrow of the seventh *Sabbath* (LXX "week"), you will count fifty days [. . .]." This passage contains several ambiguities, connected with the term "Sabbath." First, the "Sabbath of the Passover" may designate either the Saturday that has to fall within the seven days of Unleavened Bread, or the first of those days, 15 Nisan following Passover, which is a full moon, corresponding to the earlier meaning of "Sabbath" in the Bible.[100] Later, "Sabbath" can also mean a week, as understood by the LXX in the passage just quoted, the question being whether it is a "whole" week, running from Sunday to Saturday, or any period of seven consecutive days. Every possible answer has been given to these questions. The rabbinic tradition, as well as Philo and Josephus, understand the Sabbath preceding the sheaf offering as 15 Nisan (full moon);[101] only the "Boethusians" hold to the Saturday, and put the sheaf offering on the following Sunday.[102] The rabbinic tradition begins the

99. Cf. Bilha Halperin, "The Various Meanings of the Feast of the Weeks," *Beit Mikra* 136 (1993), p. 51–62. The later custom is to consume dairy products.

100. Cf. André Lemaire, "Le sabbat à l'époque royale israélite," *RB* 80 (1973), p. 161–185.

101. Cf. Philo, *Spec.leg.* 2 §162; *Ant.* 3 §250; *BMen* 65a.

102. Cf. *MMen* 10:3. Some have tried to attach these Boethusians, not to the priest Boethus, but to the Essenes (ביתוסים, corrected to בית איסים), cf. Yaakov Sussman, "The History of Halakha and the Dead Sea Scrolls," *Tarbiz* 59 (1989), p. 11–76. They are attached to the Zadokites by *AbRN* 5:2, which points in the same direction.

counting of the weeks on 16 Nisan, which leads to the fixed date of 6 (or 7) Sivan.[103] The other parties, especially the Essenes,[104] seem to hold to the more natural meaning of whole weeks, beginning on a Sunday "from the morrow of the Sabbath," whatever the meaning assigned to "Sabbath" in the expression under discussion; from this it results that Pentecost has to fall on a Sunday. However, at the time of Josephus, the question must have been debated, since he uses a prudent formulation (*Ant.* 3 §252). Rather than say simply fifty days after the presentation of the sheaf, of which he has been speaking, he stays close to his source and is careful to mention just before: "The seventh week after these offerings having elapsed." It is not clear whether this calculation begins on 16 Nisan or on the following Sunday. By means of this ambiguous expression, Josephus puts himself above any disagreements, as he often does;[105] it could well be that he is being tactful with the forerunners of the rabbinic tradition,[106] probably Pharisees. However, when he is not thinking of the need to smooth over controversies, he gives himself away. Thus, in *Ant.* 13 §252, commenting on a narrative of Nicolaus of Damascus on the immobilization of John Hyrcanus' troops for two consecutive days in time of war, he explains spontaneously that one characteristic of Pentecost is that it is celebrated on the day after Sabbath, resulting in two consecutive days of rest each year.

Unlike the other feasts, Pentecost has no tractate devoted to it in the rabbinic tradition, whether in the *Mishnah*, or any other Tannaitic collection, although certain features of the feast are mentioned by the way here or there. There is only a tractate on the first fruits *(Bikkurim)*, which makes use of various biblical data. According to Exod 23:19 the first fruits of all the produce of the earth are to be brought to the sanctuary, but *MBik* 1:3 restricts the obligation to seven kinds that characterize the Promised Land according to Deut 8:8: wheat, barley, grapes, figs, pomegranates, olive oil and date juice, in that order. It is a question only of crops harvested in the land of Israel, and the most devout make the pilgrimage each time that they are in a position to bring the first fruits of a kind, whereas others make the offerings when they come on pilgrimage for Pentecost or Tabernacles, which are the terms fixed by *MBik* 1:10 for the times of first fruits (from Exod 23:16). These first fruits are presented in a basket, decorated with the other (non-prescribed) kinds. When the

103. Cf. references in Moore II:48.

104. On the calendar of *Jubilees*, cf. chap. I, §I.2b.

105. Cf. *Ant.* 4 §81, 98, 213, 227, etc.

106. On the rivalry between FJ and Gamaliel II's enterprise at Yavneh, cf. chap. IV, §I.1.

first fruits have been brought in this way, the declaration of Deut 26:3-11 ("My father was a wandering[107] Aramaean, etc.") is made before the priest who receives them. It is noteworthy that the first fruits of wheat and grapes are brought as such, like the other kinds, and not in the form of bread and wine.

The intrinsic link between these rites and Pentecost thus appears very weak, since, according to Lev 23:17 f. it is necessary to bring for this feast, wherever one lives, two loaves made of the newly harvested wheat. However, Pentecost does indeed bear the name "day of first fruits," according to Num 28:26. So the biblical data appear inconsistent and result from the fusion of several traditions. Philo gets out of the difficulty by speaking of two distinct feasts: Pentecost proper, which is the *public* feast *par excellence* of first fruits and lasts one day,[108] and a feast of the Basket, private and less definite, lasting six months from the beginning of summer to the end of autumn, the period during which all the cultivated kinds come to maturity (*Spec. Leg.* 2 §215 f.).

The biblical Pentecost has in fact a complex position, which is both rural and linked with Passover. In the agrarian sphere, it is at the crossroads of several traditions connected with the rhythm of the crops. It is identified in Exod 23:16 as the "feast of the Harvest," that is the first fruits of the fields, but there is also a "feast of the Crops." In this way, there is one day celebrating the beginning of the first fruits, and a corresponding feast at the end of the harvest period. This system is distinct from the celebration of the first fruits of each kind, the most singular case being barley, the first sheaf of which is to be offered on the "morrow of the Sabbath" of the Passover, that is exactly seven weeks *before* Pentecost.[109] Deut 16:8 expresses it very generally ("from the day on which the sickle is put to the harvest, you will count seven weeks"). The idea that the first sheaf, or even perhaps an unleavened loaf of *barley*, should serve as global first fruits freeing for ordinary consumption the whole of the subsequent harvests, underlies the Passover at Gilgal. After that the manna ceased, and the Israelites began to eat the produce of Canaan (Josh

107. This also seems to be the understanding of FJ (*Ant.* 4 §242), but not of the LXX (cf. *BA* 5:276). The rab. trad. (Passover *Haggada*) and the Vulgate understand: "An Aramaean wanted to kill my father [. . .]," which is grammatically possible, cf. François Dreyfus, "L'actualisation de Dt 26,5," in: *Mélanges Henri Cazelles*, Paris, Desclée, 1981, p. 147–161.

108. Like FJ, Philo speaks of only one day of Pentecost, contrary to *MMoedQ* 3:4 (with *MḤag* 2:4), which states that at the time of the Temple the pilgrimage sacrifice could be presented during seven days.

109. Whence a problem of first fruits *before* Pentecost, with controversies attesting divergent customs, cf. *Tosefta kifshuṭah* 2:823 f.

5:11 f.).[110] It was also (edible) barley that Ruth gleaned in the field of Boaz (Ruth 1:22).[111] So already two concepts meet in the celebration of first fruits, to which can be added a third, with the two loaves of Lev 23:17 f. presented at Pentecost: there it is a matter of wheat *prepared* as cooked human food.

Up to this point, Pentecost is associated only with the recurrent rhythm of the solar seasons, but its chronological relation to Passover opens the door to other, more historical, considerations. As we have seen (§II.1), there is no intrinsic link in the Bible between Passover properly so called, the memorial of the deliverance from Egypt, and the more agrarian elements, such as the unleavened bread and the first sheaf. The agrarian aspects of Pentecost are clear in the Bible, but there is no decisive indication that it is also the memorial of a major event in the history of Israel, beyond the fact that the Israelites arrived at Sinai in the third month. As a result, the historicization of Pentecost, in relation to the Exodus, can take two directions, both of which are well attested: it can become a feast of the Covenant, of the gift of the Law at Sinai, which is quite distinct from Passover (cf. above §II.2), or it can be simply a completion of Passover.

The rabbinic literature emphasizes this second option, but it includes some traces of the first. In Lev 23:36, the seven days of the feast of Tabernacles are completed by an eighth, called "feast of closure."[112] Similarly, Pentecost is called "feast of closure,"[113] as if it came after seven days of Passover. The expression is also attested by Josephus, who does no more than mention the biblical sacrifices and offerings (*Ant.* 3 §252 f.), without giving them any particular historical significance. However, this "closure" comes after an interval of some seven weeks, a quite exceptional period which is particularly emphasized by the rabbinic tradition. During this time, the count is to be made daily, without interrup-

110. That is the interpretation given to the first sheaf by FJ, who states that only a handful of grilled barley grains is offered on the altar, the rest being left for the priests (*Ant.* 3 §251), which implies that they ate it. *MMen* 10:5-6, closer to Lev 23:14, says that this offering liberates the *consumption* of the year's produce, even if that produce was harvested and prepared beforehand.

111. Also the *targum* concludes that Ruth and Naomi arrived on the day of Passover, eve of the first fruits sheaf. However, in connection with Judg 7:13 (story of Gideon), FJ, forgetting the first sheaf, declares that a barley loaf is too coarse for human consumption (*Ant.* 5 §219), which is also the opinion of the rab. trad.: according to *BSoṭa* 9a, barley is animal fodder. Over time there may well have been a change in food customs.

112. The term עצרת includes the idea of stopping. The LXX renders ἐξόδιον "outcome, exit" (similarly in Num 29:35 and Deut 16:8).

113. Despite Deut 16:8's definition of the seventh day of Unleavened Bread as "closure" (עצרת).

tion, of the number of days and weeks, as suggested by Lev 23:15 ("You will count *for yourselves*"). Certain attitudes of mourning, so of abstinence, are maintained, and in particular marriages may not be solemnized, though no clear reason is given for this custom (cf. *BYeb* 62b). There is, however, a festive day in the middle of this period, in which the prohibitions are relaxed, the 33rd day after the sheaf offering, which is also the 49th day of the liturgical year beginning on 1 Nisan. There is no identifiable link between these non-biblical usages and the emergence of Christianity.[114] They seem rather to be importations from Babylonia, related to the affirmation of the weekly Sabbath against the lunar Sabbath:[115] since the calendar of reference is lunar, with veneration of each new moon, it is important to keep signs emphasizing that the cult is not lunar,[116] whence the number 7, whose square, or perfection, is 49.[117]

This ritual creates a solid link between Pentecost and Passover. On the other hand, a fairly late passage (about 250) mentions as self-evident that Pentecost commemorates the gift of the Law at Sinai. A Tannaitic commentary[118] details the chronology of the arrival at Sinai, following the information in Exod 19:1-11: the Israelites arrived on 1 Sivan, Moses went up on to the mountain on the 2nd and came down again, God spoke to him on the 3rd and the 4th, and said that He would reveal Himself on the day after the morrow, so the 6th. The targum gives the same count[119] for the revelation proper, and continues by putting the Covenant sacrifice (Exod 24:1-11) on the 7th, which amounts to dividing the gift of the Law from the Covenant. The implicit result is that Pentecost, which is not named, cannot commemorate both on the same day. The commentary cited leads to a similar result, but by reversing the sequence. To the question, what Moses may have been doing on the 5th, the answer is given that on this day he performed the Covenant sacrifice, after reading the Pentateuch up to the arrival at Sinai, and especially the commandments given to Adam, Noah, the patriarchs, and even to himself until the

114. But there is some similarity with the pre-Easter season of Lent (fasting, marriages celebrated less solemnly), whose definition wavers between a period of 40 days and one of seven weeks; by contrast the seven weeks after Easter are a specially joyful period.

115. Cf. *Search,* p. 100–102.

116. We have already seen a similar anxiety not to give rise to any suspicion of sun worship, cf. chap. V, §IV.5.

117. This meaning is known to Philo, *Vita Contempl.* §65, cf. below §2.

118. *MekhRI* II:210 f. *SOR* §5 cites a saying which states, without calculations, that the Decalogue was given on the 6th of the third month, which was a Sabbath. There is no mention of Pentecost.

119. The various forms of the Palestinian targum of Exod 19–20 are presented and discussed by Jean Potin, *La fête juive de la Pentecôte. Étude des textes liturgiques* (Lectio Divina, 65a and b), Paris, Cerf, 2 vol., 1971.

episode of Marah; it is in fact said in 24:7 that on this day Moses read the book of the Covenant, which is understood to be the reminder of the earlier occurrences of the one and only Covenant until that day. The changed order of the narration is justified by the anomaly of 24:7 in which the people declare: "We will do and we will hear." Thus the rite consecrates the acceptance of the earlier precepts ("we will do") and precedes the reception of the Law in its entirety ("we will hear"). Once again, Pentecost, which is not named but which falls on the 6th, cannot commemorate both the gift of the Law and the renewal of the Covenant. More exactly, and this is the important point here, in neither case can it celebrate the Covenant, since it falls either on the day before or the day after. There is, all the same, another opinion, according to which everything took place on the same day.

The synagogue worship for Pentecost is marked by a controversy. According to *TMeg* 3[4]:5, the majority usage is to read Deut 16:9-12, which begins with the words "seven weeks," underlining the significance of the number 7. Others, however, prescribe Exod 19:1-20, 26, which includes the Decalogue,[120] and so emphasizes the gift of the Law. The complementary reading from the Prophets is Hab 3 (*BMeg* 31a), but others say that it should be the visions in Ezek 1, a classic passage evoking the end of time *(merkaba)*, but which is not translated (is not part of the oral *targum*). According to *MḤag* 2:1, this chapter is reputed to be dangerous, since it is forbidden to teach it, even to a single disciple.[121] The normative rabbinic tradition has kept the autumn New Year (1 Tishri) as commemoration of the Creation, the gift of the Law and the last judgment (*MRSh* 1:1 f.). This is not a rabbinical innovation, however, as Philo insists on the celebration of the gift of the Law on this day, with a universalist dimension.[122] As neither he nor Josephus mentions any relation between Pentecost and the Sinai event (Law and Covenant), commentators tend to

120. In the ancient triennial cycle, commencing in Nisan (cf. chap. II, §II.5), the reading of the Ten Commandments in Exod coincides with the date of Pentecost (second year), cf. Adolf Büchler, "The reading of the Law and Prophets in a Triennial Cycle," *JQR* 5 (1893), p. 420–468. The later Babylonian usage, with the duplicated celebration outside the land of Israel, is to combine the two readings, beginning by Exod (*BMeg* 31a), and the same for the passages from the Prophets.

121. It is reported (*TḤag* 2:1) that Eleazar b. Arakh (the one who, having later gone to Emmaus in the time of Yoḥanan b. Zakkai, lost his Torah, *i.e.* adopted a Messianizing position, cf. chap. IV, §II.1), gave in the presence of his master Yoḥanan b. Zakkai a brilliant commentary on this chapter, and that he was surrounded by fire (cf. Ezek 1:4 f.; in 1:26, the throne is made of sapphires, which is close to the sapphire pavement of Exod 24:10).

122. He calls it "feast of the Trumpet," because of the *shofar* (*Spec. leg.* 2 §188 f.).

conclude that this was the common Jewish opinion,[123] and that the establishment of this connection is only a later development.

However, our observations to this point enable us to discern in the Tannaitic sources traces of Pentecost as feast of the Covenant and the gift of the Law, with a reference to their term, the last judgment, while being at the same time the feast of first fruits in their different forms.[124] These elements are residual, but were sufficiently hardy to reappear later, according to a pattern similar to that which we have already seen for the recitation of the Decalogue (chap. V, §IV.4). Truth to tell, this residue would have very little significance if it were in isolation, but we have seen that it has some connection with the marginal prehistory of the rabbinic sources (*ḥaberim*, cf. chap. V, §I.1), since it agrees very well with the importance of Pentecost for the Essenes and in Acts 2.

2. *Pentecost and Covenant among the Essenes*

The book of *Jubilees* is part of the canon of the Ethiopian Church, and fragments of it were found at Qumran. For this book, Pentecost, falling always on Sunday the 15th of the third month, is the greatest feast of the year and has no particular link with Passover.[125] Despite its interest in questions concerning the calendar, *Jub* mentions no count of seven weeks. Noah had already celebrated this feast of the Covenant with his sons. Then it was forgotten, but partly restored with the patriarchs: the covenant made with Abraham between the divided animals, the birth of Isaac, the covenant with Jacob all took place on this day. Later, it was again forgotten by the Israelites, but the angel revealed it once more to Moses and ordered him to observe Pentecost in such a way that the Covenant would be renewed each year (*Jub* 6:10). The covenant sacrifice offered by Moses at Sinai (Exod 24:1-11) took place in fact on the 15th of the third month.[126]

In *Jub* 6:21, this feast has two names and is apparently twofold also in nature: feast of the First Fruits, and feast of Oaths, or renewal of the

123. Cf. J. Potin, *La Pentecôte . . .*, p. 139.

124. In Lev 23:6 it is laid down to present as an offering for Pentecost two loaves made from the new harvest; these are leavened, despite the prohibition of leaven at the altar (Lev 2:11); Philo, *Spec. leg.* 2 §182 explains that this prohibition goes well with the similar prohibition of wine. The rab. trad. mentions these loaves only in connection with the usages of the Temple (*MMen* 10:6; 11:1).

125. This section owes much to the documentation put together by Annie Jaubert, *La notion d'Alliance dans le judaïsme aux abords de l'ère chrétienne* (Patristica Sorbonensia, 6), Paris, Seuil, 1963.

126. By inference, since according to the current text it was on the 16th that God summoned Moses on to the mountain, corresponding to Exod 24:12, after the Covenant sacrifice.

Covenant. The two aspects are mutually complementary. The archetype is the deliverance from the Deluge: a new world begins, after the chaos and disappearance of the old world; the sinners have been drowned; Noah and his sons represent the new humanity saved from the waters. This model is applied to the Israelites (5:17 f.): "If they are converted to God in justice, He will forgive all their transgressions and will pardon all their sins. It is written and decreed that He will show mercy to all those who are converted from all their faults once every year." The ritual of the feast is not set out in detail, but it involves oaths,[127] and there is a commentary (1:22 f.) in terms that recall Ezek 36:25-27: "They will not submit until they confess their own fault and those of their fathers. After that they will turn to me in all uprightness, with all their heart and all their soul [. . .] I will create in them a holy Spirit and will purify them [. . .] and they shall all be called sons of the living God." The mention of the holy Spirit (instead of the new spirit of Ezek) is characteristic: it is the sign of belonging to the community and the Covenant, by forsaking sin and by observance *in conformity* with the precepts.[128]

This rite of penitence or conversion obviously recalls the day of Atonement, which is mentioned later on in this same book (*Jub* 34:19), but without making any connection between the two.[129] A symbolic link with the first fruits is evident: just as the Covenant, whose term is the gift of the land, is renewed, so the produce of the land in the new year becomes available for consumption. The eschatological dimension appears not to go beyond this annual renewal; this may well be due to the system characteristic of *Jubilees*, which frames the whole history of the world within a fixed chronology. The development of the feast of First Fruits in a series of pentecosts, corresponding to the first fruits of wheat (bread), grapes (wine) and olives (oil), has already been mentioned several times (cf. chap. I, §I.2). There is no reason to think that the documents which have most to say about these other pentecosts (11 QT, 4 QMMT) minimize or water down the celebration of the Covenant at Pentecost. On the contrary, the example of the Therapeutae, who, according to Philo, *Vita Contempl.* §65, gave honor to the week but also to its square, shows that celebrating a series of feasts falling at fifty-day intervals does not in itself

127. Special importance (*Jub.* 36:12, 44:1 f.) is attributed to Beersheva, the Well of the Oath of Abraham in Gen 21:31, which is also a "Well of the Seven," with the same verbal play as for Pentecost. The name באר שבע[ה] can have both meanings, both suggested by the aetiological narrative which explains it. The LXX and *Ant.* 1 §212 independently translate "well of the oath."

128. For the *Spirit* is also that of the prophets, cf. chap. I, §I.3.

129. Which has astonished certain commentators, cf. Shemaryahu Talmon, "The Manual of Benedictions," *RQ* 2 (1960), p. 196–199.

weaken Pentecost. The Therapeutae held a special gathering every seven weeks, with an appropriate "banquet," but this "square" is defined as "the preparatory feast of a very great feast," that is to say the forty-nine days[130] preceding Pentecost.

In the *Damascus Document*, the expression "new Covenant," which occurs in Jer 31:31 with a purely eschatological meaning, turns up three times. In particular, the members of the community "have entered into a new Covenant in the land of Damascus" (CD 6:19, 8:21).[131] The sinners are those who have "despised the Covenant and the pact which they made in the land of Damascus";[132] strictly speaking, they are excommunicated. This Covenant is established by God with the "faithful remnant" (3:13). However, whereas Jer 31:31 draws a contrast between an old covenant and a new, there is no mention here of any "old Covenant." We should not forget that the Covenant concluded with Moses is only a renewal of that made with Noah and his sons and later forgotten. The conclusion is obvious: the "new Covenant" is a return to the law of Moses properly understood and observed, a refocusing on the Sinai event, but understood as a renewal of the forgotten Covenant, as there is never any question of a "covenant with Moses." It is hard to believe that the members of the community thought they were perfect. This is an essential question, since, besides the great historic phases of neglect of the Covenant, the transgression of each individual is a breach, or neglect, of the Covenant, giving rise to the need for reparation or renewal for the individual. This text does not mention Pentecost or a rite for periodic renewal of the Covenant, but that does not mean that its authors were not aware of them, all the more since fragments have been found at Qumran.

130. From Philo's wording it is not easy to interpret this "preparatory feast" (προέορτος) in terms of a particular day (Passover, Sheaf), cf. A. Jaubert, *Alliance*, p. 478, and more natural to see it as referring to the whole period of seven weeks; that is what Philo does for the feast of the Basket (first fruits), extending over six months (cf. above §1). However, 11 QT 18:2 f. indicates for the day of the Sheaf (the "morrow of the Sabbath," *i.e.* Sunday the 16th of the first month) the same sacrifices as those laid down for the feast of Weeks (Lev 18:18), but without explanation.

131. The exact meaning of this name remains uncertain: דמשק (Damascus) could be an anagram of מקדש (temple), or an allusion to Babylonia (exile), cf. Jerome Murphy-O'Connor, "The Judean Desert," in: Robert A. Kraft & George W. E. Nickelsburg, *Early Judaism and Its Modern Interpreters*, Philadelphia (Penn.), 1986, p. 119–156. Whatever the meaning may be, the expression does not have a primary topographical meaning, but implies a *situation* of exile even in Judaea; the implicit reference is Ezek 1–3, where God leaves His sanctuary to visit the exiles, cf. Annie Jaubert, "Le pays de Damas," *RB* 65 (1958), p. 214–248.

132. Similarly in 1 QpHab 3:2.

A fundamental aspect of this outlook is that the Covenant is not only a juridical abstraction or even the definition of a nation. This term also designates the community itself, inasmuch as it is faithful, for through it the Covenant *exists*[133] concretely; belonging to the Covenant is somewhat unstable. This way of looking at the Covenant is not new; already, in 1 Macc 1:15, "to separate oneself from the holy Covenant" was equivalent to leaving the solidarity of the community. The same meaning can be seen in Dan 11:22 f., where the "head of the Covenant" is defeated, then the Gentile king (Antiochus Epiphanes) fights against "the holy Covenant." In the Qumran *Community Rule*, to enter into the Covenant is no more and no less than to enter the community, as the rite of admission makes clear (1 QS 2:12,18). Conversely, to enter the community is to be converted to the law of Moses (5:7 f.). Several important consequences result. For one thing, Jews who are outside the community, or members who have been excluded, are outside the Covenant, and are consequently as impure as the Gentiles; this sectarian and very polemical measure,[134] closely resembles what we have seen concerning the *ḥaberim* (cf. chap. V, §I.1).

The notion of community (and not national) solidarity is very prominent. The term by which the community designates itself (*yaḥad* "together") is entirely characteristic, implying as it does the idea of communion, emphasized by many texts concerning daily life, especially all that has to do with the deliberations of the *rabbim*: "In common they will eat, in common they will bless, in common they will deliberate" (1 QS 6:2 f.); they will be instructed "in the marvellous and true mysteries in the midst of the other members of the community, in order to walk in the perfection of holiness, each in the company of his neighbor" (9:19); CD 6:20 requires that "each should love his brother as himself." This is not friendship properly so called, but responsibility. Each of the members has been entrusted with caring for the perfection of the others (CD 20:17 f.), whence the importance of fraternal correction "with humility and love that wishes the welfare of the other" (1 QS 5:25, inspired by Lev 19:17 f.).[135] The community is not a club of friends:[136] fraternal

133. The rab. trad. has preserved a trace of this concrete character: "observe a commandment" is called "make it exist" (לקיים).; likewise, Paul says νόμον ἱστάνομεν (Rom 3:31), with transitive ἵστημι.

134. In particular against interpretations of the Law judged dissident; for example, 1 QH 4:17-19 violently attacks the דורשי חלקות ("those who examine flattering, or easy things"), that is those who hold to a personal (facilitating) and not *authorized* interpretation.

135. The expression used אהבת חסד comes from Mi 6:8, where it can apply equally well to God or the neighbor. In the OT, חסד is normally an attribute of God.

136. Even though FJ, desiring to demonstrate Jewish philanthropy (cf. *Ag.Ap.* 2 §145,

charity is not an end in itself, but has its source in the concern not to share in the guilt of a brother's sin, as Ezek 3:18 explains, and thus to preserve the holiness of the community, in a word, to make the Covenant *exist*. Wrongdoers are not left to their own devices, and there is a whole procedure of warnings and excommunication, as we shall see in greater detail.

The few documents commented on here obviously form a whole, dominated by the notion of Covenant, that is, in the last analysis, the claim to be the true renewed Israel. The texts do not all have to originate in the same group. We should rather assume related, perhaps rival, currents, in accordance with the wide definition of the term "Essene" that we adopted earlier (chap. III, §IV), which is also in agreement with the diversity of groups of *ḥaberim* (chap. V, §I). One feature common to all these circles is the insistence on the regeneration of Israel by a return to the origins. Thus being a "child of Abraham" is not a simple national description, but something to live up to; to be a "son" is in the first place to be a disciple.[137] In other words, circumcision is not the guarantee of belonging to the Covenant; more exactly, true circumcision is commitment in the community (CD 16:5 f.). For all that, CD 3:2-4 states that Abraham's covenant is definitive, since he obtained merit by offering his son Isaac (cf. Gen 22:16): according to Gen 26:3, YHWH committed Himself to keep the oath made to Abraham, an idea echoed in Luke 1:73; this is the "merit of the patriarchs."[138] But this reality is looked at not from a juridical or ethnic point of view, but through providential events: despite the people's repeated infidelities, God remembers "the Covenant of the first," and He always raises up a remnant of faithful generations (CD 1:4, 6:2, cf. 1 QM 13:7 f.). The problem is obviously to identify the faithful remnant, who must "separate themselves from this wicked generation." The theme of the fathers' sin and infidelity is characteristic (cf. 1 QH 3:34). Pedigree gives no privilege, which, by the way, raises the problem

etc.), declares, that the Essenes have "more mutual affection than the other" philosophies, he does not place friendship above respect for the Law.

137. According to Gen 17:13 f., the *nation* is linked to circumcision and the Covenant. FJ, very aware of genealogy, understands that circumcision is to preserve the *nation* (γένος, *Ant.* 1 §192, cf. chap. I, §II.1, and below §IV.1) but, characteristically, he never speaks of the Covenant. *MBik* 1:4 gives an interesting controversy: for some, the proselyte cannot pronounce certain ritual formulae, since he cannot call himself a descendant of Abraham; others retort that he can, since according to Gen 17:5 Abraham is the father of many peoples (גוים, playing on the post-biblical sense of "non-Jew"), cf. *Tosefta kifshuṭah* 1:824 f.

138. This theme (זכות אבות) is classic in the rab. trad.: the patriarchs desired the land and merited it (cf. *Tanḥ re'é* §8, from Jer 3:19, etc.), the question being to know whether this right is acquired for their descendants.

of the origin of the community's priests: it is not to be taken for granted that they are such by birth (cf. below §IV.3).

It is easy to see that these questions are close to an entire body of Christian themes present throughout the NT, turning on the claim, which can properly be called sectarian, to be the true Israel. The prologue of the *Rule*, defining the community's project, says explicitly that it is a question of fixing norms for all Israel "at the end" (1 QS 1:1-5). Many commentators have already made comparisons with the NT, as we have seen in connection with the Pentecost of Acts 2 (chap. VI, §III.2). Before developing two particular aspects in the following section, we shall simply emphasize two points already discussed from another angle. The typology of Noah[139] for expressing the renewal of the Covenant leads directly to a very simple meaning given by Paul to the water of baptism: entry into the Kingdom begins with a sign of passage through death, but now the sinners are not drowned, but are delivered from their sin which is transferred to Jesus Christ (cf. chap. II, §I.4). Further, since the community of the Covenant has the monopoly of *inspired* interpretation of the law of Moses, it can only reject, or at best ignore, other communities with parallel claims, unless some particular pressure forces a confrontation. This gives a context for the reciprocal (and relatively late) fulminations to be found in the gospels and the rabbinic sources, which we associated with the reorganization of Yavneh (chap. V, §V.2), but which do not appear in properly Pauline Christianity.

IV – Initiation, Sanctions, Offices

Pentecost, when the Covenant is renewed, is also the day for receiving new members, whose admission into the community is thereby an entry into the Covenant. That is the general setting of the Pentecost of Acts 2, and it is also a cornerstone in the Essene customs (1 QS 5:8; *Jub* 6:17 f.); this likeness is hardly surprising, since we are dealing with circles which were originally alike. The procedure for admitting candidates throws light on the community's nature and structure, but it is fairly complex, and the information that we possess is scattered. For this reason we will follow the description of the Essenes given by Josephus (*J.W.* 2 §119–160). Not only is it full of details and fits in reasonably well with the documents from the Judaean wilderness,[140] but, above all, it is the only

139. Cf. Jean Daniélou, *Sacramentum futuri. Étude sur les origines de la typologie biblique*, Paris, Cerf, 1950, p. 59 f.

140. Cf. Todd S. Beall, *Josephus' Description of the Essenes Illustrated by the Dead Sea Scrolls* (SNTS, Monograph 58), Cambridge University Press, 1988.

synthesis written for outside readers, whether Jewish or not,[141] whereas the Qumran and similar texts are internal literature,[142] and we do not know what authority they possessed. It is generally admitted that Josephus had his information firsthand, from the period of his youth that he spent with Bannus, to the point where the question arises whether he may not have broken the prohibition, which he himself mentions, against divulging customs that were in principle esoteric. To his credit, he says nothing about questions concerning the calendar and feasts, nor about juridical details concerning punishments or promotions; these are two areas of major importance, on which the NT also is silent, despite some passing allusions.[143]

Also to his credit, he does mention divergent customs, the most important concerning marriage. After declaring that the Essenes disdain

141. Philo gives two descriptions of the Essenes (*Quod omnis probus*, §75–91, and a fragment of an *Apology for the Jews* preserved by Eusebius, *Praep. evang.* 8.11.1-18, still known as *Hypothetica*), which by and large agree with FJ; most often less precise, they do, however, provide some additional information. Philo calls the Essenes, whom he locates in Syria-Palestine, ϑεραπευταὶ ϑεοῦ par excellence; however, he devotes an entire treatise (*Vita Contempl.*) to describing groups of "Therapeutae," parallel to the Essenes and widely spread, but whose finest flower are to be found near Lake Mareotis, not far from Alexandria; certain descriptive details show that he had known and visited them. These Therapeutae closely resemble the Essenes, but appear to have adopted a more contemplative way of life, and to have admitted women.

142. Cf. Florentino García Martínez & Julio Trebolle Barrera, *Los hombres de Qumrán. Literatura, estructura social y concepciones religiosas*, Madrid, Edit. Trotta, 1993.

143. A description very close to that of FJ is given by Hippolytus of Rome, *Refutatio*, 9.18.3–28.2, but with notable differences, to the point where one begins to wonder if both may have depended on the same source; the technical discussions are summarized by M. Marcovitch, "The Essenes as Christians," in: *Studies in Greco-Roman Religions and Gnosticism*, Leyden, Brill, 1988, p. 144–155; Hippolytus' polemic against the Jews aims in part at showing that they are divided into sects (αἱρέσεις), arising from the multiplicity of individual interpretations which have fragmented the law of Moses (IX, 18.1 f.). For Hippolytus, we have made constant use here of the unpublished M.A. dissertation of Emmanuelle Main, *Esséniens, Pharisiens, Sadducéens chez Hippolyte. La notice de l'Elenchos*, Jerusalem, Hebrew University, 1992; the general conclusion is that Hippolytus had no other source than FJ (perhaps with variants), but may have known him through a compiler, as he introduces many expressions inspired by the NT, especially regarding their alleged belief in the resurrection of the dead, whereas FJ speaks only of the immortality of the soul (the name of the Jewish-Christian Hegesippus is often put forward, but cannot be verified). It is also possible to see in these tiny details a clever rhetoric at work: if the Essenes are really so close to the Christians in their doctrines, they have all the less excuse for not recognizing Jesus Christ risen, and there is no serious reason to think that Hippolytus had any source other than FJ. This is also the conclusion reached by Tessa Rajak, "*Ciò che Flavio Giuseppe vide*: Josephus and the Essenes," in: Fausto Parente & Joseph Sievers (Eds.), *Josephus and the History of the Greco-Roman Period. Essays in Memory of Morton Smith* (Studia Post-Biblica, 41), Leiden, Brill, 1994, p. 141–160, insisting on the ease with which FJ composed in Greek, while getting inspiration from the methods (though not the content) of other historians.

marriage (*J.W.* 2 §120), he concedes that some of them do marry, but only for purposes of procreation (2 §160). Philo too completely excludes marriage among the Essenes.[144] The Dead Sea texts strike a different note: 1 QSa 1:4 makes provision for the arrival of women and children; 1 QSa 1:9 f. authorizes marriage only after the age of twenty. CD 4:20 f. regards as equivalent to unchastity the fact of having married two women in one's lifetime,[145] and a widower may not remarry, for the sake of the Creation (Gen 1:27); divorce is not excluded, but only in the sense of separation without remarriage.[146] The feature common to both camps is the rejection of sensuality, as Josephus is careful to note (2 §161).

1. Admission; Initiation in the Name of the Trinity

We have already seen something of the admission of new members into the groups of *ḥaberim* (chap. V, §I.1); what Josephus tells us about

144. *Apud* Eusebius, *Praep. evang.* 8.11.14 f. Likewise Pliny, *Hist. nat.* 5.15.75, but he tends to know as Essenes only a colony around the Dead Sea.

145. Lit. "in their lifetime" בחייהם, where the masculine form of the suffix is not strictly limited to the male gender, and some have wished to understand it as meaning "while their wives are still alive," so that remarriage would be possible after the death of the first wife, but this meaning forces the text. In like manner, 11 QT 57:17 f. prescribes one wife at a time for the king (contrary to David and Solomon), and advocates endogamy. It is difficult to know if this principle of strict monogamy fits in with the evidence of FJ. He states that marriage is real only after a trial period, to verify the woman's fertility (*J.W.* 2 §161); that appears to imply repudiation and remarriage in case of sterility, but he gives no juridical detail establishing a distinction between "union" and "marriage" (with or without legal betrothal). In any case, it is possible to conjecture from what FJ says that if a marriage had been fruitful, any other subsequent marriage was excluded (with or without polygamy). For the rab. trad., divorce (in view of remarriage, to observe the precept to have children) is obligatory after ten years of sterility (*MYeb* 6:6).

146. The rab. trad. is aware of polygamy (*MYeb* 1:1 f., alluding to Elkanah, 1 Sam 1:1 f.), and maintains it in principle, as the scriptural arguments in favor of monogamy are regarded as heterodox (Samaritans, Sadducees, then Qaraites); in *BYeb* 65a, a sage says that *in his view*, whoever marries a second wife must repudiate the first: that is an opinion, not a tradition. Jewish polygamy is attested also by FJ (*J.W.* 1 §477, "ancestral custom") and Justin, *Dialogue*, 134.1. Philo, *Spec. leg.* 2 §135, is not very clear, and suggests rather (for reasons of morality) a repudiation before another marriage, but his lack of precision implies that for him monogamy is not a strict obligation, otherwise he would have said so; in fact, he cannot forget that the patriarchs, who were not truly monogamous, are "living laws." Cf. texts and bibliography brought together by Mordechai A. Friedman, "Polygamy—New Information from the Genizah," *Tarbiz* 43 (1973), p. 166–198. Regarding divorce, a difficult expression in Deut 24:1 (ערות דבר), gives rise to controversy (*MGiṭ* 10:9): the school of Shammai prohibits divorce, except for indecency or incest (understanding דבר ערוה with allusion to Lev 18), whereas the school of Hillel permits it even for a trivial motive; this same controversy features in Matt 19:8, where Jesus defends the same opinion as the school of Shammai.

the Essenes is comparable (*J.W.* 2 §137–142), but we must now go into further details.

Curiously enough, Josephus, who has just said that he is going to describe the three philosophical schools of the Jews, begins by saying that the Essenes are Jews "by nationality" *(genos)*. This apparent redundancy[147] has attracted various commentaries.[148] We begin with the observation that Josephus uses this same term *(genos)* when he speaks of the group or association (or "breed") of the Essenes themselves,[149] and of the Sadducees (*Ant.* 13 §297), but not of the Pharisees, whom he does not wish to describe as a closed group; so the term designates in these cases a recognized membership, which should not be assumed to be hereditary. However, he also employs the same term to indicate an ethnic origin (Hebrews, Egyptians), or royal or priestly genealogical descent; in those cases it does have an hereditary character.[150] In order to determine whether Josephus is referring, in the case of the Essenes, to a voluntary or to an hereditary membership, it is enough to observe that, in contrast to the Galilean "brigands" in their attitude to Herod, he never defines Jews in terms of heredity alone, at least in reference to the situation of his own day. On the contrary, he explains (*Ant.* 1 §191) that circumcision was given to Abraham to protect the "nation" *(genos)* from any alteration, which is for him a contemporary concern, since he makes no reference to

147. Hippolytus omits the phrase (IX, 18:3).

148. Some examples: Jerome Murphy-O'Connor, "The Essenes and Their History," *RB* 81 (1974), p. 241–244 holds that at the return from exile the Essenes had difficulty in being accepted as Jews (this view, which is contrary to the privileged status of the Hasideans in 1–2 Macc, comes from the opinion that the first redactional state of the *Community Rule* did not contain legal dispositions, but expressed an "enthusiastic," or "charismatic" spirit). Daniel R. Schwartz, "On Two Aspects of a Priestly View of Descent at Qumran," in: Laurence H. Schiffman (Ed.), *Archaeology and History in the Dead Sea Scrolls* (JSOT-ASOR Monographs, 2), Sheffield, 1990, p. 157–179, supposes that FJ introduces a sacerdotal model of legitimation. Shaye J. D. Cohen, "'ΙΟΥΔΑΙΟΣ ΤΟ ΓΕΝΟΣ and Related Expressions in Josephus," in: Fausto Parente & Joseph Sievers (Eds.), *Josephus and the History of the Greco-Roman Period. Essays in Memory of Morton Smith* (Studia Post-Biblica, 41), Leiden, Brill, 1994, p. 23–38, maintains that here FJ means that they are Judaeans, *i.e.* from the ethnic community of Judaea, but Judaea had been widely extended since John Hyrcanus and included many who had been Judaized by force; it would be bizarre if, for no apparent reason, "Judaea" meant here the narrower territory of Ezra-Nehemiah or Judas Maccabaeus, and in any case such a meaning is not very easy to draw from the actual text of FJ.

149. Whether to designate the collectivity (*Ant.* 13 §172, 15 §371), or to indicate that a particular individual belonged to the Essenes (*J.W.* 1 §78, 2 §113,119 and the parallels in *Ant.*).

150. In *Life* §1 γένος designates FJ's own family; in *Ag.Ap.* 1 §54 he points out that he is a priest by birth (ἐκ γένους). In *Ag.Ap.* 1 §30 f. he mentions the steps taken to avoid any alteration of the nation (γένος) of priests.

the Covenant. In fact, he betrays no hesitations when he is speaking of proselytes in general or even of forced conversions: the Idumaeans and other free immigrants are circumcised, since in Judaea personal status has been governed by Jewish law since the Hasmonaeans (cf. chap. VI, §I.1).

This being the case we cannot escape the simple, though unexpected conclusion: Josephus is saying that the Essenes have to be circumcised Jews![151] That does not appear to exclude proselytes *a priori*, although it is possible that Josephus may have meant circumcision *on the eighth day*. As he says nothing similar about the Pharisees and the Sadducees, it seems that the point needs to be made about the Essenes: decoded, for Josephus, entry into the Essenes should not be confused with conversion to Judaism or replace it. We saw earlier that documents from the Judaean wilderness include some Samaritan elements, and even that, according to certain rabbinic sources, Samaritans could be admitted into *ḥaberim* brotherhoods (chap. V, §I.1). In other words, Josephus, who is systematically unfavorable to the Samaritans, is implicitly taking up a position on a debatable question. Further, this same question, viewed from another angle, is at the center of the famous debate in Acts 15, where the opinion expressed by Josephus is reinterpreted: Do new members of the community have to be circumcised, that is be "Jews by nationality" before being admitted? In the context of Peter's visit to Cornelius, the question appears to concern the admission of Gentiles. This essential problem has already been discussed, in connection with the baptism of proselytes and the personality of James (chap. V, §II). It can be put in another way: Does the renewal of the Covenant in view of "all Israel" imply a renewal of Judaism itself, or not? The question of the Jewish monopoly (Jesus said, "Salvation comes from the Jews") is not really new, since the reforms of Ezra and Nehemiah already had the objective of making a very restricted group of *Jews* the true Israel, thus excluding notably their circumcised neighbors.

At the moment when he was writing the *War*, Josephus obviously had a soft spot for the Essenes, seeing in them perhaps the party of reference for the future. It is not very likely that at this time he had any very clear ideas about the Christians, since he apparently only discovered them later, at Rome around 90 (cf. chap. I, §I.1). He may, however, have got wind of them earlier, not so much from what they might have been

151. T. S. Beall, *Josephus' Description*, p. 37 understands simply that non-Jews (proselytes) were not admitted, and cites the *Rule*, which has the same requirement (1 QS 6:13 f.): "Whoever of Israel who commits himself to joining the council of the community." But the problem is precisely to determine what it means to be "of Israel," which does not necessarily mean the same thing as simply belonging to the Jewish nation.

saying—Christians, being without political impact, would not have impressed him very much—but more concretely and more seriously from the attitudes of certain brotherhoods, more or less "charismatic" as we would say today, which were directly admitting Gentiles (uncircumcised "proselytes"), thus compromising the reference he wanted for the future of the *nation*.[152]

To return to the candidates. Josephus implies that the process of initiation lasted three years (2 §137 f.). During the first year, in which the candidate remained outside the community, he was given a hatchet, a linen "girdle" and a white garment, and led the same kind of life as the Essenes. The hatchet was used for digging toilet trenches (2 §148). The linen girdle, which was much more than a simple loin-cloth, was "used" for the ablutions,[153] then for the meals, and was regarded as sacred (2 §129); it was in reality a priestly vestment, the *abneṭ* of Exod 28:39, analogous to the veil hiding the Holy of Holies (Exod 26:31).[154] The white garment was the normal garb of the Essenes, probably symbolizing purity.[155] So the sacred ritual of the meal, which was prepared by priests (cf. below), had a sacerdotal dimension (cf. chap. II, §II.5). With all these elements, the candidates were being trained in the Essene way of life, including purifications,[156] while remaining outside the community; in other words, they took their meals apart, presumably with their fellow novices. If at the time determined, they had given proof of self-mastery,[157] they

152. It is possible also that he already knew the works of Philo (from whom he clearly takes his distance at the beginning of *Ant.)*; when Philo speaks of the Essenes and the Therapeutae, he expressly says that they are disciples of Moses, but he never says that they are Jews, which fits his open attitude towards proselytism.

153. FJ's actual wording, implying that this garment is put on for the bath, is perhaps defective (or deliberately imprecise, as he often is): taking a meal in wet clothes, even sacred, seems odd, but above all purification requires that one be naked. However, FJ's expression can strictly be taken to refer to a gesture of *sanctification* (ablution of hands and feet), and not a simple purification, cf. chap. III, §IV. The rab. trad. has preserved the obligation of washing the hands before a meal, which is a priestly gesture (cf. chap. II, §II.2).

154. According to *Ant.* 3 §156, the *abneṭ*, properly wound about the body, is really the equivalent of a tunic (χιτών).

155. 1 QM 7:9-10 describes the battle dress of the priests, all the items of which are of white linen.

156. Cf. André Dupont-Sommer, "Culpabilité et rites de purification dans la secte juive de Qoumrân," *Sem* 15 (1965), p. 61–70 (63). Hippolytus has the same understanding, 32.2.

157. The term employed ἐγκράτεια is classic since Aristotle, *Eth. Nic.* 7.4 (twinned with καρτερία "strength of soul, firmness"). The proper object of this preliminary firmness appears to be in the first place sexual pleasure (cf. also Acts 24:25): earlier (2 §120), FJ has emphasized that the Essenes turn aside from pleasure (ἡδονή) as from an evil; later, speaking of married Essenes (2 §161), he mentions that they do not unite with their wives

were then allowed to come closer to the Essene life, by sharing[158] in the "purer waters" of purification, but were not yet admitted to the common exercises, in particular the meals,[159] which were taken in a place regarded as sacred, where no profane person might penetrate.[160] So there was a gradation in the purifications.

This second phase lasted two years, and if the candidates had given proof of character, they were admitted into the community, but before taking part in the meals, they had to pronounce "fearful oaths." Before discussing them, we recall that these phases are very like those in the Qumran *Community Rule* (1 QS 6:13-23), although the latter does not mention garments and has a rather different way of presenting access to the "purity," the community meal. On the other hand, the stages of admission to the *ḥaberim* brotherhoods involved the reception of certain garments (chap. V, §I.1). Basically, there is a central element common to all these groups, which is the community meal; the groups of neophytes lead the same life as the community proper, but are separated according to several stages of access to the meal, which is therefore the element that defines the community and gives its identity. It is significant that this was precisely the reproach made to Peter after his visit to Cornelius ("You have eaten with them," Acts 11:3), and that the decrees of James had among other effects that of avoiding unwanted contacts (cf. chap. V, §II.1).

Later on, without direct link with the admission of new members, Josephus distinguishes four classes of Essenes "following the seniority of their practice," then adds that if a senior touches a junior he contracts the same impurity as if he had touched a foreigner (2 §150). As we have seen, he has mentioned only two phases of initiation. His method of composition is not always very coherent, and the question has long been asked whether he means periods of initiation (first, second, third year, full members) or a gradation of purity within the community after the oaths

---

during pregnancy, to show that they do not marry for pleasure (ἡδονή), but to have children. 1 QS 4:9-11 makes similar demands.

158. Lit.: "*and* he shares"; the particle καί has here an explicative, and not an additive sense: this is the sole new thing to which the candidate is admitted.

159. The term used συμβιώσεις indicates common life in general, but the context requires that the reader understand specifically the meals.

160. The meal is thus analogous to an act of worship (communion sacrifice); there has been much discussion about whether the Qumran community regarded itself as an ordinary city (as in the *Rule*) or as a temple (as in the *Temple Scroll*), cf. Laurence H. Schiffman, "Communal Meals at Qumran," *RQ* 10 (1979), p. 45–56; both points of view can be reconciled by considering both the mobility of the Essenes, mentioned by FJ, and certain archaeological evidence, cf. above §I.2.

(priests, Levites, lay members, novices).[161] The Qumran documents do not give direct clarification, but they do show an extreme concern for hierarchy and precedence, according to various titles attesting various customs. Besides, Josephus says that the Essenes live to a very great age; in this regard, the three years of initiation do not last long, and so the novices all together more likely represent one class, the three others being degrees of seniority within the community. The degrees of impurity defined by the rabbinic tradition (*MToh* 1:1 f.) may also throw light on Josephus' four classes. The impurity of Gentiles is the strongest, corresponding to that of the novices; it is followed by two degrees of lesser impurity, then the pure state, corresponding to the fully integrated members. The correspondence may be only approximate,[162] but the important thing is to notice the increasing fragility of the degrees of purity.[163] Finally, Josephus makes no clear connection between the classes of purity and the position of priests, Levites or other community officers.

The oaths, according to Josephus, are eleven, and "it is by oaths such as these that the Essenes bind the new members" (2 §142), which may imply that the list is not fixed, or more probably, that he is making a selection. In first place is a global commitment to "venerate the divinity, and to observe justice to men." This is precisely the goal of John the Bap-

161. Cf. T. S. Beall, *Josephus' Description*, p. 99 f.

162. The admission procedure in the *Rule* is slightly different, but shows the same spirit. There are three examinations: the first, preliminary, on the rules, but without the candidate being allowed to touch the "purity"; a second, after a year, permits him to touch the dry food of the "purity," which is not liable to be contaminated; a third, after a second year, permits him to touch liquids. The distinction in matters of purity between solid and liquid foodstuffs is based on Lev 11:34 f., which indicates that a dry food becomes liable to impurity by contact with a liquid (further developed in *MMakh* 1:1 f., cf. also chap. V, §I.1). Purity is only a way of symbolizing distance from sin, or, by the same token, the reception of the Spirit, cf. 1 QS 2:11-17.

163. It may be because of this intrinsic fragility that Philo, who stresses the moral strength and the *freedom* of the Essenes (and implicitly of the Therapeutae), leaves out the systems of purification, cf. chap. I, §II.1. Even so, he preserves the conception underlying the ritual sign, as he emphasizes that the Essenes must "flee the cities, because of the crimes which city dwellers are wont to commit; they know well [. . .] that living together with such folk inflicts incurable harm on souls" (cf. similarly 1 QS 8:13 f.). For Philo, this is only a return to the tradition of Sinai, since the Law was given (most unusually) in a desert, cf. *Decal.* §5 f.; during the community banquet of the Therapeutae, two choirs expressly imitate the canticle of Exod 15 (*Vita contempl.* §84–88). This gives the clue to understanding a curious notice: in the *Hypothetica* (*apud* Eusebius, *Hist. eccl.*, 8.11.1), Philo (or whoever is the author) affirms that Moses was the founder of the Essenes; this information may not be historically exact, but it shows that for him the Essenes were not of recent date, and especially that they carry out the essence of the law of Moses (cf. 1 QS 5:8 f.); in this sense, any reforming group may bear this title, as we have already seen from another angle (cf. chap. III, §IV).

tist's preaching according to Josephus (*Ant.* 18 §116), and is not far removed from the twin commandments recalled by Jesus in Mark 12:29 par.: love of God (cf. Deut 6:5) and love of the neighbor as oneself (cf. Lev 19:18). This global commitment obviously covers everything, but needs to be made more specific by further oaths. One of them is to respect the authorities, "for it is always by the will of God that power is conferred on someone," and to carry out any offices with modesty (2 §140). In the immediate context, the authorities are those placed in various offices within the community, according to the usual understanding, but Josephus has already spoken of them (2 §134), and his repetitious formulation, based on the Essene view of providence,[164] appears to include also constituted authorities in general, which is never the case in the Qumran texts. In fact, it is not self-evident that the Essenes committed themselves to respecting (legally) the Jewish authorities in general,[165] and Josephus may be suspected of giving a slight twist to his wording in such a way as to suggest that the Essenes were also respectful of Roman authority. In the same spirit, another of the oaths was to abstain from "brigandage" (2 §142), that is not from simple robbery,[166] since a previous oath concerns theft,[167] but from revolutionary activities,[168] or from sedition in general; for Josephus, then, the Essenes distanced themselves from any Messianism of zealot type. Such an option, which would not be astonishing in the colony at Bathyra,[169] certainly goes in the direction favored by Josephus,

164. To which is attached a gift of prophecy: in *Ant.* 15 §374 the Essene Menaḥem foretells to Herod that he will be king, as God has judged him worthy.

165. Philo, *Quod omnis probus*, §91, says that the various kings who had reigned over Syria-Palestine could never, despite their continual perversities, accuse the Essenes, but that, on the contrary, they were "vanquished by them"; here he places himself strictly on the level of morality (the Essenes are "athletes of virtue"), and overlooks coercion or juridical dependence.

166. The apparent redundancy has troubled commentators, and Hippolytus, 9.23.4, already omits it.

167. The term employed κλοπή corresponds to Heb. גנב, meaning secret theft, and not raping, robbery or seizure by force (גזל, LXX ἀφαιρέω); but this case figures expressly in the Decalogue (Exod 20, LXX οὐ κλέψεις "Thou shalt not steal"), and so we must assume not a simple redundancy, but an interpretation authorized (by the community) which generalizes the precept to any form of theft, robbery or extortion (in 1 QpHab 9:5 the priests of Jerusalem are accused of robbing the people). This is not an abstract detail, as it is noteworthy that in 1 QM 7:2 (situation of eschatological warfare) certain overseers are commanded to levy booty (שלל); in 1 QM 12:11, God is even asked to do the same.

168. This meaning has been proposed by Constantin Daniel, "Les 'Hérodiens' du Nouveau Testament sont-ils des esséniens?" *RQ* 6 (1967), p. 31–53; the objections raised always assume that the "brigands" in FJ (and the NT, λῃσταί) are mere robbers, but we have seen that their politico-religious motivation was uppermost, cf. chap. III, §I.2.

169. Whose profile, or at least norm, was certainly not much different from the *ḥaberim*, cf. chap. III, §II.1. This was also Paul's final position, cf. Rom 13:1-7.

and it is a good question whether it really formed part of the practice of all the Essenes. Another of the oaths pronounced, not to reveal to the outside world anything concerning the brethren, "even under torture unto death" (2 §141), may suggest certain political implications.[170] In any case, it is a "fearful oath," which implies that the temptation could be great, *i.e.* that zealots and Essenes were indeed of a similar type.

Several of the oaths turn on honesty and the authority of the word pronounced. First, to love truth and denounce liars (2 §141), which is close to a previous oath on hatred of the unjust and support for the just, even if that involves disobedience (2 §139). The just and the unjust in question are brethren, and not people in the world, who are in all cases impure, so that once again we come across fraternal charity, which is always subordinated to the holiness of the community. Then, to keep with respect the books of the community, and transmit the teachings of the masters as one has received them (2 §142); so there is an esoteric oral tradition, distinct from writings, whether biblical or not.[171] This notion of traditional oral (esoteric) teaching is fundamental. It is an essential point in common with the Pharisees according to Josephus, and then with the *ḥaberim* and the rabbinic tradition (cf. chap. I, §I.3), which leads us again to the recognition that all these groups are of the same kind; the authority of this teaching comes from the Spirit, which the community declares that it possesses. With these oaths goes the principle, mentioned by Josephus (2 §135), that the Essenes consider that any word pronounced by them is stronger than an oath, and even that an oath is worse than perjury, since one who calls on God to guarantee what he has to say proves thereby that he speaks without authority: he lies, or at least he does not have the Spirit of the community.[172] In other words, the true Essene speaks

170. 1 QS 8:11-12 also speaks of the secret, but meaning rather esoteric teaching, which could not be divulged by chance (cf. 1 QS 9:16 f.). CD 16:7-9 lays down that if someone has taken the oath to observe some point of the Law, he ought to keep it, even at the cost of his life; this enigmatic formula, which implies that certain aspects of the Law may be optional, can acquire a fairly simple meaning in a perspective of zealot Messianizing, since a commitment to it was always based on Scripture.

171. Likewise, Philo, *Quod omnis probus*, §80 stresses the importance for the Essenes of the "ancestral laws (χρώμενοι τοῖς πατρίοις νόμοις), such that the human soul could not have conceived them without being possessed by God"; these laws train them, in the sporting sense of the term, in the moral part of philosophy. From this rather complex formulation, we can see: 1. these laws are distinct from the Pentateuch properly so called, which might have worried Philo; 2. they are however "inspired"; 3. their content is formal rather than moral, since they serve only as a "trainer." In this way, Philo erases any particularism (as also the idea of the Covenant), to lay emphasis on moral elevation. He never mentions the other parties of which Josephus writes (Pharisees, Sadducees).

172. Philo, *Decal.* §84 recommends regarding every word pronounced as an oath

with *authority*, power and assurance, just like Apollos in Acts 18:24 f., Peter in Acts 2:14 f., etc.

Certain rules of the group do not form part of the list of oaths, but can be classed with them, either because of their importance or because of the penalty attached. Thus Josephus states that they "have the greatest reverence, after God, for the name of the lawgiver;[173] whoever blasphemes it is punished by death" (2 §145). Josephus also mentions, as a common norm, the general prohibition of pronouncing the name of God, a blasphemy punishable by stoning.[174] Blasphemy is really a deviation of the oath or benediction; it is only to be expected in the case of God, but less so in that of Moses, for what could an oath sworn by Moses be? Similarly, CD 15:1-5 forbids swearing by God, even under a roundabout form,[175] and by the law of Moses. E. Qimron, on the basis of a new reading of the text,[176] shows that this prohibition is general, *except at the admission* of candidates (and of young adults up to the age of twenty). Decoded, this means that the only lawful oaths are the "fearful oaths" of the new members, and they are pronounced in the name of God *and in the name of Moses*. If to that is added the fact that entry into the Covenant is nothing else than the reception of the Holy Spirit, who presides over the actualization of the law of Moses (§III.2 above), it can immediately be seen that entry into the community, marked by a final purification, is placed under a very simple threefold sign: God, Moses and the Spirit.

(sworn by God), and advises in case of necessity to swear by a substitute (parents, heaven, etc.); Sir 23:9 warns against all oaths. However, Deut 6:13 says expressly: "It is by my name that you shall swear," maintained by *Ant.* 4 §287 and the rab. trad. (*BNed* 20a, etc.).

173. André Dupont-Sommer, *The Essene Writings from Qumran*, Gloucester (Mass.), P. Smith, 1973, p. 358, believes that this is the Teacher of Righteousness, their founder, and observes that the Pythagoreans also forbid pronouncing the name of Pythagoras; this is however rather improbable, as the "lawgiver" (νομοθέτης) always means Moses in FJ, cf. Matthias Delcor, "Contribution à l'étude de la législation des sectaires de Damas et Qoumrân," *RB* 61 (1954), p. 533–553; furthermore, it is likely that, as Philo suggests, they recognized Moses alone as their true founder.

174. *Ant.* 3 §276 and 4 §202, thus following Lev 24:16 MT "Whoever *blasphemes* (נוקב) the name of YHWH will be put to death"; the LXX has ὀνομάζων ("Whoever *names* . . ."), which Philo too appears to presuppose, *Vita Mosis* 2 §205 f.

175. Abbreviated *aleph-lamed* (for אלהים) or *aleph-dalet* (אדוני) instead of יהוה. *MBer* 9:4 mentions a temporary decree, taken against the *minim,* to greet others using the Name of God (tetragrammaton), like Boaz (Ruth 2:4); *TBer* 6:20 explains that these *minim* use the above periphrases (כנויים) for the benedictions, and thus cause the Name to be forgotten (*MSoṭa* 7:6 mentions that every priest pronounced the Name for the sacerdotal blessing in the Temple); in the context of the reorganization of Yavneh, these are certainly Jewish-Christians, contrary to the conclusion of *Tosefta kifshuṭah* 1:124.

176. Elisha Qimron, "שבועת הבנים in the Damascus Covenant 15.1-2," *JQR* 81 (1990), p. 115–188.

Josephus omits any information about the calendar and does not mention any feast of the Covenant or of Oaths, but it is not excessively risky to supply it. For one thing, the parallel documents speak of it, even Philo with his Therapeutae and their pentecosts. Further, the very possibility of blaspheming the name of Moses presupposes, to be concrete, that the Essenes had legitimate occasions for swearing oaths by this same name, which harmonizes very well with a rite of renewing the Covenant.

The points of contact between all this and the NT are obvious, one of the major elements being the power of the authoritative word. Here we will only emphasize the mobility of the ternary structure that we have just picked out. The Sermon on the Mount in its present context provides a direct illustration. At his baptism, Jesus receives the Spirit, who leads him into the wilderness to be tested. One of the aspects of this temptation scene, in a situation of urgency, is struggle between two interpretations of the same scriptural text, that of Satan and that of the Spirit.[177] Jesus emerges victorious, gathers people around him and delivers the Sermon. In it, he first recalls the requirement to respect the immutable Scripture,[178] Law and Prophets, which are to be fulfilled (today); then he makes a free commentary on the Decalogue, which becomes more demanding and at the same time more concrete (spiritual, or "inspired" sense). The result is in no way that he puts forward innovations of his own, and that was certainly not his aim; the similarities between Jesus' teaching and that of John the Baptist have been noted, and there are numerous parallels with the Qumran texts, especially the Beatitudes and the Lord's Prayer. And yet at the end, his listeners oppose the *authority* of Jesus, who has taken care to forbid all oaths, to the timidity of the *scribes*. The difference is that Jesus has both Moses and the Spirit, whereas the others have only Moses, whom they stop at reading, without any *authoritative* interpretation. When Jesus says, "it has been *said* to you," he quotes only the words of Scripture, and, paraphrasing with the help of his listeners' reaction, it is as if he said, "the scribes have *read* to you" (but have nothing else to say). So the ternary model consists of God, then the immutable Scripture (Moses and the Prophets), and finally the authorized or inspired interpreter (here Jesus); *ex hypothesi*, the Spirit who inspires Jesus at the time is the one who inspired the Scriptures, while Satan represents a deviant spirit. The whole scene is dominated by the baptism of Jesus, who is designated as Son and not simply as prophet, thus completing the Trinitarian revelation;[179] this, however, is an anticipation similar to John the Baptist's proclamation of the Lamb of God.

177. Similarly, 1 QS 3:18 distinguishes the two spirits in man.

178. Literal, cf. chap. II, §I.4.

179. John C. O'Neill, *Who Did Jesus Think He Was?* (Biblical Interpretation Series,

The trinitarian pattern is also present in the baptismal symbol, but under a different, more ritual form: to baptize in the name of the Father, and of the Son and of the Holy Spirit (Matt 28:19, cf. 1 Cor 12:3 f.). It is indeed a rite of initiation, but the Son occupies the second position, that of Moses: he is the new Moses,[180] or the incarnate (inalterable) Word. Jesus as Son is raised to the rank of divine veneration by the resurrection, through which he is the initiator of a new creation; this is a divine attribute and associates him very naturally with the perfectly biblical theme of hypostasized Wisdom. The Spirit is expressed by the life of and in the community, by its teaching and its rites.[181]

It is the second term of the triad that has undergone a major transformation, allowing a comparison with the candidates at Pentecost in Acts 2:38, to whom baptism is administered *in the name of* Jesus Christ, with a view to receiving the gift of the Spirit. Besides the meanings already seen (chap. II, §I.3), the mention of the name has the air of an oath. A little later, Peter raises up a lame man through this same name; so it is the source of an *authority*. In passing we observe that this trinitarian structure of the way God manifests Himself underlines the difference between the pre-paschal Jesus, teacher, healer, prophet, and the Risen Lord. The difficulty in putting the two together is precisely the point of the complex scene of the Transfiguration, showing the union between Jesus and Moses through Elijah, an identification which the apostles cannot conceive, since he is for them only the authorized master; that is why they are told that they will not understand until after the resurrection. That has hardly any sense for them at the time, but this synthesis later becomes the point on which their recognition of Jesus turns, as 2 Pet 1:16 f. insists.

2. *Table Fellowship and Penalties*

The oaths are fearful because they involve responsibility. So there are penalties attached to them. Josephus says only that those who are

---

11), Leiden, Brill, 1995, p. 94 f. brings together several passages (Philo, *Testament of the Twelve Patriarchs*, *Joseph and Aseneth*, etc.) containing properly Jewish allusions to the Trinity and Incarnation, but he restricts himself to ideas, without seeking to classify the various currents or to make any connection with customs.

180. It is possible that this "new Moses" is in the background of the debate over Ben Zoma, who wished that in the days of the Messiah (salvation) the deliverance from Egypt (Moses) would no longer be recalled; compromised by his incursion into paradise, this Ben Zoma may have been exhibiting symptoms of Christianity, cf. chap. V, §IV.1 and 3.

181. It is easy to see that the Creed, even in its primitive forms (cf. chap. I, §I.1), develops this pattern, from which Jesus' biography is missing.

caught in or convicted[182] of serious faults are expelled from the community, but that they remain bound by their oaths and so, not being able to touch profane food, they die of starvation (*J.W.* 2 §143). Expulsion is therefore principally a removal from the community meal. Josephus' brevity is somewhat disappointing, but it has the merit of focusing attention on what is essential. The precepts and oaths taken all together converge on food, and in particular on the community meal, which has a sacred structure:[183] according to *Ant.* 18 §22, *priests* prepare the bread and other food. Although there is no mention of meat,[184] these meals resemble communion sacrifices, eaten in the sanctuary, which fills out what has been said concerning the holiness of the garment and of the place: the community itself is the sanctuary.[185] In like manner, the *ḥaber* is one who eats ordinary food in a state of Levitical purity; this is not one commandment among others, less still a substitute for the rest, but the ex-

182. In the LXX, the verb ἁλίσκομαι corresponds to הרשע "be declared guilty" (Exod 22:8), המצא "be found" (Deut 24:7; Prov 6:31), הלכד "be caught, captured, conquered" (Prov 6:2; Zech 14:2), etc.

183. This idea of an assimilation with the "pure table" of the sanctuary (Lev 24:6), which comes from the *ḥaberim* (cf. below), is preserved by the rab. trad. (*MAb* 3:3): "If three eat at the same table and have said over it words of the Torah, it is as if they had eaten at the table of the Place, blessed be it, as it is said (Ezek 41:22): 'And he said to me: This is the table which is before YHWH.'"

184. It is not expressly excluded. Philo, *Vita contempl.*, §73, describes the banquet of the feast of the Therapeutae, and states that "the table is pure of foods containing blood"; this expression (which may mean vegetables, fish, etc.) is especially characteristic of meat ritually slaughtered for sacrifices, and in fact this banquet has every appearance of being an act of worship, cf. A. Jaubert, *L'Alliance*, p. 480. In the cases of Josephus' Essenes, it is reasonable to conjecture that the employment of priests to *prepare* the food (ποίησις βρωμάτων) implies, at least from time to time, the ritual slaughter of animals (independently of the paschal lamb).

185. Cf. CD 3:19-20: "God builds a sure house in Israel, such as never existed before until now; those who attach themselves to it firmly are destined to eternal life." Besides, "To lay a foundation of truth" (1 QS 5:3-6), is to practice the entire Law. This is also the meaning of οἰκοδομέω in the NT (cf. *TWNT* 5:139 f.): to build in "stone" the foundations of the house. The community sees itself as the temple, cf. Geza Vermes, "Car le Liban, c'est le conseil de la communauté," in: *Mélanges Robert*, Paris, 1957, p. 316–325. This is the new Jerusalem (2 Q), with future cultic organization, cf. 1 QSb 4:25-26. The liturgy and, more generally, the acts of the community bring about an assembly of angels and human beings (the term "saints" is ambiguous, cf. 1 QM 18:2, 1 QH 11:12): in *Jub* 2:17 f., the angels celebrate the Sabbath; in 6:18 the feast of Weeks is celebrated in heaven; according to 1 QS 11:7 f., the angels take part in the community council; in 1 QSa 2:8-9, it is because of the angels that the impure cannot be admitted to the council, etc. With this theme is associated that of the *merkaba* (Ezek 1), by means of which God follows His people into exile, cf. John Strugnell, "The Angelic Liturgy at Qumran," *VTSup* 7 (1960), p. 318–345 (336 f.).

pression of the quintessence of the Torah.[186] This insistence on food and table fellowship opens up vast anthropological questions, but we will only observe here that the first commandment in the Bible, after the initial blessings (including the command to increase and multiply), is a precept not to eat a certain food (Gen 2:17), whereas the last commandment given by Jesus is to "take and eat . . . drink."

The Qumran documents give many details, but they do not depart from this pattern: the penalties imposed can be defined in terms of a greater or lesser degree of removal from the "purity," the community meal. CD 9:16-23 distinguishes two areas: serious wrongs against God or the neighbor, and crimes involving money.[187] For a serious fault to be judged and punished, there have to be three witnesses, corresponding perhaps to three successive occasions. When a breach of the law has occurred, the witness must make a deposition before an officer of the court[188] in the presence of the accused. Once two testimonies have been recorded independently, whether relating to the same wrongdoing or to two successive occasions of the same nature, the one accused is excluded from the "purity," as a precautionary measure, since his guilt has not yet been legally established. In accusations concerning property, two testimonies are enough to prove the charge, but even after only one, the accused is removed from the "purity," as a similar precautionary measure.[189] In fact, Deut 19:15 requires "two or three witnesses to sustain any charge," which leaves some room for interpretation.[190] 11 QT 64:6-13 mentions two or three witnesses for the traitor, then capital punishment ("hanging"); 1 Tim 5:19 speaks of accusation by two or three witnesses; Heb 10:28 indicates that rejection of the Law attested by two or three witnesses is punishable by death. These three cases bear on repetition of the

186. Cf. chap. V, §I.1. It is especially remarkable that members at different stages of initiation do not eat together, even though that was theoretically possible, by taking certain legal steps. Jacob Neusner, *From Politics to Piety: The Emergence of Pharisaic Judaism*, Hoboken, Ktav, 1979, p. 47 f., concludes from the rabbinic sources that it is a question of a "pure food club," but does not wonder about the nature of these clubs.

187. Respectively called מות and הון, biblical terminology corresponding to נפשות and ממונות in *MSanh* 1:1, similarly ("death" and "money," representing the nature of the maximum possible penalties).

188. Called מבקר, cf. §IV.3.

189. The rabbinic system is different: there is no idea of recidivism, and the principle is that in all cases (with very rare exceptions, particularly facts that are naturally public, like births and deaths) the witness of two is sufficient to attest a single act, on condition that they can prove they were together (cf. Dan 13:36) and that they are not related (*MSanh* 3:6 f.).

190. In *Ant.* 4 §219 and *Life* §49, FJ also mentions two or three witnesses, but in *Ant.* 8 §358, regarding the trial of Naboth, he has three witnesses, whereas 1 Kgs 21:10 f. has only two. So he attests a custom which distinguished between various cases.

same act, each witness being independent and capable of giving personal testimony. John 8:17 and Rev 11:3 speak only of two witnesses, but the reference is either literary, to Zech 3:3-14, so the two Messiahs, or juridical, to the drawing up of a legal document (contract).[191]

For CD 9:23 f., the witnesses must have attained the age of majority, or of military service, normally 20, and, at least in a criminal matter, "fear God," that is be members of the community (cf. 20:15 f.), and *moreover* be partakers of the "purity," so not have committed any voluntary offense without having made up for it. Women may also testify: 1 QSa 1:9-10 makes provision for a man to marry as soon as he knows right from wrong, that is reaches his majority; he can unite with a woman, who can then testify against him and take part in discussion in the court. This case has given rise to controversies,[192] but a biblical reference suffices (Gen 2:24). The union is *ipso facto* a marriage, by which the woman attains to legal majority; her testimony against her husband no doubt chiefly concerns the domain of purity, which is an intimate matter and highly important. In that case she needs sufficient knowledge.[193] Josephus has nothing to say on this question, except that the Essenes are afraid of women's shamelessness and are convinced that none remains faithful to one husband (2 §121). Philo fires even heavier shots, when discussing the Essenes; on the other hand, he puts both Therapeutae and Therapeutrides on the same footing.[194] These two authors can hardly be regarded as feminists, but the very violence of their expressions may betray a widespread division of opinion concerning the place of women in the community.

Penal procedure is somewhat better defined in CD 9:2-8, which introduces an essential element, the warning.[195] No one may accuse another without proving that he has already warned him personally; otherwise the accuser is guilty of either carrying out a vendetta or even of being an ac-

191. This is the starting point from which the rab. trad. generalizes to all testimonies.

192. Dominique Barthélemy, *DJD* 1, London, 1956, p. 235, takes the text as it is; on the other hand, Joseph M. Baumgarten, *Studies in Qumran Law* (SJLA, 24), Leiden, Brill, 1977, p. 186 f., regards such a measure as impossible, in the name of Athenian and Roman law (he invokes also 1 Cor 14:34 and 1 Tim 3:11-12), but he is forced to correct the text.

193. A delicate subject for Paul and for the rab. trad., cf. the case of Priscilla, chap. VI, §II.1.

194. Cf. Eusebius, *Hist. eccl.* 8.11.14 f. (Essenes), and Philo, *Vita contempl.* §32 f., 68 f., 83–87.

195. תוכחה. Under the name of התריה (התראה) rab. law makes the same demand: the witness of a sinful act must have warned the guilty party *just before the act* of the penalty that he will incur, as he is presumed to have forgotten it; characteristically, if the delinquent is a *ḥaber*, the warning is no longer obligatory, since he is supposed to know the Law, and not to let himself be governed by his passions. . . .

complice.[196] The result is that the first offense generally carries no consequences, except private warning or remonstrance. Thus, in 2 Cor 13:1, Paul cites Deut 19:15, indicating that he is now on the third warning, that is the third time that the same faults have occurred; at his next visit he will have the right to punish any further backsliding. He is not talking of a criminal trial or sentence, but of excommunication. There too, the number of witnesses is understood as the "number of testimonies." The same is true in Matt 18:16, where two or three warnings have to be given before the judgment of the community and finally exclusion: to be *regarded* as a Gentile or a (Jewish) tax collector represents maximal impurity, the first of the four classes defined above, in which Gentiles and Jews that do not belong to the community are lumped together (cf. chap. V, §I.3). The impurity thus acquired, which has precise juridical consequences, symbolizes the reality of sin. It is an echo in reverse of the pedagogy of entry into the community, in which the various purifications are the outward signs of an inward distancing from sin, but without any magical effect, as Josephus emphasizes with regard to John the Baptist (*Ant.* 18 §117).

For the definition of penalties, there is first (*Jub*, 11 QT) what is laid down in the Bible, with a tendency to generalize the death penalty, as in Philo and Josephus, who even says that blasphemy of the name of Moses is a capital crime (cf. above). However, given the need for prior warning, there is a good chance that the death penalty remained purely theoretical.[197] More interesting is the list provided in 1 QS 6:24 f., defining a series of cases immediately after the rules for admitting new members (6:21-23).[198] This list concerns the incidents of common life, running from the very serious to the very trivial, but omitting any problems concerning Sabbath, sacrifices, or marriage; it concerns ethics rather than rites. The first article concerns lying about property. The next treat of relations with the neighbor, then the assembly, then sexual modesty, and finally cases of total exclusion, temporary or permanent, from the community.[199] For example, one who "turns aside from the foundation" of

196. Cf. respectively Lev 19:18; Ps.-Jon. and Neof. on Deut 32:35 (vengeance) and 1 QS 5:24 f., cf. Ezek 33:8, Sir 19:13 f.

197. In *Ag.Ap.* 2 §145, FJ insists on the extreme severity of the sanctions, which shows that according to him the customs can really be observed (and so that the death penalty is theoretical).

198. These two passages do not belong to the same level of redaction, and the list itself, with its mixture of different formulations, is an aggregate of small clauses of different origins, but bringing them all together is significant. In CD 14:18 f. are the remains of a similar list, presented as norms of community life before the coming of the Messiah son of Aaron; 4 QDb, fr. 18, 4:1 f. gives complementary details.

199. In the rab. trad., banishment is exclusion from the brotherhood, but not from the people. *BMoedQ* 16a describes a whole procedure of convocation with envoys, etc., which

the community, that is negates or denies its reason for existing, redoes two years of novitiate (1 QS 7:18), since he has thereby made himself as impure as a foreigner (the two years in 1 QS, where the procedure is a little different, correspond to the three years in Josephus). However, if a member of more than ten years standing is excluded, there is no possibility of return (cf. *J.W.* 2 §143 f.), which shows a link between seniority and access to the higher degrees of purity (cf. above, §1). It is also forbidden to help one that has been expelled (1 QS 7:24 f.), since his impurity is contagious, as Josephus also implies, even if he waters it down out of a concern for "philanthropy" (*J.W.* 2 §144). At the opposite end of the scale, the most venial faults are punished by several days or weeks of exclusion from the "purity."

A somewhat different case, connected with the question of oaths, is furnished by suspicion of theft in the camp. According to Lev 5:1, if, after official declaration, someone that knows who is to blame keeps quiet, he too is guilty, as he is assumed to be an accomplice. CD 9:10-12 clarifies the procedure by obliging the owner of the object that has disappeared to swear an "oath of malediction,"[200] that is an adaptation of the public curse laid down in Num 5:21 in the case of a suspected woman. The themes are obviously related, and the subject dealt with immediately before (Num 5:5-10), the restitution of objects lost or stolen, comes immediately afterwards in our text (CD 9:13 f.).[201] As well as these formal reasons, another motive brings the two cases together: belief in the effectiveness of curses (cf. Judg 17:2), which is a consequence of the authority of the spoken word. It is hard to know how representative is this case, but it is well illustrated by the story of Ananias and Sapphira (Acts 5:4 f.), which concerns lying about property, and in which Peter's word falls like a thunderbolt (cf. chap. VI, §III.3).

In all these cases, we have brought together all the available sources, including the NT, on the same footing, as it is clearly a question of the same culture. That does not imply uniformity, as there are obviously some notable differences in customs, as we have seen regarding admission of new members, private property, marriage, or the position of women. The model of this multiform character remains the rabbinic tradition: the reorganization of Yavneh marked out a perimeter, within

---

is attached to Num 16:12 f. (revolt of Korah) and Jer 46:16; there is a gradation of sanctions.

200. שבועת האלה, formula which features in Num 5:21.

201. A comparable technique of assimilation of neighboring cases (which is a form of *midrash*) is used in the rabbinic traditions, cf. Wilhelm Bacher, *Die exegetische Terminologie der jüdischen Traditionsliteratur*, Leipzig, 1899, I:133.

which the innumerable controversies, apart from some exceptional cases of banishment, attest both the likeness and the diversity of the brotherhoods.[202]

3. Government, Offices; Kerygma and Church

Josephus emphasizes that the Essenes are obedient in all things to their "overseers." These are elected, and collegially responsible for services for all (*J.W.* 2 §123).[203] There is no mention of a community head, elected or not, nor of anyone in charge of admission of new members. Concerning judgments, Josephus mentions only, for serious matters, assemblies of at least a hundred members; the position of the officers and priests in them is not defined, and authority in decision making comes from seniority and numbers (2 §146). These summaries allow us to distinguish two areas of obedience: day-to-day activities, which depend on the officers, including all material, technical and financial aspects, without necessarily being limited to them, and judicial matters, obviously connected with tradition and teaching, where the seniors express their opinions first, and decisions are taken by majority vote.

The same division of powers occurs also in the Qumran *Community Rule*, with some interesting nuances. First, Josephus' "overseers" have long been compared to the *Rule*'s "inspectors,"[204] in charge of the community's income (1 QS 6:20) and alms (CD 14:13 f.). However, these inspectors seem to have had very extensive powers. According to 1 QS 6:12, the inspector presides at the Council of the community, and he is the only one who can speak without asking permission of the assembly. In CD 9:18 f. the inspector acts as prosecutor in criminal charges, which goes with his role, already mentioned, of collecting the testimonies supporting the accusation. For CD 13:5 f., the inspector instructs the priests in the Law, teaches the community about the works of God, trains and examines the candidates for admission. CD 14:8 f. even mentions an inspector over all the "camps," apparently in charge of all the communities. Such an impressive omnicompetence has raised the question whether the functions of the inspector may have undergone development, which would explain their inflation.[205] It appears simpler to see in the notion of

202. Cf. Saul Lieberman, "The Discipline in the So-Called Dead Sea Manual of Discipline," *JBL* 71 (1952), p. 199–206.

203. Lit.: "indistinctly charged with services for all" ἀδιαίρετοι πρὸς ἁπάντων εἰς τὰς χρείας ἕκαστοι. Apparently there is no elective hierarchy that supplants seniority (the classes).

204. The terms ἐπιμελητής (FJ) and מבקר, פקיד (1 QS, CD) can be considered as equivalent, but nothing suggests that they constitute a *title* (they denote an *onus* and not an *honor*).

205. Cf. discussion and references in T. S. Beall, *Josephus' Description*, p. 47.

"overseer" a generic term that is purely functional, covering any sort of responsibility from garbage disposal to training of novices. In any case, the absence of titles, except for the classes of purity, would be better suited to the Essenes' mistrust of honors (2 §140) and their democratic attitude, since all are called to the same perfection;[206] this fits Josephus' concise definition, putting all the "overseers" in the same rank (*J.W.* 2:123).

The other branch of power, concerning authority in matters of teaching and law, cannot be reduced to the elected "overseers." Those who enter the community ought to "submit to the authority of the sons of Zadok, [who are] the priests that keep the Covenant, and to the authority of the majority of the members of the community."[207] This formulation is very close to the definition given by Josephus, who distinguishes the same two forms of permanent statutory authority, but here the "sons of Zadok" clearly have the same position and authority as Josephus' "elders."[208] This equivalence invites us to examine what the Essenes understood by "priest."

The term "elder" used by Josephus is rather banal;[209] its sole merit is to designate a recognized personal status (wisdom, competence, maturity), thus a moral responsibility, in contrast to an office, elective or not, implying a contractual juridical responsibility. Josephus does, however, speak of priests: in *Ant.* 18 §20, he says that the Essenes choose good men *as* priests,[210] to receive the produce of the land and prepare bread and other food. To receive and deal with the Levitical contributions tied to the land (tithes, offerings) and to prepare meals are priestly activities, suited to the sacerdotal dimension of the meals. Josephus' formulation implies that these officers exercise a priestly function, but are not really priests; he is certainly too imbued with the importance of genealogy for the legitimacy of the priesthood,[211] to allow them to be true priests. However,

206. In the OT, the term σεμνότης features only in 2 Macc 3:13, in connection with the "majesty of the Temple."

207. 1 QS 5:2-3 רוב אנשי היחד.

208. Likewise, in the rab. trad., the authority of the "elder" (זקן) is very great; also his teaching is regarded as highly dangerous if he departs from the norm, represented here by the great Sanhedrin; his case is all the more serious as he affirms that he is faithful to his masters, cf. *MSanh* 11:1-2, which makes provision for "hanging" (זקן ממרא). To be both "faithful to one's own masters" and "in contradiction with the teaching of the majority" suggests the reorganization of Yavneh, cf. chap. IV, §I.3.

209. R. Alastair Campbell, *The Elders. Seniority Within Earliest Christianity*, Edinburgh, T. & T. Clark, 1994.

210. According to the mss [A]MW; the mediaeval *epitome* E corrects to "and priests," which is a facilitating reading.

211. Cf. *Ag.Ap.* 1 §31 on the importance of archives for establishing and checking the legitimacy of the priests.

there is an analogous phenomenon among the *ḥaberim*: certain passages show that they receive tithes as such, like Levites or priests (*YMaasSh* 5:5, p. 56b), without any identifiable link with their pedigree.[212]

The passage already quoted from the *Rule* speaks unambiguously of "priests sons of Zadok." No text refers to the personal status of candidates for admission, or of any special treatment of those who may be priests or Levites by birth. On the contrary, 1 QS 1:18-19 declares that those who enter into the Covenant *will be* priests, Levites, etc.[213] In fact, the Covenant was forgotten until the arrival of "Zadok" (CD 5:2-5), and the members of the community are called to be "sons of Zadok."[214] This person is first of all literary: high priest in the time of Solomon (1 Kgs 2:35), he is in no way a descendant of Aaron and Eleazar, and not even of the tribe of Levi; he is the prototype of the *elected* priest, to the detriment of dynasties. According to Ezek 44:15, it is precisely "sons of" Zadok who become the true priests; they are not his descendants, but his moral heirs. Furthermore, with the Essenes, no situation is permanent; according to 1 QS 5:24, the position of anyone can be changed by discernment of spirits. This insistence on the reality of the priesthood comes from the central position of the Covenant, and its expression in properly cultic acts: the community identifies itself as a temple. In *Ant.* 18 §19, they offer sacrifices by themselves, being excluded[215] from the Temple for reasons

212. Likewise, it emerges from a fairly complex discussion in *BGiṭ* 30b on the Levites who receive the tithe that they are in fact *ḥaberim*, who are assimilated to the Levites. The usual explanation is that the *ḥaberim* then the sages, by their study, perform a true worship. On this transfer, cf. Sacha Stern, *Jewish Identity in Early Rabbinic Writings* (AGAJU, 23), Leiden, Brill, 1994.

213. And we in fact find them in various contexts. According to 1 QS 8:1-5, the council of the community is to comprise twelve members plus three priests (although it is not a tribunal). CD 10:4-10 defines a group of ten elected judges, four from the tribe of Levi (and Aaron), and six from Israel; they must be between 25 and 60 years of age and be versed in the texts. 4 QOrd 2-4 speaks of a tribunal of ten members and two priests. According to 1 QS 6:2 f. every council in formal session should include at least ten persons, one of whom is a priest. For the meal, the priest will reach out his hand first so that the benedictions may be pronounced over the first fruits of bread and wine, etc. The composition and role of these organisms, as well as the age limits, vary from source to source, but there are always priests or Levites. They appear to have been very numerous: at least 10% of the full members, which is certainly superior to the proportion of priests by birth among Jews in general.

214. The Teacher of Righteousness is to be (or become) the high priest son of Zadok; his precise identification remains problematic, cf. Jerome Murphy-O'Connor, "The Judean Desert," in: Robert A. Kraft & George W. E. Nickelsburg, *Early Judaism and Its Modern Interpreters*, Philadelphia (Penn.), 1986, p. 119–156, and discussion p. 140.

215. The form εἰργόμενοι is in the passive, and not the middle voice (which would have the sense of "excluding oneself"), cf. Ralph Marcus, "Pharisees, Essenes and Gnostics," *JBL* 73 (1954), p. 157–161.

of purification ritual; 1 QS 9:3 f. also mentions sacrifices. It is not easy to say clearly whether and how the Essenes offered sacrifices, at Qumran or elsewhere, and whether all the brotherhoods had the same practice.[216] We will only remark here that even if there were only a hope for a renewed sanctuary, it would imply people ready and able to carry out the temple worship at any moment; further, if, as Josephus says, priests prepared the food, communion sacrifices are involved.

The evidence is not always clear, and many aspects cannot be dealt with here, but everything points to a priesthood by promotion, rather than by birth.[217] Josephus also writes that the Essenes preferred to adopt children rather than have them themselves, which allowed them to avoid marriage (*J.W.* 2 §120). There could be no clearer evidence of their lack of interest in questions of genealogy; it may also be a reason why Josephus insists that the Essenes had to be Jews "by nationality."

These various elements throw some light on functions in the NT. First of all, Jesus is declared to be a high priest like Melchizedek[218] by Heb 7:14 f., which stresses that he does not belong at all to any priestly tribe, and that his priesthood is an office (rather than an honor) acquired by strictly personal title. The question also arises concerning *presbuteroi*, *episkopoi* and *diakonoi*, ancestors of our priests, bishops and deacons, at least regarding the titles. The first term, which is simply that of Josephus' "elders," without sacerdotal terminology, designates a status, whereas the other two represent offices, that of "overseers" and that of "servants." In

216. Cf. the discussion by T. S. Beall, *Josephus' Description*, p. 115–119. In chap. IV, §I.4, we have seen that Yoḥanan b. Zakkai kept his distance from any cult at Jerusalem. The rab. trad. has retained the custom of three daily prayers (and a fourth on the Sabbath) bearing the name of the sacrifices in the Temple and recited at the corresponding times; this is a substitute for the cult itself. Tradition has it that this custom dates from the exile after the ruin of the first Temple (567); this is going too far, but there are some signs that the custom did exist *before* 70, that is in circles which refused at least Herod's temple (and perhaps that of the Hasmonaeans before). According to *MTaan* 4:2 (and par.), at the moment when each of the 24 courses (משמרות) of priests (and Levites) came to take its week of service in the Temple, the people of their villages were constituted in "stations" (מעמדות) in their synagogues (and perhaps also at Jerusalem); they prayed, fasted and read Gen 1 as well as the precepts on the sacrifices, thus filling out the official worship. However, the texts are not very clear (cf. *Tosefta kifshuṭah* 5:1103 f.), and these stations, especially with fasting, suggest rather dissident practices (according to *MMeg* 4:3, the "station" is a gesture of mourning, requiring at least ten persons), analogous perhaps to the "vicarious fast" of the Quartodecimans, cf. above §I.2.

217. There is another pointer in the same direction in *J.W.* 4§155, where the revolutionaries (zealots) set side the high priest then in office and impose another chosen by lot with no connection with any of the traditional high priestly families.

218. That is of a non-Levitical priesthood, as is seen also in the fragment 11 QMelch, where Melchizedek, called *elohim* and king, saves and *expiates*.

Acts 20:17 f., Paul summons for the last time the "elders" of Ephesus, and tells them, in face of the external and internal dangers that he foresees, to watch over the flock over which the Holy Spirit has "placed" them as "overseers." No procedure is clearly indicated,[219] and we do not know if they had a collegial responsibility for everything, or if there was a subdivision of tasks. The same superimposing of "elders" and "overseers" also occurs in Titus 2:1. After explaining to Titus that he is to establish "elders" in each town of Crete, Paul describes the qualities required, and explains, "the 'overseer,' as God's steward, must be irreproachable"; thus "he will be able to exhort in sound doctrine and refute those who contradict." In both cases, Paul has in view the integrity of the community and of doctrine, and not material offices, which explains why responsibility is attributed to the elders, who *ex hypothesi* have personal recognized qualities.

The term "servants" is generic, since Paul attributes it to himself, (2 Cor 3:6, etc.), but there are some indications of a technical sense.[220] In 2 Tim 3:8 f., Paul demands that they be "married to one wife,"[221] like the overseers, also sober and honest, which implies that they are in charge, among other things, of wine and money. He appears also to allow this office to be given to women,[222] which implies that it is not connected with teaching, at least according to the writer's own ideas. The institution narrative of the Seven in Acts is not very explicit. It does not say clearly that they are instituted as "servants,"[223] but it indicates that "service of tables" has the same importance as "the word," and that those to be chosen must be of good reputation and "filled with the Spirit of God" (Acts 6:3).[224] Taking into account the ritual reported by Josephus, as well as allusions to the breaking of bread, it is not going too far to assume that what is

219. For example, in Acts 14:23, Paul and Barnabas, visiting the communities that they had founded, "established" (χειροτονήσαντες, perhaps indicating an imposition of hands) elders; then, with prayer and fasting, they commended "them" (the elders, or the whole group of disciples?) to the Lord.

220. Cf. the dossier in *TWNT* 2 (1935), p. 81–93.

221. It is hardly probable, in his milieu, that Paul refers here to polygamy, whose prohibition appears to go without saying; if he had meant it, he would have said so more clearly. He is certainly speaking of those who have never remarried. The argument on creation, cited by CD 4:20 f., features also in Mark 10:6 and Matt 19:4. On polygamy, cf. above §IV introd.

222. In 2 Tim 3:11, Paul speaks of "women" (and requires in particular that they be sober) between two paragraphs specifying the qualities of the "servant." The meaning often given of "deacon's wife" is not the most obvious. In Rom 16:1 Phœbe is described as "deacon" (διάκονος) of the church of Cenchreae.

223. Perhaps they never were in reality: the only two of the Seven whose acts are reported, Stephen and Philip, are in no way busied with tables, cf. chap. VI, §I.3 but cf. chap. I, §II.1.

224. WT; AT: "filled with Spirit and Wisdom."

involved is the preparation, even perhaps the conduct of community meals, in other words major community meetings.[225] Similarly, in his description of the cultic meal of the Therapeutae, Philo describes the tables as sacred, and emphasizes that the "servants" *(diakonoi)*[226] in charge of the service of the tables must be chosen with care (*Vita Cont.* §72 f.). According to Phil 1:1, each community had several "overseers" and several "servants"; whether or not that was so, the distinction between the two kinds of office is fairly clear: the latter were in charge of the working of the community, the former with its definition. In this sense, when Jesus gave his disciples power to baptize, or to forgive or retain sins (Matt 18:18; John 20:23), he was simply giving them the office of "overseer," with the power to admit new members and to exclude wrongdoers (cf. 2 Cor 13:1).

To clarify further, we need to remark first that the NT is not much concerned with community organization, and gives first place to the role of "apostle"[227] or "witness." This other side of the apostles' task is expressed by a mission given *by the Risen Christ*, which is not to be confused with the power just mentioned: "Go out to the whole world, proclaim the Good News to every creature" (Mark 16:15). They work within pre-existing groups, and they attract new members, not without stirring up contestations and divisions. In a word, they preach and proclaim a *kerygma*. In the ancient world, those who gathered in answer to such a summons were normally called an *ekklesia*; this term designates in the first place not the members of a constituted group, but an assembly precisely as "called out."[228] Thus we arrive at a twofold definition of the community: as constituted group, it is a "great number" (chap. VI, §III.4), managed by "overseers" with power to admit or exclude; as assembly convoked by the apostles' call, it is a "church" (*ekklesia*). A passage of Ignatius of Antioch, written around 100 but attesting a reality that was al-

225. In 1 Tim 5:17, the expression "presiding elders" (προεστῶτες πρεσβύτεροι) is not really technical (and cannot be confined to presiding over the assembly): it means simply that the offices have been entrusted to "elders."

226. The rab. trad. uses the Heb. equivalent (שמש) for the service of the ritual paschal meal (§II.2).

227. The rab. trad. has the equivalent שליח "emissary," and clearly states his juridical quality (*MBer* 5:5): "A man's emissary is as the man himself."

228. By a qualified herald, whose proclamation is a κήρυγμα, cf. Moulton, *s. v.* ἐκκλησία and the developments taken from classical Athenian customs in *Dict. ant.*, "ekklesia," 2:511 f. Even in Acts 19, the noisy gathering in the theater at Ephesus is brought within the norms of a duly summoned assembly (cf. v. 32 ἐκκλησία) by the presence and call to order of the responsible magistrate (γραμματεύς), who refers any further debate to a future assembly due to be held on a fixed date (cf. v. 39 ἔννομος). A merely spontaneous assemblage was regarded *a priori* as a riot or dissidence, συστροφή (Acts 19:40; 23:12; MT קשר, cf. 2 Kgs 15:15; Am 7:10).

ready customary, brings out especially well these two aspects of one and the same entity (*Ad Smyrn.* 8:2): "Where the bishop appears, let there be the 'great number,' just as where Jesus Christ is, let there be the Catholic 'Church'! It is not allowed in the absence of the bishop either to baptize or to perform the *agapê*." The juridical role of the bishop (the "overseer") is particularly clear, but that is not enough to make a Christian assembly, for it is necessary that Jesus Christ be present, that is proclaimed: that is the kerygma which founds the Church. It is of course significant that precisely the term "church" has been retained to designate the Christian assembly;[229] the office of herald is not to be confused with that of bishop, or, if you like, Paul is not to be confused with Peter.

V – Why *Christiani?*

Jesus and his disciples were from the beginning called "Nazoreans," a term which has been kept in Syriac and Hebrew, and which we must regard as Jewish-Christian. Again, as we have shown (chap. VI, §I.3), the Latin term *christiani*, given by the Romans to Messianic agitators, was pinned on the disciples at Antioch at a time of disturbance. This name has stuck in Greek and in Latin. That it should have done so is all the more remarkable in that Pauline Christianity is not strictly speaking a Messianism: "Christ" has become a mere proper name, and the Pentecost narrative of Acts 2 is careful to sidestep the final (Messianic) question of the disciples, who await the establishment of the kingship of Israel (Acts 1:6 WT). If the names of Christ (Anointed) and Christian have been preserved, even though turned aside from their primitive meaning, it can only be because they originally had an appreciable significance, *a priori* connected with an anointing. Moreover, in a culture as sensitive to signs as Judaism, we need to start by looking not for clever juggling of verses or subtle biblical allusions to a king-Messiah or a priest-Messiah, but to concrete points of reference, that is, following the method we have used until now, rites, rather than events or doctrines.

Let us say it at once: the available information is too tenuous to come to certain conclusions. We shall have to be content with presump-

229. In the NT the term ἐκκλησία has a flexibility analogous to that of πλῆθος: it can designate just as well either a local and well-defined group (Acts 8:1; Rom 16:1, etc.) or an indeterminate agglomerate of groups, analogous to a people (Matt 16:21; Acts 9:31; Eph 1:22, etc.). There is a comparable metonymy in the rab. trad.: *BSuk* 27b states that all Israel can stand in a single booth during the feast of Tabernacles (סוכות "booths"); *BPes* 78b declares that all Israel can share a single paschal lamb. The real meaning is that the little group gathered (for a feast) represents the whole people, or the whole "Catholic Church."

tions based on convergent indications, and distinguishing two parts: first concerning anointings properly so called, then some observations on the cross as a sign.

1. Christians, Anointings

The NT never speaks of ritual anointing, except of the sick (Mark 6:13; Jas 5:14). Laying on of hands is often mentioned, but in circumstances so diverse that it is difficult to draw specific implications, apart from the quite banal fact that it is an official gesture.[230] These variations have apparently had as cause or as effect a certain fluidity of usages, even for a given rite. We have an example of this in Acts 19:3, where Paul imposes both hands according to the AT, but only one hand according to the

230. In the OT, the laying on of hands is not associated with the Spirit, but rather with the conferring of a position or office, cf. Gen 48:14 (Jacob and Ephraim-Manasseh); in Num 27:18-23 Moses lays his hands on Joshua, who has already received the Spirit, but in Deut 34:9, it is this gesture that confers the Spirit (cf. the institution of the Seven in Acts 6:6). In 1 Tim 4:14 and 2 Tim 1:6 f. the imposition of hands confers or officially recognizes a charism. In Mark 10:13-16 Jesus imposes hands on children; Luke 18:15 f. omits the imposition of hands (but transfers it in Acts to the newly baptized). Jesus imposes hands as a healer (he is asked to do so, which presupposes that it is a customary gesture, cf. Mark 5:23; 7:32). For the blind man of Bethsaida, there are two phases of laying on of hands, first with saliva (suggesting the word, also anointing and/or baptism), then without, and he sees (Mark 8:22-26). The rab. trad. distinguishes (with some confusion, cf. *MSanh* 1:3 and *TSanh* 1:1) imposition of hands on an animal to be ritually slaughtered (סמיכה, cf. Lev 4:15) and institution of "elders" (סמיכות זקנים). In fact, there is an analogy in the background: in Num 8:9 f. Moses must bring forward (והקרבת, LXX προσάξεις) the Levites of the Tabernacle, then the sons of Israel lay hands on the Levites, then Aaron presents them; there is an idea of transfer or substitution, since subsequently it is they who lay hands on the head of the bulls to be sacrificed, which are a substitute for the firstborn. Likewise, in Lev 1:4 etc., the *personal* imposition of hands gives the victim its expiatory character. In Lev 16:21, by imposition of hands the high priest "puts" the people's sins on the head of the scapegoat: the gesture symbolizes a transfer of condemnation. Later Christian trad. knows the imposition of hands, especially for ordination, a subject often studied, cf. Eduard Lohse, *Die Ordination im Spätjudentum und im Neuen Testament*, Göttingen, Vandenhoeck & Ruprecht, 1951. The technical term χειροτονεῖν can signify the laying on properly so called (of one or both hands), but also the raising of the arms (or of only one); the latter is the classic way of expressing a vote by show of hands (χειροτονία), as opposed to secret ballot (ψῆφος, cf. below §2). The same expression can also designate any (religious) mission, since Justin, *Dial.* §17, 108, uses it for the Jewish emissaries sent against the Christians. The rab. trad. (*YSanh* 1:2, p. 19a, l. 42 f.) has two terms regarded as equivalent for the ordination of a *rabbi* (become *rab* in Babylonia, perhaps influenced by the term רבי [רבותא], denoting growth, dignity and even sometimes anointing). In Judaea-Galilee, the term was מני (cf. Dan 2:24 f.; 3:12; Ezra 7:25), which means literally "introduce into the count" (מניין); the recipient then has a right to vote in deliberative assemblies. In Babylonia, it was סמיכות "imposition of hands." Both terms strongly suggest two aspects of admission into a community of *rabbim* (or *ḥaberim*), or the tribunals of 10 or 12 in the Qumran documents (cf. above §IV.3 and chap. V. §I.1).

WT; it is hard to know *a priori* if this difference of one letter has any important significance.

The major fact that obliges us to study the NT more closely is the later testimony of the Christian canonico-liturgical tradition. Hippolytus of Rome, writing at the beginning of the 3rd century, but showing all the signs of strict conservatism, describes the admission of a neophyte. After being baptized (no definite minister is indicated), the candidate receives from an "elder" (priest) an anointing with oil, then is confirmed by the bishop who pours oil on the head, lays a hand on the head and makes a sign on the forehead. Having then received the Spirit, the new member enters into the people ("the order of laity") and is allowed to receive the kiss of peace, which is the first gesture of the eucharist proper (*Trad. apost.* 22.3). Of course, the mere fact of writing down a ritual in such minute detail implies that there were controversies, or at least divergent traditions. Tertullian and his spiritualizing heresy are somewhere in the background, and the Syriac tradition attests another sequence: anointing with oil by the bishop, then baptism, and finally imposition of an outward mark (the cross) that closes the rite; this arrangement is fairly parallel to the narrative of the man born blind (mud on the eyes, then washing, and finally recognition, John 9:6 f.). These variants do not, however, obscure the presence of two distinct blocks: a baptism without any specialized minister, which is none other than the conclusion of a catechumenal process, and a body of admission rites performed by the bishop or under his responsibility and consisting of one or more anointings and the imposition of a sign.

The obvious question to ask, is whether these gestures were created by the Church, or whether they go back to the first generation, that is, whether they are of Jewish origin. In a general way, the series of rituals described by Hippolytus have clear Jewish counterparts.[231] The remarkable exception is precisely the body of rites of confirmation by the bishop. The ancient Jewish sources provide no clear positive attestation. There is, however, an interesting piece of indirect evidence. Deut 6:8 appears to prescribe the wearing of phylacteries on the arm and "between the eyes,"[232] which seems to indicate the forehead. However, *MMen* 4:8 declares that wearing the phylacteries on the forehead is "the usage of the

231. Cf. Gregory Dix, *The Shape of the Liturgy*, London, Dacre Press, 1945², p. 82 f. He follows the rab. trad., especially the usages of the brotherhoods *(ḥabura)*; the fact that he believes that these sources represent Judaism in general does not affect his conclusions, which are reinforced by the Essene analogies already considered.

232. The text is really difficult, and ancient witnesses attest various usages, cf. Philo, *Spec. leg.* 4 §137 and *Ant.* 4 §213.

minim,"[233] and that they should be worn on top of the head. The reasons given for this decision are a little artificial: for example Deut 14:1 forbids the wearing, as a sign of mourning, of "baldness" (tonsure) between the eyes; so it is argued that "between the eyes" means "on top of the head."[234] But there is something on the forehead of the Jewish-Christians (*minim*) which for them attracts the phylacteries and for the rabbinic tradition repels them. The phylacteries contain "all the words," that is the essentials of the Torah.[235] That being so, comparison with the rite of confirmation described above suggests a possible answer: if someone has received an anointing with oil and the sign of the cross on the forehead, putting the phylactery on the same spot is equivalent to saying that the Torah rests on symbols that are typically Christian, or at least have become so. We have already seen something of the same kind in the matter of whitewashed walls (chap. V, §IV.2). Further, as problems with the *minim* appear only with the reorganization of Yavneh, it is tempting to establish a parallel between this question about phylacteries and the attempt by Gamaliel II to avoid the paschal lamb looking as if it were immolated on a cross (cf. above §I.1). If the comparison be justified, it would mean that both the anointing *and* the sign of the cross were of Jewish origin, at least among Essenes and *ḥaberim*.

So we need to push the investigation further, looking in the NT for tiny indications, even if we do not expect to find clear mention of these things because of concern not to publish the rites (chap. I, §I.5).

In Luke 4:18, Jesus applies to himself the verse of Isa 61:1, "The Spirit of YHWH is on me, by which He has anointed me, to proclaim good news." In Acts 10:37 f., Peter tells how Jesus, after the baptism that John proclaimed, had been anointed by God with spirit and power. A similar expression already occurs in Acts 4:26 (Jesus anointed by God), with a quotation from Ps 2:1-2, in which the kings of the earth fight against YHWH and against His anointed; the reference is royal, not sacerdotal, and allows a comparison with Pilate's notice, in which Jesus is described as king of the Jews (John 19:19). However, Jesus' own declaration, quoting Isa, has rather a prophetic reference. All these expressions, which certainly indicate an authority and a mission, do not however correspond to any clearly identifiable gesture. In the narratives

233. דרכי מינות, which can also mean "a custom that leads to the *minim*."

234. Cf. *BMen* 37b; it is possible to argue by analogy: just as the phylacteries for the יד (meaning "forearm" and "hand") are placed on the largest part (the arm), so those for the head are placed on the largest part, *i.e.* on the skull.

235. The same for the *mezuza*, not without variations and controversies, cf. chap. V, §IV.2.

of Jesus' baptism there are also some curious expressions. The Spirit is manifested, in the form of a dove, *after* Jesus has been baptized (Matt 3:16 par.). Then, according to Mark 1:8 and John 1:33, John the Baptist proclaims that the one who is to come will baptize in holy Spirit[236] (Matt 3:11 and Luke 3:16 adding fire[237]). Even if "baptize" simply means to plunge, without any technical specification, these expressions make an odd combination of the idea of immersion (in water) and the Spirit. Anyhow, there is another way of expressing the gift of the Spirit which may appear more natural. It is given by Paul in Titus 3:6: "God has poured out this Spirit on you through Jesus Christ." Similarly, Peter in his speech at Pentecost (Acts 2:17) quotes Joel 3:1 ("I will pour my spirit on all flesh").

These two formulations express two quite distinct ways of representing the gift of the Spirit, but in the last analysis neither evokes the breath of the Spirit (cf. John 3:8; 20:22), or the Spirit's sudden irruption (Acts 19:6). On the contrary, both suggest in the background a concrete gesture which is applicable not directly to the Spirit, but to something that symbolizes the Spirit, whether by "plunging in" or "pouring out." In the first case, the reference would be baptism, or at least a certain stage in the baptismal course; in the second, one might think of Ezek 36:25 f. "I will pour out over you a pure water [. . .]; I will put my Spirit in you," but this prophecy was not related to baptism, at least in the strict sense of immersion.[238]

In that case, no ritual background is readily apparent, since "pouring" is not the same as "anointing" (cf. Exod 29:7). A comparison can, however, be made with the astounding scene known as the "anointing at Bethany": a woman pours a precious perfume on the head of Jesus, who declares to his astonished disciples that she has prepared his body for burial, and that wherever the Gospel is proclaimed, what she has done will be told in memory of her (Matt 26:13; Mark 14:9). This narrative, coming just before the Last Supper and forming a kind of diptych with it, has therefore enormous importance. The parallel traditions make of it an isolated episode. According to Luke 7:38, a sinful woman bathes Jesus' feet with her tears, wipes them with her hair and anoints them with perfume.[239]

236. Cf. the dossier established by Kilian McDonnell & George T. Montague, *Christian Initiation and Baptism in the Holy Spirit: Evidence from the First Eight Centuries*, Collegeville, Minn., Liturgical Press, 1991.

237. In relation with the judgment (with destruction and purification) announced by John the Baptist, cf. Isa 4:4 etc., and also 1 QS 4:13.

238. In the NT and the earliest Fathers, cf. chap. II, §I.5.

239. The verb ἀλείφω, employed here, corresponds also in the LXX to משח (most often rendered χρίω), cf. Gen 31:13; Exod 30:31 and 40:15 (for a garment, it translates סוך, 2 Sam 12:20; Ruth 3:3).

John 11:2 recalls the supposedly well-known fact that Mary had anointed Jesus with perfume and wiped his feet with her hair, but the episode is retold only later, just before the Last Supper and in a stylized form (12:3); this is a deliberate construction, which specifies that she anointed his feet with a costly perfume. The point of the narrative, the details of the scene and the identification of the guests vary, but the episode is memorized by means of the gesture of pouring a perfume.

The ultimate meaning, connected with the proclamation of the Gospel, is centered on Jesus himself, and not on the identity of the woman, except by the fact that she is exercising a diaconal function,[240] by taking care of an aspect of the service of tables. By embalming, especially with a highly scented perfume, a corpse escapes corruption and stench, with the symbolic meaning of escaping death. From another point of view, it is also the constant quality, according to the LXX, of a sacrifice agreeable to God, which is reckoned as being of "pleasing odor,"[241] whereas, materially speaking, the technical side of sacrificing was rather the opposite.[242] By her gesture, then, the woman foretells the resurrection, or more exactly Jesus interprets it this way, just as he interprets the bread and wine of the Last Supper. More precisely still, Jesus, who until then has refused any kingship, accepts, as if taken by surprise, something that resembles a royal anointing (cf. below).

But that is not all. In 2 Cor 2:14-16, Paul says: "Through us, God spreads in every place the perfume of his knowledge. In fact, we are for God the good odor of Christ (of the Anointed), for those who are being saved and for those who are being lost; for some, an odor of death leading to death, for others an odor of life leading to life." Paul is not generally very imaginative, and the metaphor used here is certainly not without some basis in reality: it presupposes a gesture of anointing with a sweet smelling substance, both "us" and Jesus. Here we find a further dimension of the gesture performed by the woman at Bethany, which explains its permanent significance: like Jesus, the disciples present and future receive a fragrant anointing that signifies their death and their resurrection. We find too a famous expression, which designates both a rite and a reality (Rom 6:5):[243] "If we die with him, we shall live with him." Other pas-

240. Cf. the introduction to the scene in John 12:2 καὶ ἡ Μάρθα διηκόνει (cf. Luke 10:40).

241. Cf. Eph 5:2 "Christ has given himself up for us as an *offering and victim*, as a *sweet smelling* fragrance," citing Exod 29:18 LXX (cf. Ps 40:7; Ezek 20:41).

242. According to *MAb* 5:5, the first of the ten permanent miracles at the Temple was that pregnant women did not miscarry despite the smell of the sacred meats (sacrifices).

243. Which quickly became a reality of persecution. This assimilation of the disciples' destiny to that of Jesus can be compared with the mention of Pilate in the Creed,

sages also assume an anointing received by the disciples. 1 John 2:20 declares to his correspondents: "You have an anointing from the Holy One." Paul develops a similar idea in 2 Cor 1:21: "It is God who gives us the anointing, He who has marked us with His seal." In this last statement, in which Paul, as is his wont, attributes to God the existence and life of the communities, it is difficult not to suppose that he is guided by a concrete gesture. In the end, however, we have to admit that all these texts hardly convey more than a rumor of anointing, probably with a diversity of customs. All the same, one fact emerges: despite the imprecision of the narratives, there is somewhere a mark symbolizing the Spirit, which is distinct from the water of baptism.[244] In John 3:5 f. Nicodemus is invited to a twofold rebirth, from water *and* the Spirit. In Gal 3:23 f., three phases can be perceived: justification by faith is linked up with baptism, then it is followed by the sending of the Spirit (4:6), and finally by the cross. Heb 5:13 makes a distinction between the milk of beginners and the solid food of the "perfect," *i.e.* of those who have finished with the initiation, who have received the laying on of hands after the baptisms (6:2). Even in Acts 19:3, where Paul appears to say that baptism in the name of Jesus gives the Spirit, the sequel shows that "baptism in the name of Jesus" is concluded by the laying on of hands (or of *the* hand) followed by the irruption of the Spirit. All these allusions are made in passing, without bothering about a description, and the terminology used is imprecise.

Still on the subject of anointings, we need to pause a moment over the distinction between (olive) oil and perfumes, especially myrrh and balm (extracted from the sap of the balsam tree). Exod 30:23 f. gives a long description of a holy unguent intended for the consecration by anointing of the utensils of worship, as well as of Aaron and his sons as priests. This preparation is an olive oil to which is added choice perfumes in fixed proportions. The Pentateuch does not mention any properly royal anointing (Deut 18:18): the first are those of Saul and David, for which the prophet Samuel has only oil.[245] However, according to a rabbinic opin-

---

which is of Roman origin; its primary sense is not to pinpoint a date, but to point out an exemplar: "Just as Jesus did not give way under Pilate (Roman persecution), so you, stay faithful under Roman persecution," cf. Stephen Liberty, "The Importance of Pontius Pilatus in Creed and Gospel," *JTS* 45 (1944), p. 38–56.

244. Cf. the investigation by L. S. Thornton, *Confirmation. Its Place in the Baptismal Mystery*, Westminster, London, A. & C. Black, 1954.

245. Cf. 1 Sam 10:1 and 16:2 f.; in 2 Kgs 9:1 f., Elisha has king Jehu consecrated by an anointing with oil. In all these cases, a prophet acts to enthrone a king without royal pedigree. In the case of Solomon, the court was divided, and he was hastily anointed by Zadok the priest and Nathan the prophet, with (sacred) oil taken from the Tabernacle (1 Kgs 1:39), thus creating an irreversible event.

ion,[246] kings were anointed with oil of balm, the most fragrant of all.[247] The subject merits further inquiry, but suffice it to say here that, whatever the original meaning of anointing, there have certainly been contaminations at various times between that of kings and that of priests, the best example being 1 Chr 29:22, where king Solomon and the high priest Zadok are anointed together.

It is expressly laid down that the special composition of the priestly unguent sanctifies by itself, so that it cannot be either granted to a foreigner or used for private purposes (Exod 30:32 f.). That implies that there could be other, private, unctions, since the prohibition bears only on the sacred mixture. When Daniel goes into mourning, he mentions that he has fasted and abstained from anointings with oil (Dan 10:3),[248] thus implying that he was used to such unctions. It is, however, difficult to generalize: neither Philo nor Josephus mentions such practices involving anointing as characteristic of Judaism in general. In *Ant.* 12 §120 f., Josephus remarks by the way, with regard to Antioch, that Jews do not wish to use "foreign" oil, but that is not enough to infer a generalized practice of ritual anointings, since oil had other uses. In any case, it is a fact that oil, like any liquid, can easily become impure and contaminate by contact. But above all, being more easily absorbed than water, oil is more liable to render all sorts of dry substances impure, as CD 12:15-17 expresses very clearly.

There are all the same a few small signs that anointings were current practice in some circles. In *Life* §74, Josephus denounces the religious hypocrisy of his opponent John of Gischala, and in particular his lucrative traffic in olive oil intended for anointings.[249] This John, heir to

246. Cf. *YSoṭa* 8:3, p. 22c and *BKer* 5b.

247. The balsam trees of Jericho (and En-Gaddi) were famous *(opobalsamon)*, cf. *Ant.* 4 §100. FJ explains that they had been brought by the queen of Sheba (*Ant.* 8 §174), but Pliny, *Hist. nat.* 12.25.117, attaches their appearance at Jericho to a visit by Alexander (surely legendary), in the course of his march from Tyre to Alexandria (332 B.C.). They have now disappeared, but excavations at Herodian Jericho and Qumran have uncovered perfume flasks; in particular, in a cave some three km. from Qumran, an intact sealed juglet, apparently containing genuine balm, cf. Joseph Patrich and Benny Arubas, "A Juglet Containing Balsam Oil (?) From a Cave Near Qumran," *IEJ* 39 (1989), p. 43–59, with bibliography and discussion of ancient sources.

248. LXX ἔλαιον οὐκ ἠλειψάμην, MT (and Theod.) סוך לא סכתי. According to Ruth 3:3 Naomi recommends Ruth to bathe and anoint herself (וסכת, LXX ἀλείψῃ); Luc. adds χρίσῃ μύρον, ("you will anoint yourself with myrrh"), probably another translation or a gloss which has become a doublet, meant to correct the normal meaning of the first verb "anoint with oil."

249. The parallel narrative in *J.W.* 2 §591 f. is slightly different, but in the same spirit. According to *BMen* 85b, there was a shortage of legally pure oil at Laodicea (north of Arados, cf. Adolphe Neubauer, *La géographie du Talmud*, Paris, 1868, p. 209), and it was not

Ezekias and Judas the Galilean, is none other than the leader of the "brigands" who foiled Josephus' policy; he was a hard-line zealot. By contrast, when Josephus is describing the Essenes, he takes the trouble to point out, among the oaths taken by candidates, that they swore to abstain from "brigandage," *i.e.* from zealot activity; he also states that the Essenes regarded all oil as impure, to the point that any contact, even by chance, obliged them to undergo total purification (*J.W.* 2 §123). This declaration is surprising, as it seems to isolate oil among other liquids without any apparent legal reason,[250] and decides a debate which is not even formulated. In fact, it is hardly likely that the Essenes abstained from using oil lamps; at any rate, a normal quantity has been discovered at all levels at Qumran (although that does not prove the point under discussion). But above all, texts already mentioned indicate a third pentecost, feast of new oil (first fruits), at the time of the olive harvest (cf. chap. I, §I.2b); according to 11 QT 22:16, after the first fruits of oil have been offered, the whole of the production, which has been thus redeemed, becomes available for use. At most one might infer that older oil becomes impure or that oil originating elsewhere is forbidden, but certainly not a total prohibition of oil. What Josephus has to say must be regarded as tendentious, or at least incomplete, which can be very well explained by allowing a connection between the zealot spirit and anointings with oil, which he was certainly not inclined to encourage.

We have already likened the zealots to the Messianizing movements, who were trying by their activism to hasten the coming of the Kingdom or the Messiah, with or without appropriate biblical reflextions. If they practiced anointings, they too would be "messiahs" or *christoi*, and bear this sign wherever they went. For Paul, an active Messianist, the tradition that associates him with Gischala may perhaps imply that he himself was a *christos*.

The rabbinic tradition is aware of a "war anointed,"[251] whose activity is described from Deut 20:1-9; this passage is a ritual of holy war, led by a priest. Apparently, the anointed one in question is this priest, but it is not said who has instituted him. However, another passage shows that, once victorious, he carries out the office of high priest, so he is not

---

to be found at Tyre or Jerusalem, but only at *Gush Ḥalab* (Gischala) in the house of a poor man who scorned his fellow Jews.

250. Thus Christian D. Ginsburg, *The Essenes. Their History and Doctrines*, London, Longmans Green & Co., 1864 (repr. Routledge & Kegan Paul, 1955), p. 42, judged, before the recent discoveries, that they rejected anointings with oil as a luxury opposed to the simplicity of their way of life.

251. *MSoṭa* 8:1 משוח מלחמה; this participle is distinct from משיח "Messiah."

anointed *for this purpose* by one greater than he (*MMak* 2:6). The expression has a double meaning, one applicable before the war, and the other after. First he is "anointed in view of war," which has nothing exceptional about it, and may just as well apply to the eschatological war; this meaning would be well suited to zealots. The second meaning is more exceptional, "anointed by war," that is raised to a pontifical rank. Two cases are well known. First, Pinḥas "by his ardent zeal has received the inheritance of an eternal priesthood." This declaration, based on the feats performed by Pinḥas against the Midianites (Num 31:6 f.), is pronounced by the priest Mattathias, who showed a similar zeal during the Greek persecutions;[252] likewise, *TSoṭa* 7:17 declares Pinḥas "war anointed." The second case, in the same context, is Judas Maccabaeus: in 1 Macc 3:50-60 before facing the Greeks at Emmaus, he prepared his troops, following fairly closely the forms laid down in Deut 20, as if he were the priest instituted for this purpose, though he is in no way a priest, or only in a literary sense.[253] He too is "anointed by war," but with retroactive effect. But Pinḥas and Judas are simply illustrious models, who can perfectly well be brought into comparison with the zealot movements; these latter, as "anointed for war," could also hope for the consecration of being "anointed by war."

So the rumors of anointing get some further precision, with a very simple and very militant Messianic meaning; that is enough to understand in what way the rebels mentioned by Suetonius at Rome acted *impulsore Chresto.* It is enough also to affirm that the tradition reported by Hippolytus certainly has Jewish roots, but we have not yet reached firm ground, either concerning the rites themselves or concerning a link with the Covenant and Pentecost. In order to try to get a little more precision, we need now to examine the "sign" with which the forehead of the candidate is marked, namely the cross.

2. The Cross

We have already come across various allusions to the cross as a sign. The most remarkable is the shape of the paschal lamb, roasted on two spits in the form of a cross (above, §I.1). The most symbolic case is confirmation by the bishop, who anoints the forehead with oil and marks a

252. 1 Macc 2:54 ἐν τῷ ζηλῶσαι ζῆλον ἔλαβεν διαθήκην ἱερωσύνης αἰωνίας: the priesthood is the result of the effectiveness of his zeal. Mattathias omits to say that Pinḥas was already a priest, grandson of Aaron; he appears to think that he became one at that moment.

253. As can be seen by comparing 1 Macc, 2 Macc and Dan 8, cf. Étienne Nodet, "Mattathias, Samaritains et Asmonéens," *Trans* 7 (1994), p. 93–106.

cross as a seal. However, it appears difficult to find an intrinsic link between these two. It is possible to take a roundabout way by interpreting, as we have seen, the whole of baptism "in the name of Jesus" as the transfer of a debt, analogous to the transfer of the people's sins on to the scapegoat (cf. chap. II, §I.5). Whatever the exact procedure and its sacrificial aspects, the result is for the baptized the annulment of his or her debt, which is the content of Jesus' inaugural proclamation of the year of forgiveness (Luke 4:19). In strictly banking terms, a certificate of debt was annulled by drawing two lines across it in the form of a cross,[254] apparently a fairly natural gesture. In this way, the mark of a cross on the forehead, traced with the thumb, can easily represent the forgiveness of sins, that is redemption through the cross of the slaughtered lamb. The conjunction is even more natural if it can be shown that the cross on the forehead *pre-existed* any strictly Christian significance. If an anointing with oil (made with the finger) is added, it becomes possible to identify the two essential elements in the oddly matched expression "a crucified Messiah," with reference either to Jesus or to his followers ("if we die with him"). That does not, however, imply that they had this meaning at the beginning.

There is in fact a biblical model. In Ezek 9:1 f., a man clothed in linen (an angel) stands in the midst of the destroyers who are going to chastise Jerusalem, and YHWH says to him: "Go through the city, through Jerusalem, *make a mark* on the forehead of all those who groan and lament because of the abominations which are committed within her." The word for "mark," translated "sign" by the LXX, is the last letter of the Hebrew alphabet, *thaw*, which at the time that interests us was equivalent to the Greek letter *theta*, as the literal Greek translations of the 2nd century understood very well.[255] This mark on the forehead is a phylactery, whose use is very similar to that of the blood of the paschal lamb, put on the lintels of doors (Exod 12:7), and perhaps also put as a "memorial between the eyes" (13:9,16), so also on the forehead.[256] The same passage of Ezek, translated independently of the LXX, is in the background

254. As shown by various papyri of the Greek and Roman periods, cf. the sources brought together by Lieberman I, "X and Θ," p. 185–191, whose conclusions have been largely drawn on here.

255. Ezek 9:4 והתוית תו, lit. "and you will mark a mark," LXX δος τὸ σημεῖον ἐπὶ τὰ μέτωπα. Aq. and Theod. put τὸ ϑαῦ (and not ταῦ), transcription of תו. Originally, the *theta*, seventh letter, corresponded to the Heb. *ṭeṭ*, in the same position, and not to the *thaw* (corresponding to the Gk. *tau*, last letter borrowed from the Phoenician alphabet, before the special letters were added).

256. And the hand, cf. §II.1. This commentary is also given by Redaq on Ezek 9:4; he must have been using an authorized tradition, as he tries to combine this interpretation,

of Rev 7:3 f., where the angel who arises from the East holds God's seal,[257] but may not destroy anything until the elect (the 100,000) have been marked on the forehead by this seal; the same is enjoined on the angel with the fifth trumpet (Rev 9:4). An analogous idea can be perceived in Eph 4:30, "Do not grieve the Holy Spirit, *in whom* God has conferred on you a seal in view of the day of your deliverance." The constant element in these metaphors is an official seal (on the forehead). They appear to be based on more than a simple literary borrowing, as the term used (seal) is stronger than that in Ezek. In the same spirit CD 9:10-12 declares, quoting the prophecy of Ezek, that when the Anointed of Aaron and Israel arrive, those who are marked with the *thaw* on their forehead will be saved.

There is a rabbinic saying that the *thaw* of Ezek 9:4 is "like the *theta* of a vote."[258] This alludes to the mode of secret ballot by which, in the Greek tradition, the judges voted on the guilt of the accused: by a smooth (or white) pebble for acquittal, and by a black pebble, or one pierced or inscribed with a *theta* Θ, for *thanatos* "death." This same midrash expressly understands the "man in white" of Ezek as a *quaestor*, the subordinate magistrate charged, among other things, with executing the sentence, who marks a *theta* signifying the death penalty "on the forehead of the men"; beneath the metaphor, Roman evidence from the 1st century attests a juridical reality.[259] The *thaw* of Ezek was, then, capable of diametrically opposite interpretations: a sign of life and a sign of

---

where the mark of blood represents life, with an opposite view in the Talmud, where the mark of blood represents death (*BShab.* 55a), cf. below. Philo, *Spec. leg.* 1 §58, is opposed to any practice of tattooing (as a mark of slavery), which presupposes that it existed, but he makes no connection with Passover.

257. Lit.: "the imprint" (σφραγις), which has a defined and permanent character; it is the term in the LXX for טבעת and חותם, meaning a recognizable official seal (Exod 35:22; 1 Kgs 21:8; Esth 3:10, etc.). In his description of confirmation, Hippolytus uses for signing with the cross the verb σφραγίζω (which is constant in patristic literature).

258. *Lam Rabba* 2:1 has the Greek expression כתיטא בפספס (with textual corruptions), lit.: "Like a ϑῆτα in (on) a ψήφος."

259. Its usage reached as far as Rome, since Martial, *Epigr.* 7.37 alludes to it as an innovation: "Do you know the deathly mark of the *quaestor*? It is important to study *(discere)* this new *theta*." Persius, *Saturn.* 4.13 uses the expression to "mark *(praefigere)* the black *theta* on vice," to mean simply "condemn." In ancient Rome, the execution of a capital sentence was extremely ritualized, with a dimension of offering sacrifice (to the gods of the underworld), as indicated by the use of the terms *immolatio*, the technical term for the consecration of the victim by placing meal (*mola*) on its head, and *supplicium*, an offering made to placate or propitiate (cf. Th. Mommsen, *Römisches Strafrecht,* Leipzig, Karl Binding, 1899 [repr. Graz, Akademische Druck- u. Verlagsanstalt, 1955], p. 900 f.). Although we have no direct attestation of the practice, the foregoing expressions appear to imply that the condemned criminal was indeed marked.

death,[260] thanks to widely observed customs having no definite link with either Judaism or Christianity.

Tertullian affirms that this *thaw* was precisely the sign of the cross (*Against Marcion* 3.22), but this was no personal invention. Origen explains about the same time[261] that he has sought information from Jews; for one of them, the *thaw*, last letter of the alphabet, was a sign of perfection conferred on those who groaned at being among sinners, but who also had to suffer *with them* for not having protested and reacted; for another, the *thaw* symbolized those who observed the *Thorah*, of which it is the first letter. Both these opinions recur in the rabbinic tradition (*BShab* 55a); the first, which in fact understands Ezek 9 in relation to Ezek 3:18 f. (if the just do not warn sinners, they will die with them), enables the *thaw* to be understood as a sign of election and at the same time as a sign of death. This interpretation is subtle, but it is not certainly the primary meaning of Ezek 9.[262] Origen also cites the opinion of a third Jew, "one of those who believe in Christ": the shape of the *thaw* in the ancient Hebrew writing resembles the cross and prefigures the future sign on the forehead of Christians.

This information given by the Jewish-Christian on the shape of the *thaw* is exact and can even be filled out. In the palaeo-Hebrew alphabet,[263] two letters have more or less the form of a cross, that is of a simple mark: the first, *aleph*, and the last, *thaw*, both liable to alternate between + and X. This symbolism is obviously used in Rev 1:8, "I am the *alpha* and the *omega*, says the Lord God." The first and last letters of the Greek alpha-

260. Opposition perceptible in a discussion reported in *BShab* 55a, and concealed in an apparently gratuitous pun: "Rab said: 'תיו is for תחיה – thou shalt live; תיו is for תמות – thou shalt die.'"

261. *Selecta in Ezechielem*, *PG* 13.800d.

262. According to another interpretation of the same passage *(ibid.)*, the angel (Gabriel) is charged with putting a *thaw* in ink on the foreheads of the just, and a *thaw* in blood on the foreheads of the impious, so that the destroying angels may preserve the former and kill the latter. We might have expected the reverse, since ink corresponds to the procedure of the tribunal (attested by *Tanḥ*, par. *tazria* §7; the interpretation is not however arbitrary, as it is possible to understand the instrument קסת הסופר of Ezek 9:2 as "ink and scribe's pen," cf. the *hebraeus* of Field, *a. l.*), whereas blood protects, as in Exod 12. This form comes from an inversion motivated by self-censorship, cf. Lieberman I:190.

263. The rab. trad. (*BSanh* 21b) has kept a precise memory that the law was first given to Israel in (palaeo-)Hebrew letters (כתב עברי). At the time of Ezra, it was given again, and Israel chose Aramaic writing ("Assyrian," כתב אשורי, cf. *MMeg* 2:2), leaving Hebrew writing to the natives (הדיוטות, from ἰδιῶται), who are none other than the Samaritans, who have retained it. Origen, *In Psalmos II*, §2 (*PG* 12.1104) and Jerome, *Epist. 25* (*PL* 28.594) indicate that the tetragrammaton continued to be written in this way, as also in the Qumran fragments. For the Christian sources, cf. also Jean Daniélou, *Bible et liturgie* (Lex Orandi, 11), Paris, Cerf, 1951, p. 89 f.

bet express that God is the beginning and the end of all things, but in the context it applies equally well to Jesus Christ "who has freed us from sin by his blood" (cf. Rev 21:6). These letters, transposed into the first and last letters of the old Hebrew alphabet, become the two forms of the cross; in addition, no one can open the book except "a lamb standing as if slain" (5:6). It is possible to infer that the cross of the paschal lamb is superimposed on the first and last letters of the alphabet, thus providing the key to the alphabet and ultimately to Scripture itself. Thus, through a sort of symbolic pun, the cross fulfills Scripture: "All is accomplished," is precisely what Jesus says on the cross (John 19:30). All this symbolism is linked to Hebrew. In Greek, however, it is even simpler, especially if there is also an anointing with oil. Then the X is the letter *chi*, the initial of *Christos*. This is the most direct way of understanding Rev 22:4 ("And his name shall be written on their forehead"); it also gives added significance to the rabbinic interpretation of the sign as the mark of death.

The clarity of this symbolism of the cross should not, however, obscure the fact that it brings together two series of elements which are quite distinct: the instrument of Jesus' death, with three unequal branches, to which is attached the preparation of the paschal lamb, and a mark (on the forehead) in the form of a cross, upright or on its side, with four equal branches and several different meanings, direct or annexed.[264] That these two realities should come together in a common symbolism presupposes that both pre-existed independently. That is obvious for the first. As for the second, the rabbinic tradition, whose basis is close to the marginal customs of the *ḥaberim*, never takes any interest in other religions for their own sake, following in this a very biblical custom. In other words, the very energy with which it objects to placing a sign on the forehead betrays that it was familiar with such a sign, at least in these circles;[265] the prohibition of putting phylacteries on the forehead tells its own story.

The simplest conclusion to all these observations would be that Hippolytus' description of the bishop's reception of a new member, anoint-

264. The first is the model of the Latin and Greek cross; the second corresponds to the "St. Andrew's cross" (X).

265. Archaeology sheds further light on the use of the cross as a mark: ossuaries engraved with crosses and Jewish names in Hebrew and Greek (including ιησους) were discovered in 1945 near Jerusalem. They were dated between -50 and +50, and at first "Christianized," like other finds of the same nature, but a more independent examination has shown that they were strictly Jewish, crosses included, cf. Erich Dinkler, "Zur Geschichte des Kreuzsymbol," *ZThK* 48 (1951), p. 148–172, who makes a judicious comparison between these funerary crosses and the *thaw* of Ezek 9:4: mark (or talisman) for the elect presumed just who will be admitted to the life to come.

ing with oil and marking the forehead with a cross, is only a Christian reinterpretation of a gesture coming unchanged from Jewish brotherhoods of Covenant renewal, whether zealot or not. The cross, as a simple mark with a number of possible meanings, was originally an official gesture of affiliation, made by the "overseer." It would then be easy to see how such "anointed ones," brandishing the proclamation of the end and the imminent arrival of "the Anointed One" (the Messiah), could have been called *christiani* by the Roman authorities. It would be equally easy to take hold of certain aspects of Paul's religious culture, as, in all likelihood, an "anointed" Messianist. The parallel between the seal of the Spirit at baptism (Eph 1:13) and the seal of circumcision (Rom 4:11) suggests a possible blood rite. When he declares that he has not been sent to baptize, but to evangelize, "not in the wisdom of rhetoric, so that the cross of Christ will not be voided" (1 Cor 1:17), he is not necessarily expressing lack of interest in signs in themselves, but rather his sense of a mission to give them another, "fuller" meaning. The cross (a simple mark) on the forehead of one anointed already existed as a customary sign, concluding the baptismal course; by preaching, it was given the new meaning of "the cross of Christ," combining death and life (resurrection, new creation). This brought about a complete mutation of Messianism, which ceased to be centered on Jerusalem.

But these affirmations remain conditional, just like the meanings attached to the Covenant and Pentecost. The sources investigated do not allow us to claim that they are firm conclusions, but at best probable hypotheses, which make it possible to situate the Nazoreans in relation to the *christiani*, before and after Paul. But the allusions to rites are vague, and sometimes contradictory. We must not lose sight of the fact that the first disciples did not form a homogeneous group.[266]

266. Other interesting points in common between Christian and Jewish rituals (Roman Canon, dismissal of the catechumens, etc.) have been noted by Frédéric Manns, *L'Israël de Dieu. Essais sur le christianisme primitif* (Studium Biblicum Franciscanum, Analecta 42), Jerusalem, Franciscan Printing Press, 1996, p. 183 f.

Conclusions

The arguments presented in this book have often been fairly complex. This has been unavoidable, since, in the absence of direct information, we have had to make do with small indications which point in the same direction (while bearing in mind that two half-proofs do not add up to one proof). Nonetheless, the overall thesis is quite simple. The central elements of Christianity in their entirety, including the eucharist, the cross and the system of excommunication, are directly derived from Jewish "sects" of the most traditional type, claiming to represent the renewal of the true Covenant, especially in Galilee. We are here dealing with incarnation in the widest sense of the term. Jesus, embodying the full force of tradition, made disciples only in Israel, even if he did cross a number of barriers which were thought to be insuperable and worried the authorities. It was only after the troubles connected with his disappearance from the scene that a major transgression occurred, in the form of active contact with the Gentiles. But was that a betrayal or a divinely inspired move? Jesus' disciples were astounded when he told them that they would do greater works than he. In fact, despite the massive impression brought about by centuries of Christendom, the birth of Christianity was an unlikely event and the new movement was not at all well organized at first, as we have seen for ourselves when we tried to follow in the footsteps of the apostles around the complex world of Judaism within the Roman empire.

This brief conclusion seeks to review the journey taken throughout this book and to point out a series of questions which were only glimpsed in the course of our travels.

I – What We Have Seen

When events and speeches are handed down, not by an impartial official recorder, but by a highly committed oral tradition (even with the help of written notes), they are not so easy to reconstruct precisely, since memory has tried to make sense of them by a process of selection and transformation. For this reason, the method we have followed has been to look at rites and gestures. There were two reasons for this. First, rites and gestures are to be presumed to have remained stable, unless an external emergency or internal crises have arisen; this means that any development has *a priori* taken place in fits and starts, whereas ideas or outlooks develop imperceptibly, without requiring a major crisis. Secondly, even when these customs are not described as such, which is the case in the NT, they appear incidentally in the narratives; but above all they determine mental structures, as shown by the spontaneous association of entities that have no natural relationship with one another (e.g. "Spirit" and "anointing").

Rather than go over the discussions and itemize the results obtained point by point, we will, for the sake of greater clarity, group some of them around a number of themes which have recurred throughout the book.

Authority is one such theme, which has occurred in different contexts. Usually, the subject arises in connection with government and obedience, but another context is that of the word, where authority has to do rather with inspiration or assurance. This second form of authority has a remarkable feature, as we have seen with regard to the prohibition of oaths among the Essenes. Those who have received the teachings of the group and have been admitted after a suitable course of initiation, promise obedience; they are then deemed to have a powerful word. Different texts explain that, after this course of initiation, which is punctuated by various rites, they have received the Spirit. In particular, they have been put in touch with the source of the inspiration of the Scriptures, according to the community's understanding; in other words, it is possible to make the changeless texts speak to the present. It is on this basis that obedience is demanded. This attitude stands in marked contrast to that of the historians, especially Josephus, who strive for rational neutrality and retire behind their sources when the facts reported appear incredible or bizarre.

The NT loses no opportunity to show the apostles speaking with assurance and authority, or as "powerful in the Spirit." This is not, however, the same thing as independence, and Paul fears having run in vain if he loses communion with Peter and James. Jesus, who speaks and acts with authority, is an exemplary case. He never presents himself as sent in his own name, but receives baptism, then the Spirit, and he goes apart to a lonely place to pray. From this we can learn the meaning of the strange notion of "witness" in the NT, whose extreme form is "martyr." From a juridical point of view, a witness is like the historian just mentioned. His role is limited to conscientiously reporting the facts that he has observed, on the express condition that he is not in any way personally involved; the "authority" of such a witness can be summed up in terms of reliable memory and impartiality. By contrast, when Matthias is chosen to replace Judas, it is important to find someone who has been "with us" since John's baptism, in order to make him a witness of the resurrection, then the assembly prays that God will choose between the candidates presented. It is obvious that, juridically speaking, the evidence provided by such a witness is inadmissible.

Nevertheless, that is the term used on numerous occasions. It is not a question of testifying about a fact in the past (he rose on such or such a day), but of a competence, in every sense of the word, to witness to something that is true in the present (he is risen). This competence arises from a teaching already received, but also from the Spirit who brings that teaching alive. So there is a testimony, but the witness is entirely involved in what he says, because at the center is a personal experience that has been authenticated. It implies a dimension of obedience, which is very apparent in the term "apostle," meaning "sent." This meaning of "witness" appears to be very new, but an echo is to be found among the Essenes: no one may keep silent about a brother's fault, and at the same time no one may testify concerning it before the assembly, in the strictly juridical sense, unless he can prove that the culprit was duly warned. In other words, the member of the group is bound to be a committed and persuasive witness to the Law here and now, responsible for his fellow member's sanctification.

The instance just discussed, in which the witness's authority depends on his fidelity, gives a ready link with the first, and more usual, meaning of authority as connected with government and so with obedience. But precisely in this area of government, there is a noticeable lack of symmetry between Jews and Christians. Among the Jews we can observe from 90 onwards, at a time when the Holy Place in Jerusalem was beginning once again to function, though on a reduced scale and under Roman surveillance, the *non*-priestly reorganization of Yavneh under the energetic rule of Gamaliel II. It was he who undertook to federate a certain number of Essene-like brotherhoods *(ḥaberim)*, of varying antiquity and tradition (but with a particular respect for Galilean customs), in order to create a school that would serve as a point of reference for the people as a whole. The term "sanhedrin" was used for this institution—an interesting choice, as it was employed by the Romans to designate a more or less compulsory conference of entities that were independent and of equal rank. The enterprise was centered on Judaea and apparently negotiated with the Romans, but the road ahead would be long and difficult, since zealot currents remained active. Some groups refused to join or were excluded, notably the Jewish-Christians, or at least some of them, such as the Nazorean heirs of James. In Rome, Josephus was discreetly following these events from a distance. He also saw himself as one who could federate a vast *ethnos* spread throughout the Empire, where the Pharisees were in the ascendant, at least as a reference point. He did not lose sight of Jerusalem, but even he was careful to turn his Galilean past to advantage, though in a clearly priestly perspective. Perhaps he was too much of a politician and not sufficiently "inspired"; in any case, he had no following.

Among the Christians, problems of government and exclusion of heretics appear only after 150, and bring into play the authority of the church of Rome. Before that, there were clearly profound differences between Jewish-Christians, faithful to the memory of the Master and awaiting the Messiah, and the "Pauline" Christians proclaiming the resurrection. The different communities developed independently until the time of Yavneh, persecuted from time to time and from various quarters, the *christiani* appearing more dangerous than the Nazoreans. The apparent unanimity of the Jerusalem assembly (Acts 15) affirms that a reconciliation took place, at least belatedly, but cannot entirely hide the earlier tensions between Paul and James. Nor does it conceal the fact that in those turbulent early days the reference point was James. Peter, disciple of Jesus and recognized as head of the Church, cannot be compared to Gamaliel: he simply tries to maintain a link between the various centrifugal forces, in itself no mean feat. Eventually he was drawn to Rome, where, as Tacitus puts it, "all the iniquities of the world come together and exercise their fatal charm." It would certainly be anachronistic to imagine him there ruling and making laws. On the contrary, it was by their martyrdom, in circumstances which are not perfectly clear, that Peter and Paul achieved the rank of founders.

Yet Christianity is credited with having abolished the Law, a remarkable achievement when one looks at its origins, which were both marginal and very traditional. By contrast, rabbinic Judaism, issuing from a similar conservative environment, developed the Law even further, going as far as 613 precepts, and not shrinking from some innovations. That consolidation is comprehensible given the reorganization undertaken at Yavneh. But how can we explain the Christian outcome in the absence of a centralizing authority and against strong Judaizing tendencies present from the beginning and continuing for several centuries?

To do so we have to look at the nature of the Law and the precise point of the Pauline kerygma. Like any other system of rational organization, the Law exists in order to create a boundary within which life can go on; it does this by means of actions that put the performer in touch with God, who is their author. In the case of the Essenes (and the *ḥaberim*), everything comes together in sharing in the community meal, called "purity," with its overtones of worship. This notion of (Levitical) purity is essential: everything has to be ritually pure, and the participant must be free from sin, as sin always entails some ritual impurity. Already, in the biblical ritual of the Day of Atonement, sin is represented by impurity. This equivalence is not there by chance. Just as the impure contaminates, so evil too contaminates, whereas the pure and the good are inert. Therefore, the foreigner, the sinner and even the candidate awaiting admission contaminate. The source of all impurity is death, the utmost evil, and it too contaminates, whereas life is inert. In other words, celebrating the "purity" meal, which is a contact with life and with God, is a fragile achievement from every point of view. Anything that happens, whether voluntary or not, can be dangerous. From all this can come a great self-mastery, especially with the support of one's fellows, but it is also a source of tension: hope in the fulfillment of the Scriptures is concentrated on an ultimate victory of God and the sons of light over evil and the sons of darkness. That does not exclude also rivalries among brotherhoods. Finally, zealot activism, in order to hasten the end, is not far away; here we glimpse the outline of Paul, before and also, for a time, after his conversion.

Into this context breaks the kerygma, which is concise in its formulation and biblical in its content: Christ's resurrection is a victory—unhoped for but verified by experience—of life over death, and, by analogy, of the pure over the impure. Concretely, the foreigner and the Gentile, even if they do not become Jews, and even the impurity of women, cease to be dangerous, and communion is possible. Still more concretely, history and even persecution are no longer to be feared, since death has been vanquished. One of the leading themes of Acts is to show how the mission developed thanks to opposition and persecution. Once all that is projected on to the "purity," in which the role of bread and wine has been stressed, the whole system turns completely around, beginning with what is most central: forgiveness is now stronger than sin, an outcome that is nothing short of scandalous. It only needs a change of vocabulary, in terms of the kerygma, for the eucharistic elements to become a sign of resurrection and power (especially on the night of Saturday-Sunday); that is the point of the Emmaus story. So it is not surprising that this central rite, which expresses the very existence of the brotherhood (or the Church) has been maintained, along with an associated rite of access, baptism in the broad sense. But that implies "eating together," a grave transgression which ignores the barrier of impurity. So the precepts that organize purification and separation along the lines of national distinction fall into desuetude, since they no longer create communion between the members. Nonetheless, there remains a clear distinction between the community with its own rites and the world outside. All this obviously has nothing to do with any sort of liberalism, still less with watering down Judaism or integrating it into the Roman world, after the fashion of Stoics or Cynics: the *christiani* were regarded as dangerous for hundreds of years.

These transformations were not brought about by any administrative decisions, nor were they based on the objective report of witnesses concerning past events. They resulted from a proclamation directly addressed. This took two forms: the more concise proclaimed the resurrection and the cancellation of the debt; the more developed form explained that what had happened did not come out of the blue, but was the fulfillment of hopes long nourished by the Scriptures. In other words, the preaching was animated by the Spirit that inspired all Scripture. So the preachers said, but in reality their position was open to attack on all sides. For Jews of a similar background who did not accept this preaching, because of the undeniable facts that evil had not disappeared from the world, that idolatry persisted, that the enemy remained hostile, it represented a very grave danger: it confiscated the Covenant and tended to break up the Jewish people, and especially the brotherhoods, who were striving to restore the Covenant by returning to Moses. Not only did it interfere with the clear markers set up at Creation when God brought order out of chaos, but it seriously threatened the mission entrusted to the chosen people, to prepare the world for an end which was still far off. So we can understand how it was that the *minim* caused a serious crisis at Yavneh, whereas Josephus, more concerned with the national culture than with the Covenant, could afford to show a polite interest in Jesus and in the emerging Christians.

Jesus was a teacher and a healer. Later on, Peter, Barnabas and even Paul can all be seen performing healings and exorcisms. However, in the NT epistles, and even in Peter's Pentecost sermon, all these aspects have become entirely secondary. Jesus, Peter says, was accredited by signs and wonders, but he neglects to tell his listeners exactly what Jesus said and did. Everything is centered first on the kerygma, in which Jesus' resurrection shows that God is mightier than sins committed, and then on the call to conversion and baptism.

Renan, who of course could not know the discoveries that have accumulated since his time, was certainly correct to say that Christianity is an Essenism that has largely succeeded. But when he deplored the fact that Jesus proclaimed the Kingdom but what appeared instead was the Church, he showed that he was too much of a romantic and that he did not read the texts aright.

II – What Is Still to be Seen

While working on the origins of Christianity, we have caught sight of close connections both with earlier marginal Jewish groups, and also with institutions of the patristic period. Many problems, however, still remain unsolved. We mention a number of them here under three headings. First, we have had much to say about apostles, Nazoreans and other *christiani*, but very little about the historical Jesus; on this subject, certain problems of method can be extracted from the remarks already made about his first disciples. The second question concerns the surrounding Jewish environment, its relations with Greek culture and with later rabbinic traditions. A third concern would be to clarify the connection between the NT and the later history of the Church, heresies and dogmatic developments.

The Historical Jesus. This is a fashionable topic, but it gives rise to methodological complications leading sometimes to statements which come close to begging the question. The criteria employed are judicious, and we have made use of them in the course of this study. The problem lies, however, in their application. Thus, it is entirely logical to fix a criterion of disharmony ("embarrassment"), according to which, if the NT has preserved a detail about Jesus that is embarrassing for the Church, it is certainly historical, since it is hard to see how it could have been invented. The classic example given is the baptism of Jesus by John, which is regarded as aberrant from a Christian point of view and so cannot be a redactional effect. In this case, however, we have seen that the supposition is quite groundless. Likewise, it is logical to look for discontinuities: if Jesus' teaching as it is reported cannot have come from the Jewish environment or from the primitive community, if it is, that is to say, original, then it is authentic. True, but one conclusion usually drawn is that the prohibition of divorce or oaths was proper to Jesus, which implies a view of Galilean Judaism that does not accord with the evidence. Furthermore, even if such criteria, properly used, can establish that Jesus said or did such or such a thing, it is obviously an abuse of the critical method to maintain that only items so established can safely be attributed to Jesus.

We cannot go here into a detailed discussion, all the more as the underlying problem is of a different order. Study of texts and their publication has shown a major difference between the Jewish-Christian outlook, attached to the memory of an exceptional teacher who came to an unfortunate end, and the Pauline outlook, which relativizes the Law and is centered on the Risen Lord. The NT taken all together bears the strong imprint of this latter view, along with visible traces of the former, especially in the biographies of Jesus. The native Jewish soil must therefore be examined with great care. Otherwise we run the risk of projecting the Pauline Christ on to the Jesus who walked the winding roads of the Galilean heartland, thus turning him surreptitiously into someone who rose again before he had died, or a sort of extraterrestrial being who healed the sick but had no roots in time or place, and who could just as well have turned up in Cyprus, or Syria, or anywhere. From this results the obsession with discovering some esoteric or original teaching proper to Jesus, some "super-Law" that is sublimely ethical and has the added advantage of being able to eliminate sin. Such views are far removed from those of Paul, or even from Jesus' own teaching as it has come down to us: he does not shrink from insisting on the commandments of love of God and of the neighbor, or on the Golden Rule, which can hardly be treated as major innovations. This way of thinking does, it is true, have some support in the NT, but it can really be regarded as proto-Gnostic. The case of the *Gospel of Thomas*, which has pronounced Gnostic features, is enlightening: it consists solely of words of Jesus.

Let us take an example which brings together several problems. Jesus declares that whoever does not carry his cross and follow after him cannot be his disciple. We can see how such a formula could well come from later disciples at a time of persecution, by assimilating the cross of Jesus' execution to their own sufferings and having Jesus predict it for them too; in that case, the historical basis for such a statement is fairly weak (even if crucifixion was a common sight at the time). Furthermore, according to the synoptics, Jesus did not carry his own cross. But if we notice that just before, he says that no one can come to him without *hating* father, mother, wife, children, etc., another horizon opens up. As a matter of fact, Jesus himself left his family, a move which did not go smoothly, in order to enter into John's baptism; later on, he redefined his family as those who do the will of God, and here and there are signs of strong tensions between his natural family ("brothers") and his disciples. Furthermore, as we have seen, the cross as a sign *(thaw)* is in the first place a Jewish symbol of election or a mark of protection. In other words, it is not too difficult to attempt an institutional reading of Jesus' statement, which, in the setting of Essene relationships, gives it a quite different historical coloring. The primary meaning would be that those who do not leave their natural environment to journey towards the seal of entry into a new family and obey (renounce oneself) cannot be Jesus' disciples (enter into the Kingdom, or the Covenant). This presupposes a certain process brought to completion and confirmed. On this basis, which is comparable with the call of John the Baptist, the second meaning follows quite naturally. It originates in the kerygma, through which the cross of Jesus (bringing together the instrument of execution and the appearance of the paschal lamb) becomes a metaphor for the trials of the disciple which is superimposed on the sign of election.

Such a clarification gives rise, however, to other difficulties. Jesus has abandoned the Nazoreans (Nazareth) for John's baptism, but the matter is not yet done with. For one thing, he was condemned to death as a Nazorean. Then too his family came back in force after he had left the scene, since James then became the point of reference and started a long line of Nazoreans who were to play various roles. Even Paul was called a Nazorean. Later a *Gospel of the Nazoreans* states that Jesus would have refused to be baptized by John, which is highly interesting, even if the reason given appears secondary. We can at least conclude that the relations between Jesus' disciples and his family, who had an acute dynastic sense, were fairly complex and would merit serious examination. In the NT, two attempts at unification are placed under Jesus' own authority, when he appoints Peter to be head of the Church, and when he makes Mary *mother* of the beloved *disciple*. Such syntheses certainly cover over great differences among disciples or adherents of Jesus, and certainly conflicts as well. The early sources show traces of "eucharistic" meals with or without wine, with or without fish, etc. It is also significant that certain lists of "heretical" Christian groups *(haireseis)* bear more or less the same names as Jewish "heresies."

The mention of Jesus' condemnation gives rise to other difficult questions. We have seen in the gospels a superimposition and even a certain mixing together of two sorts of conflicts: those of Jesus' own time, when the main opponents were the high priest and various authorities in Jerusalem and Galilee, and those connected with the quarrel over the *minim*, some sixty years later, when the opponents were rather the "Pharisees" (using this term with caution). A clear separation of these two levels, if it were possible, would allow us better to understand the last week of Jesus' life and the precise nature of his trial.

The Jewish Context. The NT account of this trial mentions the Sanhedrin. That is an institution whose nature is far from clear. In Herod's youth, the Romans created five sanhedrins, on both sides of the Jordan, with the idea of quieting things down and making the various Jewish factions come to some agreement; there is no sign that they were meant to be permanent assemblies. At a later period, the school of Yavneh also called itself by the Greek name sanhedrin, rather than tribunal, senate, or assembly of elders. There is room for wondering if here too the Romans intervened, at the time of Gamaliel II and with his approval, in order to make the different brotherhoods come to some agreement, which would explain the various ripples which were caused. It is not enough to state that this Sanhedrin was simply the prolongation of the Jerusalem Sanhedrin, since the only early sources to suggest (and only vaguely) that this body was a permanent entity are the gospels; hence there is a risk of arguing in a circle because of the superimposition of the two conflicts.

Another apparently well-known institution turns out to be difficult to grasp: the synagogue. The primary meaning of this Greek term is a gathering that has been called together, and the first time it is used in the Bible is for the gathering of the lower waters in the course of Creation. A recent study has tried to find the origin of the term as used of a community building by tracing it back in time, from the better to the less well known. It is fully visible from the 3rd cent. A.D., from texts as well as from archaeology, but before 70, the evidence from the Jewish world in general is fairly vague, the clearest being provided by the NT. We can get a little more precision on the basis of the *holiness* of the building. Philo occasionally mentions places where Jews gather on the Sabbath, especially for teaching, but he speaks of *sacred* places called synagogues only with regard to the Essenes. Josephus also speaks of Sabbath teaching, and once or twice of places of prayer, but he expressly says that the place where the Essenes hold their community meals, which have a sacrificial aspect, is *sacred*. The rabbinic tradition also indicates that the synagogue is a *sacred* place, which is significant. Furthermore, that same tradition situates its origin at the time of the Babylonian exile, parallel to the establishment of public prayers named after the sacrifices. Such an early date would not be easy to prove, but what is important is that it shows at least that the synagogue was not regarded as a substitute for Herod's temple, but rather a parallel institution.

All these allusions appear to hang together quite well and suggest that the synagogue, as a special community building, originated as an institution proper to marginal groups (Essenes, *ḥaberim*), with a note of sacredness connected with community meals and official prayer. This is only an hypothesis to be explored, but it agrees *a priori* quite well with the data of the gospels as we have been interpreting them. Further, it would give a precise significance to the trouble that Paul took to preach *in the synagogues*. Similarly, when James declares that Moses is proclaimed every Sabbath in the synagogues of each town, it is not at all certain that he has in mind the customs and community premises of *all* the Jews in every place. His horizon may very well be limited to the rural hamlets of Judaea and Galilee. Here, we may recall that the *Mishnah* defines a town as "large" when ten men can regularly be found there who have the leisure to assure public worship; in fact, it is talking of little villages.

Paul's borrowings from the Greek world (mysteries, apotheosis, etc.), are certainly not due to any conformism, as we have seen. The question is then to determine whether they are direct borrowings, or whether they come *via* Judaism. In the former case, they would be purely accidental or ornamental, but in the latter, we might suspect something more substantial. Certain features invite us to look more closely at these cultural contacts. Thus, the Essene brotherhoods do not appear to have much in common with biblical tribes, but they do look rather like Pythagorean *thiasi*, with Platonism somewhere in the background. The Essenes were highly concerned about the Law and the Covenant, and little given to compromising contacts with foreigners, but their cult of self-mastery as well as their doctrine of an after-life, varying between resurrection and immortality, are hard to find in the Pentateuch, but have quite respectable Greek and Latin parallels. The question has to be tackled at an even earlier stage: the Maccabaean crisis ended officially in a victory over Hellenization, but there is room for regarding it as a violent reaction to what was in reality a profound and abiding Greek influence. Even anointing for war looks rather like anointing for an athletic contest.

Early Church. The Church has kept two characteristic and complementary traces of its sectarian origin: no one is born a Christian, and "Outside the Church there is no salvation." Among the rites and doctrines that are central to Christianity, we have found massive borrowings from Judaism. This has an important consequence for the history of the early Church which would need to be worked out in detail. Theology did not create these dogmas. On the contrary, dogmas and customs, more or less clearly formulated from the beginning but very stable, provoked, on the occasion of controversies, systematic reflexions inspired by different philosophical currents. These systems have always come up against an insurmountable difficulty. The Gospel proclaims events which were in themselves unlikely and where God can be recognized only by taking a risk, viewed as a movement of the Spirit. Theology has too often tried to transform them into rational structures in which history becomes subordinated to necessity, while the Spirit is gradually reduced to a function that is almost ornamental. The fact that Philo, whose vast project is strictly rational, should have passed for being a Christian from the end of the 2nd century, is instructive. It means that Christians were taking over the traditional civilizing expansion of Hellenism, but with a new apologetic which was independent of the Roman pantheon now in decline. A rationalizing attitude of this sort had some very concrete consequences: heresy hunting within, and, more generally, the conviction that, if the survival of paganism was troublesome, the survival of Judaism was strictly absurd. Now, not only did Paul profess quite different opinions, but historically, as we have seen, it was rather the birth of Pauline Christianity that bordered on the improbable.

The Jewish-Christians were, in the last analysis, the least strange of Jesus' disciples. They left traces of various sorts. First, a certain number of Greek texts survive, like the *Didache*, the *Odes of Solomon* or the *Pseudo-Clementine Homilies*, which have a very Jewish-Christian air, but may also reflect the general Christian culture of the time, and not only of groups that did not sponsor any mission to the Gentiles. More specifically, several ancient writers mention, but without giving details, different groups which were fairly marginal, whose links with Judaea disappear after 135. Finally, the most visible trace is the collection of churches known as Oriental, which claim to stem from Antioch and which are often older than the church of Rome. They were certainly not very Pauline in origin; in Acts, the episodes connected with Syria are rather marginal, and we quickly lose sight of Damascus and Antioch, not to mention Tarsus. In this regard, we can glimpse the lasting significance of the episode which Paul relates in Gal, when he lost out to emissaries of James at Antioch over table fellowship between Christians of Jewish and of Gentile origin. Nonetheless, communications with the west were maintained, and these churches came to adopt at least a gospel harmony, derived from that attested by Justin, then the NT in its final form, probably under the influence of liturgical usages. These movements of the 2nd century are not well documented, but we must suppose that the oriental liturgies, conservative as they are like every rite, have preserved very primitive elements originating in the brotherhoods, even if the traditional explanations associated with them are not necessarily primitive. That, after all, is exactly what we have seen in the case of the rabbinic traditions.

Indexes

It has been deemed useful to divide the matter into seven parts:

I. Bible and Apocrypha (with OT and NT)
II. Philo of Alexandria (but not Ps.-Philo)
III. Flavius Josephus
IV. Qumran and DSS
V. Rabbinic Sources (with Targums)
VI. All the other ancient writers, from Herodotus to Photius
VII. Modern Scholars (some of them are listed in the Abbreviations)

Within each part, the items are sorted alphabetically with the key words.

I — Bible and Apocrypha

II — Philo

III — Flavius Josephus

IV — Qumran and Dead Sea Scrolls

V — Rabbinic Sources

VI — Other Ancient Writers

VII — Modern Scholars